BEFORE CHAPTER AND VERSE

Reading the Woven Torah

Including the Full English Text of the Torah

Arranged According to its Literary Structure

Moshe Kline

For Deena

ISBN 978-965-598-271-8

Cover design by Douglas Van Dorn

Edited by Katherine Factor

Acknowledgements

"הרבה למדתי מרבותי, ומחביריי יותר מרבותי, ומתלמידי יותר מכולן"

"I have learned much from my teachers, more from my colleagues, but most from my students"

Babylonian Talmud, Taanit, 7:a

For many years I have had the pleasure of studying with a group of devoted students of the Torah, to whom I refer in the afterword. Weekly meetings have been going on for years, with members of the group spread out from Afghanistan to Wales, and from Jerusalem to California. In many respects, this book is the result of our studies. Members of the group have inspired and encouraged me to finish it. All have contributed to it in many ways, reading numerous drafts, offering countless suggestions, proofreading, designing, and more. But above all their contributions, I value their commitment to study the Torah as it presents itself, without preconditions or preconceptions. Andy Wehrle, Paul Hocking, Eliezer Blasberg, Brett Kopin, Matthew Nelson, and Doug Van Dorn, this book is yours.

And yet, with the best of intentions from all of us, the book would not have come into being without the firm hand of its editor, Katherine Factor. Like the potter who takes a heap of clay and forms it into a delightful vessel, Katherine took my thoughts and drafts, and helped fashion them into a book worthy of its content. There can be no greater praise for an editor. While we disagreed at times, our arguments were like those of Hillel and Shamai, "for the sake of heaven." Thank you, Katherine.

Several scholars have followed the development of the theory presented in this book from its earliest stages. I wish to thank Rabbi Prof. Alan Brill for his decades of encouragement and time spent evaluating earlier versions. Thanks to Rabbi Dr. David E. S. Stein for his long-term interest in the project, and especially his critique and comments on the penultimate draft. My friend, Dr. George Savran, who is still not completely convinced, has nevertheless always been a cheerful source of support.

"Rejoice, O Zebulun, on your journeys, and Issachar, in your tents." This verse is traditionally understood as depicting these brothers as partners. Zebulun engaged in commerce and supported his studious brother Issachar. My late brother, Donald, supported the studies he himself so valued. This book is dedicated to his memory.

No doubt, there will be critics who will find arguments unsatisfying, proofs lacking, and evidence weak. But I am prepared, because I have been living with my greatest critic for over fifty years. Like the angel who wrestled with Jacob, Deena has firmly grasped me by the heels lest I fly off in fantasies and fantastic speculation. She has constantly demanded I make sense, that I limit myself to ideas that are firmly based in the text. She is my Socrates, the midwife of my soul.

"Blessed are you YHWH our Elohim, king of the universe, who has sanctified us through his commandments and commanded us to engage with the Torah." This blessing is part of the morning prayers. I have been blessed with the ability to "engage with the Torah." But if any light shines forth from this book, it is the light of the Torah, and the gift of its creator. Thank you for permitting me to see these hints of splendor in the Torah.

Contents

List of Figures

Preface

The Project Origins: St. John's College

We had just completed a seminar on Paul's Letter to the Galatians that left my stomach in knots. As always, the atmosphere in the after-seminar coffee shop was electric with tutors and students continuing the discussions of Plato, Paul, and Kant, with intensity matched only by the density of the cigarette smoke. After all, this was 1963 at St. John's college, the Great Books school.

The windowless coffee shop in the basement of the majestic colonial building where twice weekly seminars on the Great Books were held was full beyond capacity. Students brimmed with learning, debating with faculty about how the book they were reading impacted the search for "the good life." In the melee I found myself next to one of my tutors, Robert Sacks.

I lost no time on coffee or hamburgers before telling him of my dismay about Paul's theory of justification through faith. It seemed totally inconsistent with Plato's concept of "the pursuit of good." Moreover, my intestines rebelled at what I understood as Paul's claim that faith is more important than actions for ultimate human good. This was the opening of a conversation that defined the course of my life, and ultimately, led me to write this book.

The upshot of the conversation was that I was not sufficiently in touch with my Jewishness. My resistance to Paul was consistent enough with my Hebrew-school-after school education; but I did not really know what it meant to follow "the law" of the Torah. I have spent the years since exploring my Jewishness through practice and study that developed into research. In the following pages I will tell you how these studies led to a new understanding of the Torah as a magnificent literary composition written to be read in two distinctly different ways—and how that fact can change not only the way you read the Torah, but how it can influence your life. But first, I want to explain how important St. John's was in shaping my thinking.

I was just sixteen when I finished high school with the title of "class nonconformist." I had chosen St. John's as much because it too was unconventional, as because of the unique education it offered: four years without electives, tests or grades grounded in reading Great Books from Homer to Einstein. The three-hundred or so students and faculty formed an intense intellectual community dedicated to developing critical thinking. The key to this ideal education was an ongoing conversation based on direct contact with the great thinkers; it was not acceptable to read commentaries. We were expected to grapple with Aristotle and Kant unaided. This was the approach that would eventually doom my attempt to study classical Jewish texts at a seminary, but more on that in a moment. There was an element of the approach to reading the western classics that eventually colored my study of Hebrew classics and led to my discoveries.

Leo Strauss taught at University of Chicago at that time but came to St. John's once a year to deliver a formal lecture. His seminal essay, *Persecution and the Art of Writing* (1954), had a tremendous influence at St. John's. In it, he explains that the great thinkers often hid their deepest, heterodox, ideas within their writings to avoid conflict with the powers that be—and a fate like that of Socrates. Critical reading thus required making the distinction between what a writer said and what they meant. The ultimate insight afforded the critical reader the "secret teaching," the holy grail of nonconformist thinking. Strauss' approach affected me profoundly. Coupled with critical reading tools I developed at St. John's, this formative era made possible the discovery of the secret teaching of the Torah, which is detailed in this book, as well as my editions of the Torah (*The Woven Torah*) and the Mishnah (*The Woven Mishnah*).

Between St. John's and Israel

By the time I graduated I had made two major commitments: one to Diana/Deena Brodkin, who was one year my junior at St. John's, and one to the rabbinical school of The Jewish Theological Seminary of America (JTS). The outcomes of these relationships were quite different. Deena and I are still married after more than half a century . . . while the Seminary and I divorced after one year.

I was committed to explore my Jewishness at the Seminary and hoped to use the tools of critical thinking I had developed at St. John's to probe the depth of the traditional texts, like the Bible, Mishnah, Talmud. But I was in for a shock. It turned out that Jewish studies, at least at the novice level, were the antithesis of what I had hoped for. There was not a single text that was approached directly, without commentary, and commentary on commentary. Suffering from the unbridled hubris of youth, without the least bit of humility, I totally rejected the traditional Jewish approach to studying the sources and left the Seminary after a year. I was not disappointed with Deena, however. We have been continuing the St. John's conversation with great enthusiasm for all our years together.

While I left the Seminary, I did not abandon the search to know myself and my roots but changed my approach. I decided to try a "back-to-nature" approach and became a farmer, growing avocados in Israel. The first significant period in Israel for this narrative took place in Karkur, where we had a small avocado plantation. Once a week I studied Talmud with my dear friend Jean Hyman. He had studied in France with a remarkable teacher, Rabbi Leon Ashkenazi. As leader of the Scouts in France— also known as Manitou (nicknamed after "the great spirit" of the Algonquians), Rabbi Ashkenazi had helped rebuild the Jewish community of France after the war. He had a unique background, combining kabbalistic knowledge received from his father who was the last chief rabbi of Algiers, and western philosophy which he studied at the Sorbonne University. Jean taught me how Rabbi Ashkenazi would tease out the philosophic underpinnings of the Talmud.

After a few years we moved to Kibbutz Lavi to pursue a more community-centered lifestyle. Eventually, as a member of Lavi, I was given time to renew my Jewish studies at the Yeshivah of the religious kibbutz movement. During that year I also had the opportunity to study directly with Rabbi Ashkenazi, who had recently moved to Israel. When I started studying with him, I had no indication that my life was about to change in a totally unpredictable way.

The Maharal

With Rabbi Ashkenazi I studied the work of the Maharal of Prague, (Rabbi Yehuda ben Betzalel Loew (1512? –1609)). I am indebted to the pioneering research of the Maharal of Prague. None of what I present in this book (or in my editions of the Torah and the Mishnah) could have come to light were it not for the groundbreaking work of the Maharal. He was amongst the important Jewish scholars of his time and had a unique approach which melded philosophy with traditional Jewish texts, opening my eyes to vistas I had never foreseen.

For me, the ancient Jewish texts appeared like the broken tablets, until I studied the Marahal's writings on *Mishnah* tractate *Avot* with Rabbi Ashkenazi. Only then did I realize that I had been missing the integrity of these texts by ignoring their literary structure. The Maharal demonstrated, for example, that an ostensible collection of ten aphorisms was in fact a meticulously composed philosophical composition based on a weave containing two warp threads and five weft threads. (It took years before I realized that these five pairs were composed to reflect or resonate with an esoteric reading of the Decalogue, presented here in Part Two.) My heart sang, I found my teacher, the Maharal, via his disciple, Rabbi Leon Ashkenazi.

Rabbi Ashkenazi encouraged me to investigate the other sixty-two tractates of the Mishnah in line with the Maharal's approach to *Mishnah* tractate *Avot*. Basically, he assigned to me a life's work: to reproduce the *Mishnah* according to its original format. He told me that the Mishnah had been studied according to its structure (which he associated with the kabbalah, an esoteric discipline of Jewish mysticism) as recently as four or five generations ago, but the knowledge of how to read the *Mishnah* in that way had been lost. The single remnant was in the Maharal's commentary on tractate *Avot*. There was philosophic, religious, depth to be recovered by identifying the formal literary structure of the Mishnah. But I was still a farmer living on kibbutz with four small children, and Rabbi Ashkenazi's assignment would take full-time concentration. How could I resolve the tension between my dream and my family's security?

There was a lengthy period during which I struggled to pursue my Jewish studies while working in the orchards of the kibbutz. But then one day I had a near-death experience. While driving a tractor I was thrown from the tractor and trapped under the wheels of a wagon attached to it. After being dragged for some distance, the wheel went over me, fracturing my pelvis and just missing my liver. I had to lie in bed motionless for six weeks to have the pelvis heal. During that time, I recognized the fragility of life and committed myself fully to the project Rabbi Ashkenazi had given me. I understood that a life's work is a precious and rare gift, one not to be refused. We left kibbutz so that I could devote more time to developing my edition of the Mishnah.

Following the hints of the Maharal—and the encouragement from Rabbi Ashkenazi—I completed an analysis of the Mishnah after about ten years, crowned by the publication of *The Woven Mishnah,* HaMishnah C'Darcah. In it, I demonstrated that over five-hundred chapters of Mishnah were constructed as weaves. Sizes vary, but all chapters adhere to certain basic principles. These are the same principles according to which the literary units of the Torah were constructed; they were constructed to be grasped two-dimensionally, warp and weft. It has been available on my website, chaver.com, for over twenty years. While developing this edition of the Mishnah, I published a few articles on the structure of Mishnaic chapters in journals and books. They are also available on chaver.com.[1]

Having completed my edition of the Mishnah, I began a similar analysis of the Torah. The goals were to identify the parts of the Torah and to investigate whether they were organized according to any identifiable pattern. The first book I had "cracked" was Leviticus. I began there because the material is similar to the *Mishnah,* since they are both largely books of laws.

The Discovery

My analysis of the Torah's principles of organization led to the discovery that all five books of the Torah are made up of previously unknown well-defined literary "Units" that share certain characteristics virtually identical to those I had found in the Mishnah. Specifically, each Unit was built as a table or weave, a two-dimensional, non-linear construct,

according to an esoteric paradigm analogous to the stone tablets of the Decalogue. This discovery made possible the reconstruction, or more properly, "translation" of the Torah which appears in my edition, *The Woven Torah,* in the Appendix. It is not a translation from language to language but rather from linear format to non-linear format. Within it I reproduce the eighty-six Units of the Torah in their two-dimensional woven format. The connections between Units lead to the identification of the formal structure of each of the five books. Since the same formatting technique was used throughout the Torah —both on the level of individual literary Units and on the level of whole books—it is most simply understood as the work of a single hand or school, which I refer to as "M."

The importance of the discovery transcends the conclusion that the Torah was composed by a single author. It makes it possible to read the Torah in a new way, as a multi-leveled, highly sophisticated composition. The new reading is guided by the structure as well as certain elements of the narrative, which can be understood as reading instructions. Thus, the Torah can be read in two distinct ways. One way is based on the linear reading of the text that considers its structure minimally, the "traditional" way. The "new" way, based on two-dimensional, table-like literary units, produces insights that are not available from the traditional way. Through the course of this book, I demonstrate that M intended that the Torah be read in both ways.

For more than two millennia, exegesis has focused exclusively on the linear reading. The goal of this book is to empower you to explore the Torah as a non-linear, woven text. . . and to become an enlightened reader of a lesser known "way."

---

[1] See: Moshe Kline, "The Literary Structure of the Mishnah" (*Erubin* Chapter X), *Alei Sefer* 14 (1987): 5-28. For a full edition of the Mishnah in which each chapter is arranged according to its non-linear structure see: http://www.chaver.com/Mishnah-New/Hebrew/Text/Shishah Sidrei Mishnah.htm.
For an introduction to the structuring of chapters of the Mishnah see:
http://www.chaver.com/Mishnah-New/English/Articles/Introduction to the Structured Mishnah.pdf.
Much of what is described there regarding chapters of the Mishnah can be applied to the Units of the Torah as well.

Introduction

In Plato's Banquet, Alcibiades--that outspoken son of outspoken Athens--compares Socrates and his speeches to certain sculptures which are very ugly from the outside, but within have most beautiful images of things divine. The works of the great writers of the past are very beautiful even from without. And yet their visible beauty is sheer ugliness, compared with the beauty of those hidden treasures which disclose themselves only after very long, never easy, but always pleasant work. This always difficult but always pleasant work is, I believe, what philosophers had in mind when they recommended education.

...Writing between the lines. This expression is clearly metaphoric. Any attempt to express its meaning in unmetaphoric language would lead to the discovery of a *terra incognita*, a field whose very dimensions are as yet unexplored and which offers ample scope for highly intriguing and even important investigations.

—Leo Strauss, *Persecution and the Art of Writing*

In other words, the Great Books contain, besides their exoteric teachings as piously summarized in textbooks, esoteric doctrines reserved only for the most intelligent and perceptive. It must be admitted that this sounds rather preposterous— but only until one has read Professor Strauss, after which it appears astonishingly plausible. ... An exoteric work contains a popular or edifying teaching that is accessible to all, and a secret or esoteric teaching that reveals itself only after careful and thoughtful study – study that to begin with is at least as concerned with literary questions as philosophic problems.

—Irving Kristol, *The Philosophers' Hidden Truth*, Commentary, Oct, 1952

Before embarking on an expedition into unchartered realms in the Five Books of Moses, a word about our preparations: I have made every possible attempt to make my reading faith neutral. My goal has been to read the Torah as a Great Book, not necessarily as a source of religious belief.

Personally, I have seen that most readers, whether scholars or laymen, believers or skeptics, come to the Torah with multiple preconceptions and beliefs which color their readings. One remarkably unexpected example, directly related to the content of this book, is the most accepted scholarly view of the Torah. It holds the Torah was melded from four or more earlier compositions. Surprisingly, part of the argument for this "documentary hypothesis" is the deity is represented by two primary names, Elohim, translated "God," and YHWH, the tetragrammaton, translated "the Lord." Starting from the view that the Torah is the source of monotheism, the critics assume that the names are equivalent and point to different sources, each of which used a single name.

We will begin from a more literary position, recognizing that the Torah is one of the Great Books. By reading the Torah very carefully, we will view vistas seen by few. To read carefully, we must try to read without prejudice. To paraphrase the language of the bartenders in the old westerns, we will have to "check our religion at the door." We will explore the significance of the author presenting the deity through two characters in the narrative.

Terra Incognita in the Torah

Herein I will detail the discovery of a *terra incognita*, a deeper understanding that is buried within the Torah. The Torah consists of the first five books of the Bible, the Five Books of Moses, or Pentateuch. With the adherents of biblical religions numbering in the billions, the Torah may be the most-read book ever composed, clear testimony to the extraordinary talent of its author. Yet, as beautiful and majestic as divine images are in the Torah, they pale when compared with "the beauty of those hidden treasures which disclose themselves only after very long, never easy, but always pleasant work."

Yes, the path to our biblical *terra incognita* is arduous, but the reward of seeing the hidden treasures of the Torah justifies the labor. You, dear reader, will learn how to identify and develop the "inner Torah" and thus be enriched by the treasure.

The Torah must be studied in a special way to reveal that which is concealed within it. Irving Kristol made the astute observation that the study which leads to the discovery of the esoteric *terra incognita* is a "study that to begin with is at least as concerned with literary questions as philosophic problems." We will be dealing extensively with literary questions, especially questions that reflect on the literary structure, so let us start with what we know about the structure of the Torah.

When we open our Bibles, we see the Torah divided into three primary divisions: the five books of Moses (Genesis, Exodus, Leviticus, Numbers and Deuteronomy); chapters; and verses. In Jewish bibles there is an additional division into weekly readings, or *parashot*. All of them, except for the division into five books, are not original divisions of the Torah.

Parsing the Torah

Even if we remove the divisions of the Torah into its chapters and verses, we will still not be looking at the text the way it was seen in ancient times. The Torah scrolls used in synagogues reflect the oldest known written form, stretching back millennia. The oldest existing example is a Dead Sea scroll from the third century BCE. The Hebrew of the scrolls found at the Dead Sea, as well as the scrolls read in synagogues today, contains no divisions between sentences, no punctuation as we know it, and the words themselves contain no vowels, all of which can be found in modern Hebrew books. So, the reader of a Torah scroll must make many more decisions about "how" to read than we do, turning the process of reading into a creative act.

First, the lack of vowels in the Torah requires the reader to decide which of the possible readings of the "non-voweled" word is most suitable. An English equivalent would be like the combination of consonants "mn." What does this stand for: man, men, mine? The reader of a Hebrew Torah scroll must scan the context to establish the most likely meaning. Next, the reader must determine where a sentence ends. Both these activities require a degree of reader involvement through trial and error to arrive at simple meanings. Thus, the experience of reading, even the meaning of "reading," in ancient times differed significantly from ours.

The ancient reader of Hebrew, having to parse out the individual words and sentences, was much more sensitive to the need to define rhetorical elements of text (the elements which confer meaning). There is no way of knowing for sure to what extent the average reader was also able to identify the larger divisions of the Torah that are of interest to us in this book. But the onus of working actively with the text from the most basic level of identifying words and sentences may hint that at least some ancient readers were competent at divining the meanings that appear to us as "between the lines."

Let us look a little more closely at the concept "rhetorical elements," because it underlies all of what we will deal with. Since the original state of the five books —as far as we know—was as undivided as the sentences within them, certain questions present themselves to anyone who wants to understand their composition: *How were the books of the Torah divided into parts? Is there a consistent set of markers which would indicate to our ancient reader how the sentences they parsed out of the unbroken flow of words should relate to other sentences to form higher order rhetorical elements, something like our paragraphs?* The discovery of internal divisions would lead to the identification of new levels of meaning based on those divisions. Unsurprisingly, I found that each book divides into well-defined literary units (hereafter "Units"). All told there are eighty-six literary Units in the Torah, as opposed to one-hundred-eighty-seven chapters that appear in our Bibles (only since the early thirteenth century.) The organization within and between these Units leads to the *terra incognita*.

The chapter divisions in our Bibles are further divided into verses, a single one-size-fits-all division. The discovery of the esoteric Torah begins with the breakthrough realization that determined that the Units of the Torah are divided on multiple levels. Each level reveals additional rhetorical elements. The first Unit of Genesis, the creation, provides the first and perhaps clearest example of how the Torah's Units are divided internally. Each of the six days of creation has a well-defined closing formula, "there was evening and morning." There can be no mistaking that the reader is meant to understand that each day is a compositional element. The days can also be subdivided into smaller elements which have additional rhetorical functions, but the clarity of the six-days division demands attention. We examine the meaning of the creation Unit closely in Part Three, but for now we want to see what it tells us about the creation of the Torah.

The six days provide a paradigm of how to read the esoteric Torah. By observing how they group themselves according to prominent characteristics, we will be led to the secret of the Torah's composition. The six days display two independent organizing principles. One is established by two sets of three consecutive days, 1-3 and 4-6. The other is found in three pairs of days, 1,4; 2,5; and 3,6. The two organizing principles interlock in such a way that they can be presented together through a chart. This chart is the key that opens the esoteric Torah. It enables the reader first to identify the divisions and subdivisions of Units, and then arrange them in a table.

The secret is that the Units of the Torah were composed two dimensionally, as tables or weaves. One principle of organization is found in the columns, or warp threads, and the other in the rows, or weft threads. The esoteric reading involves integrating these two principles. It is based on a woven format that visualizes all the subdivisions and the relationships between them as illustrated in Figure 1.

Figure 1. Woven Format of Six Days of Creation

	L	R
A	1	4
B	2	5
C	3	6

Envision the text of the six days of creation laid out in the tabular form, as you see within the lines in Figure 1 It reads in the order 1, 2, 3, 4 etc. In that respect nothing about the actual text of the Torah has been changed. And yet, everything has changed, because elements of the esoteric Torah are revealed through this format.

Have another look at the table. See those headers outside the lines that seem to be labels for the columns and rows (A-C, L, R)? They are in fact the map of the *terra incognita*. Each of them represents a concept, five in all, from the three rows and the two columns. The combination of the two days in each row produces a concept which transcends each individual day, a concept that lives "between the lines." Similarly, the three days in each column together produce a new concept. These five concepts are not found in the verse-by-verse reading; they are totally hidden. They form a "super-text" that can only be accessed by grasping the tabular format.

It is noteworthy that there are two distinct types of concepts in the super text, those formed by the rows (A-C) and those formed by the columns (L, R). The concepts in the columns are created by consecutive segments of text while the segments in the rows are nonconsecutive. This difference causes the two types to have different levels of visibility. In this specific example, the rows create an image of a three-tiered universe with the luminous transcendent above (A), the earthly immanent below (C) and a middle between them (B). The columns contain unmoving named entities in A and moving, unnamed entities in B. Each of the Torah's eighty-six Units was composed two-dimensionally, like the "world" created by divine speech in the days of creation. For reasons discussed later, I refer to this paradigm as "woven text."

The Torah and the Mishnah

The Mishnah, (the early third century compendium of Jewish Law), was composed according to the same two-dimensional woven paradigm and rules of organization as the Torah. The connection between the Torah and the Mishnah suggests that the art of constructing woven literary compositions may have been at least a component of the oral tradition traced back to Moses, as outlined in the Mishnah in Tractate Avot. For our purposes, the Mishnah is evidence that the knowledge of how to read and write woven texts continued into the early part of the third century. Since then, however, there appears to be no sign of the knowledge having been passed on. Without the guidance of previous generations, we are left to explore the terra incognita on our own.

The Torah is a Visual Document

As we learn how to read the esoteric Torah, we will need to be aware of conventions employed by its author. The most far-reaching of these is that the esoteric Torah was planned and composed as a document incorporating "visual rhetoric." This convention can be seen on all the multiple levels of planning, especially the chapter-like Units. These eighty-six Units which form the Torah are all two-dimensional and must be visualized as weaves in order to access the esoteric super-text. While it is not possible to know for sure why the Torah was constructed in this manner, the Torah was constructed to be read in two different ways by two different audiences: the many, who read it linearly without reference to the structure, and the few, who "see" the esoteric meanings embedded in the structure.

These two sets of readers are hinted at by the division of the people at Mt. Sinai. In Exodus 24:10, the people at the base of the mountain saw only smoke and lightening while the seventy elders ascended to the middle of the mountain where "they saw the deity of Israel; and there was under his feet the like of a paved work of sapphire stone, and the like of the very heaven for clearness." Could the author be telling us that the vision of the deity is based upon (under his feet) a clear view of structure, "like of a paved work of sapphire stone?" Whether or not this was the author's meaning, we now have the means to demonstrate precisely, "like of the very heaven for clearness," how the inner voice of the Torah, the terra incognita, is embedded in the woven Units of the Torah.

There is a strong hint in the Torah itself that the visualization of a text carries meaning not readily communicated orally. In Deuteronomy (26:4-8), Moses tells the Elders (the same term used for those who saw a vision of Elohim thirty-nine years earlier) to write out the "torah" ("teaching," probably Deuteronomy) on a monumental structure, the base of an altar. Moses describes the fully visualized text as "a clear explication." There is no other case in the Torah where a written text, or oral recitation, is described as "clear," not even the stone tablets. What is even more striking is the fact that the book of Deuteronomy also begins with an explication of "torah", an oral one: "took Moses upon him to expound this torah (Deut 1:5)." The same Hebrew word is used for "expound" and "explicate;" both the altar and Moses perform the same function. But there is a significant difference between them. Moses "took" upon himself to expound, in other words, he set upon expounding. There is no mention of the quality of Moses exposition. The text written on the altar, on the other hand, produced a "clear" explication. The written, visual, text was clearer than the original oral recitation from Moses' lips.

On a more granular level, the Torah employs what I call "visual" logic or rhetoric, as opposed to oral/aural rhetoric. One distinction between the two types of rhetoric determines where the "synthesis," the middle element between logical poles is placed. Speaking and most writing place the "synthesis" at the end. We must grasp the pair of opposites, like thesis and antithesis, as such to understand how the synthesis mediates between them. Thus, the order in normal oral/aural rhetoric is thesis, antithesis, synthesis.

This is not the order of the Torah, which employs visual rhetoric. In the Torah (as well as in the Mishnah), the conceptual middle, the synthesis, is found in the middle term of three, as if it is a visual bridge between the poles. In the example in Figure 1, the central pair of days B, is a conceptual middle between the heavenly above (A) and the earthly below (C). This specific convention contributed significantly to masking the esoteric Torah. Understanding the coherence, and inner meaning, of the triad is dependent on seeing the visual orientation that places the (conceptual) middle in the textual middle rather than at the end.

The Esoteric Torah Demands Creativity

"Reading" woven text is a creative endeavor. I have placed "reading" in curly quotes because the activity I am describing is not what we usually think of as reading (unless you are a poet or a code breaker). It demands much more of the reader, who is forced to discover meanings created by new contexts and juxtapositions.

In our example from the days of creation, the reader first must define the five new concepts revealed in the super-text. From that point, the "reading" is a function of the reader's creativity. The reader is challenged to integrate the new, derived, concepts with the literal meanings of each of the six days. The goal is to "see" the whole of the composition and the specific function of each segment of text in creating the picture. In that sense, reading the esoteric composition as a woven Torah is an exercise in personal creativity. The reader maintains a dialogue with the Torah while determining how the exoteric (linear) and esoteric (nonlinear) readings shed light on each other. The more clearly you integrate all the parts of the weave, the more clearly you will be able to understand each individual part. Conversely, to determine the full meaning of any individual part, it is necessary to understand its place in the context of the weave. The weave thus creates new levels of context and meaning.

Seeking M, the Author

The staggeringly meticulous structure of the Torah testifies that it was planned by a single individual, or at the most a closely-knit group of co-authors. For convenience and conformity with scholarly standards, I refer to the author as "M."[2] As extraordinary as M was as a technician, carrying out an enormously complex plan, M was also an author whose stories have captured the imagination of most of humanity. The success M has had in promulgating the exoteric Torah, pales when compared with the success M has had in hiding the esoteric Torah; it disappeared without a trace for nearly two millennia.

Why was a book written in a way that would entrance many people by its stories, while reserving for just a few, if any, its most securely hidden treasures? What secrets did M want to transmit to the very few while hiding them from the many? Answering that question is an ongoing endeavor. To better understand M, we must recognize that the Torah is a highly sophisticated composition. While the foundation of the discovery of the esoteric Torah is an awareness of its literary structure, there are other, non-structural, elements that hint at the sophistication of M's plan. Here is a brief example.

Eve and the Change of the Deity's Name

In the Garden of Eden, Eve ate from a forbidden tree and shared some with her partner as well. Consequently, they were expelled from the Garden. This story is well-known even to people with just a cursory knowledge of the Torah. How the story colors our understanding of the human condition is debated by the various biblical religions.

In this story, a normally overlooked, but most important detail is the name of the deity used in it. Throughout the Torah two main names are employed to indicate the deity, Elohim (usually "God") and YHWH (usually "the Lord.") The deity of the Garden narrative is called YHWH Elohim, a combination of the two names. The deity has a single

---

[2] Hendel and others do employ "M" referring to the collective variants of the Masoretic Text (commonly abbreviated "MT"). As I work solely with the MT and propose that an authored text can be identified despite textual variants, I use M to refer to the author, rather than the text. Purists may prefer M$_a$, with "a" for author; I think it unnecessarily cumbersome for our needs.

unified name in the Garden narrative, rather than the two distinct names found everywhere else. This integrated face of the deity disappears with the expulsion of people from the Garden. The deity never again appears in the Torah represented by the integrated name.

The Torah teaches about human nature through the Garden narrative, and it *also* teaches something about the deity and its connection to people. Human events have their parallel in the way the deity is perceived in the Torah. Human actions which lead to the expulsion from the Garden are paralleled by a change in the deity as perceived by the reader, from a state of revealed unity—YHWH Elohim—to a state in which deity presents different faces: YHWH *and* Elohim.

At no point does the Torah directly say anything about the change of divine names after the expulsion from the Garden. But that in no way implies that the change is an inconsequential matter; something about the way the reader is to perceive the deity has changed. If we limit ourselves to reading the explicit results of eating from the tree, we learn about the punishments meted out to the snake, Eve and her partner, but nothing about the change to take place in our perception of the Godhead. The method of reading the esoteric Torah focuses on the significant, implicit, information embedded in the Torah, such as the changes in the deity's names, as well as explicit meanings. If you follow the method, you will learn to give voice to the unspoken esoteric Torah, and it will empower you to be a partner in the discovery of the terra incognita in the Torah.

The Reader's Toolbox

The discovery of the principles of non-linear organization within the Torah has led to the development of two tools which can serve all who are interested in exploring the Torah as a woven composition. The first is the full structured text of the Torah, *The Woven Torah*, in English (JPS 1917 trans.) in the Appendix. In it, I have reconstructed the woven formats of all eighty-six Units according to the principles noted in the example in Figure 1. The full Hebrew text of *The Woven Torah* is available at chaver.com and academia.edu.

The second tool is a map (the subject of Part Four) of the arrangement of the Units of each of the five books. Just as each Unit has an identifiable non-linear structure, so too does each of the books.

I want to enable you—and encourage you—to use these tools to explore for yourself the terra incognita, the esoteric Torah, for its sake alone. Rabbi Meir (139-163?) stated that for one who studies the Torah for its own sake: "The Torah's secrets are revealed to him, and he becomes as an ever-increasing wellspring and as an unceasing river. He becomes modest, patient and forgiving of insults. The Torah uplifts him and makes him greater than all creations." [3] This book is about the activity of studying Torah according to a method lost for nearly two millennia. The method can transform its practitioner into an "ever-increasing wellspring." This is part of the function of the esoteric Torah. For the student of the Torah, it means undergoing a personal transformation, from being a consumer of commentaries, to becoming a creator of living tradition.

The Book

This book presents a new reading of the Torah, based on careful literary analysis, primarily of its structure. The reading is "esoteric" because it uncovers an arcane aspect of the Torah. The reader must grasp and compare large blocks of text in a visual manner to understand how they are organized. The result of this reading can be described as discovering a philosophical composition within the Torah. This composition uses the individual laws and events as threads to weave a tapestry. The images woven into the tapestry only begin to appear when the details of blocks of text have been integrated.

Learning the approach to this reading is like learning a new language. It has a vocabulary and a grammar. To learn the grammar, it is necessary to break the pattern of linear reading, because the semantic units that fit together are not necessarily consecutive.

The vocabulary consists of all the possible semantic components in the Torah, such as the days of creation, the plagues in Egypt, and the individual laws. They range in size from individual letters and words to whole books. The definition of the parts that are more than single words and less than whole books is the most important and most difficult step.

[3] Mishnah, Mesecet Avot 6:1

The grammar is the set of rules that explain how the semantic parts fit together, such as the three sets of three plagues in Egypt.

Throughout the decades that I have tried to understand the literary structure of the Torah, I have often been asked (mostly by my wife, and recently by my editor) what meaning I expect to derive from understanding structure. This book should make very clear why it is necessary to read the Torah according to its formal composition: because it reveals hidden wisdom. Rather than just giving you the tools to access the esoteric Torah (Parts II-IV), I will show how these tools can be used to explain the appearance of the deity under different names (Parts I and V). The five Parts of this book are organized in an envelope structure: Parts I and V relate to each other while also "enclosing" Parts II-IV. In Part One we see that Elohim and YHWH seem to be different characters. Parts II, III, and IV provide the means to clarify this difference. Part Five employs the tools developed in Parts II, III, and IV to explain why Elohim and YHWH are presented as different characters. The solution leads to seeing the big-picture story of the Torah: the holy YHWH is revealed in the mundane world created by Elohim.

Part One

The book of Genesis was constructed to distinguish between Elohim and YHWH by means of the patriarchal stories. For thousands of years these stories have fascinated young and old, Jew and gentile, you and me. Applying Kristol's words from above, the prologue of the Torah, Genesis 1:1-11:9, contains "a popular (exoteric) teaching accessible to all, and a secret or esoteric teaching that reveals itself only after careful and thoughtful study." The *exoteric* reading contains fable-like stories about the beginnings of the world of people, the six-day creation, the Garden of Eden, the Flood, and the Tower of Babel. The "popular" teachings relate to each of these stories as virtually independent of each other. The *esoteric* reading integrates the details of all four stories to paint a single coherent picture.

This picture has two halves, divine and human. The divine half is made up of the actions, speeches, and names, of the deity. The human half is made up of the actions, speeches, and names, of people. As you might guess from my well-balanced sentences, the two halves of the picture reflect each other. For example, the creation of Eve through separation is reflected in the separation of YHWH from Elohim.

"Careful and thoughtful study" leads to the realization that an esoteric goal of this prologue is to distinguish between Elohim and YHWH as characters in the Torah. We finish Part One with a question, *why did M need two divine characters in the narrative?*

Part Two

This is where we begin to discover the esoteric Torah, hidden for millennia. M, the author of the Torah, left a faint trail of crumbs, just enough to verify a discovery, leading to the Decalogue. The ten Words (commandments) are presented as a divine speech inscribed by the divine hand on divine tablets. They contain the secret of how a written text can reflect divine, superhuman, speech, the esoteric Torah. The secret is that divine speech can be represented by woven text.

Our first task is to define how M wanted the Decalogue divided into ten parts. We settle on the division in Torah scrolls. The second decision is to see how they were arranged on the tablets. We take Exodus 32:15 to describe that the Words (commands) were written *alternately* on the two tablets so that the odd-numbered were on one and the evens on the other.

This is the key discovery that makes possible the identification of the esoteric Decalogue, as well as the whole esoteric Torah. The tablets form a weave. The stone tablets are like warp threads set on the loom. The ten Words are then woven across the two tablets in five threads of two Words each. Each pair is an element of a composition that reveals itself when the arrangement of the Words on the tablets is accurately reproduced.

The two narratives regarding the giving of two sets of tablets demonstrate how the Decalogue was created to be seen differently by two different audiences. The people never saw the first tablets whole, and consequently had no knowledge of the secret esoteric arrangement, because Moses smashed the tablets as he entered the camp. The exoteric view sees the Decalogue as a fractured collection of laws. The coherent, intact, second set of tablets was esoteric, intended for Moses' eyes alone.

Part Three

Part Three builds upon the theory that the esoteric, woven Decalogue is the paradigm of the Torah's Units, the pattern according to which they were constructed. We first develop the tools needed to read the esoteric Torah and learn the general characteristics of the Torah's Units. We begin by explaining the labeling conventions of the woven Units as they appear in *The Woven Torah*, including a color code. Here we see the mechanics of the crucial step that transforms the exoteric linear reading into the esoteric woven reading.

An examination of examples of woven Units to clarify their characteristics—and how they are identified—adds revelatory value of the woven format. Two of the sample Units are of special interest for our study of the names, the creation Unit, Genesis I, and the Unit containing the signs (plagues) in Egypt, Exodus III. Elohim creates in distinct days, and YHWH brings about events which overturn elements of Elohim's creation, e.g., water turns to blood.

Comparing the structures of the two Units allows us to pinpoint the relationship between Elohim's acts of creation and YHWH's signs of "decreation." The decreation, YHWH's symbolic negation of the days of creation through his signs, announces the arrival of YHWH on the stage of the history of nations. By negating elements of the natural world, as it were, YHWH is revealed as supernatural.

Part Four

M did not limit the employment of weave-like organization to the level of the eighty-six woven Units. The individual Units associate in sets of Units which form higher order weaves. The patterns created by these higher-order structures establish the unique forms of all five books. In Part Four we will observe the rules, the glue, which hold the Units in sets, as well as connecting the sets to each other. We will see that it is then possible to map each book two-dimensionally, just as we map each Unit.

In Part Four we will see the visual orientation of the Torah is clearly reflected in the formats of some of its books. Leviticus is a center point: it is constructed to present the reader with the experience of the High Priest on Yom Kippur, The Day of Atonement. The reader passes through sections of Leviticus which were composed to parallel sections of the tabernacle compound. As you read, you pass through the courtyard, the holy place, and the holy of holies to reach the *imitatio Deus* of "Be holy for I am holy" in 19:1. This is followed by three sections which retrace the path going outwards and back to the community in the courtyard with an outlook to the future in the land. The association of the reader with the High Priest is yet another sign that this was to be an esoteric reading.

We will focus on Genesis as our sample book and observe in detail how it was constructed and how its structure is represented in the map in Figure 2. We will see that the whole is to be envisioned as a weave, having meaning in its columns as well as in its three rows.

Figure 2. A Structural Map of Genesis

	A		B	C	D	E	F
1	I (1:1-2:3)		V (11:10-13:4)	VI (13:5-14:24)	XI (25:12-34)	XII (26:1-33)	XVII (36:1-41:45)
2	II (2:4-4:26)	IV (11:1-9)	VII (15:1-17:27)	VIII (18:1-19:38)	XIII (26:34-28:9)	XIV (28:10-32:3)	XVIII (41:46-47:26)
3	III (5:1-10:32)		IX (20:1-22:19)	X (22:20-25:11)	XV (32:4-33:16)	XVI (33:17-35:29)	XIX (47:27-50:26)

Part Five

Part Five offers a solution to the Elohim/YHWH distinction based on the overview presented by the map of Genesis. We see that the distinctions between the two names, or characters, is the single integrating element throughout the book. By mapping the appearances of Elohim and YHWH against the map of literary Units, we discover the foundational distinction between them. We see Genesis was fashioned to establish Elohim as the revelation of the immanence of the deity and YHWH as the transcendence. We conclude that the Torah presents the revelation of the transcendent, YHWH, in the realm of the immanent, Elohim.

Bottom line: The two ways of reading the Torah produce two different perspectives on Genesis. The traditional chronological reading leads to an understanding of Genesis as a collection of histories of the patriarchs and their relationships with deity. The structural reading shifts the focus from below to above, from people to deity. The structure leads to the understanding that Genesis was composed to reveal the deity's work in the world, in the creation of the immanent, and in the revelation of the transcendent, characterized in Elohim and YHWH. The histories of the patriarchs are the means for presenting the stories of Elohim and YHWH. Structure is theology.

The Appendix

In many respects, the appendix is the most important part of the book. It contains the full color-coded text of the woven Torah, divided into its eighty-six Units. The purpose of the body of *Before Chapter and Verse* is to enable you to work with the woven text in the appendix. On the recommendation of Robert Alter, I have used the Jewish Publication Society's 1917 translation.

A Note About Names

Since we will be exploring the names Elohim (Elohim) and YHWH (YHWH) intensively, it will be beneficial to set some ground rules about how we use them. The following reading might give the impression they are different entities entirely. The Torah also gives dual names to human characters, such as: Abram and Abraham; Jacob and Israel, Jethro and Reuel. Just as Jacob and Israel are the same person, so too are Elohim and YHWH the same deity. This is supported by the fact they never interact. Even so, the Torah does make important distinctions between them, such as the fact Elohim produced the first set of stone tablets by himself, while YHWH partnered with Moses to produce the second set; YHWH partnered with Eve in producing Cain, while Elohim presented her with Seth. For clarity in the discussion, I will not translate the names but will continue to use Elohim and YHWH. To avoid confusion, I will use "deity" as the generic, rather than "God."

We are reading the Torah as a work of literature and must make an important distinction between the ways the names are used throughout the Torah. The distinction is between whether the deity is onstage or off. In the seven-day creation narrative Elohim is completely onstage, in the foreground. On the other hand, when the snake mentions Elohim to Eve, he is offstage. Usually, when a character mentions deity, the deity is offstage; but when the narrator mentions deity, he is onstage. We can learn about the differences between Elohim and YHWH from the other characters as well as directly from the narrator. But we only have a direct view of divine actions when the deity is on the stage. At other times we see him through the eyes of a character.

Part One
The Problem to be Solved by Reading the Woven Torah: Elohim and YHWH

The prolog of Genesis (1:1-11:9) introduces multiple divine names: two individual names, Elohim and YHWH, and a combined name YHWH Elohim. Each name is connected to a line of people: Elohim is connected to "the sons of Elohim;" YHWH is connected to Cain; YHWH and Elohim are both connected to Seth, whose father was Elohim's Adam, and mother was YHWH Elohim's Eve. To fully appreciate the significance of these textual phenomena, one must study the woven Torah.

Chapter 1. Introducing the Players

The Divine Names and the Plan of the Torah

One of the central concerns of the Torah is to show how YHWH, deity of Israel, is revealed in the world created by Elohim. This revelation is directed at repairing a rupture that occurred with the expulsion of people from Eden. Just as Eden conveys an image of a time/place when/where people had an intimate relationship with deity, the Eden experience also signals a time/place when/where the names YHWH (the Lord) and Elohim (God) appear united. With the expulsion from Eden, the names are separated. The rest of the Torah can be read as a plan to reconcile the divine names through the establishment of a holy state in Canaan.

Starting at Genesis 2:4, the Garden of Eden narrative is the only place in the Torah where the two names, YHWH and Elohim, appear united to represent a single character. The deity who formed the Garden and interacts with his creatures in the Garden is called YHWH Elohim, often translated "the Lord God." The result of the human Garden-of-Eden experience—and the separation from it—is paralleled by a change in the divine name; the deity never again appears as YHWH Elohim. Each half of the Edenic name is used to represent a divine character in the narrative. (It may be easier for some to speak of the names as representing "aspects" of the deity, but from the literary perspective the names represent characters.)

- Elohim represents the Godly aspects of the mundane, immanent, experienced world. These can be expressed in nature, science, law, in short, day-to-day life in the world created in six days.

- YHWH is associated with holiness, as in, "You shall be holy, for I YHWH your Elohim am holy (Lev 19:1)." He seeks to create a holy people (Exod 19:6) who can facilitate the revelation of holiness in the mundane world. The command to be holy opens Leviticus 19, the central Unit of the Torah in my reading, a Unit formatted to simulate the ark of the covenant.[4]

The Israelites are redeemed from slavery to become the living revelation of YHWH's holiness in the mundane realm of Elohim. The perfection of the nation, instituted and maintained by YHWH's laws, reveals YHWH to the world. Elohim-the-mundane and YHWH-the-holy are reunited with the simultaneous revelation of the holy, through Israel, within the world. The book of Genesis sets the stage for this reconnection by *distinguishing between Elohim and YHWH*. Jacob's oath after the ladder dream foreshadows the integration of the transcendent YHWH with the immanent Elohim: "YHWH will become Elohim for me (Gen 28:21)."

Elohim, YHWH, and YHWH Elohim

All of Genesis should be read as an introduction to the central story of the Torah, the development of the Israelite nation as the vehicle for divine revelation. Within this introduction, chapters 1:1-11:9 are a prologue to the central theme of Genesis, the histories of the fathers of the nation, and deity's connections with them. Within the prologue are four well defined Units:

- I (1:1-2:3) the Creation
- II (2:4-4:26) the Garden and history of Cain
- III (5:1-10:32) the Flood
- IV (11:1-11:9) the Tower of Babel

These four Units introduce us to Elohim and YHWH. In Unit I, only Elohim appears, to create all in six days; in IV, YHWH alone confuses the languages and disperses peoples. In II and III both names are used. We begin our exploration of these names in the following paragraphs. But later we see that we must incorporate the two names used for the first people in the analysis, Adam, created on day six by Elohim, and HaAdam fashioned by YHWH Elohim to work in the Garden of Eden. (The Hebrew "Ha" is the definite article, thus YHWH Elohim formed "the Adam.")

While various names are applied to "deity" in the Torah, the two principal names are Elohim and YHWH. Elohim is the name of the creator in the first chapter of Genesis; YHWH is best known as the name of the national deity of Israel. "Elohim" is a plural form in Hebrew but normally appears with a verb in the singular. It is also used as a generic in the plural, especially when referring to idolatry, "other gods (Elohim)." YHWH, which is related to the verb "to be" in Hebrew, is used only as a proper name. Both these names are used extensively in

Genesis. From Exodus on, the appearance of Elohim in an active role is infrequent; most of the narrative speaks of YHWH. There are various approaches and theories regarding the distinction between the names and the way they are used.

Some scholars are comfortable saying the names are essentially interchangeable. They might argue: "Since the Torah is the source of monotheism, the names must both refer to the same entity. The difference is probably just stylistic." While many biblical scholars may agree with the theology of this position, (if not the circular reasoning), the different names still disturb them formally. They propose the Torah was redacted from several older documents that used different names for the same deity. We will read the Torah as a highly polished composition that can be read in two ways, exoterically, as it has been for millennia, and esoterically, based on the discoveries to be detailed in this volume. Reading the Torah as a coherent composition leads to accepting the names as representing two different characters in the narrative.

Together, Units I-IV present the process whereby YHWH, who is absent from the Unit I creation, takes a central role in the narrative. This name first appears in Unit II (2:4): "These are the generations of the heaven and of the earth when they were created, in the day that YHWH Elohim made earth and heaven." YHWH is introduced in a name which includes the name Elohim, the creator in Unit I. This compound name appears in the opening verse of the Unit, telling us we are to hear a story about the "generations" of heaven and earth. The verse introduces us to a narrative which has two components, heaven, and earth. This introductory pair of terms is followed by narratives which focus on pairings: the first human couple, HaAdam and Eve, the pair of trees in the garden of Eden, Cain and Abel. (I explain the difference between Adam and HaAdam below.) YHWH appears for the first time as an actor independent of Elohim after the expulsion from the Garden.

The Separation of YHWH and Elohim

The split between YHWH and Elohim takes place precisely when HaAdam and Eve are banished from the Garden. The same action that changed the future of humanity also changed the future of the deity as presented in the Torah. In the Edenic state the two names are connected. In the non-Edenic state, they are separated. Eating from the tree of knowledge led to changes in both people and the name of deity.

Another instance of this parallel is the formation of Eve as a reflection of the appearance and separation of YHWH. We are first told about Elohim the creator (Unit I) and then see YHWH attached to Elohim (Unit II: 2:4-3:24). Then YHWH is separated from Elohim to become an independent name (Unit II: 4:1ff). This progression parallels the separation of Eve from HaAdam. The offspring of this specific parallel between heaven and earth is Cain, whose birth Eve describes thusly: "I have got me a man with YHWH (4:1)." The two who were separated from a partner, YHWH and Eve, are connected to each other through Cain. And further, the birth of Seth provides the first opportunity to compare YHWH and Elohim post Eden.

Eve—not the narrator—is the first to mention both YHWH and Elohim after Eden. Both mentions refer to the birth of a son. So, we see that Eve knows the difference between divine characters after the expulsion from the Garden. Eve partners with YHWH in delivering Cain. Regarding the birth of Seth, she says: "Elohim has granted me other seed in place of Abel, for Cain has killed him." The birth of Seth is the function of Elohim's "grant." YHWH and Eve partnered, but Elohim granted a son to Eve. From the perspective of the deity, YHWH is intimately associated with Eve, while Elohim lacks a personal relationship with her.

Elohim is the independent creator in Unit I while YHWH first appears connected to Elohim in the Garden narrative. This distinction also holds in the bigger picture, when comparing Units I and IV. Elohim creates at a distance in I through speech, while in IV YHWH "comes down" to see what people are up to and then to prevent them from communicating with each other.

The major distinctions are also displayed in the flood narrative. They are so sharp there that the flood story seems to be primarily a vehicle for clearly presenting YHWH and Elohim as wholly different characters. For example, YHWH sends down rain from above while Elohim brings up water from below. To prepare for the further investigation of divine names, we must first investigate the humans introduced before the flood: Adam and HaAdam, Eve, Cain, Abel and Seth. The story of these people is the window to the story of YHWH and Elohim.

In Unit I, Elohim creates "Adam" while YHWH Elohim forms "HaAdam" in Unit II. The ways they are brought into being as "first people" are quite different. "And Elohim created Adam in his own image, in the image of Elohim created he him; male and female created he them (1:27)." The word "created" is repeated three times. No material is mentioned. Adam is created from nothing. Compare this with "Then YHWH Elohim formed HaAdam of the dust of the ground and breathed into his nostrils the breath of life (2:7)."

Adam was directly created by Elohim without any means or material, but YHWH Elohim combines two components: dust of the ground and divine breath of life, to *form* HaAdam. Like YHWH Elohim who formed him, HaAdam is a compound entity. While this similarity goes unnoted by the narrator, the similarity between Elohim and Adam is noted both in Unit I and later in Unit III, Adam was created "in the image of Elohim." HaAdam is male and has no mate until Eve is made from him. Adam is created male and female. Adam is Elohim's final creation, created after all other creatures, but YHWH Elohim formed all the other creatures while searching for a mate, "a help meet for him," for HaAdam.

> And YHWH Elohim said: 'It is not good that HaAdam should be alone; I will make him a help meet for him.' And out of the ground YHWH Elohim formed every beast of the field, and every fowl of the air; and brought them unto HaAdam to see what he would call them; and whatsoever HaAdam would call every living creature, that was to be the name thereof. And HaAdam gave names to all cattle, and to the fowl of the air, and to every beast of the field; but for Adam there was not found a help meet for him. And YHWH Elohim caused a deep sleep to fall upon HaAdam, and he slept; and he took one of his ribs, and closed up the place with flesh instead thereof. And the rib, which YHWH Elohim had taken from HaAdam, made he a woman, and brought her unto HaAdam. (Gen. 2:18-22)

The significance of the other creatures being potential life partners for HaAdam is expanded by comparison with Elohim's blessing to the newly created Adam: "'Be fruitful, and multiply, and replenish the earth, and subdue it; and have dominion over the fish of the sea, and over the fowl of the air, and over every living thing that creepeth upon the earth (1:28)." Adam is to "have dominion" over the creatures while HaAdam is to see them as potential partners, equals. Adam was created as a gamekeeper gatherer and HaAdam as a farmer: "And YHWH Elohim took HaAdam and put him into the Garden of Eden to dress it and to keep it (2:15)." Figure 3 summarizes the differences between Adam and HaAdam.

Figure 3. Distinctions between Adam and HaAdam

Distinguishing Characteristics	Unit I Elohim *creates* "Adam"	Unit II YHWH Elohim *forms* "HaAdam"
Name	Adam is not a proper name, but rather the name of the class "humanity."	HaAdam is a single individual whose name includes the Hebrew definite article "*ha*" "*the* Man"
Essential nature	"And Elohim created Adam in his own image, in the image of Elohim created he him; male and female created he them (1:27)."	"Then YHWH Elohim formed HaAdam of the dust of the ground, and breathed into his nostrils the breath of life (2:7)."
Comparison with deity	Adam was created in the image of Elohim	HaAdam is a compound entity like YHWH Elohim who formed him
Mate	Adam is created male and female.	HaAdam is male and has no mate until Eve is made from him.
Place in order of creation vis-à-vis animals	Adam is Elohim's final creation, created after all other creatures.	YHWH Elohim formed all the other creatures while searching for a mate, a "help meet" for HaAdam
Relationship with earth	Commanded to conquer the land	Formed to serve the soil
Relationship to other creatures	Adam is to "have dominion" over the creatures	HaAdam is to see them as potential partners, equals
Profession	Adam was created as a gamekeeper and gatherer	HaAdam was a farmer
Central Descendant	Seth	Cain

The Descendants of Adam and HaAdam

We have established that M distinguishes between Elohim creating Adam and YHWH Elohim forming HaAdam. Each divine name is associated with differently named people. We now examine the births of the children of Adam and HaAdam to see what this might tell us about the distinctions between the divine names. Four references are relevant to this investigation:

- 4:1 And HaAdam knew Eve his wife; and she conceived and bore Cain and said: 'I have gotten a man with the help of YHWH.'
- 4:2 And again she bore his brother Abel.
- 4:25 And Adam knew his wife again; and she bore a son, and called his name Seth: 'for Elohim hath appointed me another seed instead of Abel; for Cain slew him.'
- 5:1-3 This is the book of the generations of Adam. In the day that Elohim created Adam,

in the likeness of Elohim made he him; male and female created he them, and blessed them, and called their name Adam, in the day when they were created. And Adam lived a hundred and thirty years, and begot a son in his own likeness, after his image; and called his name Seth.

Had we not distinguished between Adam and HaAdam, this investigation would be irrelevant. But having made the distinction, we cannot but notice that both are presented as fathering children. Verse 4:1 tells us that HaAdam fathered Cain. Eve names Cain and attributes his birth to "the help of YHWH." Verse 4:25 informs us that Adam fathered Seth. Here too Eve responds to the birth by naming her son and explaining the name by relating it to Elohim, "for Elohim hath appointed me another seed instead of Abel." HaAdam has a son associated with YHWH, Cain, and Adam has a son associated with Elohim, Seth. Lest there be any suspicion of a corruption in the text, 5:1-3 makes it clear that Elohim created Adam who fathered Seth. But there is a problem. In 4:25 we hear "Adam knew his wife again" and she gave birth to Seth. Why are we told "again?" There is no previous mention of Adam knowing his wife.

The solution, (thanks to Rabbi Brett Kopin), is that Eve was the "wife" of both Adam and HaAdam. But as scandalous as this sounds, the idea is supported by further details. The evidence is accessible from the simple meanings of the text, but building the case takes a bit of sleuthing.

Eve links Seth's birth with the death of Abel. What do we know about Abel's conception? "And again, she bore his brother Abel (4:2)." Nothing. There is no declaration of Abel's paternity, nor a naming, nor a reference to deity. The fact that Abel is called Cain's brother does not exclude the possibility that they have different fathers. Abel's conception, like the meaning of his Hebrew name, "vapor," "emptiness," is totally transparent. It seems likely M created the empty blank for the reader to fill in. Let us say that Adam, created by Elohim, fathered Abel. When "Adam *again* knew his wife," Eve, Elohim provides them a son to replace Abel who was killed by Cain, who was aligned with YHWH. Abel, the shepherd, was thus fathered by Adam, the gamekeeper gatherer, created by Elohim. Cain, the farmer, was fathered by HaAdam, the farmer formed by YHWH Elohim.

HaAdam knew what he was talking about when he named his wife Eve (Heb *Hava*, life), "And HaAdam called his wife's name Eve, because she was the mother of all living (3:20)." Eve was the mother of all: Cain, Abel, and Seth. Adam was the father of Abel and Seth, HaAdam was the father of Cain.

The narrative is coherent, albeit elusive. Once they are identified, the parts fit together to present a whole picture. M presents two lines of people associated with the two divine names: 1) Elohim, Adam and Seth; 2) YHWH, HaAdam and Cain. The two lines are connected through Eve, described by HaAdam as the mother of all. The existence of two lines of people associated with two divine characters prepares us to see distinctions between the divine names reflected through the lines of people. Two lines of people having a single mother, each associated with a different divine name, hints at the centrality of Eve for the future reintegration of the divine names. In the following chapter we explore how that reintegration is to be facilitated

Chapter 2. The Development of YHWH

Three Creations and Three Lines of People

Inconsistencies in distinguishing between the traditional reading of the Torah and the new, esoteric, reading we are exploring are fundamental to our understanding. In Chapter One we focused on the implications of reading Units I (1:1-2:3) and II (2:4-4:26) as two separate narratives. The implications include seeing Adam and HaAdam as different, as well as Elohim, who created Adam, as different from YHWH Elohim who formed HaAdam. Although only Elohim is reported to have created heaven and earth, YHWH Elohim's forming HaAdam and other creatures is effectively an additional creation, producing a second source of people in the narrative. The plot thickened with the appearance of the next generation, Cain, Abel, and Seth. Eve gave birth to all three, while Adam fathered Abel and Seth, and HaAdam fathered only Cain. These points bear repeating because they seem so inconsistent with the way these narratives are usually read.

We will now integrate these points into a coherent view of Units I-IV, the prologue of Genesis. The stories which appear as independent elements in these Units, (the creation, the Garden of Eden, the flood, Babel), are deceptive. They are much more closely connected than appears on the surface. The first three—from the creation to the flood—disguise a cohesive plan in which each story is crafted to play a specific part, while the fourth, the Babel narrative, reflects the three previous Units within it, as a form of summary. Each of the first three contributes to a unifying theme, the parallel literary development of deity and people through three types of creation.

M has indicated Units I-III should be read together as *a block of creation Units* by inserting the Hebrew root *b.r.a.*, "create," into the first verse of each Unit.

- I. "In the beginning Elohim *created* the heaven and the earth (1:1)"

- II. "These are the generations of the heaven and of the earth when they were *created* (2:4)"

- III. "This is the book of the generations of Adam. In the day that Elohim *created* Adam (5:1)"

To reveal M's plan, we will gather details from each of the Units. The opening verses create a three-part figure with a conceptual middle: Unit I) divine perspective; Unit III) human perspective; Unit II) the interaction between heaven and earth, divine and human. Note the need to deconstruct M's visual order with the conceptual middle in the middle (I, II, III) into oral order (I, thesis; III, antithesis; II, synthesis. (See the discussion of visual rhetoric in the Introduction). While the Units differ, each of the three establishes a new line of people. In Unit I (the first creation) Elohim creates Adam, male and female, who give rise to "the sons of Elohim (Gen 6:1)." In Unit II (the second creation) YHWH Elohim forms HaAdam and Eve who are Cain's parents. (Later, just before the flood, YHWH states that he formed HaAdam.) Cain becomes the patriarch of the line of HaAdam and Eve. In Unit III (the third creation), Elohim and YHWH independently and in unison create again. They both "wipe out" the lines of people that can be traced directly back to each of them, the sons of Elohim and the descendants of Cain. The world will be peopled by a third line, one which links to both names, Elohim and YHWH, through Seth's parents, Adam (not HaAdam) and Eve. Figure 4's flow chart summarizes how the three creation Units lead us to see ourselves as "hybrids," integrating the two divine sources, and consequently, reflecting the unrevealed source of the two divine names.

Figure 4. The Three-Creations Flow Chart

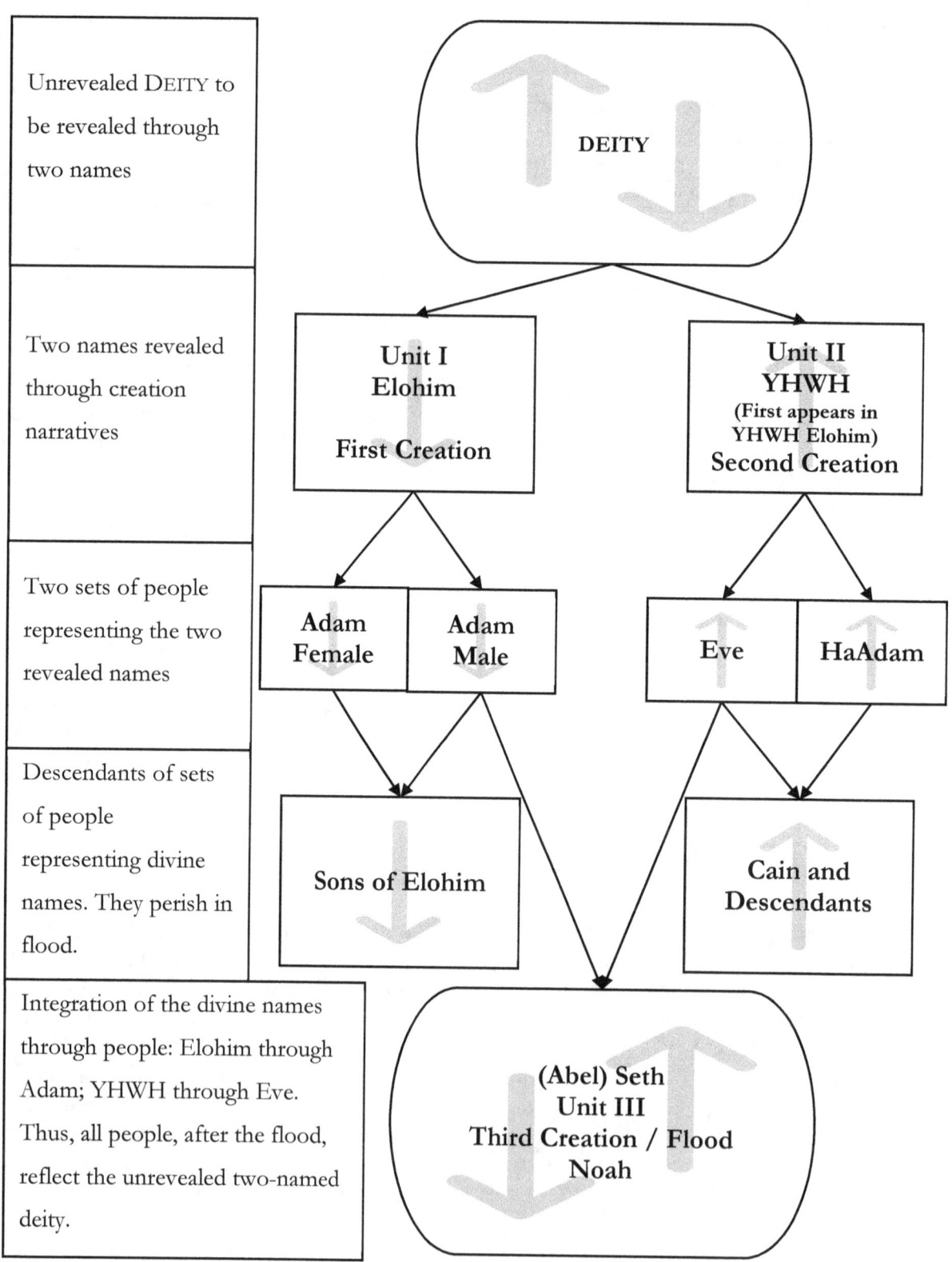

Unrevealed DEITY to be revealed through two names

Two names revealed through creation narratives

Two sets of people representing the two revealed names

Descendants of sets of people representing divine names. They perish in flood.

Integration of the divine names through people: Elohim through Adam; YHWH through Eve. Thus, all people, after the flood, reflect the unrevealed two-named deity.

DEITY

Unit I
Elohim

First Creation

Unit II
YHWH
(First appears in YHWH Elohim)
Second Creation

Adam Female | Adam Male

Eve | HaAdam

Sons of Elohim

Cain and Descendants

(Abel) Seth
Unit III
Third Creation / Flood
Noah

Figure 4 is visual evidence of a plan. The elegant integration of the three Units was planned. We can see a picture that stretches into the future when the world will be peopled solely by the descendants of Seth, people who trace their origins to both Elohim through their father Adam and YHWH through their mother Eve. We now look more closely at how M planned Units I-III as an integrated block.

Unit I (Genesis 1:1-2:3): YHWH in Potential

Even though YHWH does not appear in Unit I, an element of the narrative is linked to a future revelation. The last act attributed to Elohim in the creation narrative in Gen 2:3, "And Elohim blessed the seventh day, and *hallowed* it," is a foreshadowing of what is to become a central theme. Holiness is YHWH's most clearly revealed characteristic, "Ye shall be holy; for holy am I YHWH your Elohim (Lev 19:2)." And yet, the Hebrew root for the verb "to hallow" and the noun "holy," *k'dosh*, is never again used in the book of Genesis. The next time *k'dosh* appears is at the burning bush when Elohim tells Moses "Put off thy shoes from off thy feet, for the place whereon thou standest is *holy* ground (Exod 3:5)." Shortly thereafter, in the "Song of the Sea," M applies *holy* to YHWH for the first time, "Who is like unto thee, YHWH, among the mighty? who is like unto thee, *glorious in holiness* (Exod 15:11)." YHWH is revealed as holy when the sea divides. This is just the first of many places where YHWH is described, or describes himself, as holy.

The arrangement of the six days in two sets can also be seen as foreshadowing the coming division between Elohim and YHWH. The first three days contain single, named creations: light (day), the divider (sky), and the dry land (earth). The next three contain categories of unnamed creations: heavenly lights, water and air animals, land animals. The distinction between the two sets of days points to an underlying "divine dyad," such as "one and many," a metaphysical concept so fundamental that it underlies all of creation. The compound name YHWH Elohim may be the next iteration of this dyad.

Unit II (2:4-4:26): Parallels between YHWH and Eve

Since M has directed us to examine the development of heaven and earth, "the generations of heaven and earth," we have no choice but to employ terms regarding deity which may not normally be consistent with belief in a single, omniscient, creator deity.

In Unit II, things previously hidden and hinted at are now delineated through two parallel developments. First, the hidden, two-fold nature of deity captured in the "divine dyad" (one-and-many) in Unit I, is revealed in II by the introduction of YHWH to form a two-fold name, YHWH Elohim. Second, the amorphous gender dyad from I, "male and female," is established through detailing the formation of HaAdam (the man) and then by the formation of his woman. The parallel elaboration of deity and people can be observed by focusing on the similarities between Eve and YHWH. The most obvious similarity between YHWH and Eve is found in their names. The Hebrew forms are closely related. "YHWH" is based on the verb "to be" (*hayah*) and Eve (Chava in Hebrew) on the verb "to live," (*chayah*). Both names are proper names as opposed to the generic applied to each of their partners. Elohim is a generic plural form used for "Gods" as well for "Elohim," the single creator. Adam means "man" as well as "humanity," and HaAdam "the (individual) man." The distinction between the named and the generic may be associated with the underlying dyad of Unit I. The creations of the first three days are all singular and named, indicating an affinity to YHWH and Eve. The creations of days four to six are all plural and generic, e. g., "birds." They have an affinity to the words "Elohim," and "Adam."

Another, more complex, similarity between YHWH and Eve is based on the similar stages of their manifestation. Both Eve and YHWH are combined with characters who preceded them in the narrative. Elohim creates heaven and earth before the name YHWH Elohim appears. HaAdam names all the creatures before Eve is formed from him. Both YHWH and Eve appear from nowhere associated with characters who have already been established on M's stage. Eve's attachment to HaAdam does not end with the removal of his rib.

They were still attached, "one flesh…and were not ashamed (Gen 2:24–25)."

At this time (Unit II) YHWH and Elohim are still connected. Both pairs separate as a result of Eve and HaAdam eating the fruit and experiencing the underlying duality of reality, the separation of the self from the other, captured in the merism "knowledge of good and bad." For the human pair, their distinction one from the other was mediated by the skin in which each was robed. For the deity, the parallel is the separation of YHWH from Elohim, to be, effectively, two distinct characters in the narrative. Separation, especially in the format of redemption, will be one of YHWH's leading activities, i.e., redeeming Israel from Egypt. The birth of a new nation separated from Egypt's side, as it were, clearly resonates with the appearance of Eve separated from HaAdam and, consequently, YHWH from Elohim. The special relationship between YHWH and Eve leads directly, as we shall see, to the first events in which YHWH appears independently outside the Garden.

Drawing the parallel between Eve and YHWH implies something about M's artfulness. If we have read the first Units correctly, M is nudging us to seek parallels between the earthly and heavenly narratives. Eve and YHWH are revealed as characters in parallel ways. Ultimately, eating the fruit of the Tree separates HaAdam and Eve from Eden as well as separating YHWH from Elohim.

Who is YHWH?

Now that YHWH and Elohim have been separated, we can begin to see how they differ. Apparently, since we know so much about Elohim from the first Unit, the narrative now focuses on YHWH. M provides us with three different views of YHWH: Eve's, Cain and Abel's, and the narrator's. This is where the esoteric reading of the Torah begins to distinguish, substantially, between YHWH and Elohim.

- For Eve YHWH is a partner in reproduction, substantiating our analyses above of a special relationship between them. "And HaAdam knew Eve his wife; and she conceived and bore Cain, and said: 'I have gotten a man with the help of YHWH.'" (4:1)

- For Cain and Abel, YHWH is the deity to whom to bring offerings. "And again she bore his brother Abel. And Abel was a keeper of sheep, but Cain was a tiller of the ground. And in process of time it came to pass, that Cain brought of the fruit of the ground an offering unto YHWH. And Abel, he also brought of the firstlings of his flock and of the fat thereof. And YHWH had respect unto Abel and to his offering; but unto Cain and to his offering He had not respect. And Cain was very wroth, and his countenance fell. (4:3-5)

- Finally, the narrator introduces YHWH as the deity of morality by having him warn Cain "if thou doest not well, sin coucheth at the door; and unto thee is its desire, but thou mayest rule over it (4:7)."

None of these characteristics have previously been applied to Elohim. However, actions of YHWH Elohim can be seen as precursors to the development of YHWH as a character. YHWH Elohim's endeavor to find a mate for HaAdam resonates with YHWH partnering with Eve to produce Cain. The prohibition to eat from the Tree of Knowledge, and the punishment for violating it, present YHWH Elohim as a deity demanding fealty. Knowledge of good and bad, the foundation of morality and judgement, exits only in potential for YHWH Elohim in Eden, but outside is a reality indicated by YHWH warning Cain "sin coucheth at the door." We expand the point that YHWH Elohim is the precursor of YHWH when examining Unit III. (Logically, since we have learned about Elohim from Unit I, any difference between Elohim and YHWH Elohim should be attributed to the addition of YHWH.) But first we examine the section of II clearly meant to prepare us for III.

Cain and Seth

And Cain knew his wife; and she conceived, and bore Enoch; and he builded a city, and called the name of the city after the name of his son Enoch. And unto Enoch was born Irad; and Irad begot Mehujael; and Mehujael begot Methushael; and Methushael begot Lamech. And Lamech took unto him two wives;

the name of one was Adah, and the name of the other Zillah. And Adah bore Jabal; he was the father of such as dwell in tents and have cattle. And his brother's name was Jubal; he was the father of all such as handle the harp and pipe. And Zillah, she also bore Tubal-cain, the forger of every cutting instrument of brass and iron; and the sister of Tubal-cain was Naamah. And Lamech said unto his wives: Adah and Zillah, hear my voice; ye wives of Lamech, hearken unto my speech; for I have slain a man for wounding me, and a young man for bruising me; If Cain shall be avenged sevenfold, truly Lamech seventy and sevenfold.

And Adam knew his wife again; and she bore a son, and called his name Seth: 'for Elohim hath appointed me another seed instead of Abel; for Cain slew him.' And to Seth, to him also there was born a son; and he called his name Enosh; then began the use of the name YHWH. (Gen 4:17-26)

Unit II ends with two segments reporting births, the full line of Cain in one, and Seth and his son Enosh in the other. We should take a moment to note the existence of Seth in the narrative provides us with significant unwritten information. As we have said, the creations of Adam and HaAdam in the Hebrew narrative are associated with two different names of deity, with Adam created in the image of Elohim and HaAdam created by YHWH Elohim as a mixture of earth and divine breath. The narrative then distinguishes two lines of people coming from Adam and HaAdam, as if different breeds or "generations." We have no reason to assume these distinctly different lines of people (Adam and HaAdam) can mate with each other. The birth of Seth reveals they can. Moreover, M reveals through Seth a plan to attribute characteristics to Seth's descendants derived from YHWH through his mother Eve and from Elohim through his father, Adam. When Eve announces Seth's name, she recognizes he is from Elohim. She already knows what we only learn in the next Unit, III, just as Adam was in the image and likeness of Elohim, Seth was in the image and likeness of Adam.

The juxtaposition of Cain and Seth might seem inappropriate insofar as they represent two different lines of people, a "pure" line, Cain's, from the deity as YHWH, Cain, and Seth's from the combined name YHWH Elohim (see Figure 4). Seemingly, it would be more appropriate to describe the descendants of male and female Adam (created by Elohim) in parallel with Cain, as they are also associated with a single name of deity. The problem is, there is no elaboration of the descendants of Elohim's Adam at all, other than a generic reference to the males, "sons of Elohim," in Unit III. There are in fact only generic names, Adam, male and female, and these sons, associated with the generic name for deity, Elohim. This point is emphasized in contrast by the naming of both men and women in Cain's line. Like YHWH, those descending from the people he formed have individual names. This brings us to the explanation of why M compares Cain with Seth.

Since Cain and Seth share a mother but have different fathers, the distinctions we find between them should indicate differences between their fathers, and in parallel, between the name of deity associated with each. The most obvious of these differences is based on the extreme creativity associated with Cain's descendants. M mentions the builder of a city, "all such as handle the harp and pipe," and "the forger of every cutting instrument of brass and iron." We can add to that "poets." Lamech's speech to his wives is a poem which can be compared with the opening of Moses' closing poem: "Give ear, ye heavens, and I will speak; and let the earth hear the words of my mouth (Deut 32:1);" "hear my voice; ye wives of Lamech, hearken unto my speech (Gen 4:23)." Creativity is associated with the formation of HaAdam from the earth and the planting of a Garden in Eden. None of these creative powers are noted for Elohim's Adam.

There is no indication of the accomplishments of Adam's descendants. In fact, other than the notice of the births of Seth and Enosh we have nothing but the cryptic announcement "then began the use of the name YHWH." However, when we put that together with Eve's invocation of Elohim, we see both names are used within the space of two verses regarding Adam's descendants. This could be M's verification that Seth's descendants show characteristics associated with both names. On the other hand, no divine names are mentioned in the extensive segment relating HaAdam's descendants, who are wiped out in the flood. We can focus in on this distinction by comparing what is stated about Adam's grandson Enosh and HaAdam's grandson Enoch.

- **4:26** And to Seth, to him also there was born a son; and he called his name Enosh; *then they began to call upon the name YHWH*

- **4:17** And Cain knew his wife; and she conceived, and bore Enoch; and he builded a city, and *called the name of the city after the name of his son Enoch.*

The two verses share "to call the name." One shows the greatness of an individual who built a city named after him. The other multiplies the names of deity available to people. The comparison leads us back to where we began the Unit, in the generations of heaven and earth. Cain's line, beginning with the building of a city, highlights the earthly oriented generations. Seth's descendants are oriented to deity. This distinction is the perfect lead-in to Unit III.

Unit III (Genesis 5:1-10:32): Elohim and YHWH Defined in the Flood

The Divine Names Separate as Characters but Combine in People

At this point we have three types of people in the world: descendants of Elohim through Adam, descendants of YHWH through Cain, and descendants of Seth who combine the influences of Elohim and YHWH. We have also seen three different names for the deity, Elohim, YHWH Elohim, and YHWH. The distinctions between people are based on their connections to the three names. This reading is so different from the conventional reading that we must reflect upon it a bit. Seth's line will people the world through his descendant Noah. All the people of the world will be able to trace themselves back to Elohim, through Seth's father, Adam, as well as to YHWH through Seth's mother, Eve. What information might we be able to deduce from these simple observations?

There is a "post-Eden" distinction between Elohim and YHWH. The distinction is so sharp, we are forced to see them as distinct characters in M's book. The unified deity of the Garden narrative gives way to two divine characters, Elohim and YHWH. The significance of this division is expanded when we connect it with the parallel events taking place with people. The two lines of people who can be traced back to a single divine name will perish while the line which combines the names will people the world. The division in the godhead, expressed by the separation of the names, is paralleled by a consolidation of the divine names through people. The flood story brings about this consolidation in the human sphere, while spelling out the details of the differences between Elohim and YHWH.

Let us have a quick look at how all this meshes with what is beginning to take shape as M's plan. At some point in pre-history, before the flood, an event took place which inverted the relationship between "heaven" and "earth," between the godhead as represented by the divine names and the two lines of people, Adam and HaAdam. Simultaneously, the divine names separated while the divine human lines integrated. People, who have within themselves the two divine sources, may have the potential to help repair the division caused by Eve's action. If so, the Torah might be about the fulfilment of human potential by bringing about the reunification of the divine names

Much of what is to be said about the flood is derived from the arrangement of the Unit as it appears in *The Woven Torah*. The feature which facilitates further clarification of the names Elohim and YHWH is the appearance of parallel blocks of text which compare them. The first section we look at (Gen 5:1-6:10) relates the peopling of the world from two different perspectives, one attributed to Elohim (5:1-32) and the other YHWH (6:1-10).

The identification and comparison of parallel sections of text is one of the methods we use to "see" the esoteric Torah. The similarities and differences that surface from the comparison would, likely, escape a listener, or one reading according to an oral/aural paradigm. One of the characteristics of the Torah seen as a visual document is that it requires the reader, constantly, to compile and compare parallels. Laying them out visually, as follows, makes it much more convenient to work with them, (as seen in *The Woven Torah*). What follows is the parallel reading of 5:1-32 and 6:1-9, demonstrating how the two sections present two understandings of how the earth was populated.

Populating the Earth (5:1-6:10)

1	2
A 5:1 **This is the book of the generations of Adam**. In the day that Elohim created man, in the likeness of Elohim made He him; 5:2 male and female created He them, and blessed them, and called their name Adam, in the day when they were created. 5:3 And Adam lived a hundred and thirty years, and begot a son in his own likeness, after his image; and called his name Seth. 5:4 And the days of Adam after he begot Seth were eight hundred years; and he begot sons and daughters. 5:5 And all the days that Adam lived were nine hundred and thirty years; and he died. {S}	A 6:1 **And it came to pass, when HaAdam began to multiply on the face of the earth**, and daughters were born unto them, 6:2 that the sons of Elohim saw the daughters of HaAdam that they were good; and they took them wives, whomsoever they chose. 6:3 And YHWH said: 'My spirit shall not abide in man for ever, for that he also is flesh; therefore shall his days be a hundred and twenty years.' 6:4 The Nephilim were in the earth in those days, and also after that, when the sons of Elohim came in unto the daughters of HaAdam, and they bore children to them; the same were the mighty men that were of old, the men of renown.
B 5:6 And Seth lived a hundred and five years, and begot Enosh. ... {S} 5:9 And Enosh lived ninety years, and begot Kenan. ... {S} 5:12 And Kenan lived seventy years, and begot Mahalalel. ... {S} 5:15 And Mahalalel lived sixty and five years, and begot Jared. ... 5:18 And Jared lived a hundred sixty and two years, and begot Enoch. ...5:21 And Enoch lived sixty and five years, and begot Methuselah. 5:22 **And Enoch walked with Elohim** after he begot Methuselah three hundred years, and begot sons and daughters. 5:23 And all the days of Enoch were three hundred sixty and five years. 5:24 **And Enoch walked with Elohim, and he was not; for Elohim took him**. {S} 5:25 And Methuselah lived a hundred eighty and seven years, and begot Lamech. ... 5:28 And Lamech lived a hundred eighty and two years, and begot a son. 5:29 And he called his name Noah, saying: '**This same shall comfort us in our work and in the toil of our hands, which cometh from the ground which YHWH hath cursed.**' 5:30 And Lamech lived after he begot Noah five hundred ninety and five years, and begot sons and daughters. 5:31 And all the days of Lamech were seven hundred seventy and seven years; and he died. {S}	B 6:5 And YHWH saw that the wickedness of HaAdam was great in the earth, and that every imagination of the thoughts of his heart was only evil continually. 6:6 **And it repented YHWH that He had made HaAdam on the earth, and it grieved Him at His heart. 6:7 And YHWH said: 'I will blot out HaAdam whom I have created from the face of the earth;** both HaAdam, and beast, and creeping thing, and fowl of the air; for it repenteth Me that I have made them.' 6:8 **But Noah found grace in the eyes of YHWH.**
C 5:32 **And Noah was five hundred years old; and Noah begot Shem, Ham, and Japheth**.	C 6:9 These are the generations of Noah. Noah was in his generations a man righteous and whole-hearted; Noah walked with Elohim. **6:10 And Noah begot three sons, Shem, Ham, and Japheth.**

YHWH Elohim and YHWH

Unit III involves observing how an awareness of M's methods sheds light on the text. M has created clearly parallel borders to the text in columns 1 and 2. Both begin with reproduction in the first verse: "the generations of Adam (1A)" and "when HaAdam began to multiply (2A)." They both end with Noah's sons: "Noah begot Shem, Ham, and Japheth (1C)" and "Noah begot three sons, Shem, Ham, and Japheth (2C)." These parallels, ending with a superfluous repetition of the birth of Noah's sons, instruct us to examine the entirety of the two segments as parallel.

One specific point that comes out of reading the columns in parallel will significantly aid our investigation. It clarifies how to consider the combined name "YHWH Elohim" from Unit II when we compare the two separate names, YHWH, and Elohim in Unit III. We might think the combined name is meant to indicate a character who is a synthesis of the two, combining characteristics of both YHWH and Elohim. M, however, has made clear we should consider YHWH Elohim as a form of YHWH. (This is consistent with our evaluation above——YHWH Elohim should be viewed as a precursor to YHWH. We could also say that the unique characteristics introduced with YHWH Elohim are those of the YHWH component since Elohim has been introduced previously, in Unit I.) M demonstrates this through the words of Noah's father Lamech and YHWH. When naming Noah in column 1, Lamech says: "This same shall comfort us in our work and in the toil of our hands, which cometh from the ground which YHWH hath cursed (Gen 5:29)." Lamech considers the curse to have come from YHWH although the Garden narrative indicates it was YHWH Elohim. Lest there be any doubt the now separated YHWH has taken on the persona of YHWH Elohim, YHWH admits as much: "And YHWH said: 'I will blot out HaAdam *whom I have created* from the face of the earth (Gen 6:7).'" YHWH has taken ownership of HaAdam and his line. We now turn to the opening of the Unit.

Elohim and the Good; YHWH and the Bad

Column 1 begins with the invocation of Elohim. It is the first we have heard of him since the creation other than giving Seth to Eve by means of his male Adam. We hear only good things about Seth and his descendants. Seth continued the "likeness and image;" "Enoch walked with Elohim;" "Noah walked with Elohim." They all lived extraordinarily long lives. As in Unit I, here too Elohim is only associated with good (until 6:11ff). This contrasts with YHWH, who continues to see the bad, in column 2.

> And it came to pass, when HaAdam began to multiply on the face of the earth, and daughters were born unto them, that the sons of Elohim saw the daughters of HaAdam that they were good; and they took them wives, whomsoever they chose. And YHWH said: 'My spirit shall not abide in man forever, for that he also is flesh; therefore shall his days be a hundred and twenty years.' (Gen 6:1-3)

These verses mention all three of the lines of people that appear in Figure 4. First noted is the line of HaAdam, and specifically the women of this line. Second, we encounter Adam's line, which is referred to through the term "sons of Elohim." It could be Adam's descendants are sourced back to Elohim rather than Adam because they carried the "likeness and image." Or it could be this is a sign M left for the careful reader.

M begins this Unit by taking us back to the creation of Adam on day six. The effect of this revisiting is to impress us with the fact male Adam could pass on "his own likeness, after his image." This ability to transmit "likeness and image" is first associated with Elohim. From here we might deduce Adam and his male descendants all possessed this ability, as well as an affinity with Elohim. We could even go so far as to deduce it was sufficient for Adam to father Seth with Eve to guarantee the transmission of his fundamental characteristic, the likeness and image of Elohim. Whatever Eve would contribute to the coming generations, as the representative of YHWH, was consistent with the ability to transmit the likeness and image of Elohim.

Why the Sons of Elohim Preferred Daughters of YHWH

The third line of ancestry, the one from which all living people are descended, was founded because "the sons of Elohim saw the daughters of HaAdam that they were good; and they took them wives (Gen

6:2)." Here is yet another verification from M for the careful reader. Elohim has described all facets of creation (except the divider on day two) as "good." Now his sons are described as attracted to the daughters of HaAdam because they were "good." This appears to be a specific example of "likeness and image." Just as Elohim *sees* the good, so do his "sons": "And Elohim saw the light, that it was good (Gen 1:4);" "the sons of Elohim saw the daughters of HaAdam that they were good." There is also a more prosaic explanation for the attraction based on YHWH Elohim's words to Eve.

"And thy desire shall be to thy husband, and he shall rule over thee (Gen 3:16)." Eve's character changed after eating the fruit. She gained wisdom, sexuality, and deference to her mate. These qualities were seen as good, not only by Elohim's "sons," but also by male Adam who mated with Eve. Qualities with which Elohim blessed Adam are propitious for a match between male Adam and Eve after the Garden. Let us remember both male and female Adam were blessed regarding the whole earth "subdue it; and have dominion (Gen 1:28)." Both have strong domineering characters. The men of this line would find attractive the more submissive Eve-like daughters of HaAdam. And most important for us, we can see the attraction between male Adam and Eve, which led to the births of Abel and Seth. It was a marriage "made in heaven;" Elohim *blessed* Adam with dominance, and YHWH *punished* Eve with subservience.

YHWH attempts to mitigate what he sees as the failure of his creatures by shortening the lives of the descendants of Cain. They were to live a mere 120 years as opposed to the descendants of Adam who could live seven times as long, nearly a millennium.

The opening verses of the parallel which M created between segments columns 1 and 2 directed us to the opposing views of the third line of humanity, the descendants of male Adam and Eve. YHWH did not like this match, while Elohim had no problem with it. Next, we see YHWH's discontent was not limited to the mixing of the lines.

> And YHWH saw that the badness of HaAdam was great in the earth, and that every imagination of the thoughts of his heart was only bad continually. And it repented YHWH that he had made HaAdam on the earth, and it grieved him at his heart.
> (Gen 6:5, 6; my translation)

M tells us YHWH was now sorry he had formed his HaAdam on the earth, as an earthly creature, for as such "the thoughts of his heart was only bad continually." The details of the verses serve as the basis for another comparison between YHWH and Elohim. Elohim blessed Adam at his creation and until now has not withdrawn the blessing, although that is about to change. YHWH has continually been disappointed: by HaAdam, Eve, Cain, and their offspring. This comparison is strengthened by a strategic play on words. The Hebrew translated "repented" (*nahem*) has the same root as Noah's name and is used by Lamech in naming Noah.

"This same shall *comfort* (*nahem*) us in our work and in the toil of our hands, which cometh from the ground (*adama*) which YHWH hath cursed." The root which interests us is translated in this verse as "comfort." But the full significance of the root is that it indicates Noah's fate to alleviate YHWH's curse from the ground. YHWH, for his part, wishes to remove HaAdam from the earth: "And YHWH said: 'I will blot out HaAdam whom I have created from the face of the earth.'" Noah, on the other hand, is to blot out the effects of the curse YHWH placed on the earth. Noah was the great-grandson of Enoch, who walked with Elohim, and he himself also walked with Elohim. At this point we see Seth's descendants were worthy of walking with Elohim while YHWH decided to wipe out Cain's line, while preserving Seth's line. The significance of the parallel uses of *nahem* is made all the clearer by the serendipitous attachment of 6:8 to the end of 6:7.

> And YHWH said: 'I will blot out HaAdam whom I have created from the face of the earth; both HaAdam, and beast, and creeping thing, and fowl of the air; for it *repenteth* (nahem) me that I have made them.' But *Noah* found grace in the eyes of YHWH.
> (Gen 6:7,8)

The Hebrew root of Noah's name, "comfort," "relieve," as noted by his father, above, is contrasted here with M's use of the same root in a different form to express YHWH's regret. The parallel between the root of Noah's name and YHWH's regret shines a spotlight on a totally unexpected turn of events. No sooner has YHWH finished expressing his regret that he created life on the earth, than M makes the major announcement: "But *Noah* found grace in the eyes of YHWH." This is the final twist in the plot that makes the flood possible. YHWH has given up on his own "pure" creatures, the line of Cain's descendants, but has a fondness for a creature whose origin combines both YHWH (through Eve) and Elohim (through male Adam). To drive this point home, in Genesis 6:9,10 M creates closure with the Unit's opening "generations of Adam" by preceding the redundant recitation of Noah's sons' names with "generations."

> These are the generations of Noah. Noah was in his generations a man righteous and whole-hearted; Noah walked with Elohim.   And Noah begot three sons, Shem, Ham, and Japheth

Lest there be any suspicion Noah had a special relationship with YHWH, M immediately clarifies that "Noah walked with Elohim." The union of Eve with male Adam has now come to full fruition. There is a human creature who lives in relationship with both Elohim and YHWH. From Elohim people are in the divine "form and image"; YHWH contributes "earth and the breath of life." Each of them will now participate in the cataclysm that will rid the world of Elohim's and YHWH's separate lines of people, thereby creating a world in which they share an interest in people through Noah's sons.

YHWH has determined Eve will be the source of his connection with people rather than HaAdam. This is consistent with parallels between YHWH and Eve mentioned previously. Eve is separated from an earlier creation with a generic name, HaAdam. Similarly, the name YHWH is separated from an earlier generic name, Elohim. In this manner, Eve, not HaAdam is in the "form and image" of YHWH, a character who comes into being through separation from Elohim. Even their names resonate with each other in Hebrew, one, YHWH, based on "being" and the other, Eve, based on "living."

YHWH has given up on the experiment of creating life on the earth and threatens "'I will blot out HaAdam whom I have created from the face of the earth; both HaAdam, and beast, and creeping thing, and fowl of the air; for it repenteth me that I have made them (Gen 6:7).'" He speaks to himself because of feelings "in his heart" (6:6) about "the thoughts of his (HaAdam's) heart." M has emphasized the emotive side of YHWH in contrast to Elohim who is not described as having a heart nor insight into the hearts of people. Elohim *is* more adept at dealing with the physical, as evidenced by the construction of the world in six days, and as we are about to see, knowing how to build an ark. YHWH does not express a concrete plan to wipe out people before Elohim leads the way in the second section we examine, Gen 6:11-7:5, as we will now see.

Before the Flood (Genesis 6:11-7:5)

<table>
<tr><th>3</th><th>4</th></tr>
<tr>
<td>

6:11 And the earth was corrupt before Elohim, and the earth was filled with violence. **6:12** And Elohim saw the earth, and, behold, it was corrupt; for all flesh had corrupted their way upon the earth. {S} **6:13** And Elohim said unto Noah: 'The end of all flesh is come before Me; for the earth is filled with violence through them; and, behold, I will destroy them with the earth. **6:14** Make thee an ark of gopher wood; with rooms shalt thou make the ark, and shalt pitch it within and without with pitch. **6:15** And this is how thou shalt make it: the length of the ark three hundred cubits, the breadth of it fifty cubits, and the height of it thirty cubits. **6:16** A light shalt thou make to the ark, and to a cubit shalt thou finish it upward; and the door of the ark shalt thou set in the side thereof; with lower, second, and third stories shalt thou make it. **6:17** And I, behold, I do bring the flood of waters upon the earth, to destroy all flesh, wherein is the breath of life, from under heaven; every thing that is in the earth shall perish. **6:18** But I will establish My covenant with thee; and thou shalt come into the ark, thou, and thy sons, and thy wife, and thy sons' wives with thee. **6:19** And of every living thing of all flesh, two of every sort shalt thou bring into the ark, to keep them alive with thee; they shall be male and female. **6:20** Of the fowl after their kind, and of the cattle after their kind, of every creeping thing of the ground after its kind, two of every sort shall come unto thee, to keep them alive. **6:21** And take thou unto thee of all food that is eaten, and gather it to thee; and it shall be for food for thee, and for them.' **6:22 Thus did Noah; according to all that Elohim commanded him, so did he.**

</td>
<td>

7:1 And YHWH said unto Noah: 'Come thou and all thy house into the ark; for thee have I seen righteous before Me in this generation. **7:2** Of every clean beast thou shalt take to thee seven and seven, each with his mate; and of the beasts that are not clean two [and two], each with his mate; **7:3** of the fowl also of the air, seven and seven, male and female; to keep seed alive upon the face of all the earth. **7:4** For yet seven days, and I will cause it to rain upon the earth forty days and forty nights; and every living substance that I have made will I blot out from off the face of the earth.' **7:5 And Noah did according unto all that YHWH commanded him.**

</td>
</tr>
</table>

The second section contains one of the most problematic-seeming repetitions in the Torah. Elohim tells Noah:

> And of every living thing of all flesh, **two of every sort** shalt thou bring into the ark, to keep them alive with thee; they shall be male and female. Of the fowl after their kind, and of the cattle after their kind, of every creeping thing of the ground after its kind, **two of every sort** shall come unto thee, to keep them alive. (Gen 6:19, 20)

Right after this, YHWH tells Noah:

> Of every clean beast thou shalt take to thee seven and seven, each with his mate; and of the beasts that are not clean two [and two], each with his mate; of the fowl also of the air, seven and seven, male and female; to keep seed alive upon the face of all the earth. (Gen 7:2, 3)

Both of these similar yet different commands are carried out by Noah: "Thus did Noah; according to all that Elohim commanded him, so did he (Gen 6:22)," and "And Noah did according unto all that YHWH commanded him (Gen 7:5)." M tells us Noah heard Elohim and YHWH give him different commands and followed the wishes of both. This reinforces our observation in the narrative above, both Elohim and YHWH had close connections with Noah. We can use the parallels to further probe the relationship between the names of deity.

Both YHWH and Elohim decided, independently according to M, the creation of life had failed, and they would start over, with Noah replacing both Adam and HaAdam, as father of all. The order of events is telling in this regard. First, we learn YHWH wishes to wipe out all he has made because "every imagination of the thoughts of his heart was only evil continually." But he does not indicate a plan for carrying out this destruction. M provides a foreshadowing of what is to take place by immediately informing us "Noah found grace in the eyes of YHWH." However, it is not until Elohim gets involved that plans take form.

> And the earth was corrupt before Elohim, and the earth was filled with violence. And Elohim saw the earth, and, behold, it was corrupt; for all flesh had corrupted their way upon the earth. And Elohim said unto Noah: 'The end of all flesh is come before me; for the earth is filled with violence through them; and, behold, I will destroy them with the earth. Make thee an ark of gopher wood... (Gen 6:11-14)

Elohim saw the violent corruption on the earth and determined to wipe out all flesh, except for Noah and his family. YHWH saw the evil yearnings of the heart and Elohim saw physical violence. Elohim prepared a plan enabling him to wipe out all life except for Noah and the creatures he brought into the ark. At this point, M goes back to YHWH to see how Elohim's plan suites YHWH. In effect, YHWH says to Noah, "Go ahead with Elohim's plan but add additional clean animals." YHWH's reason for this request is revealed after the flood when Noah offers the clean animals to YHWH, who accepts them and releases the ground from his curse. Noah, and we, the readers, sense he is fulfilling the demands flowing from the two names. Besides the matter of the clean animals, Elohim and YHWH also differ in the manner each proposes to bring about destruction.

- **Elohim:** And I, behold, I do bring the flood of waters upon the earth, to destroy all flesh, wherein is the breath of life, *from under heaven*; every thing that is in the earth shall perish (Gen 6:17).

- **YHWH:** I will cause it to rain upon the earth forty days and forty nights; and every living

substance that I have made will I blot out *from off the face of the earth* (Gen 7:4).

These two statements contribute significant information about the difference between Elohim and YHWH. The flood waters came from two sources, above and below. YHWH rained down upon the earth for forty days to "blot out from off the face of the earth" what he had made. Elohim, on the other hand, released the waters of the earth to destroy all flesh "under heaven." Elohim and YHWH are associated with different perspectives. Elohim, associated with the waters on the earth, reflects an upward looking perspective from the point of view of the earth, "under heaven." YHWH, who sends down rain from above, has a downward perspective, looking at "the face of the earth." YHWH is positioned above and rains down to destroy what is on the face of the earth. Elohim is below and brings up the flood water from the earth to destroy everything under heaven. They have different perspectives: YHWH sees from above and Elohim from below.

The differences between the names are further clarified after Noah and his family come out of the ark. Both Elohim and YHWH make speeches which differ both in content and in form. Elohim speaks to Noah, but YHWH speaks to himself, "in his heart."

After the Flood (Genesis 8:15-9:17)

> And Noah builded an altar unto YHWH; and took of every clean beast, and of every clean fowl, and offered burnt-offerings on the altar. And YHWH smelled the sweet savour; and YHWH said in his heart: "I will not again curse the ground any more for HaAdam's sake; for the imagination of HaAdam's heart is evil from his youth; neither will I again smite any more every thing living, as I have done. While the earth remaineth, seedtime and harvest, and cold and heat, and summer and winter, and day and night shall not cease (Gen 8:20-22)."

There are references here to several matters associated with YHWH before the flood. YHWH requested extra clean animals and birds so Noah would be able to offer them to YHWH after the flood. YHWH's preference for animal offerings is also known from the Cain and Abel story. YHWH speaks in his heart about the hearts of men, as he does in 6:5, and 6:6. He fulfils Lamech's prophecy, Noah will be instrumental in ending the curse of the ground: "I will not again curse the ground anymore." But what proves to be the most salient single observation regarding YHWH's speech is, it is for the reader alone. Noah does not hear the speech because YHWH recited it "in his heart." There is no further contact between YHWH and Noah. In fact, the only communication between Noah and YHWH was when YHWH addressed him and requested the pure animals. But M has made sure we understand YHWH should be associated with hearts, the unseen. M shares additional knowledge about YHWH, telling us YHWH will henceforth not change the natural world, "seedtime and harvest, and cold and heat, and summer and winter, and day and night shall not cease." M has completed outlining the character YHWH, and we can summarize basic points we have learned about YHWH:

- He "resides" above because he sends down the rain and smells the rising smoke of the Olah (rising) offerings

- His realm extends to the face of the earth

- He sees the hidden, in hearts

- He can change, he no longer changes the ways of the world

- He has reduced contact with people

- He operates in creation through the female, Eve, the mother of all

- He first appears connected to Elohim and is subsequently separated

Now we look at the parallel passage following the flood, which reveals details about Elohim.

And Elohim spoke unto Noah, and to his sons with him, saying: "As for Me, behold, I establish My covenant with you, and with your seed after you; and with every living creature that is with you, the fowl, the cattle, and every beast of the earth with you; of all that go out of the ark, even every beast of the earth. And I will establish My covenant with you; neither shall all flesh be cut off any more by the waters of the flood; neither shall there any more be a flood to destroy the earth."

And Elohim said: "This is the token of the covenant which I make between me and you and every living creature that is with you, for perpetual generations: I have set my bow in the cloud, and it shall be for a token of a covenant between me and the earth. And it shall come to pass, when I bring clouds over the earth, and the bow is seen in the cloud, that I will remember my covenant, which is between me and you and every living creature of all flesh; and the waters shall no more become a flood to destroy all flesh. And the bow shall be in the cloud; and I will look upon it, that I may remember the everlasting covenant between Elohim and every living creature of all flesh that is upon the earth (Gen 9:8-16)."

The most obvious difference is that Elohim is actively interacting directly with Noah and his sons, "and every living creature of all flesh that is upon the earth." Elohim already stated his plan to establish a covenant with living creatures when instructing Noah to build the ark. He produced the flood on the earth, having a perspective looking up from below to that which is under the sky. He declares: "it shall be for a token of a covenant between me and the earth." His covenant has expanded from Noah to all the creatures, and to the whole earth. The word translated "token," *ot*, also appears in Elohim's creation of the heavenly bodies, which he refers to as "*otot*" "signs" for seasons (Gen 1:14). He engineered the building of the ark as well as the creation of all in six days. He first appears alone (in Unit I) and operates in creation through the male, through Adam.

The three Units at the beginning of Genesis present a process through which YHWH becomes an independent entity associated with the transcendent and female—through Eve. Elohim undergoes an opposite process. Starting as the independent creator of everything through speech, he becomes connected to the earth and those that dwell upon it, imminent, through a covenant that includes rational laws regulating human life, spoken to Noah and his sons. His connection to people is through male Adam. Figure 5 summarizes the distinctions we have seen between Elohim and YHWH.

Figure 5. Distinctions between Elohim and YHWH in Units I-III

	Elohim	YHWH
Name	Generic	Proper name
Attitude Toward People	Blesses	Warns
Orientation	Below	Above
Part of Tree	Says "Good"	Says "Bad"
Reason for Creating	Creates without stating reason	Creates HaAdam to work the garden
Creation of People	Creates Adam male and female in his image	Forms HaAdam from earth and breathes in divine breath of life, fashions Eve from HaAdam
Job of People	Adam's role is to subdue the earth and rule living creatures	HaAdam's role is to cultivate the garden
Gender Association	The male aspect of creation through Adam, the father of all	The female aspect of creation through Eve, the mother of all
Relationships with People	Has positive contact with Enoch, Noah and his sons	Has heartaches from people
Continuity/Law	Gives Noah and his sons Adam's blessing and establishes laws	No longer changes laws of nature
After Flood	Creates covenant	Receives offerings and removes curse
Area of Concern	Concerned with physical realm, actions	Concerned with moral realm, the heart
Form of Speeches	Public declamations	Private monologues
Field of Vision	Creates signs, universal sign, for himself, of covenant not to destroy	Sees what is hidden in hearts

We turn now to the conclusion of the prologue to the Torah, Unit IV, the Tower of Babel, where for the first time YHWH appears upon the stage fully independent of Elohim.

Unit IV (Genesis 11:1-9): Just YHWH /The Tower of Babel

The narrative of the Tower of Babel creates a hinge in the Torah. This narrative marks the point where M shifts from a universal narrative involving all of humanity to a narrative concerned with one nation amongst many. Babel is also important for our investigation as it is the first narrative devoted exclusively to the name YHWH without any mention of the name Elohim. We will now examine the connection between the structure of the story and its content.

11:1 And the whole earth was of one language and of one speech. 11:2 And it came to pass, as they journeyed east, that they found a plain in the land of Shinar; and they dwelt there. 11:3 And they said one to another: 'Come, let us make brick, and burn them thoroughly.' And they had brick for stone, and slime had they for mortar. 11:4 And they said: 'Come, let us build us a city, and a tower, with its top in heaven, and let us make us a name; lest we be scattered abroad upon the face of the whole earth.' 11:5 And YHWH came down to see the city and the tower, which the children of men builded. 11:6 And YHWH said: 'Behold, they are one people, and they have all one language; and this is what they begin to do; and now nothing will be withholden from them, which they purpose to do. 11:7 Come, let us go down, and there confound their language, that they may not understand one another's speech.'11:8 So YHWH scattered them abroad from thence upon the face of all the earth; and they left off to build the city. 11:9 Therefore was the name of it called Babel; because YHWH did there confound the language of all the earth; and from thence did YHWH scatter them abroad upon the face of all the earth.

In terms of the inclusive narrative of Genesis, Unit IV creates a transition. This Unit's story takes place in the third generation after the flood, as presaged near the end of Unit III, "And unto Eber (son of Arpachshad, son of Shem) were born two sons; the name of the one was Peleg (divide); for in his days was the earth divided (10:25)." It would be another six generations before the birth of Abram (11:26) in Unit V.

Abram's birth marks the beginning of the major narrative of the Torah, the founding of a nation, which ends with the death of Moses. Unit IV sets the table for that narrative. The Unit does so in two ways, one based on the outcome of the story and one on the divine name appearing in it. Regarding the names, it elucidates the development of YHWH, being the first Unit in which Elohim is not mentioned at all. YHWH has now become independent of Elohim in the narrative. The outcome of the story is humanity dividing into language groups which are to become nations. The

rest of the Torah describes how YHWH develops a unique relationship with one of these nations. These points are directly accessible from reading the story as it appears above. But the analysis of its form will lead us to additional understandings.

The narrative neatly divides into two parts, 11:1-4 and 5-9. These two parts are presented from different perspectives. The first, 1-4, is told from the point of view of people. The second, 5-9, is from the point of view of YHWH. The opening words, "the whole earth," tell us the first perspective is also of the earth, as well as people. The fact YHWH "came down," reinforces our earlier conclusion that YHWH is associated with heaven. So, the perspectives are those of heaven and earth, resonating with the opening verse of the creation (1:1). The people wish to go up to heaven by means of a tower, and YHWH goes down to the earth to see the tower.

Deeper analysis shows the two divisions, 1-4 and 5-9, were constructed with several parallels between them. The narrator's statement in 11:1 "the whole earth was of one language," is virtually repeated by YHWH in 11:6, "Behold, they are one people, and they have all one language." The narration describes people conversing with each other in 11:3, "And they said one to another." YHWH also speaks of them conversing in 11:7, "that they may not understand one another's speech." The parallel use of "one another" is a very strong indicator of an artfully designed text. The artfulness reaches a peak when the people's fear "lest we be scattered abroad upon the face of the whole earth (11:4)" comes to pass "So YHWH scattered them abroad from thence upon the face of all the earth (11:9)." The two divisions thus subdivide into three parallel parts in each. The following arrangement captures these structural observations.

Figure 6. The Format of Genesis IV in The Woven Torah

Number	Unity/One	Dialogue/Two	Diversity/Many
Perspective	**1x**	**1y**	**1z**
Human	11:1 And the whole earth was of *one language* and of one speech. 11:2 And it came to pass, as they journeyed east, that they found a plain in the land of Shinar; and they dwelt there.	11:3 And they **said one to another**: 'Come, let us make brick, and burn them thoroughly.' And they had brick for stone, and slime had they for mortar.	11:4 And they said: 'Come, let us build us a city, and a tower, with its top in heaven, and let us make us a name; <u>lest we be scattered abroad upon the face of the whole earth.</u>'
	2x	**2y**	**2z**
Divine	11:5 And YHWH came down to see the city and the tower, which the children of men builded. 11:6 And YHWH said: 'Behold, they are one people, and they have all *one language*; and this is what they begin to do; and now nothing will be withholden from them, which they purpose to do.	11:7 Come, let us go down, and there confound their language, that they may not understand **one another's speech**.'	11:8 <u>So YHWH scattered them abroad from thence upon the face of all the earth;</u> and they left off to build the city. 11:9 Therefore was the name of it called Babel; because YHWH did there confound the language of all the earth; and from thence did YHWH scatter them abroad upon the face of all the earth.

Figure 6 displays the way Unit IV appears in *The Woven Torah*, as a two-dimensional construct, (the focus of Part Three). The layout provides a "map" of the Unit. The two perspectives are provided by the division into two rows, Row 1 people, and row 2 YHWH. The three linguistic parallels are found in the columns, x, y, and z.

The columns indicate there is more to the parallels between the rows than just the three linguistic parallels. Each row divides each perspective, human (1) or divine (2), into three segments. The two segments of each column are related. In x, all of humanity is one people with one language. In this state, their potential is unlimited, "now nothing will be withholden from them, which they purpose to do." In column z, we find the opposite state mentioned in both segments, "scattered abroad upon the face of the whole earth." The single unified people are divided into multiple nations. The people express their fear of such an event (1z) while YHWH brings it about (2z).

The poles of the three-part structure reflect the dyad we found in the division between the first three days of creation (Unit I) and the next three, expressed as "one and many." This dyad defines poles in the Babel narrative. But this is a three-part structure; we skipped column y. The reason for skipping y was to first establish the poles, x and z. We cannot fully grasp the significance of the central segments, column y, without first recognizing there is a dichotomy between x and z. This dichotomy is crucial for understanding M's methodology, or rhetoric, throughout the Torah. M employs "visual" rhetoric as opposed to oral/aural rhetoric. The difference is in the placement of the "synthesis," or bridging element. The order "thesis, antithesis, synthesis" illuminates the pair of opposites, thesis and antithesis, to see how the synthesis bridges them. In M's visual rhetoric, the conceptual middle, the bridge, the synthesis, y, is placed in the middle between the poles, x and z.

What do we learn from focusing on y as the conceptual middle? The answer is found in M's striking parallels in 1y "they said one to another" and 2y "that they may not understand one another." Both segments refer to dialogues between individuals. The bridge between unity (x) and disunity (z) is dialogue. As long as there is dialogue (1y) human potential is limitless. To create a limit, YHWH prevents dialogue (2y) by confounding their language. Once we see the centrality of dialogue, the three-part division of the Babel story reveals itself as reflecting the organization of the previous three Units, I-III. Unit I describes a state of unity in which only the name Elohim is used, paralleling the human unity described in column x. In Unit III a universal upheaval, the flood, takes place, similar to the dispersion in column z. Both Unit III and column z end with the multiplicity of nations. These brings us to Unit II, the only Unit in which there is dialogue, and not just one. There are dialogues between the snake and Eve (3:1-5), YHWH Elohim and HaAdam (3:9-12), YHWH Elohim and Eve (3:13), and YHWH and Cain (4:9-15).

This plethora of dialogues characterizes Unit II, creating a parallel to column y in Unit IV. To be clear, there are one-way speeches in Units I and III, but no dialogue. None of the speeches of Elohim or YHWH draw a verbal response in these Units and no people speak with each other. M is using the Babel story to focus our attention on the pattern common to both the three columns of Unit IV, and across the three creation Units, I-III, taken together.

The common pattern has three parts, 1.) unity, 2.) duality, expressed through dialogue, and 3.) multiplicity. This is precisely the pattern we found in the appearance of the names, a single name, Elohim, in Unit I, a double name, YHWH Elohim in Unit II and fully separated names in Unit III. Thus, the Babel story can be viewed as a reflection of the first three Units and the development of the names. As a hinge, the story should also point towards what is to come. Considering Unit IV as the completion of the prologue shifts our attention to the narrative which follows, from Abram to the death of Moses.

The four-Unit prologue is bookended by Units in which a single name appears, Elohim in I and YHWH in IV. We have approached the appearance of YHWH developmentally in Units I-III and now see YHWH fully independent in IV. The three creation Units have served to create YHWH, from a literary perspective, as an independent entity. Furthermore, the placement of the independent Elohim (Unit I) and the independent YHWH (Unit IV) at the poles of the prologue suggests we see them as opposites.

The book of Genesis explores this polarity with such intensity that the polarity serves as a central organizing principle. In a way, Genesis itself is a prologue to the story of a nation that does not appear before Exodus. The clarification of the names in Genesis provides the foundation for the revelation of YHWH as the national deity of Israel in Exodus.

The spatial distinction between YHWH associated with heaven above and Elohim with earth below is fundamental, being the paradigm for similar distinctions. YHWH the heavenly is associated with the transcendent, intentions, the smell of sacrificial smoke ascending, potential, and the supernatural. Elohim, the immanent, is associated with flesh and blood, practical acts, actual, natural. As we see in Part Five, M constructed Genesis in a manner extending and clarifying these distinctions. M's goal is to establish YHWH as the name for the transcendent. This name will be characterized by the one divine attribute totally missing in Genesis after the creation, holiness. The development of the dichotomy between transcendent and immanent—using the names YHWH and Elohim in Genesis—prepares the way for the revelation of the transcendent through the category of holiness. But before we can appreciate how that is accomplished, we must learn how to read the Torah according to its esoteric structure: woven Units and woven Books

Part Two: The Exodus 20 Decalogue is the Key to the Woven Torah

The Torah was composed according to a paradigm of reading and writing unlike today's prose. Fortunately, visual poets and the development of hypertext and web-based alternatives to books can sensitize us to alternative means of transmitting and receiving information. In many ways, the Units of the Torah are closer to visually rich web pages than to simple linear writing. It is useful to visualize them as two-dimensional weaves to have access to *all* the meaning which M embedded in the Units. When seen this way, they offer the reader other levels of information that are inaccessible from the linear arrangement of our books and Torah scrolls. The next three Parts, II-IV, develop the tools for reading according to this unusual paradigm. (Ultimately, in Part Five, we will employ these tools further to understand M's distinctions between Elohim and YHWH).

Part Two presents the key to discovering and reading M's two-dimensional Units and multi-dimensional books. Like the key, or legend, which is included in a map to make the information in the map accessible, the key is situated in a prominent position in the Torah. It is presented as the only document Elohim ever wrote, the Decalogue, aka the Ten Commandments, engraved on two stone tablets. (I adopt the convention of referring to the ten discrete parts as "Words" since this is an accurate translation of M's own term *d'varim*, which is translated to the Greek as *logoi*.)

We begin by examining the narratives associated with the tablets. This examination leads to the conclusion that the tablets provide a paradigm of how *all* the Torah can be read in two ways, exoterically, and esoterically. The exoteric meaning being found in the conventional reading, and the esoteric meaning in a reading focused on the formal structure. Chapter 4 then examines the ways Elohim's speech in Exodus 20:2-13 can be divided into ten parts. Different religious traditions have divided them differently. The proper division leads to reading them as five consecutive pairs. In Chapter 5 we look at the ten parts as five consecutive pairs of Words. Chapter 6 explores why Elohim required two tablets.

Chapter 3. The Decalogue as Paradigm

Elohim as an Author to be Imitated

In Exodus 32:16, M presents the Decalogue as Elohim's only handwritten literary work, "And the tables were the work of Elohim, and the writing was the writing of Elohim, graven upon the tables." Consequently, according to M, the Decalogue is the ultimate work of literature, a divine text. There are also further signs of its importance. We are told, for instance, the Decalogue, as opposed to the rest of the Torah, was written on stone tablets to be placed in the ark of testimony.

This would put the tablets at the focus of the Israelite camp. The tribes were arrayed around the Tabernacle and the tablets containing the Decalogue were in the ark, within the Holy of Holies, at the focus of the camp. Once the tablets were placed within it, YHWH spoke with Moses from between the cherubim decorating the ark. It is hard to imagine how an author could show the importance of a text more emphatically. M used the unique status of the tablets, a divine composition, to embed information about how the Torah was composed and should be read.

Accessing the information requires that the reader understand the implication of M's presentation of the Decalogue as the paradigm of the highest possible form of writing. The logical implication is this is the literary form most worthy of imitation. Consequently, one could expect the rest of the Torah is influenced by the Decalogue as a work of literature. When we discover that the Decalogue is an exoteric/esoteric composition, it prepares us for reading the whole Torah as a similar composition.

The Voice in the Decalogue

Once carved in stone and placed in the ark, the divine revelation of the Decalogue at Sinai facilitated continuing divine revelation to Moses from between the cherubim (Exod 25:21–22). Even without considering a single word of the Decalogue itself, M's narrative tells us how to view the Decalogue. The Decalogue is a revelation by the divinity intended to facilitate continuing divine revelation. What does this tell us about the way M is addressing us as readers? We are to understand there is something in the Decalogue that transcends the simple understanding of its words. When properly visualized, written on two tablets, the Decalogue becomes a device to enable the hearing of a divine voice. Once we hear that voice emanating from the Decalogue, we will be able to hear it throughout M's composition.

The Two Narratives

Through the Decalogue, M provides two distinct insights into the Torah as an exoteric/esoteric composition. Both are based on a dyad of "one and many," or "the individual and the community." The first is found in the narratives detailing two different occasions when Moses received two stone tablets containing the Decalogue. The second is found in the details of the arrangement of the Words on the pair of tablets. The esoteric reading finds that "one and many" characterizes the dyad in the narratives as well as the dyad embodied by the two tablets. From our perspective, the narratives and the contents of the tablets are two witnesses testifying that the exoteric/esoteric character of the Torah is an essential part of its plan. We begin our reading with the narratives.

Let us recall some of the details surrounding them as described in Deuteronomy by Moses:

> So I turned and came down from the mount, and the mount burned with fire; and the two tables of the covenant were in my two hands. And I looked, and, behold, ye had sinned against YHWH your deity; ye had made you a molten calf; ye had turned aside quickly out of the way which YHWH had commanded you. And I took hold of the two tables, and cast them out of my two hands, *and broke them before your eyes* (Deut 9:15-17)

Moses received the first tablets on Mt. Sinai. Then he brought them down to the camp and was close enough for the people to see the tablets. But instead of showing the tablets, Moses shattered them before their eyes because they had made a golden calf. Instead of seeing whole tablets, all the people could see were fragments. The second tablets were different as they were not shattered but placed in a protective box before the people could see them.

At that time YHWH said unto me: 'Hew thee two tables of stone like unto the first, and come up unto Me into the mount; and make thee an ark of wood. And I will write on the tables the words that were on the first tables which thou didst break, and thou shalt put them in the ark.' So I made an ark of acacia-wood, and hewed two tables of stone like unto the first, and went up into the mount, having the two tables in my hand. And he wrote on the tables according to the first writing, the ten words, which YHWH spoke unto you in the mount out of the midst of the fire in the day of the assembly; and YHWH gave them unto me. And I turned and came down from the mount, and put the tables in the ark which I had made; and there they are, as YHWH commanded me. (Deut 10:1-5)

If we were to read the Torah as simply a record of historical events, we would say the deity had to engrave a second set of tablets because Moses shattered the first set. While this may be true, it does not address the fact the Torah presents us with significantly different details regarding the two sets. In other words, we are entitled to ask: Why does the Torah need two sets of tablets; what is being taught through the duplication? This is M's big tell. Once these questions have been asked, the door to the esoteric Torah has been unlocked.

By piecing together details from Moses' speech in Deuteronomy, we can deduce the two sets of tablets were intended for two different audiences. Before ascending Sinai the second time, YHWH (not Elohim) told Moses (not Bezalel who is to direct the construction of the Tabernacle) to make a box (ark) in which to place the second tablets. By divine command, only Moses was to see the second tablets. He would place them in the box as soon as he received them. The whole, coherent, tablets were for his eyes alone. The people never saw more than the fragments of the first tablets. The same text was written, word for word, letter for letter, for two different audiences. One audience, the people, would never see the Decalogue as more than shattered pieces. *Only Moses would know exactly how the ten Words were arranged on the two stone tablets.* Divine revelation delivered by Moses to the people, through human speech, delivered word-by-word, is like the shattered tablets. Word-by-word speech is sufficient for transmitting each of the laws. But the divine revelation grasped by Moses was an integrated whole, a "gestalt," like the whole tablets, which create a vision transcending the simple meaning of each of its parts.

Two Readings for Two Audiences

There are therefore two ways of reading the ten Words, an exoteric way, for the many, according to which they are grasped piece by piece, and an esoteric way, for the few, according to which they are grasped as a ten-part whole divided between two tablets. In fact, we will see the whole Torah can be read in two ways by two different audiences. The Torah was composed as an exoteric/esoteric text according to the paradigm of the Decalogue. The exoteric text is available to all through the simple meanings of the stories and laws. But a deeper meaning awaits those who read the Torah as a composition.

Details of the narratives are also significant for our investigation of the names Elohim and YHWH. Each set of tablets is associated with a different name. Elohim is associated with the exoteric and YHWH with the esoteric. The tablets that were to be presented to the people were engraved by Elohim on tablets hewn by Elohim (Exod 32:16). These are the exoteric, shattered tablets. The preparation of the esoteric, second, tablets was a joint venture carried out by Moses and YHWH together. Moses carved out the tablets at YHWH's command for YHWH to engrave. The esoteric tablets demanded an additional activity by Moses, the recipient of the esoteric divine teaching. This is the model for the study of the esoteric Torah; it requires the active participation of the recipient.

Chapter 4. The Division into Ten Words

The Jewish and Catholic Divisions

We now begin to investigate the question of how the divine speech should be divided into ten parts. Figure 7 shows the text of the Decalogue divided into fourteen possible parts. It distinguishes between the two major ways these parts were reduced to ten Words, Catholic (following Augustine) and Jewish.

Over the millennia, two ancient "schools" have been proposed based on whether the two laws that prohibit coveting, (13 and 14 below), should be considered one or two Words. One school is Jewish, and the other is Catholic. The Catholic division derives from St. Augustine and reads 13 and 14 as two Words, while Jewish sources combine them into one Word (as does Protestantism). Both sides agree that 6-12 are seven Words. The dispute is over how to see three remaining Words in the combination of parts 1-5 and 13, 14. The Jewish sources divide 1-5 into two Words, consisting of 1 and 2-5. They combine 13 and 14 for the final Word. According to the Catholic division, 1-5 form one Word and 13 and 14 are two separate Words. The results are marked in columns C=Catholic and J=Jewish in the table.

Figure 7. Jewish and Catholic Divisions of the Decalogue

	Exodus 20, 2-13	C	J
1	I am YHWH thy Elohim, who brought thee out of the land of Egypt, out of the house of bondage.	1	1
2	Thou shalt have no other Elohims before Me.		2
3	Thou shalt not make unto thee a graven image, nor any manner of likeness, of any thing that is in heaven above, or that is in the earth beneath, or that is in the water under the earth;		
4	thou shalt not bow down unto them		
5	nor serve them; for I YHWH thy Elohim am a jealous Elohim, visiting the iniquity of the fathers upon the children unto the third and fourth generation of them that hate Me; and showing mercy unto the thousandth generation of them that love Me and keep My commandments.		
6	Thou shalt not take the name of YHWH thy Elohim in vain; for YHWH will not hold him guiltless that taketh His name in vain.	2	3
7	Remember the sabbath day, to keep it holy. Six days shalt thou labour, and do all thy work; but the seventh day is a sabbath unto YHWH thy Elohim, in it thou shalt not do any manner of work, thou, nor thy son, nor thy daughter, nor thy man-servant, nor thy maid-servant, nor thy cattle, nor thy stranger that is within thy gates; for in six days YHWH made heaven and earth, the sea, and all that in them is, and rested on the seventh day; wherefore YHWH blessed the sabbath day, and hallowed it.	3	4
8	Honour thy father and thy mother, that thy days may be long upon the land which YHWH thy Elohim giveth thee.	4	5
9	Thou shalt not murder.	5	6
10	Thou shalt not commit adultery	6	7
11	Thou shalt not steal.	7	8
12	Thou shalt not bear false witness against thy neighbour.	8	9
13	Thou shalt not covet thy neighbour's house	9	10
14	thou shalt not covet thy neighbour's wife, nor his man-servant, nor his maid-servant, nor his ox, nor his ass, nor any thing that is thy neighbour's.	10	

There are some differences of opinion as to whether the opening of 1, "I am YHWH" is part of the Decalogue. St. Augustine and Philo leave the phrase out, while the Talmud takes it as the first Word (i.e.,

Commandment). But everyone who combines 13 and 14 in the table above must identify two Words before part 6, "You shall not take the name." What is clear from this is M created ambiguity by stating there were ten parts. The text does not number the Words, like the days of creation, nor can the text be divided easily. The careful reader is forced into action and must search for clues leading to M's ten-part division.

An Older Division

There is one more surprising source of division into ten, and this division may be the oldest. Figure 8 illustrates how the Decalogue is divided into ten Words in the Torah scrolls used in synagogues. The text of the Torah (written from right to left) is divided into paragraph-like divisions throughout the scroll. There are two kinds of divisions: major and minor. These are indicated in the scrolls in two ways.

Figure 8. The Divisions of the Decalogue in the Torah Scroll

אנכי יהוה אלהיך אשר הוצאתיך מארץ מצרים מבית עבדים לא יהיה לך אלהים אחרים על פני
לא תעשה לך פסל וכל תמונה אשר בשמים ממעל ואשר בארץ מתחת ואשר במים מתחת
לארץ לא תשתחוה להם ולא תעבדם כי אנכי יהוה אלהיך אל קנא פקד עון אבת על בנים על
שלשים ועל רבעים לשנאי ועשה חסד לאלפים לאהבי ולשמרי מצותי   1   לא תשא את שם
יהוה אלהיך לשוא כי לא ינקה יהוה את אשר ישא את שמו לשוא   2
זכור את יום השבת לקדשו ששת ימים תעבד ועשית כל מלאכתך ויום השביעי שבת ליהוה
אלהיך לא תעשה כל מלאכה אתה ובנך ובתך עבדך ואמתך ובהמתך וגרך אשר בשעריך כי
ששת ימים עשה יהוה את השמים ואת הארץ את הים ואת כל אשר בם וינח ביום השביעי על
כן ברך יהוה את יום השבת ויקדשהו   3   כבד את אביך ואת אמך למען יארכון ימיך על
האדמה אשר יהוה אלהיך נתן לך   4   לא תרצח   5   לא תנאף   6   לא תגנב   7
לא תענה ברעך עד שקר   8   לא תחמד בית רעך   9   לא תחמד אשת רעך ועבדו
ואמתו ושורו וחמרו וכל אשר לרעך   10

An "open" or major paragraph division begins on a new line, like the paragraph after 2 above. A "closed" or minor paragraph division, begins nine letter spaces after the preceding paragraph, on the same line, like 1 above. The illustration shows exactly how the Decalogue looks in the scrolls except for the addition of numerals I have placed after each Word. The division is like the Catholic division, with an additional flourish; there is a major paragraph break before the third Word, "Remember the Sabbath," (that is, after "2" above.) So how is one to judge which set of divisions is the one M referred to when saying there are ten?

There is another element of organization mentioned in the Torah. It relates to the way the tablets appear in iconic representations such as paintings of Moses with the tablets, and Torah scroll covers. All such representations picture a linear set on each tablet, usually 1-5 on one and 6-10 on the other, or according to the Catholic division 1-4 and 5-10. There is no obvious basis in the biblical narrative for either arrangement. But by listening carefully to M we can determine how the Words were arranged on the tablets. The arrangement provides information to help us determine M's division into ten.

M hints at the arrangement of the Words when describing the tablets in Exodus 32:15: "And Moses turned, and went down from the mount, with the two tables of the testimony in his hand; tables that were written on both their sides; on the one side and on the other were they written." The English translation "on both their sides" gives the impression each tablet had writing on both faces, front and back. The Hebrew makes this interpretation very unlikely. "Side" (עבר) in Hebrew does not appear in the Torah as "two sides of a coin" but rather in the sense of "two sides of the street." The distinction is the "sides" of the coin are on two opposite surfaces or planes, while the "sides" of the street are on a single plane. Therefore, it is unlikely M is telling us there was writing on both sides of each tablet. The addition of "on the one side and on the other they were written" locks in the single plane understanding, as appears in the story of Balaam.

And the ass saw the angel of YHWH standing in the way, with his sword drawn in his hand; and the ass turned aside out of the way, and went into the field; and Balaam smote the ass, to turn her into the way. Then the angel of YHWH stood in a hollow way between the vineyards, a fence being *on this side, and a fence on that side.* (Num 22:23-24)

Plainly, the vineyard fence "on this side …and on that side" is in a single plane. There is no case in the Torah where the phrase can be interpreted "front and back." What then could this phrase tell us about the arrangement of the Words on the tablets?

There is a solution to the puzzle. We must imagine the tablets are before us and we begin by writing the first Word on one of the tablets and then shift over to the other tablet for the second Word and then go back to the first tablet for the third Word, etc. We would wind up with the "odd" Words on one tablet and the "evens" on the other, having written on both "sides," "on one…and (then) on the other." I suggest M is saying the tablets were inscribed "alternately." The verification is heuristic. The resulting arrangement of the Words, according to the scroll division in five consecutive pairs, one Word of each pair on each tablet, reveals a woven composition. The consecutive-pairs solution indicates the two prohibitions against coveting are not a case of prolixity, but rather M's confirmation the Words should be read in consecutive pairs, as we will read them in the following chapter.

Chapter 5. Five Consecutive Pairs of Words

The Words are arranged here in consecutive pairs (A-E) in Figure 9 according to the division in Torah scrolls. The first Word in each pair is marked (1), and the second is marked (2). The pairs are marked A-E. This arrangement leads to the identification of five subjects for the five pairs. Besides pair (E), coveting, two other pairs are also obvious: both Words in pair (A) have YHWH as their subject, and pair (B) contains the only two positive commands. A bit less obvious, pair (C) contains capital crimes associated with the human body, murder, and adultery. These two crimes define the extent of human life from conception to death. The Words of the remaining pair, (D), have dishonesty in common.

The consecutive pairs arrangement reveals a composition containing two distinct types of thread paralleling the two types of thread used in weaving. Each tablet has a thread defined by the five Words inscribed on it. These two threads are like lengthwise warp threads. The five threads created by the pairs are like horizontal weft threads. There are new meanings to be discovered embedded in the warp and weft.

Figure 9. The Decalogue in Five Consecutive pairs

Tablet 1	Tablet 2
1A I am YHWH thy Elohim, who brought thee out of the land of Egypt, out of the house of bondage. Thou shalt have no other Elohims before Me. Thou shalt not make unto thee a graven image, nor any manner of likeness, of any thing that is in heaven above, or that is in the earth beneath, or that is in the water under the earth; thou shalt not bow down unto them, nor serve them; for I YHWH thy Elohim am a jealous Elohim, visiting the iniquity of the fathers upon the children unto the third and fourth generation of them that hate Me; and showing mercy unto the thousandth generation of them that love Me and keep My commandments.	**2A** Thou shalt not take the name of YHWH thy Elohim in vain; for YHWH will not hold him guiltless that taketh His name in vain.
1B Remember the sabbath day, to keep it holy. Six days shalt thou labour, and do all thy work; but the seventh day is a sabbath unto YHWH thy Elohim, in it thou shalt not do any manner of work, thou, nor thy son, nor thy daughter, nor thy man-servant, nor thy maid-servant, nor thy cattle, nor the stranger that is within thy gates,; for in six days YHWH made heaven and earth, the sea, and all that in them is, and rested on the seventh day; wherefor YHWH blessed the sabbath, and hallowed it.	**2B** Honour thy father and thy mother, that thy days may be long upon the land which YHWH thy Elohim giveth thee.
1C Thou shalt not murder.	**2C** Thou shalt not commit adultery.
1D Thou shalt not steal.	**2D** Thou shalt not bear false witness against thy neighbour.
1E Thou shalt not covet thy neighbour's house;	**2E** Thou shalt not covet thy neighbour's wife, nor his man-servant, nor his maid-servant, nor his ox, nor his ass, nor any thing that is thy neighbour's

The Weft

We have now seen the Decalogue should be read as five consecutive pairs of Words divided according to the divisions in the Torah scroll. This opens a window to an entirely new vista for exegesis. The best-known part of the Torah, the only text spoken and written by Elohim, contains additional layers of information within its literary structure. In addition to the outer text composed of laws, the divine voice transmits an additional text embedded in the structure. The embedded composition contains five new concepts based on the common elements of the pairs. The structured composition forms an image that is a vehicle for creative meditation, demanding a certain amount of reader input. Every pair of Words demands the reader formulate a concept that links them, often indicated lexically. Integrating the five new concepts is a higher-order synthesis than the two elements of a pair and thus demands even deeper reading and greater creativity from the reader.

Creative meditation can lead to seeing two overlapping images in the five pairs. One is a hierarchal flow from one subjective entity to another, from a passionate YHWH (A) to a passionate person (E). The other is an image of how two diametrically opposite wills, divine (A) and human (E), express themselves through human life (C). The phenomenon of dual imagery is not limited to the woven Decalogue; it is a major organizing principle in the Torah as a whole. After examining the two types of organization in the Decalogue, we will see how they appear in the Torah as a whole.

The Hierarchical Flow

The Decalogue can be read as five consecutive pairs of Words forming an articulate composition by taking a closer look at each pair. The goal of this second look is to determine if and how the pairs connect with each other.

Pair A: "I am," the Name

The subject of pair A is YHWH, divided between YHWH's first-person revelation of who he is, his nature, (1A) and his name (2A). Although (2A) shifts from YHWH speaking in the first person in (1A) to referring to him in the third person, the deity remains the subject.

Pair B: Remember, Honor

We identified pair (B) initially by the fact these are the only two positive commands in the Decalogue. But they also have additional similarities. They both state reasons to observe the commands which refer to YHWH: (1B) *"for* in six days YHWH made heaven and earth"; (2B) *"that* thy days may be long upon the land which YHWH thy Elohim giveth thee."* Another common element appears within these quotations; they both contain "days."

Interestingly, they point to two different directions, the past, when the world was created, and the future in the land. The connection between the creation and parents may also hint at a theme like "origins." While YHWH is connected to pair (B), he is not at the center of the stage, as he is in (A). We thus learn from the context created by the juxtaposition of pairs (A) and (B) that YHWH's relative position, foreground, or background, may be significant.

Pair C: Murder, Adultery

YHWH's movement to the background becomes more significant in the context created through (C). YHWH does not appear at all in (C); Pair C is completely about people. This fact further clarifies the difference between (A) and (B) because YHWH recedes further into the background in (C). We explored several links between the parts of (C), capital crimes, the human body, and the extent of life.

Now we are in the process of defining a context that may help us see more clearly how to grasp pair (C). The significance of the new contexts should not be underestimated. Each pair plays a part in defining a context that is not available from the linear flow of the ten Words. Pairs (A) and (C) are the immediate context of pair (B). We have noted (A) and (B) share "YHWH." Perhaps the element of time explicit in (B) and implicit in (C) (the extent of life) is what links these pairs.

But there is a clearer connection between B and C which also expands one of M's rhetorical paradigms for us, the visual paradigm of "the conceptual middle is in the middle." The visual orientation of the Torah places the logical middle, the "bridge," in the structural middle between the poles in a three-part structure, rather than at the end, where it would appear according to the oral/aural model we are most familiar within our everyday lives. We will now see the visual paradigm can be applied by extension to structures containing more than three parts.

Looking at A-C as an ordered triad according to M's method means B mediates between poles A and C, i.e., there is significant difference between A and C which is in some way bridged by B. The most obvious difference is the subject of A is YHWH, while C deals with people without any mention of YHWH. B bridges the two by connecting people with YHWH. The connection is facilitated by the positive commands. Carrying them out provides a direct link between people and the divinity since the human action is an expression of divine will. This gives the following progression: A, YHWH; B, YHWH's connection with people; C, people.

Pair D: Stealing, False Witness

Pair D verifies we are descending some sort of ladder. While C dealt directly with people, D looks at things associated with people, property (D1), and reputation (D2). Both can be included under "possessions." We can verify the suitability of this description by again using the rule of the conceptual middle to examine C-E. If we describe E as "thoughts about other peoples' property," then the resultant triad is C: others; D: others' property; E:

thoughts about others' property. This reading is summarized in Figure 10.

Figure 10. The Hierarchical Flow of the Pairs of Words

Pair	Subject of Pair
A	YHWH
B	YHWH's connection with people
C	People
D	Things connected with people
E	Thoughts about things connected with people

We have slightly modified our original descriptions of the pairs in line with information provided by their contexts. Not only are the five themes ordered hierarchically, from YHWH to the thoughts or emotions of a person, but they are also firmly attached to each other and form a five-link chain. The ten Words, arranged in pairs, demonstrate an integrated five-part vision.

According to this vision, the subjective individual in pair E is connected to YHWH in pair A through three levels of ordered intermediaries, pairs B-D. It is possible each of the intermediaries is meant to highlight an abstract category through its common subject. The Words of pair B, as noted above, have time in common; pair C, physical human life; and pair D has things attributed to people (possessions). In short, the categories are ordered: time in pair B, people in pair C, things attributed to people in pair D. At the very least, we have found the Decalogue

was constructed to be read as five hierarchically organized pairs of Words.

M's Formal Verification of the Flow

We have developed a reading according to our grasp of the five common themes defined by the pairs. Our reading found links between the pairs, which create a hierarchy, that "flows" downwards. M has used formal, "objective" literary devices to reinforce this reading. I shall refer to one of them as "the flow technique." These devices are only significant in the five-pair reading and are virtually invisible in the linear reading. They can be considered further evidence M intended the pairs to be read hierarchically.

M highlights the three-part organization of pairs C-E by a formal definition of pair D as a linking "middle" between C and E. Since part of the "objectivity" is based on Hebrew word count, I have modified the translation in Figure 11 to reflect it.

Figure 11. The Flow Technique in C-E

	1	2
C	No murder	No adultery
D	No stealing	Thou shalt not bear false witness against **thy neighbour**
E	Thou shalt not covet **thy neighbour's** house	Thou shalt not covet **thy neighbour's** wife…

The Words of pair C have a common structure in the Hebrew. Both Words contain just two words, the negation, "No," followed by a verb. D1 also has two words in the Hebrew, "No stealing." We identified the Words of E as a pair based on a linguistic link, their opening words, "Thou shalt not covet." They

also have another linguistic link, "thy neighbour." D2 also contains "thy neighbor." D has thus been marked as the middle between C and E by combining their specific literary characteristics. Like C, 1D contains only two words; like E, 2D contains language common to both Words of E. The beauty of this formal verification of the "flow" from pair to pair is it only appears in the five-pair arrangement and combines structure (C) and content (E). M, the craftsperson, was fully aware of the interdependence of form and content.

The Concentric Symmetry of the Pairs

Having determined the five pairs are ordered hierarchically, we turn to another formal literary device identified in the order of the pairs: symmetry. Several different symmetries can be seen in the structure. The first symmetry can be discerned from the fact the middle pair, C, divides the five-pair structure symmetrically: pairs A and B are connected to YHWH; pairs D and E relate to people and possessions (property and reputation). It is possible to interpret this symmetry by considering the hierarchical organization. For example, we might say the structure indicates human life, C, has both an "upper" divine aspect, A and B, as well as a "lower" mundane aspect, D and E. While this observation may be valuable in and of itself, the structure contains two more symmetries which will lead us to even more intriguing observations.

The extremities, pairs A and E, share a similarity, as do the adjacent pairs, B and D. The similarity between YHWH, as he appears in A, and the aspect of people addressed in E is that both describe emotive beings: in A, YHWH describes himself as an impassioned "jealous Elohim," while in E people are commanded to restrain their passions, "you shall not covet." The appearance of similar emotions in the extreme pairs may indicate the theme of pair E is more than "coveting." The structure is directing

us to compare YHWH himself in A with individual human personality or subjectivity in E. As we see in the following, the symmetry of pairs B and D will enable us to better understand the implied connection between A, and E.

The similarity between B and D is a function of the connection between each of them and the adjacent extreme pair, A and E. It is not difficult to see a connection between coveting, E, and dishonesty, D. The latter may well be the result of the former. In other words, D appears to stand in a relationship with E, which is the opposite of the order of the pairs, if we see D as a result of E. In general terms, we can say the actions mentioned in D are expressions of desire or will of the subject of E. The subjective individual of E expresses elements of subjectivity by means of the actions in D. We can see the same relationship between A and B. Pair B contains positive actions demanded by YHWH, the subject of A. Observing the Sabbath and honoring parents are concrete expressions of divine will since they are positive commandments. When a person observes the commandment, divine will is expressed through the person.

The physical existence of the person (C) is the focus of both divine and individual wills. Consequently, the concentric reading of the pairs is bidirectional. It is read both from the bottom up and the top down. This movement—up from a person and down from YHWH—recalls Jacob's dream. The three steps in the middle are like a ladder enabling "angels" to go up and down.

Figure 12. Comparison of Hierarchical and Concentric Readings

Pair	Hierarchical Reading	Concentric Symmetrical Reading
A	YHWH	Divine subject
B	YHWH's connection with people (time)	Expression of divine will
C	People	Physical human life
D	Things connected with people	Expression of human will
E	Thoughts about things connected with people	Human subject

As compact as the five pair composition is, it nevertheless contains two different principles of organization, one based on hierarchy and the other on symmetry. The symmetrical reading can also be described as composed of two concentric rings focused on C. The outer ring, A and E, contains

subjects, B and D expressions of the subjects' will, with C as the meeting point of the two subjects.

The conflation of organizing principles in the Decalogue may appear to be the product of an overzealous exegesis of a relatively small text. But it is in fact one of the features that emphasize the

Decalogue as the divine paradigm according to which the Torah was constructed. In broadest terms, the paradigm combines linearity with non-linearity. As we will deal intensively with the non-linear reading of the Torah in the remainder of this book, it is important that we see how prevalent the dual formatting, linear and non-linear, is in the Torah. I have dealt with this point extensively elsewhere so I will just summarize it here in a brief digression.[4]

Digression on the Concentric Organization of the Torah

Multiple levels of organization in the Torah are non-linear. The overall organization of the five books reflects the same conflation of organizing principles as the Decalogue. The whole Torah can be read linearly as a chronology, but it can also be viewed concentrically. The difference between "reading" and "viewing" is significant. When reading the Torah chronologically, it appears to be a history moving from the past to the future of Israel in Canaan. When viewing it concentrically, the chronology becomes the means to create a virtually static picture. The hierarchical ordering of the Decalogue pairs, which I have described as "flowing" is analogous to the chronological flow of the Torah. The Torah is also organized concentrically.

The first intimation that the Torah might be organized concentrically is found in the similar subject divisions of Exodus and Numbers. Both books are divided into sections that relate to the Tabernacle and sections that do not. In Exodus the division is in the middle. The first half of the book relates the exodus from Egypt to the arrival of the Israelites at Sinai. The second half relates in detail, multiple times, in fact, the construction of the tabernacle. Approximately the first quarter of Numbers contains tabernacle-related material. The narrative of the wanderings in the desert, beginning with the departure from Sinai, follows the tabernacle-related material. Nearly all of Leviticus relates to the tabernacle. The tabernacle is thus a single consistent theme spread over three books and occupying the center of the Torah. This "holy" core is more extensive than the forty-years history, divided between the first part of Exodus and the second part of Numbers, which surrounds it. Visually, we can describe the history as a "ring" surrounding the tabernacle narrative. Another ring can be seen by dividing the tabernacle material between the three books it appears in. The material in Leviticus largely deals with the functioning of the tabernacle, including sacrifices and the priests' obligations. The material in Exodus, addressing the construction of the tabernacle, and in Numbers, its maintenance, is subordinate to the core operations described in Leviticus. The ancillary Tabernacle material thus forms a "ring" around Leviticus. We can sketch the concentric arrangement as follows:

Figure 13. The Concentric Arrangement of Exodus, Leviticus, and Numbers

Exodus	(H) History
	(T) Tabernacle (ancillary)
Leviticus	Tabernacle (core)
Numbers	(T) Tabernacle (ancillary)
	(H) History

The Arrangement of the Text Reflects the Shape of the Encampment

This concentric arrangement is like the arrangement of the desert encampment as described in Numbers 2:1-3:39. At the focus of the camp stood the Tabernacle and the precincts of the priests, like Leviticus in our figure above. It was surrounded by two concentric rings of people. The inner ring was composed of the families of the Levites who served in the Tabernacle, which is parallel to our ancillary ring (T). The outer ring was composed of the twelve tribal camps of the Israelites, parallel to the ring of Israelite history (H). The concentric structure of the Torah imitates a structure described within it, the Israelite encampment in the wilderness. Thus, the Torah is organized both linearly, as a history, and

[4] See: Moshe Kline, "Structure Is Theology: The Composition of Leviticus," in *Current Issues in Priestly and Related Literature: The Legacy of Jacob Milgrom and Beyond* (eds., Roy E. Gane and Ada Taggar-Cohen; Atlanta: SBL Press, 2015), 225-264

non-linearly, in the format of the wilderness encampment, symmetrically. The two organizing principles resonate with the dual organizing principles of the Decalogue. As the Decalogue is introduced as Elohim's speech (Exod. 20:1) and writing (32:16), M makes the case that the Torah should be read as a document which at the very least is based on a divine paradigm.

The Decalogue Was Hidden in Plain Sight

The discovery that the Decalogue is composed of five pairs of Words confronts us with an exciting challenge; we are looking at a previously unknown biblical document. But it was not hidden in a cave thousands of years ago; *the document was embedded in the Torah by M in plain view!* This document is the composition which M indicates was reserved for Moses' eyes alone. The challenge is to understand what can be learned from this composition. Eventually, we will also have to address the question of why it was not known. For now, we will explore the added value of what we can learn from the five pairs of Words, as opposed to what we learn from ten individual Words.

The Difference between the Tablets

If our solution to the "puzzle" is correct, and we have divided and arranged the Words properly, we should now be able to read each tablet as a coherent composition. Since Elohim created two stone tablets, it seems each was intended to display a substantial concept. This implies the Decalogue is based on a conceptual dyad represented by the two stone tablets, a dyad so significant Elohim divided the Words between two tablets to demonstrate it. If we are to interpret the fact the stone tablets were created before they were inscribed, we might say the dyad in some way takes precedence over the details of the Words. Remember we are examining the only document presenting itself as the representation of divine speech created by the divine hand. Whatever distinction we find between the tablets carries theological significance.

The dyad must be foundational, truly a divine dyad, an Israelite yin and yang. This conceptual dyad is not the only such dyad in the Torah. As we have seen in Part One (and will see in more detail in Part Three), the days of creation reveal a dyad we characterized as "one and many" and "separate and connected." The second creation narrative also has a dyad, the two trees in the Garden of Eden.

In fact, the Tree of Life and the Tree of Knowledge of good and bad may help us clarify the tablets. We will see M has given us a good reason to compare the tablets with the trees. We will proceed by examining the divine dyad expressed through the two tablets in two ways. First, we will see what dyads might be found on the tablets. After that we read the five-Word composition on each tablet.

The Guarding Cherubim

M links the two stone tablets with the two named trees in the Garden of Eden. The connection is made by means of the appearance of cherubim in association with both the tablets and the trees. The function of the cherubim in both cases is similar. Regarding the tablets, the cherubim were attached to the cover of the ark containing the tablets. They are described with their wings outspread as "covering" the Ark (Exodus 25:20). While the Hebrew is usually understood as "cover," the Hebrew can also have the sense of "protect."

The cherubim were also placed outside of the Garden of Eden to "protect" or "guard" it (Genesis 3:24). In addition, YHWH is present in the Holy of Holies where He speaks with Moses from between the cherubim. Similarly, YHWH Elohim is present in the garden of Eden where HaAdam hears his voice "walking about." The parallel presence of the cherubim, combined with the similarity of their functions and the presence of the divine voice, suggests we look for a parallel between the two stone tablets in the ark in the middle of the camp, and the two trees in the garden.

The Trees

The function of the tree of life is to maintain the life of the person who eats from it. "And YHWH Elohim said: 'Behold, HaAdam is become as one of us, to know good and evil; and now, lest he put forth his hand, and take also of the tree of life, and eat, and live for ever '"

The effects of eating from the tree of knowledge of good and bad can be observed via the change that took place within the people who ate from it. Before eating from the tree, they were naked, but they were not ashamed. After eating they were ashamed and covered themselves with fig leaves. Shame requires the presence of another person. M specifically uses a plural reflexive form of the verb translated "were not ashamed," indicating it is a social emotion, one requiring a common set of values. These common values appeared after eating from the forbidden tree. Therefore, one of the differences between the two trees is the tree of life has a purely personal existential effect (life), while the tree of knowledge of good and bad has a social effect, on relationships.

Moreover, the name of the tree of knowledge is formulated in a manner implying the use of language— "good and bad" are linguistic attributes. Therefore, the Tree of Knowledge presupposes the use of language, which is not necessarily true of the Tree of Life. Speech, being an act of social intercourse, requires an "other." So, we have yet another indication the tree of knowledge is in some way "social" while the tree of life is personal. There is a similarity between this distinction between the trees and the distinction we saw between the two three-day cycles in the creation. The first cycle, days 1-3, like the Tree of Life, concerns separate individual entities, while the second cycle, days 4-6, like the Tree of Knowledge, concerns classes of connected entities, (stars, birds etc.)

Identifying the Trees with the Tablets

M has created yet another link between the tablets and the trees in the Garden of Eden based on the names of the trees. The names given to the two trees in the Garden are closely associated with the central pair of Words, C, the visual focus of the tablets. Word 1C prohibits murder and is thus an obvious link to the Tree of Life. To see the connection between 2C, "Thou shalt not commit adultery", and the tree of knowledge, it is only necessary to note the Hebrew word for "knowledge" is identical to the word for carnal knowledge, sexual intercourse, as in "HaAdam *knew* Eve."

We now have enough information from other divine dyads to formulate a hypothesis regarding the difference between the tablets. We can expect tablet 1, linked to the tree of life through its central Word, 1C, to embody a principle like "one" or "separate" and focus on the individual. Tablet 2 could reflect a principle of "many" or "connected" and focus on relationships. But before we examine the compositions on each of the individual tablets, we must first clarify the difference between 1E and 2E.

Pair E: A House Is Not a Possession

The same device which M used to identify the Words of E as a pair, the common verb "covet," can be a stumbling block when examining the distinction between the tablets. If we limit ourselves to examining the act prohibited in each Word here, "coveting," we are forced to say there is no real difference between 1E and 2E. This is evidently why some consider them a single Word.

Figure 14. The use of 'house' in Thread E

1E	2E
Thou shalt not covet thy neighbour's house	Thou shalt not covet thy neighbour's wife, nor his man-servant, nor his maid-servant, nor his ox, nor his ass, nor any thing that is thy neighbour's

M has used this apparent difficulty as an instruction to the careful reader. Since the actions are the same, the significant distinction between the Words must be between the objects. We are forced to ask why the "house" in 1E is not included in "anything that your fellow man has" in 2E.

"House" (*bayit*) appears twice in the Decalogue. The other appearance is in the other pole (1A) when YHWH refers to Egypt as "the *house* of bondage." It is clear, even from the limited use in the Decalogue itself, the Hebrew term has multiple meanings. Other meanings of *bayit* include "home," as used in Genesis when Abram is told to leave his father's "home," and as in Exodus, "the *house* of Levy," which like "the *house* of David," refers to family, meaning "the line of." I would like to suggest we should understand the usage here to be akin to the modern concept of "identity." Describing Egypt as "the *house* of slavery" means we identify Egypt as a place of slavery, much as we identify a Levite as belonging to the "*house* of Levy." The "house" is the source of one's identity, which defines or "contains" the individual.

We can now understand pair E as referring to two different aspects of an individual's identity. All the people and things mentioned in 2E have in common that while they belong to one person today, they can be transferred to another tomorrow. Even a wife can be divorced or widowed and marry another. They are not really an intrinsic part of one's identity but, rather, are attributed to their owner. On the other hand, one cannot escape one's family line, the "house" which is an inalienable part of one's identity. Thus, through the two prohibitions against coveting, M has pointed to two different aspects of an individual's identity, that which is intrinsic and that which is extrinsic.

This is another opportunity to marvel at M's literary skill. The common action in pair E, covet, leads to discovering the ten Words should be read as five consecutive pairs, while the difference between the objects of the same pair leads to discovering a distinction between the tablets. In fact, M has directed us to the dyad *one and many*.

One and Many

Our examination of divine dyads leads us to recognize pairs of terms such as "separate and connected" and "one and many" as foundational. M found a formal way to demonstrate these dyads in E.

Word 1E prohibits the coveting of just *one feature*, ancestry, while 2E prohibits the coveting of *many objects*. The grammatical objects of the single verb "covet" are themselves "one" in 1E and "many" in 2E.

Moreover, in 1E the "house" has been separated from "anything that your fellow man has" in 2E. At the same time, many other specifics in 2E like "his ox, or his donkey", while seemingly superfluous, are connected to "anything." Thus, in pair E, M demonstrates both "one and many" and "separate and connected."

We now have three dyads that we can divide between the tablets to help us discover why there are two tablets. Tablet 1 appears to be associated with "one", "separate", and "intrinsic," while tablet 2 relates to "many," "connected," and "extrinsic." The connection we noted between "house" and "identity" indicates a fourth useful dyad "self" in 1 and "other" in 2. These dyads give a strong sense of how the tablets differ. We will now look closely at the five-Word composition on tablet 2 and its implications for understanding the divine dyad.

Tablet 2: Relationships

Figure 15. Relationships on Tablet 2

2A
Thou shalt not take the name of YHWH thy Elohim in vain; for YHWH will not hold him guiltless that taketh His name in vain.
2B
Honour thy father and thy mother, that thy days may be long upon the land which YHWH thy Elohim giveth thee.
2C
Thou shalt not commit adultery.
2D
Thou shalt not bear false witness against thy neighbour.
2E
Thou shalt not covet thy neighbour's wife, nor his man-servant, nor his maid-servant, nor his ox, nor his ass, nor any thing that is thy neighbour's

As shown in Figure 15, Words 2B, 2C, and 2D are based on interpersonal relationships: parents and children in 2B, husband and wife in 2C, and colluding witnesses in 2D (witnessing was done in pairs or threes). Progressively less-durable connections bind together the three sets of people. Word 2B contains a blood relationship, 2C a

connection through marriage, and 2D a connection through circumstance. These three direct the careful reader to look for similar connections in 2A and 2E. The connection between YHWH and his name in 2A is clearly the strongest of them all since they are eternally inseparable. On the contrary, the connection between an owner and his property 2E is the weakest since they can easily be separated. The ordering is thus based on the intensity of the connection, from the strongest to the weakest. The Words of tablet 2 are arranged hierarchically according to the strength of the connection.

A Five-Part Social Vision

By focusing on the social connections in 2B-D, we can integrate 2A and 2E into a five-part social vision. The stability of marriage based on 2C is a precondition for multigenerational stability in 2B. This may indicate we can read tablet 2 from the bottom-up. If we do, we begin with the desire for private property in 2E. This desire in 2E leads to the development of legal institutions in 2D, which leads to the stability of marriages in 2C, which leads to familial devotion; in 2B, with concomitant social stability "that thy days may be long upon the land which YHWH thy Elohim giveth thee." A stable society can devote energy to the pursuit of wisdom, knowledge of the divine name, 2A.

Once we have read the tablet from the bottom to the top as an outline of social organization, we can just as well read it from the top-down as a series of dependencies. Divine knowledge, 2A, is dependent on familial piety and social stability, 2B, which is dependent on marital stability, etc.

The Decalogue is a five-pair composition with complex inner structuring. Each five-Word tablet is also a composition unto itself. The following chart summarizes the composition on tablet 2. This thematic organization is consistent with the description of the Words as arranged hierarchically according to the strength of relationships. The stronger the relationship—that is—the higher up on the tablet, the more elevated the stage of social development.

Figure 16. Tablet 2 as a Series of Relationships Pointing to Social Dependencies

	Relationship	Societal Dependencies
2A	Inseparable, Divine Name	Knowledge of the Divine Name Depends on
2B	Blood	Familial Piety / Social Stability Depends on
2C	Marriage	Marriage Depends on
2D	Witnesses	Law Depends on
2E	Ownership	The Desire for Property

The "social dependencies" reading summarized in Figure 16 is my attempt to find meaning in the obviously well-ordered connection hierarchy. These are new realms of exegesis that developed from the esoteric non-linear reading. Tablet 2 presents itself as an ordered five-part unit even though its five Words not consecutive in the Torah. The order itself is determined by a scale of intensity applied to relationships. The arrangement is a clear literary artifact. When probing the order to see if it contains additional meanings, (such as the foundations of social organization), we search for what information M communicates through this ordered set of Words. The key for further exploration is: the five Words on tablet 2 are a planned unit held together by a literary glue that contains "relationships" as a primary ingredient. Any further exegesis must account for this fact.

Tablet 1: Individuals

Figure 17. Tablet 1: Focus on Individuals

Tablet 1
1A
I am YHWH thy Elohim, who brought thee out of the land of Egypt, out of the house of bondage. Thou shalt have no other Elohims before Me. Thou shalt not make unto thee a graven image, nor any manner of likeness, of any thing that is in heaven above, or that is in the earth beneath, or that is in the water under the earth; thou shalt not bow down unto them, nor serve them; for I YHWH thy Elohim am a jealous Elohim, visiting the iniquity of the fathers upon the children unto the third and fourth generation of them that hate Me; and showing mercy unto the thousandth generation of them that love Me and keep My commandments.
1B
Remember the sabbath day, to keep it holy. Six days shalt thou labour, and do all thy work; but the seventh day is a sabbath unto YHWH thy Elohim, in it thou shalt not do any manner of work, thou, nor thy son, nor thy daughter, nor thy man-servant, nor thy maid-servant, nor thy cattle, nor the stranger that is within thy gates,; for in six days YHWH made heaven and earth, the sea, and all that in them is, and rested on the seventh day; wherefor YHWH blessed the sabbath
1C
Thou shalt not murder.
1D
Thou shalt not steal.
1E
Thou shalt not covet thy neighbour's house;

The investigation of tablet 1 starts with the observation it shares a formal similarity with tablet 2: both tablets define their themes through the three central Words on each tablet. On tablet 2 three social pairings, parents and children, husband and wife, and witnesses set the "relationships" theme. Words 1B, 1C, and 1D, the three central Words of tablet 1, form a single three-part image of a person. The theme is most easily grasped by applying the perspective of concentric planning we have observed above. We start from the middle 1C with a living individual whose life is sacrosanct. This physical being has two aspects to its life, subjective or spiritual (1B) and objective, material (1D). The three central Words (1B, C, D) indicate three ordered aspects of an individual, visualized as nested one within the other.

- The command to hallow the sabbath in 1B is based on a spiritual act that imitates YHWH. "Remember the sabbath day, to keep it holy... wherefor YHWH blessed the sabbath, and hallowed it." The individual who observes the sabbath is, spiritually, like YHWH and transcends the day-to-day world.

- In 1C, the spirit is embodied in the living being, reminiscent of the breath of life being breathed into a human's earthen body in (Gen. 2:7).

- Like the body being clothed by YHWH Elohim before leaving Eden (Gen. 3:21), Word 1D grants the physical living person a protective mantel, possessions.

Figuratively, the three aspects of the individual are nested like Russian dolls: property (1D) is like a garment that enshrouds the living body in (1C), which, in turn, is the garment of the spirit (1B). What they have in common is all three are aspects of an individual. They should, apparently, be grasped as an integrated entity, a whole person. How does this person connect to the framework of 1A and 1E?

If we continue the imagery of nesting, we should see 1A as nested in 1B and 1E as providing a nest for 1D. It is hard to argue against the imagery of the "house," 1E, being a nest! But still, we should look at the specifics. If 1D is a protective garment shielding the bare individual in 1C, then the clan, or family in 1E must be a super garment, for it protects and even engulfs everything pertaining to the propertied individual in 1D.

The full series is: the holy deity is the source (1A); the deity's holiness nests in the human spirit (1B), which nests in a body (1C), which nests in property (1D), which nests within the clan (1E). The rule is each element in the series after 1A is a garment, or nest, for the previous element. The divinity (1A) is "wrapped" in four garments, three belonging to an individual, and one a "house," the ultimate vessel that defines the inherent identity of the individual. As with tablet 2, here too the possibilities for exegesis are manifold.

Integrating the Two Tablets

We have discussed the concept "divine dyad" in several contexts. It reflects an inherent duality in the world and may be associated with the two divine names we are investigating. We began our exploration of the two five-Word compositions on the two tablets with the expectation of finding a divine dyad distinguishing between them. We found the dyad, "individuals and relationships," by observing the separate basis of ordering on each tablet: tablet 1 is ordered as a five-part single entity described from the inside out; tablet 2 contains five social relationships in descending order of durability. The two ordering principles are consistent with the expectations we derived from the Edenic trees and the two sets of the days of creation. Tablet 1 describes aspects of an individual and tablet 2 aspects of relationships. The order on tablet 1 presents stages in the development of a human identity. The farther down on the tablet, the more fully defined the individual. On tablet 2, the farther down on the tablet, the weaker the relationship. Placing the two together creates an interactive image. Is M saying the more well-defined the individual, the weaker the social connection? This feels counterintuitive and remains a subject for further exploration.

Summary and Conclusions of Part Two

The goal of this Part was to present the divine paradigm of woven text. M presents the tablets as the divine paradigm that reproduces divine speech through divine writing. We began with a puzzle. M says the tablets contained ten Words but does not divide them for us nor say how they were arranged on the tablets. We used the paragraph divisions within the Torah scrolls and literary indicators, together with a hint from Exodus 32:15 to solve the puzzle.

The Words should be read in consecutive pairs. This indicated they should be understood as written alternately on the tablets, with the odd numbered Words on tablet 1 and the even numbered Words on tablet 2. The five pairs produce five new concepts that can be understood both hierarchically and concentrically. Each of the tablets also proved to be ordered according to its half of the "divine dyad" represented by the two tablets, providing two more concepts, "individual" and "relationships." The seven new concepts revealed by the arrangement of pairs are like a weave containing two warp threads, the tablets, and five weft threads, the pairs. Consequently, insofar as the Words inscribed on the tablets represent divine speech, it seems M is saying the deity speaks in weaves.

The Decalogue is presented as the deity's only self-written text, a text that replicates divine speech. We have discovered the text can be read in two different ways, linearly and multi-dimensionally. In a linear way, as it has been read for millennia, it is primarily a collection of laws. But when the text is read as a two-dimensional weave, it displays multiple levels of composition via ordered relationships. Simply put, the woven format provides for the embedding of multiple additional meanings. Woven text is much richer than the literal content of its separate parts. Since none of the additional embedded meanings are literal, it demands a reader's active participation to compile them. The activated reader must partner with the author to reveal the meanings rooted in the woven structure. The reader thus becomes a partner in revelation, an ever-flowing spring. This is the fuller meaning of the narratives regarding the two sets of tablets.

The first tablets, intended for all the people, are like the universally grasped piecemeal linear reading. The shattering of the tablets into pieces prevented the people from seeing the five-pair woven structure. The formatted second tablets were hidden from the people in the box which Moses prepared before receiving them. The only individual— other than Moses— who could have seen the writing on the tablets was Joshua, who we are told accompanied Moses down the mountain when the first tablets were still intact. Moses and Joshua were thus the only ones, according to M's narrative, to possess the esoteric knowledge of divine writing.

We have been reading the Torah as a book composed by an author, M. From this perspective, the Decalogue and the stone tablets have special significance. M claims possession of a unique writing paradigm, one attributed to the deity itself. We have already seen hints the six-day creation narrative is also a woven text. In other words, not only did Elohim speak and write the Decalogue as a weave, but he also spoke the world into being according to this paradigm. We will have a closer look at the creation weave in Part Three. As we progress, we will see evidence M composed the entire Torah according to the woven format of the Decalogue. Each of its eighty-six Units is a two-dimensional weave. The Decalogue thus provides the key to the esoteric reading of the Torah. Just as the vision of the writing on the tablets was reserved for the eyes of Moses and Joshua, so too was the knowledge of the Torah's structure reserved for the few.

Part Three: The Units of the Woven Torah

Our analysis of the Exodus Decalogue and the stone-tablets narratives in the previous Part has taught us that the Torah contains text written for two different audiences, according to the divine paradigm of exoteric/esoteric writing. One audience, the public, would grasp it piecemeal, shattered, while the other, initiated individuals, could see it as a coherent whole. We will see that this description of two intended audiences applies to the whole Torah. The same technique that established the Decalogue's coherence as a composition was applied to all the Units of the Torah. As a public text, to be read in public, the Torah appears to be a linear composition. However, each of its Units was constructed as a woven text containing additional meanings for those who know how to access and read the esoteric woven format.

The woven format enabled M to embed information within the text utilizing juxtaposition of textual elements within the weave, such as the pairs of Decalogue Words noted in Part Two, as well as the arrangements on each of the two tablets. The overall "picture" or composition created by the weave, such as in the flow from pair to pair in the Decalogue, is virtually inaccessible in the linear reading. Thus, the formatted Units in *The Woven Torah* provide access to additional layers of meaning embedded in the woven structure. We will look at the formatting and notation used in *The Woven Torah* in the following examples.

This Part includes two sets of examples. The first two are short examples of Units that demonstrate how the woven format reveals meanings not easily derived from linear readings. The first is Genesis Unit XII (26:1-33), a narrative Unit detailing Isaac's interaction with Abimelech. We will see that the woven formatting was employed in legal Units as well as narratives through the second short example, Leviticus Unit XXII (27). The second set of examples consists of two Units of special interest to us. The creation weave, Genesis Unit I (1:1-2:3), details the seven days of Elohim's creation. The signs, or "decreation" weave, Exodus Unit III (6:29-11:10), demonstrates how YHWH reveals himself by changing aspects of the natural world created by Elohim. There is a set of matches between the creation Unit and the signs Unit suggesting that they were conceived to be grasped as related or parallel. Details of the six days of the creation of the natural world are negated in Egypt through the signs according to a strict ordering. The overall effect is to emphasize the signs Unit as where YHWH reveals himself through the signs, which can be conceived as a form of "decreation." The two texts totally resonate with each other. *Their interlocking provides some of the strongest evidence of how M distinguished between Elohim and YHWH.*

Chapter 6. Genesis Unit XII (26:1-33)

We begin with a narrative Unit that clearly demonstrates characteristics of woven text. Having analyzed the tablets of the Decalogue as a paradigm, we will be able to see how the paradigm can be applied in Genesis 26:1-33 (Unit XII). The Unit contains the narrative of Isaac and Abimelech, as well as Isaac's interactions with YHWH. In fact, it contains all the narratives concerning Isaac other than those which refer to his immediate family.

Genesis XII is defined as a Unit both by its own form and content as well as by the surrounding material. Unit XI closes with Jacob obtaining Esau's birthright, and Unit XIII opens with Esau's marriages and continues with Jacob once more obtaining the birthright and closes with Esau's additional marriages. Unit XII is thus surrounded by narratives about Jacob and Esau, who do not appear in this Unit at all.

The linear reading of Genesis 26:1-33 seems uneven because it jumps back and forth between its dual subjects, Isaac's interactions with YHWH and with Abimelech, and contains another disjuncture as well, about wells. The woven reading smooths out the bumps while revealing a hidden theme: Isaac's liberation from the shadow of his father Abraham. (We will use this example to get better acquainted with the formats and notation found in *The Woven Torah* from which all the examples below are drawn). To clarify the transformation of the linear text to the woven format, we will start by looking at the Unit as it appears in Bibles, with a slight modification. (Note that breaks are added where a section of narrative ends, and numbers are added to the sections).

Genesis Unit XII

1

26:1 And there was a famine in the land, beside the first famine that was in the days of Abraham. And Isaac went unto Abimelech king of the Philistines unto Gerar. 26:2 And YHWH appeared unto him, and said: 'Go not down unto Egypt; dwell in the land which I shall tell thee of. 26:3 Sojourn in this land, and I will be with thee, and will bless thee; for unto thee, and unto thy seed, I will give all these lands, and I will establish the oath which I swore unto Abraham thy father; 26:4 and I will multiply thy seed as the stars of heaven, and will give unto thy seed all these lands; and by thy seed shall all the nations of the earth bless themselves; 26:5 because that Abraham hearkened to My voice, and kept My charge, My commandments, My statutes, and My laws.'

26:6 And Isaac dwelt in Gerar. 26:7 And the men of the place asked him of his wife; and he said: 'She is my sister'; for he feared to say: 'My wife'; 'lest the men of the place should kill me for Rebekah, because she is fair to look upon.' 26:8 And it came to pass, when he had been there a long time, that Abimelech king of the Philistines looked out at a window, and saw, and, behold, Isaac was sporting with Rebekah his wife. 26:9 And Abimelech called Isaac, and said: 'Behold, of a surety she is thy wife; and how saidst thou: She is my sister?' And Isaac said unto him: 'Because I said: Lest I die because of her.' 26:10 And Abimelech said: 'What is this thou hast done unto us? one of the people might easily have lain with thy wife, and thou wouldest have brought guiltiness upon us.' 26:11 And Abimelech charged all the people, saying: 'He that toucheth this man or his wife shall surely be put to death.'

2

26:12 And Isaac sowed in that land, and found in the same year a hundredfold; and YHWH blessed him. 26:13 And the man waxed great, and grew more and more until he became very great. 26:14 And he had possessions of flocks, and possessions of herds, and a great household; and the Philistines envied him. 26:15 Now all the wells which his father's servants had digged in the days of Abraham his father, the Philistines had stopped them, and filled them with earth.

26:16 And Abimelech said unto Isaac: 'Go from us; for thou art much mightier than we.' 26:17 And Isaac departed thence, and encamped in the valley of Gerar, and dwelt there. 26:18 And Isaac digged again the wells of water, which they had digged in the days of Abraham his father; for the Philistines had stopped them after the death of Abraham; and he called their names after the names by which his father had called them. 26:19 And Isaac's servants digged in the valley, and found there a well of living water. 26:20 And the herdmen of Gerar strove with Isaac's herdmen, saying: 'The water is ours.' And he called the name of the well Esek; because they contended with him. 26:21 And they digged another well, and they strove for that also. And he called the name of it Sitnah. 26:22 And he removed from thence, and digged another well; and for that they strove not. And he called the name of it Rehoboth; and he said: 'For now YHWH hath made room for us, and we shall be fruitful in the land.'

3

26:23 And he went up from thence to Beer-sheba. 26:24 And YHWH appeared unto him the same night, and said: 'I am the Elohim of Abraham thy father. Fear not, for I am with thee, and will bless thee, and multiply thy seed for My servant Abraham's sake.' 26:25 And he builded an altar there, and called upon the name of YHWH, and pitched his tent there; and there Isaac's servants digged a well.

26:26 Then Abimelech went to him from Gerar, and Ahuzzath his friend, and Phicol the captain of his host. 26:27 And Isaac said unto them: 'Wherefore are ye come unto me, seeing ye hate me, and have sent me away from you?' 26:28 And they said: 'We saw plainly that YHWH was with thee; and we said: Let there now be an oath betwixt us, even betwixt us and thee, and let us make a covenant with thee; 26:29 that thou wilt do us no hurt, as we have not touched thee, and as we have done unto thee nothing but good, and have sent thee away in peace; thou art now the blessed of YHWH.' 26:30 And he made them a feast, and they did eat and drink. 26:31 And they rose up betimes in the morning, and swore one to another; and Isaac sent them away, and they departed from him in peace. 26:32 And it came to pass the same day, that Isaac's servants came, and told him concerning the well which they had digged, and said unto him: 'We have found water.' 26:33 And he called it Shibah. Therefore the name of the city is Beer-sheba unto this day.

I have divided the linear text into three numbered sections, 1-3. Each of these sections is a doublet, containing two scenes, with the division between the scenes marked by an empty space. A single pattern repeats in all three doublets; in the first scene of each doublet, YHWH addresses Isaac, while Abimelech addresses him in the second scene. In other words, there are three parallel pairs of scenes. The division into scenes establishes that there are two parallel story threads, one involving YHWH and one involving Abimelech. The two threads are braided or interwoven. Transforming this linear layout to the woven format has several advantages. The two scenes of each section are arranged side by side, enabling the reader to examine each of the threads independently as well as to compare them sided by side. Most significantly, it gives a direct view of a composition composed of six parts which are woven together by two warp threads and three weft threads.

Figure 18 presents a skeletal outline of how the text will be arranged as weave. Our three sections are presented as three rows, or weft threads. Each thread is divided into two parts, its two scenes. The result is that one column, warp thread, contains only YHWH's addresses to Isaac, while the other warp thread contains only the scenes which involve Abimelech. The three weft threads are marked by the same numbers we used above, 1-3. The warp threads are marked by the first two letters of the Hebrew alphabet, א (aleph) and ב (bet). Because we will eventually need to note many new divisions within the text, I have had to resort to many forms of notation. Later we will also meet the third letter of the Hebrew alphabet, ג (gimmel). (While it may take a bit of time for non-Hebrew readers to get used to these letters, anyone investigating the esoteric Torah should be able to recognize a few Hebrew letters!)

Figure 18. Skeletal Outline of Gen XII (26:1-33)

1א	1ב
1-5	6-11
2א	2ב
12-15	16-22
3א	3ב
23-25	26-33

Let us take a moment to note how the linear text of the Torah, as it appears in books and Torah scrolls, is transcribed to the tabular format of *The Woven Torah*. The most important convention regards the order in which the segments of woven text are transcribed from the linear text, 1א, 1ב, 2א, 2ב, 3א, 3ב. In broad terms, the figure indicates that the Unit is divided on two different levels. It has three major divisions, weft threads 1-3, which contain consecutive pairs of segments. Each weft thread is divided into two smaller divisions, segments א and ב. As we found in the Decalogue, there is added value in reading the two segments of the weft threads together to determine the concept which unites them. Similarly, there is information to be found by examining the three segments of the warp threads.

The multi-level division is the cornerstone of the non-linear, esoteric, reading. In the Decalogue, the multi-level division was displayed through the division into ten Words and five pairs of Words. Figure 18 shows that Genesis Unit XII contains the equivalent of six "words," textual segments, which form three pairs, 1-3. According to the tabular convention, each weft thread, pair of segments, represents a concept, as did each pair of Words in the Decalogue. In addition, each warp thread, א and ב, consisting of three non-consecutive segments, also represents a coherent theme, as did each stone tablet. A full understanding of the Unit requires the integration of the weft themes and warp themes as shown in Figure 19.

Figure 19. Thematic Outline of Gen XII

Weft Themes	Warp Themes	
Isaac and Abraham	YHWH's Blessings	Abimelech's Antipathy
1 **Isaac is Compared with Abraham**	1א 1-5	1ב 6-11
2 **Isaac's Wealth and** **a Struggle over Abraham's "Wells"**	2א 12-15	2ב 26-22
3 **Isaac Produces His Own Well** **and Becomes Independent**	3א 23-25	3ב 26-33

Figure 19 adds the general themes of the threads to the skeletal outline. These are the subjects revealed by the woven-text reading, which are inaccessible from a simple hearing or linear reading. They are the themes which the individual must integrate to access M's conceptual plan of the Unit. This is not the place for a detailed analysis, but the general lines are enlightening. M begins by comparing Isaac with his father Abraham in weft thread 1. In 2 Isaac begins to develop his independence by becoming independently wealthy. But he is still compared with Abraham through his father's wells. In thread 3 he obtains his own well and steps out of his father's shadow. The process is paralleled by YHWH's blessings in thread א. In 1א, YHWH promises to bless Isaac and be with him in the future, "I will be with thee, and will bless thee," while detailing Abraham's blessing. In 2א YHWH blesses Isaac *after* his successful hundred-fold harvest. Finally, in 3א YHWH is with Isaac, "for I am with thee."

This barebones outline of the content of the Unit is sufficient to demonstrate that the woven format reveals an otherwise hidden layer of meaning. Even more important for us at this point is that we see indications that the Unit was planned to be understood as a weave. It's clearly challenging to see these themes in the linear reading, which further demonstrates how *The Woven Torah*'s layout enhances meaning. In addition to a visualization of the literary structure of the Unit, *The Woven Torah* also contains a set of colored highlights to emphasize significant parallels between parts of the Unit. An explanation of the highlights follows Figure 20.

Figure 20. The Woven Text of Genesis Unit XII

1א

26:1 And there was a famine in the land, beside the first famine that was in the days of Abraham. And Isaac went unto Abimelech king of the Philistines unto Gerar. 26:2 And YHWH appeared unto him, and said: 'Go not down unto Egypt; dwell in the land which I shall tell thee of. 26:3 Sojourn in this land, and I will be with thee, and will bless thee; for unto thee, and unto thy seed, I will give all these lands, and I will establish the oath which I swore unto Abraham thy father; 26:4 and I will multiply thy seed as the stars of heaven, and will give unto thy seed all these lands; and by thy seed shall all the nations of the earth bless themselves; 26:5 because that Abraham hearkened to My voice, and kept My charge, My commandments, My statutes, and My laws.'

2א

A 26:12 And Isaac sowed in that land, and found in the same year a hundredfold; and YHWH blessed him. 26:13 And the man waxed great, and grew more and more until he became very great. 26:14 And he had possessions of flocks, and possessions of herds, and a great household; and the Philistines envied him.
B 26:15 Now all the wells which his father's servants had digged in the days of Abraham his father, the Philistines had stopped them, and filled them with earth.

3א

26:23 And he went up from thence to Beer-sheba. 26:24 And YHWH appeared unto him the same night, and said: 'I am the Elohim of Abraham thy father. Fear not, for I am with thee, and will bless thee, and multiply thy seed for My servant Abraham's sake.' 26:25 And he builded an altar there, and called upon the name of YHWH, and pitched his tent there; and there Isaac's servants digged a well.

1ב

26:6 And Isaac dwelt in Gerar. 26:7 And the men of the place asked him of his wife; and he said: 'She is my sister'; for he feared to say: 'My wife'; 'lest the men of the place should kill me for Rebekah, because she is fair to look upon.' 26:8 And it came to pass, when he had been there a long time, that Abimelech king of the Philistines looked out at a window, and saw, and, behold, Isaac was sporting with Rebekah his wife. 26:9 And Abimelech called Isaac, and said: 'Behold, of a surety she is thy wife; and how saidst thou: She is my sister?' And Isaac said unto him: 'Because I said: Lest I die because of her.' 26:10 And Abimelech said: 'What is this thou hast done unto us? one of the people might easily have lain with thy wife, and thou wouldest have brought guiltiness upon us.' 26:11 And Abimelech charged all the people, saying: 'He that toucheth this man or his wife shall surely be put to death.'

2ב

A 26:16 And Abimelech said unto Isaac: 'Go from us; for thou art much mightier than we.' 26:17 And Isaac departed thence, and encamped in the valley of Gerar, and dwelt there.
B 26:18 And Isaac digged again the wells of water, which they had digged in the days of Abraham his father; for the Philistines had stopped them after the death of Abraham; and he called their names after the names by which his father had called them. 26:19 And Isaac's servants digged in the valley, and found there a well of living water. 26:20 And the herdmen of Gerar strove with Isaac's herdmen, saying: 'The water is ours.' And he called the name of the well Esek; because they contended with him. 26:21 And they digged another well, and they strove for that also. And he called the name of it Sitnah. 26:22 And he removed from thence, and digged another well; and for that they strove not. And he called the name of it Rehoboth; and he said: 'For now YHWH hath made room for us, and we shall be fruitful in the land.'

3ב

26:26 Then Abimelech went to him from Gerar, and Ahuzzath his friend, and Phicol the captain of his host. 26:27 And Isaac said unto them: 'Wherefore are ye come unto me, seeing ye hate me, and have sent me away from you?' 26:28 And they said: 'We saw plainly that YHWH was with thee; and we said: Let there now be an oath betwixt us, even betwixt us and thee, and let us make a covenant with thee; 26:29 that thou wilt do us no hurt, as we have not touched thee, and as we have done unto thee nothing but good, and have sent thee away in peace; thou art now the blessed of YHWH.' 26:30 And he made them a feast, and they did eat and drink. 26:31 And they rose up betimes in the morning, and swore one to another; and Isaac sent them away, and they departed from him in peace. 26:32 And it came to pass the same day, that Isaac's servants came, and told him concerning the well which they had digged, and said unto him: 'We have found water.' 26:33 And he called it Shibah. Therefore the name of the city is Beer-sheba unto this day. {S}

One critical point before we look at the color code: up to now we spoke of two levels of division represented by the three weft threads (1-3) and their division into two segments (א and ב). Threads 2 and 3 have been further divided, making a third level of division within the Unit, "elements" A and B. This subdivision of the four segments (2א, 2ב, 3א, 3ב) is based on the observation that each of them has a narrative to which a well-story seems to have been added. Element (A) thus contains the YHWH/Abimelech narrative, while element B contains an ostensibly independent theme, "wells."

The Color Code

The Units of *The Woven Torah* (TWT) employ highlights to emphasize words and phrases that connect the components of the Units. The highlights are a guide to M's plan of the Unit. The full set of highlights appears at the beginning of TWT in the Appendix.

This highlight, light blue, is the most common, indicating horizontal parallels between segments of the same weft thread, i.e., in the same row. In threads 2 and 3 it marks the mention of wells in both segments of both threads. In thread 2 they are the wells they "had digged in the days of Abraham his father;" whereas in 3, "Isaac's servants digged a well." The distinction between Abraham's wells in 2 and Isaac's well in 3 plays a major role in integrating the segments of the Unit as noted in Figure 19.

The next highlight, green, is used to illustrate parallels between vertical segments in the same thread. In thread א it shows that YHWH blesses Isaac in all the segments of א. In ב it highlights interactions between Isaac and Abimelech in all three segments.

The last highlight we examine here has two parts that together indicate a chiasm. A chiasm (also called a chiasmus) is a literary device in which a sequence of words or ideas is presented and then repeated in reverse order. In these two-dimensional Units, a genuine X-shape is formed by the repetitions.) This color font shows the first stroke of the X of the chiasm, marking the linking oath between YHWH and Abraham in 1א and between Isaac and Abimelech in 3ב. The second stroke of the chiasm is formed by the repetition of fear, Isaac's fear of death in 1ב and YHWH telling him not to fear in 3א.

Reflection on Complexity

We are learning the rudiments of a new way of reading the Torah. It may feel more difficult than learning a new language because it is based on a text we thought we already knew well. Specifically, *we are forced to deal with new meanings based on rhetorical components identified in the new divisions we have found.* From the beginning, we ignored the division into chapters because these were not part of the original composition, and so are extrinsic to the text of the Torah. The only internal divisions that have been commonly recognized up to now are the divisions into five books. But all that changes when we read the Torah as an esoteric composition—it becomes much more multi-dimensional.

Every level of division that we identify in the terra incognita of the literary structure of the Torah reveals another level of organization that must be accounted for to understand M's plan. So far, we have examined four new levels of internal division in the Torah that do not appear in Bibles. The largest division is the Unit, roughly equivalent to the chapter. As opposed to chapter divisions, the Unit divisions are based on internal indicators that identify the Units as planning components. One of them that appears in Gen XII is a chiasm, as noted through color coding. M used it to define the boundaries or "corners" of the two-dimensional Unit.

While the Unit is the largest rhetorical component that divides the entire Torah into like components, it is not the largest rhetorical component in the Torah. We have already seen in Part One the three creation Units combine to form a planned set of Units. Most of the Units, but not all, seventy-nine of eighty-six, combine into higher level sets. We discuss the higher levels of organization in Part Four.

For now, let's concentrate on what we see when we drill down into the Unit. The major internal divisions within the Unit, the weft thread (1, 2, etc.), and its subdivision the segment (א, ב, ג) are found in all the Units. The further subdivision of segments into elements (A, B etc.) is not common to all Units, but it is nevertheless an unmistakable planning component. Altogether we have now identified five levels of internal division in the Torah: 1) book, 2) Unit, 3) weft thread, 4) segment of weft thread, 5) element of segment. In due course, we will also meet a sixth.

The identification of layer upon layer of organization, testifies to layer upon layer of planning. Gen XII could not be constructed as we have seen it in woven view, had it not been planned in meticulous detail.

Furthermore, it never would have been composed if M had not cared to demonstrate the importance of Isaac getting his own well. Most important for our understanding how the structure embeds an esoteric reading, we can see reading the weave reveals meanings inaccessible from the linear reading.

Chapter 7. Leviticus Unit **XXII (27)**

We are going to see several noteworthy matters in the last Unit of Leviticus, XXII. In this case, uniquely for the four example Units we are examining, the Unit happens to be identical to a chapter, 27. On a technical level, we will see how M makes use of our fifth level of division, elements (A, B…), to create a double weft thread. Less technically, we will see how the visual paradigm of the conceptual middle being in the middle of the structure is applied to a Unit with three warp threads. Most important in my eyes, we will increase our appreciation of the Torah as a work of exquisite literary artistry. The Unit is an apparent collection of not-clearly-related laws, but the woven format reveals how the laws are related.

Figure 21. Leviticus Unit XXII (27)

	Value		
	Fixed Value	**Intrinsic Value**	**Relative Value**

Desanctification

Priest Shall Value

א	ב	ג
27:1 And YHWH spoke unto Moses, saying: 27:2 Speak unto the children of Israel, and say unto them: When a man shall clearly utter a vow of persons unto YHWH, according to thy valuation, 27:3 then thy valuation shall be for the male from twenty years old even unto sixty years old, even thy valuation shall be fifty shekels of silver, after the shekel of the sanctuary. 27:4 And if it be a female, then thy valuation shall be thirty shekels. 27:5 And if it be from five years old even unto twenty years old, then thy valuation shall be for the male twenty shekels, and for the female ten shekels. 27:6 And if it be from a month old even unto five years old, then thy valuation shall be for the male five shekels of silver, and for the female thy valuation shall be three shekels of silver. 27:7 And if it be from sixty years old and upward: if it be a male, then thy valuation shall be fifteen shekels, and for the female ten shekels. 27:8 But if he be too poor for thy valuation, then he shall be set before the priest, and the priest shall value him; according to the means of him that vowed shall the priest value him. {S}	27:9 And if it be a beast, whereof men bring an offering unto YHWH, all that any man giveth of such unto YHWH shall be holy. 27:10 He shall not alter it, nor change it, a good for a bad, or a bad for a good; and if he shall at all change beast for beast, then both it and that for which it is changed shall be holy. 27:11 And if it be any unclean beast, of which they may not bring an offering unto YHWH, then he shall set the beast before the priest. 27:12 And the priest shall value it, whether it be good or bad; as thou the priest valuest it, so shall it be. 27:13 But if he will indeed redeem it, then he shall add the fifth part thereof unto thy valuation.	27:14 And when a man shall sanctify his house to be holy unto YHWH, then the priest shall value it, whether it be good or bad; as the priest shall value it, so shall it stand. 27:15 And if he that sanctified it will redeem his house, then he shall add the fifth part of the money of thy valuation unto it, and it shall be his.

Redeemable

2א	2ב	2ג
A 27:16 And if a man shall sanctify unto YHWH part of the field of his possession, then thy valuation shall be according to the sowing thereof; the sowing of a homer of barley shall be valued at fifty shekels of silver. 27:17 If he sanctify his field from the year of jubilee, according to thy valuation it shall stand. 27:18 But if he sanctify his field after the jubilee, then the priest shall reckon unto him the money according to the years that remain unto the year of jubilee, and an abatement shall be made from thy valuation. 27:19 And if he that sanctified the field will indeed redeem it, then he shall add the fifth part of the money of thy valuation unto it, and it shall be assured to him. 27:20 And if he will not redeem the field, or if he have sold the field to another man, it shall not be redeemed any more. 27:21 But the field, when it goeth out in the jubilee, shall be holy unto YHWH, as a field devoted; the possession thereof shall be the priest's.	A 27:26 Howbeit the firstling among beasts, which is born as a firstling to YHWH, no man shall sanctify it; whether it be ox or sheep, it is YHWH'S. 27:27 And if it be of an unclean beast, then he shall ransom it according to thy valuation, and shall add unto it the fifth part thereof; or if it be not redeemed, then it shall be sold according to thy valuation.	A 27:30 And all the tithe of the land, whether of the seed of the land, or of the fruit of the tree, is YHWH'S; it is holy unto YHWH. 27:31 And if a man will redeem aught of his tithe, he shall add unto it the fifth part thereof.

Non-Redeemable

B 27:22 And if he sanctify unto YHWH a field which he hath bought, which is not of the field of his possession; 27:23 then the priest shall reckon unto him the worth of thy valuation unto the year of jubilee; and he shall give thy valuation in that day, as a holy thing unto YHWH. 27:24 In the year of jubilee the field shall return unto him of whom it was bought, even to him to whom the possession of the land belongeth. 27:25 And all thy valuations shall be according to the shekel of the sanctuary; twenty gerahs shall be the shekel.	B 27:28 Notwithstanding, no devoted thing, that a man may devote unto YHWH of all that he hath, whether of man or beast, or of the field of his possession, shall be sold or redeemed; every devoted thing is most holy unto YHWH. 27:29 None devoted, that may be devoted of men, shall be ransomed; he shall surely be put to death.	B 27:32 And all the tithe of the herd or the flock, whatsoever passeth under the rod, the tenth shall be holy unto YHWH. 27:33 He shall not inquire whether it be good or bad, neither shall he change it; and if he change it at all, then both it and that for which it is changed shall be holy; it shall not be redeemed. 27:34 These are the commandments, which YHWH commanded Moses for the children of Israel in mount Sinai. {P}

Before we start our reading, notice another highlight from *The Woven Torah*—the delineation of A/B-type elements, like weft thread 2 in Figure 21. It helps emphasize that the division into elements is a significant planning feature and consequently must be considered when developing a reading of the Unit.

Leviticus XXII is one of the Units that have been planned on at least three different levels. The uppermost level divides the Unit into two weft threads, 1-2. Each thread is itself divided into three segments, א, ב, ג. The three segments of thread 2 are further divided into elements, A and B. The flow of the linear text is across the weft threads: 1א, 1ב, 1ג, 2אA, 2אB, etc. Each of the warp threads and weft threads has its own theme. The warp demonstrates three different types of value. Thread א deals with fixed values, predetermined by the text in holy shekels. These are "holy values" and are in opposition to the values in thread ג, which are relative or personal values. The value of the house in 1ג and the value of the tithes in 2ג are relative to the wealth of the individual. So, the extreme warp threads demonstrate absolute and relative values. Between them, in thread ב, are intrinsic values. The animals that qualify as offerings are intrinsically valuable as offerings. Their value is neither fixed by the Torah nor relative to the wealth of the person offering them. The things that are proscribed, 2 בB, are intrinsically holy once they have been proscribed. So, the columns are ordered: א, absolute monetary value; ב, intrinsic value; ג, relative monetary value, relative to the wealth of the owner. The order is conceptual.

Now let us look at the weft. The common subject of thread 1 is the value of free-will gifts to YHWH. All three segments of 1 also contain a priestly assessment of value. Thread 2 is organized on a principle of holiness. In its segments, it distinguishes between two aspects of holiness: volitional, that which requires consecration, and non-volitional, that which does not require consecration. In 2א we find the consecration of land, volitional holiness. Its counterpart, 2ג, demonstrates non-volitional holiness through tithes. The middle segment, 2ב is a true middle. It combines aspects of 2א and 2ג. Like 2ג, it has a non-volitional component, 2בA, firstlings. Like 2א, it has a volitional component, 2בB, *herem*, proscription.

Thread 2 has yet another level of order within it, represented by two sub-rows, A and B. Each of the sub-rows has a common subject, and the two subjects complement each other. In sub-row 2-A, each element includes the possibility of redeeming the holy gifts. There is no possibility of redemption in sub-row 2-B. So, row 2 has within it two organizing principles, one vertical and one horizontal. The vertical principle is "the origins of holiness." The horizontal principle is "the possibility of redemption." The thread constitutes a weave within the weave. We will see that the days of creation also create a weave within a weave. Altogether, the Unit is an elegant, meticulously planned artifact. We will probe the meanings embedded in structures more deeply in the next two examples

Chapter 8. Genesis Unit I (1:1-2:3), The Creation Weave

Elohim's Creation and M's Creation

Genesis Unit I, or "the creation weave," like the Decalogue, has a special status in the Torah as a paradigm. The same divine name that spoke the Decalogue, Elohim, creates the world in speech in six days. We read the Decalogue and its surrounding narratives as evidence that Elohim's esoteric speech is revealed in the woven structure on the two tablets. We will now see that just as Elohim spoke the Decalogue as an esoteric woven text, so too did Elohim speak the world into existence through an esoteric weave. While ten Words were needed for the Decalogue paradigm, M has Elohim speak the entire creation into being through a weave that contains just six days. Both the Decalogue, and the creation of the whole world can be grasped as esoteric woven text.

We should not be at all surprised that the creation is a paradigmatic esoteric text since it has been treated as such for at least two millennia. We will encounter some surprising, even startling ideas when we examine the creation weave. For one, M indicates that the world's origins must be considered both creation from nothing, *ex nihilo*, and from a pre-existing substance, *ex materia*.

Along with making a statement about the nature of the world, M also tells us something about authorship. Just as Elohim the author of the Decalogue is presented as the ultimate author, so too Elohim the creator of the world is presented as the ultimate creator. The limited scope of the Decalogue makes it the paradigm for authoring woven Units. The enormity of scope of the creation weave makes it the paradigm for the totality of M's enterprise, the Torah. Through his descriptions of Elohim as creator, M reveals *himself* as a creator and displays the tools of his craft. An obvious weave announces that M is a weaver of text. By following the implications of this weave, we will see the big picture view of the Torah. Elohim and M create the backdrop of imminent physical reality against which to contrast the coming revelation of transcendent holiness through the character of YHWH. Above all, we will see that the presentation of an orderly view of the physical world implies an underlying metaphysic.

The open and closed paragraphs we noted in Figure 8 in Chapter 4 are indicated in our translation in the following as well as in the Appendix. The open, major, paragraph, (Hebrew *p'tuhah*), is marked {P} and the minor or closed paragraph (Hebrew *stumah*) is marked {S}

Figure 22. Genesis Unit I (1:1- 2:3) As it Appears in The Woven Torah

1א

1:1 In the beginning God created the heaven and the earth.

2א

A 1:3 And God said: 'Let there be light.' And there was light. 1:4 And God saw the light, that it was good; and God divided the light from the darkness. 1:5 And God called the light Day, and the darkness He called Night. And there was evening and there was morning, one day. {P}

B 1:6 And God said: 'Let there be a firmament in the midst of the waters, and let it divide the waters from the waters.' 1:7 And God made the firmament, and divided the waters which were under the firmament from the waters which were above the firmament; and it was so. 1:8 And God called the firmament Heaven. And there was evening and there was morning, a second day. {P}

C i 1:9 And God said: 'Let the waters under the heaven be gathered together unto one place, and let the dry land appear.' And it was so. 1:10 And God called the dry land Earth, and the gathering together of the waters called He Seas; and God saw that it was good.

ii 1:11 And God said: 'Let the earth put forth grass, herb yielding seed, and fruit-tree bearing fruit after its kind, wherein is the seed thereof, upon the earth.' And it was so. 1:12 And the earth brought forth grass, herb yielding seed after its kind, and tree bearing fruit, wherein is the seed thereof, after its kind; and God saw that it was good. 1:13 And there was evening and there was morning, a third day. {P}

1ב

1:2 Now the earth was unformed and void, and darkness was upon the face of the deep; and the spirit of God hovered over the face of the waters.

2ב

A 1:14 And God said: 'Let there be lights in the firmament of the heaven to divide the day from the night; and let them be for signs, and for seasons, and for days and years; 1:15 and let them be for lights in the firmament of the heaven to give light upon the earth.' And it was so. 1:16 And God made the two great lights: the greater light to rule the day, and the lesser light to rule the night; and the stars. 1:17 And God set them in the firmament of the heaven to give light upon the earth, 1:18 and to rule over the day and over the night, and to divide the light from the darkness; and God saw that it was good. 1:19 And there was evening and there was morning, a fourth day. {P}

B 1:20 And God said: 'Let the waters swarm with swarms of living creatures, and let fowl fly above the earth in the open firmament of heaven.' 1:21 And God created the great sea-monsters, and every living creature that creepeth, wherewith the waters swarmed, after its kind, and every winged fowl after its kind; and God saw that it was good. 1:22 And God blessed them, saying: 'Be fruitful, and multiply, and fill the waters in the seas, and let fowl multiply in the earth.' 1:23 And there was evening and there was morning, a fifth day. {P}

C i 1:24 And God said: 'Let the earth bring forth the living creature after its kind, cattle, and creeping thing, and beast of the earth after its kind.' And it was so. 1:25 And God made the beast of the earth after its kind, and the cattle after their kind, and every thing that creepeth upon the ground after its kind; and God saw that it was good.

ii 1:26 And God said: 'Let us make man in our image, after our likeness; and let them have dominion over the fish of the sea, and over the fowl of the air, and over the cattle, and over all the earth, and over every creeping thing that creepeth upon the earth.' 1:27 And God created man in His own image, in the image of God created He him; male and female created He them. 1:28 And God blessed them; and God said unto them: 'Be fruitful, and multiply, and replenish the earth, and subdue it; and have dominion over the fish of the sea, and over the fowl of the air, and over every living thing that creepeth upon the earth.' 1:29 And God said: 'Behold, I have given you every herb yielding seed, which is upon the face of all the earth, and every tree, in which is the fruit of a tree yielding seed--to you it shall be for food; 1:30 and to every beast of the earth, and to every fowl of the air, and to every thing that creepeth upon the earth, wherein there is a living soul, [I have given] every green herb for food.' And it was so. 1:31 And God saw every thing that He had made, and, behold, it was very good. And there was evening and there was morning, the sixth day. {P}

The text of Genesis Unit I in Figure 22 introduces another color highlight, red. This one is used to indicate "bracketing" (sometimes called "inclusio"), as marked by the closing weft thread mirroring the opening thread. This is accomplished here through "the heaven and the earth" in 1א being repeated in 3א, while 1ב, "the spirit of Elohim hovered" comes to completion in 3ב "He rested from all his work."

The Structure of the Unit

Unit I of Genesis (1:1-2:3) is divided into three major horizontal divisions, weft threads 1-3. They can be viewed as thread 1) prologue, thread 2) the creation, thread 3) epilogue. This format presents the creation as a fractal of the entire Torah, which is also divided into three parts. Genesis is the prologue to the forty-year redemption story in Exodus-Numbers, while Deuteronomy is an epilogue. Moreover, just as the core of the Torah is distributed over three books, the creation itself (thread 2) is detailed through a triple thread (A-C). The strength of thread 2 resonates with Ecclesiastes 4:12 "a threefold cord is not quickly broken." We examine it closely below. The five-part figure created by the integration of the "threefold cord" (2) with the prologue (1) and the epilogue (3) bears a close conceptual resemblance to the five-part hierarchical paradigm we noted in the Decalogue. The warp too (א, ב), we will see, is connected to the Decalogue through the "divine dyad" underlying the division between the two stone tablets.

Two Three-Day Cycles

We begin by examining thread 2, which contains the days of creation, a weave within the weave, similar to the one we found in Leviticus Unit XXII. The elements of 2א (A-C) are parallel to the elements of 2ב. Many commentators have pointed out that the first three days of creation form a block that is parallel to the next three days of the creation story. The specific creations of days four to six (2ב) give expression to the parallel creations of days one to three (2א). The light that was created on day one appears from the heavenly bodies created on day four. The land creatures created on day six utilize the earth and plants created on day three. The fish and birds of day five are found in the elements of day two, the sky and water.

The days thus divide up in two different ways, as two cycles of three days each, first to third (2א) fourth to sixth (2ב) and as three pairs of days: first

(2אA) and fourth (2בA), second (2אB) and fifth (2בB), third (2אC) and sixth (2בC). The woven format integrates these two arrangements. The argument for arranging the parts in a weave like this is that *this arrangement makes more information available about what the text says than the normal linear arrangement does*. The woven format gives the reader a set of instructions, as it were, that are not otherwise available. This is the set of instructions about how the parts relate to each other. By making these instructions so (relatively) blatant in the first Unit of the Torah, M provides the guidelines for how to study all the units of the Torah. We will see now how the warp and weft unpack themselves as principles of organization.

Reading the Warp of the Six Days: One and Many

The arrangement of the first to third days and the fourth to sixth in separate warp threads indicates that we should look for something that the *first* three days have in common and something else that *the next three* have in common, as well as an identifiable relationship between the segments. On each of the first three days Elohim names a creation: first, light (2אA); second, sky (2אB); third, earth (2אC). On the other hand, each of the days in thread ב mentions a class of objects: fourth, luminaries (2בA); fifth, birds and fish (2בB); sixth, terrestrial animals and Adam, male and female (2בC). So, we can begin with the fact that *the warp indicates a distinction between singular creations and classes/ plural creations*. This distinction echoes the divine dyad which distinguishes between the stone tablets, "the individual and relationships", or "one and many."

The distinction between singular and plural is reinforced by an action that is common in all three elements of 2א, separation. Each of the first three days is associated with an act of separation: 2אA) light from darkness; 2אB) the waters above from the waters below; 2אC), the oceans from the dry land. The act of separation emphasizes uniqueness or singularity. This last observation sends us back to segment 2ב to see whether it contains a counterpart to "separation" in 2א.

As a matter of fact, each of the last three days of creation describes the "occupation" of space. The terminology is sharp: the sun, moon, and stars are placed in heaven to "rule" day and night; Adam is told to "conquer" the earth; the fish are to fill the sea. In each case the second cycle of creation in בּ "invades" or controls its first cycle parallel in א. This principle of "occupation" is clearly in opposition to the first cycle principle of "separation." Another distinction between the first three days and the last three is that the creations of the first three do not move, while the creations of the last three do. Each day of בּ hints at a different type of motion: אA, cyclical; אB, in three-dimensional space; אC, horizontal. We can see that the warp threads are opposites in several senses, based on distinctions like simple and complex; singular and plural; primary and secondary; static and dynamic. This demonstrates the characteristic of the warp, a fixed set of relationships between the vertical threads.

Reading the Weft: A Visual Hierarchy

Now let us look at the weft threads, the horizontal rows. Once the days have been arranged in a weave, more information becomes apparent; specifically, the paired days are arranged according to a visual key. On the top, in 2A, we see light and the heavenly bodies, sun, moon and stars: the upper, luminous, transcendent realm. On the bottom, 2C, we find earth and plants and the earth-bound creatures, the immanent lower world. In the middle, 2B, are the creatures that fill the space between heaven and earth, as well as the very division between above and below (second day). Suddenly, the grid clicks into place and the creation story takes on a whole new perspective. The weave comes into focus, and we see the literary tapestry as it was created on the literary loom.

The Tapestry

From this point on any further analysis must consider the image painted by the arrangement of the six individual days in the creation weave, the picture woven into the tapestry. The critical juncture is the appearance of a coherent spatial arrangement, with the stars above, the earth below, and a middle level between them at the center—the world as we see it. I consider this visualization an internal verification that the arrangement was planned. *To see the picture, we must arrange the six days, as we have, in two vertically parallel warp threads. Only then the three-tiered representation of the world as it is experienced appears.* M has demonstrated that the weave has vertical "sense," a top and bottom. This is a significant observation because it can be applied to all the woven Units: they should be viewed as having been woven on a vertical loom.

Up to this point, we dealt with an interesting literary phenomenon made up of complex parallels. Now we must acknowledge that this is more than a literary curiosity. Using just six "knots" of warp and weft, M has woven *the weave of reality*. The appearance of a clear representation of the experienced world out of the peculiar division of creation into six parts marks the text as a work of art, a tapestry woven on the literary loom by a master craftsperson. The visual hierarchy of the creation parallels the conceptual hierarchy we found in the Decalogue, with the heavenly above and the earthly below. In addition, the three-tiered hierarchy prefigures three-tiered Mt. Sinai, which itself is translated into the three parts of the tabernacle.

It is clear now that the creation story has two aspects. It is meant to appear as a linear text by having parts marked serially from one to six. Nevertheless, to understand its underlying coherence, the creation must be seen as a non-linear construct. The reader must recognize the pattern of the loom from which the text was woven. In other words, there is an additional level of meaning that can be accessed only by an active reader reading the text according to its structure, an esoteric terra incognita.

Logically, we are now confronted by the very real possibility that the creation narrative was first conceived as a two-dimensional woven text that would eventually be deconstructed into a linear text. Like the Decalogue, it was written on two "tablets" which were subsequently "shattered" into six consecutive narrative parts, "days." Reconstructing the original, coherent, woven-creation narrative is not merely a matter of arranging the parts on the page and assigning new notation to the parts, as I have. Reconstructing the weave simultaneously entails a process of discovering the meanings that might be embedded in the structure. The creation narrative is a masterful composition. It could not have been composed without a plan to create an exoteric/esoteric text. Deciphering the woven structure is inextricably connected with the search for that plan and the meanings embedded in the esoteric reading.

Our experience reading the "divine weave," the Decalogue, has prepared us to read the creation weave. We found that the Decalogue can be read as three documents. Each tablet is a coherent five-Word composition. Reading the two tablets in parallel, according to the pairs of Words, revealed the third composition, the woven Decalogue. We will take a similar approach to the creation weave. We have begun by identifying the tapestry of the six days of creation, the weave within the weave. We continue by completing the larger weave, integrating 1:1,2 and 2:1-3. Following that, we will examine the resulting full warp threads, א and ב, as the equivalents of the stone tablets.

Integrating the Prologue and the Epilogue in the Tapestry

We have completed our preliminary reading of the six creation days. We will now see how our well-known weave is transformed into one of the Torah's eighty-six Units. In general, a Unit has a clear beginning and end. In the case of Gen Unit I, we have but a few verses before the creation of light, and they are surely part of the creation story. The completion of the creation on the Sabbath also plainly closes the story. So, we have a few verses (thread 1) before the six-day weave (thread 2), and a few verses after it (thread 3). A comparison between threads 1 and 3 reveals several significant parallels.

Figure 23. Threads 1 and 3 in Genesis Unit I

1א	1ב
A In the beginning Elohim created **B** the heaven **C** and the earth	**A** Now the earth was unformed and void **B** and darkness was upon the face of the deep **C** and the spirit of Elohim hovered over the face of the waters
3א	3ב
A And the heaven **B** and the earth were finished **C** and all the host of them	**A** And on the seventh day Elohim finished His work which He had made; **B** and He rested on the seventh day from all His work which He had made. **C** And Elohim blessed the seventh day, and hallowed it; because that in it He rested from all His work which Elohim in creating had made.

Figure 23 clarifies the formal similarity between threads 1 and 3. There are three unmodified nouns and one verb in both 1א and 3א; they have a parallel laconic style. Together, they give a barebones outline of the narrative: Elohim begins to create heaven and earth in 1א and then they are finished in 3א. What comes between them in 2א is none other than the creation of heaven and earth! All three segments of א concern heaven and earth.

Segments 1ב and 3ב also have structural similarity: both contain three sentences and are more expansive than א. But this is just a formal parallel since the contents are so different. There is one connection between 1ב and 3ב that bears closer inspection though, Elohim. In 1ב we are told that Elohim's spirit was restless, "hovered." In 3ב we see Elohim at rest. This change in Elohim's demeanor surely must be significant.

In the following paragraphs, we will explore how 1 and 3 integrate with 2 to create the full creation weave. The goal is to reveal the meaning conveyed through the structured text, one that is not available from the traditional linear reading. The underlying assumption is that a *highly structured text reveals deeply embedded meaning through its principles of organization.* Genesis Unit I is constructed as a fractal. It contains three weft threads, and the segments of each thread divide into three elements. It *is highly structured.*

Viewing the creation weave according to its internal chronology seems to yield trivial results; thread 1 is before the creation and 3 after the creation. But when we examine threads 1 and 3, in light of the three-part visually hierarchical figure we found in 2, the results are no longer trivial. We might consider 1 as "above" 2A, and 3 as "below" 2C, since the tapestry of the days presents a visually hierarchical pattern. We can consider 2A as pointing to the "transcendent" by means of heavenly lights. In that case, we should think of 1 as truly transcendent, i.e., completely outside the experienced world. Following this approach, thread 3 points to that which is "more immanent" than the earth of 2C. To see what this might mean, we must examine 1 and 3 more closely.

Thread 3: Elohim Separates from the Creation

Segment 3א, is the only one in the creation weave which does not mention Elohim. It is limited to heaven and earth and their contents. Segment 3ב, on the other hand, is the only segment in which the earth is not mentioned, nor any other creation specifically. It mentions three times a "task" that Elohim had performed and then stopped on the seventh day but does not specify any objects. The underlying figure which appears when viewing thread 3 is based on the total separation of Elohim (3ב) from his creation (3א).

There is, however, a subtle linguistic connection, a one-word parallel between the segments of 3, which may be significant because it is the opening word of both segments. To grasp how strong this parallel sounds in Hebrew, we will have to change the normal English word order. The first word of both segments is "finished." Word-for-word, the two openings would read: "Finished (were) the heaven and the earth…," "Finished (was) Elohim." The parallels force us to compare two kinds of "finished," that which can describe the world, and that which can be applied to Elohim. The completion of the creation (3א) is characterized by its separation from Elohim (3ב). This explains how 3 can be "more immanent" than the earth in 2C. During the days of creation, 2, Elohim is still involved with the world, his creation. In 3 though, he is completely separated from "heaven and earth," in a literary sense. There is no element of divinity in the created world in 3א, nor mention of created entities in 3ב. The thread can be read as a summation of the goal of creation: *Elohim created in six days a mundane background (3א) against which holiness (3ב) can be revealed.* Now let us look at thread 1.

Thread 1: The Prologue

Figure 24. A Chiasm between Verse 1 and Verse 2 of Genesis Unit I

	1א	1ב
A	Elohim	Earth
B	Heaven	The Deep
C	Earth	Elohim

Segment 1א contains three nouns (all at the close of the verse in Hebrew): A) Elohim, B) heaven, C) earth. While there appears to be a significant difference in 1א between Elohim, the subject, and heaven and earth, the objects, segment 1ב suggests that all three unmodified nouns should be grasped as a set. 1ב contains three descriptions: A) "the *earth* was unformed and void"; B) "darkness was upon the face of the *deep*"; C) "the spirit of *Elohim* hovered over the face of the waters." 1ב refers to two of the nouns in 1א, Elohim and the earth. The two nouns that are repeated are the first and last parts of each triad. Elohim appears at the beginning of 1א and at the end of 1ב, while the earth appears at the end of 1א and in the beginning of 1ב. This reversal of order is known as an inverted parallel, or chiasm, from the Greek letter chi, which is shaped like an X. It is one of the most fundamental principles of organization in the Torah and is established here in its very first two verses.

The inversion is emphasized by the central terms of each triad, "heaven" and "the deep." They are opposite aspects of space, above and below. The Hebrew word translated "the deep" occurs only four other times in the Torah. In all four of those occurrences, it comes paired with "heaven." Evidently, the chiasm is not just a formal reversal of order, but rather a literary device intended to convey meaning. As a device, its function is to demonstrate that its parts form a coherent block of text, while at the same time defining limits of the block. In this case the chiasm implies, "These two segments form a single piece. They must be read together." Elohim and the earth are locked together by the chiasm. This interconnection is the opposite of what we found in thread 3, where they were completely independent of each other. That being the case, we can read the whole of the weft as pointing to a process whereby Elohim is separated from the world we experience.

Creation is not so much about the production of new entities, as about the withdrawal of Elohim from control of these entities. The threads point to stages: 1) Elohim and the world are interlocked; 2) Elohim separates Himself from the world step-by-step; 3) Elohim and the world are separate. This final stage includes the appearance of the concept "holy," which Elohim applies to the Sabbath. We might even say that holiness is the goal of creation, as expressed through the weft. This is the only mention of holiness in Genesis. It does not appear again until Elohim introduces himself to Moses in the burning bush. Immediately after the mention of sanctification of the Sabbath in Gen 2:3, the name YHWH, which is to be identified with holiness, appears for the first time, "These are the generations of the heaven and of the earth when they were created, in the day that YHWH-Elohim made earth and heaven (2:4)."

Reading the Warp: Two Modes of Creation

Since we began investigating the names Elohim and YHWH, we have encountered other significant pairings, like the trees in the garden and the two tablets. The dyad before us presents itself as the most fundamental dyad of all, the warp upon which the web of the world was woven. Consequently, threads א and ב deserve very close inspection. In our analysis of the Decalogue, we hypothesized the existence of a "divine dyad" which would explain why the Decalogue was engraved on two stone tablets, and therefore, suggested there might be a link with the days of creation. We have now seen that the creation weave is also written on two stone tablets (warp threads). The first set of tablets of the Decalogue and the detailed creation of the world are both attributed to Elohim alone, and both are based on five pairs. We have also noted that the Decalogue and the creation weave share the "divine dyad" of "one and many." We will now see the dyad unique to the creation weave.

The reading of the warp threads proceeds similarly to the reading of the tablets. We will read threads א and ב as if they are independent compositions. We justified this type of reading of the Decalogue by observing that Elohim as well as YHWH required two stone tablets to create a *visualization* of the woven Decalogue. Taking the Decalogue as M's paradigm of woven text leads to the understanding that the carved-in-stone distinction between the tablets is M's sign that warp threads in woven texts are *substantially* different, as we saw in the earlier examples. The reader is charged with determining the underlying duality of all Units which contain two warp threads by asking "what pair of concepts do these warp threads represent?"

To begin with, we can consider the two segments of thread 1 as the headers of the two threads. Although reading the two segments of thread 1 independently is obviously an unorthodox way to read, it solves a problem that occurs when reading these segments serially. The Hebrew, often translated "In the beginning Elohim created," is more suitably translated as "In the beginning of Elohim's creation." The combination of "heaven and earth" is the Hebrew equivalent of "the universe," for which there is no other term. So, an idiomatic serial reading would be "When Elohim began creating the universe, and the earth was *tohu uvohu* (unformed and void)." This reading implies that the earth, while it was formless, already existed when Elohim began to create the universe. Reading segments א and ב as parallel headers avoids this apparent contradiction. Thread א describes the creation of the universe beginning with the creation of light. Thread ב describes bringing form and order to an existent world, the first step of which is the creation of time in 2בA. This reading is strengthened by the chiasm we noted in Figure 24. The chiasm hinges on the dyad "heaven" and "the deep." Between them they define vertical space that is visualized as above, heaven, and below, the deep. They also define two perspectives, from above and from below. The three elements of 1ב are ordered from the bottom up: the earth, water upon the earth, the breath of Elohim above the water, as opposed to the top down in 1א: Elohim, heaven, earth. This may be M's way of expressing two ostensibly exclusive aspects of creation, *ex nihilo* and *ex materia*; creation from "above" is like *ex nihilo* and creation from below is like *ex materia*.

The original Hebrew of these verses offers additional support for our reading. The words translated "unformed and void," *tohu vavohu*, need clarification. Unfortunately, there are no other uses of *tohu vavohu* in the Torah to help us. In modern Hebrew, the phrase can mean "chaos." Perhaps the meaning is "inchoate." All these possibilities share the understanding that the earth existed in a very different way than we see it—but it existed. Yet, if we understand that the earth already existed, what sense do we make of 1א declaring that it presents the beginning of the creation of the earth? The answer hinges on our understanding of a single Hebrew letter.

The word in the translation we are using which must be addressed, "now," translates the Hebrew connective prefix *vav*, a single letter. As a connective, the *vav* usually means "and." The translation "now" does not convey the sense of a connective but does point to the difficulty of the Hebrew syntax. For our purpose, distinguishing between threads א and ב, the connection between them is significant. Reading "and" instead of "now" directs us to a reading which offers verse 2 as an alternative to verse 1. This reading suggests that there are two ways of considering the origins of the world as we experience it: 1) "In the beginning Elohim created," *and* 2) "the earth was." By simply reading the Hebrew connective according to its most common literal meaning, we are rewarded with M's plan of the warp. Verses 1 and 2 are the headings of the threads א and ב, and apparently relate to two different perspectives on creation, א) from above, from the immaterial, *ex nihilo*, and ב) from below, from the preexisting, *ex materia*.

One last point: Even a preliminary look at the warp threads reveals a close affinity to the Edenic trees. Thread א contains a set of dyads, like light and darkness, which are presented as opposites, or poles. The tree of good and bad is an icon of polarized thinking, aligning it with thread א. Thread ב includes the development of life, aligning it with the tree of life.

Thread א: *Ex Nihilo*

There are several possible principles of order in thread א based on characteristics of the first three days of creation. One possibility is based on the ancient concept of the four elements, fire, air, water, and earth. M has indicated that we are to see a natural progression in thread א based on the classical four elements. The key to seeing the direct correlation between the elements and the day of creation is a clarification of the Hebrew word translated "light." The word "*or*," light, can also be read as "*ur*," flame. So, we begin with light, which is related to fire on day one, and then see air that divides the waters above from waters below on day two. Earth appears on day three. The elements are ordered according to a scale of substantiality, from the insubstantial, light, to the substantial, earth. The state of the creation in

3א, "finished," is fully substantiated. Therefore, it seems we should see 1א as totally insubstantial, a concept, words. We have in fact done just that by observing that the translation should be "When Elohim began to create the universe," followed in thread א by "Elohim said: 'Let there be light.'" 1א sets the stage for the first creation—light— but is itself so insubstantial that it is placed above light.

We can only guess what M might have had in mind placing 1א above the four elements of the physical world. Nothing is created in 1א; it is pure language, words used to set the stage. In the beginning is language; these are nearly the opening words of John's gospel. There is logos, an underlying order that can be verbalized. It is realized in 2א by Elohim speaking the elements into being and giving them names. The three segments of the thread all include "heaven and earth," indicating a single process. Thread א describes the coming into being (2א) of the immanent physical universe (3א) from Elohim's words, *ex nihilo* (1א). The underlying process described by the individual steps can be characterized as "realization." The process is implemented by dyadic divisions such as upper and lower waters.

Thread ב: *Ex Materia*

We begin our reading of thread ב with a clarification of a key term, *ruakh*, "spirit." It will prove useful to note the Latin equivalent, *anima*. We will see that the creation of life on days five and six are part of an integrated triad that includes day four. What the three have in common is movement, "animation." While we found thread א was arranged according to a physical hierarchy of substantiality, thread ב is organized according to a principle of animation. The framework of 1ב and 3ב point us to poles of divine animation. In 1ב Elohim's spirit (anima) is described as "hovering," indicating a constant, in place, activity. By the time we get to 3ב, Elohim is at rest. The three intermediate steps, 2בA-C, contain three degrees of animation. It appears that we should see them as steps whereby Elohim transfers animation from himself to his creation. More precisely, Elohim's spirit, anima, animates the world.

In segment 1ב neither the earth nor space have any movement or animation associated with them. Only Elohim's anima is active. Day four introduces the various movements of the heavenly bodies: stars, planets, sun, moon. All have different periods and cycles, but they all have one thing in common: regular, unchanging, movement. They do not show the independent movement associated with life. They are locked onto their medium, the sky. Life is introduced on day five with the fish and birds. While they clearly have the freedom of movement associated with life, they also share a similarity with the heavenly bodies. Just as the stars are carried about by their element, the sky, so too can birds and fish be carried about by the currents in their environments. On day six Elohim creates the first creatures which move totally independently of their environment. From day-to-day, motion, originally attributed to Elohim's anima, is gradually transferred his creations. Finally, on day seven, Elohim is devoid of motion, at rest. The inclusive theme of thread ב is thus the introduction of animation to a previously existing inanimate world. While there are additional signs of organization within thread ב, this is the most inclusive: the cosmos comes to life and Elohim rests.

The themes we have identified in the warp threads are consistent with the dyad "inanimate" (א), and "animate" (ב), or "physical" and "spiritual." There may be other dyads that are even closer to M's categories, but the general lines are clear. The physical process of creation *ex nihilo* (א) is capped by a self-sustaining cosmos in 3א. The parallel process (ב) of creation *ex materia* details the transfer of the divine spirit to the cosmos and ends with the introduction of "holiness" in 3ב. The processes themselves are inverted, as may be hinted at in the chiasm we found in thread 1. Thread א begins with the insubstantial (1א) and ends with the substantial (3א) while ב is the reverse, beginning with the substantial (1ב) and ending with the insubstantial (3ב). Elohim creates a cosmos based on two distinct, complementary, principles: substance and spirit. Together they define the natural world. The underlying theology appears to be based on the understanding that the deity is immaterial. Therefore, the inanimate physical world must have come into being *ex nihilo*, while that which is animated shares a characteristic of the preexistent, Elohim, spirit, anima.

Physics and Metaphysics in the Creation Weave

From what we have seen, we can deduce that, the days of creation (and their objects) are not the primordial elements of reality, according to M's narrative. They are logically preceded by a weave of two sets of principles found in the warp and weft. The unique creation of each day comes to signify the unique meshing of two primary principles, as in conceptual threads, one in the warp and one in the weft. Each day is itself the knot of the two threads. There are five such principles in the six-day weave, two verticals, the sets of three days, and three horizontals—the pairs of days. The addition of the prologue, 1, and the epilogue, 3, two more horizontal principles, brings the total number of prime principles to seven— like the total number of days mentioned in the narrative. So, we have seven enumerated "days," or stages in the linear narrative, matched by seven embedded principles of organization that are inaccessible without reconstructing the creation weave.

If we take the days of creation to express aspects of the physical world, then the embedded primary principles would pertain to metaphysics since they logically precede the creation. *The exoteric reading of creation as a description of the physical world is paralleled by the esoteric weave that reveals the metaphysical underpinnings of creation.*

The weave paradigm leads to seeing the primary elements of M's metaphysics through the categories developed in the warp threads, א and ב, since the warp must be set before the weft is woven across it. M seems to indicate that consideration of the origins of the cosmos, as we experience it, will inevitably lead to a dichotomy. We cannot grasp the fullness of reality without granting that the source must be seen as both *ex nihilo*— establishing the inanimate—and *ex materia*—producing animation. Furthermore, the underlying dichotomy is inseparable from the nature of the deity represented by the name Elohim in the creation. Elohim acts through the two channels represented by threads א and ב. The inherent duality may be hinted at by a plural form in 1:26 "Let *us* make man in *our* image, after *our* likeness." It may also be indicated with the duality of "image" and "likeness." But the duality embedded in the natural world is just a preview of the duality which we are about to deal with, the natural and the supernatural. For that, we now turn to Exodus Unit III, the signs (plagues) in Egypt.

Chapter 9. Exodus Unit III (6:29-11:10): The Decreation Weave

The Signs in Egypt Are Linked to the Days of Creation

Our fourth and final example, Exodus Unit III (6:29-11:10), shares commonalities with the Creation Weave, Genesis Unit I, in that Exodus Unit III contains a complex inner weave within the weave of the Unit. The six days of creation form a three-thread weave within one weft thread of the creation weave, while nine signs (often called "plagues") form a tight weave making up the three central weft threads of the five-weft-thread Unit III in Exodus. These two inner weaves are perhaps the most accessible examples of textual weaving in the Torah, but their significance as a pair of texts far transcends the novelty of their organization: YHWH refers to elements of Elohim's creation in the signs to reveal himself through a "decreation."

The true significance of these two well-known narratives—the creation and the plagues—can only be grasped by the reader who has accessed the key to the esoteric reading of the Torah, textual weaving. Evidently, M composed these two Units to resonate in parallel. Such a reading reveals the cornerstone of M's theology, the distinction between Elohim and YHWH. The creation presents Elohim as the creator of the *natural universe*. The signs in Egypt present YHWH as the *supernatural redeemer* of Israel. M's weave of YHWH's signs is a systematic, though largely symbolic, day-by-day reversal of Elohim's creation, a decreation.

M has taken Elohim's creation of the natural world as a backdrop against which YHWH is highlighted as supernatural. The technique has YHWH create signs which demonstrate their supernatural origin by conflicting in some way with Elohim's "nature," e.g., water turned to blood. YHWH's supernatural signs deconstruct, or in terms of the Torah, "decreate" Elohim's creation. Consequently, I call Exodus Unit III the "Decreation Weave." After our reading of Exodus Unit III itself, we will turn to compare it closely with the creation.

We begin our reading of Exodus Unit III by focusing on the five-stage theme developed by the five weft threads. After that, we will read the weave created by the three sets of three signs in threads 2-4. The analysis of this weave will prepare us to compare Elohim's creation with YHWH's decreation.

Grasping the Unit as a Whole

We begin our reading with a visual overview of the entire Unit Exodus 6:29-11:10, on a single page. It is necessary to present the Unit on a single page so that you can see its contours clearly. The full-size readable text is in the Appendix. The structure provides M's guide to reading the Unit. We can see directly from Figure 25 that the Unit displays a five-part symmetry like we have seen in other five-part figures.

Figure 25. Single Page View of Exodus Unit III

1א

A 6:29 that YHWH spoke unto Moses, saying: 'I am YHWH; speak thou unto Pharaoh king of Egypt all that I speak unto thee.' **6:30** And Moses said before YHWH: 'Behold, I am of uncircumcised lips, and how shall Pharaoh hearken unto me?' **{P}**
7:1 And YHWH said unto Moses: 'See, I have set thee in Elohim's stead to Pharaoh; and Aaron thy brother shall be thy prophet. **7:2** Thou shalt speak all that I command thee; and Aaron thy brother shall speak unto Pharaoh, that he let the children of Israel go out of his land. **7:3** And I will harden Pharaoh's heart, and multiply My signs and My wonders in the land of Egypt. **7:4** But Pharaoh will not hearken unto you,
B and I will lay My hand upon Egypt, and bring forth My hosts, My people the children of Israel, out of the land of Egypt, by great judgments. **7:5** And the Egyptians shall know that I am YHWH, when I stretch forth My hand upon Egypt, and bring out the children of Israel from among them.' **7:6** And Moses and Aaron did so; as YHWH commanded them, so did they. 7:7 And Moses was fourscore years old, and Aaron fourscore and three years old, when they spoke unto Pharaoh. {P}

1ב

A 7:8 And YHWH spoke unto Moses and unto Aaron, saying: **7:9** 'When Pharaoh shall speak unto you, saying: Show a wonder for you; then thou shalt say unto Aaron: Take thy rod, and cast it down before Pharaoh, that it become a serpent.' **7:10** And Moses and Aaron went in unto Pharaoh, and they did so, as YHWH had commanded;

B and Aaron cast down his rod before Pharaoh and before his servants, and it became a serpent. **7:11** Then Pharaoh also called for the wise men and the sorcerers; and they also, the magicians of Egypt, did in like manner with their secret arts. **7:12** For they cast down every man his rod, and they became serpents; but Aaron's rod swallowed up their rods. **7:13** And Pharaoh's heart was hardened, and he hearkened not unto them; as YHWH had spoken. **{S}**

2א

A 7:14 And YHWH said unto Moses: 'Pharaoh's heart is stubborn, he refuseth to let the people go. **7:15** Get thee unto Pharaoh in the morning; lo, he goeth out unto the water; and thou shalt stand by the river's brink to meet him; and the rod which was turned to a serpent shalt thou take in thy hand. **7:16** And thou shalt say unto him: YHWH, the Elohim of the Hebrews, hath sent me unto thee, saying: Let My people go, that they may serve Me in the wilderness; and, behold, hitherto thou hast not hearkened; **7:17** thus saith YHWH: In this thou shalt know that I am YHWH--behold, I will smite with the rod that is in my hand upon the waters which are in the river, and they shall be turned to blood. **7:18** And the fish that are in the river shall die, and the river shall become foul; and the Egyptians shall loathe to drink water from the river.' **{S}**

B 7:19 And YHWH said unto Moses: 'Say unto Aaron: Take thy rod, and stretch out thy hand over the waters of Egypt, over their rivers, over their streams, and over their pools, and over all their ponds of water, that they may become blood; and there shall be blood throughout all the land of Egypt, both in vessels of wood and in vessels of stone.' **7:20** And Moses and Aaron did so, as YHWH commanded; and he lifted up the rod, and smote the waters that were in the river, in the sight of Pharaoh, and in the sight of his servants; and all the waters that were in the river were turned to blood. **7:21** And the fish that were in the river died; and the river became foul, and the Egyptians could not drink water from the river; and the blood was throughout all the land of Egypt. **7:22** And the magicians of Egypt did in like manner with their secret arts; and Pharaoh's heart was hardened, and he hearkened not unto them, as YHWH had spoken. **7:23** And Pharaoh turned and went into his house, neither did he lay even this to heart. **7:24** And all the Egyptians digged round about the river for water to drink; for they could not drink of the water of the river. **7:25** And seven days were fulfilled, after that YHWH had smitten the river. **{P}**

2ב

A 7:26 And YHWH spoke unto Moses: 'Go in unto Pharaoh, and say unto him: Thus saith YHWH: Let My people go, that they may serve Me. **7:27** And if thou refuse to let them go, behold, I will smite all thy borders with frogs. **7:28** And the river shall swarm with frogs, which shall go up and come into thy house, and into thy bed-chamber, and upon thy bed, and into the house of thy servants, and upon thy people, and into thine ovens, and into thy kneading-troughs. **7:29** And the frogs shall come up both upon thee, and upon thy people, and upon all thy servants.'

B 8:1 And YHWH said unto Moses: 'Say unto Aaron: Stretch forth thy hand with thy rod over the rivers, over the canals, and over the pools, and cause frogs to come up upon the land of Egypt.' **8:2** And Aaron stretched out his hand over the waters of Egypt; and the frogs came up, and covered the land of Egypt. **8:3** And the magicians did in like manner with their secret arts, and brought up frogs upon the land of Egypt. **8:4** Then Pharaoh called for Moses and Aaron, and said: 'Entreat YHWH, that He take away the frogs from me, and from my people; and I will let the people go, that they may sacrifice unto YHWH.' **8:5** And Moses said unto Pharaoh: 'Have thou this glory over me; against what time shall I entreat for thee, and for thy servants, and for thy people, that the frogs be destroyed from thee and thy houses, and remain in the river only?' **8:6** And he said: 'Against to-morrow.' And he said: 'Be it according to thy word; that thou mayest know that there is none like unto YHWH our Elohim. **8:7** And the frogs shall depart from thee, and from thy houses, and from thy servants, and from thy people; they shall remain in the river only.' **8:8** And Moses and Aaron went out from Pharaoh; and Moses cried unto YHWH concerning the frogs, which He had brought upon Pharaoh. **8:9** And YHWH did according to the word of Moses; and the frogs died out of the houses, out of the courts, and out of the fields. **8:10** And they gathered them together in heaps; and the land stank. **8:11** But when Pharaoh saw that there was respite, he hardened his heart, and hearkened not unto them; as YHWH had spoken. **{S}**

2ג

A

B 8:12 And YHWH said unto Moses: 'Say unto Aaron: Stretch out thy rod, and smite the dust of the earth, that it may become gnats throughout all the land of Egypt.' **8:13** And they did so; and Aaron stretched out his hand with his rod, and smote the dust of the earth, and there were gnats upon man, and upon beast; all the dust of the earth became gnats throughout all the land of Egypt. **8:14** And the magicians did so with their secret arts to bring forth gnats, but they could not; and there were gnats upon man, and upon beast. **8:15** Then the magicians said unto Pharaoh: 'This is the finger of Elohim'; and Pharaoh's heart was hardened, and he hearkened not unto them; as YHWH had spoken. **{S}**

3א

8:16 And YHWH said unto Moses: 'Rise up early in the morning, and stand before Pharaoh; lo, he cometh forth to the water; and say unto him: Thus saith YHWH: Let My people go, that they may serve Me. **8:17** Else, if thou wilt not let My people go, behold, I will send swarms of flies upon thee, and upon thy servants, and upon thy people, and into thy houses; and the houses of the Egyptians shall be full of swarms of flies, and also the ground whereon they are. **8:18** And I will set apart in that day the land of Goshen, in which My people dwell, that no swarms of flies shall be there, to the end that thou mayest know that I am YHWH in the midst of the earth. **8:19** And I will put a division between My people and thy people--by to-morrow shall this sign be.' **8:20** And YHWH did so; and there came grievous swarms of flies into the house of Pharaoh, and into his servants' houses; and in all the land of Egypt the land was ruined by reason of the swarms of flies. **8:21** And Pharaoh called for Moses and for Aaron, and said: 'Go ye, sacrifice to your Elohim in the land.' **8:22** And Moses said: 'It is not meet so to do; for we shall sacrifice the abomination of the Egyptians to YHWH our Elohim; lo, if we sacrifice the abomination of the Egyptians before their eyes, will they not stone us? **8:23** We will go three days' journey into the wilderness, and sacrifice to YHWH our Elohim, as He shall command us.' **8:24** And Pharaoh said: 'I will let you go, that ye may sacrifice to YHWH your Elohim in the wilderness; only ye shall not go very far away; entreat for me.' **8:25** And Moses said: 'Behold, I go out from thee, and I will entreat YHWH that the swarms of flies may depart from Pharaoh, from his servants, and from his people, tomorrow; only let not Pharaoh deal deceitfully any more in not letting the people go to sacrifice to YHWH.' **8:26** And Moses went out from Pharaoh, and entreated YHWH. **8:27** And YHWH did according to the word of Moses; and He removed the swarms of flies from Pharaoh, from his servants, and from his people; there remained not one. **8:28** And Pharaoh hardened his heart this time also, and he did not let the people go. **{P}**

3ב

9:1 Then YHWH said unto Moses: 'Go in unto Pharaoh, and tell him: Thus saith YHWH, the Elohim of the Hebrews: Let My people go, that they may serve Me. **9:2** For if thou refuse to let them go, and wilt hold them still, **9:3** behold, the hand of YHWH is upon thy cattle which are in the field, upon the horses, upon the asses, upon the camels, upon the herds, and upon the flocks; there shall be a very grievous murrain. **9:4** And YHWH shall make a division between the cattle of Israel and the cattle of Egypt; and there shall nothing die of all that belongeth to the children of Israel.' **9:5** And YHWH appointed a set time, saying: 'Tomorrow YHWH shall do this thing in the land.' **9:6** And YHWH did that thing on the morrow, and all the cattle of Egypt died; but of the cattle of the children of Israel died not one. **9:7** And Pharaoh sent, and, behold, there was not so much as one of the cattle of the Israelites dead. But the heart of Pharaoh was stubborn, and he did not let the people go. **{P}**

3ג

9:8 And YHWH said unto Moses and unto Aaron: 'Take to you handfuls of soot of the furnace, and let Moses throw it heavenward in the sight of Pharaoh. **9:9** And it shall become small dust over all the land of Egypt, and shall be a boil breaking forth with blains upon man and upon beast, throughout all the land of Egypt.' **9:10** And they took soot of the furnace, and stood before Pharaoh; and Moses threw it up heavenward; and it became a boil breaking forth with blains upon man and upon beast. **9:11** And the magicians could not stand before Moses because of the boils; for the boils were upon the magicians, and upon all the Egyptians. **9:12** And YHWH hardened the heart of Pharaoh, and he hearkened not unto them; as YHWH had spoken unto Moses. **{S}**

4א

A 9:13 And YHWH said unto Moses: 'Rise up early in the morning, and stand before Pharaoh, and say unto him: Thus saith YHWH, the Elohim of the Hebrews: Let My people go, that they may serve Me. **9:14** For I will this time send all My plagues upon thy person, and upon thy servants, and upon thy people, that thou mayest know that there is none like Me in all the earth. **9:15** Surely now I had put forth My hand, and smitten thee and thy people with pestilence, and thou hadst been cut off from the earth. **9:16** But in very deed for this cause have I made thee to stand, to show thee My power, and that My name may be declared throughout all the earth. **9:17** As yet exaltest thou thyself against My people, that thou wilt not let them go? **9:18** Behold, tomorrow about this time I will cause it to rain a very grievous hail, such as hath not been in Egypt since the day it was founded even until now. **9:19** Now therefore send, hasten in thy cattle and all that thou hast in the field; for every man and beast that shall be found in the field, and shall not be brought home, the hail shall come down upon them, and they shall die.' **9:20** He that feared the word of YHWH among the servants of Pharaoh made his servants and his cattle flee into the houses; **9:21** and he that regarded not the word of YHWH left his servants and his cattle in the field. **{P}**

B 9:22 And YHWH said unto Moses: 'Stretch forth thy hand toward heaven, that there may be hail in all the land of Egypt, upon man, and upon beast, and upon every herb of the field, throughout the land of Egypt.' **9:23** And Moses stretched forth his rod toward heaven; and YHWH sent thunder and hail, and fire ran down unto the earth; and YHWH caused to hail upon the land of Egypt. **9:24** So there was hail, and fire flashing up amidst the hail, very grievous, such as had not been in all the land of Egypt since it became a nation. **9:25** And the hail smote throughout all the land of Egypt all that was in the field, both man and beast; and the hail smote every herb of the field, and broke every tree of the field. **9:26** Only in the land of Goshen, where the children of Israel were, was there no hail. **9:27** And Pharaoh sent, and called for Moses and Aaron, and said unto them: 'I have sinned this time; YHWH is righteous, and I and my people are wicked. **9:28** Entreat YHWH, and let there be enough of these mighty thunderings and hail; and I will let you go, and ye shall stay no longer.' **9:29** And Moses said unto him: 'As soon as I am gone out of the city, I will spread forth my hands unto YHWH; the thunders shall cease, neither shall there be any more hail; that thou mayest know that the earth is YHWH'S. **9:30** But as for thee and thy servants, I know that ye will not yet fear YHWH Elohim.'-- **9:31** And the flax and the barley were smitten; for the barley was in the ear, and the flax was in bloom. **9:32** But the wheat and the spelt were not smitten; for they ripen late.-- **9:33** And Moses went out of the city from Pharaoh, and spread forth his hands unto YHWH; and the thunders and hail ceased, and the rain was not poured upon the earth. **9:34** And when Pharaoh saw that the rain and the hail and the thunders were ceased, he sinned yet more, and hardened his heart, he and his servants. **9:35** And the heart of Pharaoh was hardened, and he did not let the children of Israel go; as YHWH had spoken by Moses. **{P}**

4ב

A 10:1 And YHWH said unto Moses: 'Go in unto Pharaoh; for I have hardened his heart, and the heart of his servants, that I might show these My signs in the midst of them; **10:2** and that thou mayest tell in the ears of thy son, and of thy son's son, what I have wrought upon Egypt, and My signs which I have done among them; that ye may know that I am YHWH.' **10:3** And Moses and Aaron went in unto Pharaoh, and said unto him: 'Thus saith YHWH, the Elohim of the Hebrews: How long wilt thou refuse to humble thyself before Me? let My people go, that they may serve Me. **10:4** Else, if thou refuse to let My people go, behold, to-morrow will I bring locusts into thy border; **10:5** and they shall cover the face of the earth, that one shall not be able to see the earth; and they shall eat the residue of that which is escaped, which remaineth unto you from the hail, and shall eat every tree which groweth for you out of the field; **10:6** and thy houses shall be filled, and the houses of all thy servants, and the houses of all the Egyptians; as neither thy fathers nor thy fathers' fathers have seen, since the day that they were upon the earth unto this day.' And he turned, and went out from Pharaoh. **10:7** And Pharaoh's servants said unto him: 'How long shall this man be a snare unto us? let the men go, that they may serve YHWH their Elohim, knowest thou not yet that Egypt is destroyed?' **10:8** And Moses and Aaron were brought again unto Pharaoh; and he said unto them: 'Go, serve YHWH your Elohim; but who are they that shall go?' **10:9** And Moses said: 'We will go with our young and with our old, with our sons and with our daughters, with our flocks and with our herds we will go; for we must hold a feast unto YHWH.' **10:10** And he said unto them: 'So be YHWH with you, as I will let you go, and your little ones; see ye that evil is before your face. **10:11** Not so; go now ye that are men, and serve YHWH; for that is what ye desire.' And they were driven out from Pharaoh's presence. **{S}**

B 10:12 And YHWH said unto Moses: 'Stretch out thy hand over the land of Egypt for the locusts, that they may come up upon the land of Egypt, and eat every herb of the land, even all that the hail hath left.' **10:13** And Moses stretched forth his rod over the land of Egypt, and YHWH brought an east wind upon the land all that day, and all the night; and when it was morning, the east wind brought the locusts. **10:14** And the locusts went up over all the land of Egypt, and rested in all the borders of Egypt; very grievous were they; before them there were no such locusts as they, neither after them shall be such. **10:15** For they covered the face of the whole earth, so that the land was darkened; and they did eat every herb of the land, and all the fruit of the trees which the hail had left; and there remained not any green thing, either tree or herb of the field, through all the land of Egypt. **10:16** Then Pharaoh called for Moses and Aaron in haste; and he said: 'I have sinned against YHWH your Elohim, and against you. **10:17** Now therefore forgive, I pray thee, my sin only this once, and entreat YHWH your Elohim, that He may take away from me this death only.' **10:18** And he went out from Pharaoh, and entreated YHWH. **10:19** And YHWH turned an exceeding strong west wind, which took up the locusts, and drove them into the Red Sea; there remained not one locust in all the border of Egypt. **10:20** But YHWH hardened Pharaoh's heart, and he did not let the children of Israel go. **{P}**

4ג

A

B 10:21 And YHWH said unto Moses: 'Stretch out thy hand toward heaven, that there may be darkness over the land of Egypt, even darkness which may be felt.' **10:22** And Moses stretched forth his hand toward heaven; and there was a thick darkness in all the land of Egypt three days; **10:23** they saw not one another, neither rose any from his place for three days; but all the children of Israel had light in their dwellings. **10:24** And Pharaoh called unto Moses, and said: 'Go ye, serve YHWH; only let your flocks and your herds be stayed; let your little ones also go with you.' **10:25** And Moses said: 'Thou must also give into our hand sacrifices and burnt-offerings, that we may sacrifice unto YHWH our Elohim. **10:26** Our cattle also shall go with us; there shall not a hoof be left behind; for thereof must we take to serve YHWH our Elohim; and we know not with what we must serve YHWH, until we come thither.' **10:27** But YHWH hardened Pharaoh's heart, and he would not let them go. **10:28** And Pharaoh said unto him: 'Get thee from me, take heed to thyself, see my face no more; for in the day thou seest my face thou shalt die.' **10:29** And Moses said: 'Thou hast spoken well; I will see thy face again no more.' **{P}**

5א

A 11:1 And YHWH said unto Moses: 'Yet one plague more will I bring upon Pharaoh, and upon Egypt; afterwards he will let you go hence; when he shall let you go, he shall surely thrust you out hence altogether.

B 11:2 Speak now in the ears of the people, and let them ask every man of his neighbour, and every woman of her neighbour, jewels of silver, and jewels of gold.' **11:3** And YHWH gave the people favour in the sight of the Egyptians.
C Moreover the man Moses was very great in the land of Egypt, in the sight of Pharaoh's servants, and in the sight of the people. **{S}**

5ב

A 11:4 And Moses said: 'Thus saith YHWH: About midnight will I go out into the midst of Egypt; **11:5** and all the first-born in the land of Egypt shall die, from the first-born of Pharaoh that sitteth upon his throne, even unto the first-born of the maid-servant that is behind the mill; and all the first-born of cattle. **11:6** And there shall be a great cry throughout all the land of Egypt, such as there hath been none like it, nor shall be like it any more. **11:7** But against any of the children of Israel shall not a dog whet his tongue, against man or beast; that ye may know how that YHWH doth put a difference between the Egyptians and Israel. **11:8** And all these thy servants shall come down unto me, and bow down unto me, saying: Get thee out, and all the people that follow thee; and after that I will go out.' And he went out from Pharaoh in hot anger. **{S}**
B 11:9 And YHWH said unto Moses: 'Pharaoh will not hearken unto you; that My wonders may be multiplied in the land of Egypt.'

C11:10 And Moses and Aaron did all these wonders before Pharaoh; and YHWH hardened Pharaoh's heart, and he did not let the children of Israel go out of his land. **{S}**

Even before we look at the content of Exodus Unit III, there are significant points to observe from the structure visible in Figure 25. First, we see that the Unit has an "envelope" structure created by threads 1 and 5. These two threads have just *two* segments while the middle three weft threads all have *three* segments (based on internal literary indicators). We will see that the contents of the envelope, weft threads 2-4, are nine signs, or wonders, made up of three sets of three. The symmetry established by the envelope is further developed by threads 2 and 4, the second and penultimate. Even in the microtext we can see that these two threads are both composed of two sub-threads, which is not true of the central thread, 3. The symmetry defined by threads 2 and 4 is further emphasized by a lacuna; elements 2λA and 4λA are both empty. We see the reason for this emptiness below.

The result of these formal observations is that we can see the same paradigm of concentric symmetry in this Exodus Unit as we previously saw in the Creation Weave, the Decalogue and across the books of the Torah. The use of repeating structural paradigms on different levels of organization is one of the signs that the Torah was meticulously planned. It also presents the careful reader with a tool for mining meanings embedded deep within the esoteric Torah. Each instance in which the paradigm is employed displays a set of formal relationships between its parts that can be applied to exploring a further instance of the same paradigm.

Our previous experience with five-part structures has taught us that they can be viewed as processes. More precisely, the three intermediate parts provided graduated steps between the poles established by the envelope, the first and fifth parts. Consequently, having understood M's method of organization, we now have a way of making at least an educated guess about how our Unit should be read. Threads 1 and 5 are likely to present poles, bridged by threads 2-4. According to this hypothesis, we should begin reading by comparing threads 1 and 5 to establish the framework.

Consistent with the overall theme in the Unit of divine "signs," each of the five threads has a different degree of *signi*fication vis-a-vis their common theme, insurrection. Threads 1 and 5 present the poles: a symbolic insurrection in thread 1, and a fully realized insurrection in thread 5. Thread 1 is almost purely symbolic. It takes place in

a setting that includes only Pharaoh and his court. The effects of the first sign do not extend beyond the seat of authority and its symbolic staves, symbols of authority. Aaron turns his staff into a living symbol, and this is followed by Pharaoh's councilor-magicians, who also turn their staffs into living symbols. When Aaron's staff swallows those of Pharaohs' councilor-magicians, the act itself is symbolic, indicating, perhaps, that Aaron serves a higher authority. No real damage is done, nor is the creation of a living symbol a unique power bestowed upon Aaron. It is, apparently, within the job description of all higher-level authorities. YHWH himself similarly engages in pure symbolism in thread 1. He tells Moses that he, Moses, will appear to Pharaoh as a god, and Aaron will appear as Moses' prophet (7:1). The fact that the structure begins with pure symbolism is totally fitting for a Unit devoted to signs.

In thread 5 we learn that Pharaoh's antagonist, Moses, has achieved fame throughout the land, "the man Moses was very great in the land of Egypt, in the sight of Pharaoh's servants, and in the sight of the people (11:3)." Moreover, Moses then threatens Pharaoh that his people will change their allegiance, "And all these thy servants shall come down unto me, and bow down unto me (11:8)." What began as a duel of symbols in thread 1, has turned into a true popular revolution, with the threat embodied in the warning concerning the impending death of the firstborn. We can already see that thread 5 "realizes" something which exists symbolically, in potential, in thread 1, a political challenge to Pharaoh. Again, using our experience gained from similar structures, we can predict that threads 2-4 are graduated steps leading from thread 1 to 5. The full five-part Unit would then present a five-step process of civil insurrection initiated through a masked threat in thread 1. Here is a summary of the intermediate stages of the insurgency in threads 2-4.

- **Thread 2, the first triad (blood, frogs, lice)**
  Thread 2 has common elements with thread 1, the living staff symbol. All three of the signs are brought about by Aaron by means of his staff and are then imitated by Pharaoh's councilor-magicians. The effects are largely symbolic, creating more nuisance than damage. While bodies of water turned to blood, water was still to be had by digging; frogs in one's dinner plate might be

unhygienic and disgusting, but no worse. One significant change from thread 1 is in the circle of people affected. While thread 1 was limited to Pharaoh's court, the three "annoyances" of thread 2 affect the entire population. The stench of rotting fish and frogs that filled the air of Egypt may indicate a general malaise that the people began to perceive. Something is rotten in Egypt.

- **Thread 3 (mixture, bovine disease, boils)**

  Thread 3 is significantly different from the first two. As opposed to thread 2, it cannot be understood as a duel between Aaron and Pharaoh's councilor-magicians. Actual damage is caused by the loss of personal property, death of livestock. The text emphasizes the distinction between the Egyptians who suffer and the Israelites who are unaffected. While the distinction between the two peoples may have been implied in the earlier stages through Aaron's superior mastery of matter, it becomes explicit in this stage. YHWH himself declares he will distinguish between Egyptian and Israelite. This point is further emphasized by Moses when he tells Pharaoh that the Israelite form of worship is abhorrent to the Egyptians. The basis for

sedition is prepared in this triad by the separation of one part of the population from the other. This theme is further developed in thread 4.

- **Thread 4 (hail, locust, darkness)**

  The seeds of Pharaoh's political downfall, sown in thread 3, take root in thread 4. The warning before the hail makes a unique appeal to the citizenry not to fall into the trap set for Pharaoh. "He that feared the word of YHWH among the servants of Pharaoh made his servants and his cattle flee into the houses; and he that regarded not the word of YHWH left his servants and his cattle in the field (9:20,21)." Egyptian society has undergone a change that threatens its very existence, "And Pharaoh's servants said unto him: 'How long shall this man be a snare unto us? let the men go, that they may serve YHWH their Elohim, *knowest thou not yet that Egypt is destroyed?* (10:7)'"

We can now verify that our previous readings of five-part literary structures have indeed led us to an inclusive political reading of the Decreation. Egypt, as a pharaonic state, is being dissolved. The process of sedition outlined above is summarized in Figure 26.

Figure 26. Five Stages of Sedition in Five Threads

Thread	Signs		Effect
1.	Prologue (6:29-7:13)		A purely symbolic threat to Pharaoh's authority, restricted to an audience consisting of Pharaoh and his advisors.
2.	Blood (7:14-25), Frogs (7:26-8:11), Lice (8:12-15)		Largely symbolic, lacking real damage, but causing a stench and an itch
3.	Mixture (8:16-28), Pestilence (9:1-7), Boils (9:8-12)		Both symbolic, distinguishing between Israel and Egypt, and causing significant damage, death of herds
4.	Hail (9:13-35), Locust (10:1-20), Darkness (10:21-29)		Largely non-symbolic, inflicting regime destabilizing damage
5.	Epilogue (11:1-10),		A non-symbolic threat to Pharaoh's hegemony supported by the people of Egypt

Seeing YHWH's signs associated with a process of civil breakdown and revolt teaches us something about the nature of YHWH; it is within YHWH's power to foment civil insurrection. But why did YHWH need all these signs to carry out the plan? To answer that question, we would have to know more about his plan. Fortunately, he shares his plan with us. By listening very carefully to what YHWH says, we can learn not only his intent in multiplying his signs but also how M wants the Torah to be read. YHWH's words appear in the introduction to his eighth "sign," the plague of locust.

> And YHWH said to Moses, "Come into Pharaoh, for I Myself have hardened his heart and the heart of his servants, so that I may set these signs of Mine in his midst, and so that you may tell in the hearing of your son and your son's son how I toyed with Egypt, and My signs that I set upon them, and you shall know that I am YHWH." (Exod 10:1-2)

This speech needs clarification. YHWH implies that Pharaoh would have released the Israelite slaves at an earlier stage had YHWH not hardened Pharaoh's heart. YHWH states directly that he intervened in order "that I may set *these signs of mine* in his midst." YHWH began with a plan which required that he bring about a specific set of signs. The plan necessitated divine intervention *to guarantee Pharaoh's unwillingness to release his slaves*. If Pharaoh released them too soon, YHWH would not be able to display all his intended signs. This reasoning gives us insight into M's view of history, as presented in the Torah.

M's View of History

A divine plan precedes the events which determine history. The events themselves are engineered to carry out the plan. The deity is like an author, working from an outline, developing characters according to the needs of the plot. The story itself is the history presented in the Torah. It is a text which contains signs appearing in this order: blood, frogs, lice, mixture, bovine plague, boils, hail, locust, darkness, and the death of the firstborn. The plan required the enunciation of them all, in this order, with the surrounding narrative which appears in the Torah, including dialogues between YHWH and Moses, responses by Pharaoh's councilors, and more. In other words, history is significant only insofar as it provides the means to reveal the details of the divine plan as described in the Torah. YHWH hardened Pharaoh's heart *so that* the Torah would be an accurate representation of the divine plan. YHWH's speech also reveals the function of the plan.

The Function of the Signs

It was in YHWH's power to have initiated a single sign to bring about the release of the Israelites; but YHWH chose to harden Pharaoh's heart to complete his plan to display the different signs. These were not for the benefit of convincing Pharaoh, nor for the expediency of the redemption. The signs were planned to create a text that would be studied by future generations, a text which could lead to knowledge of YHWH.

YHWH says that his signs are directed to two different audiences for two different purposes. One audience includes Pharaoh and, perhaps, his councilors; the other includes future generations of Israelites. Insofar as the Torah presents itself as the record of these signs, it can be read in two diverse ways by two audiences, one reading from the perspective of Pharaoh, and one from the perspective of Israel.

Pharaoh's point of view is linear. As a participant in the events, he would have had only limited knowledge of the details presented by the Torah. He did not hear the parts of YHWH's speeches that were not meant for his ears, nor did he hear the voice of the narrator who speaks in the Torah. In the guise of a prophet, he only heard Aaron repeat words that Moses, in the guise of a god, originally heard from YHWH. Pharaoh's knowledge of YHWH as a communicator through language was thus third hand. However, he experienced the events with a pressing immediacy that surely transcended the art of any author to reproduce. Sign after sign, he had to take stock and weigh his options, for as he gradually learned, he was fighting for the very existence of his kingdom. He read the signs as indications of his opponent's power, growing from sign to sign until he recognized YHWH as the supreme power. Any reading that focuses on the events related in the text as a display of YHWH's power can thus be characterized as "pharaonic." Such a reading will emphasize the forces brought into play at each stage. Future generations of Israelites were commanded to read the signs differently.

As opposed to the pharaonic reading, the "Israelite" reading is non-linear and meta-historical. It takes advantage of all the rich details available in the literary record which were not available to Pharaoh. The goal of this reading is literary-theological: to understand YHWH's nature as revealed through his signs as described in the Torah. This is in keeping with YHWH's avowed purpose in multiplying his signs while redeeming his people. The Israelite reading distinguishes between two aspects of the Torah, —the apparent historical, and the literary. Whatever the historical events may have been, they are to be conceptualized by means of the literary record, the Torah, which is meta-historical. This reading views the text as a whole fabric in which each detail is essential. YHWH produced the signs in Egypt *so that* they would appear in the Torah and be retold from generation to generation. By studying this text, Israelites are to obtain knowledge of YHWH. The text is thus the primary means to obtain divine knowledge because YHWH reveals himself through the text, not through history. History, Pharaoh's reading, was merely the means by which the Torah was produced.

An Israelite Reading

The Torah thus distinguishes between two readings of the events, Pharaoh's, and Israel's. Pharaoh was to read the events in a way that would convince him YHWH's power freed the Israelites. These same freed Israelites were to read the events in such a way as to learn about the nature of YHWH. The close study of the events by generation after generation, as

prescribed by YHWH, has become the study of a written text. The non-linear characteristics of this document reveal an extremely sophisticated author who addressed an equally sophisticated readership. Much of the meaning embedded in the text is dependent on close reading, paying attention to precise linguistic and formal details.

M has provided for two readings, an exoteric linear reading for the eyes of Pharaoh, or Pharaoh-like readers, and an esoteric non-linear reading for the eyes of the Israelites, or Israelite-like readers. M employs the signs narrative as a device to distinguish between Elohim and YHWH. We will now see how *M reveals details about YHWH through the signs in Egypt, by contrasting them with Elohim's signs in the creation.* Through all the details of the analysis, keep in mind the final goal is to grasp the knowledge of the nature of YHWH.

Analyzing the Signs

The central structure of nine signs must be visualized as a weave to be fully understood. In fact, it and the six days of creation are the clearest examples of woven text in the Torah. Before I present the nine-sign weave, I will list the signs consecutively with some of the characteristics of each one. The list shows how the table is developed.

Figure 27. Three Cycles of Signs in Threads 2-4 of Exodus Unit III

Cycle	Thread	Sign	Instruction to Moses	Agent
First	2	Blood	Get thee unto Pharaoh in the morning	Aaron
		Frogs	Go in unto Pharaoh	Aaron
		Lice	Say unto Aaron: Stretch out thy rod	Aaron
Second	3	Mixture	Rise up early in the morning and stand before Pharaoh	YHWH
		Cattle plague	Go in unto Pharaoh	YHWH
		Boils	Take to you handfuls of soot	Moses and Aaron
Third	4	Hail	Rise up early in the morning and stand before Pharaoh	Moses
		Locusts	Go in unto Pharaoh	Moses
		Darkness	Stretch out thy hand	Moses

In Figure 27, I have divided the nine signs into three cycles. Each cycle repeats a set of three different instructions to Moses. In the first sign of each cycle, YHWH tells Moses to stand before Pharaoh in the morning. In the second sign of each cycle, YHWH

tells Moses to go to Pharaoh. (To be consistent with the old JPS translation, I have used "go." However, the Hebrew is better translated here as "come.") The third sign in each cycle has no introduction; YHWH simply tells Moses how to bring it about.

In respect of these three different instructions, each of the three cycles is identical to the others; the three instructions appear in the same order in each cycle. There is, however, another element that distinguishes one cycle from the other, the agent who brings about the sign. Aaron brings about all three signs in the first cycle. Similarly, all three signs in the third cycle are brought about by Moses. The middle cycle has a combination of agents. YHWH himself brings about two signs, and one is brought about by Aaron and Moses together. We now have two different means of classifying the signs. We can divide them into three groups according to the three different instructions, and we can divide them by agents. Representing them in a weave, as in Figure 28, demonstrates the two different methods of grouping simultaneously.

Figure 28. The Nine Sign Weave

Stage/Thread		א	ב	ג
	Instruction→ Agent↓	Go to Pharaoh in the morning	Come	None
2	Aaron	Blood	Frogs	Lice
3	Mixed	Mixture	Livestock Plague	Boils
4	Moses	Hail	Locust	Darkness

At this point, the main value of the weave in Figure 28 is methodological. It indicates that each thread of the weave, warp and weft, should be examined as a three-sign set, six sets in all. The three weft threads can then be compared with each other. So too, the three warp threads can be compared. Aaron performs in weft thread 2 by pointing at the ground. All three of these signs have their source in the ground. In weft thread 4, Moses points to the sky to initiate each sign. These signs come out of the sky. The signs in the middle thread come neither from the ground nor from the sky, but from between them. So, there is a clear spatial theme in the organization of the signs expressed by the relative positioning of the weft threads. The three-part spatial organization is the inverse of the pattern created by the days of creation. While the creation weave created an image of the world as experienced, with the sky above and the earth below, the signs weave projects an image of an upside-down world.

The warp threads draw our attention to the introductions, and consequently, the "actors" in each scene. In the first warp thread, (א), YHWH tells Moses to go to Pharaoh in the morning. In the second warp thread, (ב), YHWH invites Moses to come with him to Pharaoh. Here I must clarify a point. The Hebrew verb that appears in the introductions to the three signs in the middle warp thread is *bo*, "come," even though it is often mistakenly translated in this context as "go." The importance of properly understanding this verb is that it positions the speaker, YHWH. Moses is told to "come" to Pharaoh, thereby implying that either YHWH is with Pharaoh, or that he will go with Moses to Pharaoh. Thus, there is a contrast with the first warp thread, where Moses is apparently sent to Pharaoh without YHWH. In the third warp thread, (ג), Moses does not go to Pharaoh at all; he is with YHWH. This gives us the following arrangement of players: first warp thread, Moses and Pharaoh; second warp thread, YHWH, Moses, and Pharaoh; third warp thread, Moses and YHWH. These observations are summarized in Figure 29

Figure 29. Decreation Weave Players

According to Warp Threads

Instruction➜	א	ב	ג
	Go to Pharaoh in the morning	Come	None
Players	Moses, Pharoah	YHWH, Moses, Pharoah	YHWH, Moses

Since Moses is common to all three, he can be omitted in considering the unique characteristics of the warp threads. This leaves the following arrangement: first warp thread, Pharaoh; second warp thread, YHWH and Pharaoh; third warp thread, YHWH. The middle warp thread is a combination of the two adjacent warp threads. This is a strikingly clear example of the visual rhetoric we noted earlier; the structural middle is the conceptual middle. The same is true of the weft threads, where the middle weft thread also combines the poles, Moses and Aaron.

The signs of the first warp thread, the bodies of water changing to blood, the invasion of mixed things, and the hail all pointedly take place by the light of day in the morning. These three signs bring about changes in the three levels of the created world: the lower waters (2), the upper waters (4) (that fall to the ground), and the biosphere between them (3). This is the mundane world over which Pharaoh claims mastery; hence, he alone appears in this warp thread.

Next, we are going to look at the third warp thread, (ג). There is an important methodological point that explains why we skip from the first warp thread to the third warp thread. We have noted that the central warp thread and the central weft thread combine elements of the extremities i.e. Pharaoh on one extreme, YHWH on the other, and both in the middle. Therefore, we should first study the extremes and then see how they combine in the middle.

The most obvious difference between the signs of the first warp thread and the third warp thread, (lice, boils, and darkness), is visibility. Lice are virtually invisible, boils have no visible cause, and darkness is the negation of visibility. These stand in sharp contrast with the signs of thread (א), all of which are associated with morning, the light of day. The invisible signs were brought about without any visible warning from the invisible deity, YHWH.

These three signs directly affect individuals, as opposed to the cataclysmic changes of the first three signs. Even darkness, which might appear to be an objective change, is reported in terms of individual blindness: "people did not see one another." The verb used to bring it about, *veyamosh*, literally means "was made palpable." The palpable darkness prevented individuals from interacting, "people did not see one other." It was so bad that (literally) "for three days they could not get up *from under themselves*." We can sharpen the comparison between the first warp thread and the third by examining the order within each warp thread.

We have already noted that the first warp thread reproduces a picture drawn by the first days of the creation in which the primal world consists of three levels, the upper and lower waters and the firmament between them. This is the objective world clearly seen by the light of day. The third warp thread deals with personal experience, the itch of a mite, the discomfort of a skin eruption, and isolating "darkness." These three signs are ordered experientially. They begin with an itch caused by the smallest of visible creatures, followed by a skin eruption that could have either an external or internal or psychosomatic cause. Finally, there is a darkness of the spirit. The order is "internalization," from the outside inward. It points to experience that forces an unmediated confrontation between the individual and YHWH. The extreme warp threads have defined the separate realms of "public events" and "private experience," or perhaps, "objective" and "subjective" realities.

The substantial, public, Pharaonic world of the first warp thread meets the third warp thread's private world of the spirit in the central warp thread. The common metaphor for the combination of the body-public and the private spirit is animal life, or simply life; the Hebrew for "animals," *chayot*, can also be read as "life," *chayut*. The central warp thread is made up of frogs, livestock, and locust. It seethes and swarms with life—and death. From the lower world of the first weft thread, rise hordes of frogs. From the upper world of the third weft thread come down swarms of locust. In the middle are masses of domesticated flocks and herds. Clearly, the middle warp thread contains living creatures, which join the objective physicality of the first warp thread with the hidden spirit of the third warp thread. Pharaoh, the hero of the first warp thread, is presented as the ostensible master of matter. The invisible YHWH who appears by himself in the third warp thread is the master of the spirit. YHWH and Pharaoh, spirit and flesh, meet in the middle warp thread.

We deal below with the one-to-one correspondence of the signs and the days of creation, but first let us ponder why the decreation weave has three warp threads as opposed to the two warp threads of the creation weave. It seems that our distinction between *materia* and *anima* in the warp of creation is paralleled by the first two warp threads of the signs. We have just seen the emphasis on anima in thread (ב) of the signs. Thread (א) of the signs contains no enunciated life forms, although the "mixture" of 3א, captured in a single Hebrew word, is often interpreted as a mixture of animals or insects. However, reading the signs in parallel with the days of creation reveals that "mixture" parallels and inverts the "separation" between above and below created on day two. This combines with the reference to lower waters in 2א and upper waters in 4א to create an image equivalent to the development of the physical world on days 1-3, although inverted. If this is an accurate understanding of M's plan, then warp thread (ג), subjectivity, the realm of individuals in the signs weave, would be the added thread. Pharoah's absence in the introductions to the signs in warp thread (ג) is telling. Pharoah is at home in the objective world of Elohim's creation, threads א and ב in the signs weave. He is foreign to YHWH's unique concern with the human spirit, the spirit that can be lost in oppressive darkness. The association of YHWH with subjectivity is consistent with

YHWH's pre-deluge concerns with the machinations of the human heart, as we saw in Part One.

Creation and Decreation

The upside-down world of Exodus Unit III, in which the three-tiered hierarchy of creation is inverted, is symptomatic of the overall thrust of the signs, which is to cause Egypt to return to primal disorder. Each of the weft threads of creation is in some way symbolically "undone" in reverse order. In weft thread 4, the last of the nine signs, darkness, negates day one, light. On the same weft thread, lights fall out of the sky in the form of fiery hail, in opposition to day four during which the lights were placed in the sky. On the "earth" thread, 2, the bodies of water formed on day 3 turn to blood and the creatures created from the earth on day six are attacked by the very earth which gave birth to them in the form of lice. On the middle level, weft thread 3, the "divider" of day 2 is negated by "mixture." The living creatures, first mentioned in day five, lose their ability to move because of the boils.

The capstone of the comparison between the creation and the decreation is provided by the parallels between the prologues and epilogues of both structures, threads 1 and 3 in the creation, and threads 1 and 5 in the decreation. The first word in the Torah, *rashit*, beginning, echoes in thread 5 of the signs through the Hebrew word for firstborn, *behor*. Both words are used in the Torah in reference to first fruits. So, the death of "the beginnings," the firstborn, is an inversion of the introduction of the creation weave. In the introduction of the signs, where Aaron changes a staff to a serpent, YHWH says that he will withdraw from Egypt his *tzvaot*, "hosts." The same word, *tzvaot*, is mentioned in the conclusion of creation. In the creation, they are the hosts of heaven and earth created by Elohim, while in the decreation they are YHWH's hosts. The connections between the signs and the days of creation are summarized in Figure 30.

Figure 30. Signs in Egypt Negate Days of Creation

1 **Introduction**	Divine "hosts" leaves Egypt	
2 **Earth** **(Below)**	2א Gatherings of water turn to blood	2ג Earth produces lice which attack men and beasts
3 **Middle**	3א Divider becomes Mixture	3ג Life is paralyzed
4 **Luminescent** **(Above)**	4א Fiery Hail Lights fall from sky	4ג Darkness replaces Light
5 **Epilogue**	Death of the first born ("beginnings" are destroyed)	

Distinctions Between Elohim's Creation and YHWH's Decreation

M has utilized the visual tapestry of creation, embedded in the weft of the creation weave, to deconstruct creation. As interesting as the "decreation" is as a literary phenomenon, it is even more important for our attempt to understand M's narrative. The decreation, which takes place in Egypt, can only be fully grasped after the creation weave has been analyzed, as we did in the previous chapter. M used the reversal of the creation weave as a model for the breakdown of the state and the return to primal chaos in Egypt. The signs are a step-by-step reversal of creation, within a limited context; each sign brings Egypt closer to chaos. We can understand this by connecting the signs in Egypt to the creation weave. However, as M has pointed out, this reading of events was not intended for Pharaoh, but rather for future generations of Israelites who could connect the redemption in Egypt to the creation narrative to learn about the nature of YHWH revealed against the background of Elohim's nature and deeds. We can note a few of the differences which our analysis has revealed.

The correlation between Elohim's creation and YHWH's decreation reveals the cornerstone of M's theology. Elohim represents the creator who implemented a plan to create a self-maintaining world. After the completion of the creation, Elohim and the created world were independent of each other. Order in the created world was to be maintained by the heavenly lights from above, and by Adam, (created as/in the image of Elohim) from below. While Elohim created through an evolutionary progression of days, YHWH is revealed through a two-fold revolution. He attacks the order of the world created by Elohim, as well as the political order of Egypt maintained by Pharaoh. It is as if YHWH took up Elohim's creation narrative as a guide to bringing about disorder in the world. Finally, we interpreted the addition of a third warp thread as demonstrating that YHWH, in contrast to Elohim, relates to human subjectivity. We close this chapter with the highlights of the differences between Elohim and YHWH indicated by the creation and decreation. These highlights are summarized in Figure 31

- The days of creation present the figure of a *natural* order based on the four primal elements: fire (light) days one and four; air and water days two and five; earth days three and six. YHWH is presented through his signs in Egypt as the source of the *supernatural*.

- Elohim's creation is hierarchical, from the top down; YHWH decreates from the bottom up.

- In Elohim's creation, the function of people, Adam, is to maintain order in the world, like Pharaoh. In YHWH's new order, the function of Israel is to serve YHWH, as HaAdam served YHWH Elohim in the Garden of Eden by maintaining it.

- As pictured through the paired creation days, Elohim's world is based on a prime dyad, "inanimate/animate," or similar. YHWH's revelation, through the tripled signs, introduces a third realm, the subjective.

- YHWH directly brings about two signs, mixture, and bovine plague, placed in the middle between those oriented towards the earth, brought about by Aaron, and those brought about by Moses from the sky. YHWH is revealed in the middle, at the meeting point of heaven and earth.

- Elohim creates his ordered world without any intermediary; YHWH asks Moses and Aaron to mediate between him and Pharaoh to bring chaos to Egypt.

Figure 31. Summary of Distinctions Between the Creation and Decreation Weaves

	Elohim: Days of Creation	**YHWH: Signs in Egypt**
Purpose	Separate Elohim from the World	Reveal YHWH in the World
Method	Evolutionary Creates Order through Nature	Revolutionary Breaks Down Order through the Supernatural
Visually Hierarchical Organization	From the Top Down	From the Bottom Up
Warp	Polar Inanimate and Animate	Contains Third Category Inanimate – Animate - Subjective
Place of Deity	Outside of World	In the Middle Between Heaven and Earth
Function of People	Maintain the World	Serve YHWH
Intermediation	Elohim Creates Directly	YHWH Decreates with Intermediation of Moses and Aaron

Part Four: Mapping the Books of the Torah

When reflecting on the complexity of M's plan in Part Three, we noted six levels of division within the Torah. Each division introduces a rhetorical component that contributes meaning to the esoteric reading of the Torah.

The Torah is divided into five books

   The five books are divided into eighty-six *Units*

      Each Unit is subdivided into warp *threads* and weft *threads*

         The threads themselves are divided into *segments*

            Segments may be divided into *elements*

               Elements may be divided into *parts*

In the Units we have examined, we broke down the Torah to its smallest structurally significant components. This breakdown led to a "reweaving," a seeing how the components coalesce in Units to create the images M wove. In this Part we continue the process of putting the components of the Torah together. This entails the iteration of three more levels of organization. By the time we finish this Part, we will be acquainted with at least eight levels of meaningful organization in the Torah.

The complexity of the plan was sufficient to guarantee that much of the meaning M embedded in the structure would remain hidden from most hearers or readers. Reading according to the structure would then lead to an esoteric reading—designed for the few. The esoteric character of the reading increases exponentially as we add the levels of order we are about to explore. Seeing new vistas in the Torah is the reward for successfully identifying the eighty-six Units. Identifying them is a precondition for understanding how they group themselves.

We will now see how the Units fit together in thematically related "sets" and how the alignment of the sets defines the formal and thematic structure of each of the five books. In Chapter 10, we examine the map of the Torah, which is made up of its eighty-six Units. In Chapter 11, we closely examine the map of Genesis. This examination will prepare us to study the distribution of the names Elohim and YHWH in Genesis in Part Five.

Chapter 10. Structural Map of the Torah

Sets of Units & the Color Indications

The structural map, Figure 32, has been designed to demonstrate connections between Units within each of the five books. There are two types of connections.

- **One type of connection consists of sets of Units,** noted by upper case Roman letters in the map. Sets can be made up of consecutive Units, such as seen in Genesis A, or alternating Units (like the Words on each tablet), such as those seen in Genesis B, as we will see in more detail below. The organization of Units in sets is one of the significant indicators of authorial intent in the Torah. They make clear that the individual Units were constructed and arranged to fit together in higher-order structures like pieces of Lego.

Genesis A	Genesis B
I	V
1:1-2:3	11:10-13:4
II	VII
2:4-4:26	15:1-17:27
III	IX
5:1-10:32	20:1-22:19

- **The second type of connection is noted by means of colors.** Every set of Units in the Torah, except for one, is paired with another set. The pairings are indicated by similar colors, such as Genesis B and E, and C and D. The paired sets elucidate the thematic structures of the books.

Figure 32. Structural Map of the Torah

GENESIS

A		B	C	D	E	F
I 1:1-2:3		V 11:10-13:4	VI 13:5-14:24	XI 25:12-34	XII 26:1-33	XVII 36:1-41:45
II 2:4-4:26	IV 11:1-9	VII 15:1-17:27	VIII 18:1-19:38	XIII 26:34-28:9	XIV 28:10-32:3	XVIII 41:46-47:26
III 5:1-10:32		IX 20:1-22:19	X 22:20-25:11	XV 32:4-33:16	XVI 33:17-35:29	XIX 47:27-50:26

EXODUS

A
I 1:1-4:18	II 4:19-6:28
III 6:29-11:10	IV 12:1-13:16

V
13:17-15:21

B
VI 15:22-17:16	VII 18:1-20:23
VIII 21:1-22:16	IX 22:17-23:19

X
23:20-24:18

C
XI 25:1-27:21	XII 28:1-43
XIII 29:1-30:10	XIV 30:11-31:17

XV
31:18-34:35

D
XVI 35:1-36:7	XVII 36:8-38:20
XVIII 38:21-39:31	XIX 39:32-40:38

LEVITICUS

A	B	C	D		E	F	G
I 1-3	IV 8-10	VII 13:1-46	X 16		XVI 22:1-25	XIX 24	XXII 27
II 4-5	V 11	VIII 13:47-14:57	XI 17	XIII 19	XV 21	XVIII 23	XXI 26
III 6-7	VI 12	IX 15	XII 18		XIV 20	XVII 22:26-33	XX 25

NUMBERS

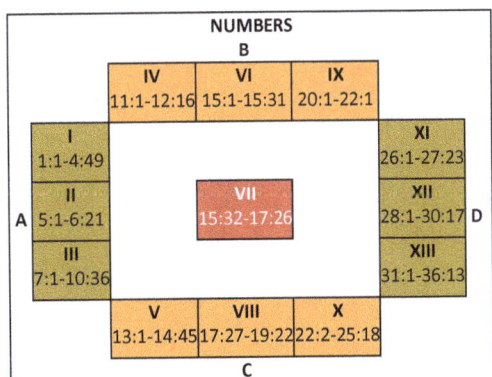

DEUTERONOMY

A	B	C	D	
V 9:1-10:11	VI 10:12-11:32	IX 25:5-27:26	XII 31:1-32:47	
III 5:1-6:3	IV 6:4-8:18	VIII 21:10-25:4	XI 28:69-30:20	XIII 32:48-34:12
I 1:1-:23	II 4:1-49	VII 12:1-21:9	X 28:1-28:68	

The Paired Sets

Figure 33. Two Pairs of Intertwined Sets in Genesis

B ↔	C	D ↔	E
V =	VI	XI =	XII
11:10-	13:5-	25:	26:
13:4	14:24	12-34	1-33
VII =	VIII	XIII =	XIV
15:1-	18:1-	26:34-	28:10-
17:27	19:38	28:9	32:3
IX =	X	XV =	XVI
20:1-	22:20-	32:4-	33:17-
22:19	25:11	33:16	35:29

It is interesting to observe that each of the books, except Exodus, is constructed entirely from sets of three Units each, and one unattached, "independent," Unit. The triads come in two varieties, simple and intertwined. Simple triads contain three consecutive Units. In Figure 33, the intertwined triads are indicated by ↔ at the top of the columns and = between paired Units. For example, numbers of Units in Genesis D (Units XI, XIII and XV) alternate with the Units of E (XII, XIV, XIV). The alternation reflects a shift in focus, back and forth, between two themes. Triad D contains three Units that deal exclusively with family, specifically the relationship between Jacob and Esau. Triad E contains interactions and alliances between members of the family and powers outside the family, both human and divine. The fact that the themes alternate makes the linear reading bumpy, seemingly disorganized.

The sets paired by intertwining are Genesis B/C and D/E, Numbers B/C and Deuteronomy A/B. The non-intertwined pairs of triad sets are Genesis A/F; Leviticus A/G, B/F, D/E; Numbers A/D; Deuteronomy C/D.

Exodus is unique and contains four sets of four Units each. They, too, are paired, A/B and C/D. The consistent use of paired sets across the whole Torah is another strong indicator that it is a well-planned composition.

Independent Units

There are seven "independent" Units in the Torah which are not attached to other Units in a set. Every book has one, except Exodus, which has three, further emphasizing Exodus as different from the other books. The details of how these independent Units are used in each book, and their distribution across the five books, contribute to the view that the whole Torah is an integrated, planned composition.

Five of the Units come at the centers of books. In two books, Genesis and Deuteronomy, the independent Unit is not in a center. The fact that these two books differ from the other three in the placement of the independent Units reinforces the thesis that the three central books were composed as a three-part core surrounded by prologue-like and epilogue-like books. The prologue has the independent Unit near the beginning, the epilogue has it at the end, and the central Units have it in the centers. Exodus has three "centers." Examining them demonstrates one of the literary functions common to the independent Units of Exodus, Leviticus, and Numbers: creating foci.

Three Centers of Exodus

The three "centers" of Exodus are: Units V (13:17-15:21), X (23:20-24:18), and XV (31:18-34:35). All three Units function as textual dividers. Unit X divides the book in half, and Units V and XV further divide each half in half again. Unit X, which contains the covenant between YHWH and Israel (24:4-8) and the mystical vision of the deity (24:10,11) is the pivot between non-tabernacle (1:1-23:19) and tabernacle (25:1-40:35) related material. Unit V contains the crossing of the Reed Sea. It separates the events in Egypt (Units I-IV) from the events outside of Egypt (VI-IX) in the first half of Exodus. Unit XV contains the narrative of the golden calf and marks the line between the heavenly tabernacle (XI-XIV) and the earthly (XVI-XIX). These three divider Units divide the other Units of the book into four sets of four Units each.

The Roles of Independent Units in the Structures of the Books of the Torah

The independent Units of Leviticus and Numbers are similar to Exodus X in that they define the center points of these books. Together with Deuteronomy XIII, these independent Units also define literary structures which imitate formal structures defined within the text itself. Leviticus is constructed from three concentric rings of text so that the reader replicates the experience of the High Priest on the Day of Atonement, going into and out of the Holy of Holies. The central Unit, XIII (Lev. 19), represents the Ark of the Covenant at the center. This explains why it contains references to the Decalogue as well as sixteen first-person divine revelations in the form "I am YHWH," paralleling YHWH's speeches to Moses from between the cherubim on the ark.

The Book of Numbers, containing thirteen Units, was constructed to reflect the way the tribes camped in groups of three tribes each, around the tabernacle, the holy center. Unit VII, containing the Korach narrative, focuses on who should be in the holy center. The independent Unit of Deuteronomy is XIII, its last Unit. The other twelve Units are grouped in two sets of six Units. Since Unit XIII contains Moses' blessings to the tribes, it can be viewed as parallel to Moses facing the twelve tribes divided in two sets of six, as they were to divide to receive blessings and curses (Deut 27:12,13). The place of Unit XIII at the end of Deuteronomy, and consequently, at the end of the Torah, may indicate that part of its function is to mark the end. This is reinforced by the placement of the independent Unit of Genesis IV, the Tower of Babel narrative. Near the beginning of Genesis, it marks the transition of the narrative from the universal to the particular. Following it, Unit V begins the story of the covenant with Abraham and his descendants, which occupies the rest of the Torah.

Not all the information I am giving you here is necessary for our narrow goal of understanding the use of the names Elohim and YHWH, primarily in Genesis. But we also have a broader goal, learning how to read and interpret M's esoteric text. My own explorations have only scratched the surface. The additional information is meant to help and guide you in exploring the *terra incognita* on your own.

Chapter 11. The Map of the Genesis Weave

This is an important juncture in our progress, so a little reflection is not out of place before we look at what this chapter holds. We began with the challenge of understanding why the names Elohim and YHWH are both used to refer to deity. I asserted that the puzzle is soluble but there is a prerequisite for understanding the solution, learning how to read the esoteric Torah. Through our reading of the Decalogue, we have understood that M had a divine paradigm of woven writing. We then saw examples of how M applied the paradigm to the construction of the Torah's eighty-six Units. The Units, while they differ somewhat from each other in their dimensions, are all on the same order of size and have the same function, dividing the Torah into coherent woven compositions. We have now gone a step further and have begun to see how the Units associate with each other to establish the formal structures of books. In this chapter we will see that the same two-dimensional paradigm of woven text in the Units was also applied to the weaving of an entire book, Genesis.

The solution to our two-name puzzle is found by reading Genesis according to its weave. All our previous chapters have prepared us for this stage. We have developed an understanding of M's systematic use of structural paradigms and visual rhetoric. Genesis itself is an iteration of textual weaving, but at a higher level than we have seen. The divisions of the threads of warp and weft are now replaced by whole Units to create the weave of the whole book. The book is thus a weave of weaves. Eventually, we will see that M embedded the distinctions between YHWH and Elohim in the warp threads of Genesis. To get there, we will first have to identify the characteristics that suggest how Genesis should be read as a weave, by drilling down into the details behind its arrangement.

Genesis contains nineteen Units divided into six sets of three, marked A–F, and a single independent Unit, IV (11:1–9). Set A consists of the creation narratives, each of which has "create" in its opening verse. The remaining five sets, B–F, encompass the patriarchal narratives: Abraham (B-C), Isaac-Jacob (D-E), and Joseph (F). All three patriarchal narratives share certain characteristics that mark

them as planned blocks. Each of the three narratives begins with two "generations of": Shem and Terach (B), Ishmael and Isaac (D), and Esau and Jacob (F). Each block also ends with two deaths and burials in Hebron: C, Unit X—23:19, and 25:9; E, Unit XVI—35:19, and -29; F, Unit XIX—50:13, 26. However, they do differ in size. The Joseph narrative (F) has three Units, while the other two have six Units each. This creates an almost symmetrical structure consisting of three Units in the opening and closing blocks (A and F), the "bookends," and six Units in each of the two middle narratives (B-C and D-E). This structural symmetry leads to the discovery of conceptual symmetry.

The two three-Unit sets, A and F, have a common theme expressed as a pair of poles. The theme is "kingship," expressed through heavenly kingship in A, and the earthly kingship of Pharaoh and Joseph in F. The two six-Unit blocks, the Abraham narrative and the Isaac-Jacob narrative, also reveal a conceptual pattern by means of a structural pattern. They have been constructed similarly. Each of them is composed of two intertwined threads, B/C and D/E. Both large narratives alternate Units having two different themes—alliances, and family.

Unit V in B contains the original alliance between Abram and YHWH, as well as a temporary alliance with Pharaoh mediated by Sarai. In VI, the focus shifts to Abram's interactions with his nephew, Lot. This pattern is repeated twice in VII-X. The result is that the three alternating Units of B, (V, VII, IX) share a common theme, alliances, and the three parallel Units of C, (VI, VIII, X), also share a common theme, family, specifically, children of Abraham's brothers. This exact pattern of alternating themes repeats itself in the second six-Unit narrative, D/E, utilizing the same themes, alliances and family. However, the second block reverses the order. It begins with family in XI (D) and shifts to alliances in XII (E). Regarding these themes, the six-Unit intertwined blocks are thus mirrored images. The family thread is second in B/C and first in D/E. Figure 34 is a more detailed map of Genesis containing the points we have just seen, as well as others we are about to see.

Figure 34. The Literary Structure of the Book of Genesis

	Creation Narratives		Abraham Narrative		Isaac-Jacob Narrative		Joseph Narrative
	A		B	C	D	E	F
	Divine Kingship Elohim and YHWH		Covenants (With deity and Abimelech) and Altars	Brothers' Children (Lot and Rebecca)	Brothers (Jacob and Esau)	Covenants (With deity and Abimelech) and Altars	Human Kingship Joseph and Pharaoh, and Esau's kings
1	**I** **1:1-2:3** *"Elohim **created**"* Days of creation		**V** **11:10-13:4** Generations of Shem and Terach YHWH and Pharaoh send Abraham to Canaan Abraham builds Altar at Beit El	**VI** **13:5-14:24** Lot gets captured and Abraham saves him	**XI** **25:12-34** Generations of Ishmael and Isaac Jacob buys birthright from Esau	**XII** **26:1-33** Isaac wants to go to Egypt like Abraham but YHWH makes a covenant with him and Isaac stays near Abimelech with whom he also makes a covenant	**XVII** **36:1-41:45** Generations of Esau and Jacob Joseph and Dreams
2	**II** **2:4-4:26** *"… when they were created"* HaAdam and Eve, Cain and Abel	**IV** **11.1-9)** Tower of Babel	**VII** **15:1-17:27** Covenants between YHWH and Abram, Elohim and Abraham, Birth of Ishmael	**VIII** **18:1-19:38** Destruction of Sodom and saving of Lot	**XIII** **26:34-28:9** Jacob impersonates Esau	**XIV** **28:10-32:3** Jacob's Ladder at Beit El, Jacob marries Levan's daughters and makes a covenant with him	**XVIII** **41:46-47:26** Joseph's brothers come to Egypt
3	**III** **5:1-10:32** *"on the day Elohim created Adam"* Noah		**IX** **20:1-22:19** Covenant with Abimelech Binding Isaac on Altar	**X** **22:20-25:11** Obtaining Rebecca for Isaac Deaths of Sarah and Abraham	**XV** **32:4-33:16** Jacob makes peace with Esau	**XVI** **33:17-35:29** Rape of Dinah Jacob returns to Beit El to build an Altar Deaths of Rachel and Isaac	**XIX** **47:27-50:26** Deaths of Jacob and Joseph

Three Ring Structure

Figure 35. Concentric Rings in Genesis

A	B	C	D	E	F
Kingship	Covenants	Family	Family	Covenants	Kingship

As in the maps of the other books of the Torah, background colors, blue, green and yellow, used in the map of Genesis indicate that the pairs of sets which have similar colors have related themes. Thus, three major themes appear in the following sets of Units:

- A and F are kingship

- B and E are covenants

- C and D are the Abrahamic family

According to the map, these themes are concentric, ring-like. A/F, kingship, is the outer ring; B/E, covenants, is the middle ring; and C/D, family, is the inner. In other words, the reversal of thematic order in D/E (from B/C)is to create symmetry and place the family at the center of the book. Shortly, we will see the details underlying the three-ring arrangement of Units in Genesis, but first, we should have a look at other examples of concentric plans focused on a family. These examples are evidence that M considered the family, or at least certain families, a core subject on which to build a narrative.

We will have a look at two other structures that feature concentric arrangements around families, or family related material. These two additional structures are also further indications of M's proclivity for working with paradigmatic structures, simple patterns that are used on multiple levels of planning. We have examined parts of one of these examples in Genesis Unit III, the flood. It is a virtual template for the structure of Genesis. The other example is an entire book of the Torah, Leviticus, also constructed with three rings and with family in the center ring. Together, the two examples help verify that we have grasped Genesis according to M's esoteric design. Visualizing the design is of utmost importance for revealing the distinctions between Elohim and YHWH

Two More Family-Centered Structures

In Figure 36 we see that the six weft threads of Genesis Unit III form a pattern of three concentric subjects. Threads 1 and 6 detail the generations of humanity before and after the flood. They are separate from threads 2-5 which encompass the flood story, from the events which led to the flood and the building of the ark in 2, to the results of the flood in 5. Within this "flood" block of four weft threads, 3 and 4 give the details of the flood itself. The abstract format is like the format we have discovered for the whole book of Genesis—three concentric rings. But the similarities are more than abstract.

Figure 36. Links Between Genesis III and the Concentric Structure of Genesis

Outline of Genesis Unit III			Link between Genesis III and Triads of book	Outline of Genesis	
Stages of Unit III Narrative	א	ב		Genesis Triad	Theme
1 **Generations** Prologue to Flood	1א 5:1-32	1ב 6:1-10	In the day that Elohim created man, in the likeness of Elohim made he him (5:1)	A	Divine Kingship
2 **Before the Flood**	2א 6:11-22	2ב 7:1-5	But I will establish My covenant with you (6:18)	B	Covenants
3 **Beginning of Flood**	3א 7:6-10	3ב 7:11-16	In the selfsame day entered Noah, and Shem, and Ham, and Japheth, the sons of Noah, and Noah's wife, and the three wives of his sons with them, into the ark (7:13)	C	Family
4 **End of Flood**	4א 7:17-8:5	4ב 8:6-14	and Noah only was left, and they that were with him in the ark. (7:23)	D	Family
5 **After the Flood**	5א 8:15-22	5ב 9:1-17	As for Me, behold, I establish My covenant with you, and with your seed after you; (9:9)	E	Covenants
6 **Generations** Epilogue to Flood	6א 9:18-29	6ב 10:1-32	And the beginning of his (Nimrod) kingdom was Babel, and Erech, and Accad, and Calneh, in the land of Shinar. (10:10)	F	Human Kingship

Both the book of Genesis and its Unit III have a formal focus consisting of a multi-generational family. Noah's family is physically enclosed in the ark in threads 3 and 4. The parallel in Genesis, threads C and D, focus on the Abrahamic family itself. Covenants characterize threads B and E in the map of Genesis. In thread 2 of the flood, the structural parallel of thread B in the book, we find: "But I will establish my *covenant* with thee; and thou shalt come into the ark, thou, and thy sons, and thy wife, and thy sons' wives with thee (6:18)." Similarly, in thread 5, which is parallel to E, "And Elohim spoke unto Noah, and to his sons with him, saying: "As for me, behold, I establish my covenant with you, and with your seed after you; and with every living creature that is with you, the fowl, the cattle, and every beast of the earth with you; of all that go out of the ark, even every beast of the earth (9:8-10).""" In short, the six weft threads of Genesis III establish a pattern repeated by the six sets of Units of Genesis.

Before we turn to the next parallel concentric structure, we should note an aspect of how we visualized the parallels between the Unit and the book in Figure 36. The outline of Genesis Unit III is arranged, as are all eighty-six Units of the Torah, with vertical warp threads, א and ב, across which are woven six horizontal weft threads, 1-6. M established the vertical warp of all the Units of the Torah in Genesis Unit I by creating the "picture" of a three-tiered reality. The picture would not appear as representative of the experienced world unless the days were arranged as we saw them earlier, creating a vertical warp. However, we have not yet determined the proper orientation of the map of Genesis. In the outline of Genesis in Figure 36, the orientation has been rotated 90 degrees, so that the sets of triads are horizontal rather than vertical, as they appear in the map of Figure 34. We will address the significance of this observation in Chapter 12. For now, we turn to the structure of Leviticus.

Figure 37. The Literary Structure of Leviticus

A	B	C	D		E	F	G
I (1-3)	IV (8-10)	VII (13.1-46)	X (16)	XIII (19)	XIV (20)	XVII (22.26-33)	XX (25)
II (4-5)	V (11)	VIII (13.47-14.57)	XI (17)		XV (21)	XVIII (23)	XXI (26)
III (6-7)	VI (12)	IX (15)	XII (18)		XVI (22.1-25)	XIX (24)	XXII (27)

The Literary structure of Leviticus, as seen in Figure 37, is very similar to the structure we have seen in Genesis.[5] The specific characteristic that interests us is based on the concentric pairs of sets, A and G, B and F, D and E. Each of these pairs, or rings, was marked by M with a different "tag," indicating a theme associated with the ring. The three themes indicated by the tags are: "place" in A/G, "time" in B/F and "family" in D/E. The family theme is established by the extensive references to family relationships in these sets of Units as seen in Figure 38.

Figure 38. Family Relationships in the Central Ring of Leviticus

D	E
Unit X	**Unit XIV**
sons, brother, household (3x), father	sons, progeny (3x), family, father (6x), mother (5x), wife (2x), daughter-in-law, half-sister (2x), aunt (3x), uncle, sister-in-law
Unit XI	**Unit XV**
Anomalous[6]	sons (3x), mother (2x), father (3x), daughter (2x), sister (2x), brother, husband, wife, widow, divorcee, progeny (3x)
Unit XII	**Unit XVI**
relative, father (9x), mother (5x), sister (4x), wife (4x), granddaughter, son (2x), half-sister, paternal aunt, maternal aunt, uncle, daughter-in-law, sister-in-law	sons (2x), progeny (3x), child, daughter (2x), father (2x)

One additional characteristic of the three-ring structure of Leviticus is associated with the structure of the Tabernacle. The three areas of the Tabernacle are divided between the courtyard outside the tent, and the two areas within the tent. The outer room of the tent is the holy place and the inner room, the holy of holies, containing the Ark of the Covenant. Content of the Units of Leviticus shows that M associated the theme of the outer ring (A/G) with the courtyard, the middle ring (B/F) with the holy place, and the inner ring (D/E) with the holy of holies. Consequently, we can say that the family-related material is "placed" in the holy of holies theme.

Our reading of Genesis III very closely parallels our description of Leviticus as relating to the Tabernacle. It too has an outer ring, threads 1 and 6, which are outside the story of the flood in threads 2-

---

[5] I have written extensively about Leviticus elsewhere. See note 3.
[6] See note 3.

5, like the courtyard outside the tent. Threads 2 and 5 provide transitions "into" and "out" of the flood, like the holy place provides a transitional room into the holy of holies.

The two additional concentric structures show that M's arrangement of Genesis matches the arrangements of Genesis Unit III and the book of Leviticus, both of which place the family in the center, in the holy of holies, as it were. Whatever significance we might want to attribute to the centrality of family, the fact that it is a recurring theme justifies our understanding of the rings of Genesis. But there is also internal evidence, within Genesis that substantiates our arrangement of the Units in three rings

A detailed reading of all the relationships between Units in Genesis would fill a book of its own, if not more. So, we will limit ourselves to just one example to show how tightly the book is organized. One of the more perplexing incidents in Genesis involves Abram presenting his wife, Sarai, to the Egyptians as his sister. Later, after his name has been changed to Abraham, and his wife's to Sarah, he does the same thing with Abimelech the king of Gerar. Like father like son, Isaac also presents his wife in Gerar as his sister. We will now see that these three incidents combine with the rape of Dina to establish the central ring, B/E, as focused on covenants.

The four Units in which these incidents take place are the four "corner" Units of the ring: Sarai in V, Sarah in IX, Rebekah in XII and Dinah in XVI. The first three are similar in that they are represented as their husbands' sisters. The full significance of their being "sisters" can be understood by considering the fate of Sarai in Egypt. Abram, and likely many others, went to Egypt to secure grain at a time of famine. When he arrives with his extended household:

...the Egyptians beheld the woman that she was very fair. And the princes of Pharaoh saw her, and praised her to Pharaoh; and the woman was taken into Pharaoh's house. And he dealt well with Abram for her sake; and he had sheep, and oxen, and he-asses, and men-servants, and maid-servants, and she-asses, and camels. (12:14-16).

Pharaoh allies with Abram because of Sarai. We may assume that his "princes" deemed Abram, from amongst the multitude who came from Canaan for supplies, worthy of an alliance. Compare this with Hamor's speech to the people of Shechem after the rape of Dinah:

...These men are peaceable with us; therefore let them dwell in the land, and trade therein; for, behold, the land is large enough for them; let us take their daughters to us for wives, and let us give them our daughters. Only on this condition will the men consent unto us to dwell with us, to become one people, if every male among us be circumcised, as they are circumcised. (34:20-22)

Hamor argues that his marriage to Dinah, which can only be accomplished through the circumcision of all their males, will benefit their city. Thus, the rape of Dinah is also presented in the framework of creating an alliance. All four cases present marriage as a basis for covenants. This is sufficient evidence, combined with the discovery of the family centered three-ring paradigm to verify the layout of Genesis as presented in Figure 34.

Part Five: The Solution: The Map of Elohim and YHWH

If we are to read the composition of Genesis as a weave, we will have to identify the themes of rows 1-3. But even before we approach that analysis, we have some observations to make. We earlier distinguished between warp threads and weft threads to demonstrate that Units are better represented as weaves than as tables. In weaving, weft threads are there to be seen, while warp threads are hidden within the weave. The distinction is crucial to the solution of our opening problem.

Chapter 12. The Orientation of the Map

In M's first weave, the creation, the weft thread containing the days forms the tapestry of the cosmos. The warp threads of the "divine dyad" are embedded in the weave, but not directly accessible in the visualization. That is the character of weaves: the warp is there to hold the weft without drawing attention to itself.

Figure 39. The Unit Map of Genesis

	A		B	C	D	E	F
1	I (1:1-2:3)		V (11:10-13:4)	VI (13:5-14:24)	XI (25:12-34)	XII (26:1-33)	XVII (36:1-41:45)
2	II (2:4-4:26)	IV (11.1-9)	VII (15:1-17:27)	VIII (18:1-19:38)	XIII (26:34-28:9)	XIV (28:10-32:3)	XVIII (41:46-47:26)
3	III (5:1-10:32)		IX (20:1-22:19)	X (22:20-25:11)	XV (32:4-33:16)	XVI (33:17-35:29)	XIX (47:27-50:26)

Returning to the book of Genesis, we have identified its weft threads in A-F. Until now, we have read woven Units as if they were woven on a vertical loom with warp threads running vertically and weft threads horizontally. This orientation is consistent with the appearance of the tapestry of the cosmos in Genesis Unit I. Days one and four are above, and three and six are below. This forms the image of the luminescent above and the earth below. Orientation is not arbitrary; it is part of the plan.

Through an act of pure literary genius, M utilized the very same signs that established the orientation of the Units with a vertical warp to establish the orientation of the book of Genesis with a horizontal warp. Before looking at the details, let us look at the source of our analogy in ancient weaving.

Figure 40. Horizontal and Vertical Looms Circa 1200 BCE [7]

Fig. 16A.—Weavers at work as represented in the Tomb of Nefer-ronpet, Superintendent of
Weavers at Thebes. Date about 1200 B.C. From a drawing by Mr. N. de G. Davies.

Figure 40 illustrates weavers at work circa 1200 BCE. It is a sketch of a painting in an Egyptian tomb of that period. The picture shows two types of looms. On the right is a vertical loom with vertical warp. On the left are two horizontal looms with a horizontal warp. M was aware of both types and considered it proper to weave smaller compositions on a vertical loom and a larger composition, a whole book, on a horizontal loom. The significance of this for us will soon be apparent, but first, back to M's stroke of genius (one of many).

How did M manage to use the same signs to indicate to the reader that the warp threads of Units are vertical, while the warp threads of the whole book are horizontal? Elements of the days of creation appear in the corners of the book to establish the orientation. The parallels are in the framework, threads A and F of the book. In thread A, Units I and III have parallels to days one and three and in thread F Unit XVII contains an element from day four while Unit XIX resonates with day six, as indicated in Figure 41.

---

[7] H. Ling Roth, "Ancient Egyptian and Greek Looms," *Project Gutenberg*, June 8, 2008, https://www.gutenberg.org/files/25731/25731-h/25731-h.htm (accessed June 5, 2021)

Figure 41. Days of Creation in Corners of Genesis

	A	F
1	Like Day 1 Unit I Days	Like Day 4 Unit XVII Eleven stars, and the sun and the moon
2	Unit II	Unit XVIII
3	Like Day 3 Unit III Waters upon the earth recede to reveal the dry land	Like day 6 XIX (47:27-50:26) Were fruitful and multiplied

Starting from the end, on day six, Elohim tells Adam to be fruitful and multiply and fill the land. In Unit XIX, the last Unit of F, the narrator says that the children of Israel were fruitful and multiplied extensively in the Land of Goshen. Next, on day four, Elohim creates the large lights and the stars. In the parallel Unit of F, XVII, Joseph dreams that eleven stars, and the sun and the moon bow down to him. In another parallel between these elements, Elohim says the Sun and moon will rule over day and night. Joseph's brothers, using the same Hebrew term, ask him whether his first dream implied that he wished to rule over them. Then, the specific creation of the first day is light, called "day." The parallel Unit I in A, is divided into seven "days." And finally, on the third day of creation, the waters upon the earth recede to reveal the dry land. The exact same receding of the waters upon the earth takes place in the parallel Unit III of A, the Noah narrative. The four textual clues we have identified "pin" the four corners of the creation weave to the four "corners" of the Book of Genesis! M has instructed us to orient the book as we have, with row 1 above and row 3 below as in Figure 39. While the orientation may at first seem trivial, we are about to see that it is anything but trivial.

Chapter 13. The Warp of the Map

While the weaver's art includes hiding the warp threads, they nevertheless establish the frame which holds the weave together. In the book of Genesis, the warp is established by the names Elohim and YHWH (as well as other things). Over the generations knowledge of woven text and so knowledge of the warp (as well as the weft!) has completely disappeared, leaving much confusion regarding the variations in the names. However, we will now see that the familial narratives of Genesis were woven across a warp of divine names. We noted earlier that the weaving analogy implies that the categories of the warp must be defined before the weft is woven. In the case of Genesis, we can infer that M began to plan the book to distinguish between the names (amongst other things) and fashioned the individual narratives to carry out this goal. We can now test this theory.

We begin by examining the appearances of Elohim and YHWH after Babel. In doing so, it is important, to distinguish between appearances of the divine characters "on the stage" as the active character, as opposed to *references* to them by other characters. The following chart summarizes the active appearances of Elohim and YHWH in Units V-XIX, according to the map of the book which we have derived from its literary structure.

Figure 42. Map of Appearances of Elohim and YHWH in Genesis after Babel

	B	C	D	E	F
1	**V** (11:10-13:4) Y speaks to Abram 12:1 Y appears to Abram 12:7 Y afflicts Pharaoh 12:17	**VI** (13:5-14:24) Y promises the land to Abram and many descendants 13:14	**XI** (25:12-34) Y answers Yitzhak's request 25:21 Y tells Rivka she has twins 25:23	**XII** (26:1-33) Y appears to Yitzhak and says don't go down 26:1 Y blesses Yitzhak 26:12 Y appears to Yitzhak at night and blesses him 26:24	**XVII** (36:1-41:45) Y kills Er 38:7 Y kills Onan 38:10 Y was with Joseph 39:2 Y was with Joseph 39:21
2	**VII** (15:1-17:27) Y speaks to Abram in vision, Covenant between the parts 15:1. Y appears to Abram and makes conditional covenant 17:1 E speaks to Abram and changes his name to Abraham and makes a commitment that Abraham will father nations 17:3 E speaks to Abraham and commands the covenant of circumcision 17:9 E speaks to Abraham and changes Sari's name to Sarah 17:15	**VIII** (18:1-19:38) Y appears to Abraham as anashim 18:1 Y asks why Sarah laughed 18:13 Y speaks to himself about Abraham 18:15 Y speaks to himself about Sodom 18:20 Y speaks to Abraham about Sodom Y leaves Abraham 18:33 Y rains down brimstone from heaven 19:24 E while destroying the cities remembers Abraham and saves Lot 19:29	**XIII** (26:34-28:9)	**XIV** (28:10-32:3) Y appears to Yaakov on a ladder 28:13 Y sees that Leah is hated 29:31 E hears Leah 30:17 E remembers Rachel 30:22 Y tells Yaakov to go home 31:3	**XVIII** (41:46-47:26) E speaks to Israel in a night vision 46:2
3	**IX** (20:1-22:19) E comes to Abimelech in a dream 20:2 Y remembers (פקד) Sarah 21:1 E speaks to Abraham about Sarah 21:12 E hears the voice of the boy 21:17 E opens Hagar's eyes 21:19 E is with the boy 21:20 E tries Abraham and says to him 22:1	**X** (22:20-25:11) E blesses Yitzhak 25:11	**XV** (32:4-33:16)	**XVI** (33:17-35:29) E tells Yaakov to go to Beit El 35:1 E appears to Yaakov on his way from Padan Aram 35:9 E changes Yaakov to Israel 35:10	**XIX** (47:27-50:26)

The results are astounding. Only YHWH appears in row 1, and, with one exception, only Elohim appears in row 3. Both appear in the middle, in row 2. Clearly, the structure of the book as presented above contains a conceptually significant horizontal component as well as the vertical component defined by the sets of Units. The warp consists of YHWH acting above, Elohim below, and both acting in the middle. We have noted throughout our analysis that the Torah utilizes visual rhetoric. M stressed this point by describing the six-day creation in a manner that produces a visualization of the world as we experience it. To reproduce the visual plan accurately the days must be ordered in two parallel columns, with days one to three in one column, and four to six in the other. The result is: that which is visually above in the world is above in the text and that which is visually below in the world is below in the text. The text itself then becomes a visual representation of the world it describes, as well as a key for reading Genesis according to its formal structure.

The story of the world that was created in six days and the Torah itself are both visually oriented. This insight reinforces the discovery that Genesis was formatted, as displayed above, to reveal characteristics of YHWH and Elohim. In fact, the creation paradigm itself explains the relationships between the three rows of Units: row 1 relates to the transcendent, the above, row 3 to the immanent, the below, and row 2 forms an interface between them. Of course, our concepts of immanent and transcendent may not be directly applicable but approximations. A closer look at the distinctions between the rows will help clarify the concepts M embedded within them, which I have labelled here with immanent and transcendent.

One of the fundamental observations which allowed us to divide all of Genesis after Babel into three patriarchal narratives concerns the cycle of life. Each narrative begins with a Unit containing a double use of "generations" and ends with a Unit containing two deaths. According to the map, the "generations" or births, appear in row 1, YHWH's precinct. The deaths, on the other hand, appear in row 3, Elohim's realm. Having discovered the key to the wisdom that M embedded in Genesis' structure, we can now search the Units of row 1 for YHWH's characteristics and row 3 for Elohim's. The terms of this search will be broader than when we merely searched out the appearances of YHWH and Elohim on the stage. Each name now has a full warp thread that is marked as being associated with it. So, we will seek out the unique characteristics of threads 1 and 3, to fill in our knowledge of YHWH and Elohim. Once they are identified, we can test our observations in thread 2.

YHWH's Thread

Figure 43. Common Elements of YHWH's Thread

V (11:10-13:4)	VI (13:5-14:24)	XI (25:12-34)	XII (26:1-33)	XVII (36:1-41:45)
11:10 These are the generations of 12:2 And I will make of thee a great nation 13:2 And Abram was very rich in cattle, in silver, and in gold.	13:5 And Lot also, who went with Abram, had flocks, and herds, and tents. 13:6 And the land was not able to bear them, that they might dwell together; for their substance was great, so that they could not dwell together. 13:14 And YHWH said unto Abram, after that Lot was separated from him: 'Lift up now thine eyes, and look from the place where thou art, northward and southward and eastward and westward; 13:15 for all the land which thou seest, to thee will I give it, and to thy seed for ever. 14:22 And Abram said to the king of Sodom: 'I have lifted up my hand unto YHWH, Elohim Most High, Maker of heaven and earth, 14:23 that I will not take a thread nor a shoe-latchet nor aught that is thine, lest thou shouldest say: I have made Abram rich	25:12 Now these are the generations of 25:33 And Jacob said: 'Swear to me first'; and he swore unto him; and he sold his birthright unto Jacob. 25:34 And Jacob gave Esau bread and pottage of lentils; and he did eat and drink, and rose up, and went his way. So Esau despised his birthright.	26:3 Sojourn in this land, and I will be with thee, and will bless thee; for unto thee, and unto thy seed, I will give all these lands, and I will establish the oath which I swore unto Abraham thy father; 26:4 and I will multiply thy seed as the stars of heaven, and will give unto thy seed all these lands; and by thy seed shall all the nations of the earth bless themselves 26:12 And Isaac sowed in that land, and found in the same year a hundredfold; and YHWH blessed him. 26:13 And the man waxed great, and grew more and more until he became very great. 26:14 And he had possessions of flocks, and possessions of herds, and a great household; and the Philistines envied him. 26:16 And Abimelech said unto Isaac: 'Go from us; for thou art much mightier than we.' 26:17 And Isaac departed thence, and encamped in the valley of Gerar, and dwelt there. 26:23 And he went up from thence to Beer-sheba. 26:24 And YHWH appeared unto him the same night, and said: 'I am the Elohim of Abraham thy father. Fear not, for I am with thee, and will bless thee, and multiply thy seed	36:1 Now these are the generations of 36:6 And Esau took his wives, and his sons, and his daughters, and all the souls of his house, and his cattle, and all his beasts, and all his possessions, which he had gathered in the land of Canaan; and went into a land away from his brother Jacob. 36:7 For their substance was too great for them to dwell together; and the land of their sojournings could not bear them because of their cattle. 39:2 And YHWH was with Joseph, and he was a prosperous man 39:5 And it came to pass from the time that he appointed him overseer in his house, and over all that he had, that YHWH blessed the Egyptian's house for Joseph's sake; and the blessing of YHWH was upon all that he had, in the house and in the field. 39:21 But YHWH was with Joseph, and showed kindness unto him, and gave him favour in the sight of the keeper of the prison.

In addition to the "generations" theme, thread 1 features expansive wealth. Abram became "very rich in cattle, in silver, and in gold (V)" in Egypt. Next, in Unit VI, we learn: "And Lot also, who went with

Abram, had flocks, and herds, and tents. And the land was not able to bear them, that they might dwell together; for their substance was great, so that they could not dwell together." The need to separate because of great wealth repeats in XII "And Abimelech said unto Isaac: 'Go from us; for thou art much mightier than we'" and XVII, "For their

substance was too great for them to dwell together." YHWH even blessed Egyptians with great wealth "for Joseph's sake." YHWH's realm contains generations, multiplication of descendants, and expansive wealth. The counterpart in Elohim's sphere is quite striking.

Elohim's Thread

Figure 44. Common Elements of Elohim's Thread

IX (20:1-22:19)	X (22:20-25:11)	XV (32:4-33:16)	XVI (33:17-35:29)	XIX (47:27-50:26)
20:3 But Elohim came to Abimelech in a dream of the night, and said to him: 'Behold, thou shalt die 20:11 And Abraham said: 'Because I thought: Surely the fear of Elohim is not in this place 21:16 And she went, and sat her down over against him a good way off, as it were a bow-shot; for she said: 'Let me not look upon the death of the child.' 22:2 And He said: 'Take now thy son, thine only son, whom thou lovest, even Isaac, and get thee into the land of Moriah; and offer him there for a burnt-offering 22:10 And Abraham stretched forth his hand, and took the knife to slay his son. 22:12 And he said: 'Lay not thy hand upon the lad, neither do thou any thing unto him; for now I know that thou art a Elohim-fearing man	23:2 And Sarah died in Kiriatharba--the same is Hebron--in the land of Canaan; and Abraham came to mourn for Sarah, and to weep for her. 25:8 And Abraham expired, and died in a good old age, an old man, and full of years; and was gathered to his people. **25:11** And it came to pass after the death of Abraham, that Elohim blessed Isaac his son	32:8 Then Jacob was greatly afraid and was distressed. 32:12 Deliver me, I pray Thee, from the hand of my brother, from the hand of Esau; for I fear him, lest he come and smite me, the mother with the children. 32:31 And Jacob called the name of the place Peniel: 'for I have seen Elohim face to face, and my life is preserved.'	34:30 And Jacob said to Simeon and Levi: 'Ye have troubled me, to make me odious unto the inhabitants of the land, even unto the Canaanites and the Perizzites; and, I being few in number, they will gather themselves together against me and smite me; and I shall be destroyed, I and my house.' 35:8 And Deborah Rebekah's nurse died, and she was buried below Beth-el under the oak 35:19 And Rachel died, and was buried in the way to Ephrath 35:29 And Isaac expired, and died, and was gathered unto his people, old and full of days; and Esau and Jacob his sons buried him.	47:29 And the time drew near that Israel must die 49:33 And when Jacob made an end of charging his sons, he gathered up his feet into the bed, and expired, and was gathered unto his people. 50:15 And when Joseph's brethren saw that their father was dead, they said: 'It may be that Joseph will hate us, and will fully requite us all the evil which we did unto him.' 50:26 So Joseph died, being a hundred and ten years old. And they embalmed him, and he was put in a coffin in Egypt.

3

Death and fear unite all the Units of thread 3, from fear of Elohim, to fear of fratricide. Elohim's limiting realm of death and fear stands in sharp contrast to the expansiveness of life and wealth in YHWH's row 1. What has happened in M's narrative regarding Elohim, who was described as seeing only "good" in the days of creation? And how has YHWH been transformed in the narrative from the fear-inspiring deity who saw the bad in people's hearts before the flood, to the source of "good"?

They seem to have exchanged identities. There may be a formal verification of this reversal in one consistent rule in all of thread 1. Only one name of the deity is active in the Units of the thread. However, in Unit I the name is Elohim, whereas in the other Units of the thread it is YHWH. There does seem to be a reversal after Unit I. We return to this point after looking at further distinctions between the names in threads 1 and 3.

Figure 45. Comparing YHWH's and Elohim's Blessings

YHWH Blesses in Thread 1	Elohim Blesses in Thread 3
13:14 And YHWH said unto Abram, after that Lot was separated from him: 'Lift up now thine eyes, and look from the place where thou art, northward and southward and eastward and westward; 13:15 for all the land which thou seest, to thee will I give it, and to thy seed for ever. 13:16 And I will make thy seed as the dust of the earth; so that if a man can number the dust of the earth, then shall thy seed also be numbered.	25:11 And it came to pass after the death of Abraham, that Elohim blessed Isaac his son
26:2 And YHWH appeared unto him, and said: 'Go not down unto Egypt; dwell in the land which I shall tell thee of. 26:3 Sojourn in this land, and I will be with thee, and will bless thee; for unto thee, and unto thy seed, I will give all these lands, and I will establish the oath which I swore unto Abraham thy father; 26:4 and I will multiply thy seed as the stars of heaven, and will give unto thy seed all these lands; and by thy seed shall all the nations of the earth bless themselves; 26:5 because that Abraham hearkened to My voice, and kept My charge, My commandments, My statutes, and My laws.	35:9 And Elohim appeared unto Jacob again, when he came from Paddan-aram, and blessed him. 35:10 And Elohim said unto him: 'Thy name is Jacob: thy name shall not be called any more Jacob, but Israel shall be thy name'; and He called his name Israel. 35:11 And Elohim said unto him: 'I am El Shadai. Be fruitful and multiply; a nation and a company of nations shall be of thee, and kings shall come out of thy loins; 35:12 and the land which I gave unto Abraham and Isaac, to thee I will give it, and to thy seed after thee will I give the land.'

Elohim and YHWH bless in different ways. YHWH's blessings can be characterized as expansive compared with Elohim's. YHWH promises Abram all the land he can see and descendants as numerous as the dust of the earth. He promises Isaac multiple lands and progeny as numerous as the stars. Elohim is much more laconic. He merely blesses Isaac, without any content. When blessing Jacob, Elohim does not promise multitudinous descendants, but rather "a company of nations shall be of thee, and kings shall come out of thy loins." Elohim emphasizes nations rather than individuals. We can extend this comparison by comparing appearances of Elohim and YHWH in the shared row, thread 2.

The Middle Thread, Elohim and YHWH

Figure 46. The Middle Thread: YHWH and Elohim

VII (15:1-17:27)	VIII (18:1-19:38)	XIII (26:34-28:9)	XIV (28:10-32:3)	XVIII (41:46-47:26)
YHWH speaks to Abram in vision, Covenant between the parts 15:1. YHWH appears to Abram and makes conditional covenant 17:1 Elohim speaks to Abram and changes his name to Abraham and makes a commitment that Abraham will father nations 17:3 Elohim speaks to Abraham and commands the covenant of circumcision 17:9 Elohim speaks to Abraham and changes Sari's name to Sarah 17:15 Elohim goes "up" from Abraham 17:22	YHWH appears to Abraham as anashim 18:1 YHWH asks why Sarah laughed 18:13 YHWH speaks to himself about Abraham 18:15 YHWH speaks to himself about Sodom 18:20 YHWH speaks to Abraham about Sodom YHWH leaves Abraham 18:33 YHWH rains down brimstone from heaven 19:24 Elohim while destroying the cities remembers Abraham and saves Lot 19:29		YHWH appears to Yaakov on a ladder 28:13 YHWH sees that Leah is hated 29:31 Elohim hears Leah 30:17 Elohim remembers Rachel 30:22 YHWH tells Yaakov to go home 31:3	Elohim speaks to Israel in a night vision 46:2

The very first blessing in thread 2, in Unit VII, has a special value for us because it verifies the tension we noted between the rewards of thread 1 and the fear of thread 3: "After these things the word of YHWH came unto Abram in a vision, saying: 'Fear not, Abram, I am thy shield, thy reward shall be exceeding great (15:1).'" In this blessing M has demonstrated that thread 2 is to be considered a conceptual middle between threads 1 and 3, incorporating characteristics of both. Amongst those characteristics are active appearances by both YHWH and Elohim. The continuation of Unit VII contains extremely important consecutive appearances by both.

- And when Abram was ninety years old and nine, YHWH appeared to Abram, and said unto him: 'I am El Shadai; walk before me, and be thou wholehearted. And I will make my covenant between me and thee, and will multiply thee exceedingly (17:1,2).

- And Abram fell on his face; and Elohim talked with him, saying: 'As for Me, behold, My covenant is with thee, and thou shalt be the father of a multitude of nations. Neither shall thy name any more be called Abram, but thy name shall be Abraham; for the father of a multitude of nations have I made thee. And I will make thee exceeding fruitful, and I will make nations of thee, and kings shall come out of thee (17:3-6).

The importance of this comparison between YHWH and Elohim is highlighted by the phrase in 17:4 translated "as for me." This is as close as M ever comes to indicating that one of the names (divine characters) is aware of the other. YHWH has just proposed a covenant with Abram linked to Abram's behavior, "walk before Me, and be thou wholehearted," i. e. "be like Noah." Now Elohim speaks for the first time since concluding a covenant with all flesh after the flood and opens with the same words which precede the declaration of his covenant with Noah, "As for me, behold, I establish my covenant with you (9:9)." There too, after the flood, Elohim's covenant is paralleled by an earlier speech by YHWH: "YHWH said in his heart: 'I will not again curse the ground any more for man's sake; for the imagination of man's heart is evil from his youth

(8:21).'" In both the flood narrative and the Abraham narrative, M forces the reader to compare Elohim and YHWH.

In addition, at the precise moment when the name of deity interacting with Abram changes, so too does Abram's name change to Abraham. Elohim introduces this change at the same time as proposing a covenant with Abraham that differs from YHWH's. While YHWH demanded "wholeheartedness," Elohim makes no such demand, at least not immediately. The demand he does make is more limited. Following Elohim's declaration of the covenant when changing Abram's name, he details its two sides.

> And I will establish My covenant between Me and thee and thy seed after thee throughout their generations for an everlasting covenant, to be Elohim unto thee and to thy seed after thee. And I will give unto thee, and to thy seed after thee, the land of thy sojournings, all the land of Canaan, for an everlasting possession; and I will be their Elohim. (17:7,8)

> And Elohim said unto Abraham: 'And as for thee, thou shalt keep My covenant, thou, and thy seed after thee throughout their generations. This is My covenant, which ye shall keep, between Me and you and thy seed after thee: every male among you shall be circumcised. And ye shall be circumcised in the flesh of your foreskin; and it shall be a token of a covenant betwixt Me and you. (17:9-11)

The two sides of the agreement are: Elohim will give Abraham's descendants "the land of Canaan, for an everlasting possession," while they will "be circumcised." To see just how different this is from YHWH's covenant, we need to return to YHWH's words earlier in the Unit:

> In that day YHWH made a covenant with Abram, saying: 'Unto thy seed have I given this land, from the river of Egypt unto the great river, the river Euphrates; the Kenite, and the

Kenizzite, and the Kadmonite, and the Hittite, and the Perizzite, and the Rephaim, and the Amorite, and the Canaanite, and the Girgashite, and the Jebusite.' (15:18-21)

Our dyad of "expansive and limited" accurately describes the differences between YHWH's and Elohim's covenants in Unit VII. YHWH's demands are limitless, "be thou wholehearted," and the reward is proportionate "from the river of Egypt unto the great river, the river Euphrates." Elohim requires just one limited act of limiting the flesh, circumcision, and promises just the land of Canaan. We should note that Elohim's demand is of the flesh as opposed to YHWH's demand of "wholeheartedness." This is an accurate reflection of the distinction between them we found in the flood Unit.

Unit VIII, the next Unit of thread 2, contains just a cameo appearance by Elohim, compared with the presence of YHWH. Nevertheless, it is important verification of our previous identification of the realm associated with each name. Like his bringing down rain from the heavens for forty days, "YHWH caused to rain upon Sodom and upon Gomorrah brimstone and fire from YHWH out of heaven (19:24)." M has made sure that we understand that YHWH is associated with heaven above. Elohim joins YHWH in the destruction of Sodom just as he did in the flood, from below:

> And Abraham got up early in the morning to the place where he had stood before YHWH. And he looked out toward Sodom and Gomorrah, and toward all the land of the Plain, and beheld, and, lo, the smoke of the land went up as the smoke of a furnace. And it came to pass, *when Elohim destroyed the cities* of the Plain, that Elohim remembered Abraham, and sent Lot out of the midst of the overthrow, when He overthrew the cities in which Lot dwelt. (19:27-29)

Here M reinforces the above and below perspectives associated with YHWH and Elohim by referring to the hill where Abraham met with YHWH. It is to be the vantage from which he views Elohim's "overthrow" of the cities below. Elohim's place is below, and YHWH's is above. This is precisely what we see in the map of Genesis, YHWH above and Elohim below.

Another Unit in thread 2, XIV, also includes a visualization of the relative positions of Elohim and YHWH. "And he dreamed, and behold a ladder set up on the earth, and the top of it reached to heaven; and behold the angels of Elohim ascending and descending on it (28:12)." In Jacob's vision of the ladder, angels ascend from Elohim, placing Elohim at the bottom of the ladder. We are then told YHWH's position relative to the ladder to heaven, "And, behold, YHWH stood upon it (28:13)." Again, we see Elohim below and YHWH above, just as the warp threads in the weave of Genesis present them. We see below, Jacob's words in his response to YHWH's proposed covenant hint at the significance of the distinction between the names.

And, behold, YHWH stood upon it, and said: 'I am YHWH, the Elohim of Abraham thy father, and the Elohim of Isaac. The land whereon thou liest, to thee will I give it, and to thy seed. And thy seed shall be as the dust of the earth, and thou shalt spread abroad to the west, and to the east, and to the north, and to the south. And in thee and in thy seed shall all the families of the earth be blessed. And, behold, I am with thee, and will keep thee whithersoever thou goest, and will bring thee back into this land; for I will not leave thee, until I have done that which I have spoken to thee of.' And Jacob awaked out of his sleep, and he said: 'Surely YHWH is in this place; and I knew it not.' And he was afraid, and said: 'How full of awe is this place! this is none other than the house of Elohim, and this is the gate of heaven.' And Jacob rose up early in the morning, and took the stone that he had put under his head, and set it up for a pillar, and poured oil upon the top of it. And he called the name of that place Beth-el, but the name of the city was Luz at the first. And Jacob vowed a vow, saying: 'If Elohim will be with me, and will keep me in this way that I go, and

will give me bread to eat, and raiment to put on, so that I come back to my father's house in peace, then shall YHWH be Elohim for me, and this stone, which I have set up for a pillar, shall be Elohim's house; and of all that thou shalt give me I will surely give the tenth unto thee.' (28:13-22)

This narrative is where M reveals how the story of YHWH is to develop further. First of all, it is a new kind of covenant. YHWH presents his offer, and then Jacob presents his side, which contains conditions. The exchange also involves Elohim in Jacob's vow. The substance of the narrative is dependent upon our knowing that Jacob is aware of a distinction between Elohim and YHWH. This significant information is disclosed by means of Jacob's dream. He visualizes a reality which is composed of Elohim below, YHWH above, and a ladder between them. YHWH is then presented through his most expansive promises, including "*all the families of the earth*." YHWH has a plan to influence the entire lower world, which until now has been associated with Elohim on the earth. Jacob and his descendants are to become the means whereby the heavenly YHWH is to be revealed within the imminent world. Jacob is the ladder in the dream through which YHWH is to descend. M makes this point in the most subtle way, by describing YHWH's position ambivalently. "And, behold, YHWH stood upon it (him) (28:13)." The Hebrew pronominal suffix referring to the object upon which YHWH stood can refer to either the ladder or Jacob as antecedent. YHWH is either on top of the ladder or on top of Jacob. Identifying Jacob with the ladder removes the ambivalence.

While YHWH spoke in a dream, Jacob "awaked out of his sleep" and spoke. He was struck by the fact that "YHWH is in this place; and I knew it not (28:16)." He was shocked that YHWH could be in a place that was "the house of Elohim." YHWH the heavenly, transcendent, should not be in a place. "And he was afraid, and said: 'How full of awe is this place! This is none other than the house of Elohim, and this is (also) the gate of heaven!'" We should remember that the Hebrew "*yera*" is both fear and awe. According to our reading above, it is most applicable to the realm of Elohim, thus "the house of Elohim." But it is also the "gate of heaven" where stands the base of the ladder stretching to heaven and YHWH.

The most fascinating aspect of this extraordinary narrative is Jacob's response to YHWH's dream covenant, "dream" both because of when it took place, and because of its content. It took place at night while Jacob slept and promised all that a person could "dream" of attaining. Apparently, Jacob is not immediately tempted to throw in his lot with YHWH, who promises, "And, behold, I am with thee, and will keep thee whithersoever thou goest, and will bring thee back into this land." Evidently, Jacob is not satisfied that the heavenly YHWH, of grandiose promises, is truly capable of dealing with the minutia of human existence associated with Elohim's physical world. YHWH has to prove himself to Jacob by "dressing up" in the persona of Elohim, as Jacob (the voice) needed to dress up in the persona of Esau (the body). This reading is consistent with our observations concerning the causes of the flood in Part One. YHWH wished to destroy people because of the thoughts of their hearts while Elohim was angered by the corruption of the flesh. YHWH is associated with that which is hidden in the heart and Elohim with the visible flesh.

Jacob has extremely modest requests, food and clothing and a trip home: "If Elohim will be with me, and will keep me in this way that I go, and will give me *bread to eat*, and *raiment to put on*, so that I come back to my father's house in peace, then shall YHWH be Elohim for me." This modest request is associated with Elohim, who, as we saw, provides more modest blessings than YHWH. But what could Jacob mean by "then shall YHWH be Elohim for me?" Here lies the key to the story and the turning point of the Torah. The full realization of this covenant will be delayed until YHWH redeems the Israelites from Egypt to become their Elohim. However, the next time YHWH appears to Jacob is also the last, in 31:1 "And YHWH said unto Jacob: 'Return unto the land of thy fathers.'" The command creates closure with YHWH's first words to Abram, telling him to leave his father's home. The story of YHWH's involvement with the patriarchs is complete. Afterward all of Jacob's contacts with deity are with Elohim. YHWH has become Elohim, according to Jacob's oath. Joseph, whom Israel "loved more than all his children," was totally ignorant of the name YHWH. Thus, Genesis ends with the dominance of Elohim and the need for YHWH to be reintroduced at the burning bush.

Chapter 14. When YHWH Becomes Elohim: Creative Reading

The distinction between Elohim and YHWH is inseparable from the formal plan of Genesis. The demonstration may have implications regarding authorship—Genesis is a coherent composition, not a patch-quilt. While this could be a significant finding, it was not the goal of the demonstration. The goal was to demonstrate the value of studying the Torah according to its woven structure. The tools we developed in Parts Two to Four to study the Torah as a woven text helped us to deepen our understanding of the difference between Elohim and YHWH as well as their combined function as an organizing principle. But of course, I have much more to say, and you surely have questions you would like me to address. Nevertheless, there is enough in this book to enable others to continue developing a reading of *The Woven Torah*. Still, it would certainly be dereliction of duty for me not to address the fundamental theological question, even if only superficially.

We have seen considerable evidence that M composed Genesis in a manner designed to highlight the distinction between Elohim and YHWH. How are we to interpret the indications that the names Elohim and YHWH are presented as if they were two significantly distinct divine characters in the book? Is M some form of dualist? These are the questions I feel compelled to address. In short: M has answered these questions in every Unit of the Torah. The Torah was composed to be read in two ways. M has associated the two readings with the two names. The dual readings of the Torah may reflect the apparent dualism implied by Elohim and YHWH. Even though there are two distinct ways of reading, as a linear text and as a woven text, there is only one text.

I see the two stone-tablet narratives as crucial for understanding the different expressions of Elohim's and YHWH's ways of writing and reading. Elohim speaks the Decalogue and produces carved and engraved tablets by himself. Ultimately, these tablets are shattered before the eyes of the whole camp. YHWH, on the other hand, partnered with Moses; Moses was to carve out the tablets for YHWH to write on. These are the tablets that Moses hid in a box (Deut 10:1), never showing them (that we know of). Elohim is associated with the linear reading, which is like M's shattered tablets (Units), when the Torah is read verse-by-verse. YHWH is associated with the esoteric reading, based on the woven structure. For Elohim, writing is a reproduction of speech, like the first tablets. For YHWH, it is the reproduction of writing, like the second tablets.

Elohim, the independent creator in Genesis Unit I, plans and creates the structure of reality in a manner that can be deconstructed by YHWH with the assistance of Moses and Aaron, "And Moses and Aaron did all these wonders before Pharaoh (Exod 11:10)." The linear reading of the Torah establishes a baseline, like Elohim's creation. The structured reading uncovers "signs" and "wonders," which, in turn, reveal the hand of an author who invites the reader to partner in discovering and revealing the signs and wonders. Supernatural, heavenly, YHWH promises unbounded riches to those who hear his voice; M, similarly, promises unbounded creative delight to those who read the woven Torah. By participating in the revelation of the esoteric Torah, the creative reader partners in the revelation of the holy, YHWH, thus changing the reality defined by Elohim. This is the realization of Jacob's dream, when YHWH, the holy, becomes part of our world.

Afterword: Weaving it All Together

This afterword was an unplanned, delightful product of ongoing study with my student-colleagues while reviewing parts of the book. With deepest appreciation I dedicate this addition to these pioneers of the esoteric Torah who have helped clarify that this kind of study is expansive. Our study has led to weaving the five books together into a new map, a veritable tapestry, presenting an all-encompassing view of the woven Torah, presented in Figure 47. The details revealed through the tapestry indicate that *the entire Torah was planned and composed as an integrated artifact.*

Figure 47. The Torah Weave

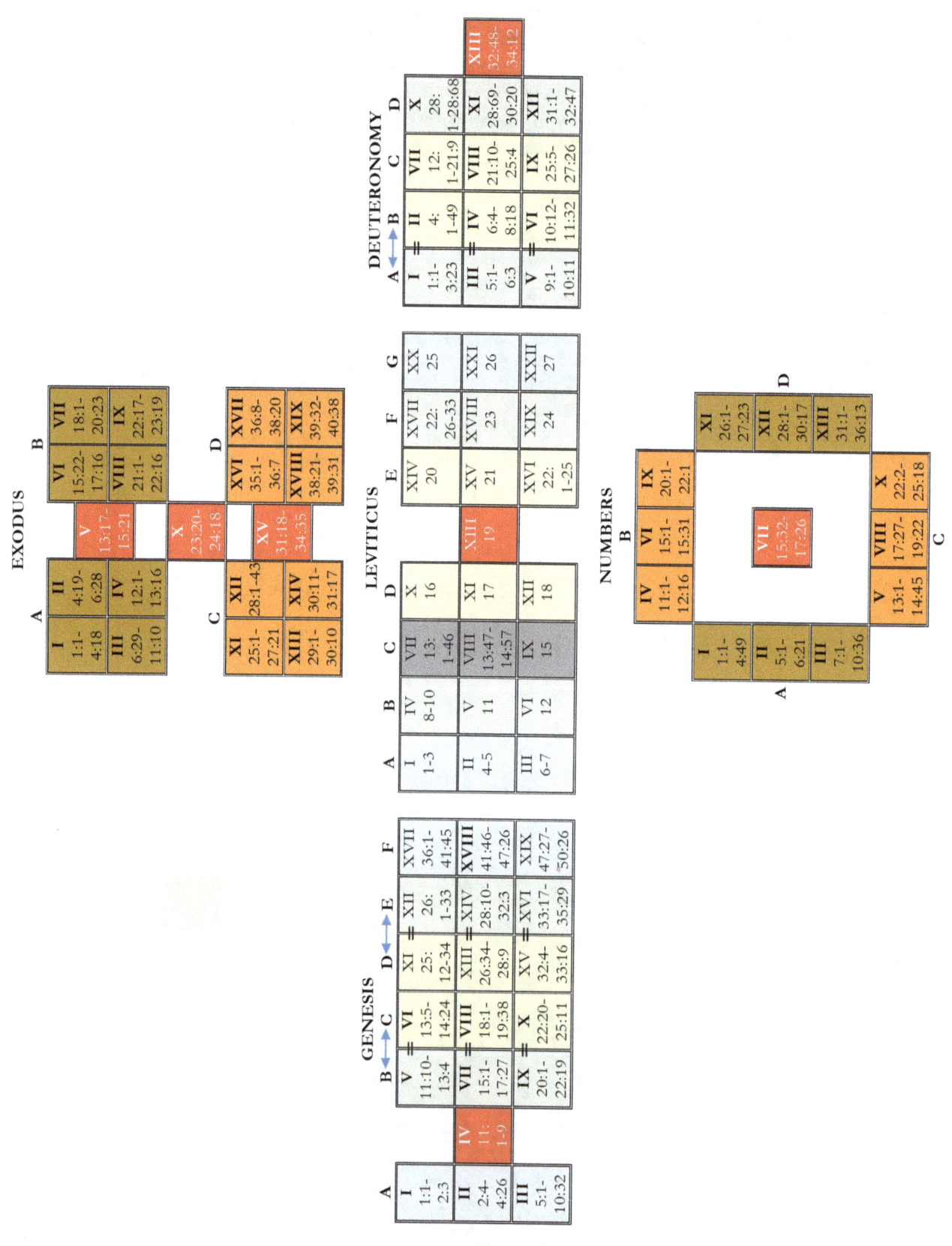

Up to now we have noted four distinct levels of textual weaving within the Torah. The six days of creation and the Decalogue, included in the first level, are weaves within Units. The second level contains the eighty-six woven Units, presented in Part Three. The third level is defined by the weaves formed by subdivisions of books, like the interwoven double triads in Genesis. The woven books themselves, described in Part Four, form the fourth level. When I began writing *The Esoteric Woven Torah*, I thought this fourth level, woven books, was M's ultimate creation. But now we must add a fifth level of organization, the integration of the five books of the Torah in the Torah tapestry.

Two Arrangements

The tapestry can be seen as two distinct arrangements of books, representing two different ways of conceptualizing the relationships between the five books of the Torah. One arrangement contains two interlocking sets of three books each: Genesis, Leviticus, and Deuteronomy, the horizontal component:

Genesis	Leviticus	Deuteronomy

and Exodus, Leviticus, and Numbers, the vertical.

Exodus
Leviticus
Numbers

In this arrangement, Leviticus has a double role as the center of both the horizontal and vertical triads. Interestingly, both threads have the same number of Units, divided similarly between the books in each thread. Both Genesis and Exodus have nineteen Units, while Numbers and Deuteronomy both have thirteen. Consequently, each thread has thirty-two Units, plus twenty-two in Leviticus.

The second arrangement is comparable with Ezekiel's vision of the divine chariot. Four books (creatures) surround Leviticus (the divine throne) in the center. This visualization is outlined in Figure 48.

Figure 48. Chariot View of Tapestry

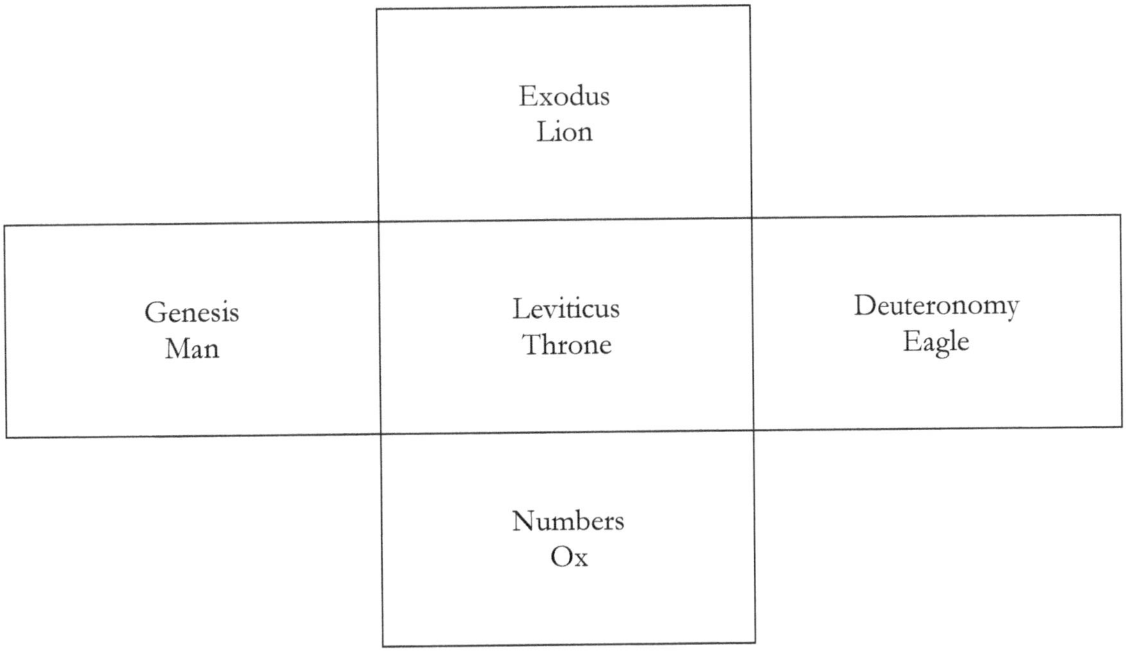

A complete understanding of the tapestry could lead to the integration of these two arrangements and warrant an additional publication. So, with your indulgence, for now I will paint a broad stroke picture to weave together the books of the Torah.

Weave Arrangement

In attempting to conceptualize what meanings may be embedded in the intersecting triads arrangement, we can apply what we have learned about textual weaves. All through our investigation of woven text we have considered continuity as the primary distinguishing characteristic of weft threads. They contain a continuous, unbroken flow of text, although usually divided into segments. The vertical triad, Exodus, Leviticus, and Numbers, fulfills the conditions of a weft thread since they are a continuous flow of text broken into three components, books, and defined by the forty-year journey. Similarly, the horizontal triad, Genesis, Leviticus, and Deuteronomy, may fulfill the conditions of a warp thread, being a group of noncontiguous segments. However, they also must demonstrate some type of coherence as a set of segments.

All three books of the horizontal thread are composed of triads, except for one unattached Unit in each book. The formal structures of these three books clarify they were planned together as a multi-book composition. A single set of (conceptual) warp threads span the three books, integrating them into a single extended weave. The coherence of the three-book plan is established by the set of concepts that distinguishes between the three warp threads that connect the books.

As we have seen in Genesis, a fundamental dyad, close to "transcendent and immanent," distinguishes between the outer threads (1 and 3), while the middle thread (2) is an interface, or connection, between the two. However, there is a difference between Genesis and Deuteronomy; the outer threads are reversed. In Genesis, the transcendent orientation is above, in thread (1), and the immanent below, in thread (3). In Deuteronomy, however, the imminent is above (1) and the transcendent below (3).

Leviticus was designed to lock itself to Genesis on one side and Deuteronomy on the other by a remarkable device. The first half of Leviticus is like Genesis because the map of the book places the "transcendent" above (1) and the "immanent" below (3). The second half of Leviticus, like all of Deuteronomy, has the immanent oriented above (1) and the transcendent below (3). Leviticus XIII (19) is the divider, as noted in Figure 49.

Figure 49. Interlocking Genesis, Leviticus, and Deuteronomy

Warp Thread	Genesis	Leviticus First Half		Leviticus Second Half	Deuteronomy
			Leviticus Unit XIII (19)		
1	Oriented to the transcendent			Oriented to the immanent	
2	Interface			Interface	
3	Oriented to the immanent			Oriented to the transcendent	

The tight structural integration of these three books, based on a three-thread warp, identifies them as the warp of the Torah tapestry. Further, characteristics of Genesis and Deuteronomy may point to the conceptual plan of the warp. The forty-year narrative detailed in Exodus and Numbers is the central story of the Torah. Genesis is a prologue to this story, and Deuteronomy, looking to the future settlement of the nation in Canaan, is an epilogue. Consequently, they form a timeline. They also have another set of characteristics to apply to the timeline.

Genesis is about individuals and Deuteronomy is about a nation. In this respect, an earlier analysis of Leviticus is enlightening.[8] The first half of Leviticus focuses on individuals and the second half on the nation. This fits precisely with Figure 49 and can explain the inversion of orientation after Leviticus

---

[8] See FN 3

XIII (19) while maintaining a conceptual consistency. Individuals are grounded in the immanent physical (3 in Figure 49) and "lift up their eyes" to the transcendent (1) in aspiration. The nation, on the other hand, is founded on the acceptance of a common deity and calendar, the transcendent, (1) and aspires (raises its eyes) to material continuity in its land (3). This explanation is, of course, hypothetical and deserves further expansion and clarification. But no matter how we may explain the inversion, Genesis, Leviticus, and Deuteronomy form a tightly planned block and represent the warp of the Torah through their three common horizontal threads.

Chariot Arrangement

In the second arrangement, four books are seen surrounding Leviticus, like the four faces of Ezekiel's chariot supporting the divine throne (Leviticus) in the center.

> I looked, and lo, a stormy wind came sweeping out of the north—a huge cloud and flashing fire, surrounded by a radiance…

Each of them had a human face [at the front]; each of the four had the face of a lion on the right; each of the four had the face of an ox on the left; and each of the four had the face of an eagle [at the back…

Above the expanse over their heads was the semblance of a throne, in appearance like sapphire; and on top, upon this semblance of a throne, there was the semblance of a human form.

Ezekiel 1

Ezekiel describes an arrangement like Figure 50 I have added the cardinal direction associated with each of the faces. Since Ezekiel sees the chariot coming from the North, Man, facing him, is the South face, with the East, the Lion, to its right and the West, the face of the Ox, to its left. The faces are mapped to the directions in Figure 50 according to the ancient practice of having East, the orient, oriented to the top of the map.

Figure 50. Ezekiel's Chariot

	Exodus Lion East	
Deuteronomy Eagle North	Leviticus Throne Source	Genesis Man South
	Numbers Ox West	

It is surprising that the Torah, a book about YHWH's revelation in the world, can be seen as a structural parallel to Ezekiel's divine chariot. But there are further parallels that raise the level of surprise to astonishment. Two individual books, Exodus and Numbers, are formatted according to the chariot paradigm. Looking at Figure 47, both of these books are divided into four quadrants, A-D, like the chariot figure. Both contain a vision of the deity at their center. Unit X in Exodus contains the narrative of the elders seeing the deity; in Numbers VII, the deity reveals himself to the nation at the tent of meeting (16:19). The vision of the elders in Exodus is startlingly similar to Ezekiel's.

- Above the expanse over their heads was the semblance of a throne, in appearance like sapphire; and on top, upon this semblance of a throne, there was the semblance of a human form. (Ezekiel 1:26)
- Then went up Moses, and Aaron, Nadab, and Abihu, and seventy of the elders of Israel; and they saw the deity of Israel; and there was under his feet the like of a paved work of sapphire stone, and the like of the very heaven for clearness. (Exodus 24:10)

It appears that the Torah and Ezekiel's chariot represent a single paradigm, according to which YHWH is revealed through a five-part figure consisting of the deity carried or supported by four "faces." The parallel between the Torah tapestry and Ezekiel's vision invites our attention, and fascinating questions come to mind: Is there a correlation between the faces and the books of the Torah? What could this tell us about the plan of the Torah? How does the chariot arrangement of the Torah connect to the weave arrangement? All these tantalizing questions will have to wait for a future study to address them. For now, I close with a proposal to integrate the warp and weft of the weave arrangement.

In broadest terms, there is a substantive difference between the two intersecting threads of the weave arrangement. Only the books of the vertical, weft, thread contain miracles and wonders, such as the signs in Egypt and the dividing of the sea. Also, the appearance of YHWH in clouds, fire, and smoke is limited to this thread. Perhaps the distinction is that the vertical thread is associated with the supernatural, as opposed to the "natural" horizontal warp thread, in Genesis and Deuteronomy, at least after the Tower of Babel narrative.

Alternatively, we can identify the vertical thread as characterized by YHWH's gradual revelation in the world, coming down from heaven to the mountain in Exodus, to the center of the camp in Numbers, in Unit VII. If the weft presents a picture of the revelation of the supernatural in the world, the horizontal warp might establish the natural foundations against which the supernatural appears. We have seen in ch. 9 that YHWH's grand appearance on the stage of nations takes place through the signs in Egypt. They are perceived as reversing the natural course of things, specifically against the background of the days of creation, e.g., the light of day one becomes darkness. The warp: Genesis, Leviticus, and Deuteronomy sets the foundation of the weave by establishing the natural created world.

Since these are to be the closing words of the book, I will try to tie together the Torah tapestry and the distinction we have explored between Elohim and YHWH. The horizontal triad may represent the natural world of cause and effect associated with Elohim since the days of creation. The vertical thread contains the supernatural, miraculous revelation of YHWH. The Torah tapestry thus integrates Elohim and YHWH. Perhaps the study of the Torah as a tapestry is meant to present the student with a path that leads to the Edenic integration of YHWH Elohim.

Appendix: The Woven Torah

Keys to Reading *The Woven Torah*

While presented as an appendix, what follows is the most important part of this book, the full text of the Torah's eighty-six Units in woven format. What has preceded is essentially an extended introduction intended to whet your appetite and provide you with the tools for studying the Torah according to its woven structure. To provide for the broadest readership, the text appears here in English translation, from the JPS 1917 edition. The Hebrew version appears on my website, chaver.com, as well as on academia.edu. I hope to publish a supplementary volume soon with the Hebrew text and additional detailed studies. Although the explanation of how the traditional linear text of the Torah is transformed into the woven format appears in Part Three, for convenience, I have summarized the main points here together with the color code.

Division of the Books into Units

The Woven Torah is divided according to its inner literary structure. Each book is divided into *Units*. There are eighty-six Units in the Torah, as opposed to one hundred eighty-seven chapters. The Units are marked by Roman Numerals. Each book of the Torah has its own inner structure which is determined by the way its Units group together in sets of Units. The sets appear on the <u>map of the books</u>, Figure 47, marked by upper case Latin characters.

Arrangement of the Units as Weaves

For convenience, the common chapter and verse numbers appear before each verse. Each Unit is arranged according to its inner structure as a table, or more properly, a weave. It is divided into major and minor divisions. The major divisions are the rows, or weft threads, which are marked by Arabic numerals. The weft threads are subdivided, where necessary, into segments. There are up to three segments in a weft thread, and they are marked by Hebrew letters, א(aleph) ב(bet) ג(gimmel). These segments can have up to two further subdivisions. The first level of subdivision within the segment is marked by upper case Latin characters. The second level is marked by lower case Roman numerals in parenthesis. The order of the linear text is across weft threads, 1א, 1ב, 1ג, 2א, 2ב, etc.

Color Coding

The color coding is used primarily to indicate linguistic hooks between parts of the Unit. However, they also point to more substantive connections and should be utilized to gain an appreciation of the Unit as a literary construct.

Horizontal Links

There are two types of horizontal links. The first type is:

Direct parallels between all segments of a horizontal thread are highlighted by this color. This often points to the common theme of the thread.

There is another set of highlights sometimes used within a three-part thread. To understand this highlight, it is necessary to keep in mind that the Torah was designed as a visual document, containing visual logic, rather than oral/aural logic. This distinction is expressed in the order of elements in a triad. In speech, the synthetic middle comes last: thesis, antithesis, and finally synthesis. It is necessary to present the poles first in order to grasp the middle as a synthesis. The is not the case in a visual presentation, like the Torah. The conceptual middle is in the middle. This rule applies to more than just the parts of a three-part thread. It also applies the threads themselves. A thread which is positioned between two other threads should be read as a conceptual middle between them. Here are the colors which point to the linguistic pattern that is sometimes employed in a three-part row to note the linguistic middle.

Key words in the first and second segments are marked by this color. Key words in the second and third segments are marked by this color. The result is that the middle segment will have words marked with both colors.

Vertical Links

Two types of vertical highlighting are employed, one for links between multiple segments of warp threads and one for links between parts of a single segment.

This highlight is used to indicate a repeating word or phrase within multiple segments of a warp thread (column).

This highlight is used to marked parallels between parts of a single segment.

Boundary Links

Boundary links refer to connections between the opening and closing weft threads There are two types of highlighting employed to mark linguistic indicators of the boundaries of a Unit, closure and chiasm.

Closure between the first weft thread and the last is marked by this color.

Two colors are employed to mark a chiasm.

This color indicates the half chiasm created by the connection between the upper left segment (first segment of first weft thread) and the lower right segment (last segment of last weft thread).

This color indicates the connection between the upper right (last segment of first weft thread) and lower left (first segment of last weft thread) half of the chiasm.

Genesis

Genesis Unit I (1:-2:3)

1א

1:1 In the beginning God created the heaven and the earth.

1ב

1:2 Now the earth was unformed and void, and darkness was upon the face of the deep; and the spirit of God hovered over the face of the waters.

2א

A 1:3 And God said: 'Let there be light.' And there was light. 1:4 And God saw the light, that it was good; and God divided the light from the darkness. 1:5 And God called the light Day, and the darkness He called Night. And there was evening and there was morning, one day. {P}

B 1:6 And God said: 'Let there be a firmament in the midst of the waters, and let it divide the waters from the waters.' 1:7 And God made the firmament, and divided the waters which were under the firmament from the waters which were above the firmament; and it was so. 1:8 And God called the firmament Heaven. And there was evening and there was morning, a second day. {P}

C i 1:9 And God said: 'Let the waters under the heaven be gathered together unto one place, and let the dry land appear.' And it was so. 1:10 And God called the dry land Earth, and the gathering together of the waters called He Seas; and God saw that it was good.

ii 1:11 And God said: 'Let the earth put forth grass, herb yielding seed, and fruit-tree bearing fruit after its kind, wherein is the seed thereof, upon the earth.' And it was so. 1:12 And the earth brought forth grass, herb yielding seed after its kind, and tree bearing fruit, wherein is the seed thereof, after its kind; and God saw that it was good. 1:13 And there was evening and there was morning, a third day. {P}

2ב

A 1:14 And God said: 'Let there be lights in the firmament of heaven to divide the day from the night; and let them be for signs, and for seasons, and for days and years; 1:15 and let them be for lights in the firmament of the heaven to give light upon the earth.' And it was so. 1:16 And God made the two great lights: the greater light to rule the day, and the lesser light to rule the night; and the stars. 1:17 And God set them in the firmament of the heaven to give light upon the earth, 1:18 and to rule over the day and over the night, and to divide the light from the darkness; and God saw that it was good. 1:19 And there was evening and there was morning, a fourth day. {P}

B 1:20 And God said: 'Let the waters swarm with swarms of living creatures, and let fowl fly above the earth in the open firmament of heaven.' 1:21 And God created the great sea-monsters, and every living creature that creepeth, wherewith the waters swarmed, after its kind, and every winged fowl after its kind; and God saw that it was good. 1:22 And God blessed them, saying: 'Be fruitful, and multiply, and fill the waters in the seas, and let fowl multiply in the earth.' 1:23 And there was evening and there was morning, a fifth day. {P}

C i 1:24 And God said: 'Let the earth bring forth the living creature after its kind, cattle, and creeping thing, and beast of the earth after its kind.' And it was so. 1:25 And God made the beast of the earth after its kind, and the cattle after their kind, and every thing that creepeth upon the ground after its kind; and God saw that it was good.

ii 1:26 And God said: 'Let us make man in our image, after our likeness; and let them have dominion over the fish of the sea, and over the fowl of the air, and over the cattle, and over all the earth, and over every creeping thing that creepeth upon the earth.' 1:27 And God created man in His own image, in the image of God created He him; male and female created He them. 1:28 And God blessed them; and God said unto them: 'Be fruitful, and multiply, and replenish the earth, and subdue it; and have dominion over the fish of the sea, and over the fowl of the air, and over every living thing that creepeth upon the earth.' 1:29 And God said: 'Behold, I have given you every herb yielding seed, which is upon the face of all the earth, and every tree, in which is the fruit of a tree yielding seed--to you it shall be for food; 1:30 and to every beast of the earth, and to every fowl of the air, and to every thing that creepeth upon the earth, wherein there is a living soul, [I have given] every green herb for food.' And it was so. 1:31 And God saw every thing that He had made, and, behold, it was very good. And there was evening and there was morning, the sixth day. {P}

3א

2:1 And the heaven and the earth were finished, and all the host of them.

3ב

2:2 And on the seventh day God finished His work which He had made; and He rested on the seventh day from all His work which He had made. 2:3 And God blessed the seventh day, and hallowed it; because that in it He rested from all His work which God in creating had made. {P}

Genesis Unit II (2:4-4:26)

א

A 2:4 These are the generations of the heaven and of the earth when they were created, in the day that the LORD God made earth and heaven. 2:5 No shrub of the field was yet in the earth, and no herb of the field had yet sprung up; for the LORD God had not caused it to rain upon the earth, and there was not a man to till the ground; 2:6 but there went up a mist from the earth, and watered the whole face of the ground. 2:7 Then the LORD God formed man of the dust of the ground, and breathed into his nostrils the breath of life; and man became a living soul.

B 2:8 And the LORD God planted a garden eastward, in Eden; and there He put the man whom He had formed. 2:9 And out of the ground made the LORD God to grow every tree that is pleasant to the sight, and good for food; the tree of life also in the midst of the garden, and the tree of the knowledge of good and evil. 2:10 And a river went out of Eden to water the garden; and from thence it was parted, and became four heads. 2:11 The name of the first is Pishon; that is it which compasseth the whole land of Havilah, where there is gold; 2:12 and the gold of that land is good; there is bdellium and the onyx stone. 2:13 And the name of the second river is Gihon; the same is it that compasseth the whole land of Cush. 2:14 And the name of the third river is Tigris; that is it which goeth toward the east of Asshur. And the fourth river is the Euphrates. 2:15 And the LORD God took the man, and put him into the garden of Eden to dress it and to keep it. 2:16 And the LORD God commanded the man, saying: 'Of every tree of the garden thou mayest freely eat; 2:17 but of the tree of the knowledge of good and evil, thou shalt not eat of it; for in the day that thou eatest thereof thou shalt surely die.'

ב

A 2:18 And the LORD God said: 'It is not good that the man should be alone; I will make him a help meet for him.' 2:19 And out of the ground the LORD God formed every beast of the field, and every fowl of the air; and brought them unto the man to see what he would call them; and whatsoever the man would call every living creature, that was to be the name thereof. 2:20 And the man gave names to all cattle, and to the fowl of the air, and to every beast of the field; but for Adam there was not found a help meet for him.

B 2:21 And the LORD God caused a deep sleep to fall upon the man, and he slept; and He took one of his ribs, and closed up the place with flesh instead thereof. 2:22 And the rib, which the LORD God had taken from the man, made He a woman, and brought her unto the man. 2:23 And the man said: 'This is now bone of my bones, and flesh of my flesh; she shall be called Woman, because she was taken out of Man.' 2:24 Therefore shall a man leave his father and his mother, and shall cleave unto his wife, and they shall be one flesh. 2:25 And they were both naked, the man and his wife, and were not ashamed.

2א

A 3:1 Now the serpent was more subtle than any beast of the field which the LORD God had made. And he said unto the woman: 'Yea, hath God said: Ye shall not eat of any tree of the garden?' 3:2 And the woman said unto the serpent: 'Of the fruit of the trees of the garden we may eat; 3:3 but of the fruit of the tree which is in the midst of the garden, God hath said: Ye shall not eat of it, neither shall ye touch it, lest ye die.' 3:4 And the serpent said unto the woman: 'Ye shall not surely die; 3:5 for God doth know that in the day ye eat thereof, then your eyes shall be opened, and ye shall be as God, knowing good and evil.' 3:6 And when the woman saw that the tree was good for food, and that it was a delight to the eyes, and that the tree was to be desired to make one wise, she took of the fruit thereof, and did eat; and she gave also unto her husband with her, and he did eat. 3:7 And the eyes of them both were opened, and they knew that they were naked; and they sewed fig-leaves together, and made themselves girdles.

B 3:8 And they heard the voice of the LORD God walking in the garden toward the cool of the day; and the man and his wife hid themselves from the presence of the LORD God amongst the trees of the garden. 3:9 And the LORD God called unto the man, and said unto him: 'Where art thou?' 3:10 And he said: 'I heard Thy voice in the garden, and I was afraid, because I was naked; and I hid myself.' 3:11 And He said: 'Who told thee that thou wast naked? Hast thou eaten of the tree, whereof I commanded thee that thou shouldest not eat?' 3:12 And the man said: 'The woman whom Thou gavest to be with me, she gave me of the tree, and I did eat.' 3:13 And the LORD God said unto the woman: 'What is this thou hast done?' And the woman said: 'The serpent beguiled me, and I did eat.' 3:14 And the LORD God said unto the serpent: 'Because thou hast done this, cursed art thou from among all cattle, and from among all beasts of the field; upon thy belly shalt thou go, and dust shalt thou eat all the days of thy life. 3:15 And I will put enmity between thee and the woman, and between thy seed and her seed; they shall bruise thy head, and thou shalt bruise their heel.' {S} 3:16 Unto the woman He said: 'I will greatly multiply thy pain and thy travail; in pain thou shalt bring forth children; and thy desire shall be to thy husband, and he shall rule over thee.' {S} 3:17 And unto Adam He said: 'Because thou hast hearkened unto the voice of thy wife, and hast eaten of the tree, of which I commanded thee, saying: Thou shalt not eat of it; cursed is the ground for thy sake; in toil shalt thou eat of it all the days of thy life. 3:18 Thorns also and thistles shall it bring forth to thee; and thou shalt eat the herb of the field. 3:19 In the sweat of thy face shalt thou eat bread, till thou return unto the ground; for out of it wast thou taken; for dust thou art, and unto dust shalt thou return.' 3:20 And the man called his wife's name Eve; because she was the mother of all living. 3:21 And the LORD God made for Adam and for his wife garments of skins, and clothed them. {P} 3:22 And the LORD God said: 'Behold, the man is become as one of us, to know good and evil; and now, lest he put forth his hand, and take also of the tree of life, and eat, and live for ever.' 3:23 Therefore the LORD God sent him forth from the garden of Eden, to till the ground from whence he was taken. 3:24 So He drove out the man; and He placed at the east of the garden of Eden the cherubim, and the flaming sword which turned every way, to keep the way to the tree of life. {S}

3א

4:17 And Cain knew his wife; and she conceived, and bore Enoch; and he builded a city, and called the name of the city after the name of his son Enoch. 4:18 And unto Enoch was born Irad; and Irad begot Mehujael; and Mehujael begot Methushael; and Methushael begot Lamech. 4:19 And Lamech took unto him two wives; the name of one was Adah, and the name of the other Zillah. 4:20 And Adah bore Jabal; he was the father of such as dwell in tents and have cattle. 4:21 And his brother's name was Jubal; he was the father of all such as handle the harp and pipe. 4:22 And Zillah, she also bore Tubal-cain, the forger of every cutting instrument of brass and iron; and the sister of Tubal-cain was Naamah. 4:23 And Lamech said unto his wives: Adah and Zillah, hear my voice; ye wives of Lamech, hearken unto my speech; for I have slain a man for wounding me, and a young man for bruising me; 4:24 If Cain shall be avenged sevenfold, truly Lamech seventy and sevenfold.

2ב

A 4:1 And the man knew Eve his wife; and she conceived and bore Cain, and said: 'I have gotten a man with the help of the LORD.' 4:2 And again she bore his brother Abel. And Abel was a keeper of sheep, but Cain was a tiller of the ground. 4:3 And in process of time it came to pass, that Cain brought of the fruit of the ground an offering unto the LORD. 4:4 And Abel, he also brought of the firstlings of his flock and of the fat thereof. And the LORD had respect unto Abel and to his offering; 4:5 but unto Cain and to his offering He had not respect. And Cain was very wroth, and his countenance fell. 4:6 And the LORD said unto Cain: 'Why art thou wroth? and why is thy countenance fallen? 4:7 If thou doest well, shall it not be lifted up? and if thou doest not well, sin coucheth at the door; and unto thee is its desire, but thou mayest rule over it.' 4:8 And Cain spoke unto Abel his brother. And it came to pass, when they were in the field, that Cain rose up against Abel his brother, and slew him.

B 4:9 And the LORD said unto Cain: 'Where is Abel thy brother?' And he said: 'I know not; am I my brother's keeper?' 4:10 And He said: 'What hast thou done? the voice of thy brother's blood crieth unto Me from the ground. 4:11 And now cursed art thou from the ground, which hath opened her mouth to receive thy brother's blood from thy hand. 4:12 When thou tillest the ground, it shall not henceforth yield unto thee her strength; a fugitive and a wanderer shalt thou be in the earth.' 4:13 And Cain said unto the LORD: 'My punishment is greater than I can bear. 4:14 Behold, Thou hast driven me out this day from the face of the land; and from Thy face shall I be hid; and I shall be a fugitive and a wanderer in the earth; and it will come to pass, that whosoever findeth me will slay me.' 4:15 And the LORD said unto him: 'Therefore whosoever slayeth Cain, vengeance shall be taken on him sevenfold.' And the LORD set a sign for Cain, lest any finding him should smite him. 4:16 And Cain went out from the presence of the LORD, and dwelt in the land of Nod, on the east of Eden.

3ב

4:25 And Adam knew his wife again; and she bore a son, and called his name Seth: 'for God hath appointed me another seed instead of Abel; for Cain slew him.' 4:26 And to Seth, to him also there was born a son; and he called his name Enosh; then began men to call upon the name of the LORD. {S}

Genesis Unit III (5:1-10:32)

א1

A 5:1 This is the book of the generations of Adam. In the day that God created man, in the likeness of God made He him; 5:2 male and female created He them, and blessed them, and called their name Adam, in the day when they were created. 5:3 And Adam lived a hundred and thirty years, and begot a son in his own likeness, after his image; and called his name Seth. 5:4 And the days of Adam after he begot Seth were eight hundred years; and he begot sons and daughters. 5:5 And all the days that Adam lived were nine hundred and thirty years; and he died. {S}

B 5:6 And Seth lived a hundred and five years, and begot Enosh. 5:7 And Seth lived after he begot Enosh eight hundred and seven years, and begot sons and daughters. 5:8 And all the days of Seth were nine hundred and twelve years; and he died. {S} 5:9 And Enosh lived ninety years, and begot Kenan. 5:10 And Enosh lived after he begot Kenan eight hundred and fifteen years, and begot sons and daughters. 5:11 And all the days of Enosh were nine hundred and five years; and he died. {S} 5:12 And Kenan lived seventy years, and begot Mahalalel. 5:13 And Kenan lived after he begot Mahalalel eight hundred and forty years, and begot sons and daughters. 5:14 And all the days of Kenan were nine hundred and ten years; and he died. {S} 5:15 And Mahalalel lived sixty and five years, and begot Jared. 5:16 And Mahalalel lived after he begot Jared eight hundred and thirty years, and begot sons and daughters. 5:17 And all the days of Mahalalel were eight hundred ninety and five years; and he died. {S} 5:18 And Jared lived a hundred sixty and two years, and begot Enoch. 5:19 And Jared lived after he begot Enoch eight hundred years, and begot sons and daughters. 5:20 And all the days of Jared were nine hundred sixty and two years; and he died. {S} 5:21 And Enoch lived sixty and five years, and begot Methuselah. 5:22 And Enoch walked with God after he begot Methuselah three hundred years, and begot sons and daughters. 5:23 And all the days of Enoch were three hundred sixty and five years. 5:24 And Enoch walked with God, and he was not; for God took him. {S} 5:25 And Methuselah lived a hundred eighty and seven years, and begot Lamech. 5:26 And Methuselah lived after he begot Lamech seven hundred eighty and two years, and begot sons and daughters. 5:27 And all the days of Methuselah were nine hundred sixty and nine years; and he died. {S} 5:28 And Lamech lived a hundred eighty and two years, and begot a son. 5:29 And he called his name Noah, saying: 'This same shall comfort us in our work and in the toil of our hands, which cometh from the ground which the LORD hath cursed.' 5:30 And Lamech lived after he begot Noah five hundred ninety and five years, and begot sons and daughters. 5:31 And all the days of Lamech were seven hundred seventy and seven years; and he died. {S}
C 5:32 And Noah was five hundred years old; and Noah begot Shem, Ham, and Japheth.

א2

6:11 And the earth was corrupt before God, and the earth was filled with violence. 6:12 And God saw the earth, and, behold, it was corrupt; for all flesh had corrupted their way upon the earth. {S} 6:13 And God said unto Noah: 'The end of all flesh is come before Me; for the earth is filled with violence through them; and, behold, I will destroy them with the earth. 6:14 Make thee an ark of gopher wood; with rooms shalt thou make the ark, and shalt pitch it within and without with pitch. 6:15 And this is how thou shalt make it: the length of the ark three hundred cubits, the breadth of it fifty cubits, and the height of it thirty cubits. 6:16 A light shalt thou make to the ark, and to a cubit shalt thou finish it upward; and the door of the ark shalt thou set in the side thereof; with lower, second, and third stories shalt thou make it. 6:17 And I, behold, I do bring the flood of waters upon the earth, to destroy all flesh, wherein is the breath of life, from under heaven; every thing that is in the earth shall perish. 6:18 But I will establish My covenant with thee; and thou shalt come into the ark, thou, and thy sons, and thy wife, and thy sons' wives with thee. 6:19 And of every living thing of all flesh, two of every sort shalt thou bring into the ark, to keep them alive with thee; they shall be male and female. 6:20 Of the fowl after their kind, and of the cattle after their kind, of every creeping thing of the ground after its kind, two of every sort shall come unto thee, to keep them alive. 6:21 And take thou unto thee of all food that is eaten, and gather it to thee; and it shall be for food for thee, and for them.' 6:22 Thus did Noah; according to all that God commanded him, so did he.

ב1

A 6:1 And it came to pass, when men began to multiply on the face of the earth, and daughters were born unto them, 6:2 that the sons of God saw the daughters of men that they were fair; and they took them wives, whomsoever they chose. 6:3 And the LORD said: 'My spirit shall not abide in man for ever, for that he also is flesh; therefore shall his days be a hundred and twenty years.' 6:4 The Nephilim were in the earth in those days, and also after that, when the sons of God came in unto the daughters of men, and they bore children to them; the same were the mighty men that were of old, the men of renown. {P}

B 6:5 And the LORD saw that the wickedness of man was great in the earth, and that every imagination of the thoughts of his heart was only evil continually. 6:6 And it repented the LORD that He had made man on the earth, and it grieved Him at His heart. 6:7 And the LORD said: 'I will blot out man whom I have created from the face of the earth; both man, and beast, and creeping thing, and fowl of the air; for it repenteth Me that I have made them.' 6:8 But Noah found grace in the eyes of the LORD. {P}

C 6:9 These are the generations of Noah. Noah was in his generations a man righteous and whole-hearted; Noah walked with God. 6:10 And Noah begot three sons, Shem, Ham, and Japheth.

ב2

7:1 And the LORD said unto Noah: 'Come thou and all thy house into the ark; for thee have I seen righteous before Me in this generation. 7:2 Of every clean beast thou shalt take to thee seven and seven, each with his mate; and of the beasts that are not clean two [and two], each with his mate; 7:3 of the fowl also of the air, seven and seven, male and female; to keep seed alive upon the face of all the earth. 7:4 For yet seven days, and I will cause it to rain upon the earth forty days and forty nights; and every living substance that I have made will I blot out from off the face of the earth.' 7:5 And Noah did according unto all that the LORD commanded him.

3א

A 7:6 And Noah was six hundred years old when the flood of waters was upon the earth.

B 7:7 And Noah went in, and his sons, and his wife, and his sons' wives with him, into the ark, because of the waters of the flood. 7:8 Of clean beasts, and of beasts that are not clean, and of fowls, and of every thing that creepeth upon the ground, 7:9 there went in two and two unto Noah into the ark, male and female, as God commanded Noah. 7:10 And it came to pass after the seven days, that the waters of the flood were upon the earth.

4א

A 7:17 And the flood was forty days upon the earth; and the waters increased, and bore up the ark, and it was lifted up above the earth. 7:18 And the waters prevailed, and increased greatly upon the earth; and the ark went upon the face of the waters. 7:19 And the waters prevailed exceedingly upon the earth; and all the high mountains that were under the whole heaven were covered. 7:20 Fifteen cubits upward did the waters prevail; and the mountains were covered. 7:21 And all flesh perished that moved upon the earth, both fowl, and cattle, and beast, and every swarming thing that swarmeth upon the earth, and every man; 7:22 all in whose nostrils was the breath of the spirit of life, whatsoever was in the dry land, died. 7:23 And He blotted out every living substance which was upon the face of the ground, both man, and cattle, and creeping thing, and fowl of the heaven; and they were blotted out from the earth; and Noah only was left, and they that were with him in the ark.
B 7:24 And the waters prevailed upon the earth a hundred and fifty days. 8:1 And God remembered Noah, and every living thing, and all the cattle that were with him in the ark; and God made a wind to pass over the earth, and the waters assuaged; 8:2 the fountains also of the deep and the windows of heaven were stopped, and the rain from heaven was restrained. 8:3 And the waters returned from off the earth continually; and after the end of a hundred and fifty days the waters decreased.
C 8:4 And the ark rested in the seventh month, on the seventeenth day of the month, upon the mountains of Ararat. 8:5 And the waters decreased continually until the tenth month; in the tenth month, on the first day of the month, were the tops of the mountains seen.

3ב

A 7:11 In the six hundredth year of Noah's life, in the second month, on the seventeenth day of the month, on the same day were all the fountains of the great deep broken up, and the windows of heaven were opened. 7:12 And the rain was upon the earth forty days and forty nights.
B 7:13 In the selfsame day entered Noah, and Shem, and Ham, and Japheth, the sons of Noah, and Noah's wife, and the three wives of his sons with them, into the ark; 7:14 they, and every beast after its kind, and all the cattle after their kind, and every creeping thing that creepeth upon the earth after its kind, and every fowl after its kind, every bird of every sort. 7:15 And they went in unto Noah into the ark, two and two of all flesh wherein is the breath of life. 7:16 And they that went in, went in male and female of all flesh, as God commanded him; and the LORD shut him in.

4ב

A 8:6 And it came to pass at the end of forty days, that Noah opened the window of the ark which he had made. 8:7 And he sent forth a raven, and it went forth to and fro, until the waters were dried up from off the earth. 8:8 And he sent forth a dove from him, to see if the waters were abated from off the face of the ground. 8:9 But the dove found no rest for the sole of her foot, and she returned unto him to the ark, for the waters were on the face of the whole earth; and he put forth his hand, and took her, and brought her in unto him into the ark.

B 8:10 And he stayed yet other seven days; and again he sent forth the dove out of the ark. 8:11 And the dove came in to him at eventide; and lo in her mouth an olive-leaf freshly plucked; so Noah knew that the waters were abated from off the earth.

C 8:12 And he stayed yet other seven days; and sent forth the dove; and she returned not again unto him any more. 8:13 And it came to pass in the six hundred and first year, in the first month, the first day of the month, the waters were dried up from off the earth; and Noah removed the covering of the ark, and looked, and behold, the face of the ground was dried. 8:14 And in the second month, on the seven and twentieth day of the month, was the earth dry. {S}

5א

A 8:15 And God spoke unto Noah, saying: 8:16 'Go forth from the ark, thou, and thy wife, and thy sons, and thy sons' wives with thee. 8:17 Bring forth with thee every living thing that is with thee of all flesh, both fowl, and cattle, and every creeping thing that creepeth upon the earth; that they may swarm in the earth, and be fruitful, and multiply upon the earth.' 8:18 And Noah went forth, and his sons, and his wife, and his sons' wives with him; 8:19 every beast, every creeping thing, and every fowl, whatsoever moveth upon the earth, after their families; went forth out of the ark.

B 8:20 And Noah builded an altar unto the LORD; and took of every clean beast, and of every clean fowl, and offered burnt-offerings on the altar. 8:21 And the LORD smelled the sweet savour; and the LORD said in His heart: 'I will not again curse the ground any more for man's sake; for the imagination of man's heart is evil from his youth; neither will I again smite any more every thing living, as I have done. 8:22 While the earth remaineth, seedtime and harvest, and cold and heat, and summer and winter, and day and night shall not cease.'

6א

9:18 And the sons of Noah, that went forth from the ark, were Shem, and Ham, and Japheth; and Ham is the father of Canaan. 9:19 These three were the sons of Noah, and of these was the whole earth overspread. 9:20 And Noah the husbandman began, and planted a vineyard. 9:21 And he drank of the wine, and was drunken; and he was uncovered within his tent. 9:22 And Ham, the father of Canaan, saw the nakedness of his father, and told his two brethren without. 9:23 And Shem and Japheth took a garment, and laid it upon both their shoulders, and went backward, and covered the nakedness of their father; and their faces were backward, and they saw not their father's nakedness. 9:24 And Noah awoke from his wine, and knew what his youngest son had done unto him. 9:25 And he said: Cursed be Canaan; a servant of servants shall he be unto his brethren. 9:26 And he said: Blessed be the LORD, the God of Shem; and let Canaan be their servant. 9:27 God enlarge Japheth, and he shall dwell in the tents of Shem; and let Canaan be their servant. 9:28 And Noah lived after the flood three hundred and fifty years. 9:29 And all the days of Noah were nine hundred and fifty years; and he died. {P}

5ב

A 9:1 And God blessed Noah and his sons, and said unto them: 'Be fruitful and multiply, and replenish the earth. 9:2 And the fear of you and the dread of you shall be upon every beast of the earth, and upon every fowl of the air, and upon all wherewith the ground teemeth, and upon all the fishes of the sea: into your hand are they delivered. 9:3 Every moving thing that liveth shall be for food for you; as the green herb have I given you all. 9:4 Only flesh with the life thereof, which is the blood thereof, shall ye not eat. 9:5 And surely your blood of your lives will I require; at the hand of every beast will I require it; and at the hand of man, even at the hand of every man's brother, will I require the life of man. 9:6 Whoso sheddeth man's blood, by man shall his blood be shed; for in the image of God made He man. 9:7 And you, be ye fruitful, and multiply; swarm in the earth, and multiply therein.' {S}

B 9:8 And God spoke unto Noah, and to his sons with him, saying: 9:9 'As for Me, behold, I establish My covenant with you, and with your seed after you; 9:10 and with every living creature that is with you, the fowl, the cattle, and every beast of the earth with you; of all that go out of the ark, even every beast of the earth. 9:11 And I will establish My covenant with you; neither shall all flesh be cut off any more by the waters of the flood; neither shall there any more be a flood to destroy the earth.' 9:12 And God said: 'This is the token of the covenant which I make between Me and you and every living creature that is with you, for perpetual generations: 9:13 I have set My bow in the cloud, and it shall be for a token of a covenant between Me and the earth. 9:14 And it shall come to pass, when I bring clouds over the earth, and the bow is seen in the cloud, 9:15 that I will remember My covenant, which is between Me and you and every living creature of all flesh; and the waters shall no more become a flood to destroy all flesh. 9:16 And the bow shall be in the cloud; and I will look upon it, that I may remember the everlasting covenant between God and every living creature of all flesh that is upon the earth.' 9:17 And God said unto Noah: 'This is the token of the covenant which I have established between Me and all flesh that is upon the earth.' {P}

6ב

10:1 Now these are the generations of the sons of Noah: Shem, Ham, and Japheth; and unto them were sons born after the flood. 10:2 The sons of Japheth: Gomer, and Magog, and Madai, and Javan, and Tubal, and Meshech, and Tiras. 10:3 And the sons of Gomer: Ashkenaz, and Riphath, and Togarmah. 10:4 And the sons of Javan: Elishah, and Tarshish, Kittim, and Dodanim. 10:5 Of these were the isles of the nations divided in their lands, every one after his tongue, after their families, in their nations. 10:6 And the sons of Ham: Cush, and Mizraim, and Put, and Canaan. 10:7 And the sons of Cush: Seba, and Havilah, and Sabtah, and Raamah, and Sabteca; and the sons of Raamah: Sheba, and Dedan. 10:8 And Cush begot Nimrod; he began to be a mighty one in the earth. 10:9 He was a mighty hunter before the LORD; wherefore it is said: 'Like Nimrod a mighty hunter before the LORD.' 10:10 And the beginning of his kingdom was Babel, and Erech, and Accad, and Calneh, in the land of Shinar. 10:11 Out of that land went forth Asshur, and builded Nineveh, and Rehoboth-ir, and Calah, 10:12 and Resen between Nineveh and Calah--the same is the great city. 10:13 And Mizraim begot Ludim, and Anamim, and Lehabim, and Naphtuhim, 10:14 and Pathrusim, and Casluhim--whence went forth the Philistines--and Caphtorim. {S} 10:15 And Canaan begot Zidon his firstborn, and Heth; 10:16 and the Jebusite, and the Amorite, and the Girgashite; 10:17 and the Hivite, and the Arkite, and the Sinite; 10:18 and the Arvadite, and the Zemarite, and the Hamathite; and afterward were the families of the Canaanite spread abroad. 10:19 And the border of the Canaanite was from Zidon, as thou goest toward Gerar, unto Gaza; as thou goest toward Sodom and Gomorrah and Admah and Zeboiim, unto Lasha. 10:20 These are the sons of Ham, after their families, after their tongues, in their lands, in their nations. {S} 10:21 And unto Shem, the father of all the children of Eber, the elder brother of Japheth, to him also were children born. 10:22 The sons of Shem: Elam, and Asshur, and Arpachshad, and Lud, and Aram. 10:23 And the sons of Aram: Uz, and Hul, and Gether, and Mash. 10:24 And Arpachshad begot Shelah; and Shelah begot Eber. 10:25 And unto Eber were born two sons; the name of the one was Peleg; for in his days was the earth divided; and his brother's name was Joktan. 10:26 And Joktan begot Almodad, and Sheleph, and Hazarmaveth, and Jerah; 10:27 and Hadoram, and Uzal, and Diklah; 10:28 and Obal, and Abimael, and Sheba; 10:29 and Ophir, and Havilah, and Jobab; all these were the sons of Joktan. 10:30 And their dwelling was from Mesha, as thou goest toward Sephar, unto the mountain of the east. 10:31 These are the sons of Shem, after their families, after their tongues, in their lands, after their nations. 10:32 These are the families of the sons of Noah, after their generations, in their nations; and of these were the nations divided in the earth after the flood. {P}

Genesis Unit IV (11:1-11:9)

1א

11:1 And the whole earth was of one language and of one speech. **11:2** And it came to pass, as they journeyed east, that they found a plain in the land of Shinar; and they dwelt there.

2א

11:5 And the LORD came down to see the city and the tower, which the children of men builded. **11:6** And the LORD said: 'Behold, they are one people, and they have all one language; and this is what they begin to do; and now nothing will be withholden from them, which they purpose to do.

1ב

11:3 And they said one to another: 'Come, let us make brick, and burn them thoroughly.' And they had brick for stone, and slime had they for mortar.

2ב

11:7 Come, let us go down, and there confound their language, that they may not understand one another's speech.'

1ג

11:4 And they said: 'Come, let us build us a city, and a tower, with its top in heaven, and let us make us a name; lest we be scattered abroad upon the face of the whole earth.'

2ג

11:8 So the LORD scattered them abroad from thence upon the face of all the earth; and they left off to build the city. **11:9** Therefore was the name of it called Babel; because the LORD did there confound the language of all the earth; and from thence did the LORD scatter them abroad upon the face of all the earth. {P}

Genesis Unit V (11:10-13:4)

א1

11:10 These are the generations of Shem. Shem was a hundred years old, and begot Arpachshad two years after the flood. 11:11 And Shem lived after he begot Arpachshad five hundred years, and begot sons and daughters. {S} 11:12 And Arpachshad lived five and thirty years, and begot Shelah. 11:13 And Arpachshad lived after he begot Shelah four hundred and three years, and begot sons and daughters. {S} 11:14 And Shelah lived thirty years, and begot Eber. 11:15 And Shelah lived after he begot Eber four hundred and three years, and begot sons and daughters. {S} 11:16 And Eber lived four and thirty years, and begot Peleg. 11:17 And Eber lived after he begot Peleg four hundred and thirty years, and begot sons and daughters. {S} 11:18 And Peleg lived thirty years, and begot Reu. 11:19 And Peleg lived after he begot Reu two hundred and nine years, and begot sons and daughters. {S} 11:20 And Reu lived two and thirty years, and begot Serug. 11:21 And Reu lived after he begot Serug two hundred and seven years, and begot sons and daughters. {S} 11:22 And Serug lived thirty years, and begot Nahor. 11:23 And Serug lived after he begot Nahor two hundred years, and begot sons and daughters. {S} 11:24 And Nahor lived nine and twenty years, and begot Terah. 11:25 And Nahor lived after he begot Terah a hundred and nineteen years, and begot sons and daughters. {S} 11:26 And Terah lived seventy years, and begot Abram, Nahor, and Haran.

א2

A 12:1 Now the LORD said unto Abram: 'Get thee out of thy country, and from thy kindred, and from thy father's house, unto the land that I will show thee. 12:2 And I will make of thee a great nation, and I will bless thee, and make thy name great; and be thou a blessing. 12:3 And I will bless them that bless thee, and him that curseth thee will I curse; and in thee shall all the families of the earth be blessed.' 12:4 So Abram went, as the LORD had spoken unto him; and Lot went with him; and Abram was seventy and five years old when he departed out of Haran. 12:5 And Abram took Sarai his wife, and Lot his brother's son, and all their substance that they had gathered, and the souls that they had gotten in Haran; and they went forth to go into the land of Canaan; and into the land of Canaan they came. 12:6 And Abram passed through the land unto the place of Shechem, unto the terebinth of Moreh. And the Canaanite was then in the land. 12:7 And the LORD appeared unto Abram, and said: 'Unto thy seed will I give this land'; and he builded there an altar unto the LORD, who appeared unto him.

B 12:8 And he removed from thence unto the mountain on the east of Beth-el, and pitched his tent, having Beth-el on the west, and Ai on the east; and he builded there an altar unto the LORD, and called upon the name of the LORD. 12:9 And Abram journeyed, going on still toward the South. {P}

ב1

11:27 Now these are the generations of Terah. Terah begot Abram, Nahor, and Haran; and Haran begot Lot. 11:28 And Haran died in the presence of his father Terah in the land of his nativity, in Ur of the Chaldees. 11:29 And Abram and Nahor took them wives: the name of Abram's wife was Sarai; and the name of Nahor's wife, Milcah, the daughter of Haran, the father of Milcah, and the father of Iscah. 11:30 And Sarai was barren; she had no child. 11:31 And Terah took Abram his son, and Lot the son of Haran, his son's son, and Sarai his daughter-in-law, his son Abram's wife; and they went forth with them from Ur of the Chaldees, to go into the land of Canaan; and they came unto Haran, and dwelt there. 11:32 And the days of Terah were two hundred and five years; and Terah died in Haran. {P}

ב2

A 12:10 And there was a famine in the land; and Abram went down into Egypt to sojourn there; for the famine was sore in the land. 12:11 And it came to pass, when he was come near to enter into Egypt, that he said unto Sarai his wife: 'Behold now, I know that thou art a fair woman to look upon. 12:12 And it will come to pass, when the Egyptians shall see thee, that they will say: This is his wife; and they will kill me, but thee they will keep alive. 12:13 Say, I pray thee, thou art my sister; that it may be well with me for thy sake, and that my soul may live because of thee.' 12:14 And it came to pass, that, when Abram was come into Egypt, the Egyptians beheld the woman that she was very fair. 12:15 And the princes of Pharaoh saw her, and praised her to Pharaoh; and the woman was taken into Pharaoh's house. 12:16 And he dealt well with Abram for her sake; and he had sheep, and oxen, and he-asses, and men-servants, and maid-servants, and she-asses, and camels. 12:17 And the LORD plagued Pharaoh and his house with great plagues because of Sarai Abram's wife. 12:18 And Pharaoh called Abram, and said: 'What is this that thou hast done unto me? why didst thou not tell me that she was thy wife? 12:19 Why saidst thou: She is my sister? so that I took her to be my wife; now therefore behold thy wife, take her, and go thy way.' 12:20 And Pharaoh gave men charge concerning him; and they brought him on the way, and his wife, and all that he had. 13:1 And Abram went up out of Egypt, he, and his wife, and all that he had, and Lot with him, into the South. 13:2 And Abram was very rich in cattle, in silver, and in gold.

B 13:3 And he went on his journeys from the South even to Beth-el, unto the place where his tent had been at the beginning, between Beth-el and Ai; 13:4 unto the place of the altar, which he had made there at the first; and Abram called there on the name of the LORD.

Genesis Unit VI (13:5-14:24)

1א

A 13:5 And Lot also, who went with Abram, had flocks, and herds, and tents. 13:6 And the land was not able to bear them, that they might dwell together; for their substance was great, so that they could not dwell together. 13:7 And there was a strife between the herdmen of Abram's cattle and the herdmen of Lot's cattle. And the Canaanite and the Perizzite dwelt then in the land. 13:8 And Abram said unto Lot: 'Let there be no strife, I pray thee, between me and thee, and between my herdmen and thy herdmen; for we are brethren. 13:9 Is not the whole land before thee? separate thyself, I pray thee, from me; if thou wilt take the left hand, then I will go to the right; or if thou take the right hand, then I will go to the left.' 13:10 And Lot lifted up his eyes, and beheld all the plain of the Jordan, that it was well watered every where, before the LORD destroyed Sodom and Gomorrah, like the garden of the LORD, like the land of Egypt, as thou goest unto Zoar. 13:11 So Lot chose him all the plain of the Jordan; and Lot journeyed east; and they separated themselves the one from the other.

B 13:12 Abram dwelt in the land of Canaan, and Lot dwelt in the cities of the Plain, and moved his tent as far as Sodom. 13:13 Now the men of Sodom were wicked and sinners against the LORD exceedingly.

2א

A 14:1 And it came to pass in the days of Amraphel king of Shinar, Arioch king of Ellasar, Chedorlaomer king of Elam, and Tidal king of Goiim, 14:2 that they made war with Bera king of Sodom, and with Birsha king of Gomorrah, Shinab king of Admah, and Shemeber king of Zeboiim, and the king of Bela--the same is Zoar. 14:3 All these came as allies unto the vale of Siddim--the same is the Salt Sea. 14:4 Twelve years they served Chedorlaomer, and in the thirteenth year they rebelled. 14:5 And in the fourteenth year came Chedorlaomer and the kings that were with him, and smote the Rephaim in Ashteroth-karnaim, and the Zuzim in Ham, and the Emim in Shaveh-kiriathaim, 14:6 and the Horites in their mount Seir, unto El-paran, which is by the wilderness. 14:7 And they turned back, and came to En-mishpat--the same is Kadesh--and smote all the country of the Amalekites, and also the Amorites, that dwelt in Hazazon-tamar. 14:8 And there went out the king of Sodom, and the king of Gomorrah, and the king of Admah, and the king of Zeboiim, and the king of Bela--the same is Zoar; and they set the battle in array against them in the vale of Siddim; 14:9 against Chedorlaomer king of Elam, and Tidal king of Goiim, and Amraphel king of Shinar, and Arioch king of Ellasar; four kings against the five. 14:10 Now the vale of Siddim was full of slime pits; and the kings of Sodom and Gomorrah fled, and they fell there, and they that remained fled to the mountain.

B 14:11 And they took all the goods of Sodom and Gomorrah, and all their victuals, and went their way. 14:12 And they took Lot, Abram's brother's son, who dwelt in Sodom, and his goods, and departed.

1ב

A 13:14 And the LORD said unto Abram, after that Lot was separated from him: 'Lift up now thine eyes, and look from the place where thou art, northward and southward and eastward and westward; 13:15 for all the land which thou seest, to thee will I give it, and to thy seed for ever. 13:16 And I will make thy seed as the dust of the earth; so that if a man can number the dust of the earth, then shall thy seed also be numbered. 13:17 Arise, walk through the land in the length of it and in the breadth of it; for unto thee will I give it.'

B 13:18 And Abram moved his tent, and came and dwelt by the terebinths of Mamre, which are in Hebron, and built there an altar unto the LORD. {P}

2ב

A 14:13 And there came one that had escaped, and told Abram the Hebrew--now he dwelt by the terebinths of Mamre the Amorite, brother of Eshcol, and brother of Aner; and these were confederate with Abram. 14:14 And when Abram heard that his brother was taken captive, he led forth his trained men, born in his house, three hundred and eighteen, and pursued as far as Dan. 14:15 And he divided himself against them by night, he and his servants, and smote them, and pursued them unto Hobah, which is on the left hand of Damascus. 14:16 And he brought back all the goods, and also brought back his brother Lot, and his goods, and the women also, and the people. 14:17 And the king of Sodom went out to meet him, after his return from the slaughter of Chedorlaomer and the kings that were with him, at the vale of Shaveh--the same is the King's Vale. 14:18 And Melchizedek king of Salem brought forth bread and wine; and he was priest of God the Most High. 14:19 And he blessed him, and said: 'Blessed be Abram of God Most High, Maker of heaven and earth; 14:20 and blessed be God the Most High, who hath delivered thine enemies into thy hand.' And he gave him a tenth of all.

B 14:21 And the king of Sodom said unto Abram: 'Give me the persons, and take the goods to thyself.' 14:22 And Abram said to the king of Sodom: 'I have lifted up my hand unto the LORD, God Most High, Maker of heaven and earth, 14:23 that I will not take a thread nor a shoe-latchet nor aught that is thine, lest thou shouldest say: I have made Abram rich; 14:24 save only that which the young men have eaten, and the portion of the men which went with me, Aner, Eshcol, and Mamre, let them take their portion.' {S}

Genesis Unit VII (15:1-17:27)

א1

15:1 After these things the word of the LORD came unto Abram in a vision, saying: 'Fear not, Abram, I am thy shield, thy reward shall be exceeding great.' 15:2 And Abram said: 'O Lord GOD, what wilt Thou give me, seeing I go hence childless, and he that shall be possessor of my house is Eliezer of Damascus?' 15:3 And Abram said: 'Behold, to me Thou hast given no seed, and, lo, one born in my house is to be mine heir.' 15:4 And, behold, the word of the LORD came unto him, saying: 'This man shall not be thine heir; but he that shall come forth out of thine own bowels shall be thine heir.' 15:5 And He brought him forth abroad, and said: 'Look now toward heaven, and count the stars, if thou be able to count them'; and He said unto him: 'So shall thy seed be.' 15:6 And he believed in the LORD; and He counted it to him for righteousness. 15:7 And He said unto him: 'I am the LORD that brought thee out of Ur of the Chaldees, to give thee this land to inherit it.' 15:8 And he said: 'O Lord GOD, whereby shall I know that I shall inherit it?' 15:9 And He said unto him: 'Take Me a heifer of three years old, and a she-goat of three years old, and a ram of three years old, and a turtle-dove, and a young pigeon.' 15:10 And he took him all these, and divided them in the midst, and laid each half over against the other; but the birds divided he not. 15:11 And the birds of prey came down upon the carcasses, and Abram drove them away. 15:12 And it came to pass, that, when the sun was going down, a deep sleep fell upon Abram; and, lo, a dread, even a great darkness, fell upon him. 15:13 And He said unto Abram: 'Know of a surety that thy seed shall be a stranger in a land that is not theirs, and shall serve them; and they shall afflict them four hundred years; 15:14 and also that nation, whom they shall serve, will I judge; and afterward shall they come out with great substance. 15:15 But thou shalt go to thy fathers in peace; thou shalt be buried in a good old age. 15:16 And in the fourth generation they shall come back hither; for the iniquity of the Amorite is not yet full.' 15:17 And it came to pass, that, when the sun went down, and there was thick darkness, behold a smoking furnace, and a flaming torch that passed between these pieces. 15:18 In that day the LORD made a covenant with Abram, saying: 'Unto thy seed have I given this land, from the river of Egypt unto the great river, the river Euphrates; 15:19 the Kenite, and the Kenizzite, and the Kadmonite, 15:20 and the Hittite, and the Perizzite, and the Rephaim, 15:21 and the Amorite, and the Canaanite, and the Girgashite, and the Jebusite.' {S}

א2

A 17:1 And when Abram was ninety years old and nine, the LORD appeared to Abram, and said unto him: 'I am God Almighty; walk before Me, and be thou wholehearted. 17:2 And I will make My covenant between Me and thee, and will multiply thee exceedingly.' 17:3 And Abram fell on his face; and God talked with him, saying: 17:4 'As for Me, behold, My covenant is with thee, and thou shalt be the father of a multitude of nations. 17:5 Neither shall thy name any more be called Abram, but thy name shall be Abraham; for the father of a multitude of nations have I made thee. 17:6 And I will make thee exceeding fruitful, and I will make nations of thee, and kings shall come out of thee. 17:7 And I will establish My covenant between Me and thee and thy seed after thee throughout their generations for an everlasting covenant, to be a God unto thee and to thy seed after thee. 17:8 And I will give unto thee, and to thy seed after thee, the land of thy sojournings, all the land of Canaan, for an everlasting possession; and I will be their God.'

B 17:9 And God said unto Abraham: 'And as for thee, thou shalt keep My covenant, thou, and thy seed after thee throughout their generations. 17:10 This is My covenant, which ye shall keep, between Me and you and thy seed after thee: every male among you shall be circumcised. 17:11 And ye shall be circumcised in the flesh of your foreskin; and it shall be a token of a covenant betwixt Me and you. 17:12 And he that is eight days old shall be circumcised among you, every male throughout your generations, he that is born in the house, or bought with money of any foreigner, that is not of thy seed. 17:13 He that is born in thy house, and he that is bought with thy money, must needs be circumcised; and My covenant shall be in your flesh for an everlasting covenant. 17:14 And the uncircumcised male who is not circumcised in the flesh of his foreskin, that soul shall be cut off from his people; he hath broken My covenant.' {S}

ב1

16:1 Now Sarai Abram's wife bore him no children; and she had a handmaid, an Egyptian, whose name was Hagar. 16:2 And Sarai said unto Abram: 'Behold now, the LORD hath restrained me from bearing; go in, I pray thee, unto my handmaid; it may be that I shall be builded up through her.' And Abram hearkened to the voice of Sarai. 16:3 And Sarai Abram's wife took Hagar the Egyptian, her handmaid, after Abram had dwelt ten years in the land of Canaan, and gave her to Abram her husband to be his wife. 16:4 And he went in unto Hagar, and she conceived; and when she saw that she had conceived, her mistress was despised in her eyes. 16:5 And Sarai said unto Abram: 'My wrong be upon thee: I gave my handmaid into thy bosom; and when she saw that she had conceived, I was despised in her eyes: the LORD judge between me and thee.' 16:6 But Abram said unto Sarai: 'Behold, thy maid is in thy hand; do to her that which is good in thine eyes.' And Sarai dealt harshly with her, and she fled from her face. 16:7 And the angel of the LORD found her by a fountain of water in the wilderness, by the fountain in the way to Shur. 16:8 And he said: 'Hagar, Sarai's handmaid, whence camest thou? and whither goest thou?' And she said: 'I flee from the face of my mistress Sarai.' 16:9 And the angel of the LORD said unto her: 'Return to thy mistress, and submit thyself under her hands.' 16:10 And the angel of the LORD said unto her: 'I will greatly multiply thy seed, that it shall not be numbered for multitude.' 16:11 And the angel of the LORD said unto her: 'Behold, thou art with child, and shalt bear a son; and thou shalt call his name Ishmael, because the LORD hath heard thy affliction. 16:12 And he shall be a wild ass of a man: his hand shall be against every man, and every man's hand against him; and he shall dwell in the face of all his brethren.' 16:13 And she called the name of the LORD that spoke unto her, Thou art a God of seeing; for she said: 'Have I even here seen Him that seeth Me?' 16:14 Wherefore the well was called 'Beer-lahai-roi; behold, it is between Kadesh and Bered. 16:15 And Hagar bore Abram a son; and Abram called the name of his son, whom Hagar bore, Ishmael. 16:16 And Abram was fourscore and six years old, when Hagar bore Ishmael to Abram. {S}

ב2

A 17:15 And God said unto Abraham: 'As for Sarai thy wife, thou shalt not call her name Sarai, but Sarah shall her name be. 17:16 And I will bless her, and moreover I will give thee a son of her; yea, I will bless her, and she shall be a mother of nations; kings of peoples shall be of her.' 17:17 Then Abraham fell upon his face, and laughed, and said in his heart: 'Shall a child be born unto him that is a hundred years old? and shall Sarah, that is ninety years old, bear?' 17:18 And Abraham said unto God: 'Oh that Ishmael might live before Thee!' 17:19 And God said: 'Nay, but Sarah thy wife shall bear thee a son; and thou shalt call his name Isaac; and I will establish My covenant with him for an everlasting covenant for his seed after him. 17:20 And as for Ishmael, I have heard thee; behold, I have blessed him, and will make him fruitful, and will multiply him exceedingly; twelve princes shall he beget, and I will make him a great nation. 17:21 But My covenant will I establish with Isaac, whom Sarah shall bear unto thee at this set time in the next year.' 17:22 And He left off talking with him, and God went up from Abraham.

B 17:23 And Abraham took Ishmael his son, and all that were born in his house, and all that were bought with his money, every male among the men of Abraham's house, and circumcised the flesh of their foreskin in the selfsame day, as God had said unto him. 17:24 And Abraham was ninety years old and nine, when he was circumcised in the flesh of his foreskin. 17:25 And Ishmael his son was thirteen years old, when he was circumcised in the flesh of his foreskin. 17:26 In the selfsame day was Abraham circumcised, and Ishmael his son. 17:27 And all the men of his house, those born in the house, and those bought with money of a foreigner, were circumcised with him. {P}

Genesis Unit VIII (18:1-19:38)

א

A 18:1 And the LORD appeared unto him by the terebinths of Mamre, as he sat in the tent door in the heat of the day; 18:2 and he lifted up his eyes and looked, and, lo, three men stood over against him; and when he saw them, he ran to meet them from the tent door, and bowed down to the earth, 18:3 and said: 'My lord, if now I have found favour in thy sight, pass not away, I pray thee, from thy servant. 18:4 Let now a little water be fetched, and wash your feet, and recline yourselves under the tree. 18:5 And I will fetch a morsel of bread, and stay ye your heart; after that ye shall pass on; forasmuch as ye are come to your servant.' And they said: 'So do, as thou hast said.' 18:6 And Abraham hastened into the tent unto Sarah, and said: 'Make ready quickly three measures of fine meal, knead it, and make cakes.' 18:7 And Abraham ran unto the herd, and fetched a calf tender and good, and gave it unto the servant; and he hastened to dress it. 18:8 And he took curd, and milk, and the calf which he had dressed, and set it before them; and he stood by them under the tree, and they did eat.

B 18:9 And they said unto him: 'Where is Sarah thy wife?' And he said: 'Behold, in the tent.' 18:10 And He said: 'I will certainly return unto thee when the season cometh round; and, lo, Sarah thy wife shall have a son.' And Sarah heard in the tent door, which was behind him.-- 18:11 Now Abraham and Sarah were old, and well stricken in age; it had ceased to be with Sarah after the manner of women.-- 18:12 And Sarah laughed within herself, saying: 'After I am waxed old shall I have pleasure, my lord being old also?' 18:13 And the LORD said unto Abraham: 'Wherefore did Sarah laugh, saying: Shall I of a surety bear a child, who am old? 18:14 Is any thing too hard for the LORD. At the set time I will return unto thee, when the season cometh round, and Sarah shall have a son.' 18:15 Then Sarah denied, saying: 'I laughed not'; for she was afraid. And He said: 'Nay; but thou didst laugh.'

ב

A 18:16 And the men rose up from thence, and looked out toward Sodom; and Abraham went with them to bring them on the way. 18:17 And the LORD said: 'Shall I hide from Abraham that which I am doing; 18:18 seeing that Abraham shall surely become a great and mighty nation, and all the nations of the earth shall be blessed in him? 18:19 For I have known him, to the end that he may command his children and his household after him, that they may keep the way of the LORD, to do righteousness and justice; to the end that the LORD may bring upon Abraham that which He hath spoken of him.'

B 18:20 And the LORD said: 'Verily, the cry of Sodom and Gomorrah is great, and, verily, their sin is exceeding grievous. 18:21 I will go down now, and see whether they have done altogether according to the cry of it, which is come unto Me; and if not, I will know.' 18:22 And the men turned from thence, and went toward Sodom; but Abraham stood yet before the LORD. 18:23 And Abraham drew near, and said: 'Wilt Thou indeed sweep away the righteous with the wicked? 18:24 Peradventure there are fifty righteous within the city; wilt Thou indeed sweep away and not forgive the place for the fifty righteous that are therein? 18:25 That be far from Thee to do after this manner, to slay the righteous with the wicked, that so the righteous should be as the wicked; that be far from Thee; shall not the Judge of all the earth do justly?' 18:26 And the LORD said: 'If I find in Sodom fifty righteous within the city, then I will forgive all the place for their sake.' 18:27 And Abraham answered and said: 'Behold now, I have taken upon me to speak unto the LORD, who am but dust and ashes. 18:28 Peradventure there shall lack five of the fifty righteous; wilt Thou destroy all the city for lack of five?' And He said: 'I will not destroy it, if I find there forty and five.' 18:29 And he spoke unto Him yet again, and said: 'Peradventure there shall be forty found there.' And He said: 'I will not do it for the forty's sake.' 18:30 And he said: 'Oh, let not the LORD be angry, and I will speak. Peradventure there shall thirty be found there.' And He said: 'I will not do it, if I find thirty there.' 18:31 And he said: 'Behold now, I have taken upon me to speak unto the LORD. Peradventure there shall be twenty found there.' And He said: 'I will not destroy it for the twenty's sake.' 18:32 And he said: 'Oh, let not the LORD be angry, and I will speak yet but this once. Peradventure ten shall be found there.' And He said: 'I will not destroy it for the ten's sake.' 18:33 And the LORD went His way, as soon as He had left off speaking to Abraham; and Abraham returned unto his place.

א2

A 19:1 And the two angels came to Sodom at even; and Lot sat in the gate of Sodom; and Lot saw them, and rose up to meet them; and he fell down on his face to the earth; 19:2 and he said: 'Behold now, my lords, turn aside, I pray you, into your servant's house, and tarry all night, and wash your feet, and ye shall rise up early, and go on your way.' And they said: 'Nay; but we will abide in the broad place all night.' 19:3 And he urged them greatly; and they turned in unto him, and entered into his house; and he made them a feast, and did bake unleavened bread, and they did eat.

B 19:4 But before they lay down, the men of the city, even the men of Sodom, compassed the house round, both young and old, all the people from every quarter. 19:5 And they called unto Lot, and said unto him: 'Where are the men that came in to thee this night? bring them out unto us, that we may know them.' 19:6 And Lot went out unto them to the door, and shut the door after him. 19:7 And he said: 'I pray you, my brethren, do not so wickedly. 19:8 Behold now, I have two daughters that have not known man; let me, I pray you, bring them out unto you, and do ye to them as is good in your eyes; only unto these men do nothing; forasmuch as they are come under the shadow of my roof.' 19:9 And they said: 'Stand back.' And they said: 'This one fellow came in to sojourn, and he will needs play the judge; now will we deal worse with thee, than with them.' And they pressed sore upon the man, even Lot, and drew near to break the door. 19:10 But the men put forth their hand, and brought Lot into the house to them, and the door they shut. 19:11 And they smote the men that were at the door of the house with blindness, both small and great; so that they wearied themselves to find the door. 19:12 And the men said unto Lot: 'Hast thou here any besides? son-in-law, and thy sons, and thy daughters, and whomsoever thou hast in the city; bring them out of the place; 19:13 for we will destroy this place, because the cry of them is waxed great before the LORD; and the LORD hath sent us to destroy it.' 19:14 And Lot went out, and spoke unto his sons-in-law, who married his daughters, and said: 'Up, get you out of this place; for the LORD will destroy the city.' But he seemed unto his sons-in-law as one that jested. 19:15 And when the morning arose, then the angels hastened Lot, saying: 'Arise, take thy wife, and thy two daughters that are here; lest thou be swept away in the iniquity of the city.' 19:16 But he lingered; and the men laid hold upon his hand, and upon the hand of his wife, and upon the hand of his two daughters; the LORD being merciful unto him. And they brought him forth, and set him without the city. 19:17 And it came to pass, when they had brought them forth abroad, that he said: 'Escape for thy life; look not behind thee, neither stay thou in all the Plain; escape to the mountain, lest thou be swept away.' 19:18 And Lot said unto them: 'Oh, not so, my lord; 19:19 behold now, thy servant hath found grace in thy sight, and thou hast magnified thy mercy, which thou hast shown unto me in saving my life; and I cannot escape to the mountain, lest the evil overtake me, and I die. 19:20 Behold now, this city is near to flee unto, and it is a little one; oh, let me escape thither--is it not a little one?--and my soul shall live.' 19:21 And he said unto him: 'See, I have accepted thee concerning this thing also, that I will not overthrow the city of which thou hast spoken. 19:22 Hasten thou, escape thither; for I cannot do any thing till thou be come thither.'--Therefore the name of the city was called Zoar.-- 19:23 The sun was risen upon the earth when Lot came unto Zoar. 19:24 Then the LORD caused to rain upon Sodom and upon Gomorrah brimstone and fire from the LORD out of heaven; 19:25 and He overthrow those cities, and all the Plain, and all the inhabitants of the cities, and that which grew upon the ground. 19:26 But his wife looked back from behind him, and she became a pillar of salt.

ב2

A 19:27 And Abraham got up early in the morning to the place where he had stood before the LORD. 19:28 And he looked out toward Sodom and Gomorrah, and toward all the land of the Plain, and beheld, and, lo, the smoke of the land went up as the smoke of a furnace. 19:29 And it came to pass, when God destroyed the cities of the Plain, that God remembered Abraham, and sent Lot out of the midst of the overthrow, when He overthrew the cities in which Lot dwelt.

B 19:30 And Lot went up out of Zoar, and dwelt in the mountain, and his two daughters with him; for he feared to dwell in Zoar; and he dwelt in a cave, he and his two daughters. 19:31 And the first-born said unto the younger: 'Our father is old, and there is not a man in the earth to come in unto us after the manner of all the earth. 19:32 Come, let us make our father drink wine, and we will lie with him, that we may preserve seed of our father.' 19:33 And they made their father drink wine that night. And the first-born went in, and lay with her father; and he knew not when she lay down, nor when she arose. 19:34 And it came to pass on the morrow, that the first-born said unto the younger: 'Behold, I lay yesternight with my father. Let us make him drink wine this night also; and go thou in, and lie with him, that we may preserve seed of our father.' 19:35 And they made their father drink wine that night also. And the younger arose, and lay with him; and he knew not when she lay down, nor when she arose. 19:36 Thus were both the daughters of Lot with child by their father. 19:37 And the first-born bore a son, and called his name Moab--the same is the father of the Moabites unto this day. 19:38 And the younger, she also bore a son, and called his name Ben-ammi--the same is the father of the children of Ammon unto this day. {S}

Genesis Unit IX (20:1-22:19)

א

20:1 And Abraham journeyed from thence toward the land of the South, and dwelt between Kadesh and Shur; and he sojourned in Gerar. 20:2 And Abraham said of Sarah his wife: 'She is my sister.' And Abimelech king of Gerar sent, and took Sarah. 20:3 But God came to Abimelech in a dream of the night, and said to him: 'Behold, thou shalt die, because of the woman whom thou hast taken; for she is a man's wife.' 20:4 Now Abimelech had not come near her; and he said: 'my Lord, wilt Thou slay even a righteous nation? 20:5 Said he not himself unto me: She is my sister? and she, even she herself said: He is my brother. In the simplicity of my heart and the innocency of my hands have I done this.' 20:6 And God said unto him in the dream: 'Yea, I know that in the simplicity of thy heart thou hast done this, and I also withheld thee from sinning against Me. Therefore suffered I thee not to touch her. 20:7 Now therefore restore the man's wife; for he is a prophet, and he shall pray for thee, and thou shalt live; and if thou restore her not, know thou that thou shalt surely die, thou, and all that are thine.' 20:8 And Abimelech rose early in the morning, and called all his servants, and told all these things in their ears; and the men were sore afraid. 20:9 Then Abimelech called Abraham, and said unto him: 'What hast thou done unto us? and wherein have I sinned against thee, that thou hast brought on me and on my kingdom a great sin? thou hast done deeds unto me that ought not to be done.' 20:10 And Abimelech said unto Abraham: 'What sawest thou, that thou hast done this thing?' 20:11 And Abraham said: 'Because I thought: Surely the fear of God is not in this place; and they will slay me for my wife's sake. 20:12 And moreover she is indeed my sister, the daughter of my father, but not the daughter of my mother; and so she became my wife. 20:13 And it came to pass, when God caused me to wander from my father's house, that I said unto her: This is thy kindness which thou shalt show unto me; at every place whither we shall come, say of me: He is my brother.' 20:14 And Abimelech took sheep and oxen, and men-servants and women-servants, and gave them unto Abraham, and restored him Sarah his wife. 20:15 And Abimelech said: 'Behold, my land is before thee: dwell where it pleaseth thee.' 20:16 And unto Sarah he said: 'Behold, I have given thy brother a thousand pieces of silver; behold, it is for thee a covering of the eyes to all that are with thee; and before all men thou art righted.' 20:17 And Abraham prayed unto God; and God healed Abimelech, and his wife, and his maid-servants; and they bore children. 20:18 For the LORD had fast closed up all the wombs of the house of Abimelech, because of Sarah Abraham's wife. {S}

ב

21:1 And the LORD remembered Sarah as He had said, and the LORD did unto Sarah as He had spoken. 21:2 And Sarah conceived, and bore Abraham a son in his old age, at the set time of which God had spoken to him. 21:3 And Abraham called the name of his son that was born unto him, whom Sarah bore to him, Isaac. 21:4 And Abraham circumcised his son Isaac when he was eight days old, as God had commanded him. 21:5 And Abraham was a hundred years old, when his son Isaac was born unto him. 21:6 And Sarah said: 'God hath made laughter for me; every one that heareth will laugh on account of me.' 21:7 And she said: 'Who would have said unto Abraham, that Sarah should give children suck? for I have borne him a son in his old age.' 21:8 And the child grew, and was weaned. And Abraham made a great feast on the day that Isaac was weaned. 21:9 And Sarah saw the son of Hagar the Egyptian, whom she had borne unto Abraham, making sport. 21:10 Wherefore she said unto Abraham: 'Cast out this bondwoman and her son; for the son of this bondwoman shall not be heir with my son, even with Isaac.' 21:11 And the thing was very grievous in Abraham's sight on account of his son. 21:12 And God said unto Abraham: 'Let it not be grievous in thy sight because of the lad, and because of thy bondwoman; in all that Sarah saith unto thee, hearken unto her voice; for in Isaac shall seed be called to thee. 21:13 And also of the son of the bondwoman will I make a nation, because he is thy seed.' 21:14 And Abraham arose up early in the morning, and took bread and a bottle of water, and gave it unto Hagar, putting it on her shoulder, and the child, and sent her away; and she departed, and strayed in the wilderness of Beer-sheba. 21:15 And the water in the bottle was spent, and she cast the child under one of the shrubs. 21:16 And she went, and sat her down over against him a good way off, as it were a bow-shot; for she said: 'Let me not look upon the death of the child.' And she sat over against him, and lifted up her voice, and wept. 21:17 And God heard the voice of the lad; and the angel of God called to Hagar out of heaven, and said unto her: 'What aileth thee, Hagar? fear not; for God hath heard the voice of the lad where he is. 21:18 Arise, lift up the lad, and hold him fast by thy hand; for I will make him a great nation.' 21:19 And God opened her eyes, and she saw a well of water; and she went, and filled the bottle with water, and gave the lad drink. 21:20 And God was with the lad, and he grew; and he dwelt in the wilderness, and became an archer. 21:21 And he dwelt in the wilderness of Paran; and his mother took him a wife out of the land of Egypt. {P}

א2

A 21:22 And it came to pass at that time, that Abimelech and Phicol the captain of his host spoke unto Abraham, saying: 'God is with thee in all that thou doest. 21:23 Now therefore swear unto me here by God that thou wilt not deal falsely with me, nor with my son, nor with my son's son; but according to the kindness that I have done unto thee, thou shalt do unto me, and to the land wherein thou hast sojourned.' 21:24 And Abraham said: 'I will swear.'

B 21:25 And Abraham reproved Abimelech because of the well of water, which Abimelech's servants had violently taken away. 21:26 And Abimelech said: 'I know not who hath done this thing; neither didst thou tell me, neither yet heard I of it, but to-day.' 21:27 And Abraham took sheep and oxen, and gave them unto Abimelech; and they two made a covenant.

C 21:28 And Abraham set seven ewe-lambs of the flock by themselves. 21:29 And Abimelech said unto Abraham: 'What mean these seven ewe-lambs which thou hast set by themselves?' 21:30 And he said: 'Verily, these seven ewe-lambs shalt thou take of my hand, that it may be a witness unto me, that I have digged this well.' 21:31 Wherefore that place was called Beer-sheba; because there they swore both of them. 21:32 So they made a covenant at Beer-sheba; and Abimelech rose up, and Phicol the captain of his host, and they returned into the land of the Philistines. 21:33 And Abraham planted a tamarisk-tree in Beer-sheba, and called there on the name of the LORD, the Everlasting God. 21:34 And Abraham sojourned in the land of the Philistines many days. {P}

ב2

A 22:1 And it came to pass after these things, that God did prove Abraham, and said unto him: 'Abraham'; and he said: 'Here am I.' 22:2 And He said: 'Take now thy son, thine only son, whom thou lovest, even Isaac, and get thee into the land of Moriah; and offer him there for a burnt-offering upon one of the mountains which I will tell thee of.' 22:3 And Abraham rose early in the morning, and saddled his ass, and took two of his young men with him, and Isaac his son; and he cleaved the wood for the burnt-offering, and rose up, and went unto the place of which God had told him. 22:4 On the third day Abraham lifted up his eyes, and saw the place afar off. 22:5 And Abraham said unto his young men: 'Abide ye here with the ass, and I and the lad will go yonder; and we will worship, and come back to you.' 22:6 And Abraham took the wood of the burnt-offering, and laid it upon Isaac his son; and he took in his hand the fire and the knife; and they went both of them together. 22:7 And Isaac spoke unto Abraham his father, and said: 'My father.' And he said: 'Here am I, my son.' And he said: 'Behold the fire and the wood; but where is the lamb for a burnt-offering?' 22:8 And Abraham said: 'God will provide Himself the lamb for a burnt-offering, my son.' So they went both of them together. 22:9 And they came to the place which God had told him of; and Abraham built the altar there, and laid the wood in order, and bound Isaac his son, and laid him on the altar, upon the wood. 22:10 And Abraham stretched forth his hand, and took the knife to slay his son.

B 22:11 And the angel of the LORD called unto him out of heaven, and said: 'Abraham, Abraham.' And he said: 'Here am I.' 22:12 And he said: 'Lay not thy hand upon the lad, neither do thou any thing unto him; for now I know that thou art a God-fearing man, seeing thou hast not withheld thy son, thine only son, from Me.' 22:13 And Abraham lifted up his eyes, and looked, and behold behind him a ram caught in the thicket by his horns. And Abraham went and took the ram, and offered him up for a burnt-offering in the stead of his son. 22:14 And Abraham called the name of that place Adonai-jireh; as it is said to this day: 'In the mount where the LORD is seen.'

C 22:15 And the angel of the LORD called unto Abraham a second time out of heaven, 22:16 and said: 'By Myself have I sworn, saith the LORD, because thou hast done this thing, and hast not withheld thy son, thine only son, 22:17 that in blessing I will bless thee, and in multiplying I will multiply thy seed as the stars of the heaven, and as the sand which is upon the seashore; and thy seed shall possess the gate of his enemies; 22:18 and in thy seed shall all the nations of the earth be blessed; because thou hast hearkened to My voice.' 22:19 So Abraham returned unto his young men, and they rose up and went together to Beer-sheba; and Abraham dwelt at Beer-sheba. {P}

Genesis Unit X (22:20-25:11)

א

22:20 And it came to pass after these things, that it was told Abraham, saying: 'Behold, Milcah, she also hath borne children unto thy brother Nahor: 22:21 Uz his first-born, and Buz his brother, and Kemuel the father of Aram; 22:22 and Chesed, and Hazo, and Pildash, and Jidlaph, and Bethuel.' 22:23 And Bethuel begot Rebekah; these eight did Milcah bear to Nahor, Abraham's brother. 22:24 And his concubine, whose name was Reumah, she also bore Tebah, and Gaham, and Tahash, and Maacah. {P}

ב

23:1 And the life of Sarah was a hundred and seven and twenty years; these were the years of the life of Sarah. 23:2 And Sarah died in Kiriatharba--the same is Hebron--in the land of Canaan; and Abraham came to mourn for Sarah, and to weep for her. 23:3 And Abraham rose up from before his dead, and spoke unto the children of Heth, saying: 23:4 'I am a stranger and a sojourner with you: give me a possession of a burying-place with you, that I may bury my dead out of my sight.' 23:5 And the children of Heth answered Abraham, saying unto him: 23:6 'Hear us, my lord: thou art a mighty prince among us; in the choice of our sepulchres bury thy dead; none of us shall withhold from thee his sepulchre, but that thou mayest bury thy dead.' 23:7 And Abraham rose up, and bowed down to the people of the land, even to the children of Heth. 23:8 And he spoke with them, saying: 'If it be your mind that I should bury my dead out of my sight, hear me, and entreat for me to Ephron the son of Zohar, 23:9 that he may give me the cave of Machpelah, which he hath, which is in the end of his field; for the full price let him give it to me in the midst of you for a possession of a burying-place.' 23:10 Now Ephron was sitting in the midst of the children of Heth; and Ephron the Hittite answered Abraham in the hearing of the children of Heth, even of all that went in at the gate of his city, saying: 23:11 'Nay, my lord, hear me: the field give I thee, and the cave that is therein, I give it thee; in the presence of the sons of my people give I it thee; bury thy dead.' 23:12 And Abraham bowed down before the people of the land. 23:13 And he spoke unto Ephron in the hearing of the people of the land, saying: 'But if thou wilt, I pray thee, hear me: I will give the price of the field; take it of me, and I will bury my dead there.' 23:14 And Ephron answered Abraham, saying unto him: 23:15 'My lord, hearken unto me: a piece of land worth four hundred shekels of silver, what is that betwixt me and thee? bury therefore thy dead.' 23:16 And Abraham hearkened unto Ephron; and Abraham weighed to Ephron the silver, which he had named in the hearing of the children of Heth, four hundred shekels of silver, current money with the merchant. 23:17 So the field of Ephron, which was in Machpelah, which was before Mamre, the field, and the cave which was therein, and all the trees that were in the field, that were in all the border thereof round about, were made sure 23:18 unto Abraham for a possession in the presence of the children of Heth, before all that went in at the gate of his city. 23:19 And after this, Abraham buried Sarah his wife in the cave of the field of Machpelah before Mamre--the same is Hebron--in the land of Canaan. 23:20 And the field, and the cave that is therein, were made sure unto Abraham for a possession of a burying-place by the children of Heth. {S}

2א

A 24:1 And Abraham was old, well stricken in age; and the LORD had blessed Abraham in all things. 24:2 And Abraham said unto his servant, the elder of his house, that ruled over all that he had: 'Put, I pray thee, thy hand under my thigh. 24:3 And I will make thee swear by the LORD, the God of heaven and the God of the earth, that thou shalt not take a wife for my son of the daughters of the Canaanites, among whom I dwell. 24:4 But thou shalt go unto my country, and to my kindred, and take a wife for my son, even for Isaac.' 24:5 And the servant said unto him: 'Peradventure the woman will not be willing to follow me unto this land; must I needs bring thy son back unto the land from whence thou camest?' 24:6 And Abraham said unto him: 'Beware thou that thou bring not my son back thither. 24:7 The LORD, the God of heaven, who took me from my father's house, and from the land of my nativity, and who spoke unto me, and who swore unto me, saying: Unto thy seed will I give this land; He will send His angel before thee, and thou shalt take a wife for my son from thence. 24:8 And if the woman be not willing to follow thee, then thou shalt be clear from this my oath; only thou shalt not bring my son back thither.' 24:9 And the servant put his hand under the thigh of Abraham his master, and swore to him concerning this matter.

B 24:10 And the servant took ten camels, of the camels of his master, and departed; having all goodly things of his master's in his hand; and he arose, and went to Aram-naharaim, unto the city of Nahor. 24:11 And he made the camels to kneel down without the city by the well of water at the time of evening, the time that women go out to draw water. 24:12 And he said: 'O LORD, the God of my master Abraham, send me, I pray Thee, good speed this day, and show kindness unto my master Abraham. 24:13 Behold, I stand by the fountain of water; and the daughters of the men of the city come out to draw water. 24:14 So let it come to pass, that the damsel to whom I shall say: Let down thy pitcher, I pray thee, that I may drink; and she shall say: Drink, and I will give thy camels drink also; let the same be she that Thou hast appointed for Thy servant, even for Isaac; and thereby shall I know that Thou hast shown kindness unto my master.' 24:15 And it came to pass, before he had done speaking, that, behold, Rebekah came out, who was born to Bethuel the son of Milcah, the wife of Nahor, Abraham's brother, with her pitcher upon her shoulder. 24:16 And the damsel was very fair to look upon, a virgin, neither had any man known her; and she went down to the fountain, and filled her pitcher, and came up. 24:17 And the servant ran to meet her, and said: 'Give me to drink, I pray thee, a little water of thy pitcher.' 24:18 And she said: 'Drink, my lord'; and she hastened, and let down her pitcher upon her hand, and gave him drink. 24:19 And when she had done giving him drink, she said: 'I will draw for thy camels also, until they have done drinking.' 24:20 And she hastened, and emptied her pitcher into the trough, and ran again unto the well to draw, and drew for all his camels. 24:21 And the man looked stedfastly on her; holding his peace, to know whether the LORD had made his journey prosperous or not. 24:22 And it came to pass, as the camels had done drinking, that the man took a golden ring of half a shekel weight, and two bracelets for her hands of ten shekels weight of gold; 24:23 and said: 'Whose daughter art thou? tell me, I pray thee. Is there room in thy father's house for us to lodge in?' 24:24 And she said unto him: 'I am the daughter of Bethuel the son of Milcah, whom she bore unto Nahor.' 24:25 She said moreover unto him: 'We have both straw and provender enough, and room to lodge in.' 24:26 And the man bowed his head, and prostrated himself before the LORD. 24:27 And he said: 'Blessed be the LORD, the God of my master Abraham, who hath not forsaken His mercy and His truth toward my master; as for me, the LORD hath led me in the way to the house of my master's brethren.'

2ב

A 24:28 And the damsel ran, and told her mother's house according to these words. 24:29 And Rebekah had a brother, and his name was Laban; and Laban ran out unto the man, unto the fountain. 24:30 And it came to pass, when he saw the ring, and the bracelets upon his sister's hands, and when he heard the words of Rebekah his sister, saying: 'Thus spoke the man unto me,' that he came unto the man; and, behold, he stood by the camels at the fountain. 24:31 And he said: 'Come in, thou blessed of the LORD; wherefore standest thou without? for I have cleared the house, and made room for the camels.' 24:32 And the man came into the house, and he ungirded the camels; and he gave straw and provender for the camels, and water to wash his feet and the feet of the men that were with him. 24:33 And there was set food before him to eat; but he said: 'I will not eat, until I have told mine errand.' And he said: 'Speak on.' 24:34 And he said: 'I am Abraham's servant. 24:35 And the LORD hath blessed my master greatly; and he is become great; and He hath given him flocks and herds, and silver and gold, and men-servants and maid-servants, and camels and asses. 24:36 And Sarah my master's wife bore a son to my master when she was old; and unto him hath he given all that he hath. 24:37 And my master made me swear, saying: Thou shalt not take a wife for my son of the daughters of the Canaanites, in whose land I dwell. 24:38 But thou shalt go unto my father's house, and to my kindred, and take a wife for my son. 24:39 And I said unto my master: Peradventure the woman will not follow me. 24:40 And he said unto me: The LORD, before whom I walk, will send His angel with thee, and prosper thy way; and thou shalt take a wife for my son of my kindred, and of my father's house; 24:41 then shalt thou be clear from my oath, when thou comest to my kindred; and if they give her not to thee, thou shalt be clear from my oath.

B 24:42 And I came this day unto the fountain, and said: O LORD, the God of my master Abraham, if now Thou do prosper my way which I go: 24:43 behold, I stand by the fountain of water; and let it come to pass, that the maiden that cometh forth to draw, to whom I shall say: Give me, I pray thee, a little water from thy pitcher to drink; 24:44 and she shall say to me: Both drink thou, and I will also draw for thy camels; let the same be the woman whom the LORD hath appointed for my master's son. 24:45 And before I had done speaking to my heart, behold, Rebekah came forth with her pitcher on her shoulder; and she went down unto the fountain, and drew. And I said unto her: Let me drink, I pray thee. 24:46 And she made haste, and let down her pitcher from her shoulder, and said: Drink, and I will give thy camels drink also. So I drank, and she made the camels drink also. 24:47 And I asked her, and said: Whose daughter art thou? And she said: The daughter of Bethuel, Nahor's son, whom Milcah bore unto him. And I put the ring upon her nose, and the bracelets upon her hands. 24:48 And I bowed my head, and prostrated myself before the LORD, and blessed the LORD, the God of my master Abraham, who had led me in the right way to take my master's brother's daughter for his son. 24:49 And now if ye will deal kindly and truly with my master, tell me; and if not, tell me; that I may turn to the right hand, or to the left.' 24:50 Then Laban and Bethuel answered and said: 'The thing proceedeth from the LORD; we cannot speak unto thee bad or good. 24:51 Behold, Rebekah is before thee, take her, and go, and let her be thy master's son's wife, as the LORD hath spoken.' 24:52 And it came to pass, that, when Abraham's servant heard their words, he bowed himself down to the earth unto the LORD.

3א

24:53 And the servant brought forth jewels of silver, and jewels of gold, and raiment, and gave them to Rebekah; he gave also to her brother and to her mother precious things. 24:54 And they did eat and drink, he and the men that were with him, and tarried all night; and they rose up in the morning, and he said: 'Send me away unto my master.' 24:55 And her brother and her mother said: 'Let the damsel abide with us a few days, at the least ten; after that she shall go.' 24:56 And he said unto them: 'Delay me not, seeing the LORD hath prospered my way; send me away that I may go to my master.' 24:57 And they said: 'We will call the damsel, and inquire at her mouth.' 24:58 And they called Rebekah, and said unto her: 'Wilt thou go with this man?' And she said: 'I will go.' 24:59 And they sent away Rebekah their sister, and her nurse, and Abraham's servant, and his men. 24:60 And they blessed Rebekah, and said unto her: 'Our sister, be thou the mother of thousands of ten thousands, and let thy seed possess the gate of those that hate them.'

4א

25:1 And Abraham took another wife, and her name was Keturah. 25:2 And she bore him Zimran, and Jokshan, and Medan, and Midian, and Ishbak, and Shuah. 25:3 And Jokshan begot Sheba, and Dedan. And the sons of Dedan were Asshurim, and Letushim, and Leummim. 25:4 And the sons of Midian: Ephah, and Epher, and Hanoch, and Abida, and Eldaah. All these were the children of Keturah. 25:5 And Abraham gave all that he had unto Isaac. 25:6 But unto the sons of the concubines, that Abraham had, Abraham gave gifts; and he sent them away from Isaac his son, while he yet lived, eastward, unto the east country.

3ב

24:61 And Rebekah arose, and her damsels, and they rode upon the camels, and followed the man. And the servant took Rebekah, and went his way. 24:62 And Isaac came from the way of Beer-lahai-roi; for he dwelt in the land of the South. 24:63 And Isaac went out to meditate in the field at the eventide; and he lifted up his eyes, and saw, and, behold, there were camels coming. 24:64 And Rebekah lifted up her eyes, and when she saw Isaac, she alighted from the camel. 24:65 And she said unto the servant: 'What man is this that walketh in the field to meet us?' And the servant said: 'It is my master.' And she took her veil, and covered herself. 24:66 And the servant told Isaac all the things that he had done. 24:67 And Isaac brought her into his mother Sarah's tent, and took Rebekah, and she became his wife; and he loved her. And Isaac was comforted for his mother. {P}

4ב

25:7 And these are the days of the years of Abraham's life which he lived, a hundred threescore and fifteen years. 25:8 And Abraham expired, and died in a good old age, an old man, and full of years; and was gathered to his people. 25:9 And Isaac and Ishmael his sons buried him in the cave of Machpelah, in the field of Ephron the son of Zohar the Hittite, which is before Mamre; 25:10 the field which Abraham purchased of the children of Heth; there was Abraham buried, and Sarah his wife. 25:11 And it came to pass after the death of Abraham, that God blessed Isaac his son; and Isaac dwelt by Beer-lahai-roi. {P}

Genesis Unit XI (25:12-25:34)

1א

25:12 Now these are the generations of Ishmael, Abraham's son, whom Hagar the Egyptian, Sarah's handmaid, bore unto Abraham. 25:13 And these are the names of the sons of Ishmael, by their names, according to their generations: the first-born of Ishmael, Nebaioth; and Kedar, and Adbeel, and Mibsam, 25:14 and Mishma, and Dumah, and Massa; 25:15 Hadad, and Tema, Jetur, Naphish, and Kedem; 25:16 these are the sons of Ishmael, and these are their names, by their villages, and by their encampments; twelve princes according to their nations. 25:17 And these are the years of the life of Ishmael, a hundred and thirty and seven years; and he expired and died; and was gathered unto his people. 25:18 And they dwelt from Havilah unto Shur that is before Egypt, as thou goest toward Asshur: over against all his brethren he did settle. {P}

2א

25:20 And Isaac was forty years old when he took Rebekah, the daughter of Bethuel the Aramean, of Paddan-aram, the sister of Laban the Aramean, to be his wife. 25:21 And Isaac entreated the LORD for his wife, because she was barren; and the LORD let Himself be entreated of him, and Rebekah his wife conceived. 25:22 And the children struggled together within her; and she said: 'If it be so, wherefore do I live?' And she went to inquire of the LORD. 25:23 And the LORD said unto her: Two nations are in thy womb, and two peoples shall be separated from thy bowels; and the one people shall be stronger than the other people; and the elder shall serve the younger. 25:24 And when her days to be delivered were fulfilled, behold, there were twins in her womb. 25:25 And the first came forth ruddy, all over like a hairy mantle; and they called his name Esau. 25:26 And after that came forth his brother, and his hand had hold on Esau's heel; and his name was called Jacob. And Isaac was threescore years old when she bore them.

1ב

25:19 And these are the generations of Isaac, Abraham's son: Abraham begot Isaac.

2ב

25:27 And the boys grew; and Esau was a cunning hunter, a man of the field; and Jacob was a quiet man, dwelling in tents. 25:28 Now Isaac loved Esau, because he did eat of his venison; and Rebekah loved Jacob. 25:29 And Jacob sod pottage; and Esau came in from the field, and he was faint. 25:30 And Esau said to Jacob: 'Let me swallow, I pray thee, some of this red, red pottage; for I am faint.' Therefore was his name called Edom. 25:31 And Jacob said: 'Sell me first thy birthright.' 25:32 And Esau said: 'Behold, I am at the point to die; and what profit shall the birthright do to me?' 25:33 And Jacob said: 'Swear to me first'; and he swore unto him; and he sold his birthright unto Jacob. 25:34 And Jacob gave Esau bread and pottage of lentils; and he did eat and drink, and rose up, and went his way. So Esau despised his birthright. {P}

Genesis Unit XII (26:1-26:33)

1א

26:1 And there was a famine in the land, beside the first famine that was in the days of Abraham. And Isaac went unto Abimelech king of the Philistines unto Gerar. 26:2 And the LORD appeared unto him, and said: 'Go not down unto Egypt; dwell in the land which I shall tell thee of. 26:3 Sojourn in this land, and I will be with thee, and will bless thee; for unto thee, and unto thy seed, I will give all these lands, and I will establish the oath which I swore unto Abraham thy father; 26:4 and I will multiply thy seed as the stars of heaven, and will give unto thy seed all these lands; and by thy seed shall all the nations of the earth bless themselves; 26:5 because that Abraham hearkened to My voice, and kept My charge, My commandments, My statutes, and My laws.'

2א

A 26:12 And Isaac sowed in that land, and found in the same year a hundredfold; and the LORD blessed him. 26:13 And the man waxed great, and grew more and more until he became very great. 26:14 And he had possessions of flocks, and possessions of herds, and a great household; and the Philistines envied him.
B 26:15 Now all the wells which his father's servants had digged in the days of Abraham his father, the Philistines had stopped them, and filled them with earth.

3א

26:23 And he went up from thence to Beer-sheba. 26:24 And the LORD appeared unto him the same night, and said: 'I am the God of Abraham thy father. Fear not, for I am with thee, and will bless thee, and multiply thy seed for My servant Abraham's sake.' 26:25 And he builded an altar there, and called upon the name of the LORD, and pitched his tent there; and there Isaac's servants digged a well.

1ב

26:6 And Isaac dwelt in Gerar. 26:7 And the men of the place asked him of his wife; and he said: 'She is my sister'; for he feared to say: 'My wife'; 'lest the men of the place should kill me for Rebekah, because she is fair to look upon.' 26:8 And it came to pass, when he had been there a long time, that Abimelech king of the Philistines looked out at a window, and saw, and, behold, Isaac was sporting with Rebekah his wife. 26:9 And Abimelech called Isaac, and said: 'Behold, of a surety she is thy wife; and how saidst thou: She is my sister?' And Isaac said unto him: 'Because I said: Lest I die because of her.' 26:10 And Abimelech said: 'What is this thou hast done unto us? one of the people might easily have lain with thy wife, and thou wouldest have brought guiltiness upon us.' 26:11 And Abimelech charged all the people, saying: 'He that toucheth this man or his wife shall surely be put to death.'

2ב

A 26:16 And Abimelech said unto Isaac: 'Go from us; for thou art much mightier than we.' 26:17 And Isaac departed thence, and encamped in the valley of Gerar, and dwelt there.
B 26:18 And Isaac digged again the wells of water, which they had digged in the days of Abraham his father; for the Philistines had stopped them after the death of Abraham; and he called their names after the names by which his father had called them. 26:19 And Isaac's servants digged in the valley, and found there a well of living water. 26:20 And the herdmen of Gerar strove with Isaac's herdmen, saying: 'The water is ours.' And he called the name of the well Esek; because they contended with him. 26:21 And they digged another well, and they strove for that also. And he called the name of it Sitnah. 26:22 And he removed from thence, and digged another well; and for that they strove not. And he called the name of it Rehoboth; and he said: 'For now the LORD hath made room for us, and we shall be fruitful in the land.'

3ב

26:26 Then Abimelech went to him from Gerar, and Ahuzzath his friend, and Phicol the captain of his host. 26:27 And Isaac said unto them: 'Wherefore are ye come unto me, seeing ye hate me, and have sent me away from you?' 26:28 And they said: 'We saw plainly that the LORD was with thee; and we said: Let there now be an oath betwixt us, even betwixt us and thee, and let us make a covenant with thee; 26:29 that thou wilt do us no hurt, as we have not touched thee, and as we have done unto thee nothing but good, and have sent thee away in peace; thou art now the blessed of the LORD.' 26:30 And he made them a feast, and they did eat and drink. 26:31 And they rose up betimes in the morning, and swore one to another; and Isaac sent them away, and they departed from him in peace. 26:32 And it came to pass the same day, that Isaac's servants came, and told him concerning the well which they had digged, and said unto him: 'We have found water.' 26:33 And he called it Shibah. Therefore the name of the city is Beer-sheba unto this day. {S}

Genesis Unit XIII (26:34-28:9)

1

26:34 And when Esau was forty years old, he took to wife Judith the daughter of Beeri the Hittite, and Basemath the daughter of Elon the Hittite. 26:35 And they were a bitterness of spirit unto Isaac and to Rebekah. {S}

2א

27:1 And it came to pass, that when Isaac was old, and his eyes were dim, so that he could not see, he called Esau his elder son, and said unto him: 'My son'; and he said unto him: 'Here am I.' 27:2 And he said: 'Behold now, I am old, I know not the day of my death. 27:3 Now therefore take, I pray thee, thy weapons, thy quiver and thy bow, and go out to the field, and take me venison; 27:4 and make me savoury food, such as I love, and bring it to me, that I may eat; that my soul may bless thee before I die.'

2ב

27:5 And Rebekah heard when Isaac spoke to Esau his son. And Esau went to the field to hunt for venison, and to bring it. 27:6 And Rebekah spoke unto Jacob her son, saying: 'Behold, I heard thy father speak unto Esau thy brother, saying: 27:7 Bring me venison, and make me savoury food, that I may eat, and bless thee before the LORD before my death. 27:8 Now therefore, my son, hearken to my voice according to that which I command thee. 27:9 Go now to the flock, and fetch me from thence two good kids of the goats; and I will make them savoury food for thy father, such as he loveth; 27:10 and thou shalt bring it to thy father, that he may eat, so that he may bless thee before his death.' 27:11 And Jacob said to Rebekah his mother: 'Behold, Esau my brother is a hairy man, and I am a smooth man. 27:12 My father peradventure will feel me, and I shall seem to him as a mocker; and I shall bring a curse upon me, and not a blessing.' 27:13 And his mother said unto him: 'Upon me be thy curse, my son; only hearken to my voice, and go fetch me them.' 27:14 And he went, and fetched, and brought them to his mother; and his mother made savoury food, such as his father loved. 27:15 And Rebekah took the choicest garments of Esau her elder son, which were with her in the house, and put them upon Jacob her younger son. 27:16 And she put the skins of the kids of the goats upon his hands, and upon the smooth of his neck. 27:17 And she gave the savoury food and the bread, which she had prepared, into the hand of her son Jacob.

3א

27:18 And he came unto his father, and said: 'My father'; and he said: 'Here am I; who art thou, my son?' 27:19 And Jacob said unto his father: 'I am Esau thy first-born; I have done according as thou badest me. Arise, I pray thee, sit and eat of my venison, that thy soul may bless me.' 27:20 And Isaac said unto his son: 'How is it that thou hast found it so quickly, my son?' And he said: 'Because the LORD thy God sent me good speed.' 27:21 And Isaac said unto Jacob: 'Come near, I pray thee, that I may feel thee, my son, whether thou be my very son Esau or not.' 27:22 And Jacob went near unto Isaac his father; and he felt him, and said: 'The voice is the voice of Jacob, but the hands are the hands of Esau.' 27:23 And he discerned him not, because his hands were hairy, as his brother Esau's hands; so he blessed him. 27:24 And he said: 'Art thou my very son Esau?' And he said: 'I am.' 27:25 And he said: 'Bring it near to me, and I will eat of my son's venison, that my soul may bless thee.' And he brought it near to him, and he did eat; and he brought him wine, and he drank. 27:26 And his father Isaac said unto him: 'Come near now, and kiss me, my son.' 27:27 And he came near, and kissed him. And he smelled the smell of his raiment, and blessed him, and said: See, the smell of my son is as the smell of a field which the LORD hath blessed. 27:28 So God give thee of the dew of heaven, and of the fat places of the earth, and plenty of corn and wine. 27:29 Let peoples serve thee, and nations bow down to thee. Be lord over thy brethren, and let thy mother's sons bow down to thee. Cursed be every one that curseth thee, and blessed be every one that blesseth thee.

3ב

27:30 And it came to pass, as soon as Isaac had made an end of blessing Jacob, and Jacob was yet scarce gone out from the presence of Isaac his father, that Esau his brother came in from his hunting. 27:31 And he also made savoury food, and brought it unto his father; and he said unto his father: 'Let my father arise, and eat of his son's venison, that thy soul may bless me.' 27:32 And Isaac his father said unto him: 'Who art thou?' And he said: 'I am thy son, thy first-born, Esau.' 27:33 And Isaac trembled very exceedingly, and said: 'Who then is he that hath taken venison, and brought it me, and I have eaten of all before thou camest, and have blessed him? yea, and he shall be blessed.' 27:34 When Esau heard the words of his father, he cried with an exceeding great and bitter cry, and said unto his father: 'Bless me, even me also, O my father.' 27:35 And he said: 'Thy brother came with guile, and hath taken away thy blessing.' 27:36 And he said: 'Is not he rightly named Jacob? for he hath supplanted me these two times: he took away my birthright; and, behold, now he hath taken away my blessing.' And he said: 'Hast thou not reserved a blessing for me?' 27:37 And Isaac answered and said unto Esau: 'Behold, I have made him thy lord, and all his brethren have I given to him for servants; and with corn and wine have I sustained him; and what then shall I do for thee, my son?' 27:38 And Esau said unto his father: 'Hast thou but one blessing, my father? bless me, even me also, O my father.' And Esau lifted up his voice, and wept. 27:39 And Isaac his father answered and said unto him: Behold, of the fat places of the earth shall be thy dwelling, and of the dew of heaven from above; 27:40 And by thy sword shalt thou live, and thou shalt serve thy brother; and it shall come to pass when thou shalt break loose, that thou shalt shake his yoke from off thy neck. 27:41 And Esau hated Jacob because of the blessing wherewith his father blessed him. And Esau said in his heart: 'Let the days of mourning for my father be at hand; then will I slay my brother Jacob.'

4א

27:42 And the words of Esau her elder son were told to Rebekah; and she sent and called Jacob her younger son, and said unto him: 'Behold, thy brother Esau, as touching thee, doth comfort himself, purposing to kill thee. 27:43 Now therefore, my son, hearken to my voice; and arise, flee thou to Laban my brother to Haran; 27:44 and tarry with him a few days, until thy brother's fury turn away; 27:45 until thy brother's anger turn away from thee, and he forget that which thou hast done to him; then I will send, and fetch thee from thence; why should I be bereaved of you both in one day?'

4ב

27:46 And Rebekah said to Isaac: 'I am weary of my life because of the daughters of Heth. If Jacob take a wife of the daughters of Heth, such as these, of the daughters of the land, what good shall my life do me?' 28:1 And Isaac called Jacob, and blessed him, and charged him, and said unto him: 'Thou shalt not take a wife of the daughters of Canaan. 28:2 Arise, go to Paddan-aram, to the house of Bethuel thy mother's father; and take thee a wife from thence of the daughters of Laban thy mother's brother. 28:3 And God Almighty bless thee, and make thee fruitful, and multiply thee, that thou mayest be a congregation of peoples; 28:4 and give thee the blessing of Abraham, to thee, and to thy seed with thee; that thou mayest inherit the land of thy sojournings, which God gave unto Abraham.' 28:5 And Isaac sent away Jacob; and he went to Paddan-aram unto Laban, son of Bethuel the Aramean, the brother of Rebekah, Jacob's and Esau's mother.

5

28:6 Now Esau saw that Isaac had blessed Jacob and sent him away to Paddan-aram, to take him a wife from thence; and that as he blessed him he gave him a charge, saying: 'Thou shalt not take a wife of the daughters of Canaan'; 28:7 and that Jacob hearkened to his father and his mother, and was gone to Paddan-aram; 28:8 and Esau saw that the daughters of Canaan pleased not Isaac his father; 28:9 so Esau went unto Ishmael, and took unto the wives that he had Mahalath the daughter of Ishmael Abraham's son, the sister of Nebaioth, to be his wife. {S}

Genesis Unit XIV (28:10-32:3)

1

28:10 And Jacob went out from Beer-sheba, and went toward Haran. 28:11 And he lighted upon the place, and tarried there all night, because the sun was set; and he took one of the stones of the place, and put it under his head, and lay down in that place to sleep. 28:12 And he dreamed, and behold a ladder set up on the earth, and the top of it reached to heaven; and behold the angels of God ascending and descending on it. 28:13 And, behold, the LORD stood beside him, and said: 'I am the LORD, the God of Abraham thy father, and the God of Isaac. The land whereon thou liest, to thee will I give it, and to thy seed. 28:14 And thy seed shall be as the dust of the earth, and thou shalt spread abroad to the west, and to the east, and to the north, and to the south. And in thee and in thy seed shall all the families of the earth be blessed. 28:15 And, behold, I am with thee, and will keep thee whithersoever thou goest, and will bring thee back into this land; for I will not leave thee, until I have done that which I have spoken to thee of.' 28:16 And Jacob awaked out of his sleep, and he said: 'Surely the LORD is in this place; and I knew it not.' 28:17 And he was afraid, and said: 'How full of awe is this place! this is none other than the house of God, and this is the gate of heaven.' 28:18 And Jacob rose up early in the morning, and took the stone that he had put under his head, and set it up for a pillar, and poured oil upon the top of it. 28:19 And he called the name of that place Beth-el, but the name of the city was Luz at the first. 28:20 And Jacob vowed a vow, saying: 'If God will be with me, and will keep me in this way that I go, and will give me bread to eat, and raiment to put on, 28:21 so that I come back to my father's house in peace, then shall the LORD be my God, 28:22 and this stone, which I have set up for a pillar, shall be God's house; and of all that Thou shalt give me I will surely give the tenth unto Thee.'

2א

29:1 Then Jacob went on his journey, and came to the land of the children of the east. 29:2 And he looked, and behold a well in the field, and, lo, three flocks of sheep lying there by it.--For out of that well they watered the flocks. And the stone upon the well's mouth was great. 29:3 And thither were all the flocks gathered; and they rolled the stone from the well's mouth, and watered the sheep, and put the stone back upon the well's mouth in its place.-- 29:4 And Jacob said unto them: 'My brethren, whence are ye?' And they said: 'Of Haran are we.' 29:5 And he said unto them: 'Know ye Laban the son of Nahor?' And they said: 'We know him.' 29:6 And he said unto them: 'Is it well with him?' And they said: 'It is well; and, behold, Rachel his daughter cometh with the sheep.' 29:7 And he said: 'Lo, it is yet high day, neither is it time that the cattle should be gathered together; water ye the sheep, and go and feed them.' 29:8 And they said: 'We cannot, until all the flocks be gathered together, and they roll the stone from the well's mouth; then we water the sheep.' 29:9 While he was yet speaking with them, Rachel came with her father's sheep; for she tended them. 29:10 And it came to pass, when Jacob saw Rachel the daughter of Laban his mother's brother, and the sheep of Laban his mother's brother, that Jacob went near, and rolled the stone from the well's mouth, and watered the flock of Laban his mother's brother. 29:11 And Jacob kissed Rachel, and lifted up his voice, and wept. 29:12 And Jacob told Rachel that he was her father's brother, and that he was Rebekah's son; and she ran and told her father. 29:13 And it came to pass, when Laban heard the tidings of Jacob his sister's son, that he ran to meet him, and embraced him, and kissed him, and brought him to his house. And he told Laban all these things. 29:14 And Laban said to him: 'Surely thou art my bone and my flesh.' And he abode with him the space of a month. 29:15 And Laban said unto Jacob: 'Because thou art my brother, shouldest thou therefore serve me for nought? tell me, what shall thy wages be?' 29:16 Now Laban had two daughters: the name of the elder was Leah, and the name of the younger was Rachel. 29:17 And Leah's eyes were weak; but Rachel was of beautiful form and fair to look upon. 29:18 And Jacob loved Rachel; and he said: 'I will serve thee seven years for Rachel thy younger daughter.' 29:19 And Laban said: 'It is better that I give her to thee, than that I should give her to another man; abide with me.' 29:20 And Jacob served seven years for Rachel; and they seemed unto him but a few days, for the love he had to her. 29:21 And Jacob said unto Laban: 'Give me my wife, for my days are filled, that I may go in unto her.' 29:22 And Laban gathered together all the men of the place, and made a feast. 29:23 And it came to pass in the evening, that he took Leah his daughter, and brought her to him; and he went in unto her. 29:24 And Laban gave Zilpah his handmaid unto his daughter Leah for a handmaid. 29:25 And it came to pass in the morning that, behold, it was Leah; and he said to Laban: 'What is this thou hast done unto me? did not I serve with thee for Rachel? wherefore then hast thou beguiled me?' 29:26 And Laban said: 'It is not so done in our place, to give the younger before the first-born. 29:27 Fulfil the week of this one, and we will give thee the other also for the service which thou shalt serve with me yet seven other years.' 29:28 And Jacob did so, and fulfilled her week; and he gave him Rachel his daughter to wife. 29:29 And Laban gave to Rachel his daughter Bilhah his handmaid to be her handmaid. 29:30 And he went in also unto Rachel, and he loved Rachel more than Leah, and served with him yet seven other years.

2ב

29:31 And the LORD saw that Leah was hated, and he opened her womb; but Rachel was barren. 29:32 And Leah conceived, and bore a son, and she called his name Reuben; for she said: 'Because the LORD hath looked upon my affliction; for now my husband will love me.' 29:33 And she conceived again, and bore a son; and said: 'Because the LORD hath heard that I am hated, He hath therefore given me this son also.' And she called his name Simeon. 29:34 And she conceived again, and bore a son; and said: 'Now this time will my husband be joined unto me, because I have borne him three sons.' Therefore was his name called Levi. 29:35 And she conceived again, and bore a son; and she said: 'This time will I praise the LORD.' Therefore she called his name Judah; and she left off bearing. 30:1 And when Rachel saw that she bore Jacob no children, Rachel envied her sister; and she said unto Jacob: 'Give me children, or else I die.' 30:2 And Jacob's anger was kindled against Rachel; and he said: 'Am I in God's stead, who hath withheld from thee the fruit of the womb?' 30:3 And she said: 'Behold my maid Bilhah, go in unto her; that she may bear upon my knees, and I also may be builded up through her.' 30:4 And she gave him Bilhah her handmaid to wife; and Jacob went in unto her. 30:5 And Bilhah conceived, and bore Jacob a son. 30:6 And Rachel said: 'God hath judged me, and hath also heard my voice, and hath given me a son.' Therefore called she his name Dan. 30:7 And Bilhah Rachel's handmaid conceived again, and bore Jacob a second son. 30:8 And Rachel said: 'With mighty wrestlings have I wrestled with my sister, and have prevailed.' And she called his name Naphtali. 30:9 When Leah saw that she had left off bearing, she took Zilpah her handmaid, and gave her to Jacob to wife. 30:10 And Zilpah Leah's handmaid bore Jacob a son. 30:11 And Leah said: 'Fortune is come!' And she called his name Gad. 30:12 And Zilpah Leah's handmaid bore Jacob a second son. 30:13 And Leah said: 'Happy am I! for the daughters will call me happy.' And she called his name Asher. 30:14 And Reuben went in the days of wheat harvest, and found mandrakes in the field, and brought them unto his mother Leah. Then Rachel said to Leah: 'Give me, I pray thee, of thy son's mandrakes.' 30:15 And she said unto her: 'Is it a small matter that thou hast taken away my husband? and wouldest thou take away my son's mandrakes also?' And Rachel said: 'Therefore he shall lie with thee to-night for thy son's mandrakes.' 30:16 And Jacob came from the field in the evening, and Leah went out to meet him, and said: 'Thou must come in unto me; for I have surely hired thee with my son's mandrakes.' And he lay with her that night. 30:17 And God hearkened unto Leah, and she conceived, and bore Jacob a fifth son. 30:18 And Leah said: 'God hath given me my hire, because I gave my handmaid to my husband. And she called his name Issachar. 30:19 And Leah conceived again, and bore a sixth son to Jacob. 30:20 And Leah said: 'God hath endowed me with a good dowry; now will my husband dwell with me, because I have borne him six sons.' And she called his name Zebulun. 30:21 And afterwards she bore a daughter, and called her name Dinah. 30:22 And God remembered Rachel, and God hearkened to her, and opened her womb. 30:23 And she conceived, and bore a son, and said: 'God hath taken away my reproach.' 30:24 And she called his name Joseph, saying: 'The LORD add to me another son.'

א3

30:25 And it came to pass, when Rachel had borne Joseph, that Jacob said unto Laban: 'Send me away, that I may go unto mine own place, and to my country. 30:26 Give me my wives and my children for whom I have served thee, and let me go; for thou knowest my service wherewith I have served thee.' 30:27 And Laban said unto him: 'If now I have found favour in thine eyes--I have observed the signs, and the LORD hath blessed me for thy sake.' 30:28 And he said: 'Appoint me thy wages, and I will give it.' 30:29 And he said unto him: 'Thou knowest how I have served thee, and how thy cattle have fared with me. 30:30 For it was little which thou hadst before I came, and it hath increased abundantly; and the LORD hath blessed thee whithersoever I turned. And now when shall I provide for mine own house also?' 30:31 And he said: 'What shall I give thee?' And Jacob said: 'Thou shalt not give me aught; if thou wilt do this thing for me, I will again feed thy flock and keep it. 30:32 I will pass through all thy flock to-day, removing from thence every speckled and spotted one, and every dark one among the sheep, and the spotted and speckled among the goats; and of such shall be my hire. 30:33 So shall my righteousness witness against me hereafter, when thou shalt come to look over my hire that is before thee: every one that is not speckled and spotted among the goats, and dark among the sheep, that if found with me shall be counted stolen.' 30:34 And Laban said: 'Behold, would it might be according to thy word.' 30:35 And he removed that day the he-goats that were streaked and spotted, and all the she-goats that were speckled and spotted, every one that had white in it, and all the dark ones among the sheep, and gave them into the hand of his sons. 30:36 And he set three days' journey betwixt himself and Jacob. And Jacob fed the rest of Laban's flocks. 30:37 And Jacob took him rods of fresh poplar, and of the almond and of the plane-tree; and peeled white streaks in them, making the white appear which was in the rods. 30:38 And he set the rods which he had peeled over against the flocks in the gutters in the watering-troughs where the flocks came to drink; and they conceived when they came to drink. 30:39 And the flocks conceived at the sight of the rods, and the flocks brought forth streaked, speckled, and spotted. 30:40 And Jacob separated the lambs--he also set the faces of the flocks toward the streaked and all the dark in the flock of Laban--and put his own droves apart, and put them not unto Laban's flock. 30:41 And it came to pass, whensoever the stronger of the flock did conceive, that Jacob laid the rods before the eyes of the flock in the gutters, that they might conceive among the rods; 30:42 but when the flock were feeble, he put them not in; so the feebler were Laban's, and the stronger Jacob's.

ב3

30:43 And the man increased exceedingly, and had large flocks, and maid-servants and men-servants, and camels and asses. 31:1 And he heard the words of Laban's sons, saying: 'Jacob hath taken away all that was our father's; and of that which was our father's hath he gotten all this wealth.' 31:2 And Jacob beheld the countenance of Laban, and, behold, it was not toward him as beforetime. 31:3 And the LORD said unto Jacob: 'Return unto the land of thy fathers, and to thy kindred; and I will be with thee.' 31:4 And Jacob sent and called Rachel and Leah to the field unto his flock, 31:5 and said unto them: 'I see your father's countenance, that it is not toward me as beforetime; but the God of my father hath been with me. 31:6 And ye know that with all my power I have served your father. 31:7 And your father hath mocked me, and changed my wages ten times; but God suffered him not to hurt me. 31:8 If he said thus: The speckled shall be thy wages; then all the flock bore speckled; and if he said thus: The streaked shall be thy wages; then bore all the flock streaked. 31:9 Thus God hath taken away the cattle of your father, and given them to me. 31:10 And it came to pass at the time that the flock conceived, that I lifted up mine eyes, and saw in a dream, and, behold, the he-goats which leaped upon the flock were streaked, speckled, and grizzled. 31:11 And the angel of God said unto me in the dream: Jacob; and I said: Here am I. 31:12 And he said: Lift up now thine eyes, and see, all the he-goats which leap upon the flock are streaked, speckled, and grizzled; for I have seen all that Laban doeth unto thee. 31:13 I am the God of Beth-el, where thou didst anoint a pillar, where thou didst vow a vow unto Me. Now arise, get thee out from this land, and return unto the land of thy nativity.' 31:14 And Rachel and Leah answered and said unto him: 'Is there yet any portion or inheritance for us in our father's house? 31:15 Are we not accounted by him strangers? for he hath sold us, and hath also quite devoured our price. 31:16 For all the riches which God hath taken away from our father, that is ours and our children's. Now then, whatsoever God hath said unto thee, do.' 31:17 Then Jacob rose up, and set his sons and his wives upon the camels; 31:18 and he carried away all his cattle, and all his substance which he had gathered, the cattle of his getting, which he had gathered in Paddan-aram, to go to Isaac his father unto the land of Canaan.

4א

31:19 Now Laban was gone to shear his sheep. And Rachel stole the teraphim that were her father's. 31:20 And Jacob outwitted Laban the Aramean, in that he told him not that he fled. 31:21 So he fled with all that he had; and he rose up, and passed over the River, and set his face toward the mountain of Gilead. 31:22 And it was told Laban on the third day that Jacob was fled. 31:23 And he took his brethren with him, and pursued after him seven days' journey; and he overtook him in the mountain of Gilead. 31:24 And God came to Laban the Aramean in a dream of the night, and said unto him: 'Take heed to thyself that thou speak not to Jacob either good or bad.' 31:25 And Laban came up with Jacob. Now Jacob had pitched his tent in the mountain; and Laban with his brethren pitched in the mountain of Gilead. 31:26 And Laban said to Jacob: 'What hast thou done, that thou hast outwitted me, and carried away my daughters as though captives of the sword? 31:27 Wherefore didst thou flee secretly, and outwit me; and didst not tell me, that I might have sent thee away with mirth and with songs, with tabret and with harp; 31:28 and didst not suffer me to kiss my sons and my daughters? now hast thou done foolishly. 31:29 It is in the power of my hand to do you hurt; but the God of your father spoke unto me yesternight, saying: Take heed to thyself that thou speak not to Jacob either good or bad. 31:30 And now that thou art surely gone, because thou sore longest after thy father's house, wherefore hast thou stolen my gods?' 31:31 And Jacob answered and said to Laban: 'Because I was afraid; for I said: Lest thou shouldest take thy daughters from me by force. 31:32 With whomsoever thou findest thy gods, he shall not live; before our brethren discern thou what is thine with me, and take it to thee.'--For Jacob knew not that Rachel had stolen them.-- 31:33 And Laban went into Jacob's tent, and into Leah's tent, and into the tent of the two maid-servants; but he found them not. And he went out of Leah's tent, and entered into Rachel's tent. 31:34 Now Rachel had taken the teraphim, and put them in the saddle of the camel, and sat upon them. And Laban felt about all the tent, but found them not. 31:35 And she said to her father: 'Let not my lord be angry that I cannot rise up before thee; for the manner of women is upon me.' And he searched, but found not the teraphim.

4ב

31:36 And Jacob was wroth, and strove with Laban. And Jacob answered and said to Laban: 'What is my trespass? what is my sin, that thou hast hotly pursued after me? 31:37 Whereas thou hast felt about all my stuff, what hast thou found of all thy household stuff? Set it here before my brethren and thy brethren, that they may judge betwixt us two. 31:38 These twenty years have I been with thee; thy ewes and thy she-goats have not cast their young, and the rams of thy flocks have I not eaten. 31:39 That which was torn of beasts I brought not unto thee; I bore the loss of it; of my hand didst thou require it, whether stolen by day or stolen by night. 31:40 Thus I was: in the day the drought consumed me, and the frost by night; and my sleep fled from mine eyes. 31:41 These twenty years have I been in thy house: I served thee fourteen years for thy two daughters, and six years for thy flock; and thou hast changed my wages ten times. 31:42 Except the God of my father, the God of Abraham, and the Fear of Isaac, had been on my side, surely now hadst thou sent me away empty. God hath seen mine affliction and the labour of my hands, and gave judgment yesternight.' 31:43 And Laban answered and said unto Jacob: 'The daughters are my daughters, and the children are my children, and the flocks are my flocks, and all that thou seest is mine; and what can I do this day for these my daughters, or for their children whom they have borne? 31:44 And now come, let us make a covenant, I and thou; and let it be for a witness between me and thee.' 31:45 And Jacob took a stone, and set it up for a pillar. 31:46 And Jacob said unto his brethren: 'Gather stones'; and they took stones, and made a heap. And they did eat there by the heap. 31:47 And Laban called it Jegar-sahadutha; but Jacob called it Galeed. 31:48 And Laban said: 'This heap is witness between me and thee this day.' Therefore was the name of it called Galeed; 31:49 and Mizpah, for he said: 'The LORD watch between me and thee, when we are absent one from another. 31:50 If thou shalt afflict my daughters, and if thou shalt take wives beside my daughters, no man being with us; see, God is witness betwixt me and thee.' 31:51 And Laban said to Jacob: 'Behold this heap, and behold the pillar, which I have set up betwixt me and thee. 31:52 This heap be witness, and the pillar be witness, that I will not pass over this heap to thee, and that thou shalt not pass over this heap and this pillar unto me, for harm. 31:53 The God of Abraham, and the God of Nahor, the God of their father, judge betwixt us.' And Jacob swore by the Fear of his father Isaac. 31:54 And Jacob offered a sacrifice in the mountain, and called his brethren to eat bread; and they did eat bread, and tarried all night in the mountain. 32:1 And early in the morning Laban rose up, and kissed his sons and his daughters, and blessed them. And Laban departed, and returned unto his place.

5

32:2 And Jacob went on his way, and the angels of God met him. 32:3 And Jacob said when he saw them: 'This is God's camp.' And he called the name of that place Mahanaim. {P}

Genesis Unit XV (32:4-33:16)

1א

A 32:4 And Jacob sent messengers before him to Esau his brother unto the land of Seir, the field of Edom. 32:5 And he commanded them, saying: 'Thus shall ye say unto my lord Esau: Thus saith thy servant Jacob: I have sojourned with Laban, and stayed until now. 32:6 And I have oxen, and asses and flocks, and men-servants and maid-servants; and I have sent to tell my lord, that I may find favour in thy sight.' 32:7 And the messengers returned to Jacob, saying: 'We came to thy brother Esau, and moreover he cometh to meet thee, and four hundred men with him.' 32:8 Then Jacob was greatly afraid and was distressed. And he divided the people that was with him, and the flocks, and the herds, and the camels, into two camps. 32:9 And he said: 'If Esau come to the one camp, and smite it, then the camp which is left shall escape.'

B 32:10 And Jacob said: 'O God of my father Abraham, and God of my father Isaac, O LORD, who saidst unto me: Return unto thy country, and to thy kindred, and I will do thee good; 32:11 I am not worthy of all the mercies, and of all the truth, which Thou hast shown unto Thy servant; for with my staff I passed over this Jordan; and now I am become two camps. 32:12 Deliver me, I pray Thee, from the hand of my brother, from the hand of Esau; for I fear him, lest he come and smite me, the mother with the children. 32:13 And Thou saidst: I will surely do thee good, and make thy seed as the sand of the sea, which cannot be numbered for multitude.'

2א

32:25 And Jacob was left alone; and there wrestled a man with him until the breaking of the day. 32:26 And when he saw that he prevailed not against him, he touched the hollow of his thigh; and the hollow of Jacob's thigh was strained, as he wrestled with him. 32:27 And he said: 'Let me go, for the day breaketh.' And he said: 'I will not let thee go, except thou bless me.' 32:28 And he said unto him: 'What is thy name?' And he said: 'Jacob.' 32:29 And he said: 'Thy name shall be called no more Jacob, but Israel; for thou hast striven with God and with men, and hast prevailed.' 32:30 And Jacob asked him, and said: 'Tell me, I pray thee, thy name.' And he said: 'Wherefore is it that thou dost ask after my name?' And he blessed him there. 32:31 And Jacob called the name of the place Peniel: 'for I have seen God face to face, and my life is preserved.' 32:32 And the sun rose upon him as he passed over Peniel, and he limped upon his thigh. 32:33 Therefore the children of Israel eat not the sinew of the thigh-vein which is upon the hollow of the thigh, unto this day; because he touched the hollow of Jacob's thigh, even in the sinew of the thigh-vein.

1ב

A 32:14 And he lodged there that night; and took of that which he had with him a present for Esau his brother: 32:15 two hundred she-goats and twenty he-goats, two hundred ewes and twenty rams, 32:16 thirty milch camels and their colts, forty kine and ten bulls, twenty she-asses and ten foals. 32:17 And he delivered them into the hand of his servants, every drove by itself; and said unto his servants: 'Pass over before me, and put a space betwixt drove and drove.' 32:18 And he commanded the foremost, saying: 'When Esau my brother meeteth thee, and asketh thee, saying: Whose art thou? and whither goest thou? and whose are these before thee? 32:19 then thou shalt say: They are thy servant Jacob's; it is a present sent unto my lord, even unto Esau; and, behold, he also is behind us.' 32:20 And he commanded also the second, and the third, and all that followed the droves, saying: 'In this manner shall ye speak unto Esau, when ye find him; 32:21 and ye shall say: Moreover, behold, thy servant Jacob is behind us.' For he said: 'I will appease him with the present that goeth before me, and afterward I will see his face; peradventure he will accept me.'

B 32:22 So the present passed over before him; and he himself lodged that night in the camp. 32:23 And he rose up that night, and took his two wives, and his two handmaids, and his eleven children, and passed over the ford of the Jabbok. 32:24 And he took them, and sent them over the stream, and sent over that which he had.

2ב

33:1 And Jacob lifted up his eyes and looked, and, behold, Esau came, and with him four hundred men. And he divided the children unto Leah, and unto Rachel, and unto the two handmaids. 33:2 And he put the handmaids and their children foremost, and Leah and her children after, and Rachel and Joseph hindermost. 33:3 And he himself passed over before them, and bowed himself to the ground seven times, until he came near to his brother. 33:4 And Esau ran to meet him, and embraced him, and fell on his neck, and kissed him; and they wept. 33:5 And he lifted up his eyes, and saw the women and the children; and said: 'Who are these with thee?' And he said: 'The children whom God hath graciously given thy servant.' 33:6 Then the handmaids came near, they and their children, and they bowed down. 33:7 And Leah also and her children came near, and bowed down; and after came Joseph near and Rachel, and they bowed down. 33:8 And he said: 'What meanest thou by all this camp which I met?' And he said: 'To find favour in the sight of my lord.' 33:9 And Esau said: 'I have enough; my brother, let that which thou hast be thine.' 33:10 And Jacob said: 'Nay, I pray thee, if now I have found favour in thy sight, then receive my present at my hand; forasmuch as I have seen thy face, as one seeth the face of God, and thou wast pleased with me. 33:11 Take, I pray thee, my gift that is brought to thee; because God hath dealt graciously with me, and because I have enough.' And he urged him, and he took it. 33:12 And he said: 'Let us take our journey, and let us go, and I will go before thee.' 33:13 And he said unto him: 'My lord knoweth that the children are tender, and that the flocks and herds giving suck are a care to me; and if they overdrive them one day, all the flocks will die. 33:14 Let my lord, I pray thee, pass over before his servant; and I will journey on gently, according to the pace of the cattle that are before me and according to the pace of the children, until I come unto my lord unto Seir.' 33:15 And Esau said: 'Let me now leave with thee some of the folk that are with me.' And he said: 'What needeth it? let me find favour in the sight of my lord.' 33:16 So Esau returned that day on his way unto Seir.

Genesis Unit XVI (33:17-35:29)

א1

33:17 And Jacob journeyed to Succoth, and built him a house, and made booths for his cattle. Therefore the name of the place is called Succoth. {S}

א2

34:1 And Dinah the daughter of Leah, whom she had borne unto Jacob, went out to see the daughters of the land. 34:2 And Shechem the son of Hamor the Hivite, the prince of the land, saw her; and he took her, and lay with her, and humbled her. 34:3 And his soul did cleave unto Dinah the daughter of Jacob, and he loved the damsel, and spoke comfortingly unto the damsel. 34:4 And Shechem spoke unto his father Hamor, saying: 'Get me this damsel to wife.' 34:5 Now Jacob heard that he had defiled Dinah his daughter; and his sons were with his cattle in the field; and Jacob held his peace until they came. 34:6 And Hamor the father of Shechem went out unto Jacob to speak with him. 34:7 And the sons of Jacob came in from the field when they heard it; and the men were grieved, and they were very wroth, because he had wrought a vile deed in Israel in lying with Jacob's daughter; which thing ought not to be done. 34:8 And Hamor spoke with them, saying 'The soul of my son Shechem longeth for your daughter. I pray you give her unto him to wife. 34:9 And make ye marriages with us; give your daughters unto us, and take our daughters unto you. 34:10 And ye shall dwell with us; and the land shall be before you; dwell and trade ye therein, and get you possessions therein.' 34:11 And Shechem said unto her father and unto her brethren: 'Let me find favour in your eyes, and what ye shall say unto me I will give. 34:12 Ask me never so much dowry and gift, and I will give according as ye shall say unto me; but give me the damsel to wife.' 34:13 And the sons of Jacob answered Shechem and Hamor his father with guile, and spoke, because he had defiled Dinah their sister, 34:14 and said unto them: 'We cannot do this thing, to give our sister to one that is uncircumcised; for that were a reproach unto us. 34:15 Only on this condition will we consent unto you: if ye will be as we are, that every male of you be circumcised; 34:16 then will we give our daughters unto you, and we will take your daughters to us, and we will dwell with you, and we will become one people. 34:17 But if ye will not hearken unto us, to be circumcised; then will we take our daughter, and we will be gone.' 34:18 And their words pleased Hamor, and Shechem Hamor's son. 34:19 And the young man deferred not to do the thing, because he had delight in Jacob's daughter. And he was honoured above all the house of his father.

ב1

33:18 And Jacob came in peace to the city of Shechem, which is in the land of Canaan, when he came from Paddan-aram; and encamped before the city. 33:19 And he bought the parcel of ground, where he had spread his tent, at the hand of the children of Hamor, Shechem's father, for a hundred pieces of money. 33:20 And he erected there an altar, and called it El-elohe-Israel. {S}

ב2

34:20 And Hamor and Shechem his son came unto the gate of their city, and spoke with the men of their city, saying: 34:21 'These men are peaceable with us; therefore let them dwell in the land, and trade therein; for, behold, the land is large enough for them; let us take their daughters to us for wives, and let us give them our daughters. 34:22 Only on this condition will the men consent unto us to dwell with us, to become one people, if every male among us be circumcised, as they are circumcised. 34:23 Shall not their cattle and their substance and all their beasts be ours? only let us consent unto them, and they will dwell with us.' 34:24 And unto Hamor and unto Shechem his son hearkened all that went out of the gate of his city; and every male was circumcised, all that went out of the gate of his city. 34:25 And it came to pass on the third day, when they were in pain, that two of the sons of Jacob, Simeon and Levi, Dinah's brethren, took each man his sword, and came upon the city unawares, and slew all the males. 34:26 And they slew Hamor and Shechem his son with the edge of the sword, and took Dinah out of Shechem's house, and went forth. 34:27 The sons of Jacob came upon the slain, and spoiled the city, because they had defiled their sister. 34:28 They took their flocks and their herds and their asses, and that which was in the city and that which was in the field; 34:29 and all their wealth, and all their little ones and their wives, took they captive and spoiled, even all that was in the house. 34:30 And Jacob said to Simeon and Levi: 'Ye have troubled me, to make me odious unto the inhabitants of the land, even unto the Canaanites and the Perizzites; and, I being few in number, they will gather themselves together against me and smite me; and I shall be destroyed, I and my house.' 34:31 And they said: 'Should one deal with our sister as with a harlot?' {P}

אג

A 35:1 And God said unto Jacob: 'Arise, go up to Beth-el, and dwell there; and make there an altar unto God, who appeared unto thee when thou didst flee from the face of Esau thy brother.' 35:2 Then Jacob said unto his household, and to all that were with him: 'Put away the strange gods that are among you, and purify yourselves, and change your garments; 35:3 and let us arise, and go up to Beth-el; and I will make there an altar unto God, who answered me in the day of my distress, and was with me in the way which I went.' 35:4 And they gave unto Jacob all the foreign gods which were in their hand, and the rings which were in their ears; and Jacob hid them under the terebinth which was by Shechem.

B 35:5 And they journeyed; and a terror of God was upon the cities that were round about them, and they did not pursue after the sons of Jacob.

בג

A 35:6 So Jacob came to Luz, which is in the land of Canaan--the same is Beth-el--he and all the people that were with him. 35:7 And he built there an altar, and called the place El-beth-el, because there God was revealed unto him, when he fled from the face of his brother. 35:8 And Deborah Rebekah's nurse died, and she was buried below Beth-el under the oak; and the name of it was called Allon-bacuth. {P}

B 35:9 And God appeared unto Jacob again, when he came from Paddan-aram, and blessed him. 35:10 And God said unto him: 'Thy name is Jacob; thy name shall not be called any more Jacob, but Israel shall be thy name'; and He called his name Israel. 35:11 And God said unto him: 'I am God Almighty. Be fruitful and multiply; a nation and a company of nations shall be of thee, and kings shall come out of thy loins; 35:12 and the land which I gave unto Abraham and Isaac, to thee I will give it, and to thy seed after thee will I give the land.' 35:13 And God went up from him in the place where He spoke with him. 35:14 And Jacob set up a pillar in the place where He spoke with him, a pillar of stone, and he poured out a drink-offering thereon, and poured oil thereon. 35:15 And Jacob called the name of the place where God spoke with him, Beth-el.

אד

A 35:16 And they journeyed from Beth-el; and there was still some way to come to Ephrath; and Rachel travailed, and she had hard labour. 35:17 And it came to pass, when she was in hard labour, that the mid-wife said unto her: 'Fear not; for this also is a son for thee.' 35:18 And it came to pass, as her soul was in departing--for she died--that she called his name Ben-oni; but his father called him Benjamin. 35:19 And Rachel died, and was buried in the way to Ephrath--the same is Beth-lehem. 35:20 And Jacob set up a pillar upon her grave; the same is the pillar of Rachel's grave unto this day.

B 35:21 And Israel journeyed, and spread his tent beyond Migdal-eder. 35:22 And it came to pass, while Israel dwelt in that land, that Reuben went and lay with Bilhah his father's concubine; and Israel heard of it. {P}

בד

A Now the sons of Jacob were twelve: 35:23 the sons of Leah: Reuben, Jacob's first-born, and Simeon, and Levi, and Judah, and Issachar, and Zebulun; 35:24 the sons of Rachel: Joseph and Benjamin; 35:25 and the sons of Bilhah, Rachel's handmaid: Dan and Naphtali; 35:26 and the sons of Zilpah, Leah's handmaid: Gad and Asher. These are the sons of Jacob, that were born to him in Paddan-aram.

B 35:27 And Jacob came unto Isaac his father to Mamre, to Kiriatharba--the same is Hebron--where Abraham and Isaac sojourned. 35:28 And the days of Isaac were a hundred and fourscore years. 35:29 And Isaac expired, and died, and was gathered unto his people, old and full of days; and Esau and Jacob his sons buried him. {P}

Genesis Unit XVII (36:1-41:45)

א

A 36:1 Now these are the generations of Esau--the same is Edom. 36:2 Esau took his wives of the daughters of Canaan; Adah the daughter of Elon the Hittite, and Oholibamah the daughter of Anah, the daughter of Zibeon the Hivite, 36:3 and Basemath Ishmael's daughter, sister of Nebaioth. 36:4 And Adah bore to Esau Eliphaz; and Basemath bore Reuel; 36:5 and Oholibamah bore Jeush, and Jalam, and Korah. These are the sons of Esau, that were born unto him in the land of Canaan.

B 36:6 And Esau took his wives, and his sons, and his daughters, and all the souls of his house, and his cattle, and all his beasts, and all his possessions, which he had gathered in the land of Canaan; and went into a land away from his brother Jacob. 36:7 For their substance was too great for them to dwell together; and the land of their sojournings could not bear them because of their cattle. 36:8 And Esau dwelt in the mountain-land of Seir--Esau is Edom.

C 36:9 And these are the generations of Esau the father of a the Edomites in the mountain-land of Seir. 36:10 These are the names of Esau's sons: Eliphaz the son of Adah the wife of Esau, Reuel the son of Basemath the wife of Esau. 36:11 And the sons of Eliphaz were Teman, Omar, Zepho, and Gatam, and Kenaz. 36:12 And Timna was concubine to Eliphaz Esau's son; and she bore to Eliphaz Amalek. These are the sons of Adah Esau's wife. 36:13 And these are the sons of Reuel: Nahath, and Zerah, Shammah, and Mizzah. These were the sons of Basemath Esau's wife. 36:14 And these were the sons of Oholibamah the daughter of Anah, the daughter of Zibeon, Esau's wife; and she bore to Esau Jeush, and Jalam, and Korah.

D 36:15 These are the chiefs of the sons of Esau: the sons of Eliphaz the first-born of Esau: the chief of Teman, the chief of Omar, the chief of Zepho, the chief of Kenaz, 36:16 the chief of Korah, the chief of Gatam, the chief of Amalek. These are the chiefs that came of Eliphaz in the land of Edom. These are the sons of Adah. 36:17 And these are the sons of Reuel Esau's son: the chief of Nahath, the chief of Zerah, the chief of Shammah, the chief of Mizzah. These are the chiefs that came of Reuel in the land of Edom. These are the sons of Basemath Esau's wife. 36:18 And these are the sons of Oholibamah Esau's wife: the chief of Jeush, the chief of Jalam, the chief of Korah. These are the chiefs that came of Oholibamah the daughter of Anah, Esau's wife. 36:19 These are the sons of Esau, and these are their chiefs; the same is Edom. {S}

E 36:20 These are the sons of Seir the Horite, the inhabitants of the land: Lotan and Shobal and Zibeon and Anah, 36:21 and Dishon and Ezer and Dishan. These are the chiefs that came of the Horites, the children of Seir in the land of Edom. 36:22 And the children of Lotan were Hori and Hemam; and Lotan's sister was Timna. 36:23 And these are the children of Shobal: Alvan and Manahath and Ebal, Shepho and Onam. 36:24 And these are the children of Zibeon: Aiah and Anah--this is Anah who found the hot springs in the wilderness, as he fed the asses of Zibeon his father. 36:25 And these are the children of Anah: Dishon and Oholibamah the daughter of Anah. 36:26 And these are the children of Dishon: Hemdan and Eshban and Ithran and Cheran. 36:27 These are the children of Ezer: Bilhan and Zaavan and Akan. 36:28 These are the children of Dishan: Uz and Aran. 36:29 These are the chiefs that came of the Horites: the chief of Lotan, the chief of Shobal, the chief of Zibeon, the chief of Anah, 36:30 the chief of Dishon, the chief of Ezer, the chief of Dishan. These are the chiefs that came of the Horites, according to their chiefs in the land of Seir. {P}

ב

A 37:2 These are the generations of Jacob. Joseph, being seventeen years old, was feeding the flock with his brethren, being still a lad even with the sons of Bilhah, and with the sons of Zilpah, his father's wives; and Joseph brought evil report of them unto their father. 37:3 Now Israel loved Joseph more than all his children, because he was the son of his old age; and he made him a coat of many colours. 37:4 And when his brethren saw that their father loved him more than all his brethren, they hated him, and could not speak peaceably unto him.

B 37:5 And Joseph dreamed a dream, and he told it to his brethren; and they hated him yet the more. 37:6 And he said unto them: 'Hear, I pray you, this dream which I have dreamed: 37:7 for, behold, we were binding sheaves in the field, and, lo, my sheaf arose, and also stood upright; and, behold, your sheaves came round about, and bowed down to my sheaf.' 37:8 And his brethren said to him: 'Shalt thou indeed reign over us? or shalt thou indeed have dominion over us?' And they hated him yet the more for his dreams, and for his words.

C 37:9 And he dreamed yet another dream, and told it to his brethren, and said: 'Behold, I have dreamed yet a dream: and, behold, the sun and the moon and eleven stars bowed down to me.' 37:10 And he told it to his father, and to his brethren; and his father rebuked him, and said unto him: 'What is this dream that thou hast dreamed? Shall I and thy mother and thy brethren indeed come to bow down to thee to the earth?' 37:11 And his brethren envied him; but his father kept the saying in mind.

D 37:12 And his brethren went to feed their father's flock in Shechem. 37:13 And Israel said unto Joseph: 'Do not thy brethren feed the flock in Shechem? come, and I will send thee unto them.' And he said to him: 'Here am I.' 37:14 And he said to him: 'Go now, see whether it is well with thy brethren, and well with the flock; and bring me back word.' So he sent him out of the vale of Hebron, and he came to Shechem.

E 37:15 And a certain man found him, and, behold, he was wandering in the field. And the man asked him, saying: 'What seekest thou?' 37:16 And he said: 'I seek my brethren. Tell me, I pray thee, where they are feeding the flock.' 37:17 And the man said: 'They are departed hence; for I heard them say: Let us go to Dothan.' And Joseph went after his brethren, and found them in Dothan. 37:18 And they saw him afar off, and before he came near unto them, they conspired against him to slay him. 37:19 And they said one to another: 'Behold, this dreamer cometh. 37:20 Come now therefore, and let us slay him, and cast him into one of the pits, and we will say: An evil beast hath devoured him; and we shall see what will become of his dreams.' 37:21 And Reuben heard it, and delivered him out of their hand; and said: 'Let us not take his life.' 37:22 And Reuben said unto them: 'Shed no blood; cast him into this pit that is in the wilderness, but lay no hand upon him'--that he might deliver him out of their hand, to restore him to his father.

F36:31 And these are the kings that reigned in the land of Edom, before there reigned any king over the children of Israel. 36:32 And Bela the son of Beor reigned in Edom; and the name of his city was Dinhabah. 36:33 And Bela died, and Jobab the son of Zerah of Bozrah reigned in his stead. 36:34 And Jobab died, and Husham of the land of the Temanites reigned in his stead. 36:35 And Husham died, and Hadad the son of Bedad, who smote Midian in the field of Moab, reigned in his stead; and the name of his city was Avith. 36:36 And Hadad died, and Samlah of Masrekah reigned in his stead. 36:37 And Samlah died, and Shaul of Rehoboth by the River reigned in his stead. 36:38 And Shaul died, and Baal-hanan the son of Achbor reigned in his stead. 36:39 And Baal-hanan the son of Achbor died, and Hadar reigned in his stead; and the name of the city was Pau; and his wife's name was Mehetabel, the daughter of Matred, the daughter of Me-zahab.

G36:40 And these are the names of the chiefs that came of Esau, according to their families, after their places, by their names: the chief of Timna, the chief of Alvah, the chief of Jetheth; 36:41 the chief of Oholibamah, the chief of Elah, the chief of Pinon; 36:42 the chief of Kenaz, the chief of Teman, the chief of Mibzar; 36:43 the chief of Magdiel, the chief of Iram. These are the chiefs of Edom, according to their habitations in the land of their possession. This is Esau the father of the Edomites. {P}

H37:1 And Jacob dwelt in the land of his father's sojournings, in the land of Canaan.

F37:23 And it came to pass, when Joseph was come unto his brethren, that they stripped Joseph of his coat, the coat of many colours that was on him; 37:24 and they took him, and cast him into the pit--and the pit was empty, there was no water in it. 37:25 And they sat down to eat bread; and they lifted up their eyes and looked, and, behold, a caravan of Ishmaelites came from Gilead, with their camels bearing spicery and balm and ladanum, going to carry it down to Egypt. 37:26 And Judah said unto his brethren: 'What profit is it if we slay our brother and conceal his blood? 37:27 Come, and let us sell him to the Ishmaelites, and let not our hand be upon him; for he is our brother, our flesh.' And his brethren hearkened unto him.

G37:28 And there passed by Midianites, merchantmen; and they drew and lifted up Joseph out of the pit, and sold Joseph to the Ishmaelites for twenty shekels of silver. And they brought Joseph into Egypt. 37:29 And Reuben returned unto the pit; and, behold, Joseph was not in the pit; and he rent his clothes. 37:30 And he returned unto his brethren, and said: 'The child is not; and as for me, whither shall I go?' 37:31 And they took Joseph's coat, and killed a he-goat, and dipped the coat in the blood; 37:32 and they sent the coat of many colours, and they brought it to their father; and said: 'This have we found. Know now whether it is thy son's coat or not.' 37:33 And he knew it, and said: 'It is my son's coat; an evil beast hath devoured him; Joseph is without doubt torn in pieces.' 37:34 And Jacob rent his garments, and put sackcloth upon his loins, and mourned for his son many days. 37:35 And all his sons and all his daughters rose up to comfort him; but he refused to be comforted; and he said: 'Nay, but I will go down to the grave to my son mourning.' And his father wept for him

H. 37:36 And the Midianites sold him into Egypt unto Potiphar, an officer of Pharaoh's, the captain of the guard. {P}

2א

A 38:1 And it came to pass at that time, that Judah went down from his brethren, and turned in to a certain Adullamite, whose name was Hirah. 38:2 And Judah saw there a daughter of a certain Canaanite whose name was Shua; and he took her, and went in unto her. 38:3 And she conceived, and bore a son; and he called his name Er. 38:4 And she conceived again, and bore a son; and she called his name Onan. 38:5 And she yet again bore a son, and called his name Shelah; and he was at Chezib, when she bore him. 38:6 And Judah took a wife for Er his first-born, and her name was Tamar. 38:7 And Er, Judah's first-born, was wicked in the sight of the LORD; and the LORD slew him. 38:8 And Judah said unto Onan: 'Go in unto thy brother's wife, and perform the duty of a husband's brother unto her, and raise up seed to thy brother.' 38:9 And Onan knew that the seed would not be his; and it came to pass when he went in unto his brother's wife, that he spilled it on the ground, lest he should give seed to his brother. 38:10 And the thing which he did was evil in the sight of the LORD; and He slew him also. 38:11 Then said Judah to Tamar his daughter-in-law: 'Remain a widow in thy father's house, till Shelah my son be grown up'; for he said: 'Lest he also die, like his brethren.' And Tamar went and dwelt in her father's house.

B 38:12 And in process of time Shua's daughter, the wife of Judah, died; and Judah was comforted, and went up unto his sheep-shearers to Timnah, he and his friend Hirah the Adullamite. 38:13 And it was told Tamar, saying: 'Behold, thy father-in-law goeth up to Timnah to shear his sheep.' 38:14 And she put off from her the garments of her widowhood, and covered herself with her veil, and wrapped herself, and sat in the entrance of Enaim, which is by the way to Timnah; for she saw that Shelah was grown up, and she was not given unto him to wife. 38:15 When Judah saw her, he thought her to be a harlot; for she had covered her face. 38:16 And he turned unto her by the way, and said: 'Come, I pray thee, let me come in unto thee'; for he knew not that she was his daughter-in-law. And she said: 'What wilt thou give me, that thou mayest come in unto me?' 38:17 And he said: 'I will send thee a kid of the goats from the flock.' And she said: 'Wilt thou give me a pledge, till thou send it?' 38:18 And he said: 'What pledge shall I give thee?' And she said: 'Thy signet and thy cord, and thy staff that is in thy hand.' And he gave them to her, and came in unto her, and she conceived by him. 38:19 And she arose, and went away, and put off her veil from her, and put on the garments of her widowhood. 38:20 And Judah sent the kid of the goats by the hand of his friend the Adullamite, to receive the pledge from the woman's hand; but he found her not. 38:21 Then he asked the men of her place, saying: 'Where is the harlot, that was at Enaim by the wayside?' And they said: 'There hath been no harlot here.' 38:22 And he returned to Judah, and said: 'I have not found her; and also the men of the place said: There hath been no harlot here.' 38:23 And Judah said: 'Let her take it, lest we be put to shame; behold, I sent this kid, and thou hast not found her.' 38:24 And it came to pass about three months after, that it was told Judah, saying: 'Tamar thy daughter-in-law hath played the harlot; and moreover, behold, she is with child by harlotry.' And Judah said: 'Bring her forth, and let her be burnt.' 38:25 When she was brought forth, she sent to her father-in-law, saying: 'By the man, whose these are, am I with child'; and she said: 'Discern, I pray thee, whose are these, the signet, and the cords, and the staff.' 38:26 And Judah acknowledged them, and said: 'She is more righteous than I; forasmuch as I gave her not to Shelah my son.' And he knew her again no more.

C 38:27 And it came to pass in the time of her travail, that, behold, twins were in her womb. 38:28 And it came to pass, when she travailed, that one put out a hand; and the midwife took and bound upon his hand a scarlet thread, saying: 'This came out first.' 38:29 And it came to pass, as he drew back his hand, that, behold his brother came out; and she said: 'Wherefore hast thou made a breach for thyself?' Therefore his name was called Perez. 38:30 And afterward came out his brother, that had the scarlet thread upon his hand; and his name was called Zerah. {S}

2ב

A 39:1 And Joseph was brought down to Egypt; and Potiphar, an officer of Pharaoh's, the captain of the guard, an Egyptian, bought him of the hand of the Ishmaelites, that had brought him down thither. 39:2 And the LORD was with Joseph, and he was a prosperous man; and he was in the house of his master the Egyptian. 39:3 And his master saw that the LORD was with him, and that the LORD made all that he did to prosper in his hand. 39:4 And Joseph found favour in his sight, and he ministered unto him. And he appointed him overseer over his house, and all that he had he put into his hand. 39:5 And it came to pass from the time that he appointed him overseer in his house, and over all that he had, that the LORD blessed the Egyptian's house for Joseph's sake; and the blessing of the LORD was upon all that he had, in the house and in the field. 39:6 And he left all that he had in Joseph's hand; and, having him, he knew not aught save the bread which he did eat. And Joseph was of beautiful form, and fair to look upon.

B 39:7 And it came to pass after these things, that his master's wife cast her eyes upon Joseph; and she said: 'Lie with me.' 39:8 But he refused, and said unto his master's wife: 'Behold, my master, having me, knoweth not what is in the house, and he hath put all that he hath into my hand; 39:9 he is not greater in this house than I; neither hath he kept back any thing from me but thee, because thou art his wife. How then can I do this great wickedness, and sin against God?' 39:10 And it came to pass, as she spoke to Joseph day by day, that he hearkened not unto her, to lie by her, or to be with her. 39:11 And it came to pass on a certain day, when he went into the house to do his work, and there was none of the men of the house there within, 39:12 that she caught him by his garment, saying: 'Lie with me.' And he left his garment in her hand, and fled, and got him out. 39:13 And it came to pass, when she saw that he had left his garment in her hand, and was fled forth, 39:14 that she called unto the men of her house, and spoke unto them, saying: 'See, he hath brought in a Hebrew unto us to mock us; he came in unto me to lie with me, and I cried with a loud voice. 39:15 And it came to pass, when he heard that I lifted up my voice and cried, that he left his garment by me, and fled, and got him out.' 39:16 And she laid up his garment by her, until his master came home. 39:17 And she spoke unto him according to these words, saying: 'The Hebrew servant, whom thou hast brought unto us, came in unto me to mock me. 39:18 And it came to pass, as I lifted up my voice and cried, that he left his garment by me, and fled out.' 39:19 And it came to pass, when his master heard the words of his wife, which she spoke unto him, saying: 'After this manner did thy servant to me'; that his wrath was kindled. 39:20 And Joseph's master took him, and put him into the prison, the place where the king's prisoners were bound; and he was there in the prison.

C 39:21 But the LORD was with Joseph, and showed kindness unto him, and gave him favour in the sight of the keeper of the prison. 39:22 And the keeper of the prison committed to Joseph's hand all the prisoners that were in the prison; and whatsoever they did there, he was the doer of it. 39:23 The keeper of the prison looked not to any thing that was under his hand, because the LORD was with him; and that which he did, the LORD made it to prosper. {P}

3א

A 40:1 And it came to pass after these things, that the butler of the king of Egypt and his baker offended their lord the king of Egypt. 40:2 And Pharaoh was wroth against his two officers, against the chief of the butlers, and against the chief of the bakers. 40:3 And he put them in ward in the house of the captain of the guard, into the prison, the place where Joseph was bound. 40:4 And the captain of the guard charged Joseph to be with them, and he ministered unto them; and they continued a season in ward. 40:5 And they dreamed a dream both of them, each man his dream, in one night, each man according to the interpretation of his dream, the butler and the baker of the king of Egypt, who were bound in the prison. 40:6 And Joseph came in unto them in the morning, and saw them, and, behold, they were sad. 40:7 And he asked Pharaoh's officers that were with him in the ward of his master's house, saying: 'Wherefore look ye so sad to-day?' 40:8 And they said unto him: 'We have dreamed a dream, and there is none that can interpret it.' And Joseph said unto them: 'Do not interpretations belong to God? tell it me, I pray you.' 40:9 And the chief butler told his dream to Joseph, and said to him: 'In my dream, behold, a vine was before me; 40:10 and in the vine were three branches; and as it was budding, its blossoms shot forth, and the clusters thereof brought forth ripe grapes, 40:11 and Pharaoh's cup was in my hand; and I took the grapes, and pressed them into Pharaoh's cup, and I gave the cup into Pharaoh's hand.' 40:12 And Joseph said unto him: 'This is the interpretation of it: the three branches are three days; 40:13 within yet three days shall Pharaoh lift up thy head, and restore thee unto thine office; and thou shalt give Pharaoh's cup into his hand, after the former manner when thou wast his butler. 40:14 But have me in thy remembrance when it shall be well with thee, and show kindness, I pray thee, unto me, and make mention of me unto Pharaoh, and bring me out of this house. 40:15 For indeed I was stolen away out of the land of the Hebrews; and here also have I done nothing that they should put me into the dungeon.' 40:16 When the chief baker saw that the interpretation was good, he said unto Joseph: 'I also saw in my dream, and, behold, three baskets of white bread were on my head; 40:17 and in the uppermost basket there was of all manner of baked food for Pharaoh; and the birds did eat them out of the basket upon my head.' 40:18 And Joseph answered and said: 'This is the interpretation thereof: the three baskets are three days; 40:19 within yet three days shall Pharaoh lift up thy head from off thee, and shall hang thee on a tree; and the birds shall eat thy flesh from off thee.' 40:20 And it came to pass the third day, which was Pharaoh's birthday, that he made a feast unto all his servants; and he lifted up the head of the chief butler and the head of the chief baker among his servants. 40:21 And he restored the chief butler back unto his butlership; and he gave the cup into Pharaoh's hand. 40:22 But he hanged the chief baker, as Joseph had interpreted to them. 40:23 Yet did not the chief butler remember Joseph, but forgot him. {P}

B 41:1 And it came to pass at the end of two full years, that Pharaoh dreamed: and, behold, he stood by the river. 41:2 And, behold, there came up out of the river seven kine, well-favoured and fat-fleshed; and they fed in the reed-grass. 41:3 And, behold, seven other kine came up after them out of the river, ill favoured and lean-fleshed; and stood by the other kine upon the brink of the river. 41:4 And the ill-favoured and lean-fleshed kine did eat up the seven well-favoured and fat kine. So Pharaoh awoke. 41:5 And he slept and dreamed a second time: and, behold, seven ears of corn came up upon one stalk, rank and good. 41:6 And, behold, seven ears, thin and blasted with the east wind, sprung up after them. 41:7 And the thin ears swallowed up the seven rank and full ears. And Pharaoh awoke, and, behold, it was a dream. 41:8 And it came to pass in the morning that his spirit was troubled; and he sent and called for all the magicians of Egypt, and all the wise men thereof; and Pharaoh told them his dream; but there was none that could interpret them unto Pharaoh. 41:9 Then spoke the chief butler unto Pharaoh, saying: 'I make mention of my faults this day: 41:10 Pharaoh was wroth with his servants, and put me in the ward of the house of the captain of the guard, me and the chief baker. 41:11 And we dreamed a dream in one night, I and he; we dreamed each man according to the interpretation of his dream. 41:12 And there was with us there a young man, a Hebrew, servant to the captain of the guard; and we told him, and he interpreted to us our dreams; to each man according to his dream he did interpret. 41:13 And it came to pass, as he interpreted to us, so it was: I was restored unto mine office, and he was hanged.'

3ב

A 41:14 Then Pharaoh sent and called Joseph, and they brought him hastily out of the dungeon. And he shaved himself, and changed his raiment, and came in unto Pharaoh. 41:15 And Pharaoh said unto Joseph: 'I have dreamed a dream, and there is none that can interpret it; and I have heard say of thee, that when thou hearest a dream thou canst interpret it.' 41:16 And Joseph answered Pharaoh, saying: 'It is not in me; God will give Pharaoh an answer of peace.' 41:17 And Pharaoh spoke unto Joseph: 'In my dream, behold, I stood upon the brink of the river. 41:18 And, behold, there came up out of the river seven kine, fat-fleshed and well-favoured; and they fed in the reed-grass. 41:19 And, behold, seven other kine came up after them, poor and very ill-favoured and lean-fleshed, such as I never saw in all the land of Egypt for badness. 41:20 And the lean and ill-favoured kine did eat up the first seven fat kine. 41:21 And when they had eaten them up, it could not be known that they had eaten them; but they were still ill-favoured as at the beginning. So I awoke. 41:22 And I saw in my dream, and, behold, seven ears came up upon one stalk, full and good. 41:23 And, behold, seven ears, withered, thin, and blasted with the east wind, sprung up after them. 41:24 And the thin ears swallowed up the seven good ears. And I told it unto the magicians; but there was none that could declare it to me.' 41:25 And Joseph said unto Pharaoh: 'The dream of Pharaoh is one; what God is about to do He hath declared unto Pharaoh. 41:26 The seven good kine are seven years; and the seven good ears are seven years: the dream is one. 41:27 And the seven lean and ill-favoured kine that came up after them are seven years, and also the seven empty ears blasted with the east wind; they shall be seven years of famine. 41:28 That is the thing which I spoke unto Pharaoh: what God is about to do He hath shown unto Pharaoh. 41:29 Behold, there come seven years of great plenty throughout all the land of Egypt. 41:30 And there shall arise after them seven years of famine; and all the plenty shall be forgotten in the land of Egypt; and the famine shall consume the land; 41:31 and the plenty shall not be known in the land by reason of that famine which followeth; for it shall be very grievous. 41:32 And for that the dream was doubled unto Pharaoh twice, it is because the thing is established by God, and God will shortly bring it to pass. 41:33 Now therefore let Pharaoh look out a man discreet and wise, and set him over the land of Egypt. 41:34 Let Pharaoh do this, and let him appoint overseers over the land, and take up the fifth part of the land of Egypt in the seven years of plenty. 41:35 And let them gather all the food of these good years that come, and lay up corn under the hand of Pharaoh for food in the cities, and let them keep it. 41:36 And the food shall be for a store to the land against the seven years of famine, which shall be in the land of Egypt; that the land perish not through the famine.' 41:37 And the thing was good in the eyes of Pharaoh, and in the eyes of all his servants.

B 41:38 And Pharaoh said unto his servants: 'Can we find such a one as this, a man in whom the spirit of God is?' 41:39 And Pharaoh said unto Joseph: 'Forasmuch as God hath shown thee all this, there is none so discreet and wise as thou. 41:40 Thou shalt be over my house, and according unto thy word shall all my people be ruled; only in the throne will I be greater than thou.' 41:41 And Pharaoh said unto Joseph: 'See, I have set thee over all the land of Egypt.' 41:42 And Pharaoh took off his signet ring from his hand, and put it upon Joseph's hand, and arrayed him in vestures of fine linen, and put a gold chain about his neck. 41:43 And he made him to ride in the second chariot which he had; and they cried before him: 'Abrech'; and he set him over all the land of Egypt. 41:44 And Pharaoh said unto Joseph: 'I am Pharaoh, and without thee shall no man lift up his hand or his foot in all the land of Egypt.' 41:45 And Pharaoh called Joseph's name Zaphenath-paneah; and he gave him to wife Asenath the daughter of Poti-phera priest of On. And Joseph went out over the land of Egypt.--

Genesis Unit XVIII (41:46-47:26)

א1

41:46 And Joseph was thirty years old when he stood before Pharaoh king of Egypt.--And Joseph went out from the presence of Pharaoh, and went throughout all the land of Egypt. 41:47 And in the seven years of plenty the earth brought forth in heaps. 41:48 And he gathered up all the food of the seven years which were in the land of Egypt, and laid up the food in the cities; the food of the field, which was round about every city, laid he up in the same. 41:49 And Joseph laid up corn as the sand of the sea, very much, until they left off numbering; for it was without number.

ב1

41:50 And unto Joseph were born two sons before the year of famine came, whom Asenath the daughter of Poti-phera priest of On bore unto him. 41:51 And Joseph called the name of the first-born Manasseh: 'for God hath made me forget all my toil, and all my father's house.' 41:52 And the name of the second called he Ephraim: 'for God hath made me fruitful in the land of my affliction.'

ג1

41:53 And the seven years of plenty, that was in the land of Egypt, came to an end. 41:54 And the seven years of famine began to come, according as Joseph had said; and there was famine in all lands; but in all the land of Egypt there was bread. 41:55 And when all the land of Egypt was famished, the people cried to Pharaoh for bread; and Pharaoh said unto all the Egyptians: 'Go unto Joseph; what he saith to you, do.' 41:56 And the famine was over all the face of the earth; and Joseph opened all the storehouses, and sold unto the Egyptians; and the famine was sore in the land of Egypt.

א2

41:57 And all countries came into Egypt to Joseph to buy corn; because the famine was sore in all the earth. 42:1 Now Jacob saw that there was corn in Egypt, and Jacob said unto his sons: 'Why do ye look one upon another?' 42:2 And he said: 'Behold, I have heard that there is corn in Egypt. Get you down thither, and buy for us from thence; that we may live, and not die.' 42:3 And Joseph's ten brethren went down to buy corn from Egypt. 42:4 But Benjamin, Joseph's brother, Jacob sent not with his brethren; for he said: 'Lest peradventure harm befall him.' 42:5 And the sons of Israel came to buy among those that came; for the famine was in the land of Canaan. 42:6 And Joseph was the governor over the land; he it was that sold to all the people of the land. And Joseph's brethren came, and bowed down to him with their faces to the earth. 42:7 And Joseph saw his brethren, and he knew them, but made himself strange unto them, and spoke roughly with them; and he said unto them: 'Whence come ye?' And they said: 'From the land of Canaan to buy food.' 42:8 And Joseph knew his brethren, but they knew him not. 42:9 And Joseph remembered the dreams which he dreamed of them, and said unto them: 'Ye are spies; to see the nakedness of the land ye are come.' 42:10 And they said unto him: 'Nay, my lord, but to buy food are thy servants come. 42:11 We are all one man's sons; we are upright men, thy servants are no spies.' 42:12 And he said unto them: 'Nay, but to see the nakedness of the land ye are come.' 42:13 And they said: 'We thy servants are twelve brethren, the sons of one man in the land of Canaan; and, behold, the youngest is this day with our father, and one is not.' 42:14 And Joseph said unto them: 'That is it that I spoke unto you, saying: Ye are spies. 42:15 Hereby ye shall be proved, as Pharaoh liveth, ye shall not go forth hence, except your youngest brother come hither. 42:16 Send one of you, and let him fetch your brother, and ye shall be bound, that your words may be proved, whether there be truth in you; or else, as Pharaoh liveth, surely ye are spies.' 42:17 And he put them all together into ward three days.

ב2

42:18 And Joseph said unto them the third day. 'This do, and live; for I fear God: 42:19 if ye be upright men, let one of your brethren be bound in your prison-house; but go ye, carry corn for the famine of your houses; 42:20 and bring your youngest brother unto me; so shall your words be verified, and ye shall not die.' And they did so. 42:21 And they said one to another: 'We are verily guilty concerning our brother, in that we saw the distress of his soul, when he besought us, and we would not hear; therefore is this distress come upon us.' 42:22 And Reuben answered them, saying: 'Spoke I not unto you, saying: Do not sin against the child; and ye would not hear? therefore also, behold, his blood is required.' 42:23 And they knew not that Joseph understood them; for the interpreter was between them. 42:24 And he turned himself about from them, and wept; and he returned to them, and spoke to them, and took Simeon from among them, and bound him before their eyes.

ג2

42:25 Then Joseph commanded to fill their vessels with corn, and to restore every man's money into his sack, and to give them provision for the way; and thus was it done unto them. 42:26 And they laded their asses with their corn, and departed thence. 42:27 And as one of them opened his sack to give his ass provender in the lodging-place, he espied his money; and, behold, it was in the mouth of his sack. 42:28 And he said unto his brethren: 'My money is restored; and, lo, it is even in my sack.' And their heart failed them, and they turned trembling one to another, saying: 'What is this that God hath done unto us?'

3א

A 42:29 And they came unto Jacob their father unto the land of Canaan, and told him all that had befallen them, saying: 42:30 'The man, the lord of the land, spoke roughly with us, and took us for spies of the country. 42:31 And we said unto him: We are upright men; we are no spies. 42:32 We are twelve brethren, sons of our father; one is not, and the youngest is this day with our father in the land of Canaan. 42:33 And the man, the lord of the land, said unto us: Hereby shall I know that ye are upright men: leave one of your brethren with me, and take corn for the famine of your houses, and go your way. 42:34 And bring your youngest brother unto me; then shall I know that ye are no spies, but that ye are upright men; so will I deliver you your brother, and ye shall traffic in the land.' 42:35 And it came to pass as they emptied their sacks, that, behold, every man's bundle of money was in his sack; and when they and their father saw their bundles of money, they were afraid. 42:36 And Jacob their father said unto them: 'Me have ye bereaved of my children: Joseph is not, and Simeon is not, and ye will take Benjamin away; upon me are all these things come.' 42:37 And Reuben spoke unto his father, saying: 'Thou shalt slay my two sons, if I bring him not to thee; deliver him into my hand, and I will bring him back to thee.' 42:38 And he said: 'My son shall not go down with you; for his brother is dead, and he only is left; if harm befall him by the way in which ye go, then will ye bring down my gray hairs with sorrow to the grave.'

B 43:1 And the famine was sore in the land. 43:2 And it came to pass, when they had eaten up the corn which they had brought out of Egypt, that their father said unto them: 'Go again, buy us a little food.' 43:3 And Judah spoke unto him, saying: 'The man did earnestly forewarn us, saying: Ye shall not see my face, except your brother be with you. 43:4 If thou wilt send our brother with us, we will go down and buy thee food; 43:5 but if thou wilt not send him, we will not go down, for the man said unto us: Ye shall not see my face, except your brother be with you.' 43:6 And Israel said: 'Wherefore dealt ye so ill with me, as to tell the man whether ye had yet a brother?' 43:7 And they said: 'The man asked straitly concerning ourselves, and concerning our kindred, saying: Is your father yet alive? have ye another brother? and we told him according to the tenor of these words; could we in any wise know that he would say: Bring your brother down?' 43:8 And Judah said unto Israel his father: 'Send the lad with me, and we will arise and go, that we may live, and not die, both we, and thou, and also our little ones. 43:9 I will be surety for him; of my hand shalt thou require him; if I bring him not unto thee, and set him before thee, then let me bear the blame for ever. 43:10 For except we had lingered, surely we had now returned a second time.' 43:11 And their father Israel said unto them: 'If it be so now, do this: take of the choice fruits of the land in your vessels, and carry down the man a present, a little balm, and a little honey, spicery and ladanum, nuts, and almonds; 43:12 and take double money in your hand; and the money that was returned in the mouth of your sacks carry back in your hand; peradventure it was an oversight; 43:13 take also your brother, and arise, go again unto the man; 43:14 and God Almighty give you mercy before the man, that he may release unto you your other brother and Benjamin. And as for me, if I be bereaved of my children, I am bereaved.' 43:15 And the men took that present, and they took double money in their hand, and Benjamin; and rose up, and went down to Egypt, and stood before Joseph.

3ב

A 43:16 And when Joseph saw Benjamin with them, he said to the steward of his house: 'Bring the men into the house, and kill the beasts, and prepare the meat; for the men shall dine with me at noon.' 43:17 And the man did as Joseph bade; and the man brought the men into Joseph's house. 43:18 And the men were afraid, because they were brought into Joseph's house; and they said: 'Because of the money that was returned in our sacks at the first time are we brought in; that he may seek occasion against us, and fall upon us, and take us for bondmen, and our asses.' 43:19 And they came near to the steward of Joseph's house, and they spoke unto him at the door of the house, 43:20 and said: 'Oh my lord, we came indeed down at the first time to buy food. 43:21 And it came to pass, when we came to the lodging-place, that we opened our sacks, and, behold, every man's money was in the mouth of his sack, our money in full weight; and we have brought it back in our hand. 43:22 And other money have we brought down in our hand to buy food. We know not who put our money in our sacks.' 43:23 And he said: 'Peace be to you, fear not; your God, and the God of your father, hath given you treasure in your sacks; I had your money.' And he brought Simeon out unto them. 43:24 And the man brought the men into Joseph's house, and gave them water, and they washed their feet; and he gave their asses provender. 43:25 And they made ready the present against Joseph's coming at noon; for they heard that they should eat bread there.

B 43:26 And when Joseph came home, they brought him the present which was in their hand into the house, and bowed down to him to the earth. 43:27 And he asked them of their welfare, and said: 'Is your father well, the old man of whom ye spoke? Is he yet alive?' 43:28 And they said: 'Thy servant our father is well, he is yet alive.' And they bowed the head, and made obeisance. 43:29 And he lifted up his eyes, and saw Benjamin his brother, his mother's son, and said: 'Is this your youngest brother of whom ye spoke unto me?' And he said: 'God be gracious unto thee, my son.' 43:30 And Joseph made haste; for his heart yearned toward his brother; and he sought where to weep; and he entered into his chamber, and wept there. 43:31 And he washed his face, and came out; and he refrained himself, and said: 'Set on bread.' 43:32 And they set on for him by himself, and for them by themselves, and for the Egyptians, that did eat with him, by themselves; because the Egyptians might not eat bread with the Hebrews; for that is an abomination unto the Egyptians. 43:33 And they sat before him, the firstborn according to his birthright, and the youngest according to his youth; and the men marvelled one with another. 43:34 And portions were taken unto them from before him; but Benjamin's portion was five times so much as any of theirs. And they drank, and were merry with him.

3ג

A 44:1 And he commanded the steward of his house, saying: 'Fill the men's sacks with food, as much as they can carry, and put every man's money in his sack's mouth. 44:2 And put my goblet, the silver goblet, in the sack's mouth of the youngest, and his corn money.' And he did according to the word that Joseph had spoken. 44:3 As soon as the morning was light, the men were sent away, they and their asses. 44:4 And when they were gone out of the city, and were not yet far off, Joseph said unto his steward: 'Up, follow after the men; and when thou dost overtake them, say unto them: Wherefore have ye rewarded evil for good? 44:5 Is not this it in which my lord drinketh, and whereby he indeed divineth? ye have done evil in so doing.' 44:6 And he overtook them, and he spoke unto them these words. 44:7 And they said unto him: 'Wherefore speaketh my lord such words as these? Far be it from thy servants that they should do such a thing. 44:8 Behold, the money, which we found in our sacks' mouths, we brought back unto thee out of the land of Canaan; how then should we steal out of thy lord's house silver or gold? 44:9 With whomsoever of thy servants it be found, let him die, and we also will be my lord's bondmen.' 44:10 And he said: 'Now also let it be according unto your words: he with whom it is found shall be my bondman; and ye shall be blameless.' 44:11 Then they hastened, and took down every man his sack to the ground, and opened every man his sack. 44:12 And he searched, beginning at the eldest, and leaving off at the youngest; and the goblet was found in Benjamin's sack. 44:13 And they rent their clothes, and laded every man his ass, and returned to the city.

B 44:14 And Judah and his brethren came to Joseph's house, and he was yet there; and they fell before him on the ground. 44:15 And Joseph said unto them: 'What deed is this that ye have done? know ye not that such a man as I will indeed divine?' 44:16 And Judah said: 'What shall we say unto my lord? what shall we speak? or how shall we clear ourselves? God hath found out the iniquity of thy servants; behold, we are my lord's bondmen, both we, and he also in whose hand the cup is found.' 44:17 And he said: 'Far be it from me that I should do so; the man in whose hand the goblet is found, he shall be my bondman; but as for you, get you up in peace unto your father.' {S}

מד

44:18 Then Judah came near unto him, and said: 'Oh my lord, let thy servant, I pray thee, speak a word in my lord's ears, and let not thine anger burn against thy servant; for thou art even as Pharaoh. 44:19 My lord asked his servants, saying: Have ye a father, or a brother? 44:20 And we said unto my lord: We have a father, an old man, and a child of his old age, a little one; and his brother is dead, and he alone is left of his mother, and his father loveth him. 44:21 And thou saidst unto thy servants: Bring him down unto me, that I may set mine eyes upon him. 44:22 And we said unto my lord: The lad cannot leave his father; for if he should leave his father, his father would die. 44:23 And thou saidst unto thy servants: Except your youngest brother come down with you, ye shall see my face no more. 44:24 And it came to pass when we came up unto thy servant my father, we told him the words of my lord. 44:25 And our father said: Go again, buy us a little food. 44:26 And we said: We cannot go down; if our youngest brother be with us, then will we go down; for we may not see the man's face, except our youngest brother be with us. 44:27 And thy servant my father said unto us: Ye know that my wife bore me two sons; 44:28 and the one went out from me, and I said: Surely he is torn in pieces; and I have not seen him since; 44:29 and if ye take this one also from me, and harm befall him, ye will bring down my gray hairs with sorrow to the grave. 44:30 Now therefore when I come to thy servant my father, and the lad is not with us; seeing that his soul is bound up with the lad's soul; 44:31 it will come to pass, when he seeth that the lad is not with us, that he will die; and thy servants will bring down the gray hairs of thy servant our father with sorrow to the grave. 44:32 For thy servant became surety for the lad unto my father, saying: If I bring him not unto thee, then shall I bear the blame to my father for ever. 44:33 Now therefore, let thy servant, I pray thee, abide instead of the lad a bondman to my lord; and let the lad go up with his brethren. 44:34 For how shall I go up to my father, if the lad be not with me? lest I look upon the evil that shall come on my father.'

מה

45:1 Then Joseph could not refrain himself before all them that stood by him; and he cried: 'Cause every man to go out from me.' And there stood no man with him, while Joseph made himself known unto his brethren. 45:2 And he wept aloud; and the Egyptians heard, and the house of Pharaoh heard. 45:3 And Joseph said unto his brethren: 'I am Joseph; doth my father yet live?' And his brethren could not answer him; for they were affrighted at his presence. 45:4 And Joseph said unto his brethren: 'Come near to me, I pray you.' And they came near. And he said: 'I am Joseph your brother, whom ye sold into Egypt. 45:5 And now be not grieved, nor angry with yourselves, that ye sold me hither; for God did send me before you to preserve life. 45:6 For these two years hath the famine been in the land; and there are yet five years, in which there shall be neither plowing nor harvest. 45:7 And God sent me before you to give you a remnant on the earth, and to save you alive for a great deliverance. 45:8 So now it was not you that sent me hither, but God; and He hath made me a father to Pharaoh, and lord of all his house, and ruler over all the land of Egypt. 45:9 Hasten ye, and go up to my father, and say unto him: Thus saith thy son Joseph: God hath made me lord of all Egypt; come down unto me, tarry not. 45:10 And thou shalt dwell in the land of Goshen, and thou shalt be near unto me, thou, and thy children, and thy children's children, and thy flocks, and thy herds, and all that thou hast; 45:11 and there will I sustain thee; for there are yet five years of famine; lest thou come to poverty, thou, and thy household, and all that thou hast. 45:12 And, behold, your eyes see, and the eyes of my brother Benjamin, that it is my mouth that speaketh unto you. 45:13 And ye shall tell my father of all my glory in Egypt, and of all that ye have seen; and ye shall hasten and bring down my father hither.' 45:14 And he fell upon his brother Benjamin's neck, and wept; and Benjamin wept upon his neck. 45:15 And he kissed all his brethren, and wept upon them; and after that his brethren talked with him.

מו

45:16 And the report thereof was heard in Pharaoh's house, saying: 'Joseph's brethren are come'; and it pleased Pharaoh well, and his servants. 45:17 And Pharaoh said unto Joseph: 'Say unto thy brethren: This do ye: lade your beasts, and go, get you unto the land of Canaan; 45:18 and take your father and your households, and come unto me; and I will give you the good of the land of Egypt, and ye shall eat the fat of the land. 45:19 Now thou art commanded, this do ye: take you wagons out of the land of Egypt for your little ones, and for your wives, and bring your father, and come. 45:20 Also regard not your stuff; for the good things of all the land of Egypt are yours.' 45:21 And the sons of Israel did so; and Joseph gave them wagons, according to the commandment of Pharaoh, and gave them provision for the way. 45:22 To all of them he gave each man changes of raiment; but to Benjamin he gave three hundred shekels of silver, and five changes of raiment. 45:23 And to his father he sent in like manner ten asses laden with the good things of Egypt, and ten she-asses laden with corn and bread and victual for his father by the way. 45:24 So he sent his brethren away, and they departed; and he said unto them: 'See that ye fall not out by the way.' 45:25 And they went up out of Egypt, and came into the land of Canaan unto Jacob their father. 45:26 And they told him, saying: 'Joseph is yet alive, and he is ruler over all the land of Egypt.' And his heart fainted, for he believed them not. 45:27 And they told him all the words of Joseph, which he had said unto them; and when he saw the wagons which Joseph had sent to carry him, the spirit of Jacob their father revived. 45:28 And Israel said: 'It is enough; Joseph my son is yet alive; I will go and see him before I die.'

5א

A 46:1 And Israel took his journey with all that he had, and came to Beer-sheba, and offered sacrifices unto the God of his father Isaac. 46:2 And God spoke unto Israel in the visions of the night, and said: 'Jacob, Jacob.' And he said: 'Here am I.' 46:3 And He said: 'I am God, the God of thy father; fear not to go down into Egypt; for I will there make of thee a great nation. 46:4 I will go down with thee into Egypt; and I will also surely bring thee up again; and Joseph shall put his hand upon thine eyes.' 46:5 And Jacob rose up from Beer-sheba; and the sons of Israel carried Jacob their father, and their little ones, and their wives, in the wagons which Pharaoh had sent to carry him. 46:6 And they took their cattle, and their goods, which they had gotten in the land of Canaan, and came into Egypt, Jacob, and all his seed with him; 46:7 his sons, and his sons' sons with him, his daughters, and his sons' daughters, and all his seed brought he with him into Egypt. {S}

B 46:8 And these are the names of the children of Israel, who came into Egypt, Jacob and his sons: Reuben, Jacob's first-born. 46:9 And the sons of Reuben: Hanoch, and Pallu, and Hezron, and Carmi. 46:10 And the sons of Simeon: Jemuel, and Jamin, and Ohad, and Jachin, and Zohar, and Shaul the son of a Canaanitish woman. 46:11 And the sons of Levi: Gershon, Kohath, and Merari. 46:12 And the sons of Judah: Er, and Onan, and Shelah, and Perez, and Zerah; but Er and Onan died in the land of Canaan. And the sons of Perez were Hezron and Hamul. 46:13 And the sons of Issachar: Tola, and Puvah, and Iob, and Shimron. 46:14 And the sons of Zebulun: Sered, and Elon, and Jahleel. 46:15 These are the sons of Leah, whom she bore unto Jacob in Paddan-aram, with his daughter Dinah; all the souls of his sons and his daughters were thirty and three. 46:16 And the sons of Gad: Ziphion, and Haggi, Shuni, and Ezbon, Eri, and Arodi, and Areli. 46:17 And the sons of Asher: Imnah, and Ishvah, and Ishvi, and Beriah, and Serah their sister; and the sons of Beriah: Heber, and Malchiel. 46:18 These are the sons of Zilpah, whom Laban gave to Leah his daughter, and these she bore unto Jacob, even sixteen souls. 46:19 The sons of Rachel Jacob's wife: Joseph and Benjamin. 46:20 And unto Joseph in the land of Egypt were born Manasseh and Ephraim, whom Asenath the daughter of Poti-phera priest of On bore unto him. 46:21 And the sons of Benjamin: Bela, and Becher, and Ashbel, Gera, and Naaman, Ehi, and Rosh, Muppim, and Huppim, and Ard. 46:22 These are the sons of Rachel, who were born to Jacob; all the souls were fourteen. 46:23 And the sons of Dan: Hushim. 46:24 And the sons of Naphtali: Jahzeel, and Guni, and Jezer, and Shillem. 46:25 These are the sons of Bilhah, whom Laban gave unto Rachel his daughter, and these she bore unto Jacob; all the souls were seven. 46:26 All the souls belonging to Jacob that came into Egypt, that came out of his loins, besides Jacob's sons' wives, all the souls were threescore and six. 46:27 And the sons of Joseph, who were born to him in Egypt, were two souls; all the souls of the house of Jacob, that came into Egypt, were threescore and ten. {S}

5ב

A 46:28 And he sent Judah before him unto Joseph, to show the way before him unto Goshen; and they came into the land of Goshen. 46:29 And Joseph made ready his chariot, and went up to meet Israel his father, to Goshen; and he presented himself unto him, and fell on his neck, and wept on his neck a good while. 46:30 And Israel said unto Joseph: 'Now let me die, since I have seen thy face, that thou art yet alive.'

B 46:31 And Joseph said unto his brethren, and unto his father's house: 'I will go up, and tell Pharaoh, and will say unto him: My brethren, and my father's house, who were in the land of Canaan, are come unto me; 46:32 and the men are shepherds, for they have been keepers of cattle; and they have brought their flocks, and their herds, and all that they have. 46:33 And it shall come to pass, when Pharaoh shall call you, and shall say: What is your occupation? 46:34 that ye shall say: Thy servants have been keepers of cattle from our youth even until now, both we, and our fathers; that ye may dwell in the land of Goshen; for every shepherd is an abomination unto the Egyptians.'

5ג

A 47:1 Then Joseph went in and told Pharaoh, and said: 'My father and my brethren, and their flocks, and their herds, and all that they have, are come out of the land of Canaan; and, behold, they are in the land of Goshen.' 47:2 And from among his brethren he took five men, and presented them unto Pharaoh. 47:3 And Pharaoh said unto his brethren: 'What is your occupation?' And they said unto Pharaoh: 'Thy servants are shepherds, both we, and our fathers.' 47:4 And they said unto Pharaoh: 'To sojourn in the land are we come; for there is no pasture for thy servants' flocks; for the famine is sore in the land of Canaan. Now therefore, we pray thee, let thy servants dwell in the land of Goshen.' 47:5 And Pharaoh spoke unto Joseph, saying: 'Thy father and thy brethren are come unto thee; 47:6 the land of Egypt is before thee; in the best of the land make thy father and thy brethren to dwell; in the land of Goshen let them dwell. And if thou knowest any able men among them, then make them rulers over my cattle.'

B 47:7 And Joseph brought in Jacob his father, and set him before Pharaoh. And Jacob blessed Pharaoh. 47:8 And Pharaoh said unto Jacob: 'How many are the days of the years of thy life?' 47:9 And Jacob said unto Pharaoh: 'The days of the years of my sojournings are a hundred and thirty years; few and evil have been the days of the years of my life, and they have not attained unto the days of the years of the life of my fathers in the days of their sojournings.' 47:10 And Jacob blessed Pharaoh, and went out from the presence of Pharaoh. 47:11 And Joseph placed his father and his brethren, and gave them a possession in the land of Egypt, in the best of the land, in the land of Rameses, as Pharaoh had commanded. 47:12 And Joseph sustained his father, and his brethren, and all his father's household, with bread, according to the want of their little ones.

6א

47:13 And there was no bread in all the land; for the famine was very sore, so that the land of Egypt and the land of Canaan languished by reason of the famine. 47:14 And Joseph gathered up all the money that was found in the land of Egypt, and in the land of Canaan, for the corn which they bought; and Joseph brought the money into Pharaoh's house. 47:15 And when the money was all spent in the land of Egypt, and in the land of Canaan, all the Egyptians came unto Joseph, and said: 'Give us bread; for why should we die in thy presence? for our money faileth.' 47:16 And Joseph said: 'Give your cattle, and I will give you [bread] for your cattle, if money fail.' 47:17 And they brought their cattle unto Joseph. And Joseph gave them bread in exchange for the horses, and for the flocks, and for the herds, and for the asses; and he fed them with bread in exchange for all their cattle for that year.

6ב

47:18 And when that year was ended, they came unto him the second year, and said unto him: 'We will not hide from my lord, how that our money is all spent; and the herds of cattle are my lord's; there is nought left in the sight of my lord, but our bodies, and our lands. 47:19 Wherefore should we die before thine eyes, both we and our land? buy us and our land for bread, and we and our land will be bondmen unto Pharaoh; and give us seed, that we may live, and not die, and that the land be not desolate.' 47:20 So Joseph bought all the land of Egypt for Pharaoh; for the Egyptians sold every man his field, because the famine was sore upon them; and the land became Pharaoh's. 47:21 And as for the people, he removed them city by city, from one end of the border of Egypt even to the other end thereof. 47:22 Only the land of the priests bought he not, for the priests had a portion from Pharaoh, and did eat their portion which Pharaoh gave them; wherefore they sold not their land.

6ג

47:23 Then Joseph said unto the people: 'Behold, I have bought you this day and your land for Pharaoh. Lo, here is seed for you, and ye shall sow the land. 47:24 And it shall come to pass at the ingatherings, that ye shall give a fifth unto Pharaoh, and four parts shall be your own, for seed of the field, and for your food, and for them of your households, and for food for your little ones.' 47:25 And they said: 'Thou hast saved our lives. Let us find favour in the sight of my lord, and we will be Pharaoh's bondmen.' 47:26 And Joseph made it a statute concerning the land of Egypt unto this day, that Pharaoh should have the fifth; only the land of the priests alone became not Pharaoh's.

Genesis Unit XIX (47:27-50:26)

א

A 47:27 And Israel dwelt in the land of Egypt, in the land of Goshen; and they got them possessions therein, and were fruitful, and multiplied exceedingly. 47:28 And Jacob lived in the land of Egypt seventeen years; so the days of Jacob, the years of his life, were a hundred forty and seven years.

ב

A 48:1 And it came to pass after these things, that one said to Joseph: 'Behold, thy father is sick.' And he took with him his two sons, Manasseh and Ephraim. 48:2 And one told Jacob, and said: 'Behold, thy son Joseph cometh unto thee.' And Israel strengthened himself, and sat upon the bed. 48:3 And Jacob said unto Joseph: 'God Almighty appeared unto me at Luz in the land of Canaan, and blessed me, 48:4 and said unto me: Behold, I will make thee fruitful, and multiply thee, and I will make of thee a company of peoples; and will give this land to thy seed after thee for an everlasting possession. 48:5 And now thy two sons, who were born unto thee in the land of Egypt before I came unto thee into Egypt, are mine; Ephraim and Manasseh, even as Reuben and Simeon, shall be mine. 48:6 And thy issue, that thou begettest after them, shall be thine; they shall be called after the name of their brethren in their inheritance. 48:7 And as for me, when I came from Paddan, Rachel died unto me in the land of Canaan in the way, when there was still some way to come unto Ephrath; and I buried her there in the way to Ephrath--the same is Beth-lehem.'

ג

A 49:1 And Jacob called unto his sons, and said: 'Gather yourselves together, that I may tell you that which shall befall you in the end of days. 49:2 Assemble yourselves, and hear, ye sons of Jacob; and hearken unto Israel your father. 49:3 Reuben, thou art my first-born, my might, and the first-fruits of my strength; the excellency of dignity, and the excellency of power. 49:4 Unstable as water, have not thou the excellency; because thou wentest up to thy father's bed; then defiledst thou it--he went up to my couch. {P}
49:5 Simeon and Levi are brethren; weapons of violence their kinship. 49:6 Let my soul not come into their council; unto their assembly let my glory not be united; for in their anger they slew men, and in their self-will they houghed oxen. 49:7 Cursed be their anger, for it was fierce, and their wrath, for it was cruel; I will divide them in Jacob, and scatter them in Israel. {P}
49:8 Judah, thee shall thy brethren praise; thy hand shall be on the neck of thine enemies; thy father's sons shall bow down before thee. 49:9 Judah is a lion's whelp; from the prey, my son, thou art gone up. He stooped down, he couched as a lion, and as a lioness; who shall rouse him up? 49:10 The sceptre shall not depart from Judah, nor the ruler's staff from between his feet, as long as men come to Shiloh; and unto him shall the obedience of the peoples be. 49:11 Binding his foal unto the vine, and his ass's colt unto the choice vine; he washeth his garments in wine, and his vesture in the blood of grapes; 49:12 His eyes shall be red with wine, and his teeth white with milk. {P}
49:13 Zebulun shall dwell at the shore of the sea, and he shall be a shore for ships, and his flank shall be upon Zidon. {P}
49:14 Issachar is a large-boned ass, couching down between the sheep-folds. 49:15 For he saw a resting-place that it was good, and the land that it was pleasant; and he bowed his shoulder to bear, and became a servant under task-work. {S} 49:16 Dan shall judge his people, as one of the tribes of Israel. 49:17 Dan shall be a serpent in the way, a horned snake in the path, that biteth the horse's heels, so that his rider falleth backward. 49:18 I wait for Thy salvation, O LORD. {S} 49:19 Gad, a troop shall troop upon him; but he shall troop upon their heel. {S} 49:20 As for Asher, his bread shall be fat, and he shall yield royal dainties. {S} 49:21 Naphtali is a hind let loose: he giveth goodly words. {S} 49:22 Joseph is a fruitful vine, a fruitful vine by a fountain; its branches run over the wall. 49:23 The archers have dealt bitterly with him, and shot at him, and hated him; 49:24 But his bow abode firm, and the arms of his hands were made supple, by the hands of the Mighty One of Jacob, from thence, from the Shepherd, the Stone of Israel, 49:25 Even by the God of thy father, who shall help thee, and by the Almighty, who shall bless thee, with blessings of heaven above, blessings of the deep that coucheth beneath, blessings of the breasts, and of the womb. 49:26 The blessings of thy father are mighty beyond the blessings of my progenitors unto the utmost bound of the everlasting hills; they shall be on the head of Joseph, and on the crown of the head of the prince among his brethren. {P}
49:27 Benjamin is a wolf that raveneth; in the morning he devoureth the prey, and at even he divideth the spoil.' 49:28 All these are the twelve tribes of Israel, and this is it that their father spoke unto them and blessed them; every one according to his blessing he blessed them

B 47:29 And the time drew near that Israel must die; and he called his son Joseph, and said unto him: 'If now I have found favour in thy sight, put, I pray thee, thy hand under my thigh, and deal kindly and truly with me; bury me not, I pray thee, in Egypt. 47:30 But when I sleep with my fathers, thou shalt carry me out of Egypt, and bury me in their burying-place.' And he said: 'I will do as thou hast said.' 47:31 And he said: 'Swear unto me.' And he swore unto him. And Israel bowed down upon the bed's head. {P}

B 48:8 And Israel beheld Joseph's sons, and said: 'Who are these?' 48:9 And Joseph said unto his father: 'They are my sons, whom God hath given me here.' And he said: 'Bring them, I pray thee, unto me, and I will bless them.' 48:10 Now the eyes of Israel were dim for age, so that he could not see. And he brought them near unto him; and he kissed them, and embraced them. 48:11 And Israel said unto Joseph: 'I had not thought to see thy face; and, lo, God hath let me see thy seed also.' 48:12 And Joseph brought them out from between his knees; and he fell down on his face to the earth. 48:13 And Joseph took them both, Ephraim in his right hand toward Israel's left hand, and Manasseh in his left hand toward Israel's right hand, and brought them near unto him. 48:14 And Israel stretched out his right hand, and laid it upon Ephraim's head, who was the younger, and his left hand upon Manasseh's head, guiding his hands wittingly; for Manasseh was the first-born. 48:15 And he blessed Joseph, and said: 'The God before whom my fathers Abraham and Isaac did walk, the God who hath been my shepherd all my life long unto this day, 48:16 the angel who hath redeemed me from all evil, bless the lads; and let my name be named in them, and the name of my fathers Abraham and Isaac; and let them grow into a multitude in the midst of the earth.' 48:17 And when Joseph saw that his father was laying his right hand upon the head of Ephraim, it displeased him, and he held up his father's hand, to remove it from Ephraim's head unto Manasseh's head. 48:18 And Joseph said unto his father: 'Not so, my father, for this is the first-born; put thy right hand upon his head.' 48:19 And his father refused, and said: 'I know it, my son, I know it; he also shall become a people, and he also shall be great; howbeit his younger brother shall be greater than he, and his seed shall become a multitude of nations.' 48:20 And he blessed them that day, saying: 'By thee shall Israel bless, saying: God make thee as Ephraim and as Manasseh.' And he set Ephraim before Manasseh. 48:21 And Israel said unto Joseph: 'Behold, I die; but God will be with you, and bring you back unto the land of your fathers. 48:22 Moreover I have given to thee one portion above thy brethren, which I took out of the hand of the Amorite with my sword and with my bow.' {P}

B . 49:29 And he charged them, and said unto them: 'I am to be gathered unto my people; bury me with my fathers in the cave that is in the field of Ephron the Hittite, 49:30 in the cave that is in the field of Machpelah, which is before Mamre, in the land of Canaan, which Abraham bought with the field from Ephron the Hittite for a possession of a burying-place. 49:31 There they buried Abraham and Sarah his wife; there they buried Isaac and Rebekah his wife; and there I buried Leah. 49:32 The field and the cave that is therein, which was purchased from the children of Heth.' 49:33 And when Jacob made an end of charging his sons, he gathered up his feet into the bed, and expired, and was gathered unto his people.

א
50:1 And Joseph fell upon his father's face, and wept upon him, and kissed him. 50:2 And Joseph commanded his servants the physicians to embalm his father. And the physicians embalmed Israel. 50:3 And forty days were fulfilled for him; for so are fulfilled the days of embalming. And the Egyptians wept for him threescore and ten days. 50:4 And when the days of weeping for him were past, Joseph spoke unto the house of Pharaoh, saying: 'If now I have found favour in your eyes, speak, I pray you, in the ears of Pharaoh, saying: 50:5 My father made me swear, saying: Lo, I die; in my grave which I have digged for me in the land of Canaan, there shalt thou bury me. Now therefore let me go up, I pray thee, and bury my father, and I will come back.' 50:6 And Pharaoh said: 'Go up, and bury thy father, according as he made thee swear.' 50:7 And Joseph went up to bury his father; and with him went up all the servants of Pharaoh, the elders of his house, and all the elders of the land of Egypt, 50:8 and all the house of Joseph, and his brethren, and his father's house; only their little ones, and their flocks, and their herds, they left in the land of Goshen. 50:9 And there went up with him both chariots and horsemen; and it was a very great company. 50:10 And they came to the threshing-floor of Atad, which is beyond the Jordan, and there they wailed with a very great and sore wailing; and he made a mourning for his father seven days. 50:11 And when the inhabitants of the land, the Canaanites, saw the mourning in the floor of Atad, they said: 'This is a grievous mourning to the Egyptians.' Wherefore the name of it was called Abel-mizraim, which is beyond the Jordan. 50:12 And his sons did unto him according as he commanded them. 50:13 For his sons carried him into the land of Canaan, and buried him in the cave of the field of Machpelah, which Abraham bought with the field, for a possession of a burying-place, of Ephron the Hittite, in front of Mamre.

ב
50:14 And Joseph returned into Egypt, he, and his brethren, and all that went up with him to bury his father, after he had buried his father. 50:15 And when Joseph's brethren saw that their father was dead, they said: 'It may be that Joseph will hate us, and will fully requite us all the evil which we did unto him.' 50:16 And they sent a message unto Joseph, saying: 'Thy father did command before he died, saying: 50:17 So shall ye say unto Joseph: Forgive, I pray thee now, the transgression of thy brethren, and their sin, for that they did unto thee evil. And now, we pray thee, forgive the transgression of the servants of the God of thy father.' And Joseph wept when they spoke unto him. 50:18 And his brethren also went and fell down before his face; and they said: 'Behold, we are thy bondmen.' 50:19 And Joseph said unto them: 'Fear not; for am I in the place of God? 50:20 And as for you, ye meant evil against me; but God meant it for good, to bring to pass, as it is this day, to save much people alive. 50:21 Now therefore fear ye not; I will sustain you, and your little ones.' And he comforted them, and spoke kindly unto them.

ג
50:22 And Joseph dwelt in Egypt, he, and his father's house; and Joseph lived a hundred and ten years. 50:23 And Joseph saw Ephraim's children of the third generation; the children also of Machir the son of Manasseh were born upon Joseph's knees. 50:24 And Joseph said unto his brethren: 'I die; but God will surely remember you, and bring you up out of this land unto the land which He swore to Abraham, to Isaac, and to Jacob.' 50:25 And Joseph took an oath of the children of Israel, saying: 'God will surely remember you, and ye shall carry up my bones from hence.' 50:26 So Joseph died, being a hundred and ten years old. And they embalmed him, and he was put in a coffin in Egypt. {P}

Exodus

Exodus Unit I (1:1-4:18)

א1

A 1:1 Now these are the names of the sons of Israel, who came into Egypt with Jacob; every man came with his household: 1:2 Reuben, Simeon, Levi, and Judah; 1:3 Issachar, Zebulun, and Benjamin; 1:4 Dan and Naphtali, Gad and Asher. 1:5 And all the souls that came out of the loins of Jacob were seventy souls; and Joseph was in Egypt already. 1:6 And Joseph died, and all his brethren, and all that generation. 1:7 And the children of Israel were fruitful, and increased abundantly, and multiplied, and waxed exceeding mighty; and the land was filled with them. {P}

B 1:8 Now there arose a new king over Egypt, who knew not Joseph. 1:9 And he said unto his people: 'Behold, the people of the children of Israel are too many and too mighty for us; 1:10 come, let us deal wisely with them, lest they multiply, and it come to pass, that, when there befalleth us any war, they also join themselves unto our enemies, and fight against us, and get them up out of the land.' 1:11 Therefore they did set over them taskmasters to afflict them with their burdens. And they built for Pharaoh store-cities, Pithom and Raamses. 1:12 But the more they afflicted them, the more they multiplied and the more they spread abroad. And they were adread because of the children of Israel. 1:13 And the Egyptians made the children of Israel to serve with rigour. 1:14 And they made their lives bitter with hard service, in mortar and in brick, and in all manner of service in the field; in all their service, wherein they made them serve with rigour.

C 1:15 And the king of Egypt spoke to the Hebrew midwives, of whom the name of the one was Shiphrah, and the name of the other Puah; 1:16 and he said: 'When ye do the office of a midwife to the Hebrew women, ye shall look upon the birthstool: if it be a son, then ye shall kill him; but if it be a daughter, then she shall live.' 1:17 But the midwives feared God, and did not as the king of Egypt commanded them, but saved the men-children alive. 1:18 And the king of Egypt called for the midwives, and said unto them: 'Why have ye done this thing, and have saved the men-children alive?' 1:19 And the midwives said unto Pharaoh: 'Because the Hebrew women are not as the Egyptian women; for they are lively, and are delivered ere the midwife come unto them.' 1:20 And God dealt well with the midwives; and the people multiplied, and waxed very mighty. 1:21 And it came to pass, because the midwives feared God, that He made them houses. 1:22 And Pharaoh charged all his people, saying: 'Every son that is born ye shall cast into the river, and every daughter ye shall save alive.' {P}

א2

2:23 And it came to pass in the course of those many days that the king of Egypt died; and the children of Israel sighed by reason of the bondage, and they cried, and their cry came up unto God by reason of the bondage. 2:24 And God heard their groaning, and God remembered His covenant with Abraham, with Isaac, and with Jacob. 2:25 And God saw the children of Israel, and God took cognizance of them. {S}

ב1

A 2:1 And there went a man of the house of Levi, and took to wife a daughter of Levi. 2:2 And the woman conceived, and bore a son; and when she saw him that he was a goodly child, she hid him three months. 2:3 And when she could not longer hide him, she took for him an ark of bulrushes, and daubed it with slime and with pitch; and she put the child therein, and laid it in the flags by the river's brink. 2:4 And his sister stood afar off, to know what would be done to him. 2:5 And the daughter of Pharaoh came down to bathe in the river; and her maidens walked along by the river-side; and she saw the ark among the flags, and sent her handmaid to fetch it. 2:6 And she opened it, and saw it, even the child; and behold a boy that wept. And she had compassion on him, and said: 'This is one of the Hebrews' children.' 2:7 Then said his sister to Pharaoh's daughter: 'Shall I go and call thee a nurse of the Hebrew women, that she may nurse the child for thee?' 2:8 And Pharaoh's daughter said to her: 'Go.' And the maiden went and called the child's mother. 2:9 And Pharaoh's daughter said unto her: 'Take this child away, and nurse it for me, and I will give thee thy wages.' And the woman took the child, and nursed it. 2:10 And the child grew, and she brought him unto Pharaoh's daughter, and he became her son. And she called his name Moses, and said: 'Because I drew him out of the water.'

B 2:11 And it came to pass in those days, when Moses was grown up, that he went out unto his brethren, and looked on their burdens; and he saw an Egyptian smiting a Hebrew, one of his brethren. 2:12 And he looked this way and that way, and when he saw that there was no man, he smote the Egyptian, and hid him in the sand. 2:13 And he went out the second day, and, behold, two men of the Hebrews were striving together; and he said to him that did the wrong: 'Wherefore smitest thou thy fellow?' 2:14 And he said: 'Who made thee a ruler and a judge over us? thinkest thou to kill me, as thou didst kill the Egyptian?' And Moses feared, and said: 'Surely the thing is known.' 2:15 Now when Pharaoh heard this thing, he sought to slay Moses. But Moses fled from the face of Pharaoh, and dwelt in the land of Midian; and he sat down by a well.

C 2:16 Now the priest of Midian had seven daughters; and they came and drew water, and filled the troughs to water their father's flock. 2:17 And the shepherds came and drove them away; but Moses stood up and helped them, and watered their flock. 2:18 And when they came to Reuel their father, he said: 'How is it that ye are come so soon to-day?' 2:19 And they said: 'An Egyptian delivered us out of the hand of the shepherds, and moreover he drew water for us, and watered the flock.' 2:20 And he said unto his daughters: 'And where is he? Why is it that ye have left the man? call him, that he may eat bread.' 2:21 And Moses was content to dwell with the man; and he gave Moses Zipporah his daughter. 2:22 And she bore a son, and he called his name Gershom; for he said: 'I have been a stranger in a strange land.' {P}

ב2

3:1 Now Moses was keeping the flock of Jethro his father-in-law, the priest of Midian; and he led the flock to the farthest end of the wilderness, and came to the mountain of God, unto Horeb. 3:2 And the angel of the LORD appeared unto him in a flame of fire out of the midst of a bush; and he looked, and, behold, the bush burned with fire, and the bush was not consumed. 3:3 And Moses said: 'I will turn aside now, and see this great sight, why the bush is not burnt.' 3:4 And when the LORD saw that he turned aside to see, God called unto him out of the midst of the bush, and said: 'Moses, Moses.' And he said: 'Here am I.' 3:5 And He said: 'Draw not nigh hither; put off thy shoes from off thy feet, for the place whereon thou standest is holy ground.'

אג

בג

A 3:6 Moreover He said: 'I am the God of thy father, the God of Abraham, the God of Isaac, and the God of Jacob.' And Moses hid his face; for he was afraid to look upon God. 3:7 And the LORD said: 'I have surely seen the affliction of My people that are in Egypt, and have heard their cry by reason of their taskmasters; for I know their pains; 3:8 and I am come down to deliver them out of the hand of the Egyptians, and to bring them up out of that land unto a good land and a large, unto a land flowing with milk and honey; unto the place of the Canaanite, and the Hittite, and the Amorite, and the Perizzite, and the Hivite, and the Jebusite. 3:9 And now, behold, the cry of the children of Israel is come unto Me; moreover I have seen the oppression wherewith the Egyptians oppress them. 3:10 Come now therefore, and I will send thee unto Pharaoh, that thou mayest bring forth My people the children of Israel out of Egypt.' 3:11 And Moses said unto God: 'Who am I, that I should go unto Pharaoh, and that I should bring forth the children of Israel out of Egypt?' 3:12 And He said: 'Certainly I will be with thee; and this shall be the token unto thee, that I have sent thee: when thou hast brought forth the people out of Egypt, ye shall serve God upon this mountain.'

B 3:13 And Moses said unto God: 'Behold, when I come unto the children of Israel, and shall say unto them: The God of your fathers hath sent me unto you; and they shall say to me: What is His name? what shall I say unto them?' 3:14 And God said unto Moses: 'I AM THAT I AM'; and He said: 'Thus shalt thou say unto the children of Israel: I AM hath sent me unto you.' 3:15 And God said moreover unto Moses: 'Thus shalt thou say unto the children of Israel: The LORD, the God of your fathers, the God of Abraham, the God of Isaac, and the God of Jacob, hath sent me unto you; this is My name for ever, and this is My memorial unto all generations.

C 3:16 Go, and gather the elders of Israel together, and say unto them: The LORD, the God of your fathers, the God of Abraham, of Isaac, and of Jacob, hath appeared unto me, saying: I have surely remembered you, and seen that which is done to you in Egypt. 3:17 And I have said: I will bring you up out of the affliction of Egypt unto the land of the Canaanite, and the Hittite, and the Amorite, and the Perizzite, and the Hivite, and the Jebusite, unto a land flowing with milk and honey. 3:18 And they shall hearken to thy voice. And thou shalt come, thou and the elders of Israel, unto the king of Egypt, and ye shall say unto him: The LORD, the God of the Hebrews, hath met with us. And now let us go, we pray thee, three days' journey into the wilderness, that we may sacrifice to the LORD our God. 3:19 And I know that the king of Egypt will not give you leave to go, except by a mighty hand. 3:20 And I will put forth My hand, and smite Egypt with all My wonders which I will do in the midst thereof. And after that he will let you go. 3:21 And I will give this people favour in the sight of the Egyptians.

D And it shall come to pass, that, when ye go, ye shall not go empty; 3:22 but every woman shall ask of her neighbour, and of her that sojourneth in her house, jewels of silver, and jewels of gold, and raiment; and ye shall put them upon your sons, and upon your daughters; and ye shall spoil the Egyptians.'

A 4:1 And Moses answered and said: 'But, behold, they will not believe me, nor hearken unto my voice; for they will say: The LORD hath not appeared unto thee.' 4:2 And the LORD said unto him: 'What is that in thy hand?' And he said: 'A rod.' 4:3 And He said: 'Cast it on the ground.' And he cast it on the ground, and it became a serpent; and Moses fled from before it. 4:4 And the LORD said unto Moses: 'Put forth thy hand, and take it by the tail--and he put forth his hand, and laid hold of it, and it became a rod in his hand-- 4:5 that they may believe that the LORD, the God of their fathers, the God of Abraham, the God of Isaac, and the God of Jacob, hath appeared unto thee.' 4:6 And the LORD said furthermore unto him: 'Put now thy hand into thy bosom.' And he put his hand into his bosom; and when he took it out, behold, his hand was leprous, as white as snow. 4:7 And He said: 'Put thy hand back into thy bosom.--And he put his hand back into his bosom; and when he took it out of his bosom, behold, it was turned again as his other flesh.-- 4:8 And it shall come to pass, if they will not believe thee, neither hearken to the voice of the first sign, that they will believe the voice of the latter sign. 4:9 And it shall come to pass, if they will not believe even these two signs, neither hearken unto thy voice, that thou shalt take of the water of the river, and pour it upon the dry land; and the water which thou takest out of the river shall become blood upon the dry land.'

B 4:10 And Moses said unto the LORD: 'Oh Lord, I am not a man of words, neither heretofore, nor since Thou hast spoken unto Thy servant; for I am slow of speech, and of a slow tongue.' 4:11 And the LORD said unto him: 'Who hath made man's mouth? or who maketh a man dumb, or deaf, or seeing, or blind? is it not I the LORD? 4:12 Now therefore go, and I will be with thy mouth, and teach thee what thou shalt speak.'

C 4:13 And he said: 'Oh Lord, send, I pray Thee, by the hand of him whom Thou wilt send.' 4:14 And the anger of the LORD was kindled against Moses, and He said: 'Is there not Aaron thy brother the Levite? I know that he can speak well. And also, behold, he cometh forth to meet thee; and when he seeth thee, he will be glad in his heart. 4:15 And thou shalt speak unto him, and put the words in his mouth; and I will be with thy mouth, and with his mouth, and will teach you what ye shall do. 4:16 And he shall be thy spokesman unto the people; and it shall come to pass, that he shall be to thee a mouth, and thou shalt be to him in God's stead. 4:17 And thou shalt take in thy hand this rod, wherewith thou shalt do the signs.' {P}

D 4:18 And Moses went and returned to Jethro his father-in-law, and said unto him: 'Let me go, I pray thee, and return unto my brethren that are in Egypt, and see whether they be yet alive.' And Jethro said to Moses: 'Go in peace.'

Exodus Unit II (4:19-6:28)

1א

A 4:19 And the LORD said unto Moses in Midian: 'Go, return into Egypt; for all the men are dead that sought thy life.' 4:20 And Moses took his wife and his sons, and set them upon an ass, and he returned to the land of Egypt; and Moses took the rod of God in his hand.

B 4:21 And the LORD said unto Moses: 'When thou goest back into Egypt, see that thou do before Pharaoh all the wonders which I have put in thy hand; but I will harden his heart, and he will not let the people go. 4:22 And thou shalt say unto Pharaoh: Thus saith the LORD: Israel is My son, My first-born. 4:23 And I have said unto thee: Let My son go, that he may serve Me; and thou hast refused to let him go. Behold, I will slay thy son, thy first-born.'--

C 4:24 And it came to pass on the way at the lodging-place, that the LORD met him, and sought to kill him. 4:25 Then Zipporah took a flint, and cut off the foreskin of her son, and cast it at his feet; and she said: 'Surely a bridegroom of blood art thou to me.' 4:26 So He let him alone. Then she said: 'A bridegroom of blood in regard of the circumcision.' {P}

1ב

A 4:27 And the LORD said to Aaron: 'Go into the wilderness to meet Moses.' And he went, and met him in the mountain of God, and kissed him. 4:28 And Moses told Aaron all the words of the LORD wherewith He had sent him, and all the signs wherewith He had charged him.

B 4:29 And Moses and Aaron went and gathered together all the elders of the children of Israel. 4:30 And Aaron spoke all the words which the LORD had spoken unto Moses, and did the signs in the sight of the people. 4:31 And the people believed; and when they heard that the LORD had remembered the children of Israel, and that He had seen their affliction, then they bowed their heads and worshipped.

C 5:1 And afterward Moses and Aaron came, and said unto Pharaoh: 'Thus saith the LORD, the God of Israel: Let My people go, that they may hold a feast unto Me in the wilderness.' 5:2 And Pharaoh said: 'Who is the LORD, that I should hearken unto His voice to let Israel go? I know not the LORD, and moreover I will not let Israel go.' 5:3 And they said: 'The God of the Hebrews hath met with us. Let us go, we pray thee, three days' journey into the wilderness, and sacrifice unto the LORD our God; lest He fall upon us with pestilence, or with the sword.' 5:4 And the king of Egypt said unto them: 'Wherefore do ye, Moses and Aaron, cause the people to break loose from their work? get you unto your burdens.' 5:5 And Pharaoh said: 'Behold, the people of the land are now many, and will ye make them rest from their burdens?'

2א

A 5:6 And the same day Pharaoh commanded the taskmasters of the people, and their officers, saying: 5:7 'Ye shall no more give the people straw to make brick, as heretofore. Let them go and gather straw for themselves. 5:8 And the tale of the bricks, which they did make heretofore, ye shall lay upon them; ye shall not diminish aught thereof; for they are idle; therefore they cry, saying: Let us go and sacrifice to our God. 5:9 Let heavier work be laid upon the men, that they may labour therein; and let them not regard lying words.'

B 5:10 And the taskmasters of the people went out, and their officers, and they spoke to the people, saying: 'Thus saith Pharaoh: I will not give you straw. 5:11 Go yourselves, get you straw where ye can find it; for nought of your work shall be diminished.' 5:12 So the people were scattered abroad throughout all the land of Egypt to gather stubble for straw. 5:13 And the taskmasters were urgent, saying: 'Fulfil your work, your daily task, as when there was straw.'

2ב

A 5:14 And the officers of the children of Israel, whom Pharaoh's taskmasters had set over them, were beaten, saying: 'Wherefore have ye not fulfilled your appointed task in making brick both yesterday and today as heretofore?'

B 5:15 Then the officers of the children of Israel came and cried unto Pharaoh, saying: 'Wherefore dealest thou thus with thy servants? 5:16 There is no straw given unto thy servants, and they say to us: Make brick; and, behold, thy servants are beaten, but the fault is in thine own people.' 5:17 But he said: 'Ye are idle, ye are idle; therefore ye say: Let us go and sacrifice to the LORD. 5:18 Go therefore now, and work; for there shall no straw be given you, yet shall ye deliver the tale of bricks.' 5:19 And the officers of the children of Israel did see that they were set on mischief, when they said: 'Ye shall not diminish aught from your bricks, your daily task.'

א3

A 5:20 And they met Moses and Aaron, who stood in the way, as they came forth from Pharaoh; 5:21 and they said unto them: 'The LORD look upon you, and judge; because ye have made our savour to be abhorred in the eyes of Pharaoh, and in the eyes of his servants, to put a sword in their hand to slay us.'

B 5:22 And Moses returned unto the LORD, and said: 'Lord, wherefore hast Thou dealt ill with this people? why is it that Thou hast sent me? 5:23 For since I came to Pharaoh to speak in Thy name, he hath dealt ill with this people; neither hast Thou delivered Thy people at all.' 6:1 And the LORD said unto Moses: 'Now shalt thou see what I will do to Pharaoh; for by a strong hand shall he let them go, and by a strong hand shall he drive them out of his land.' {S}

C 6:2 And God spoke unto Moses, and said unto him: 'I am the LORD; 6:3 and I appeared unto Abraham, unto Isaac, and unto Jacob, as God Almighty, but by My name YHWH I made Me not known to them. 6:4 And I have also established My covenant with them, to give them the land of Canaan, the land of their sojournings, wherein they sojourned. 6:5 And moreover I have heard the groaning of the children of Israel, whom the Egyptians keep in bondage; and I have remembered My covenant. 6:6 Wherefore say unto the children of Israel: I am the LORD, and I will bring you out from under the burdens of the Egyptians, and I will deliver you from their bondage, and I will redeem you with an outstretched arm, and with great judgments; 6:7 and I will take you to Me for a people, and I will be to you a God; and ye shall know that I am the LORD your God, who brought you out from under the burdens of the Egyptians. 6:8 And I will bring you in unto the land, concerning which I lifted up My hand to give it to Abraham, to Isaac, and to Jacob; and I will give it you for a heritage: I am the LORD.'

D 6:9 And Moses spoke so unto the children of Israel; but they hearkened not unto Moses for impatience of spirit, and for cruel bondage. {P}

ב3

A 6:10 And the LORD spoke unto Moses, saying: 6:11 'Go in, speak unto Pharaoh king of Egypt, that he let the children of Israel go out of his land.' 6:12 And Moses spoke before the LORD, saying: 'Behold, the children of Israel have not hearkened unto me; how then shall Pharaoh hear me, who am of uncircumcised lips?' {P}

B 6:13 And the LORD spoke unto Moses and unto Aaron, and gave them a charge unto the children of Israel, and unto Pharaoh king of Egypt, to bring the children of Israel out of the land of Egypt. {S}

C 6:14 These are the heads of their fathers' houses: the sons of Reuben the first-born of Israel: Hanoch, and Pallu, Hezron, and Carmi. These are the families of Reuben. 6:15 And the sons of Simeon: Jemuel, and Jamin, and Ohad, and Jachin, and Zohar, and Shaul the son of a Canaanitish woman. These are the families of Simeon. 6:16 And these are the names of the sons of Levi according to their generations: Gershon and Kohath, and Merari. And the years of the life of Levi were a hundred thirty and seven years. 6:17 The sons of Gershon: Libni and Shimei, according to their families. 6:18 And the sons of Kohath: Amram, and Izhar, and Hebron, and Uzziel. And the years of the life of Kohath were a hundred thirty and three years. 6:19 And the sons of Merari: Mahli and Mushi. These are the families of the Levites according to their generations. 6:20 And Amram took him Jochebed his father's sister to wife; and she bore him Aaron and Moses. And the years of the life of Amram were a hundred and thirty and seven years. 6:21 And the sons of Izhar: Korah, and Nepheg, and Zichri. 6:22 And the sons of Uzziel: Mishael, and Elzaphan, and Sithri. 6:23 And Aaron took him Elisheba, the daughter of Amminadab, the sister of Nahshon, to wife; and she bore him Nadab and Abihu, Eleazar and Ithamar. 6:24 And the sons of Korah: Assir, and Elkanah, and Abiasaph; these are the families of the Korahites. 6:25 And Eleazar Aaron's son took him one of the daughters of Putiel to wife; and she bore him Phinehas. These are the heads of the fathers' houses of the Levites according to their families.

D 6:26 These are that Aaron and Moses, to whom the LORD said: 'Bring out the children of Israel from the land of Egypt according to their hosts.' 6:27 These are they that spoke to Pharaoh king of Egypt, to bring out the children of Israel from Egypt. These are that Moses and Aaron.

Exodus Unit III (6:29-11:10)

א1

A 6:29 And the LORD spoke unto Moses, saying: 'I am the LORD; speak thou unto Pharaoh king of Egypt all that I speak unto thee.' 6:30 And Moses said before the LORD: 'Behold, I am of uncircumcised lips, and how shall Pharaoh hearken unto me?' {P} 7:1 And the LORD said unto Moses: 'See, I have set thee in God's stead to Pharaoh; and Aaron thy brother shall be thy prophet. 7:2 Thou shalt speak all that I command thee; and Aaron thy brother shall speak unto Pharaoh, that he let the children of Israel go out of his land. 7:3 And I will harden Pharaoh's heart, and multiply My signs and My wonders in the land of Egypt. 7:4 But Pharaoh will not hearken unto you,

B and I will lay My hand upon Egypt, and bring forth My hosts, My people the children of Israel, out of the land of Egypt, by great judgments. 7:5 And the Egyptians shall know that I am the LORD, when I stretch forth My hand upon Egypt, and bring out the children of Israel from among them.' 7:6 And Moses and Aaron did so; as the LORD commanded them, so did they. 7:7 And Moses was fourscore years old, and Aaron fourscore and three years old, when they spoke unto Pharaoh. {P}

א2

A 7:14 And the LORD said unto Moses: 'Pharaoh's heart is stubborn, he refuseth to let the people go. 7:15 Get thee unto Pharaoh in the morning; lo, he goeth out unto the water; and thou shalt stand by the river's brink to meet him; and the rod which was turned to a serpent shalt thou take in thy hand. 7:16 And thou shalt say unto him: The LORD, the God of the Hebrews, hath sent me unto thee, saying: Let My people go, that they may serve Me in the wilderness; and, behold, hitherto thou hast not hearkened; 7:17 thus saith the LORD: In this thou shalt know that I am the LORD--behold, I will smite with the rod that is in my hand upon the waters which are in the river, and they shall be turned to blood. 7:18 And the fish that are in the river shall die, and the river shall become foul; and the Egyptians shall loathe to drink water from the river.' {S}

B 7:19 And the LORD said unto Moses: 'Say unto Aaron: Take thy rod, and stretch out thy hand over the waters of Egypt, over their rivers, over their streams, and over their pools, and over all their ponds of water, that they may become blood; and there shall be blood throughout all the land of Egypt, both in vessels of wood and in vessels of stone.' 7:20 And Moses and Aaron did so, as the LORD commanded; and he lifted up the rod, and smote the waters that were in the river, in the sight of Pharaoh, and in the sight of his servants; and all the waters that were in the river were turned to blood. 7:21 And the fish that were in the river died; and the river became foul, and the Egyptians could not drink water from the river; and the blood was throughout all the land of Egypt. 7:22 And the magicians of Egypt did in like manner with their secret arts; and Pharaoh's heart was hardened, and he hearkened not unto them; as the LORD had spoken. 7:23 And Pharaoh turned and went into his house, neither did he lay even this to heart. 7:24 And all the Egyptians digged round about the river for water to drink; for they could not drink of the water of the river. 7:25 And seven days were fulfilled, after that the LORD had smitten the river. {P}

ב1

A 7:8 And the LORD spoke unto Moses and unto Aaron, saying: 7:9 'When Pharaoh shall speak unto you, saying: Show a wonder for you; then thou shalt say unto Aaron: Take thy rod, and cast it down before Pharaoh, that it become a serpent.' 7:10 And Moses and Aaron went in unto Pharaoh, and they did so, as the LORD had commanded;

B and Aaron cast down his rod before Pharaoh and before his servants, and it became a serpent. 7:11 Then Pharaoh also called for the wise men and the sorcerers; and they also, the magicians of Egypt, did in like manner with their secret arts. 7:12 For they cast down every man his rod, and they became serpents; but Aaron's rod swallowed up their rods. 7:13 And Pharaoh's heart was hardened, and he hearkened not unto them; as the LORD had spoken. {S}

ב2

A 7:26 And the LORD spoke unto Moses: 'Go in unto Pharaoh, and say unto him: Thus saith the LORD: Let My people go, that they may serve Me. 7:27 And if thou refuse to let them go, behold, I will smite all thy borders with frogs. 7:28 And the river shall swarm with frogs, which shall go up and come into thy house, and into thy bed-chamber, and upon thy bed, and into the house of thy servants, and upon thy people, and into thine ovens, and into thy kneading-troughs. 7:29 And the frogs shall come up both upon thee, and upon thy people, and upon all thy servants.'

B 8:1 And the LORD said unto Moses: 'Say unto Aaron: Stretch forth thy hand with thy rod over the rivers, over the canals, and over the pools, and cause frogs to come up upon the land of Egypt.' 8:2 And Aaron stretched out his hand over the waters of Egypt; and the frogs came up, and covered the land of Egypt. 8:3 And the magicians did in like manner with their secret arts, and brought up frogs upon the land of Egypt. 8:4 Then Pharaoh called for Moses and Aaron, and said: 'Entreat the LORD, that He take away the frogs from me, and from my people; and I will let the people go, that they may sacrifice unto the LORD.' 8:5 And Moses said unto Pharaoh: 'Have thou this glory over me; against what time shall I entreat for thee, and for thy servants, and for thy people, that the frogs be destroyed from thee and thy houses, and remain in the river only?' 8:6 And he said: 'Against to-morrow.' And he said: 'Be it according to thy word; that thou mayest know that there is none like unto the LORD our God. 8:7 And the frogs shall depart from thee, and from thy houses, and from thy servants, and from thy people; they shall remain in the river only.' 8:8 And Moses and Aaron went out from Pharaoh; and Moses cried unto the LORD concerning the frogs, which He had brought upon Pharaoh. 8:9 And the LORD did according to the word of Moses; and the frogs died out of the houses, out of the courts, and out of the fields. 8:10 And they gathered them together in heaps; and the land stank. 8:11 But when Pharaoh saw that there was respite, he hardened his heart, and hearkened not unto them; as the LORD had spoken. {S}

ב3

A

B 8:12 And the LORD said unto Moses: 'Say unto Aaron: Stretch out thy rod, and smite the dust of the earth, that it may become gnats throughout all the land of Egypt.' 8:13 And they did so; and Aaron stretched out his hand with his rod, and smote the dust of the earth, and there were gnats upon man, and upon beast; all the dust of the earth became gnats throughout all the land of Egypt. 8:14 And the magicians did so with their secret arts to bring forth gnats, but they could not; and there were gnats upon man, and upon beast. 8:15 Then the magicians said unto Pharaoh: 'This is the finger of God'; and Pharaoh's heart was hardened, and he hearkened not unto them; as the LORD had spoken. {S}

3א

8:16 And the LORD said unto Moses: 'Rise up early in the morning, and stand before Pharaoh; lo, he cometh forth to the water; and say unto him: Thus saith the LORD: Let My people go, that they may serve Me. 8:17 Else, if thou wilt not let My people go, behold, I will send swarms of flies upon thee, and upon thy servants, and upon thy people, and into thy houses; and the houses of the Egyptians shall be full of swarms of flies, and also the ground whereon they are. 8:18 And I will set apart in that day the land of Goshen, in which My people dwell, that no swarms of flies shall be there; to the end that thou mayest know that I am the LORD in the midst of the earth. 8:19 And I will put a division between My people and thy people--by to-morrow shall this sign be.' 8:20 And the LORD did so; and there came grievous swarms of flies into the house of Pharaoh, and into his servants' houses; and in all the land of Egypt the land was ruined by reason of the swarms of flies. 8:21 And Pharaoh called for Moses and for Aaron, and said: 'Go ye, sacrifice to your God in the land.' 8:22 And Moses said: 'It is not meet so to do; for we shall sacrifice the abomination of the Egyptians to the LORD our God; lo, if we sacrifice the abomination of the Egyptians before their eyes, will they not stone us? 8:23 We will go three days' journey into the wilderness, and sacrifice to the LORD our God, as He shall command us.' 8:24 And Pharaoh said: 'I will let you go, that ye may sacrifice to the LORD your God in the wilderness; only ye shall not go very far away; entreat for me.' 8:25 And Moses said: 'Behold, I go out from thee, and I will entreat the LORD that the swarms of flies may depart from Pharaoh, from his servants, and from his people, tomorrow; only let not Pharaoh deal deceitfully any more in not letting the people go to sacrifice to the LORD.' 8:26 And Moses went out from Pharaoh, and entreated the LORD. 8:27 And the LORD did according to the word of Moses; and He removed the swarms of flies from Pharaoh, from his servants, and from his people; there remained not one. 8:28 And Pharaoh hardened his heart this time also, and he did not let the people go. {P}

3ב

9:1 Then the LORD said unto Moses: 'Go in unto Pharaoh, and tell him: Thus saith the LORD, the God of the Hebrews: Let My people go, that they may serve Me. 9:2 For if thou refuse to let them go, and wilt hold them still, 9:3 behold, the hand of the LORD is upon thy cattle which are in the field, upon the horses, upon the asses, upon the camels, upon the herds, and upon the flocks; there shall be a very grievous murrain. 9:4 And the LORD shall make a division between the cattle of Israel and the cattle of Egypt; and there shall nothing die of all that belongeth to the children of Israel.' 9:5 And the LORD appointed a set time, saying: 'Tomorrow the LORD shall do this thing in the land.' 9:6 And the LORD did that thing on the morrow, and all the cattle of Egypt died; but of the cattle of the children of Israel died not one. 9:7 And Pharaoh sent, and, behold, there was not so much as one of the cattle of the Israelites dead. But the heart of Pharaoh was stubborn, and he did not let the people go. {P}

3ג

9:8 And the LORD said unto Moses and unto Aaron: 'Take to you handfuls of soot of the furnace, and let Moses throw it heavenward in the sight of Pharaoh. 9:9 And it shall become small dust over all the land of Egypt, and shall be a boil breaking forth with blains upon man and upon beast, throughout all the land of Egypt.' 9:10 And they took soot of the furnace, and stood before Pharaoh; and Moses threw it up heavenward; and it became a boil breaking forth with blains upon man and upon beast. 9:11 And the magicians could not stand before Moses because of the boils; for the boils were upon the magicians, and upon all the Egyptians. 9:12 And the LORD hardened the heart of Pharaoh, and he hearkened not unto them; as the LORD had spoken unto Moses. {S}

4א

A 9:13 And the LORD said unto Moses: 'Rise up early in the morning, and stand before Pharaoh, and say unto him: Thus saith the LORD, the God of the Hebrews: Let My people go, that they may serve Me. 9:14 For I will this time send all My plagues upon thy person, and upon thy servants, and upon thy people; that thou mayest know that there is none like Me in all the earth. 9:15 Surely now I had put forth My hand, and smitten thee and thy people with pestilence, and thou hadst been cut off from the earth. 9:16 But in very deed for this cause have I made thee to stand, to show thee My power, and that My name may be declared throughout all the earth. 9:17 As yet exaltest thou thyself against My people, that thou wilt not let them go? 9:18 Behold, tomorrow about this time I will cause it to rain a very grievous hail, such as hath not been in Egypt since the day it was founded even until now. 9:19 Now therefore send, hasten in thy cattle and all that thou hast in the field; for every man and beast that shall be found in the field, and shall not be brought home, the hail shall come down upon them, and they shall die.' 9:20 He that feared the word of the LORD among the servants of Pharaoh made his servants and his cattle flee into the houses; 9:21 and he that regarded not the word of the LORD left his servants and his cattle in the field. {P}

B 9:22 And the LORD said unto Moses: 'Stretch forth thy hand toward heaven, that there may be hail in all the land of Egypt, upon man, and upon beast, and upon every herb of the field, throughout the land of Egypt.' 9:23 And Moses stretched forth his rod toward heaven; and the LORD sent thunder and hail, and fire ran down unto the earth; and the LORD caused to hail upon the land of Egypt. 9:24 So there was hail, and fire flashing up amidst the hail, very grievous, such as had not been in all the land of Egypt since it became a nation. 9:25 And the hail smote throughout all the land of Egypt all that was in the field, both man and beast; and the hail smote every herb of the field, and broke every tree of the field. 9:26 Only in the land of Goshen, where the children of Israel were, was there no hail. 9:27 And Pharaoh sent, and called for Moses and Aaron, and said unto them: 'I have sinned this time; the LORD is righteous, and I and my people are wicked. 9:28 Entreat the LORD, and let there be enough of these mighty thunderings and hail; and I will let you go, and ye shall stay no longer.' 9:29 And Moses said unto him: 'As soon as I am gone out of the city, I will spread forth my hands unto the LORD; the thunders shall cease, neither shall there be any more hail; that thou mayest know that the earth is the LORD'S. 9:30 But as for thee and thy servants, I know that ye will not yet fear the LORD God.'-- 9:31 And the flax and the barley were smitten; for the barley was in the ear, and the flax was in bloom. 9:32 But the wheat and the spelt were not smitten; for they ripen late.-- 9:33 And Moses went out of the city from Pharaoh, and spread forth his hands unto the LORD; and the thunders and hail ceased, and the rain was not poured upon the earth. 9:34 And when Pharaoh saw that the rain and the hail and the thunders were ceased, he sinned yet more, and hardened his heart, he and his servants. 9:35 And the heart of Pharaoh was hardened, and he did not let the children of Israel go; as the LORD had spoken by Moses. {P}

4ב

A 10:1 And the LORD said unto Moses: 'Go in unto Pharaoh; for I have hardened his heart, and the heart of his servants, that I might show these My signs in the midst of them; 10:2 and that thou mayest tell in the ears of thy son, and of thy son's son, what I have wrought upon Egypt, and My signs which I have done among them; that ye may know that I am the LORD.' 10:3 And Moses and Aaron went in unto Pharaoh, and said unto him: 'Thus saith the LORD, the God of the Hebrews: How long wilt thou refuse to humble thyself before Me? let My people go, that they may serve Me. 10:4 Else, if thou refuse to let My people go, behold, to-morrow will I bring locusts into thy border; 10:5 and they shall cover the face of the earth, that one shall not be able to see the earth; and they shall eat the residue of that which is escaped, which remaineth unto you from the hail, and shall eat every tree which groweth for you out of the field; 10:6 and thy houses shall be filled, and the houses of all thy servants, and the houses of all the Egyptians; as neither thy fathers nor thy fathers' fathers have seen, since the day that they were upon the earth unto this day.' And he turned, and went out from Pharaoh. 10:7 And Pharaoh's servants said unto him: 'How long shall this man be a snare unto us? let the men go, that they may serve the LORD their God, knowest thou not yet that Egypt is destroyed?' 10:8 And Moses and Aaron were brought again unto Pharaoh; and he said unto them: 'Go, serve the LORD your God; but who are they that shall go?' 10:9 And Moses said: 'We will go with our young and with our old, with our sons and with our daughters, with our flocks and with our herds we will go; for we must hold a feast unto the LORD.' 10:10 And he said unto them: 'So be the LORD with you, as I will let you go, and your little ones; see ye that evil is before your face. 10:11 Not so; go now ye that are men, and serve the LORD; for that is what ye desire.' And they were driven out from Pharaoh's presence. {S}

B 10:12 And the LORD said unto Moses: 'Stretch out thy hand over the land of Egypt for the locusts, that they may come up upon the land of Egypt, and eat every herb of the land, even all that the hail hath left.' 10:13 And Moses stretched forth his rod over the land of Egypt, and the LORD brought an east wind upon the land all that day, and all the night; and when it was morning, the east wind brought the locusts. 10:14 And the locusts went up over all the land of Egypt, and rested in all the borders of Egypt; very grievous were they; before them there were no such locusts as they, neither after them shall be such. 10:15 For they covered the face of the whole earth, so that the land was darkened; and they did eat every herb of the land, and all the fruit of the trees which the hail had left; and there remained not any green thing, either tree or herb of the field, through all the land of Egypt. 10:16 Then Pharaoh called for Moses and Aaron in haste; and he said: 'I have sinned against the LORD your God, and against you. 10:17 Now therefore forgive, I pray thee, my sin only this once, and entreat the LORD your God, that He may take away from me this death only.' 10:18 And he went out from Pharaoh, and entreated the LORD. 10:19 And the LORD turned an exceeding strong west wind, which took up the locusts, and drove them into the Red Sea; there remained not one locust in all the border of Egypt. 10:20 But the LORD hardened Pharaoh's heart, and he did not let the children of Israel go. {P}

4ג

A

B 10:21 And the LORD said unto Moses: 'Stretch out thy hand toward heaven, that there may be darkness over the land of Egypt, even darkness which may be felt.' 10:22 And Moses stretched forth his hand toward heaven; and there was a thick darkness in all the land of Egypt three days; 10:23 they saw not one another, neither rose any from his place for three days; but all the children of Israel had light in their dwellings. 10:24 And Pharaoh called unto Moses, and said: 'Go ye, serve the LORD; only let your flocks and your herds be stayed; let your little ones also go with you.' 10:25 And Moses said: 'Thou must also give into our hand sacrifices and burnt-offerings, that we may sacrifice unto the LORD our God. 10:26 Our cattle also shall go with us; there shall not a hoof be left behind; for thereof must we take to serve the LORD our God; and we know not with what we must serve the LORD, until we come thither.' 10:27 But the LORD hardened Pharaoh's heart, and he would not let them go. 10:28 And Pharaoh said unto him: 'Get thee from me, take heed to thyself, see my face no more; for in the day thou seest my face thou shalt die.' 10:29 And Moses said: 'Thou hast spoken well; I will see thy face again no more.' {P}

אה

בה

A 11:1 And the LORD said unto Moses: 'Yet one plague more will I bring upon Pharaoh, and upon Egypt; afterwards he will let you go hence; when he shall let you go, he shall surely thrust you out hence altogether.

A 11:4 And Moses said: 'Thus saith the LORD: About midnight will I go out into the midst of Egypt; 11:5 and all the first-born in the land of Egypt shall die, from the first-born of Pharaoh that sitteth upon his throne, even unto the first-born of the maid-servant that is behind the mill; and all the first-born of cattle. 11:6 And there shall be a great cry throughout all the land of Egypt, such as there hath been none like it, nor shall be like it any more. 11:7 But against any of the children of Israel shall not a dog whet his tongue, against man or beast; that ye may know how that the LORD doth put a difference between the Egyptians and Israel. 11:8 And all these thy servants shall come down unto me, and bow down unto me, saying: Get thee out, and all the people that follow thee; and after that I will go out.' And he went out from Pharaoh in hot anger. {S}

B 11:2 Speak now in the ears of the people, and let them ask every man of his neighbour, and every woman of her neighbour, jewels of silver, and jewels of gold.' 11:3 And the LORD gave the people favour in the sight of the Egyptians.
C Moreover the man Moses was very great in the land of Egypt, in the sight of Pharaoh's servants, and in the sight of the people. {S}

B 11:9 And the LORD said unto Moses: 'Pharaoh will not hearken unto you; that My wonders may be multiplied in the land of Egypt.'

C11:10 And Moses and Aaron did all these wonders before Pharaoh; and the LORD hardened Pharaoh's heart, and he did not let the children of Israel go out of his land. {S}

Exodus Unit IV (12:1-13:16)

א1

A 12:1 And the LORD spoke unto Moses and Aaron in the land of Egypt, saying: 12:2 'This month shall be unto you the beginning of months; it shall be the first month of the year to you. 12:3 Speak ye unto all the congregation of Israel, saying: In the tenth day of this month they shall take to them every man a lamb, according to their fathers' houses, a lamb for a household; 12:4 and if the household be too little for a lamb, then shall he and his neighbour next unto his house take one according to the number of the souls; according to every man's eating ye shall make your count for the lamb. 12:5 Your lamb shall be without blemish, a male of the first year; ye shall take it from the sheep, or from the goats; 12:6 and ye shall keep it unto the fourteenth day of the same month; and the whole assembly of the congregation of Israel shall kill it at dusk. 12:7 And they shall take of the blood, and put it on the two side-posts and on the lintel, upon the houses wherein they shall eat it. 12:8 And they shall eat the flesh in that night, roast with fire, and unleavened bread; with bitter herbs they shall eat it. 12:9 Eat not of it raw, nor sodden at all with water, but roast with fire; its head with its legs and with the inwards thereof. 12:10 And ye shall let nothing of it remain until the morning; but that which remaineth of it until the morning ye shall burn with fire. 12:11 And thus shall ye eat it: with your loins girded, your shoes on your feet, and your staff in your hand; and ye shall eat it in haste--it is the LORD'S passover. 12:12 For I will go through the land of Egypt in that night, and will smite all the first-born in the land of Egypt, both man and beast; and against all the gods of Egypt I will execute judgments: I am the LORD. 12:13 And the blood shall be to you for a token upon the houses where ye are; and when I see the blood, I will pass over you, and there shall no plague be upon you to destroy you, when I smite the land of Egypt.

B 12:14 And this day shall be unto you for a memorial, and ye shall keep it a feast to the LORD; throughout your generations ye shall keep it a feast by an ordinance for ever. 12:15 Seven days shall ye eat unleavened bread; howbeit the first day ye shall put away leaven out of your houses; for whosoever eateth leavened bread from the first day until the seventh day, that soul shall be cut off from Israel. 12:16 And in the first day there shall be to you a holy convocation, and in the seventh day a holy convocation; no manner of work shall be done in them, save that which every man must eat, that only may be done by you. 12:17 And ye shall observe the feast of unleavened bread; for in this selfsame day have I brought your hosts out of the land of Egypt; therefore shall ye observe this day throughout your generations by an ordinance for ever. 12:18 In the first month, on the fourteenth day of the month at even, ye shall eat unleavened bread, until the one and twentieth day of the month at even. 12:19 Seven days shall there be no leaven found in your houses; for whosoever eateth that which is leavened, that soul shall be cut off from the congregation of Israel, whether he be a sojourner, or one that is born in the land. 12:20 Ye shall eat nothing leavened; in all your habitations shall ye eat unleavened bread.' {P}

א2

A 12:29 And it came to pass at midnight, that the LORD smote all the firstborn in the land of Egypt, from the first-born of Pharaoh that sat on his throne unto the first-born of the captive that was in the dungeon; and all the first-born of cattle.

B 12:30 And Pharaoh rose up in the night, he, and all his servants, and all the Egyptians; and there was a great cry in Egypt; for there was not a house where there was not one dead. 12:31 And he called for Moses and Aaron by night and said: 'Rise up, get you forth from among my people, both ye and the children of Israel; and go, serve the LORD, as ye have said. 12:32 Take both your flocks and your herds, as ye have said, and be gone; and bless me also.'

C 12:33 And the Egyptians were urgent upon the people, to send them out of the land in haste; for they said: 'We are all dead men.' 12:34 And the people took their dough before it was leavened, their kneading-troughs being bound up in their clothes upon their shoulders.

ב1

A 12:21 Then Moses called for all the elders of Israel, and said unto them: 'Draw out, and take you lambs according to your families, and kill the passover lamb. 12:22 And ye shall take a bunch of hyssop, and dip it in the blood that is in the basin, and strike the lintel and the two side-posts with the blood that is in the basin; and none of you shall go out of the door of his house until the morning. 12:23 For the LORD will pass through to smite the Egyptians; and when He seeth the blood upon the lintel, and on the two side-posts, the LORD will pass over the door, and will not suffer the destroyer to come in unto your houses to smite you.

B 12:24 And ye shall observe this thing for an ordinance to thee and to thy sons for ever. 12:25 And it shall come to pass, when ye be come to the land which the LORD will give you, according as He hath promised, that ye shall keep this service. 12:26 And it shall come to pass, when your children shall say unto you: What mean ye by this service? 12:27 that ye shall say: It is the sacrifice of the LORD'S passover, for that He passed over the houses of the children of Israel in Egypt, when He smote the Egyptians, and delivered our houses.' And the people bowed the head and worshipped. 12:28 And the children of Israel went and did so; as the LORD had commanded Moses and Aaron, so did they. {S}

ב2

A 12:35 And the children of Israel did according to the word of Moses; and they asked of the Egyptians jewels of silver, and jewels of gold, and raiment. 12:36 And the LORD gave the people favour in the sight of the Egyptians, so that they let them have what they asked. And they despoiled the Egyptians. {P}

B 12:37 And the children of Israel journeyed from Rameses to Succoth, about six hundred thousand men on foot, beside children. 12:38 And a mixed multitude went up also with them; and flocks, and herds, even very much cattle.

C 12:39 And they baked unleavened cakes of the dough which they brought forth out of Egypt, for it was not leavened; because they were thrust out of Egypt, and could not tarry, neither had they prepared for themselves any victual.

א3

A 12:40 Now the time that the children of Israel dwelt in Egypt was four hundred and thirty years. 12:41 And it came to pass at the end of four hundred and thirty years, even the selfsame day it came to pass, that all the host of the LORD went out from the land of Egypt. 12:42 It was a night of watching unto the LORD for bringing them out from the land of Egypt; this same night is a night of watching unto the LORD for all the children of Israel throughout their generations. {P}

B 12:43 And the LORD said unto Moses and Aaron: 'This is the ordinance of the passover: there shall no alien eat thereof; 12:44 but every man's servant that is bought for money, when thou hast circumcised him, then shall he eat thereof. 12:45 A sojourner and a hired servant shall not eat thereof. 12:46 In one house shall it be eaten; thou shalt not carry forth aught of the flesh abroad out of the house; neither shall ye break a bone thereof. 12:47 All the congregation of Israel shall keep it. 12:48 And when a stranger shall sojourn with thee, and will keep the passover to the LORD, let all his males be circumcised, and then let him come near and keep it; and he shall be as one that is born in the land; but no uncircumcised person shall eat thereof. 12:49 One law shall be to him that is homeborn, and unto the stranger that sojourneth among you.' 12:50 Thus did all the children of Israel; as the LORD commanded Moses and Aaron, so did they.
C {S} 12:51 And it came to pass the selfsame day that the LORD did bring the children of Israel out of the land of Egypt by their hosts. {P}

D13:1 And the LORD spoke unto Moses, saying: 13:2 'Sanctify unto Me all the first-born, whatsoever openeth the womb among the children of Israel, both of man and of beast, it is Mine.'

ב3

A 13:3 And Moses said unto the people: 'Remember this day, in which ye came out from Egypt, out of the house of bondage; for by strength of hand the LORD brought you out from this place; there shall no leavened bread be eaten

B . 13:4 This day ye go forth in the month Abib. 13:5 And it shall be when the LORD shall bring thee into the land of the Canaanite, and the Hittite, and the Amorite, and the Hivite, and the Jebusite, which He swore unto thy fathers to give thee, a land flowing with milk and honey, that thou shalt keep this service in this month. 13:6 Seven days thou shalt eat unleavened bread, and in the seventh day shall be a feast to the LORD. 13:7 Unleavened bread shall be eaten throughout the seven days; and there shall no leavened bread be seen with thee, neither shall there be leaven seen with thee, in all thy borders.

C 13:8 And thou shalt tell thy son in that day, saying: It is because of that which the LORD did for me when I came forth out of Egypt. 13:9 And it shall be for a sign unto thee upon thy hand, and for a memorial between thine eyes, that the law of the LORD may be in thy mouth; for with a strong hand hath the LORD brought thee out of Egypt. 13:10 Thou shalt therefore keep this ordinance in its season from year to year. {P}
D13:11 And it shall be when the LORD shall bring thee into the land of the Canaanite, as He swore unto thee and to thy fathers, and shall give it thee, 13:12 that thou shalt set apart unto the LORD all that openeth the womb; every firstling that is a male, which thou hast coming of a beast, shall be the LORD'S. 13:13 And every firstling of an ass thou shalt redeem with a lamb; and if thou wilt not redeem it, then thou shalt break its neck; and all the first-born of man among thy sons shalt thou redeem. 13:14 And it shall be when thy son asketh thee in time to come, saying: What is this? that thou shalt say unto him: By strength of hand the LORD brought us out from Egypt, from the house of bondage; 13:15 and it came to pass, when Pharaoh would hardly let us go that the LORD slew all the firstborn in the land of Egypt, both the first-born of man, and the first-born of beast; therefore I sacrifice to the LORD all that openeth the womb, being males; but all the first-born of my sons I redeem. 13:16 And it shall be for a sign upon thy hand, and for frontlets between thine eyes; for by strength of hand the LORD brought us forth out of Egypt.' {S}

Exodus Unit V (13:17-15:21)

א1

13:17 And it came to pass, when Pharaoh had let the people go, that God led them not by the way of the land of the Philistines, although that was near; for God said: 'Lest peradventure the people repent when they see war, and they return to Egypt.' 13:18 But God led the people about, by the way of the wilderness by the Red Sea; and the children of Israel went up armed out of the land of Egypt.

א2

A 14:1 And the LORD spoke unto Moses, saying: 14:2 'Speak unto the children of Israel, that they turn back and encamp before Pi-hahiroth, between Migdol and the sea, before Baal-zephon, over against it shall ye encamp by the sea. 14:3 And Pharaoh will say of the children of Israel: They are entangled in the land, the wilderness hath shut them in. 14:4 And I will harden Pharaoh's heart, and he shall follow after them; and I will get Me honour upon Pharaoh, and upon all his host; and the Egyptians shall know that I am the LORD.' And they did so. 14:5 And it was told the king of Egypt that the people were fled; and the heart of Pharaoh and of his servants was turned towards the people, and they said: 'What is this we have done, that we have let Israel go from serving us?' 14:6 And he made ready his chariots, and took his people with him. 14:7 And he took six hundred chosen chariots, and all the chariots of Egypt, and captains over all of them. 14:8 And the LORD hardened the heart of Pharaoh king of Egypt, and he pursued after the children of Israel;

B for the children of Israel went out with a high hand. 14:9 And the Egyptians pursued after them, all the horses and chariots of Pharaoh, and his horsemen, and his army, and overtook them encamping by the sea, beside Pi-hahiroth, in front of Baal-zephon. 14:10 And when Pharaoh drew nigh

ב1

13:19 And Moses took the bones of Joseph with him; for he had straitly sworn the children of Israel, saying: 'God will surely remember you; and ye shall carry up my bones away hence with you.'

ב2

A the children of Israel lifted up their eyes, and, behold, the Egyptians were marching after them; and they were sore afraid; and the children of Israel cried out unto the LORD. 14:11 And they said unto Moses: 'Because there were no graves in Egypt, hast thou taken us away to die in the wilderness? wherefore hast thou dealt thus with us, to bring us forth out of Egypt? 14:12 Is not this the word that we spoke unto thee in Egypt, saying: Let us alone, that we may serve the Egyptians? For it were better for us to serve the Egyptians, than that we should die in the wilderness.' 14:13 And Moses said unto the people: 'Fear ye not, stand still, and see the salvation of the LORD, which He will work for you to-day; for whereas ye have seen the Egyptians to-day, ye shall see them again no more for ever. 14:14 The LORD will fight for you, and ye shall hold your peace.' {P}

B 14:15 And the LORD said unto Moses: 'Wherefore criest thou unto Me? speak unto the children of Israel, that they go forward. 14:16 And lift thou up thy rod, and stretch out thy hand over the sea, and divide it; and the children of Israel shall go into the midst of the sea on dry ground. 14:17 And I, behold, I will harden the hearts of the Egyptians, and they shall go in after them; and I will get Me honour upon Pharaoh, and upon all his host, upon his chariots, and upon his horsemen. 14:18 And the Egyptians shall know that I am the LORD, when I have gotten Me honour upon Pharaoh, upon his chariots, and upon his horsemen.'

ג1

13:20 And they took their journey from Succoth, and encamped in Etham, in the edge of the wilderness. 13:21 And the LORD went before them by day in a pillar of cloud, to lead them the way; and by night in a pillar of fire, to give them light; that they might go by day and by night: 13:22 the pillar of cloud by day, and the pillar of fire by night, departed not from before the people. {P}

ג2

A 14:19 And the angel of God, who went before the camp of Israel, removed and went behind them; and the pillar of cloud removed from before them, and stood behind them; 14:20 and it came between the camp of Egypt and the camp of Israel; and there was the cloud and the darkness here, yet gave it light by night there; and the one came not near the other all the night. 14:21 And Moses stretched out his hand over the sea; and the LORD caused the sea to go back by a strong east wind all the night, and made the sea dry land, and the waters were divided. 14:22 And the children of Israel went into the midst of the sea upon the dry ground; and the waters were a wall unto them on their right hand, and on their left. 14:23 And the Egyptians pursued, and went in after them into the midst of the sea, all Pharaoh's horses, his chariots, and his horsemen. 14:24 And it came to pass in the morning watch, that the LORD looked forth upon the host of the Egyptians through the pillar of fire and of cloud, and discomfited the host of the Egyptians. 14:25 And He took off their chariot wheels, and made them to drive heavily; so that the Egyptians said: 'Let us flee from the face of Israel; for the LORD fighteth for them against the Egyptians.' {P}

B 14:26 And the LORD said unto Moses: 'Stretch out thy hand over the sea, that the waters may come back upon the Egyptians, upon their chariots, and upon their horsemen.' 14:27 And Moses stretched forth his hand over the sea, and the sea returned to its strength when the morning appeared; and the Egyptians fled against it; and the LORD overthrew the Egyptians in the midst of the sea. 14:28 And the waters returned, and covered the chariots, and the horsemen, even all the host of Pharaoh that went in after them into the sea; there remained not so much as one of them. 14:29 But the children of Israel walked upon dry land in the midst of the sea; and the waters were a wall unto them on their right hand, and on their left.

אצ

A 14:30 Thus the LORD saved Israel that day out of the hand of the Egyptians; and Israel saw the Egyptians dead upon the sea-shore. 14:31 And Israel saw the great work which the LORD did upon the Egyptians, and the people feared the LORD; and they believed in the LORD, and in His servant Moses. {P}

B 15:1 Then sang Moses and the children of Israel this song unto the LORD, and spoke, saying: I will sing unto the LORD, for He is highly exalted; the horse and his rider hath He thrown into the sea. 15:2 The LORD is my strength and song, and He is become my salvation; this is my God, and I will glorify Him; my father's God, and I will exalt Him. 15:3 The LORD is a man of war, The LORD is His name. 15:4 Pharaoh's chariots and his host hath He cast into the sea, and his chosen captains are sunk in the Red Sea. 15:5 The deeps cover them--they went down into the depths like a stone.

בצ

A 15:6 Thy right hand, O LORD, glorious in power, Thy right hand, O LORD, dasheth in pieces the enemy. 15:7 And in the greatness of Thine excellency Thou overthrowest them that rise up against Thee; Thou sendest forth Thy wrath, it consumeth them as stubble. 15:8 And with the blast of Thy nostrils the waters were piled up--the floods stood upright as a heap; the deeps were congealed in the heart of the sea. 15:9 The enemy said: 'I will pursue, I will overtake, I will divide the spoil; my lust shall be satisfied upon them; I will draw my sword, my hand shall destroy them.' 15:10 Thou didst blow with Thy wind, the sea covered them; they sank as lead in the mighty waters.

B 15:11 Who is like unto Thee, O LORD, among the mighty? who is like unto Thee, glorious in holiness, fearful in praises, doing wonders? 15:12 Thou stretchedst out Thy right hand--the earth swallowed them. 15:13 Thou in Thy love hast led the people that Thou hast redeemed; Thou hast guided them in Thy strength to Thy holy habitation. 15:14 The peoples have heard, they tremble; pangs have taken hold on the inhabitants of Philistia. 15:15 Then were the chiefs of Edom affrighted; the mighty men of Moab, trembling taketh hold upon them; all the inhabitants of Canaan are melted away. 15:16 Terror and dread falleth upon them; by the greatness of Thine arm they are as still as a stone;

גצ

A till Thy people pass over, O LORD, till the people pass over that Thou hast gotten. 15:17 Thou bringest them in, and plantest them in the mountain of Thine inheritance, the place, O LORD, which Thou hast made for Thee to dwell in, the sanctuary, O Lord, which Thy hands have established. 15:18 The LORD shall reign for ever and ever. 15:19 For the horses of Pharaoh went in with his chariots and with his horsemen into the sea, and the LORD brought back the waters of the sea upon them; but the children of Israel walked on dry land in the midst of the sea. {P}

B 15:20 And Miriam the prophetess, the sister of Aaron, took a timbrel in her hand; and all the women went out after her with timbrels and with dances. 15:21 And Miriam sang unto them: Sing ye to the LORD, for He is highly exalted: the horse and his rider hath He thrown into the sea. {S}

Exodus Unit VI (15:22-17:16)

1א

15:22 And Moses led Israel onward from the Red Sea, and they went out into the wilderness of Shur; and they went three days in the wilderness, and found no water. 15:23 And when they came to Marah, they could not drink of the waters of Marah, for they were bitter. Therefore the name of it was called Marah. 15:24 And the people murmured against Moses, saying: 'What shall we drink?' 15:25 And he cried unto the LORD; and the LORD showed him a tree, and he cast it into the waters, and the waters were made sweet. There He made for them a statute and an ordinance, and there He proved them;

2א

A 16:1 And they took their journey from Elim, and all the congregation of the children of Israel came unto the wilderness of Sin, which is between Elim and Sinai, on the fifteenth day of the second month after their departing out of the land of Egypt. 16:2 And the whole congregation of the children of Israel murmured against Moses and against Aaron in the wilderness; 16:3 and the children of Israel said unto them: 'Would that we had died by the hand of the LORD in the land of Egypt, when we sat by the flesh-pots, when we did eat bread to the full; for ye have brought us forth into this wilderness, to kill this whole assembly with hunger.' {S} 16:4 Then said the LORD unto Moses: 'Behold, I will cause to rain bread from heaven for you; and the people shall go out and gather a day's portion every day, that I may prove them, whether they will walk in My law, or not. 16:5 And it shall come to pass on the sixth day that they shall prepare that which they bring in, and it shall be twice as much as they gather daily.'

B 16:6 And Moses and Aaron said unto all the children of Israel: 'At even, then ye shall know that the LORD hath brought you out from the land of Egypt; 16:7 and in the morning, then ye shall see the glory of the LORD; for that He hath heard your murmurings against the LORD; and what are we, that ye murmur against us?' 16:8 And Moses said: 'This shall be, when the LORD shall give you in the evening flesh to eat, and in the morning bread to the full; for that the LORD heareth your murmurings which ye murmur against Him; and what are we? your murmurings are not against us, but against the LORD.' 16:9 And Moses said unto Aaron: 'Say unto all the congregation of the children of Israel: Come near before the LORD; for He hath heard your murmurings.' 16:10 And it came to pass, as Aaron spoke unto the whole congregation of the children of Israel, that they looked toward the wilderness, and, behold, the glory of the LORD appeared in the cloud. {P}

C 16:11 And the LORD spoke unto Moses, saying: 16:12 'I have heard the murmurings of the children of Israel. Speak unto them, saying: At dusk ye shall eat flesh, and in the morning ye shall be filled with bread; and ye shall know that I am the LORD your God.' 16:13 And it came to pass at even, that the quails came up, and covered the camp; and in the morning there was a layer of dew round about the camp. 16:14 And when the layer of dew was gone up, behold upon the face of the wilderness a fine, scale-like thing, fine as the hoar-frost on the ground. 16:15 And when the children of Israel saw it, they said one to another: 'What is it?'--for they knew not what it was. And Moses said unto them: 'It is the bread which the LORD hath given you to eat.

1ב

15:26 and He said: 'If thou wilt diligently hearken to the voice of the LORD thy God, and wilt do that which is right in His eyes, and wilt give ear to His commandments, and keep all His statutes, I will put none of the diseases upon thee, which I have put upon the Egyptians; for I am the LORD that healeth thee.' {S} 15:27 And they came to Elim, where were twelve springs of water, and three score and ten palm-trees; and they encamped there by the waters.

2ב

A 16:16 This is the thing which the LORD hath commanded: Gather ye of it every man according to his eating; an omer a head, according to the number of your persons, shall ye take it, every man for them that are in his tent.' 16:17 And the children of Israel did so, and gathered some more, some less. 16:18 And when they did mete it with an omer, he that gathered much had nothing over, and he that gathered little had no lack; they gathered every man according to his eating. 16:19 And Moses said unto them: 'Let no man leave of it till the morning.' 16:20 Notwithstanding they hearkened not unto Moses; but some of them left of it until the morning, and it bred worms, and rotted; and Moses was wroth with them. 16:21 And they gathered it morning by morning, every man according to his eating; and as the sun waxed hot, it melted. 16:22 And it came to pass that on the sixth day they gathered twice as much bread, two omers for each one; and all the rulers of the congregation came and told Moses.

B 16:23 And he said unto them: 'This is that which the LORD hath spoken: To-morrow is a solemn rest, a holy sabbath unto the LORD. Bake that which ye will bake, and seethe that which ye will seethe; and all that remaineth over lay up for you to be kept until the morning.' 16:24 And they laid it up till the morning, as Moses bade; and it did not rot, neither was there any worm therein. 16:25 And Moses said: 'Eat that to-day; for to-day is a sabbath unto the LORD; to-day ye shall not find it in the field. 16:26 Six days ye shall gather it; but on the seventh day is the sabbath, in it there shall be none.' 16:27 And it came to pass on the seventh day, that there went out some of the people to gather, and they found none. {S} 16:28 And the LORD said unto Moses: 'How long refuse ye to keep My commandments and My laws? 16:29 See that the LORD hath given you the sabbath; therefore He giveth you on the sixth day the bread of two days; abide ye every man in his place, let no man go out of his place on the seventh day.' 16:30 So the people rested on the seventh day.

C 16:31 And the house of Israel called the name thereof Manna; and it was like coriander seed, white; and the taste of it was like wafers made with honey. 16:32 And Moses said: 'This is the thing which the LORD hath commanded: Let an omerful of it be kept throughout your generations; that they may see the bread wherewith I fed you in the wilderness, when I brought you forth from the land of Egypt.' 16:33 And Moses said unto Aaron: 'Take a jar, and put an omerful of manna therein, and lay it up before the LORD, to be kept throughout your generations.' 16:34 As the LORD commanded Moses, so Aaron laid it up before the Testimony, to be kept. 16:35 And the children of Israel did eat the manna forty years, until they came to a land inhabited; they did eat the manna, until they came unto the borders of the land of Canaan. 16:36 Now an omer is the tenth part of an ephah. {P}

אג

17:1 And all the congregation of the children of Israel journeyed from the wilderness of Sin, by their stages, according to the commandment of the LORD, and encamped in Rephidim; and there was no water for the people to drink. 17:2 Wherefore the people strove with Moses, and said: 'Give us water that we may drink.' And Moses said unto them: 'Why strive ye with me? wherefore do ye try the LORD?' 17:3 And the people thirsted there for water; and the people murmured against Moses, and said: 'Wherefore hast thou brought us up out of Egypt, to kill us and our children and our cattle with thirst?' 17:4 And Moses cried unto the LORD, saying: 'What shall I do unto this people? they are almost ready to stone me.' 17:5 And the LORD said unto Moses: 'Pass on before the people, and take with thee of the elders of Israel; and thy rod, wherewith thou smotest the river, take in thy hand, and go. 17:6 Behold, I will stand before thee there upon the rock in Horeb; and thou shalt smite the rock, and there shall come water out of it, that the people may drink.' And Moses did so in the sight of the elders of Israel. 17:7 And the name of the place was called Massah, and Meribah, because of the striving of the children of Israel, and because they tried the LORD, saying: 'Is the LORD among us, or not?' {P}

בג

17:8 Then came Amalek, and fought with Israel in Rephidim. 17:9 And Moses said unto Joshua: 'Choose us out men, and go out, fight with Amalek; tomorrow I will stand on the top of the hill with the rod of God in my hand.' 17:10 So Joshua did as Moses had said to him, and fought with Amalek; and Moses, Aaron, and Hur went up to the top of the hill. 17:11 And it came to pass, when Moses held up his hand, that Israel prevailed; and when he let down his hand, Amalek prevailed. 17:12 But Moses' hands were heavy; and they took a stone, and put it under him, and he sat thereon; and Aaron and Hur stayed up his hands, the one on the one side, and the other on the other side; and his hands were steady until the going down of the sun. 17:13 And Joshua discomfited Amalek and his people with the edge of the sword. {P}
17:14 And the LORD said unto Moses: 'Write this for a memorial in the book, and rehearse it in the ears of Joshua: for I will utterly blot out the remembrance of Amalek from under heaven.' 17:15 And Moses built an altar, and called the name of it Adonai-nissi. 17:16 And he said: 'The hand upon the throne of the LORD: the LORD will have war with Amalek from generation to generation.' {P}

Exodus Unit VII (18:1-20:22)

1א

18:1 Now Jethro, the priest of Midian, Moses' father-in-law, heard of all that God had done for Moses, and for Israel His people, how that the LORD had brought Israel out of Egypt. 18:2 And Jethro, Moses' father-in-law, took Zipporah, Moses' wife, after he had sent her away, 18:3 and her two sons; of whom the name of the one was Gershom; for he said: 'I have been a stranger in a strange land'; 18:4 and the name of the other was Eliezer: 'for the God of my father was my help, and delivered me from the sword of Pharaoh.' 18:5 And Jethro, Moses' father-in-law, came with his sons and his wife unto Moses into the wilderness where he was encamped, at the mount of God; 18:6 and he said unto Moses: 'I thy father-in-law Jethro am coming unto thee, and thy wife, and her two sons with her.' 18:7 And Moses went out to meet his father-in-law, and bowed down and kissed him; and they asked each other of their welfare; and they came into the tent. 18:8 And Moses told his father-in-law all that the LORD had done unto Pharaoh and to the Egyptians for Israel's sake, all the travail that had come upon them by the way, and how the LORD delivered them. 18:9 And Jethro rejoiced for all the goodness which the LORD had done to Israel, in that He had delivered them out of the hand of the Egyptians. 18:10 And Jethro said: 'Blessed be the LORD, who hath delivered you out of the hand of the Egyptians, and out of the hand of Pharaoh; who hath delivered the people from under the hand of the Egyptians. 18:11 Now I know that the LORD is greater than all gods; yea, for that they dealt proudly against them.' 18:12 And Jethro, Moses' father-in-law, took a burnt-offering and sacrifices for God; and Aaron came, and all the elders of Israel, to eat bread with Moses' father-in-law before God.

2א

A 19:1 In the third month after the children of Israel were gone forth out of the land of Egypt, the same day came they into the wilderness of Sinai. 19:2 And when they were departed from Rephidim, and were come to the wilderness of Sinai, they encamped in the wilderness; and there Israel encamped before the mount. 19:3 And Moses went up unto God, and the LORD called unto him out of the mountain, saying: 'Thus shalt thou say to the house of Jacob, and tell the children of Israel: 19:4 Ye have seen what I did unto the Egyptians, and how I bore you on eagles' wings, and brought you unto Myself. 19:5 Now therefore, if ye will hearken unto My voice indeed, and keep My covenant, then ye shall be Mine own treasure from among all peoples; for all the earth is Mine; 19:6 and ye shall be unto Me a kingdom of priests, and a holy nation. These are the words which thou shalt speak unto the children of Israel.'

3א

A 19:10 And the LORD said unto Moses: 'Go unto the people, and sanctify them to-day and to-morrow, and let them wash their garments, 19:11 and be ready against the third day; for the third day the LORD will come down in the sight of all the people upon mount Sinai.
B 19:12 And thou shalt set bounds unto the people round about, saying: Take heed to yourselves, that ye go not up into the mount, or touch the border of it; whosoever toucheth the mount shall be surely put to death; 19:13 no hand shall touch him, but he shall surely be stoned, or shot through; whether it be beast or man, it shall not live; when the ram's horn soundeth long, they shall come up to the mount.'

1ב

18:13 And it came to pass on the morrow, that Moses sat to judge the people; and the people stood about Moses from the morning unto the evening. 18:14 And when Moses' father-in-law saw all that he did to the people, he said: 'What is this thing that thou doest to the people? why sittest thou thyself alone, and all the people stand about thee from morning unto even?' 18:15 And Moses said unto his father-in-law: 'Because the people come unto me to inquire of God; 18:16 when they have a matter, it cometh unto me; and I judge between a man and his neighbour, and I make them know the statutes of God, and His laws.' 18:17 And Moses' father-in-law said unto him: 'The thing that thou doest is not good. 18:18 Thou wilt surely wear away, both thou, and this people that is with thee; for the thing is too heavy for thee; thou art not able to perform it thyself alone. 18:19 Hearken now unto my voice, I will give thee counsel, and God be with thee: be thou for the people before God, and bring thou the causes unto God. 18:20 And thou shalt teach them the statutes and the laws, and shalt show them the way wherein they must walk, and the work that they must do. 18:21 Moreover thou shalt provide out of all the people able men, such as fear God, men of truth, hating unjust gain; and place such over them, to be rulers of thousands, rulers of hundreds, rulers of fifties, and rulers of tens. 18:22 And let them judge the people at all seasons; and it shall be, that every great matter they shall bring unto thee, but every small matter they shall judge themselves; so shall they make it easier for thee and bear the burden with thee. 18:23 If thou shalt do this thing, and God command thee so, then thou shalt be able to endure, and all this people also shall go to their place in peace.' 18:24 So Moses hearkened to the voice of his father-in-law, and did all that he had said. 18:25 And Moses chose able men out of all Israel, and made them heads over the people, rulers of thousands, rulers of hundreds, rulers of fifties, and rulers of tens. 18:26 And they judged the people at all seasons: the hard causes they brought unto Moses, but every small matter they judged themselves. 18:27 And Moses let his father-in-law depart; and he went his way into his own land. {P}

2ב

19:7 And Moses came and called for the elders of the people, and set before them all these words which the LORD commanded him. 19:8 And all the people answered together, and said: 'All that the LORD hath spoken we will do.' And Moses reported the words of the people unto the LORD. 19:9 And the LORD said unto Moses: 'Lo, I come unto thee in a thick cloud, that the people may hear when I speak with thee, and may also believe thee for ever.' And Moses told the words of the people unto the LORD.

3ב

A B 19:14 And Moses went down from the mount unto the people, and sanctified the people; and they washed their garments. 19:15 And he said unto the people: 'Be ready against the third day; come not near a woman.'

B 19:16 And it came to pass on the third day, when it was morning, that there were thunders and lightnings and a thick cloud upon the mount, and the voice of a horn exceeding loud; and all the people that were in the camp trembled. 19:17 And Moses brought forth the people out of the camp to meet God; and they stood at the nether part of the mount. 19:18 Now mount Sinai was altogether on smoke, because the LORD descended upon it in fire; and the smoke thereof ascended as the smoke of a furnace, and the whole mount quaked greatly. 19:19 And when the voice of the horn waxed louder and louder, Moses spoke, and God answered him by a voice.

4א

A 19:20 And the LORD came down upon mount Sinai, to the top of the mount; and the LORD called Moses to the top of the mount; and Moses went up. 19:21 And the LORD said unto Moses: 'Go down, charge the people, lest they break through unto the LORD to gaze, and many of them perish. 19:22 And let the priests also, that come near to the LORD, sanctify themselves, lest the LORD break forth upon them.' 19:23 And Moses said unto the LORD: 'The people cannot come up to mount Sinai; for thou didst charge us, saying: Set bounds about the mount, and sanctify it.' 19:24 And the LORD said unto him: 'Go, get thee down, and thou shalt come up, thou, and Aaron with thee; but let not the priests and the people break through to come up unto the LORD, lest He break forth upon them.' 19:25 So Moses went down unto the people, and told them. {S}

B 20:1 And God spoke all these words, saying: {S} 20:2 I am the LORD thy God, who brought thee out of the land of Egypt, out of the house of bondage. Thou shalt have no other gods before Me. 20:3 Thou shalt not make unto thee a graven image, nor any manner of likeness, of any thing that is in heaven above, or that is in the earth beneath, or that is in the water under the earth; 20:4 thou shalt not bow down unto them, nor serve them; for I the LORD thy God am a jealous God, visiting the iniquity of the fathers upon the children unto the third and fourth generation of them that hate Me; 20:5 and showing mercy unto the thousandth generation of them that love Me and keep My commandments. {S} 20:6 Thou shalt not take the name of the LORD thy God in vain; for the LORD will not hold him guiltless that taketh His name in vain. {P}

20:7 Remember the sabbath day, to keep it holy. 20:8 Six days shalt thou labour, and do all thy work; 20:9 but the seventh day is a sabbath unto the LORD thy God, in it thou shalt not do any manner of work, thou, nor thy son, nor thy daughter, nor thy man-servant, nor thy maid-servant, nor thy cattle, nor thy stranger that is within thy gates; 20:10 for in six days the LORD made heaven and earth, the sea, and all that in them is, and rested on the seventh day; wherefore the LORD blessed the sabbath day, and hallowed it. {S} 20:11 Honour thy father and thy mother, that thy days may be long upon the land which the LORD thy God giveth thee. {S} 20:12 Thou shalt not murder. {S} Thou shalt not commit adultery. {S} Thou shalt not steal. {S} Thou shalt not bear false witness against thy neighbour. {S} 20:13 Thou shalt not covet thy neighbour's house; {S} thou shalt not covet thy neighbour's wife, nor his man-servant, nor his maid-servant, nor his ox, nor his ass, nor any thing that is thy neighbour's. {P}

4ב

A 20:14 And all the people perceived the thunderings, and the lightnings, and the voice of the horn, and the mountain smoking; and when the people saw it, they trembled, and stood afar off. 20:15 And they said unto Moses: 'Speak thou with us, and we will hear; but let not God speak with us, lest we die.' 20:16 And Moses said unto the people: 'Fear not; for God is come to prove you, and that His fear may be before you, that ye sin not.' 20:17 And the people stood afar off; but Moses drew near unto the thick darkness where God was. {S}

B 20:18 And the LORD said unto Moses: Thus thou shalt say unto the children of Israel: Ye yourselves have seen that I have talked with you from heaven. 20:19 Ye shall not make with Me--gods of silver, or gods of gold, ye shall not make unto you. 20:20 An altar of earth thou shalt make unto Me, and shalt sacrifice thereon thy burnt-offerings, and thy peace-offerings, thy sheep, and thine oxen; in every place where I cause My name to be mentioned I will come unto thee and bless thee. 20:21 And if thou make Me an altar of stone, thou shalt not build it of hewn stones; for if thou lift up thy tool upon it, thou hast profaned it. 20:22 Neither shalt thou go up by steps unto Mine altar, that thy nakedness be not uncovered thereon. {P}

Exodus Unit VIII (21:1-22:16)

1א

21:1 Now these are the ordinances which thou shalt set before them. 21:2 If thou buy a Hebrew servant, six years he shall serve; and in the seventh he shall go out free for nothing. 21:3 If he come in by himself, he shall go out by himself; if he be married, then his wife shall go out with him. 21:4 If his master give him a wife, and she bear him sons or daughters; the wife and her children shall be her master's, and he shall go out by himself. 21:5 But if the servant shall plainly say: I love my master, my wife, and my children; I will not go out free; 21:6 then his master shall bring him unto God, and shall bring him to the door, or unto the door-post; and his master shall bore his ear through with an awl; and he shall serve him for ever. {S}

2א

A 21:12 He that smiteth a man, so that he dieth, shall surely be put to death. 21:13 And if a man lie not in wait, but God cause it to come to hand; then I will appoint thee a place whither he may flee. {S} 21:14 And if a man come presumptuously upon his neighbour, to slay him with guile; thou shalt take him from Mine altar, that he may die. {S}

B 21:15 And he that smiteth his father, or his mother, shall be surely put to death. {S}

3א

A 21:18 And if men contend, and one smite the other with a stone, or with his fist, and he die not, but keep his bed; 21:19 if he rise again, and walk abroad upon his staff, then shall he that smote him be quit; only he shall pay for the loss of his time, and shall cause him to be thoroughly healed. {S}

B 21:20 And if a man smite his bondman, or his bondwoman, with a rod, and he die under his hand, he shall surely be punished. 21:21 Notwithstanding if he continue a day or two, he shall not be punished; for he is his money. {S}

4א

A 21:28 And if an ox gore a man or a woman, that they die, the ox shall be surely stoned, and its flesh shall not be eaten; but the owner of the ox shall be quit. 21:29 But if the ox was wont to gore in time past, and warning hath been given to its owner, and he hath not kept it in, but it hath killed a man or a woman; the ox shall be stoned, and its owner also shall be put to death. 21:30 If there be laid on him a ransom, then he shall give for the redemption of his life whatsoever is laid upon him. 21:31 Whether it have gored a son, or have gored a daughter, according to this judgment shall it be done unto him. 21:32 If the ox gore a bondman or a bondwoman, he shall give unto their master thirty shekels of silver, and the ox shall be stoned. {S}

B 21:33 And if a man shall open a pit, or if a man shall dig a pit and not cover it, and an ox or an ass fall therein, 21:34 the owner of the pit shall make it good; he shall give money unto the owner of them, and the dead beast shall be his. {S}

5א

22:4 If a man cause a field or vineyard to be eaten, and shall let his beast loose, and it feed in another man's field; of the best of his own field, and of the best of his own vineyard, shall he make restitution. {S}

6א

22:6 If a man deliver unto his neighbour money or stuff to keep, and it be stolen out of the man's house; if the thief be found, he shall pay double. 22:7 If the thief be not found, then the master of the house shall come near unto God, to see whether he have not put his hand unto his neighbour's goods. 22:8 For every matter of trespass, whether it be for ox, for ass, for sheep, for raiment, or for any manner of lost thing, whereof one saith: 'This is it,' the cause of both parties shall come before God; he whom God shall condemn shall pay double unto his neighbour. {S}

7א

22:13 And if a man borrow aught of his neighbour, and it be hurt, or die, the owner thereof not being with it, he shall surely make restitution. 22:14 If the owner thereof be with it, he shall not make it good; if it be a hireling, he loseth his hire. {S}

1ב

21:7 And if a man sell his daughter to be a maid-servant, she shall not go out as the men-servants do. 21:8 If she please not her master, who hath espoused her to himself, then shall he let her be redeemed; to sell her unto a foreign people he shall have no power, seeing he hath dealt deceitfully with her. 21:9 And if he espouse her unto his son, he shall deal with her after the manner of daughters. 21:10 If he take him another wife, her food, her raiment, and her conjugal rights, shall he not diminish. 21:11 And if he do not these three unto her, then shall she go out for nothing, without money. {S}

2ב

A 21:16 And he that stealeth a man, and selleth him, or if he be found in his hand, he shall surely be put to death. {S}

B 21:17 And he that curseth his father or his mother, shall surely be put to death. {S}

3ב

A 21:22 And if men strive together, and hurt a woman with child, so that her fruit depart, and yet no harm follow, he shall be surely fined, according as the woman's husband shall lay upon him; and he shall pay as the judges determine. 21:23 But if any harm follow, then thou shalt give life for life, 21:24 eye for eye, tooth for tooth, hand for hand, foot for foot, 21:25 burning for burning, wound for wound, stripe for stripe. {S}

B 21:26 And if a man smite the eye of his bondman, or the eye of his bondwoman, and destroy it, he shall let him go free for his eye's sake. 21:27 And if he smite out his bondman's tooth, or his bondwoman's tooth, he shall let him go free for his tooth's sake. {P}

4ב

A 21:35 And if one man's ox hurt another's, so that it dieth; then they shall sell the live ox, and divide the price of it; and the dead also they shall divide. 21:36 Or if it be known that the ox was wont to gore in time past, and its owner hath not kept it in; he shall surely pay ox for ox, and the dead beast shall be his own. {S}

B 21:37 If a man steal an ox, or a sheep, and kill it, or sell it, he shall pay five oxen for an ox, and four sheep for a sheep. 22:1 If a thief be found breaking in, and be smitten so that he dieth, there shall be no bloodguiltiness for him. 22:2 If the sun be risen upon him, there shall be bloodguiltiness for him--he shall make restitution; if he have nothing, then he shall be sold for his theft. 22:3 If the theft be found in his hand alive, whether it be ox, or ass, or sheep, he shall pay double. {S}

5ב

22:5 If fire break out, and catch in thorns, so that the shocks of corn, or the standing corn, or the field are consumed; he that kindled the fire shall surely make restitution. {S}

6ב

22:9 If a man deliver unto his neighbour an ass, or an ox, or a sheep, or any beast, to keep, and it die, or be hurt, or driven away, no man seeing it; 22:10 the oath of the LORD shall be between them both, to see whether he have not put his hand unto his neighbour's goods; and the owner thereof shall accept it, and he shall not make restitution. 22:11 But if it be stolen from him, he shall make restitution unto the owner thereof. 22:12 If it be torn in pieces, let him bring it for witness; he shall not make good that which was torn. {P}

7ב

22:15 And if a man entice a virgin that is not betrothed, and lie with her, he shall surely pay a dowry for her to be his wife. 22:16 If her father utterly refuse to give her unto him, he shall pay money according to the dowry of virgins. {S}

Exodus Unit IX (22:17-23:19)

1א
22:17 Thou shalt not suffer a sorceress to live.

2א
22:20 And a stranger shalt thou not wrong, neither shalt thou oppress him; for ye were strangers in the land of Egypt.

3א
22:27 Thou shalt not revile God, nor curse a ruler of thy people.

4א
A 23:1 Thou shalt not utter a false report; put not thy hand with the wicked to be an unrighteous witness.
B 23:2 Thou shalt not follow a multitude to do evil; neither shalt thou bear witness in a cause to turn aside after a multitude to pervert justice;
C 23:3 neither shalt thou favour a poor man in his cause. {S}

5א
23:10 And six years thou shalt sow thy land, and gather in the increase thereof; 23:11 but the seventh year thou shalt let it rest and lie fallow, that the poor of thy people may eat; and what they leave the beast of the field shall eat. In like manner thou shalt deal with thy vineyard, and with thy oliveyard.

1ב
22:18 Whosoever lieth with a beast shall surely be put to death. {S}

2ב
22:21 Ye shall not afflict any widow, or fatherless child. 22:22 If thou afflict them in any wise--for if they cry at all unto Me, I will surely hear their cry-- 22:23 My wrath shall wax hot, and I will kill you with the sword; and your wives shall be widows, and your children fatherless. {P}

3ב
22:28 Thou shalt not delay to offer of the fulness of thy harvest, and of the outflow of thy presses. The first-born of thy sons shalt thou give unto Me. 22:29 Likewise shalt thou do with thine oxen, and with thy sheep; seven days it shall be with its dam; on the eighth day thou shalt give it Me.

4ב
A 23:4 If thou meet thine enemy's ox or his ass going astray, thou shalt surely bring it back to him again. {S}
B 23:5 If thou see the ass of him that hateth thee lying under its burden, thou shalt forbear to pass by him; thou shalt surely release it with him. {S}
C 23:6 Thou shalt not wrest the judgment of thy poor in his cause.

5ב
23:12 Six days thou shalt do thy work, but on the seventh day thou shalt rest; that thine ox and thine ass may have rest, and the son of thy handmaid, and the stranger, may be refreshed. 23:13 And in all things that I have said unto you take ye heed; and make no mention of the name of other gods, neither let it be heard out of thy mouth.

1ג
22:19 He that sacrificeth unto the gods, save unto the LORD only, shall be utterly destroyed.

2ג
22:24 If thou lend money to any of My people, even to the poor with thee, thou shalt not be to him as a creditor; neither shall ye lay upon him interest. 22:25 If thou at all take thy neighbour's garment to pledge, thou shalt restore it unto him by that the sun goeth down; 22:26 for that is his only covering, it is his garment for his skin; wherein shall he sleep? and it shall come to pass, when he crieth unto Me, that I will hear; for I am gracious. {S}

3ג
22:30 And ye shall be holy men unto Me; therefore ye shall not eat any flesh that is torn of beasts in the field; ye shall cast it to the dogs. {S}

4ג
A 23:7 Keep thee far from a false matter; and the innocent and righteous slay thou not; for I will not justify the wicked.
B 23:8 And thou shalt take no gift; for a gift blindeth them that have sight, and perverteth the words of the righteous.

C 23:9 And a stranger shalt thou not oppress; for ye know the heart of a stranger, seeing ye were strangers in the land of Egypt.

5ג
23:14 Three times thou shalt keep a feast unto Me in the year. 23:15 The feast of unleavened bread shalt thou keep; seven days thou shalt eat unleavened bread, as I commanded thee, at the time appointed in the month Abib--for in it thou camest out from Egypt; and none shall appear before Me empty; 23:16 and the feast of harvest, the first-fruits of thy labours, which thou sowest in the field; and the feast of ingathering, at the end of the year, when thou gatherest in thy labours out of the field. 23:17 Three times in the year all thy males shall appear before the Lord GOD. 23:18 Thou shalt not offer the blood of My sacrifice with leavened bread; neither shall the fat of My feast remain all night until the morning. 23:19 The choicest first-fruits of thy land thou shalt bring into the house of the LORD thy God. Thou shalt not seethe a kid in its mother's milk. {P}

Exodus Unit X (23:20-24:18)

1א

23:20 Behold, I send an angel before thee, to keep thee by the way, and to bring thee into the place which I have prepared. 23:21 Take heed of him, and hearken unto his voice; be not rebellious against him; for he will not pardon your transgression; for My name is in him. 23:22 But if thou shalt indeed hearken unto his voice, and do all that I speak; then I will be an enemy unto thine enemies, and an adversary unto thine adversaries.

1ב

23:23 For Mine angel shall go before thee, and bring thee in unto the Amorite, and the Hittite, and the Perizzite, and the Canaanite, the Hivite, and the Jebusite; and I will cut them off. 23:24 Thou shalt not bow down to their gods, nor serve them, nor do after their doings; but thou shalt utterly overthrow them, and break in pieces their pillars. 23:25 And ye shall serve the LORD your God, and He will bless thy bread, and thy water; and I will take sickness away from the midst of thee. {S} 23:26 None shall miscarry, nor be barren, in thy land; the number of thy days I will fulfil. 23:27 I will send My terror before thee, and will discomfit all the people to whom thou shalt come, and I will make all thine enemies turn their backs unto thee.

1ג

23:28 And I will send the hornet before thee, which shall drive out the Hivite, the Canaanite, and the Hittite, from before thee. 23:29 I will not drive them out from before thee in one year, lest the land become desolate, and the beasts of the field multiply against thee. 23:30 By little and little I will drive them out from before thee, until thou be increased, and inherit the land. 23:31 And I will set thy border from the Red Sea even unto the sea of the Philistines, and from the wilderness unto the River; for I will deliver the inhabitants of the land into your hand; and thou shalt drive them out before thee. 23:32 Thou shalt make no covenant with them, nor with their gods. 23:33 They shall not dwell in thy land--lest they make thee sin against Me, for thou wilt serve their gods--for they will be a snare unto thee. {P}

2א

24:1 And unto Moses He said: 'Come up unto the LORD, thou, and Aaron, Nadab, and Abihu, and seventy of the elders of Israel; and worship ye afar off; 24:2 and Moses alone shall come near unto the LORD; but they shall not come near; neither shall the people go up with him.' 24:3 And Moses came and told the people all the words of the LORD, and all the ordinances; and all the people answered with one voice, and said: 'All the words which the LORD hath spoken will we do.'

2ב

24:4 And Moses wrote all the words of the LORD, and rose up early in the morning, and builded an altar under the mount, and twelve pillars, according to the twelve tribes of Israel. 24:5 And he sent the young men of the children of Israel, who offered burnt-offerings, and sacrificed peace-offerings of oxen unto the LORD. 24:6 And Moses took half of the blood, and put it in basins; and half of the blood he dashed against the altar. 24:7 And he took the book of the covenant, and read in the hearing of the people; and they said: 'All that the LORD hath spoken will we do, and obey.' 24:8 And Moses took the blood, and sprinkled it on the people, and said: 'Behold the blood of the covenant, which the LORD hath made with you in agreement with all these words.'

2ג

24:9 Then went up Moses, and Aaron, Nadab, and Abihu, and seventy of the elders of Israel; 24:10 and they saw the God of Israel; and there was under His feet the like of a paved work of sapphire stone, and the like of the very heaven for clearness. 24:11 And upon the nobles of the children of Israel He laid not His hand; and they beheld God, and did eat and drink. {S}

3א

24:12 And the LORD said unto Moses: 'Come up to Me into the mount and be there; and I will give thee the tables of stone, and the law and the commandment, which I have written, that thou mayest teach them.' 24:13 And Moses rose up, and Joshua his minister; and Moses went up into the mount of God.

3ב

24:14 And unto the elders he said: 'Tarry ye here for us, until we come back unto you; and, behold, Aaron and Hur are with you; whosoever hath a cause, let him come near unto them.' 24:15 And Moses went up into the mount, and the cloud covered the mount.

3ג

24:16 And the glory of the LORD abode upon mount Sinai, and the cloud covered it six days; and the seventh day He called unto Moses out of the midst of the cloud. 24:17 And the appearance of the glory of the LORD was like devouring fire on the top of the mount in the eyes of the children of Israel. 24:18 And Moses entered into the midst of the cloud, and went up into the mount; and Moses was in the mount forty days and forty nights. {P}

Exodus Unit XI (25:1-27:21)

1

25:1 And the LORD spoke unto Moses, saying: 25:2 'Speak unto the children of Israel, that they take for Me an offering; of every man whose heart maketh him willing ye shall take My offering. 25:3 And this is the offering which ye shall take of them: gold, and silver, and brass; 25:4 and blue, and purple, and scarlet, and fine linen, and goats' hair; 25:5 and rams' skins dyed red, and sealskins, and acacia-wood; 25:6 oil for the light, spices for the anointing oil, and for the sweet incense; 25:7 onyx stones, and stones to be set, for the ephod, and for the breastplate. 25:8 And let them make Me a sanctuary, that I may dwell among them. 25:9 According to all that I show thee, the pattern of the tabernacle, and the pattern of all the furniture thereof, even so shall ye make it.{S}

2א

A 25:10 And they shall make an ark of acacia-wood: two cubits and a half shall be the length thereof, and a cubit and a half the breadth thereof, and a cubit and a half the height thereof. 25:11 And thou shalt overlay it with pure gold, within and without shalt thou overlay it, and shalt make upon it a crown of gold round about. 25:12 And thou shalt cast four rings of gold for it, and put them in the four feet thereof; and two rings shall be on the one side of it, and two rings on the other side of it. 25:13 And thou shalt make staves of acacia-wood, and overlay them with gold. 25:14 And thou shalt put the staves into the rings on the sides of the ark, wherewith to bear the ark. 25:15 The staves shall be in the rings of the ark; they shall not be taken from it. 25:16 And thou shalt put into the ark the testimony which I shall give thee. 25:17 And thou shalt make an ark-cover of pure gold: two cubits and a half shall be the length thereof, and a cubit and a half the breadth thereof. 25:18 And thou shalt make two cherubim of gold; of beaten work shalt thou make them, at the two ends of the ark-cover. 25:19 And make one cherub at the one end, and one cherub at the other end; of one piece with the ark-cover shall ye make the cherubim of the two ends thereof. 25:20 And the cherubim shall spread out their wings on high, screening the ark-cover with their wings, with their faces one to another; toward the ark-cover shall the faces of the cherubim be. 25:21 And thou shalt put the ark-cover above upon the ark; and in the ark thou shalt put the testimony that I shall give thee. 25:22 And there I will meet with thee, and I will speak with thee from above the ark-cover, from between the two cherubim which are upon the ark of the testimony, of all things which I will give thee in commandment unto the children of Israel. {P}

B 25:23 And thou shalt make a table of acacia-wood: two cubits shall be the length thereof, and a cubit the breadth thereof, and a cubit and a half the height thereof. 25:24 And thou shalt overlay it with pure gold, and make thereto a crown of gold round about. 25:25 And thou shalt make unto it a border of a handbreadth round about, and thou shalt make a golden crown to the border thereof round about. 25:26 And thou shalt make for it four rings of gold, and put the rings in the four corners that are on the four feet thereof. 25:27 Close by the border shall the rings be, for places for the staves to bear the table. 25:28 And thou shalt make the staves of acacia-wood, and overlay them with gold, that the table may be borne with them. 25:29 And thou shalt make the dishes thereof, and the pans thereof, and the jars thereof, and the bowls thereof, wherewith to pour out; of pure gold shalt thou make them. 25:30 And thou shalt set upon the table showbread before Me alway. {P}

C 25:31 And thou shalt make a candlestick of pure gold: of beaten work shall the candlestick be made, even its base, and its shaft; its cups, its knops, and its flowers, shall be of one piece with it. 25:32 And there shall be six branches going out of the sides thereof: three branches of the candlestick out of the one side thereof, and three branches of the candlestick out of the other side thereof; 25:33 three cups made like almond-blossoms in one branch, a knop and a flower; and three cups made like almond-blossoms in the other branch, a knop and a flower; so for the six branches going out of the candlestick. 25:34 And in the candlestick four cups made like almond-blossoms, the knops thereof, and the flowers thereof. 25:35 And a knop under two branches of one piece with it, and a knop under two branches of one piece with it, and a knop under two branches of one piece with it, for the six branches going out of the candlestick. 25:36 Their knops and their branches shall be of one piece with it; the whole of it one beaten work of pure gold. 25:37 And thou shalt make the lamps thereof, seven; and they shall light the lamps thereof, to give light over against it. 25:38 And the tongs thereof, and the snuffdishes thereof, shall be of pure gold. 25:39 Of a talent of pure gold shall it be made, with all these vessels. 25:40 And see that thou make them after their pattern, which is being shown thee in the mount. {S}

2ב

A 26:1 Moreover thou shalt make the tabernacle with ten curtains: of fine twined linen, and blue, and purple, and scarlet, with cherubim the work of the skilful workman shalt thou make them. 26:2 The length of each curtain shall be eight and twenty cubits, and the breadth of each curtain four cubits; all the curtains shall have one measure. 26:3 Five curtains shall be coupled together one to another; and the other five curtains shall be coupled one to another. 26:4 And thou shalt make loops of blue upon the edge of the one curtain that is outmost in the first set; and likewise shalt thou make in the edge of the curtain that is outmost in the second set. 26:5 Fifty loops shalt thou make in the one curtain, and fifty loops shalt thou make in the edge of the curtain that is in the second set; the loops shall be opposite one to another. 26:6 And thou shalt make fifty clasps of gold, and couple the curtains one to another with the clasps, that the tabernacle may be one whole.

B 26:7 And thou shalt make curtains of goats' hair for a tent over the tabernacle; eleven curtains shalt thou make them. 26:8 The length of each curtain shall be thirty cubits, and the breadth of each curtain four cubits; the eleven curtains shall have one measure. 26:9 And thou shalt couple five curtains by themselves, and six curtains by themselves, and shalt double over the sixth curtain in the forefront of the tent. 26:10 And thou shalt make fifty loops on the edge of the one curtain that is outmost in the first set, and fifty loops upon the edge of the curtain which is outmost in the second set. 26:11 And thou shalt make fifty clasps of brass, and put the clasps into the loops, and couple the tent together, that it may be one. 26:12 And as for the overhanging part that remaineth of the curtains of the tent, the half curtain that remaineth over shall hang over the back of the tabernacle. 26:13 And the cubit on the one side, and the cubit on the other side, of that which remaineth over in the length of the curtains of the tent, shall hang over the sides of the tabernacle on this side and on that side, to cover it. 26:14 And thou shalt make a covering for the tent of rams' skins dyed red and a covering of sealskins above. {P}

C 26:15 And thou shalt make the boards for the tabernacle of acacia-wood, standing up. 26:16 Ten cubits shall be the length of a board, and a cubit and a half the breadth of each board. 26:17 Two tenons shall there be in each board, joined one to another; thus shalt thou make for all the boards of the tabernacle. 26:18 And thou shalt make the boards for the tabernacle, twenty boards for the south side southward: 26:19 And thou shalt make forty sockets of silver under the twenty boards: two sockets under one board for its two tenons, and two sockets under another board for its two tenons; 26:20 and for the second side of the tabernacle, on the north side, twenty boards. 26:21 And their forty sockets of silver: two sockets under one board, and two sockets under another board. 26:22 And for the hinder part of the tabernacle westward thou shalt make six boards. 26:23 And two boards shalt thou make for the corners of the tabernacle in the hinder part. 26:24 And they shall be double beneath, and in like manner they shall be complete unto the top thereof unto the first ring; thus shall it be for them both; they shall be for the two corners. 26:25 Thus there shall be eight boards, and their sockets of silver, sixteen sockets: two sockets under one board, and two sockets under another board. 26:26 And thou shalt make bars of acacia-wood: five for the boards of the one side of the tabernacle, 26:27 and five bars for the boards of the other side of the tabernacle, and five bars for the boards of the side of the tabernacle, for the hinder part westward; 26:28 and the middle bar in the midst of the boards, which shall pass through from end to end. 26:29 And thou shalt overlay the boards with gold, and make their rings of gold for holders for the bars; and thou shalt overlay the bars with gold. 26:30 And thou shalt rear up the tabernacle according to the fashion thereof which hath been shown thee in the mount. {S}

3א

26:31 And thou shalt make a veil of blue, and purple, and scarlet, and fine twined linen; with cherubim the work of the skilful workman shall it be made. 26:32 And thou shalt hang it upon four pillars of acacia overlaid with gold, their hooks being of gold, upon four sockets of silver. 26:33 And thou shalt hang up the veil under the clasps, and shalt bring in thither within the veil the ark of the testimony; and the veil shall divide unto you between the holy place and the most holy. 26:34 And thou shalt put the ark-cover upon the ark of the testimony in the most holy place. 26:35 And thou shalt set the table without the veil, and the candlestick over against the table on the side of the tabernacle toward the south; and thou shalt put the table on the north side.

4א

27:1 And thou shalt make the altar of acacia-wood, five cubits long, and five cubits broad; the altar shall be four-square; and the height thereof shall be three cubits. 27:2 And thou shalt make the horns of it upon the four corners thereof; the horns thereof shall be of one piece with it; and thou shalt overlay it with brass. 27:3 And thou shalt make its pots to take away its ashes, and its shovels, and its basins, and its flesh-hooks, and its fire-pans; all the vessels thereof thou shalt make of brass. 27:4 And thou shalt make for it a grating of network of brass; and upon the net shalt thou make four brazen rings in the four corners thereof. 27:5 And thou shalt put it under the ledge round the altar beneath, that the net may reach halfway up the altar. 27:6 And thou shalt make staves for the altar, staves of acacia-wood, and overlay them with brass. 27:7 And the staves thereof shall be put into the rings, and the staves shall be upon the two sides of the altar, in bearing it. 27:8 Hollow with planks shalt thou make it; as it hath been shown thee in the mount, so shall they make it. {S}

3ב

26:36 And thou shalt make a screen for the door of the Tent, of blue, and purple, and scarlet, and fine twined linen, the work of the weaver in colours. 26:37 And thou shalt make for the screen five pillars of acacia, and overlay them with gold; their hooks shall be of gold; and thou shalt cast five sockets of brass for them. {S}

4ב

27:9 And thou shalt make the court of the tabernacle: for the south side southward there shall be hangings for the court of fine twined linen a hundred cubits long for one side. 27:10 And the pillars thereof shall be twenty, and their sockets twenty, of brass; the hooks of the pillars and their fillets shall be of silver. 27:11 And likewise for the north side in length there shall be hangings a hundred cubits long, and the pillars thereof twenty, and their sockets twenty, of brass; the hooks of the pillars and their fillets of silver. 27:12 And for the breadth of the court on the west side shall be hangings of fifty cubits: their pillars ten, and their sockets ten. 27:13 And the breadth of the court on the east side eastward shall be fifty cubits. 27:14 The hangings for the one side [of the gate] shall be fifteen cubits: their pillars three, and their sockets three. 27:15 And for the other side shall be hangings of fifteen cubits: their pillars three, and their sockets three. 27:16 And for the gate of the court shall be a screen of twenty cubits, of blue, and purple, and scarlet, and fine twined linen, the work of the weaver in colours: their pillars four, and their sockets four. 27:17 All the pillars of the court round about shall be filleted with silver; their hooks of silver, and their sockets of brass. 27:18 The length of the court shall be a hundred cubits, and the breadth fifty every where, and the height five cubits, of fine twined linen, and their sockets of brass. 27:19 All the instruments of the tabernacle in all the service thereof, and all the pins thereof, and all the pins of the court, shall be of brass. {S}

5

27:20 And thou shalt command the children of Israel, that they bring unto thee pure olive oil beaten for the light, to cause a lamp to burn continually. 27:21 In the tent of meeting, without the veil which is before the testimony, Aaron and his sons shall set it in order, to burn from evening to morning before the LORD; it shall be a statute for ever throughout their generations on the behalf of the children of Israel. {S}

Exodus Unit XII (28:1-43)

1

28:1 And bring thou near unto thee Aaron thy brother, and his sons with him, from among the children of Israel, that they may minister unto Me in the priest's office, even Aaron, Nadab and Abihu, Eleazar and Ithamar, Aaron's sons. 28:2 And thou shalt make holy garments for Aaron thy brother, for splendour and for beauty. 28:3 And thou shalt speak unto all that are wise-hearted, whom I have filled with the spirit of wisdom, that they make Aaron's garments to sanctify him, that he may minister unto Me in the priest's office. 28:4 And these are the garments which they shall make: a breastplate, and an ephod, and a robe, and a tunic of chequer work, a mitre, and a girdle; and they shall make holy garments for Aaron thy brother, and his sons, that he may minister unto Me in the priest's office. 28:5 And they shall take the gold, and the blue, and the purple, and the scarlet, and the fine linen. {P}

2א

28:6 And they shall make the ephod of gold, of blue, and purple, scarlet, and fine twined linen, the work of the skilful workman. 28:7 It shall have two shoulder-pieces joined to the two ends thereof, that it may be joined together. 28:8 And the skilfully woven band, which is upon it, wherewith to gird it on, shall be like the work thereof and of the same piece: of gold, of blue, and purple, and scarlet, and fine twined linen. 28:9 And thou shalt take two onyx stones, and grave on them the names of the children of Israel: 28:10 six of their names on the one stone, and the names of the six that remain on the other stone, according to their birth. 28:11 With the work of an engraver in stone, like the engravings of a signet, shalt thou engrave the two stones, according to the names of the children of Israel; thou shalt make them to be inclosed in settings of gold. 28:12 And thou shalt put the two stones upon the shoulder-pieces of the ephod, to be stones of memorial for the children of Israel; and Aaron shall bear their names before the LORD upon his two shoulders for a memorial. {S} 28:13 And thou shalt make settings of gold; 28:14 and two chains of pure gold; of plaited thread shalt thou make them, of wreathen work; and thou shalt put the wreathen chains on the settings. {S}

2ב

28:15 And thou shalt make a breastplate of judgment, the work of the skilful workman; like the work of the ephod thou shalt make it: of gold, of blue, and purple, and scarlet, and fine twined linen, shalt thou make it. 28:16 Four-square it shall be and double: a span shall be the length thereof, and a span the breadth thereof. 28:17 And thou shalt set in it settings of stones, four rows of stones: a row of carnelian, topaz, and smaragd shall be the first row; 28:18 and the second row a carbuncle, a sapphire, and an emerald; 28:19 and the third row a jacinth, an agate, and an amethyst; 28:20 and the fourth row a beryl, and an onyx, and a jasper; they shall be inclosed in gold in their settings. 28:21 And the stones shall be according to the names of the children of Israel, twelve, according to their names; like the engravings of a signet, every one according to his name, they shall be for the twelve tribes. 28:22 And thou shalt make upon the breastplate plaited chains of wreathen work of pure gold. 28:23 And thou shalt make upon the breastplate two rings of gold, and shalt put the two rings on the two ends of the breastplate. 28:24 And thou shalt put the two wreathen chains of gold on the two rings at the ends of the breastplate. 28:25 And the other two ends of the two wreathen chains thou shalt put on the two settings, and put them on the shoulder-pieces of the ephod, in the forepart thereof. 28:26 And thou shalt make two rings of gold, and thou shalt put them upon the two ends of the breastplate, upon the edge thereof, which is toward the side of the ephod inward. 28:27 And thou shalt make two rings of gold, and shalt put them on the two shoulder-pieces of the ephod underneath, in the forepart thereof, close by the coupling thereof, above the skilfully woven band of the ephod. 28:28 And they shall bind the breastplate by the rings thereof unto the rings of the ephod with a thread of blue, that it may be upon the skilfully woven band of the ephod, and that the breastplate be not loosed from the ephod. 28:29 And Aaron shall bear the names of the children of Israel in the breastplate of judgment upon his heart, when he goeth in unto the holy place, for a memorial before the LORD continually. 28:30 And thou shalt put in the breastplate of judgment the Urim and the Thummim; and they shall be upon Aaron's heart, when he goeth in before the LORD; and Aaron shall bear the judgment of the children of Israel upon his heart before the LORD continually. {S}

3א

28:31 And thou shalt make the robe of the ephod all of blue. 28:32 And it shall have a hole for the head in the midst thereof; it shall have a binding of woven work round about the hole of it, as it were the hole of a coat of mail that it be not rent. 28:33 And upon the skirts of it thou shalt make pomegranates of blue, and of purple, and of scarlet, round about the skirts thereof; and bells of gold between them round about: 28:34 a golden bell and a pomegranate, a golden bell and a pomegranate, upon the skirts of the robe round about. 28:35 And it shall be upon Aaron to minister; and the sound thereof shall be heard when he goeth in unto the holy place before the LORD, and when he cometh out, that he die not. {S}

3ב

28:36 And thou shalt make a plate of pure gold, and engrave upon it, like the engravings of a signet: HOLY TO THE LORD. 28:37 And thou shalt put it on a thread of blue, and it shall be upon the mitre; upon the forefront of the mitre it shall be. 28:38 And it shall be upon Aaron's forehead, and Aaron shall bear the iniquity committed in the holy things, which the children of Israel shall hallow, even in all their holy gifts; and it shall be always upon his forehead, that they may be accepted before the LORD. 28:39 And thou shalt weave the tunic in chequer work of fine linen, and thou shalt make a mitre of fine linen, and thou shalt make a girdle, the work of the weaver in colours.

4

28:40 And for Aaron's sons thou shalt make tunics, and thou shalt make for them girdles, and head-tires shalt thou make for them, for splendour and for beauty. 28:41 And thou shalt put them upon Aaron thy brother, and upon his sons with him; and shalt anoint them, and consecrate them, and sanctify them, that they may minister unto Me in the priest's office. 28:42 And thou shalt make them linen breeches to cover the flesh of their nakedness; from the loins even unto the thighs they shall reach. 28:43 And they shall be upon Aaron, and upon his sons, when they go in unto the tent of meeting, or when they come near unto the altar to minister in the holy place; that they bear not iniquity, and die; it shall be a statute for ever unto him and unto his seed after him. {S}

Exodus Unit XIII (29:1-30:10)

1א

29:1 And this is the thing that thou shalt do unto them to hallow them, to minister unto Me in the priest's office: take one young bullock and two rams without blemish, 29:2 and unleavened bread, and cakes unleavened mingled with oil, and wafers unleavened spread with oil; of fine wheaten flour shalt thou make them. 29:3 And thou shalt put them into one basket, and bring them in the basket, with the bullock and the two rams.

2א

A 29:10 And thou shalt bring the bullock before the tent of meeting; and Aaron and his sons shall lay their hands upon the head of the bullock. 29:11 And thou shalt kill the bullock before the LORD, at the door of the tent of meeting. 29:12 And thou shalt take of the blood of the bullock, and put it upon the horns of the altar with thy finger; and thou shalt pour out all the remaining blood at the base of the altar. 29:13 And thou shalt take all the fat that covereth the inwards, and the lobe above the liver, and the two kidneys, and the fat that is upon them, and make them smoke upon the altar. 29:14 But the flesh of the bullock, and its skin, and its dung, shalt thou burn with fire without the camp; it is a sin-offering.

B 29:15 Thou shalt also take the one ram; and Aaron and his sons shall lay their hands upon the head of the ram. 29:16 And thou shalt slay the ram, and thou shalt take its blood, and dash it round about against the altar. 29:17 And thou shalt cut the ram into its pieces, and wash its inwards, and its legs, and put them with its pieces, and with its head. 29:18 And thou shalt make the whole ram smoke upon the altar; it is a burnt-offering unto the LORD; it is a sweet savour, an offering made by fire unto the LORD.

3א

29:26 And thou shalt take the breast of Aaron's ram of consecration, and wave it for a wave-offering before the LORD; and it shall be thy portion. 29:27 And thou shalt sanctify the breast of the wave-offering, and the thigh of the heave-offering, which is waved, and which is heaved up, of the ram of consecration, even of that which is Aaron's, and of that which is his sons'. 29:28 And it shall be for Aaron and his sons as a due for ever from the children of Israel; for it is a heave-offering; and it shall be a heave-offering from the children of Israel of their sacrifices of peace-offerings, even their heave-offering unto the LORD.

4א

29:31 And thou shalt take the ram of consecration, and seethe its flesh in a holy place. 29:32 And Aaron and his sons shall eat the flesh of the ram, and the bread that is in the basket, at the door of the tent of meeting. 29:33 And they shall eat those things wherewith atonement was made, to consecrate and to sanctify them; but a stranger shall not eat thereof, because they are holy. 29:34 And if aught of the flesh of the consecration, or of the bread, remain unto the morning, then thou shalt burn the remainder with fire; it shall not be eaten, because it is holy.

1ב

29:4 And Aaron and his sons thou shalt bring unto the door of the tent of meeting, and shalt wash them with water. 29:5 And thou shalt take the garments, and put upon Aaron the tunic, and the robe of the ephod, and the ephod, and the breastplate, and gird him with the skilfully woven band of the ephod. 29:6 And thou shalt set the mitre upon his head, and put the holy crown upon the mitre. 29:7 Then shalt thou take the anointing oil, and pour it upon his head, and anoint him. 29:8 And thou shalt bring his sons, and put tunics upon them. 29:9 And thou shalt gird them with girdles, Aaron and his sons, and bind head-tires on them; and they shall have the priesthood by a perpetual statute; and thou shalt consecrate Aaron and his sons.

2ב

A 29:19 And thou shalt take the other ram; and Aaron and his sons shall lay their hands upon the head of the ram. 29:20 Then shalt thou kill the ram, and take of its blood, and put it upon the tip of the right ear of Aaron, and upon the tip of the right ear of his sons, and upon the thumb of their right hand, and upon the great toe of their right foot, and dash the blood against the altar round about. 29:21 And thou shalt take of the blood that is upon the altar, and of the anointing oil, and sprinkle it upon Aaron, and upon his garments, and upon his sons, and upon the garments of his sons with him; and he and his garments shall be hallowed, and his sons and his sons' garments with him.

B 29:22 Also thou shalt take of the ram the fat, and the fat tail, and the fat that covereth the inwards, and the lobe of the liver, and the two kidneys, and the fat that is upon them, and the right thigh; for it is a ram of consecration; 29:23 and one loaf of bread, and one cake of oiled bread, and one wafer, out of the basket of unleavened bread that is before the LORD. 29:24 And thou shalt put the whole upon the hands of Aaron, and upon the hands of his sons; and shalt wave them for a wave-offering before the LORD. 29:25 And thou shalt take them from their hands, and make them smoke on the altar upon the burnt-offering, for a sweet savour before the LORD; it is an offering made by fire unto the LORD.

3ב

29:29 And the holy garments of Aaron shall be for his sons after him, to be anointed in them, and to be consecrated in them. 29:30 Seven days shall the son that is priest in his stead put them on, even he who cometh into the tent of meeting to minister in the holy place.

4ב

29:35 And thus shalt thou do unto Aaron, and to his sons, according to all that I have commanded thee; seven days shalt thou consecrate them. 29:36 And every day shalt thou offer the bullock of sin-offering, beside the other offerings of atonement; and thou shalt do the purification upon the altar when thou makest atonement for it; and thou shalt anoint it, to sanctify it. 29:37 Seven days thou shalt make atonement for the altar, and sanctify it; thus shall the altar be most holy; whatsoever toucheth the altar shall be holy. {S}

Exodus Unit XIV (30:11-31:17)

א1

29:38 Now this is that which thou shalt offer upon the altar: two lambs of the first year day by day continually. 29:39 The one lamb thou shalt offer in the morning; and the other lamb thou shalt offer at dusk. 29:40 And with the one lamb a tenth part of an ephah of fine flour mingled with the fourth part of a hin of beaten oil; and the fourth part of a hin of wine for a drink-offering. 29:41 And the other lamb thou shalt offer at dusk, and shalt do thereto according to the meal-offering of the morning, and according to the drink-offering thereof, for a sweet savour, an offering made by fire unto the LORD. 29:42 It shall be a continual burnt-offering throughout your generations at the door of the tent of meeting before the LORD, where I will meet with you, to speak there unto thee. 29:43 And there I will meet with the children of Israel; and [the Tent] shall be sanctified by My glory. 29:44 And I will sanctify the tent of meeting, and the altar; Aaron also and his sons will I sanctify, to minister to Me in the priest's office. 29:45 And I will dwell among the children of Israel, and will be their God. 29:46 And they shall know that I am the LORD their God, that brought them forth out of the land of Egypt, that I may dwell among them. I am the LORD their God. {P}

ב1

30:1 And thou shalt make an altar to burn incense upon; of acacia-wood shalt thou make it. 30:2 A cubit shall be the length thereof, and a cubit the breadth thereof; foursquare shall it be; and two cubits shall be the height thereof; the horns thereof shall be of one piece with it. 30:3 And thou shalt overlay it with pure gold, the top thereof, and the sides thereof round about, and the horns thereof; and thou shalt make unto it a crown of gold round about. 30:4 And two golden rings shalt thou make for it under the crown thereof, upon the two ribs thereof, upon the two sides of it shalt thou make them; and they shall be for places for staves wherewith to bear it. 30:5 And thou shalt make the staves of acacia-wood, and overlay them with gold. 30:6 And thou shalt put it before the veil that is by the ark of the testimony, before the ark-cover that is over the testimony, where I will meet with thee. 30:7 And Aaron shall burn thereon incense of sweet spices; every morning, when he dresseth the lamps, he shall burn it. 30:8 And when Aaron lighteth the lamps at dusk, he shall burn it, a perpetual incense before the LORD throughout your generations. 30:9 Ye shall offer no strange incense thereon, nor burnt-offering, nor meal-offering; and ye shall pour no drink-offering thereon. 30:10 And Aaron shall make atonement upon the horns of it once in the year; with the blood of the sin-offering of atonement once in the year shall he make atonement for it throughout your generations; it is most holy unto the LORD.' {P}

א2

30:11 And the LORD spoke unto Moses, saying: 30:12 'When thou takest the sum of the children of Israel, according to their number, then shall they give every man a ransom for his soul unto the LORD, when thou numberest them; that there be no plague among them, when thou numberest them. 30:13 This they shall give, every one that passeth among them that are numbered, half a shekel after the shekel of the sanctuary--the shekel is twenty gerahs--half a shekel for an offering to the LORD. 30:14 Every one that passeth among them that are numbered, from twenty years old and upward, shall give the offering of the LORD. 30:15 The rich shall not give more, and the poor shall not give less, than the half shekel, when they give the offering of the LORD, to make atonement for your souls. 30:16 And thou shalt take the atonement money from the children of Israel, and shalt appoint it for the service of the tent of meeting, that it may be a memorial for the children of Israel before the LORD, to make atonement for your souls.' {P}

ב2

30:17 And the LORD spoke unto Moses, saying: 30:18 'Thou shalt also make a laver of brass, and the base thereof of brass, whereat to wash; and thou shalt put it between the tent of meeting and the altar, and thou shalt put water therein. 30:19 And Aaron and his sons shall wash their hands and their feet thereat; 30:20 when they go into the tent of meeting, they shall wash with water, that they die not; or when they come near to the altar to minister, to cause an offering made by fire to smoke unto the LORD; 30:21 so they shall wash their hands and their feet, that they die not; and it shall be a statute for ever to them, even to him and to his seed throughout their generations.' {P}

‏3א

30:22 Moreover the LORD spoke unto Moses, saying: 30:23 'Take thou also unto thee the chief spices, of flowing myrrh five hundred shekels, and of sweet cinnamon half so much, even two hundred and fifty, and of sweet calamus two hundred and fifty, 30:24 and of cassia five hundred, after the shekel of the sanctuary, and of olive oil a hin. 30:25 And thou shalt make it a holy anointing oil, a perfume compounded after the art of the perfumer; it shall be a holy anointing oil. 30:26 And thou shalt anoint therewith the tent of meeting, and the ark of the testimony, 30:27 and the table and all the vessels thereof, and the candlestick and the vessels thereof, and the altar of incense, 30:28 and the altar of burnt-offering with all the vessels thereof, and the laver and the base thereof. 30:29 And thou shalt sanctify them, that they may be most holy; whatsoever toucheth them shall be holy. 30:30 And thou shalt anoint Aaron and his sons, and sanctify them, that they may minister unto Me in the priest's office. 30:31 And thou shalt speak unto the children of Israel, saying: This shall be a holy anointing oil unto Me throughout your generations. 30:32 Upon the flesh of man shall it not be poured, neither shall ye make any like it, according to the composition thereof; it is holy, and it shall be holy unto you. 30:33 Whosoever compoundeth any like it, or whosoever putteth any of it upon a stranger, he shall be cut off from his people.' {S}

‏4א

31:1 And the LORD spoke unto Moses, saying: 31:2 'See, I have called by name Bezalel the son of Uri, the son of Hur, of the tribe of Judah; 31:3 and I have filled him with the spirit of God, in wisdom, and in understanding, and in knowledge, and in all manner of workmanship, 31:4 to devise skilful works, to work in gold, and in silver, and in brass, 31:5 and in cutting of stones for setting, and in carving of wood, to work in all manner of workmanship. 31:6 And I, behold, I have appointed with him Oholiab, the son of Ahisamach, of the tribe of Dan; and in the hearts of all that are wise-hearted I have put wisdom, that they may make all that I have commanded thee: 31:7 the tent of meeting, and the ark of the testimony, and the ark-cover that is thereupon, and all the furniture of the Tent; 31:8 and the table and its vessels, and the pure candlestick with all its vessels, and the altar of incense; 31:9 and the altar of burnt-offering with all its vessels, and the laver and its base; 31:10 and the plaited garments, and the holy garments for Aaron the priest, and the garments of his sons, to minister in the priest's office; 31:11 and the anointing oil, and the incense of sweet spices for the holy place; according to all that I have commanded thee shall they do.' {P}

‏3ב

30:34 And the LORD said unto Moses: 'Take unto thee sweet spices, stacte, and onycha, and galbanum; sweet spices with pure frankincense; of each shall there be a like weight. 30:35 And thou shalt make of it incense, a perfume after the art of the perfumer, seasoned with salt, pure and holy. 30:36 And thou shalt beat some of it very small, and put of it before the testimony in the tent of meeting, where I will meet with thee; it shall be unto you most holy. 30:37 And the incense which thou shalt make, according to the composition thereof ye shall not make for yourselves; it shall be unto thee holy for the LORD. 30:38 Whosoever shall make like unto that, to smell thereof, he shall be cut off from his people.' {S}

‏4ב

31:12 And the LORD spoke unto Moses, saying: 31:13 'Speak thou also unto the children of Israel, saying: Verily ye shall keep My sabbaths, for it is a sign between Me and you throughout your generations, that ye may know that I am the LORD who sanctify you. 31:14 Ye shall keep the sabbath therefore, for it is holy unto you; every one that profaneth it shall surely be put to death; for whosoever doeth any work therein, that soul shall be cut off from among his people. 31:15 Six days shall work be done; but on the seventh day is a sabbath of solemn rest, holy to the LORD; whosoever doeth any work in the sabbath day, he shall surely be put to death. 31:16 Wherefore the children of Israel shall keep the sabbath, to observe the sabbath throughout their generations, for a perpetual covenant. 31:17 It is a sign between Me and the children of Israel for ever; for in six days the LORD made heaven and earth, and on the seventh day He ceased from work and rested.' {S}

Exodus Unit XV (31:18-34:35)

א1

A 31:18 And He gave unto Moses, when He had made an end of speaking with him upon mount Sinai, the two tables of the testimony, tables of stone, written with the finger of God.

B 32:1 And when the people saw that Moses delayed to come down from the mount, the people gathered themselves together unto Aaron, and said unto him: 'Up, make us a god who shall go before us; for as for this Moses, the man that brought us up out of the land of Egypt, we know not what is become of him.' 32:2 And Aaron said unto them: 'Break off the golden rings, which are in the ears of your wives, of your sons, and of your daughters, and bring them unto me.' 32:3 And all the people broke off the golden rings which were in their ears, and brought them unto Aaron. 32:4 And he received it at their hand, and fashioned it with a graving tool, and made it a molten calf; and they said: 'This is thy god, O Israel, which brought thee up out of the land of Egypt.' 32:5 And when Aaron saw this, he built an altar before it; and Aaron made proclamation, and said: 'To-morrow shall be a feast to the LORD.' 32:6 And they rose up early on the morrow, and offered burnt-offerings, and brought peace-offerings; and the people sat down to eat and to drink, and rose up to make merry. {P}

C 32:7 And the LORD spoke unto Moses: 'Go, get thee down; for thy people, that thou broughtest up out of the land of Egypt, have dealt corruptly; 32:8 they have turned aside quickly out of the way which I commanded them; they have made them a molten calf, and have worshipped it, and have sacrificed unto it, and said: This is thy god, O Israel, which brought thee up out of the land of Egypt.' 32:9 And the LORD said unto Moses: 'I have seen this people, and, behold, it is a stiffnecked people. 32:10 Now therefore let Me alone, that My wrath may wax hot against them, and that I may consume them; and I will make of thee a great nation.' 32:11 And Moses besought the LORD his God, and said: 'LORD, why doth Thy wrath wax hot against Thy people, that Thou hast brought forth out of the land of Egypt with great power and with a mighty hand? 32:12 Wherefore should the Egyptians speak, saying: For evil did He bring them forth, to slay them in the mountains, and to consume them from the face of the earth? Turn from Thy fierce wrath, and repent of this evil against Thy people. 32:13 Remember Abraham, Isaac, and Israel, Thy servants, to whom Thou didst swear by Thine own self, and saidst unto them: I will multiply your seed as the stars of heaven, and all this land that I have spoken of will I give unto your seed, and they shall inherit it for ever.' 32:14 And the LORD repented of the evil which He said He would do unto His people. {P}

א2

33:1 And the LORD spoke unto Moses: 'Depart, go up hence, thou and the people that thou hast brought up out of the land of Egypt, unto the land of which I swore unto Abraham, to Isaac, and to Jacob, saying: Unto thy seed will I give it-- 33:2 and I will send an angel before thee; and I will drive out the Canaanite, the Amorite, and the Hittite, and the Perizzite, the Hivite, and the Jebusite-- 33:3 unto a land flowing with milk and honey; for I will not go up in the midst of thee; for thou art a stiffnecked people; lest I consume thee in the way.' 33:4 And when the people heard these evil tidings, they mourned; and no man did put on him his ornaments. 33:5 And the LORD said unto Moses: 'Say unto the children of Israel: Ye are a stiffnecked people; if I go up into the midst of thee for one moment, I shall consume thee; therefore now put off thy ornaments from thee, that I may know what to do unto thee.' 33:6 And the children of Israel stripped themselves of their ornaments from mount Horeb onward.

ב1

A 32:15 And Moses turned, and went down from the mount, with the two tables of the testimony in his hand; tables that were written on both their sides; on the one side and on the other were they written. 32:16 And the tables were the work of God, and the writing was the writing of God, graven upon the tables.

B 32:17 And when Joshua heard the noise of the people as they shouted, he said unto Moses: 'There is a noise of war in the camp.' 32:18 And he said: 'It is not the voice of them that shout for mastery, neither is it the voice of them that cry for being overcome, but the noise of them that sing do I hear.' 32:19 And it came to pass, as soon as he came nigh unto the camp, that he saw the calf and the dancing; and Moses' anger waxed hot, and he cast the tables out of his hands, and broke them beneath the mount. 32:20 And he took the calf which they had made, and burnt it with fire, and ground it to powder, and strewed it upon the water, and made the children of Israel drink of it. 32:21 And Moses said unto Aaron: 'What did this people unto thee, that thou hast brought a great sin upon them?' 32:22 And Aaron said: 'Let not the anger of my lord wax hot; thou knowest the people, that they are set on evil. 32:23 So they said unto me: Make us a god, which shall go before us; for as for this Moses, the man that brought us up out of the land of Egypt, we know not what is become of him. 32:24 And I said unto them: Whosoever hath any gold, let them break it off; so they gave it me; and I cast it into the fire, and there came out this calf.'

C 32:25 And when Moses saw that the people were broken loose--for Aaron had let them loose for a derision among their enemies-- 32:26 then Moses stood in the gate of the camp, and said: 'Whoso is on the LORD'S side, let him come unto me.' And all the sons of Levi gathered themselves together unto him. 32:27 And he said unto them: 'Thus saith the LORD, the God of Israel: Put ye every man his sword upon his thigh, and go to and fro from gate to gate throughout the camp, and slay every man his brother, and every man his companion, and every man his neighbour.' 32:28 And the sons of Levi did according to the word of Moses; and there fell of the people that day about three thousand men. 32:29 And Moses said: 'Consecrate yourselves to-day to the LORD, for every man hath been against his son and against his brother; that He may also bestow upon you a blessing this day.' 32:30 And it came to pass on the morrow, that Moses said unto the people: 'Ye have sinned a great sin; and now I will go up unto the LORD, peradventure I shall make atonement for your sin.' 32:31 And Moses returned unto the LORD, and said: 'Oh, this people have sinned a great sin, and have made them a god of gold. 32:32 Yet now, if Thou wilt forgive their sin--; and if not, blot me, I pray Thee, out of Thy book which Thou hast written.' 32:33 And the LORD said unto Moses: 'Whosoever hath sinned against Me, him will I blot out of My book. 32:34 And now go, lead the people unto the place of which I have spoken unto thee; behold, Mine angel shall go before thee; nevertheless in the day when I visit, I will visit their sin upon them.' 32:35 And the LORD smote the people, because they made the calf, which Aaron made. {S}

ב2

33:7 Now Moses used to take the tent and to pitch it without the camp, afar off from the camp; and he called it the tent of meeting. And it came to pass, that every one that sought the LORD went out unto the tent of meeting, which was without the camp. 33:8 And it came to pass, when Moses went out unto the Tent, that all the people rose up, and stood, every man at his tent door, and looked after Moses, until he was gone into the Tent. 33:9 And it came to pass, when Moses entered into the Tent, the pillar of cloud descended, and stood at the door of the Tent; and [the LORD] spoke with Moses. 33:10 And when all the people saw the pillar of cloud stand at the door of the Tent, all the people rose up and worshipped, every man at his tent door. 33:11 And the LORD spoke unto Moses face to face, as a man speaketh unto his friend. And he would return into the camp; but his minister Joshua, the son of Nun, a young man, departed not out of the Tent. {P}

‫ג‬א

33:12 And Moses said unto the LORD: 'See, Thou sayest unto me: Bring up this people; and Thou hast not let me know whom Thou wilt send with me. Yet Thou hast said: I know thee by name, and thou hast also found grace in My sight. 33:13 Now therefore, I pray Thee, if I have found grace in Thy sight, show me now Thy ways, that I may know Thee, to the end that I may find grace in Thy sight; and consider that this nation is Thy people.' 33:14 And He said: 'My presence shall go with thee, and I will give thee rest.' 33:15 And he said unto Him: 'If Thy presence go not with me, carry us not up hence. 33:16 For wherein now shall it be known that I have found grace in Thy sight, I and Thy people? is it not in that Thou goest with us, so that we are distinguished, I and Thy people, from all the people that are upon the face of the earth?' {P}

‫ד‬א

34:1 And the LORD said unto Moses: 'Hew thee two tables of stone like unto the first; and I will write upon the tables the words that were on the first tables, which thou didst break. 34:2 And be ready by the morning, and come up in the morning unto mount Sinai, and present thyself there to Me on the top of the mount. 34:3 And no man shall come up with thee, neither let any man be seen throughout all the mount; neither let the flocks nor herds feed before that mount.' 34:4 And he hewed two tables of stone like unto the first; and Moses rose up early in the morning, and went up unto mount Sinai, as the LORD had commanded him, and took in his hand two tables of stone. 34:5 And the LORD descended in the cloud, and stood with him there, and proclaimed the name of the LORD. 34:6 And the LORD passed by before him, and proclaimed: 'The LORD, the LORD, God, merciful and gracious, long-suffering, and abundant in goodness and truth; 34:7 keeping mercy unto the thousandth generation, forgiving iniquity and transgression and sin; and that will by no means clear the guilty; visiting the iniquity of the fathers upon the children, and upon the children's children, unto the third and unto the fourth generation.'

‫ה‬א

34:27 And the LORD said unto Moses: 'Write thou these words, for after the tenor of these words I have made a covenant with thee and with Israel.' 34:28 And he was there with the LORD forty days and forty nights; he did neither eat bread, nor drink water. And he wrote upon the tables the words of the covenant, the ten words. 34:29 And it came to pass, when Moses came down from mount Sinai with the two tables of the testimony in Moses' hand, when he came down from the mount, that Moses knew not that the skin of his face sent forth beams while He talked with him.

‫ג‬ב

33:17 And the LORD said unto Moses: 'I will do this thing also that thou hast spoken, for thou hast found grace in My sight, and I know thee by name.' 33:18 And he said: 'Show me, I pray Thee, Thy glory.' 33:19 And He said: 'I will make all My goodness pass before thee, and will proclaim the name of the LORD before thee; and I will be gracious to whom I will be gracious, and will show mercy on whom I will show mercy.' 33:20 And He said: 'Thou canst not see My face, for man shall not see Me and live.' 33:21 And the LORD said: 'Behold, there is a place by Me, and thou shalt stand upon the rock. 33:22 And it shall come to pass, while My glory passeth by, that I will put thee in a cleft of the rock, and will cover thee with My hand until I have passed by. 33:23 And I will take away My hand, and thou shalt see My back; but My face shall not be seen.' {P}

‫ד‬ב

34:8 And Moses made haste, and bowed his head toward the earth, and worshipped. 34:9 And he said: 'If now I have found grace in Thy sight, O Lord, let the Lord, I pray Thee, go in the midst of us; for it is a stiffnecked people; and pardon our iniquity and our sin, and take us for Thine inheritance.' 34:10 And He said: 'Behold, I make a covenant; before all thy people I will do marvels, such as have not been wrought in all the earth, nor in any nation; and all the people among which thou art shall see the work of the LORD that I am about to do with thee, that it is tremendous. 34:11 Observe thou that which I am commanding thee this day; behold, I am driving out before thee the Amorite, and the Canaanite, and the Hittite, and the Perizzite, and the Hivite, and the Jebusite. 34:12 Take heed to thyself, lest thou make a covenant with the inhabitants of the land whither thou goest, lest they be for a snare in the midst of thee. 34:13 But ye shall break down their altars, and dash in pieces their pillars, and ye shall cut down their Asherim. 34:14 For thou shalt bow down to no other god; for the LORD, whose name is Jealous, is a jealous God; 34:15 lest thou make a covenant with the inhabitants of the land, and they go astray after their gods, and do sacrifice unto their gods, and they call thee, and thou eat of their sacrifice; 34:16 and thou take of their daughters unto thy sons, and their daughters go astray after their gods, and make thy sons go astray after their gods. 34:17 Thou shalt make thee no molten gods. 34:18 The feast of unleavened bread shalt thou keep. Seven days thou shalt eat unleavened bread, as I commanded thee, at the time appointed in the month Abib, for in the month Abib thou camest out from Egypt. 34:19 All that openeth the womb is Mine; and of all thy cattle thou shalt sanctify the males, the firstlings of ox and sheep. 34:20 And the firstling of an ass thou shalt redeem with a lamb; and if thou wilt not redeem it, then thou shalt break its neck. All the first-born of thy sons thou shalt redeem. And none shall appear before Me empty. 34:21 Six days thou shalt work, but on the seventh day thou shalt rest; in plowing time and in harvest thou shalt rest. 34:22 And thou shalt observe the feast of weeks, even of the first-fruits of wheat harvest, and the feast of ingathering at the turn of the year. 34:23 Three times in the year shall all thy males appear before the Lord GOD, the God of Israel. 34:24 For I will cast out nations before thee, and enlarge thy borders; neither shall any man covet thy land, when thou goest up to appear before the LORD thy God three times in the year. 34:25 Thou shalt not offer the blood of My sacrifice with leavened bread; neither shall the sacrifice of the feast of the passover be left unto the morning. 34:26 The choicest first-fruits of thy land thou shalt bring unto the house of the LORD thy God. Thou shalt not seethe a kid in its mother's milk.' {P}

‫ה‬ב

34:30 And when Aaron and all the children of Israel saw Moses, behold, the skin of his face sent forth beams; and they were afraid to come nigh him. 34:31 And Moses called unto them; and Aaron and all the rulers of the congregation returned unto him; and Moses spoke to them. 34:32 And afterward all the children of Israel came nigh, and he gave them in commandment all that the LORD had spoken with him in mount Sinai. 34:33 And when Moses had done speaking with them, he put a veil on his face. 34:34 But when Moses went in before the LORD that He might speak with him, he took the veil off, until he came out; and he came out, and spoke unto the children of Israel that which he was commanded. 34:35 And the children of Israel saw the face of Moses, that the skin of Moses' face sent forth beams; and Moses put the veil back upon his face, until he went in to speak with Him. {S}

Exodus Unit XVI (35:1-36:7)

1א

35:1 And Moses assembled all the congregation of the children of Israel, and said unto them: 'These are the words which the LORD hath commanded, that ye should do them. 35:2 Six days shall work be done, but on the seventh day there shall be to you a holy day, a sabbath of solemn rest to the LORD; whosoever doeth any work therein shall be put to death. 35:3 Ye shall kindle no fire throughout your habitations upon the sabbath day.' {P}

2א

35:10 And let every wise-hearted man among you come, and make all that the LORD hath commanded: 35:11 the tabernacle, its tent, and its covering, its clasps, and its boards, its bars, its pillars, and its sockets; 35:12 the ark, and the staves thereof, the ark-cover, and the veil of the screen; 35:13 the table, and its staves, and all its vessels, and the showbread; 35:14 the candlestick also for the light, and its vessels, and its lamps, and the oil for the light; 35:15 and the altar of incense, and its staves, and the anointing oil, and the sweet incense, and the screen for the door, at the door of the tabernacle; 35:16 the altar of burnt-offering, with its grating of brass, its staves, and all its vessels, the laver and its base; 35:17 the hangings of the court, the pillars thereof, and their sockets, and the screen for the gate of the court; 35:18 the pins of the tabernacle, and the pins of the court, and their cords; 35:19 the plaited garments, for ministering in the holy place, the holy garments for Aaron the priest, and the garments of his sons, to minister in the priest's office.'

3א

35:30 And Moses said unto the children of Israel: 'See, the LORD hath called by name Bezalel the son of Uri, the son of Hur, of the tribe of Judah. 35:31 And He hath filled him with the spirit of God, in wisdom, in understanding, and in knowledge, and in all manner of workmanship. 35:32 And to devise skilful works, to work in gold, and in silver, and in brass, 35:33 and in cutting of stones for setting, and in carving of wood, to work in all manner of skilful workmanship. 35:34 And He hath put in his heart that he may teach, both he, and Oholiab, the son of Ahisamach, of the tribe of Dan. 35:35 Them hath He filled with wisdom of heart, to work all manner of workmanship, of the craftsman, and of the skilful workman, and of the weaver in colours, in blue, and in purple, in scarlet, and in fine linen, and of the weaver, even of them that do any workmanship, and of those that devise skilful works. 36:1 And Bezalel and Oholiab shall work, and every wise-hearted man, in whom the LORD hath put wisdom and understanding to know how to work all the work for the service of the sanctuary, according to all that the LORD hath commanded.' 36:2 And Moses called Bezalel and Oholiab, and every wise-hearted man, in whose heart the LORD had put wisdom, even every one whose heart stirred him up to come unto the work to do it.

1ב

35:4 And Moses spoke unto all the congregation of the children of Israel, saying: 'This is the thing which the LORD commanded, saying: 35:5 Take ye from among you an offering unto the LORD, whosoever is of a willing heart, let him bring it, the LORD'S offering: gold, and silver, and brass; 35:6 and blue, and purple, and scarlet, and fine linen, and goats' hair; 35:7 and rams' skins dyed red, and sealskins, and acacia-wood; 35:8 and oil for the light, and spices for the anointing oil, and for the sweet incense; 35:9 and onyx stones, and stones to be set, for the ephod, and for the breastplate.

2ב

35:20 And all the congregation of the children of Israel departed from the presence of Moses. 35:21 And they came, every one whose heart stirred him up, and every one whom his spirit made willing, and brought the LORD'S offering, for the work of the tent of meeting, and for all the service thereof, and for the holy garments. 35:22 And they came, both men and women, as many as were willing-hearted, and brought nose-rings, and ear-rings, and signet-rings, and girdles, all jewels of gold; even every man that brought an offering of gold unto the LORD. 35:23 And every man, with whom was found blue, and purple, and scarlet, and fine linen, and goats' hair, and rams' skins dyed red, and sealskins, brought them. 35:24 Every one that did set apart an offering of silver and brass brought the LORD'S offering; and every man, with whom was found acacia-wood for any work of the service, brought it. 35:25 And all the women that were wise-hearted did spin with their hands, and brought that which they had spun, the blue, and the purple, the scarlet, and the fine linen. 35:26 And all the women whose heart stirred them up in wisdom spun the goats' hair. 35:27 And the rulers brought the onyx stones, and the stones to be set, for the ephod, and for the breastplate; 35:28 and the spice, and the oil, for the light, and for the anointing oil, and for the sweet incense. 35:29 The children of Israel brought a freewill-offering unto the LORD; every man and woman, whose heart made them willing to bring for all the work, which the LORD had commanded by the hand of Moses to be made. {P}

3ב

36:3 And they received of Moses all the offering, which the children of Israel had brought for the work of the service of the sanctuary, wherewith to make it. And they brought yet unto him freewill-offerings every morning. 36:4 And all the wise men, that wrought all the work of the sanctuary, came every man from his work which they wrought. 36:5 And they spoke unto Moses, saying: 'The people bring much more than enough for the service of the work, which the LORD commanded to make.' 36:6 And Moses gave commandment, and they caused it to be proclaimed throughout the camp, saying: 'Let neither man nor woman make any more work for the offering of the sanctuary.' So the people were restrained from bringing. 36:7 For the stuff they had was sufficient for all the work to make it, and too much. {S}

Exodus Unit XVII (36:8-38:20)

א1

A 36:8 And every wise-hearted man among them that wrought the work made the tabernacle with ten curtains: of fine twined linen, and blue, and purple, and scarlet, with cherubim the work of the skilful workman made he them. 36:9 The length of each curtain was eight and twenty cubits, and the breadth of each curtain four cubits; all the curtains had one measure. 36:10 And he coupled five curtains one to another; and the other five curtains he coupled one to another. 36:11 And he made loops of blue upon the edge of the one curtain that was outmost in the first set; likewise he made in the edge of the curtain that was outmost in the second set. 36:12 Fifty loops made he in the one curtain, and fifty loops made he in the edge of the curtain that was in the second set; the loops were opposite one to another. 36:13 And he made fifty clasps of gold, and coupled the curtains one to another with the clasps; so the tabernacle was one. {P}

B 36:14 And he made curtains of goats' hair for a tent over the tabernacle; eleven curtains he made them. 36:15 The length of each curtain was thirty cubits, and four cubits the breadth of each curtain; the eleven curtains had one measure. 36:16 And he coupled five curtains by themselves, and six curtains by themselves. 36:17 And he made fifty loops on the edge of the curtain that was outmost in the first set, and fifty loops made he upon the edge of the curtain which was outmost in the second set. 36:18 And he made fifty clasps of brass to couple the tent together, that it might be one. 36:19 And he made a covering for the tent of rams' skins dyed red, and a covering of sealskins above. {S}

C 36:20 And he made the boards for the tabernacle of acacia-wood, standing up. 36:21 Ten cubits was the length of a board, and a cubit and a half the breadth of each board. 36:22 Each board had two tenons, joined one to another. Thus did he make for all the boards of the tabernacle. 36:23 And he made the boards for the tabernacle; twenty boards for the south side southward. 36:24 And he made forty sockets of silver under the twenty boards: two sockets under one board for its two tenons, and two sockets under another board for its two tenons. 36:25 And for the second side of the tabernacle, on the north side, he made twenty boards, 36:26 and their forty sockets of silver: two sockets under one board, and two sockets under another board. 36:27 And for the hinder part of the tabernacle westward he made six boards. 36:28 And two boards made he for the corners of the tabernacle in the hinder part; 36:29 that they might be double beneath, and in like manner they should be complete unto the top thereof unto the first ring. Thus he did to both of them in the two corners. 36:30 And there were eight boards, and their sockets of silver, sixteen sockets: under every board two sockets. 36:31 And he made bars of acacia-wood: five for the boards of the one side of the tabernacle, 36:32 and five bars for the boards of the other side of the tabernacle, and five bars for the boards of the tabernacle for the hinder part westward. 36:33 And he made the middle bar to pass through in the midst of the boards from the one end to the other. 36:34 And he overlaid the boards with gold, and made their rings of gold for holders for the bars, and overlaid the bars with gold.

D 36:35 And he made the veil of blue, and purple, and scarlet, and fine twined linen; with the cherubim the work of the skilful workman made he it. 36:36 And he made thereunto four pillars of acacia, and overlaid them with gold, their hooks being of gold; and he cast for them four sockets of silver. 36:37 And he made a screen for the door of the Tent, of blue, and purple, and scarlet, and fine twined linen, the work of the weaver in colours; 36:38 and the five pillars of it with their hooks; and he overlaid their capitals and their fillets with gold; and their five sockets were of brass. {P}

ב1

A 37:1 And Bezalel made the ark of acacia-wood: two cubits and a half was the length of it, and a cubit and a half the breadth of it, and a cubit and a half the height of it. 37:2 And he overlaid it with pure gold within and without, and made a crown of gold to it round about. 37:3 And he cast for it four rings of gold, in the four feet thereof: even two rings on the one side of it, and two rings on the other side of it. 37:4 And he made staves of acacia-wood, and overlaid them with gold. 37:5 And he put the staves into the rings on the sides of the ark, to bear the ark.

B 37:6 And he made an ark-cover of pure gold: two cubits and a half was the length thereof, and a cubit and a half the breadth thereof. 37:7 And he made two cherubim of gold: of beaten work made he them, at the two ends of the ark-cover: 37:8 one cherub at the one end, and one cherub at the other end; of one piece with the ark-cover made he the cherubim at the two ends thereof. 37:9 And the cherubim spread out their wings on high, screening the ark-cover with their wings, with their faces one to another; toward the ark-cover were the faces of the cherubim. {P}

C 37:10 And he made the table of acacia-wood: two cubits was the length thereof, and a cubit the breadth thereof, and a cubit and a half the height thereof. 37:11 And he overlaid it with pure gold, and made thereto a crown of gold round about. 37:12 And he made unto it a border of a hand-breadth round about, and made a golden crown to the border thereof round about. 37:13 And he cast for it four rings of gold, and put the rings in the four corners that were on the four feet thereof. 37:14 Close by the border were the rings, the holders for the staves to bear the table. 37:15 And he made the staves of acacia-wood, and overlaid them with gold, to bear the table. 37:16 And he made the vessels which were upon the table, the dishes thereof, and the pans thereof, and the bowls thereof, and the jars thereof, wherewith to pour out, of pure gold. {P}

D 37:17 And he made the candlestick of pure gold: of beaten work made he the candlestick, even its base, and its shaft; its cups, its knops, and its flowers, were of one piece with it. 37:18 And there were six branches going out of the sides thereof: three branches of the candlestick out of the one side thereof, and three branches of the candlestick out of the other side thereof; 37:19 three cups made like almond-blossoms in one branch, a knop and a flower; and three cups made like almond-blossoms in the other branch, a knop and a flower. So for the six branches going out of the candlestick. 37:20 And in the candlestick were four cups made like almond-blossoms, the knops thereof, and the flowers thereof; 37:21 and a knop under two branches of one piece with it, and a knop under two branches of one piece with it, and a knop under two branches of one piece with it, for the six branches going out of it. 37:22 Their knops and their branches were of one piece with it; the whole of it was one beaten work of pure gold. 37:23 And he made the lamps thereof, seven, and the tongs thereof, and the snuffdishes thereof, of pure gold. 37:24 Of a talent of pure gold made he it, and all the vessels thereof. {P}

2א

37:25 And he made the altar of incense of acacia-wood: a cubit was the length thereof, and a cubit the breadth thereof, four-square; and two cubits was the height thereof; the horns thereof were of one piece with it. **37:26** And he overlaid it with pure gold, the top thereof, and the sides thereof round about, and the horns of it; and he made unto it a crown of gold round about. **37:27** And he made for it two golden rings under the crown thereof, upon the two ribs thereof, upon the two sides of it, for holders for staves wherewith to bear it. **37:28** And he made the staves of acacia-wood, and overlaid them with gold. **37:29** And he made the holy anointing oil, and the pure incense of sweet spices, after the art of the perfumer. {S}

3א

38:8 And he made the laver of brass, and the base thereof of brass, of the mirrors of the serving women that did service at the door of the tent of meeting. {S}

2ב

38:1 And he made the altar of burnt-offering of acacia-wood: five cubits was the length thereof, and five cubits the breadth thereof, four-square, and three cubits the height thereof. **38:2** And he made the horns thereof upon the four corners of it; the horns thereof were of one piece with it; and he overlaid it with brass. **38:3** And he made all the vessels of the altar, the pots, and the shovels, and the basins, the flesh-hooks, and the fire-pans; all the vessels thereof made he of brass. **38:4** And he made for the altar a grating of network of brass, under the ledge round it beneath, reaching halfway up. **38:5** And he cast four rings for the four ends of the grating of brass, to be holders for the staves. **38:6** And he made the staves of acacia-wood, and overlaid them with brass. **38:7** And he put the staves into the rings on the sides of the altar, wherewith to bear it; he made it hollow with planks. {S}

3ב

38:9 And he made the court; for the south side southward the hangings of the court were of fine twined linen, a hundred cubits. **38:10** Their pillars were twenty, and their sockets twenty, of brass; the hooks of the pillars and their fillets were of silver. **38:11** And for the north side a hundred cubits, their pillars twenty, and their sockets twenty, of brass; the hooks of the pillars and their fillets of silver. **38:12** And for the west side were hangings of fifty cubits, their pillars ten, and their sockets ten; the hooks of the pillars and their fillets of silver. **38:13** And for the east side eastward fifty cubits. **38:14** The hangings for the one side [of the gate] were fifteen cubits; their pillars three, and their sockets three. **38:15** And so for the other side; on this hand and that hand by the gate of the court were hangings of fifteen cubits; their pillars three, and their sockets three. **38:16** All the hangings of the court round about were of fine twined linen. **38:17** And the sockets for the pillars were of brass; the hooks of the pillars and their fillets of silver; and the overlaying of their capitals of silver; and all the pillars of the court were filleted with silver. **38:18** And the screen for the gate of the court was the work of the weaver in colours, of blue, and purple, and scarlet, and fine twined linen; and twenty cubits was the length, and the height in the breadth was five cubits, answerable to the hangings of the court. **38:19** And their pillars were four, and their sockets four, of brass; their hooks of silver, and the overlaying of their capitals and their fillets of silver. **38:20** And all the pins of the tabernacle, and of the court round about, were of brass. {S}

Exodus Unit XVIII (38:21-39:31)

1א

38:21 These are the accounts of the tabernacle, even the tabernacle of the testimony, as they were rendered according to the commandment of Moses, through the service of the Levites, by the hand of Ithamar, the son of Aaron the priest.-- 38:22 And Bezalel the son of Uri, the son of Hur, of the tribe of Judah, made all that the LORD commanded Moses. 38:23 And with him was Oholiab, the son of Ahisamach, of the tribe of Dan, a craftsman, and a skilful workman, and a weaver in colours, in blue, and in purple, and in scarlet, and fine linen.-- {S}

2א

A 39:2 And he made the ephod of gold, blue, and purple, and scarlet, and fine twined linen. 39:3 And they did beat the gold into thin plates, and cut it into threads, to work it in the blue, and in the purple, and in the scarlet, and in the fine linen, the work of the skilful workman. 39:4 They made shoulder-pieces for it, joined together; at the two ends was it joined together. 39:5 And the skilfully woven band, that was upon it, wherewith to gird it on, was of the same piece and like the work thereof: of gold, of blue, and purple, and scarlet, and fine twined linen, as the LORD commanded Moses. {S}

B 39:6 And they wrought the onyx stones, inclosed in settings of gold, graven with the engravings of a signet, according to the names of the children of Israel. 39:7 And he put them on the shoulder-pieces of the ephod, to be stones of memorial for the children of Israel, as the LORD commanded Moses. {P}

C 39:8 And he made the breastplate, the work of the skilful workman, like the work of the ephod: of gold, of blue, and purple, and scarlet, and fine twined linen. 39:9 It was four-square; they made the breastplate double; a span was the length thereof, and a span the breadth thereof, being double. 39:10 And they set in it four rows of stones: a row of carnelian, topaz, and smaragd was the first row. 39:11 And the second row, a carbuncle, a sapphire, and an emerald. 39:12 And the third row, a jacinth, an agate, and an amethyst. 39:13 And the fourth row, a beryl, an onyx, and a jasper; they were inclosed in fittings of gold in their settings. 39:14 And the stones were according to the names of the children of Israel, twelve, according to their names, like the engravings of a signet, every one according to his name, for the twelve tribes. 39:15 And they made upon the breastplate plaited chains, of wreathen work of pure gold. 39:16 And they made two settings of gold, and two gold rings; and put the two rings on the two ends of the breastplate. 39:17 And they put the two wreathen chains of gold on the two rings at the ends of the breastplate. 39:18 And the other two ends of the two wreathen chains they put on the two settings, and put them on the shoulder-pieces of the ephod, in the forepart thereof. 39:19 And they made two rings of gold, and put them upon the two ends of the breastplate, upon the edge thereof, which was toward the side of the ephod inward. 39:20 And they made two rings of gold, and put them on the two shoulder-pieces of the ephod underneath, in the forepart thereof, close by the coupling thereof, above the skilfully woven band of the ephod. 39:21 And they did bind the breastplate by the rings thereof unto the rings of the ephod with a thread of blue, that it might be upon the skilfully woven band of the ephod, and that the breastplate might not be loosed from the ephod; as the LORD commanded Moses. {P}

1ב

38:24 All the gold that was used for the work in all the work of the sanctuary, even the gold of the offering, was twenty and nine talents, and seven hundred and thirty shekels, after the shekel of the sanctuary. 38:25 And the silver of them that were numbered of the congregation was a hundred talents, and a thousand seven hundred and three-score and fifteen shekels, after the shekel of the sanctuary: 38:26 a beka a head, that is, half a shekel, after the shekel of the sanctuary, for every one that passed over to them that are numbered, from twenty years old and upward, for six hundred thousand and three thousand and five hundred and fifty men. 38:27 And the hundred talents of silver were for casting the sockets of the sanctuary, and the sockets of the veil: a hundred sockets for the hundred talents, a talent for a socket. 38:28 And of the thousand seven hundred seventy and five shekels he made hooks for the pillars, and overlaid their capitals, and made fillets for them. 38:29 And the brass of the offering was seventy talents and two thousand and four hundred shekels. 38:30 And therewith he made the sockets to the door of the tent of meeting, and the brazen altar, and the brazen grating for it, and all the vessels of the altar, 38:31 and the sockets of the court round about, and the sockets of the gate of the court, and all the pins of the tabernacle, and all the pins of the court round about. 39:1 And of the blue, and purple, and scarlet, they made plaited garments, for ministering in the holy place, and made the holy garments for Aaron, as the LORD commanded Moses. {P}

2ב

A 39:22 And he made the robe of the ephod of woven work, all of blue; 39:23 and the hole of the robe in the midst thereof, as the hole of a coat of mail, with a binding round about the hole of it, that it should not be rent. 39:24 And they made upon the skirts of the robe pomegranates of blue, and purple, and scarlet, and twined linen. 39:25 And they made bells of pure gold, and put the bells between the pomegranates upon the skirts of the robe round about, between the pomegranates: 39:26 a bell and a pomegranate, a bell and a pomegranate, upon the skirts of the robe round about, to minister in; as the LORD commanded Moses. {S}

B 39:27 And they made the tunics of fine linen of woven work for Aaron, and for his sons, 39:28 and the mitre of fine linen, and the goodly head-tires of fine linen, and the linen breeches of fine twined linen, 39:29 and the girdle of fine twined linen, and blue, and purple, and scarlet, the work of the weaver in colours; as the LORD commanded Moses. {S}

C 39:30 And they made the plate of the holy crown of pure gold, and wrote upon it a writing, like the engravings of a signet: HOLY TO THE LORD. 39:31 And they tied unto it a thread of blue, to fasten it upon the mitre above; as the LORD commanded Moses. {S}

Exodus Unit XIX (39:32-40:38)

1

39:32 Thus was finished all the work of the tabernacle of the tent of meeting; and the children of Israel did according to all that the LORD commanded Moses, so did they. {P}

2א

39:33 And they brought the tabernacle unto Moses, the Tent, and all its furniture, its clasps, its boards, its bars, and its pillars, and its sockets; 39:34 and the covering of rams' skins dyed red, and the covering of sealskins, and the veil of the screen; 39:35 the ark of the testimony, and the staves thereof, and the ark-cover; 39:36 the table, all the vessels thereof, and the showbread; 39:37 the pure candlestick, the lamps thereof, even the lamps to be set in order, and all the vessels thereof, and the oil for the light; 39:38 and the golden altar, and the anointing oil, and the sweet incense, and the screen for the door of the Tent; 39:39 the brazen altar, and its grating of brass, its staves, and all its vessels, the laver and its base; 39:40 the hangings of the court, its pillars, and its sockets, and the screen for the gate of the court, the cords thereof, and the pins thereof, and all the instruments of the service of the tabernacle of the tent of meeting; 39:41 the plaited garments for ministering in the holy place; the holy garments for Aaron the priest, and the garments of his sons, to minister in the priest's office. 39:42 According to all that the LORD commanded Moses, so the children of Israel did all the work. 39:43 And Moses saw all the work, and, behold, they had done it; as the LORD had commanded, even so had they done it. And Moses blessed them. {P}

2ב

40:1 And the LORD spoke unto Moses, saying: 40:2 'On the first day of the first month shalt thou rear up the tabernacle of the tent of meeting. 40:3 And thou shalt put therein the ark of the testimony, and thou shalt screen the ark with the veil. 40:4 And thou shalt bring in the table, and set in order the bread that is upon it; and thou shalt bring in the candlestick, and light the lamps thereof. 40:5 And thou shalt set the golden altar for incense before the ark of the testimony, and put the screen of the door to the tabernacle. 40:6 And thou shalt set the altar of burnt-offering before the door of the tabernacle of the tent of meeting. 40:7 And thou shalt set the laver between the tent of meeting and the altar, and shalt put water therein. 40:8 And thou shalt set up the court round about, and hang up the screen of the gate of the court. 40:9 And thou shalt take the anointing oil, and anoint the tabernacle, and all that is therein, and shalt hallow it, and all the furniture thereof; and it shall be holy. 40:10 And thou shalt anoint the altar of burnt-offering, and all its vessels, and sanctify the altar; and the altar shall be most holy. 40:11 And thou shalt anoint the laver and its base, and sanctify it. 40:12 And thou shalt bring Aaron and his sons unto the door of the tent of meeting, and shalt wash them with water. 40:13 And thou shalt put upon Aaron the holy garments; and thou shalt anoint him, and sanctify him, that he may minister unto Me in the priest's office. 40:14 And thou shalt bring his sons, and put tunics upon them. 40:15 And thou shalt anoint them, as thou didst anoint their father, that they may minister unto Me in the priest's office; and their anointing shall be to them for an everlasting priesthood throughout their generations.' 40:16 Thus did Moses; according to all that the LORD commanded him, so did he. {S}

2ג

40:17 And it came to pass in the first month in the second year, on the first day of the month, that the tabernacle was reared up. 40:18 And Moses reared up the tabernacle, and laid its sockets, and set up the boards thereof, and put in the bars thereof, and reared up its pillars. 40:19 And he spread the tent over the tabernacle, and put the covering of the tent above upon it; as the LORD commanded Moses. {S} 40:20 And he took and put the testimony into the ark, and set the staves on the ark, and put the ark-cover above upon the ark. 40:21 And he brought the ark into the tabernacle, and set up the veil of the screen, and screened the ark of the testimony; as the LORD commanded Moses. {S} 40:22 And he put the table in the tent of meeting, upon the side of the tabernacle northward, without the veil. 40:23 And he set a row of bread in order upon it before the LORD; as the LORD commanded Moses. {S} 40:24 And he put the candlestick in the tent of meeting, over against the table, on the side of the tabernacle southward. 40:25 And he lighted the lamps before the LORD; as the LORD commanded Moses. {S} 40:26 And he put the golden altar in the tent of meeting before the veil; 40:27 and he burnt thereon incense of sweet spices; as the LORD commanded Moses. {S} 40:28 And he put the screen of the door to the tabernacle. 40:29 And the altar of burnt-offering he set at the door of the tabernacle of the tent of meeting, and offered upon it the burnt-offering and the meal-offering; as the LORD commanded Moses. {S} 40:30 And he set the laver between the tent of meeting and the altar, and put water therein, wherewith to wash; 40:31 that Moses and Aaron and his sons might wash their hands and their feet thereat; 40:32 when they went into the tent of meeting, and when they came near unto the altar, they should wash; as the LORD commanded Moses. {S} 40:33 And he reared up the court round about the tabernacle and the altar, and set up the screen of the gate of the court.

3

So Moses finished the work. {P} 40:34 Then the cloud covered the tent of meeting, and the glory of the LORD filled the tabernacle. 40:35 And Moses was not able to enter into the tent of meeting, because the cloud abode thereon, and the glory of the LORD filled the tabernacle.-- 40:36 And whenever the cloud was taken up from over the tabernacle, the children of Israel went onward, throughout all their journeys. 40:37 But if the cloud was not taken up, then they journeyed not till the day that it was taken up. 40:38 For the cloud of the LORD was upon the tabernacle by day, and there was fire therein by night, in the sight of all the house of Israel, throughout all their journeys.-- {P}

Leviticus

Leviticus Unit I (1:1-3:17)

א1

1:1 And the LORD called unto Moses, and spoke unto him out of the tent of meeting, saying: 1:2 Speak unto the children of Israel, and say unto them: When any man of you bringeth an offering unto the LORD, ye shall bring your offering of the cattle, even of the herd or of the flock. 1:3 If his offering be a burnt-offering of the herd, he shall offer it a male without blemish; he shall bring it to the door of the tent of meeting, that he may be accepted before the LORD. 1:4 And he shall lay his hand upon the head of the burnt-offering; and it shall be accepted for him to make atonement for him. 1:5 And he shall kill the bullock before the LORD; and Aaron's sons, the priests, shall present the blood, and dash the blood round about against the altar that is at the door of the tent of meeting. 1:6 And he shall flay the burnt-offering, and cut it into its pieces. 1:7 And the sons of Aaron the priest shall put fire upon the altar, and lay wood in order upon the fire. 1:8 And Aaron's sons, the priests, shall lay the pieces, and the head, and the suet, in order upon the wood that is on the fire which is upon the altar; 1:9 but its inwards and its legs shall he wash with water; and the priest shall make the whole smoke on the altar, for a burnt-offering, an offering made by fire, of a sweet savour unto the LORD. {S}

א2

2:1 And when any one bringeth a meal-offering unto the LORD, his offering shall be of fine flour; and he shall pour oil upon it, and put frankincense thereon. 2:2 And he shall bring it to Aaron's sons the priests; and he shall take thereout his handful of the fine flour thereof, and of the oil thereof, together with all the frankincense thereof; and the priest shall make the memorial-part thereof smoke upon the altar, an offering made by fire, of a sweet savour unto the LORD. 2:3 But that which is left of the meal-offering shall be Aaron's and his sons'; it is a thing most holy of the offerings of the LORD made by fire. {S}

ב1

1:10 And if his offering be of the flock, whether of the sheep, or of the goats, for a burnt-offering, he shall offer it a male without blemish. 1:11 And he shall kill it on the side of the altar northward before LORD; and Aaron's sons, the priests, shall dash its blood against the altar round about. 1:12 And he shall cut it into its pieces; and the priest shall lay them, with its head and its suet, in order on the wood that is on the fire which is upon the altar. 1:13 But the inwards and the legs shall he wash with water; and the priest shall offer the whole, and make it smoke upon the altar; it is a burnt-offering, an offering made by fire, of a sweet savour unto the LORD. {P}

ב2

2:4 And when thou bringest a meal-offering baked in the oven, it shall be unleavened cakes of fine flour mingled with oil, or unleavened wafers spread with oil. {S} 2:5 And if thy offering be a meal-offering baked on a griddle, it shall be of fine flour unleavened, mingled with oil. 2:6 Thou shalt break it in pieces, and pour oil thereon; it is a meal-offering. {S} 2:7 And if thy offering be a meal-offering of the stewing-pan, it shall be made of fine flour with oil. 2:8 And thou shalt bring the meal-offering that is made of these things unto the LORD; and it shall be presented unto the priest, and he shall bring it unto the altar. 2:9 And the priest shall take off from the meal-offering the memorial-part thereof, and shall make it smoke upon the altar--an offering made by fire, of a sweet savour unto the LORD. 2:10 But that which is left of the meal-offering shall be Aaron's and his sons'; it is a thing most holy of the offerings of the LORD made by fire. 2:11 No meal-offering, which ye shall bring unto the LORD, shall be made with leaven; for ye shall make no leaven, nor any honey, smoke as an offering made by fire unto the LORD. 2:12 As an offering of first-fruits ye may bring them unto the LORD; but they shall not come up for a sweet savour on the altar. 2:13 And every meal-offering of thine shalt thou season with salt; neither shalt thou suffer the salt of the covenant of thy God to be lacking from thy meal-offering; with all thy offerings thou shalt offer salt. {S}

ג1

1:14 And if his offering to the LORD be a burnt-offering of fowls, then he shall bring his offering of turtle-doves, or of young pigeons. 1:15 And the priest shall bring it unto the altar, and pinch off its head, and make it smoke on the altar; and the blood thereof shall be drained out on the side of the altar. 1:16 And he shall take away its crop with the feathers thereof, and cast it beside the altar on the east part, in the place of the ashes. 1:17 And he shall rend it by the wings thereof, but shall not divide it asunder; and the priest shall make it smoke upon the altar, upon the wood that is upon the fire; it is a burnt-offering, an offering made by fire, of a sweet savour unto the LORD. {S}

ג2

2:14 And if thou bring a meal-offering of first-fruits unto the LORD, thou shalt bring for the meal-offering of thy first-fruits corn in the ear parched with fire, even groats of the fresh ear. 2:15 And thou shalt put oil upon it, and lay frankincense thereon; it is a meal-offering. 2:16 And the priest shall make the memorial part of it smoke, even of the groats thereof, and of the oil thereof, with all the frankincense thereof; it is an offering made by fire unto the LORD. {P}

3א

3:1 And if his offering be a sacrifice of peace-offerings: if he offer of the herd, whether male or female, he shall offer it without blemish before the LORD. 3:2 And he shall lay his hand upon the head of his offering, and kill it at the door of the tent of meeting; and Aaron's sons the priests shall dash the blood against the altar round about. 3:3 And he shall present of the sacrifice of peace-offerings an offering made by fire unto the LORD: the fat that covereth the inwards, and all the fat that is upon the inwards, 3:4 and the two kidneys, and the fat that is on them, which is by the loins, and the lobe above the liver, which he shall take away hard by the kidneys. 3:5 And Aaron's sons shall make it smoke on the altar upon the burnt-offering, which is upon the wood that is on the fire; it is an offering made by fire, of a sweet savour unto the LORD. {P}

3ב

3:6 And if his offering for a sacrifice of peace-offerings unto the LORD be of the flock, male or female, he shall offer it without blemish. 3:7 If he bring a lamb for his offering, then shall he present it before the LORD. 3:8 And he shall lay his hand upon the head of his offering, and kill it before the tent of meeting; and Aaron's sons shall dash the blood thereof against the altar round about. 3:9 And he shall present of the sacrifice of peace-offerings an offering made by fire unto the LORD: the fat thereof, the fat tail entire, which he shall take away hard by the rump-bone; and the fat that covereth the inwards, and all the fat that is upon the inwards, 3:10 and the two kidneys, and the fat that is upon them, which is by the loins, and the lobe above the liver, which he shall take away by the kidneys. 3:11 And the priest shall make it smoke upon the altar; it is the food of the offering made by fire unto the LORD. {P}

3ג

3:12 And if his offering be a goat, then he shall present it before the LORD. 3:13 And he shall lay his hand upon the head of it, and kill it before the tent of meeting; and the sons of Aaron shall dash the blood thereof against the altar round about. 3:14 And he shall present thereof his offering, even an offering made by fire unto the LORD: the fat that covereth the inwards, and all the fat that is upon the inwards, 3:15 and the two kidneys, and the fat that is upon them, which is by the loins, and the lobe above the liver, which he shall take away by the kidneys. 3:16 And the priest shall make them smoke upon the altar; it is the food of the offering made by fire, for a sweet savour; all the fat is the LORD'S. 3:17 It shall be a perpetual statute throughout your generations in all your dwellings, that ye shall eat neither fat nor blood. {P}

Leviticus Unit II (4:1-5:26)

א

A 4:1 And the LORD spoke unto Moses, saying: 4:2 Speak unto the children of Israel, saying: If any one shall sin through error, in any of the things which the LORD hath commanded not to be done, and shall do any one of them: 4:3 if the anointed priest shall sin so as to bring guilt on the people, then let him offer for his sin, which he hath sinned, a young bullock without blemish unto the LORD for a sin-offering. 4:4 And he shall bring the bullock unto the door of the tent of meeting before the LORD; and he shall lay his hand upon the head of the bullock, and kill the bullock before the LORD. 4:5 And the anointed priest shall take of the blood of the bullock, and bring it to the tent of meeting. 4:6 And the priest shall dip his finger in the blood, and sprinkle of the blood seven times before the LORD, in front of the veil of the sanctuary. 4:7 And the priest shall put of the blood upon the horns of the altar of sweet incense before the LORD, which is in the tent of meeting; and all the remaining blood of the bullock shall he pour out at the base of the altar of burnt-offering, which is at the door of the tent of meeting. 4:8 And all the fat of the bullock of the sin-offering he shall take off from it; the fat that covereth the inwards, and all the fat that is upon the inwards, 4:9 and the two kidneys, and the fat that is upon them, which is by the loins, and the lobe above the liver, which he shall take away by the kidneys, 4:10 as it is taken off from the ox of the sacrifice of peace-offerings; and the priest shall make them smoke upon the altar of burnt-offering. 4:11 But the skin of the bullock, and all its flesh, with its head, and with its legs, and its inwards, and its dung, 4:12 even the whole bullock shall he carry forth without the camp unto a clean place, where the ashes are poured out, and burn it on wood with fire; where the ashes are poured out shall it be burnt. {P}

B 4:13 And if the whole congregation of Israel shall err, the thing being hid from the eyes of the assembly, and do any of the things which the LORD hath commanded not to be done, and are guilty: 4:14 when the sin wherein they have sinned is known, then the assembly shall offer a young bullock for a sin-offering, and bring it before the tent of meeting. 4:15 And the elders of the congregation shall lay their hands upon the head of the bullock before the LORD; and the bullock shall be killed before the LORD. 4:16 And the anointed priest shall bring of the blood of the bullock to the tent of meeting. 4:17 And the priest shall dip his finger in the blood, and sprinkle it seven times before the LORD, in front of the veil. 4:18 And he shall put of the blood upon the horns of the altar which is before the LORD, that is in the tent of meeting, and all the remaining blood shall he pour out at the base of the altar of burnt-offering, which is at the door of the tent of meeting. 4:19 And all the fat thereof shall he take off from it, and make it smoke upon the altar. 4:20 Thus shall he do with the bullock; as he did with the bullock of the sin-offering, so shall he do with this; and the priest shall make atonement for them, and they shall be forgiven. 4:21 And he shall carry forth the bullock without the camp, and burn it as he burned the first bullock; it is the sin-offering for the assembly. {P}

ב

4:22 When a ruler sinneth, and doeth through error any one of all the things which the LORD his God hath commanded not to be done, and is guilty: 4:23 if his sin, wherein he hath sinned, be known to him, he shall bring for his offering a goat, a male without blemish. 4:24 And he shall lay his hand upon the head of the goat, and kill it in the place where they kill the burnt-offering before the LORD; it is a sin-offering. 4:25 And the priest shall take of the blood of the sin-offering with his finger, and put it upon the horns of the altar of burnt-offering, and the remaining blood thereof shall he pour out at the base of the altar of burnt-offering. 4:26 And all the fat thereof shall he make smoke upon the altar, as the fat of the sacrifice of peace-offerings; and the priest shall make atonement for him as concerning his sin, and he shall be forgiven. {P}

ג

A 4:27 And if any one of the common people sin through error, in doing any of the things which the LORD hath commanded not to be done, and be guilty: 4:28 if his sin, which he hath sinned, be known to him, then he shall bring for his offering a goat, a female without blemish, for his sin which he hath sinned. 4:29 And he shall lay his hand upon the head of the sin-offering, and kill the sin-offering in the place of burnt-offering. 4:30 And the priest shall take of the blood thereof with his finger, and put it upon the horns of the altar of burnt-offering, and all the remaining blood thereof shall he pour out at the base of the altar. 4:31 And all the fat thereof shall he take away, as the fat is taken away from off the sacrifice of peace-offerings; and the priest shall make it smoke upon the altar for a sweet savour unto the LORD; and the priest shall make atonement for him, and he shall be forgiven. {P}

B 4:32 And if he bring a lamb as his offering for a sin-offering, he shall bring it a female without blemish. 4:33 And he shall lay his hand upon the head of the sin-offering, and kill it for a sin-offering in the place where they kill the burnt-offering. 4:34 And the priest shall take of the blood of the sin-offering with his finger, and put it upon the horns of the altar of burnt-offering, and all the remaining blood thereof shall he pour out at the base of the altar. 4:35 And all the fat thereof shall he take away, as the fat of the lamb is taken away from the sacrifice of peace-offerings; and the priest shall make them smoke on the altar, upon the offerings of the LORD made by fire; and the priest shall make atonement for him as touching his sin that he hath sinned, and he shall be forgiven. {P}

2א

5:1 And if any one sin, in that he heareth the voice of adjuration, he being a witness, whether he hath seen or known, if he do not utter it, then he shall bear his iniquity; 5:2 or if any one touch any unclean thing, whether it be the carcass of an unclean beast, or the carcass of unclean cattle, or the carcass of unclean swarming things, and be guilty, it being hidden from him that he is unclean; 5:3 or if he touch the uncleanness of man, whatsoever his uncleanness be wherewith he is unclean, and it be hid from him; and, when he knoweth of it, be guilty; 5:4 or if any one swear clearly with his lips to do evil, or to do good, whatsoever it be that a man shall utter clearly with an oath, and it be hid from him; and, when he knoweth of it, be guilty in one of these things; 5:5 and it shall be, when he shall be guilty in one of these things, that he shall confess that wherein he hath sinned; 5:6 and he shall bring his forfeit unto the LORD for his sin which he hath sinned, a female from the flock, a lamb or a goat, for a sin-offering; and the priest shall make atonement for him as concerning his sin.

2ב

5:7 And if his means suffice not for a lamb, then he shall bring his forfeit for that wherein he hath sinned, two turtle-doves, or two young pigeons, unto the LORD: one for a sin-offering, and the other for a burnt-offering. 5:8 And he shall bring them unto the priest, who shall offer that which is for the sin-offering first, and pinch off its head close by its neck, but shall not divide it asunder. 5:9 And he shall sprinkle of the blood of the sin-offering upon the side of the altar; and the rest of the blood shall be drained out at the base of the altar; it is a sin-offering. 5:10 And he shall prepare the second for a burnt-offering, according to the ordinance; and the priest shall make atonement for him as concerning his sin which he hath sinned, and he shall be forgiven. {S}

2ג

5:11 But if his means suffice not for two turtledoves, or two young pigeons, then he shall bring his offering for that wherein he hath sinned, the tenth part of an ephah of fine flour for a sin-offering; he shall put no oil upon it, neither shall he put any frankincense thereon; for it is a sin-offering. 5:12 And he shall bring it to the priest, and the priest shall take his handful of it as the memorial-part thereof, and make it smoke on the altar, upon the offerings of the LORD made by fire; it is a sin-offering. 5:13 And the priest shall make atonement for him as touching his sin that he hath sinned in any of these things, and he shall be forgiven; and the remnant shall be the priest's, as the meal-offering. {S}

3א

5:14 And the LORD spoke unto Moses, saying: 5:15 If any one commit a trespass, and sin through error, in the holy things of the LORD, then he shall bring his forfeit unto the LORD, a ram without blemish out of the flock, according to thy valuation in silver by shekels, after the shekel of the sanctuary, for a guilt-offering. 5:16 And he shall make restitution for that which he hath done amiss in the holy thing, and shall add the fifth part thereto, and give it unto the priest; and the priest shall make atonement for him with the ram of the guilt-offering, and he shall be forgiven. {P}

3ב

5:17 And if any one sin, and do any of the things which the LORD hath commanded not to be done, though he know it not, yet is he guilty, and shall bear his iniquity. 5:18 And he shall bring a ram without blemish out of the flock, according to thy valuation, for a guilt-offering, unto the priest; and the priest shall make atonement for him concerning the error which he committed, though he knew it not, and he shall be forgiven. 5:19 It is a guilt-offering--he is certainly guilty before the LORD. {P}

3ג

5:20 And the LORD spoke unto Moses, saying: 5:21 If any one sin, and commit a trespass against the LORD, and deal falsely with his neighbour in a matter of deposit, or of pledge, or of robbery, or have oppressed his neighbour; 5:22 or have found that which was lost, and deal falsely therein, and swear to a lie; in any of all these that a man doeth, sinning therein; 5:23 then it shall be, if he hath sinned, and is guilty, that he shall restore that which he took by robbery, or the thing which he hath gotten by oppression, or the deposit which was deposited with him, or the lost thing which he found, 5:24 or any thing about which he hath sworn falsely, he shall even restore it in full, and shall add the fifth part more thereto; unto him to whom it apperaineth shall he give it, in the day of his being guilty. 5:25 And he shall bring his forfeit unto the LORD, a ram without blemish out of the flock, according to thy valuation, for a guilt-offering, unto the priest. 5:26 And the priest shall make atonement for him before the LORD, and he shall be forgiven, concerning whatsoever he doeth so as to be guilty thereby. {P}

Leviticus Unit III (6:1-7:38)

1א

6:1 And the LORD spoke unto Moses, saying: 6:2 Command Aaron and his sons, saying: This is the law of the burnt-offering: it is that which goeth up on its firewood upon the altar all night unto the morning; and the fire of the altar shall be kept burning thereby. 6:3 And the priest shall put on his linen garment, and his linen breeches shall he put upon his flesh; and he shall take up the ashes whereto the fire hath consumed the burnt-offering on the altar, and he shall put them beside the altar. 6:4 And he shall put off his garments, and put on other garments, and carry forth the ashes without the camp unto a clean place. 6:5 And the fire upon the altar shall be kept burning thereby, it shall not go out; and the priest shall kindle wood on it every morning; and he shall lay the burnt-offering in order upon it, and shall make smoke thereon the fat of the peace-offerings. 6:6 Fire shall be kept burning upon the altar continually; it shall not go out. {S}

2א

6:17 And the LORD spoke unto Moses, saying: 6:18 Speak unto Aaron and to his sons, saying: This is the law of the sin-offering: in the place where the burnt-offering is killed shall the sin-offering be killed before the LORD; it is most holy. 6:19 The priest that offereth it for sin shall eat it; in a holy place shall it be eaten, in the court of the tent of meeting. 6:20 Whatsoever shall touch the flesh thereof shall be holy; and when there is sprinkled of the blood thereof upon any garment, thou shalt wash that whereon it was sprinkled in a holy place. 6:21 But the earthen vessel wherein it is sodden shall be broken; and if it be sodden in a brazen vessel, it shall be scoured, and rinsed in water. 6:22 Every male among the priests may eat thereof; it is most holy. 6:23 And no sin-offering, whereof any of the blood is brought into the tent of meeting to make atonement in the holy place, shall be eaten; it shall be burnt with fire. {P}

1ב

6:7 And this is the law of the meal-offering: the sons of Aaron shall offer it before the LORD, in front of the altar. 6:8 And he shall take up therefrom his handful, of the fine flour of the meal-offering, and of the oil thereof, and all the frankincense which is upon the meal-offering, and shall make the memorial-part thereof smoke upon the altar for a sweet savour unto the LORD. 6:9 And that which is left thereof shall Aaron and his sons eat; it shall be eaten without leaven in a holy place; in the court of the tent of meeting they shall eat it. 6:10 It shall not be baked with leaven. I have given it as their portion of My offerings made by fire; it is most holy, as the sin-offering, and as the guilt-offering. 6:11 Every male among the children of Aaron may eat of it, as a due for ever throughout your generations, from the offerings of the LORD made by fire; whatsoever toucheth them shall be holy. {P}

2ב

7:1 And this is the law of the guilt-offering: it is most holy. 7:2 In the place where they kill the burnt-offering shall they kill the guilt-offering: and the blood thereof shall be dashed against the altar round about. 7:3 And he shall offer of it all the fat thereof: the fat tail, and the fat that covereth the inwards, 7:4 and the two kidneys, and the fat that is on them, which is by the loins, and the lobe above the liver, which he shall take away by the kidneys. 7:5 And the priest shall make them smoke upon the altar for an offering made by fire unto the LORD; it is a guilt-offering. 7:6 Every male among the priests may eat thereof; it shall be eaten in a holy place; it is most holy.

1ג

6:12 And the LORD spoke unto Moses, saying: 6:13 This is the offering of Aaron and of his sons, which they shall offer unto the LORD in the day when he is anointed: the tenth part of an ephah of fine flour for a meal-offering perpetually, half of it in the morning, and half thereof in the evening. 6:14 On a griddle it shall be made with oil; when it is soaked, thou shalt bring it in; in broken pieces shalt thou offer the meal-offering for a sweet savour unto the LORD. 6:15 And the anointed priest that shall be in his stead from among his sons shall offer it, it is a due for ever; it shall be wholly made to smoke unto the LORD. 6:16 And every meal-offering of the priest shall be wholly made to smoke; it shall not be eaten. {P}

2ג

7:7 As is the sin-offering, so is the guilt-offering; there is one law for them; the priest that maketh atonement therewith, he shall have it. 7:8 And the priest that offereth any man's burnt-offering, even the priest shall have to himself the skin of the burnt-offering which he hath offered. 7:9 And every meal-offering that is baked in the oven, and all that is dressed in the stewing-pan, and on the griddle, shall be the priest's that offereth it. 7:10 And every meal-offering, mingled with oil, or dry, shall all the sons of Aaron have, one as well as another. {P}

7:11 And this is the law of the sacrifice of peace-offerings, which one may offer unto the LORD. 7:12 If he offer it for a thanksgiving, then he shall offer with the sacrifice of thanksgiving unleavened cakes mingled with oil, and unleavened wafers spread with oil, and cakes mingled with oil, of fine flour soaked. 7:13 With cakes of leavened bread he shall present his offering with the sacrifice of his peace-offerings for thanksgiving. 7:14 And of it he shall present one out of each offering for a gift unto the LORD; it shall be the priest's that dasheth the blood of the peace-offerings against the altar. 7:15 And the flesh of the sacrifice of his peace-offerings for thanksgiving shall be eaten on the day of his offering; he shall not leave any of it until the morning. 7:16 But if the sacrifice of his offering be a vow, or a freewill-offering, it shall be eaten on the day that he offereth his sacrifice; and on the morrow that which remaineth of it may be eaten. 7:17 But that which remaineth of the flesh of the sacrifice on the third day shall be burnt with fire. 7:18 And if any of the flesh of the sacrifice of his peace-offerings be at all eaten on the third day, it shall not be accepted, neither shall it be imputed unto him that offereth it; it shall be an abhorred thing, and the soul that eateth of it shall bear his iniquity. 7:19 And the flesh that toucheth any unclean thing shall not be eaten; it shall be burnt with fire. And as for the flesh, every one that is clean may eat thereof. 7:20 But the soul that eateth of the flesh of the sacrifice of peace-offerings, that pertain unto the LORD, having his uncleanness upon him, that soul shall be cut off from his people. 7:21 And when any one shall touch any unclean thing, whether it be the uncleanness of man, or an unclean beast, or any unclean detestable thing, and eat of the flesh of the sacrifice of peace-offerings, which pertain unto the LORD, that soul shall be cut off from his people. {P}

7:22 And the LORD spoke unto Moses, saying: 7:23 Speak unto the children of Israel, saying: Ye shall eat no fat, of ox, or sheep, or goat. 7:24 And the fat of that which dieth of itself, and the fat of that which is torn of beasts, may be used for any other service; but ye shall in no wise eat of it. 7:25 For whosoever eateth the fat of the beast, of which men present an offering made by fire unto the LORD, even the soul that eateth it shall be cut off from his people. 7:26 And ye shall eat no manner of blood, whether it be of fowl or of beast, in any of your dwellings. 7:27 Whosoever it be that eateth any blood, that soul shall be cut off from his people.

7:28 And the LORD spoke unto Moses, saying: 7:29 Speak unto the children of Israel, saying: He that offereth his sacrifice of peace-offerings unto the LORD shall bring his offering unto the LORD out of his sacrifice of peace-offerings. 7:30 His own hands shall bring the offerings of the LORD made by fire: the fat with the breast shall he bring, that the breast may be waved for a wave-offering before the LORD. 7:31 And the priest shall make the fat smoke upon the altar; but the breast shall be Aaron's and his sons'. 7:32 And the right thigh shall ye give unto the priest for a heave-offering out of your sacrifices of peace-offerings. 7:33 He among the sons of Aaron, that offereth the blood of the peace-offerings, and the fat, shall have the right thigh for a portion. 7:34 For the breast of waving and the thigh of heaving have I taken of the children of Israel out of their sacrifices of peace-offerings, and have given them unto Aaron the priest and unto his sons as a due for ever from the children of Israel. 7:35 This is the consecrated portion of Aaron, and the consecrated portion of his sons, out of the offerings of the LORD made by fire, in the day when they were presented to minister unto the LORD in the priest's office; 7:36 which the LORD commanded to be given them of the children of Israel, in the day that they were anointed. It is a due for ever throughout their generations. 7:37 This is the law of the burnt-offering, of the meal-offering, and of the sin-offering, and of the guilt-offering, and of the consecration-offering, and of the sacrifice of peace-offerings; 7:38 which the LORD commanded Moses in mount Sinai, in the day that he commanded the children of Israel to present their offerings unto the LORD, in the wilderness of Sinai. {P}

Leviticus Unit IV (8:1-10:20)

א

A 8:1 And the LORD spoke unto Moses, saying: 8:2 'Take Aaron and his sons with him, and the garments, and the anointing oil, and the bullock of the sin-offering, and the two rams, and the basket of unleavened bread; 8:3 and assemble thou all the congregation at the door of the tent of meeting.' 8:4 And Moses did as the LORD commanded him; and the congregation was assembled at the door of the tent of meeting. 8:5 And Moses said unto the congregation: 'This is the thing which the LORD hath commanded to be done.'

B 8:6 And Moses brought Aaron and his sons, and washed them with water. 8:7 And he put upon him the tunic, and girded him with the girdle, and clothed him with the robe, and put the ephod upon him, and he girded him with the skilfully woven band of the ephod, and bound it unto him therewith. 8:8 And he placed the breastplate upon him; and in the breastplate he put the Urim and the Thummim. 8:9 And he set the mitre upon his head; and upon the mitre, in front, did he set the golden plate, the holy crown; as the LORD commanded Moses.

C 8:10 And Moses took the anointing oil, and anointed the tabernacle and all that was therein, and sanctified them. 8:11 And he sprinkled thereof upon the altar seven times, and anointed the altar and all its vessels, and the laver and its base, to sanctify them. 8:12 And he poured of the anointing oil upon Aaron's head, and anointed him, to sanctify him. 8:13 And Moses brought Aaron's sons, and clothed them with tunics, and girded them with girdles, and bound head-tires upon them; as the LORD commanded Moses.

D 8:14 And the bullock of the sin-offering was brought; and Aaron and his sons laid their hands upon the head of the bullock of the sin-offering. 8:15 And when it was slain, Moses took the blood, and put it upon the horns of the altar round about with his finger, and purified the altar, and poured out the remaining blood at the base of the altar, and sanctified it, to make atonement for it. 8:16 And he took all the fat that was upon the inwards, and the lobe of the liver, and the two kidneys, and their fat, and Moses made it smoke upon the altar. 8:17 But the bullock, and its skin, and its flesh, and its dung, were burnt with fire without the camp; as the LORD commanded Moses.

E 8:18 And the ram of the burnt-offering was presented; and Aaron and his sons laid their hands upon the head of the ram. 8:19 And when it was killed, Moses dashed the blood against the altar round about. 8:20 And when the ram was cut into its pieces, Moses made the head, and the pieces, and the suet smoke. 8:21 And when the inwards and the legs were washed with water, Moses made the whole ram smoke upon the altar; it was a burnt-offering for a sweet savour; it was an offering made by fire unto the LORD; as the LORD commanded Moses.

F 8:22 And the other ram was presented, the ram of consecration, and Aaron and his sons laid their hands upon the head of the ram. 8:23 And when it was slain, Moses took of the blood thereof, and put it upon the tip of Aaron's right ear, and upon the thumb of his right hand, and upon the great toe of his right foot. 8:24 And Aaron's sons were brought, and Moses put of the blood upon the tip of their right ear, and upon the thumb of their right hand, and upon the great toe of their right foot; and Moses dashed the blood against the altar round about. 8:25 And he took the fat, and the fat tail, and all the fat that was upon the inwards, and the lobe of the liver, and the two kidneys, and their fat, and the right thigh. 8:26 And out of the basket of unleavened bread, that was before the LORD, he took one unleavened cake, and one cake of oiled bread, and one wafer, and placed them on the fat, and upon the right thigh. 8:27 And he put the whole upon the hands of Aaron, and upon the hands of his sons, and waved them for a wave-offering before the LORD. 8:28 And Moses took them from off their hands, and made them smoke on the altar upon the burnt-offering; they were a consecration-offering for a sweet savour; it was an offering made by fire unto the LORD. 8:29 And Moses took the breast, and waved it for a wave-offering before the LORD; it was Moses' portion of the ram of consecration; as the LORD commanded Moses.

G 8:30 And Moses took of the anointing oil, and of the blood which was upon the altar, and sprinkled it upon Aaron, and upon his garments, and upon his sons, and upon his sons' garments with him, and sanctified Aaron, and his garments, and his sons, and his sons' garments with him. 8:31 And Moses said unto Aaron and to his sons: 'Boil the flesh at the door of the tent of meeting; and there eat it and the bread that is in the basket of consecration, as I commanded, saying: Aaron and his sons shall eat it. 8:32 And that which remaineth of the flesh and of the bread shall ye burn with fire. 8:33 And ye shall not go out from the door of the tent of meeting seven days, until the days of your consecration be fulfilled; for He shall consecrate you seven days. 8:34 As hath been done this day, so the LORD hath commanded to do, to make atonement for you. 8:35 And at the door of the tent of meeting shall ye abide day and night seven days, and keep the charge of the LORD, that ye die not; for so I am commanded. 8:36 And Aaron and his sons did all the things which the LORD commanded by the hand of Moses.

{S}

ב

A 9:1 And it came to pass on the eighth day, that Moses called Aaron and his sons, and the elders of Israel; 9:2 and he said unto Aaron: 'Take thee a bull-calf for a sin-offering, and a ram for a burnt-offering, without blemish, and offer them before the LORD. 9:3 And unto the children of Israel thou shalt speak, saying: Take ye a he-goat for a sin-offering; and a calf and a lamb, both of the first year, without blemish, for a burnt-offering; 9:4 and an ox and a ram for peace-offerings, to sacrifice before the LORD; and a meal-offering mingled with oil; for to-day the LORD appeareth unto you.' 9:5 And they brought that which Moses commanded before the tent of meeting;

B and all the congregation drew near and stood before the LORD. 9:6 And Moses said: 'This is the thing which the LORD commanded that ye should do; that the glory of the LORD may appear unto you.'

C 9:7 And Moses said unto Aaron: 'Draw near unto the altar, and offer thy sin-offering, and thy burnt-offering, and make atonement for thyself, and for the people; and present the offering of the people, and make atonement for them; as the LORD commanded.'

D 9:8 So Aaron drew near unto the altar, and slew the calf of the sin-offering, which was for himself. 9:9 And the sons of Aaron presented the blood unto him; and he dipped his finger in the blood, and put it upon the horns of the altar, and poured out the blood at the base of the altar. 9:10 But the fat, and the kidneys, and the lobe of the liver of the sin-offering, he made smoke upon the altar; as the LORD commanded Moses. 9:11 And the flesh and the skin were burnt with fire without the camp.

E 9:12 And he slew the burnt-offering; and Aaron's sons delivered unto him the blood, and he dashed it against the altar round about. 9:13 And they delivered the burnt-offering unto him, piece by piece, and the head; and he made them smoke upon the altar. 9:14 And he washed the inwards and the legs, and made them smoke upon the burnt-offering on the altar.

F 9:15 And the people's offering was presented; and he took the goat of the sin-offering which was for the people, and slew it, and offered it for sin, as the first. 9:16 And the burnt-offering was presented; and he offered it according to the ordinance. 9:17 And the meal-offering was presented; and he filled his hand therefrom, and made it smoke upon the altar, besides the burnt-offering of the morning. 9:18 He slew also the ox and the ram, the sacrifice of peace-offerings, which was for the people; and Aaron's sons delivered unto him the blood, and he dashed it against the altar round about, 9:19 and the fat of the ox, and of the ram, the fat tail, and that which covereth the inwards, and the kidneys, and the lobe of the liver. 9:20 And they put the fat upon the breasts, and he made the fat smoke upon the altar. 9:21 And the breasts and the right thigh Aaron waved for a wave-offering before the LORD; as Moses commanded.

G 9:22 And Aaron lifted up his hands toward the people, and blessed them; and he came down from offering the sin-offering, and the burnt-offering, and the peace-offerings. 9:23 And Moses and Aaron went into the tent of meeting, and came out, and blessed the people; and the glory of the LORD appeared unto all the people. 9:24 And there came forth fire from before the LORD, and consumed upon the altar the burnt-offering and the fat; and when all the people saw it, they shouted, and fell on their faces.

2א

A 10:1 And Nadab and Abihu, the sons of Aaron, took each of them his censer, and put fire therein, and laid incense thereon, and offered strange fire before the LORD, which He had not commanded them. 10:2 And there came forth fire from before the LORD, and devoured them, and they died before the LORD. 10:3 Then Moses said unto Aaron: 'This is it that the LORD spoke, saying: Through them that are nigh unto Me I will be sanctified, and before all the people I will be glorified.' And Aaron held his peace. 10:4 And Moses called Mishael and Elzaphan, the sons of Uzziel the uncle of Aaron, and said unto them: 'Draw near, carry your brethren from before the sanctuary out of the camp.' 10:5 So they drew near, and carried them in their tunics out of the camp, as Moses had said. 10:6 And Moses said unto Aaron, and unto Eleazar and unto Ithamar, his sons: 'Let not the hair of your heads go loose, neither rend your clothes, that ye die not, and that He be not wroth with all the congregation; but let your brethren, the whole house of Israel, bewail the burning which the LORD hath kindled. 10:7 And ye shall not go out from the door of the tent of meeting, lest ye die; for the anointing oil of the LORD is upon you.' And they did according to the word of Moses. {P}

B 10:8 And the LORD spoke unto Aaron, saying: 10:9 'Drink no wine nor strong drink, thou, nor thy sons with thee, when ye go into the tent of meeting, that ye die not; it shall be a statute forever throughout your generations. 10:10 And that ye may put difference between the holy and the common, and between the unclean and the clean; 10:11 and that ye may teach the children of Israel all the statutes which the LORD hath spoken unto them by the hand of Moses.' {P}

2ב

A 10:12 And Moses spoke unto Aaron, and unto Eleazar and unto Ithamar, his sons that were left: 'Take the meal-offering that remaineth of the offerings of the LORD made by fire, and eat it without leaven beside the altar; for it is most holy. 10:13 And ye shall eat it in a holy place, because it is thy due, and thy sons' due, of the offerings of the LORD made by fire; for so I am commanded. 10:14 And the breast of waving and the thigh of heaving shall ye eat in a clean place; thou, and thy sons, and thy daughters with thee; for they are given as thy due, and thy sons' due, out of the sacrifices of the peace-offerings of the children of Israel. 10:15 The thigh of heaving and the breast of waving shall they bring with the offerings of the fat made by fire, to wave it for a wave-offering before the LORD; and it shall be thine, and thy sons' with thee, as a due for ever; as the LORD hath commanded.'

B 10:16 And Moses diligently inquired for the goat of the sin-offering, and, behold, it was burnt; and he was angry with Eleazar and with Ithamar, the sons of Aaron that were left, saying: 10:17 'Wherefore have ye not eaten the sin-offering in the place of the sanctuary, seeing it is most holy, and He hath given it you to bear the iniquity of the congregation, to make atonement for them before the LORD? 10:18 Behold, the blood of it was not brought into the sanctuary within; ye should certainly have eaten it in the sanctuary, as I commanded.' 10:19 And Aaron spoke unto Moses: 'Behold, this day have they offered their sin-offering and their burnt-offering before the LORD, and there have befallen me such things as these; and if I had eaten the sin-offering to-day, would it have been well-pleasing in the sight of the LORD? 10:20 And when Moses heard that, it was well-pleasing in his sight. {P}

Leviticus Unit V (11:1-47)

א1

A 11:1 And the LORD spoke unto Moses and to Aaron, saying unto them: 11:2 Speak unto the children of Israel, saying: These are the living things which ye may eat among all the beasts that are on the earth. 11:3 Whatsoever parteth the hoof, and is wholly cloven-footed, and cheweth the cud, among the beasts, that may ye eat. 11:4 Nevertheless these shall ye not eat of them that only chew the cud, or of them that only part the hoof: the camel, because he cheweth the cud but parteth not the hoof, he is unclean unto you. 11:5 And the rock-badger, because he cheweth the cud but parteth not the hoof, he is unclean unto you. 11:6 And the hare, because she cheweth the cud but parteth not the hoof, she is unclean unto you. 11:7 And the swine, because he parteth the hoof, and is cloven-footed, but cheweth not the cud, he is unclean unto you. 11:8 Of their flesh ye shall not eat, and their carcasses ye shall not touch; they are unclean unto you.
B 11:9 These may ye eat of all that are in the waters: whatsoever hath fins and scales in the waters, in the seas, and in the rivers, them may ye eat. 11:10 And all that have not fins and scales in the seas, and in the rivers, of all that swarm in the waters, and of all the living creatures that are in the waters, they are a detestable thing unto you, 11:11 and they shall be a detestable thing unto you; ye shall not eat of their flesh, and their carcasses ye shall have in detestation. 11:12 Whatsoever hath no fins nor scales in the waters, that is a detestable thing unto you.
C 11:13 And these ye shall have in detestation among the fowls; they shall not be eaten, they are a detestable thing: the great vulture, and the bearded vulture, and the ospray; 11:14 and the kite, and the falcon after its kinds; 11:15 every raven after its kinds; 11:16 and the ostrich, and the night-hawk, and the sea-mew, and the hawk after its kinds; 11:17 and the little owl, and the cormorant, and the great owl; 11:18 and the horned owl, and the pelican, and the carrion-vulture; 11:19 and the stork, and the heron after its kinds, and the hoopoe, and the bat.

D11:20 All winged swarming things that go upon all fours are a detestable thing unto you. 11:21 Yet these may ye eat of all winged swarming things that go upon all fours, which have jointed legs above their feet, wherewith to leap upon the earth; 11:22 even these of them ye may eat: the locust after its kinds, and the bald locust after its kinds, and the cricket after its kinds, and the grasshopper after its kinds. 11:23 But all winged swarming things, which have four feet, are a detestable thing unto you.

א2

11:41 And every swarming thing that swarmeth upon the earth is a detestable thing; it shall not be eaten. 11:42 Whatsoever goeth upon the belly, and whatsoever goeth upon all fours, or whatsoever hath many feet, even all swarming things that swarm upon the earth, them ye shall not eat; for they are a detestable

ב1

A 11:24 And by these ye shall become unclean; whosoever toucheth the carcass of them shall be unclean until even. 11:25 And whosoever beareth aught of the carcass of them shall wash his clothes, and be unclean until the even. 11:26 Every beast which parteth the hoof, but is not cloven footed, nor cheweth the cud, is unclean unto you; every one that toucheth them shall be unclean. 11:27 And whatsoever goeth upon its paws, among all beasts that go on all fours, they are unclean unto you; whoso toucheth their carcass shall be unclean until the even. 11:28 And he that beareth the carcass of them shall wash his clothes, and be unclean until the even; they are unclean unto you. {S}

B 11:29 And these are they which are unclean unto you among the swarming things that swarm upon the earth: the weasel, and the mouse, and the great lizard after its kinds, 11:30 and the gecko, and the land-crocodile, and the lizard, and the sand-lizard, and the chameleon. 11:31 These are they which are unclean to you among all that swarm; whosoever doth touch them, when they are dead, shall be unclean until the even.

C 11:32 And upon whatsoever any of them, when they are dead, doth fall, it shall be unclean; whether it be any vessel of wood, or raiment, or skin, or sack, whatsoever vessel it be, wherewith any work is done, it must be put into water, and it shall be unclean until the even; then shall it be clean. 11:33 And every earthen vessel whereinto any of them falleth, whatsoever is in it shall be unclean, and it ye shall break. 11:34 All food therein which may be eaten, that on which water cometh, shall be unclean; and all drink in every such vessel that may be drunk shall be unclean. 11:35 And every thing whereupon any part of their carcass falleth shall be unclean; whether oven, or range for pots, it shall be broken in pieces; they are unclean, and shall be unclean unto you. 11:36 Nevertheless a fountain or a cistern wherein is a gathering of water shall be clean; but he who toucheth their carcass shall be unclean. 11:37 And if aught of their carcass fall upon any sowing seed which is to be sown, it is clean. 11:38 But if water be put upon the seed, and aught of their carcass fall thereon, it is unclean unto you. {S}
D11:39 And if any beast, of which ye may eat, die, he that toucheth the carcass thereof shall be unclean until the even. 11:40 And he that eateth of the carcass of it shall wash his clothes, and be unclean until the even; he also that beareth the carcass of it shall wash his clothes, and be unclean until the even.

ב2

11:43 Ye shall not make yourselves detestable with any swarming thing that swarmeth, neither shall ye make yourselves unclean with them, that ye should be defiled thereby. 11:44 For I am the LORD your God; sanctify yourselves therefore, and be ye holy; for I am holy; neither shall ye defile yourselves with any manner of swarming thing that moveth upon the earth. 11:45 For I am the LORD that brought you up out of the land of Egypt, to be your God; ye shall therefore be holy, for I am holy. 11:46 This is the law of the beast, and of the fowl, and of every living creature that moveth in the waters, and of every creature that swarmeth upon the earth; 11:47 to make a difference between the unclean and the clean, and between the living thing that may be eaten and the living thing that may not be eaten. {P}thing.

Leviticus Unit VI (12:1-8)

1א

12:1 And the LORD spoke unto Moses, saying: 12:2 Speak unto the children of Israel, saying: If a woman be delivered, and bear a man-child, then she shall be unclean seven days; as in the days of the impurity of her sickness shall she be unclean. 12:3 And in the eighth day the flesh of his foreskin shall be circumcised. 12:4 And she shall continue in the blood of purification three and thirty days; she shall touch no hallowed thing, nor come into the sanctuary, until the days of her purification be fulfilled.

2א

12:6 And when the days of her purification are fulfilled, for a son, or for a daughter, she shall bring a lamb of the first year for a burnt-offering, and a young pigeon, or a turtle-dove, for a sin-offering, unto the door of the tent of meeting, unto the priest. 12:7 And he shall offer it before the LORD, and make atonement for her; and she shall be cleansed from the fountain of her blood. This is the law for her that beareth, whether a male or a female.

1ב

12:5 But if she bear a maid-child, then she shall be unclean two weeks, as in her impurity; and she shall continue in the blood of purification threescore and six days.

2ב

12:8 And if her means suffice not for a lamb, then she shall take two turtle-doves, or two young pigeons: the one for a burnt-offering, and the other for a sin-offering; and the priest shall make atonement for her, and she shall be clean. {P}

Leviticus Unit VII (13:1-46)

1א

A 13:1 And the LORD spoke unto Moses and unto Aaron, saying: 13:2 When a man shall have in the skin of his flesh a rising, or a scab, or a bright spot, and it become in the skin of his flesh the plague of leprosy, then he shall be brought unto Aaron the priest, or unto one of his sons the priests. 13:3 And the priest shall look upon the plague in the skin of the flesh; and if the hair in the plague be turned white, and the appearance of the plague be deeper than the skin of his flesh, it is the plague of leprosy; and the priest shall look on him, and pronounce him unclean. 13:4 And if the bright spot be white in the skin of his flesh, and the appearance thereof be not deeper than the skin, and the hair thereof be not turned white, then the priest shall shut up him that hath the plague seven days. 13:5 And the priest shall look on him the seventh day; and, behold, if the plague stay in its appearance, and the plague be not spread in the skin, then the priest shall shut him up seven days more. 13:6 And the priest shall look on him again the seventh day; and, behold, if the plague be dim, and the plague be not spread in the skin, then the priest shall pronounce him clean: it is a scab; and he shall wash his clothes, and be clean. 13:7 But if the scab spread abroad in the skin, after that he hath shown himself to the priest for his cleansing, he shall show himself to the priest again. 13:8 And the priest shall look, and, behold, if the scab be spread in the skin, then the priest shall pronounce him unclean: it is leprosy. {P}

B 13:9 When the plague of leprosy is in a man, then he shall be brought unto the priest. 13:10 And the priest shall look, and, behold, if there be a white rising in the skin, and it have turned the hair white, and there be quick raw flesh in the rising, 13:11 it is an old leprosy in the skin of his flesh, and the priest shall pronounce him unclean; he shall not shut him up; for he is unclean. 13:12 And if the leprosy break out abroad in the skin, and the leprosy cover all the skin of him that hath the plague from his head even to his feet, as far as appeareth to the priest; 13:13 then the priest shall look; and, behold, if the leprosy have covered all his flesh, he shall pronounce him clean that hath the plague; it is all turned white: he is clean. 13:14 But whensoever raw flesh appeareth in him, he shall be unclean. 13:15 And the priest shall look on the raw flesh, and pronounce him unclean; the raw flesh is unclean: it is leprosy. 13:16 But if the raw flesh again be turned into white, then he shall come unto the priest; 13:17 and the priest shall look on him; and, behold, if the plague be turned into white, then the priest shall pronounce him clean that hath the plague: he is clean. {P}

2א

A 13:29 And when a man or woman hath a plague upon the head or upon the beard, 13:30 then the priest shall look on the plague; and, behold, if the appearance thereof be deeper than the skin, and there be in it yellow thin hair, then the priest shall pronounce him unclean: it is a scall, it is leprosy of the head or of the beard. 13:31 And if the priest look on the plague of the scall, and, behold, the appearance thereof be not deeper than the skin, and there be no black hair in it, then the priest shall shut up him that hath the plague of the scall seven days. 13:32 And in the seventh day the priest shall look on the plague; and, behold, if the scall be not spread, and there be in it no yellow hair, and the appearance of the scall be not deeper than the skin, 13:33 then he shall be shaven, but the scall shall he not shave; and the priest shall shut up him that hath the scall seven days more. 13:34 And in the seventh day the priest shall look on the scall; and, behold, if the scall be not spread in the skin, and the appearance thereof be not deeper than the skin, then the priest shall pronounce him clean; and he shall wash his clothes, and be clean. 13:35 But if the scall spread abroad in the skin after his cleansing, 13:36 then the priest shall look on him; and, behold, if the scall be spread in the skin, the priest shall not seek for the yellow hair: he is unclean. 13:37 But if the scall stay in its appearance, and black hair be grown up therein; the scall is healed, he is clean; and the priest shall pronounce him clean. {S}

B 13:38 And if a man or a woman have in the skin of their flesh bright spots, even white bright spots; 13:39 then the priest shall look; and, behold, if the bright spots in the skin of their flesh be of a dull white, it is a tetter, it hath broken out in the skin: he is clean. {S}

2ב

A 13:18 And when the flesh hath in the skin thereof a boil, and it is healed, 13:19 and in the place of the boil there is a white rising, or a bright spot, reddish-white, then it shall be shown to the priest. 13:20 And the priest shall look; and, behold, if the appearance thereof be lower than the skin, and the hair thereof be turned white, then the priest shall pronounce him unclean: it is the plague of leprosy, it hath broken out in the boil. 13:21 But if the priest look on it, and, behold, there be no white hairs therein, and it be not lower than the skin, but be dim, then the priest shall shut him up seven days. 13:22 And if it spread abroad in the skin, then the priest shall pronounce him unclean: it is a plague. 13:23 But if the bright spot stay in its place, and be not spread, it is the scar of the boil; and the priest shall pronounce him clean. {S}

B 13:24 Or when the flesh hath in the skin thereof a burning by fire, and the quick flesh of the burning become a bright spot, reddish-white, or white; 13:25 then the priest shall look upon it; and, behold, if the hair in the bright spot be turned white, and the appearance thereof be deeper than the skin, it is leprosy, it hath broken out in the burning; and the priest shall pronounce him unclean: it is the plague of leprosy. 13:26 But if the priest look on it, and, behold, there be no white hair in the bright spot, and it be no lower than the skin, but be dim; then the priest shall shut him up seven days. 13:27 And the priest shall look upon him the seventh day; if it spread abroad in the skin, then the priest shall pronounce him unclean: it is the plague of leprosy. 13:28 And if the bright spot stay in its place, and be not spread in the skin, but be dim, it is the rising of the burning, and the priest shall pronounce him clean; for it is the scar of the burning. {P}

2ב

A 13:40 And if a man's hair be fallen off his head, he is bald; yet is he clean. 13:41 And if his hair be fallen off from the front part of his head, he is forehead-bald; yet is he clean. 13:42 But if there be in the bald head, or the bald forehead, a reddish-white plague, it is leprosy breaking out in his bald head, or his bald forehead. 13:43 Then the priest shall look upon him; and, behold, if the rising of the plague be reddish-white in his bald head, or in his bald forehead, as the appearance of leprosy in the skin of the flesh, 13:44 he is a leprous man, he is unclean; the priest shall surely pronounce him unclean: his plague is in his head.

B 13:45 And the leper in whom the plague is, his clothes shall be rent, and the hair of his head shall go loose, and he shall cover his upper lip, and shall cry: 'Unclean, unclean.' 13:46 All the days wherein the plague is in him he shall be unclean; he is unclean; he shall dwell alone; without the camp shall his dwelling be. {S}

Leviticus Unit VIII (13:47-14:67)

1א

13:47 And when the plague of leprosy is in a garment, whether it be a woolen garment, or a linen garment; 13:48 or in the warp, or in the woof, whether they be of linen, or of wool; or in a skin, or in any thing made of skin. 13:49 If the plague be greenish or reddish in the garment, or in the skin, or in the warp, or in the woof, or in any thing of skin, it is the plague of leprosy, and shall be shown unto the priest. 13:50 And the priest shall look upon the plague, and shut up that which hath the plague seven days.

1ב

13:51 And he shall look on the plague on the seventh day: if the plague be spread in the garment, or in the warp, or in the woof, or in the skin, whatever service skin is used for, the plague is a malignant leprosy: it is unclean. 13:52 And he shall burn the garment, or the warp, or the woof, whether it be of wool or of linen, or any thing of skin, wherein the plague is; for it is a malignant leprosy; it shall be burnt in the fire. 13:53 And if the priest shall look, and, behold, the plague be not spread in the garment, or in the warp, or in the woof, or in any thing of skin; 13:54 then the priest shall command that they wash the thing wherein the plague is, and he shall shut it up seven days more. 13:55 And the priest shall look, after that the plague is washed; and, behold, if the plague have not changed its colour, and the plague be not spread, it is unclean; thou shalt burn it in the fire; it is a fret, whether the bareness be within or without.

1ג

13:56 And if the priest look, and, behold, the plague be dim after the washing thereof, then he shall rend it out of the garment, or out of the skin, or out of the warp, or out of the woof. 13:57 And if it appear still in the garment, or in the warp, or in the woof, or in any thing of skin, it is breaking out, thou shalt burn that wherein the plague is with fire. 13:58 And the garment, or the warp, or the woof, or whatsoever thing of skin it be, which thou shalt wash, if the plague be departed from them, then it shall be washed the second time, and shall be clean. 13:59 This is the law of the plague of leprosy in a garment of wool or linen, or in the warp, or in the woof, or in any thing of skin, to pronounce it clean, or to pronounce it unclean. {P}

2א

14:1 And the LORD spoke unto Moses, saying: 14:2 This shall be the law of the leper in the day of his cleansing: he shall be brought unto the priest. 14:3 And the priest shall go forth out of the camp; and the priest shall look, and, behold, if the plague of leprosy be healed in the leper; 14:4 then shall the priest command to take for him that is to be cleansed two living clean birds, and cedar-wood, and scarlet, and hyssop. 14:5 And the priest shall command to kill one of the birds in an earthen vessel over running water. 14:6 As for the living bird, he shall take it, and the cedar-wood, and the scarlet, and the hyssop, and shall dip them and the living bird in the blood of the bird that was killed over the running water. 14:7 And he shall sprinkle upon him that is to be cleansed from the leprosy seven times, and shall pronounce him clean, and shall let go the living bird into the open field. 14:8 And he that is to be cleansed shall wash his clothes, and shave off all his hair, and bathe himself in water, and he shall be clean; and after that he may come into the camp, but shall dwell outside his tent seven days. 14:9 And it shall be on the seventh day, that he shall shave all his hair off his head and his beard and his eyebrows, even all his hair he shall shave off; and he shall wash his clothes, and he shall bathe his flesh in water, and he shall be clean.

2ב

14:10 And on the eighth day he shall take two he-lambs without blemish, and one ewe-lamb of the first year without blemish, and three tenth parts of an ephah of fine flour for a meal-offering, mingled with oil, and one log of oil. 14:11 And the priest that cleanseth him shall set the man that is to be cleansed, and those things, before the LORD, at the door of the tent of meeting. 14:12 And the priest shall take one of the he-lambs, and offer him for a guilt-offering, and the log of oil, and wave them for a wave-offering before the LORD. 14:13 And he shall kill the he-lamb in the place where they kill the sin-offering and the burnt-offering, in the place of the sanctuary; for as the sin-offering is the priest's, so is the guilt-offering; it is most holy. 14:14 And the priest shall take of the blood of the guilt-offering, and the priest shall put it upon the tip of the right ear of him that is to be cleansed, and upon the thumb of his right hand, and upon the great toe of his right foot. 14:15 And the priest shall take of the log of oil, and pour it into the palm of his own left hand. 14:16 And the priest shall dip his right finger in the oil that is in his left hand, and shall sprinkle of the oil with his finger seven times before the LORD. 14:17 And of the rest of the oil that is in his hand shall the priest put upon the tip of the right ear of him that is to be cleansed, and upon the thumb of his right hand, and upon the great toe of his right foot, upon the blood of the guilt-offering. 14:18 And the rest of the oil that is in the priest's hand he shall put upon the head of him that is to be cleansed; and the priest shall make atonement for him before the LORD. 14:19 And the priest shall offer the sin-offering, and make atonement for him that is to be cleansed because of his uncleanness; and afterward he shall kill the burnt-offering. 14:20 And the priest shall offer the burnt-offering and the meal-offering upon the altar; and the priest shall make atonement for him, and he shall be clean. {S}

2ג

14:21 And if he be poor, and his means suffice not, then he shall take one he-lamb for a guilt-offering to be waved, to make atonement for him, and one tenth part of an ephah of fine flour mingled with oil for a meal-offering, and a log of oil; 14:22 and two turtle-doves, or two young pigeons, such as his means suffice for; and the one shall be a sin-offering, and the other a burnt-offering. 14:23 And on the eighth day he shall bring them for his cleansing unto the priest, unto the door of the tent of meeting, before the LORD. 14:24 And the priest shall take the lamb of the guilt-offering, and the log of oil, and the priest shall wave them for a wave-offering before the LORD. 14:25 And he shall kill the lamb of the guilt-offering, and the priest shall take of the blood of the guilt-offering, and put it upon the tip of the right ear of him that is to be cleansed, and upon the thumb of his right hand, and upon the great toe of his right foot. 14:26 And the priest shall pour of the oil into the palm of his own left hand. 14:27 And the priest shall sprinkle with his right finger some of the oil that is in his left hand seven times before the LORD. 14:28 And the priest shall put of the oil that is in his hand upon the tip of the right ear of him that is to be cleansed, and upon the thumb of his right hand, and upon the great toe of his right foot, upon the place of the blood of the guilt-offering. 14:29 And the rest of the oil that is in the priest's hand he shall put upon the head of him that is to be cleansed, to make atonement for him before the LORD. 14:30 And he shall offer one of the turtle-doves, or of the young pigeons, such as his means suffice for; 14:31 even such as his means suffice for, the one for a sin-offering, and the other for a burnt-offering, with the meal-offering; and the priest shall make atonement for him that is to be cleansed before the LORD. 14:32 This is the law of him in whom is the plague of leprosy, whose means suffice not for that which pertaineth to his cleansing. {P}

א3

14:33 And the LORD spoke unto Moses and unto Aaron, saying: 14:34 When ye are come into the land of Canaan, which I give to you for a possession, and I put the plague of leprosy in a house of the land of your possession; 14:35 then he that owneth the house shall come and tell the priest, saying: 'There seemeth to me to be as it were a plague in the house.' 14:36 And the priest shall command that they empty the house, before the priest go in to see the plague, that all that is in the house be not made unclean; and afterward the priest shall go in to see the house. 14:37 And he shall look on the plague, and, behold, if the plague be in the walls of the house with hollow streaks, greenish or reddish, and the appearance thereof be lower than the wall; 14:38 then the priest shall go out of the house to the door of the house, and shut up the house seven days.

ב3

14:39 And the priest shall come again the seventh day, and shall look; and, behold, if the plague be spread in the walls of the house; 14:40 then the priest shall command that they take out the stones in which the plague is, and cast them into an unclean place without the city. 14:41 And he shall cause the house to be scraped within round about, and they shall pour out the mortar that they scrape off without the city into an unclean place. 14:42 And they shall take other stones, and put them in the place of those stones; and he shall take other mortar, and shall plaster the house. 14:43 And if the plague come again, and break out in the house, after that the stones have been taken out, and after the house hath been scraped, and after it is plastered; 14:44 then the priest shall come in and look; and, behold, if the plague be spread in the house, it is a malignant leprosy in the house: it is unclean. 14:45 And he shall break down the house, the stones of it, and the timber thereof, and all the mortar of the house; and he shall carry them forth out of the city into an unclean place. 14:46 Moreover he that goeth into the house all the while that it is shut up shall be unclean until the even. 14:47 And he that lieth in the house shall wash his clothes; and he that eateth in the house shall wash his clothes.

ג3

14:48 And if the priest shall come in, and look, and, behold, the plague hath not spread in the house, after the house was plastered; then the priest shall pronounce the house clean, because the plague is healed. 14:49 And he shall take to cleanse the house two birds, and cedar-wood, and scarlet, and hyssop. 14:50 And he shall kill one of the birds in an earthen vessel over running water. 14:51 And he shall take the cedar-wood, and the hyssop, and the scarlet, and the living bird, and dip them in the blood of the slain bird, and in the running water, and sprinkle the house seven times. 14:52 And he shall cleanse the house with the blood of the bird, and with the running water, and with the living bird, and with the cedar-wood, and with the hyssop, and with the scarlet. 14:53 But he shall let go the living bird out of the city into the open field; so shall he make atonement for the house; and it shall be clean. 14:54 This is the law for all manner of plague of leprosy, and for a scall; 14:55 and for the leprosy of a garment, and for a house; 14:56 and for a rising, and for a scab, and for a bright spot; 14:57 to teach when it is unclean, and when it is clean; this is the law of leprosy. {P}

Leviticus Unit IX (15:1-33)

א1

15:1 And the LORD spoke unto Moses and to Aaron, saying: 15:2 Speak unto the children of Israel, and say unto them: When any man hath an issue out of his flesh, his issue is unclean. 15:3 And this shall be his uncleanness in his issue: whether his flesh run with his issue, or his flesh be stopped from his issue, it is his uncleanness. 15:4 Every bed whereon he that hath the issue lieth shall be unclean; and every thing whereon he sitteth shall be unclean. 15:5 And whosoever toucheth his bed shall wash his clothes, and bathe himself in water, and be unclean until the even. 15:6 And he that sitteth on any thing whereon he that hath the issue sat shall wash his clothes, and bathe himself in water, and be unclean until the even. 15:7 And he that toucheth the flesh of him that hath the issue shall wash his clothes, and bathe himself in water, and be unclean until the even. 15:8 And if he that hath the issue spit upon him that is clean, then he shall wash his clothes, and bathe himself in water, and be unclean until the even. 15:9 And what saddle soever he that hath the issue rideth upon shall be unclean. 15:10 And whosoever toucheth any thing that was under him shall be unclean until the even; and he that beareth those things shall wash his clothes, and bathe himself in water, and be unclean until the even. 15:11 And whomsoever he that hath the issue toucheth, without having rinsed his hands in water, he shall wash his clothes, and bathe himself in water, and be unclean until the even. 15:12 And the earthen vessel, which he that hath the issue toucheth, shall be broken; and every vessel of wood shall be rinsed in water. 15:13 And when he that hath an issue is cleansed of his issue, then he shall number to himself seven days for his cleansing, and wash his clothes; and he shall bathe his flesh in running water, and shall be clean. 15:14 And on the eighth day he shall take to him two turtle-doves, or two young pigeons, and come before the LORD unto the door of the tent of meeting, and give them unto the priest. 15:15 And the priest shall offer them, the one for a sin-offering, and the other for a burnt-offering; and the priest shall make atonement for him before the LORD for his issue. {S}

א2

15:19 And if a woman have an issue, and her issue in her flesh be blood, she shall be in her impurity seven days; and whosoever toucheth her shall be unclean until the even. 15:20 And every thing that she lieth upon in her impurity shall be unclean; every thing also that she sitteth upon shall be unclean. 15:21 And whosoever toucheth her bed shall wash his clothes, and bathe himself in water, and be unclean until the even. 15:22 And whosoever toucheth any thing that she sitteth upon shall wash his clothes, and bathe himself in water, and be unclean until the even. 15:23 And if he be on the bed, or on any thing whereon she sitteth, when he toucheth it, he shall be unclean until the even. 15:24 And if any man lie with her, and her impurity be upon him, he shall be unclean seven days; and every bed whereon he lieth shall be unclean. {S}

ב1

15:16 And if the flow of seed go out from a man, then he shall bathe all his flesh in water, and be unclean until the even. 15:17 And every garment, and every skin, whereon is the flow of seed, shall be washed with water, and be unclean until the even. 15:18 The woman also with whom a man shall lie carnally, they shall both bathe themselves in water, and be unclean until the even. {P}

ב2

15:25 And if a woman have an issue of her blood many days not in the time of her impurity, or if she have an issue beyond the time of her impurity; all the days of the issue of her uncleanness she shall be as in the days of her impurity: she is unclean. 15:26 Every bed whereon she lieth all the days of her issue shall be unto her as the bed of her impurity; and every thing whereon she sitteth shall be unclean, as the uncleanness of her impurity. 15:27 And whosoever toucheth those things shall be unclean, and shall wash his clothes, and bathe himself in water, and be unclean until the even. 15:28 But if she be cleansed of her issue, then she shall number to herself seven days, and after that she shall be clean. 15:29 And on the eighth day she shall take unto her two turtle-doves, or two young pigeons, and bring them unto the priest, to the door of the tent of meeting. 15:30 And the priest shall offer the one for a sin-offering, and the other for a burnt-offering; and the priest shall make atonement for her before the LORD for the issue of her uncleanness. 15:31 Thus shall ye separate the children of Israel from their uncleanness; that they die not in their uncleanness, when they defile My tabernacle that is in the midst of them. 15:32 This is the law of him that hath an issue, and of him from whom the flow of seed goeth out, so that he is unclean thereby; 15:33 and of her that is sick with her impurity, and of them that have an issue, whether it be a man, or a woman; and of him that lieth with her that is unclean. {P}

Leviticus Unit X (16:1-34)

1א

16:1 And the LORD spoke unto Moses, after the death of the two sons of Aaron, when they drew near before the LORD, and died; 16:2 and the LORD said unto Moses: 'Speak unto Aaron thy brother, that he come not at all times into the holy place within the veil, before the ark-cover which is upon the ark; that he die not; for I appear in the cloud upon the ark-cover.

1ב

16:3 Herewith shall Aaron come into the holy place: with a young bullock for a sin-offering, and a ram for a burnt-offering. 16:4 He shall put on the holy linen tunic, and he shall have the linen breeches upon his flesh, and shall be girded with the linen girdle, and with the linen mitre shall he be attired; they are the holy garments; and he shall bathe his flesh in water, and put them on. 16:5 And he shall take of the congregation of the children of Israel two he-goats for a sin-offering, and one ram for a burnt-offering. 16:6 And Aaron shall present the bullock of the sin-offering, which is for himself, and make atonement for himself, and for his house. 16:7 And he shall take the two goats, and set them before the LORD at the door of the tent of meeting. 16:8 And Aaron shall cast lots upon the two goats: one lot for the LORD, and the other lot for Azazel. 16:9 And Aaron shall present the goat upon which the lot fell for the LORD, and offer him for a sin-offering. 16:10 But the goat, on which the lot fell for Azazel, shall be set alive before the LORD, to make atonement over him, to send him away for Azazel into the wilderness. 16:11 And Aaron shall present the bullock of the sin-offering, which is for himself, and shall make atonement for himself, and for his house, and shall kill the bullock of the sin-offering which is for himself. 16:12 And he shall take a censer full of coals of fire from off the altar before the LORD, and his hands full of sweet incense beaten small, and bring it within the veil. 16:13 And he shall put the incense upon the fire before the LORD, that the cloud of the incense may cover the ark-cover that is upon the testimony, that he die not. 16:14 And he shall take of the blood of the bullock, and sprinkle it with his finger upon the ark-cover on the east; and before the ark-cover shall he sprinkle of the blood with his finger seven times. 16:15 Then shall he kill the goat of the sin-offering, that is for the people, and bring his blood within the veil, and do with his blood as he did with the blood of the bullock, and sprinkle it upon the ark-cover, and before the ark-cover. 16:16 And he shall make atonement for the holy place, because of the uncleannesses of the children of Israel, and because of their transgressions, even all their sins; and so shall he do for the tent of meeting, that dwelleth with them in the midst of their uncleannesses. 16:17 And there shall be no man in the tent of meeting when he goeth in to make atonement in the holy place, until he come out, and have made atonement for himself, and for his household, and for all the assembly of Israel. 16:18 And he shall go out unto the altar that is before the LORD, and make atonement for it; and shall take of the blood of the bullock, and of the blood of the goat, and put it upon the horns of the altar round about. 16:19 And he shall sprinkle of the blood upon it with his finger seven times, and cleanse it, and hallow it from the uncleannesses of the children of Israel. 16:20 And when he hath made an end of atoning for the holy place, and the tent of meeting, and the altar, he shall present the live goat. 16:21 And Aaron shall lay both his hands upon the head of the live goat, and confess over him all the iniquities of the children of Israel, and all their transgressions, even all their sins; and he shall put them upon the head of the goat, and shall send him away by the hand of an appointed man into the wilderness. 16:22 And the goat shall bear upon him all their iniquities unto a land which is cut off; and he shall let go the goat in the wilderness.

1ג

16:23 And Aaron shall come into the tent of meeting, and shall put off the linen garments, which he put on when he went into the holy place, and shall leave them there. 16:24 And he shall bathe his flesh in water in a holy place and put on his other vestments, and come forth, and offer his burnt-offering and the burnt-offering of the people, and make atonement for himself and for the people. 16:25 And the fat of the sin-offering shall he make smoke upon the altar. 16:26 And he that letteth go the goat for Azazel shall wash his clothes, and bathe his flesh in water, and afterward he may come into the camp. 16:27 And the bullock of the sin-offering, and the goat of the sin-offering, whose blood was brought in to make atonement in the holy place, shall be carried forth without the camp; and they shall burn in the fire their skins, and their flesh, and their dung. 16:28 And he that burneth them shall wash his clothes, and bathe his flesh in water, and afterward he may come into the camp.

2א

16:29 And it shall be a statute for ever unto you: in the seventh month, on the tenth day of the month, ye shall afflict your souls, and shall do no manner of work, the home-born, or the stranger that sojourneth among you. 16:30 For on this day shall atonement be made for you, to cleanse you; from all your sins shall ye be clean before the LORD. 16:31 It is a sabbath of solemn rest unto you, and ye shall afflict your souls; it is a statute for ever.

2ב

16:32 And the priest, who shall be anointed and who shall be consecrated to be priest in his father's stead, shall make the atonement, and shall put on the linen garments, even the holy garments. 16:33 And he shall make atonement for the most holy place, and he shall make atonement for the tent of meeting and for the altar; and he shall make atonement for the priests and for all the people of the assembly.

2ג

16:34 And this shall be an everlasting statute unto you, to make atonement for the children of Israel because of all their sins once in the year.' And he did as the LORD commanded Moses. {P}

Leviticus Unit XI (17:1-16)

1א

17:1 And the LORD spoke unto Moses, saying: 17:2 Speak unto Aaron, and unto his sons, and unto all the children of Israel, and say unto them: This is the thing which the LORD hath commanded, saying: 17:3 What man soever there be of the house of Israel, that killeth an ox, or lamb, or goat, in the camp, or that killeth it without the camp, 17:4 and hath not brought it unto the door of the tent of meeting, to present it as an offering unto the LORD before the tabernacle of the LORD, blood shall be imputed unto that man; he hath shed blood; and that man shall be cut off from among his people. 17:5 To the end that the children of Israel may bring their sacrifices, which they sacrifice in the open field, even that they may bring them unto the LORD, unto the door of the tent of meeting, unto the priest, and sacrifice them for sacrifices of peace-offerings unto the LORD. 17:6 And the priest shall dash the blood against the altar of the LORD at the door of the tent of meeting, and make the fat smoke for a sweet savour unto the LORD. 17:7 And they shall no more sacrifice their sacrifices unto the satyrs, after whom they go astray. This shall be a statute for ever unto them throughout their generations.

1ב

17:8 And thou shalt say unto them: Whatsoever man there be of the house of Israel, or of the strangers that sojourn among them, that offereth a burnt-offering or sacrifice, 17:9 and bringeth it not unto the door of the tent of meeting, to sacrifice it unto the LORD, even that man shall be cut off from his people.

1ג

17:10 And whatsoever man there be of the house of Israel, or of the strangers that sojourn among them, that eateth any manner of blood, I will set My face against that soul that eateth blood, and will cut him off from among his people. 17:11 For the life of the flesh is in the blood; and I have given it to you upon the altar to make atonement for your souls; for it is the blood that maketh atonement by reason of the life. 17:12 Therefore I said unto the children of Israel: No soul of you shall eat blood, neither shall any stranger that sojourneth among you eat blood.

2א

17:13 And whatsoever man there be of the children of Israel, or of the strangers that sojourn among them, that taketh in hunting any beast or fowl that may be eaten, he shall pour out the blood thereof, and cover it with dust. 17:14 For as to the life of all flesh, the blood thereof is all one with the life thereof;

2ב

therefore I said unto the children of Israel: Ye shall eat the blood of no manner of flesh; for the life of all flesh is the blood thereof; whosoever eateth it shall be cut off.

2ג

17:15 And every soul that eateth that which dieth of itself, or that which is torn of beasts, whether he be home-born or a stranger, he shall wash his clothes, and bathe himself in water, and be unclean until the even; then shall he be clean. 17:16 But if he wash them not, nor bathe his flesh, then he shall bear his iniquity. {P}

Leviticus Unit XII (18:1-30)

א1

18:1 And the LORD spoke unto Moses, saying: 18:2 Speak unto the children of Israel, and say unto them: I am the LORD your God.

ב1

18:3 After the doings of the land of Egypt, wherein ye dwelt, shall ye not do; and after the doings of the land of Canaan, whither I bring you, shall ye not do; neither shall ye walk in their statutes. 18:4 Mine ordinances shall ye do, and My statutes shall ye keep, to walk therein: I am the LORD your God.

ג1

18:5 Ye shall therefore keep My statutes, and Mine ordinances, which if a man do, he shall live by them: I am the LORD. {S}

א2

18:6 None of you shall approach to any that is near of kin to him, to uncover their nakedness. I am the LORD. {S} 18:7 The nakedness of thy father, and the nakedness of thy mother, shalt thou not uncover: she is thy mother; thou shalt not uncover her nakedness. {S} 18:8 The nakedness of thy father's wife shalt thou not uncover: it is thy father's nakedness. {S} 18:9 The nakedness of thy sister, the daughter of thy father, or the daughter of thy mother, whether born at home, or born abroad, even their nakedness thou shalt not uncover. {S} 18:10 The nakedness of thy son's daughter, or of thy daughter's daughter, even their nakedness thou shalt not uncover; for theirs is thine own nakedness. {S} 18:11 The nakedness of thy father's wife's daughter, begotten of thy father, she is thy sister, thou shalt not uncover her nakedness. {S} 18:12 Thou shalt not uncover the nakedness of thy father's sister: she is thy father's near kinswoman. {S} 18:13 Thou shalt not uncover the nakedness of thy mother's sister; for she is thy mother's near kinswoman. {S} 18:14 Thou shalt not uncover the nakedness of thy father's brother, thou shalt not approach to his wife: she is thine aunt. {S} 18:15 Thou shalt not uncover the nakedness of thy daughter-in-law: she is thy son' wife; thou shalt not uncover her nakedness. {S} 18:16 Thou shalt not uncover the nakedness of thy brother's wife: it is thy brother's nakedness. {S}

ב2

18:17 Thou shalt not uncover the nakedness of a woman and her daughter; thou shalt not take her son's daughter, or her daughter's daughter, to uncover her nakedness: they are near kinswomen; it is lewdness. 18:18 And thou shalt not take a woman to her sister, to be a rival to her, to uncover her nakedness, beside the other in her lifetime. 18:19 And thou shalt not approach unto a woman to uncover her nakedness, as long as she is impure by her uncleanness. 18:20 And thou shalt not lie carnally with thy neighbour's wife, to defile thyself with her. 18:21 And thou shalt not give any of thy seed to set them apart to Molech, neither shalt thou profane the name of thy God: I am the LORD.

ג2

18:22 Thou shalt not lie with mankind, as with womankind; it is abomination. 18:23 And thou shalt not lie with any beast to defile thyself therewith; neither shall any woman stand before a beast, to lie down thereto; it is perversion.

א3

18:24 Defile not ye yourselves in any of these things; for in all these the nations are defiled, which I cast out from before you. 18:25 And the land was defiled, therefore I did visit the iniquity thereof upon it, and the land vomited out her inhabitants.

ב3

18:26 Ye therefore shall keep My statutes and Mine ordinances, and shall not do any of these abominations; neither the home-born, nor the stranger that sojourneth among you-- 18:27 for all these abominations have the men of the land done, that were before you, and the land is defiled-- 18:28 that the land vomit not you out also, when ye defile it, as it vomited out the nation that was before you. 18:29 For whosoever shall do any of these abominations, even the souls that do them shall be cut off from among their people.

ג3

18:30 Therefore shall ye keep My charge, that ye do not any of these abominable customs, which were done before you, and that ye defile not yourselves therein: I am the LORD your God. {P}

Leviticus Unit XIII (19:1-37)

1א

A 19:1 And the LORD spoke unto Moses, saying: 19:2 Speak unto all the congregation of the children of Israel, and say unto them: Ye shall be holy; for holy am I the LORD your God.

B 19:3 Ye shall fear every man his mother, and his father, and ye shall keep My sabbaths: I am the LORD your God.

C 19:4 Turn ye not unto the idols, nor make to yourselves molten gods: I am the LORD your God.

D i 19:5 And when ye offer a sacrifice of peace-offerings unto the LORD, ye shall offer it that ye may be accepted. 19:6 It shall be eaten the same day ye offer it, and on the morrow; and if aught remain until the third day, it shall be burnt with fire. 19:7 And if it be eaten at all on the third day, it is a vile thing; it shall not be accepted. 19:8 But every one that eateth it shall bear his iniquity, because he hath profaned the holy thing of the LORD; and that soul shall be cut off from his people.

ii 19:9 And when ye reap the harvest of your land, thou shalt not wholly reap the corner of thy field, neither shalt thou gather the gleaning of thy harvest. 19:10 And thou shalt not glean thy vineyard, neither shalt thou gather the fallen fruit of thy vineyard; thou shalt leave them for the poor and for the stranger: I am the LORD your God.

1ב

A 19:11 Ye shall not steal; neither shall ye deal falsely, nor lie one to another. 19:12 And ye shall not swear by My name falsely, so that thou profane the name of thy God: I am the LORD.

B 19:13 Thou shalt not oppress thy neighbour, nor rob him; the wages of a hired servant shall not abide with thee all night until the morning. 19:14 Thou shalt not curse the deaf, nor put a stumbling-block before the blind, but thou shalt fear thy God: I am the LORD.

C i 19:15 Ye shall do no unrighteousness in judgment; thou shalt not respect the person of the poor, nor favour the person of the mighty; but in righteousness shalt thou judge thy neighbour. 19:16 Thou shalt not go up and down as a talebearer among thy people; neither shalt thou stand idly by the blood of thy neighbour: I am the LORD.

D i 19:17 Thou shalt not hate thy brother in thy heart; thou shalt surely rebuke thy neighbour, and not bear sin because of him. 19:18 Thou shalt not take vengeance, nor bear any grudge against the children of thy people, but thou shalt love thy neighbour as thyself: I am the LORD.

ii 19:19 Ye shall keep My statutes.

2א

Thou shalt not let thy cattle gender with a diverse kind;

thou shalt not sow thy field with two kinds of seed;

neither shall there come upon thee a garment of two kinds of stuff mingled together.

2ב

19:20 And whosoever lieth carnally with a woman, that is a bondmaid, designated for a man, and not at all redeemed, nor was freedom given her; there shall be inquisition; they shall not be put to death, because she was not free.

19:21 And he shall bring his forfeit unto the LORD, unto the door of the tent of meeting, even a ram for a guilt-offering. 19:22 And the priest shall make atonement for him with the ram of the guilt-offering before the LORD for his sin which he hath sinned;

and he shall be forgiven for his sin which he hath sinned. {P}

2ג

19:23 And when ye shall come into the land, and shall have planted all manner of trees for food, then ye shall count the fruit thereof as forbidden; three years shall it be as forbidden unto you; it shall not be eaten.

19:24 And in the fourth year all the fruit thereof shall be holy, for giving praise unto the LORD.

19:25 But in the fifth year may ye eat of the fruit thereof, that it may yield unto you more richly the increase thereof: I am the LORD your God.

3א

A 19:26 Ye shall not eat with the blood; neither shall ye practise divination nor soothsaying. 19:27 Ye shall not round the corners of your heads, neither shalt thou mar the corners of thy beard. 19:28 Ye shall not make any cuttings in your flesh for the dead, nor imprint any marks upon you: I am the LORD.

B 19:29 Profane not thy daughter, to make her a harlot, lest the land fall into harlotry, and the land become full of lewdness. 19:30 Ye shall keep My sabbaths, and reverence My sanctuary: I am the LORD.

C 19:31 Turn ye not unto the ghosts, nor unto familiar spirits; seek them not out, to be defiled by them: I am the LORD your God.

3ב

A 19:32 Thou shalt rise up before the hoary head, and honour the face of the old man, and thou shalt fear thy God: I am the LORD. {S}

B 19:33 And if a stranger sojourn with thee in your land, ye shall not do him wrong. 19:34 The stranger that sojourneth with you shall be unto you as the home-born among you, and thou shalt love him as thyself; for ye were strangers in the land of Egypt: I am the LORD your God.

C 19:35 Ye shall do no unrighteousness in judgment, in meteyard, in weight, or in measure. 19:36 Just balances, just weights, a just ephah, and a just hin, shall ye have: I am the LORD your God, who brought you out of the land of Egypt. 19:37 And ye shall observe all My statutes, and all Mine ordinances, and do them: I am the LORD. {P}

Leviticus Unit XIV (20:1-27)

א1

20:1 And the LORD spoke unto Moses, saying: 20:2 Moreover, thou shalt say to the children of Israel: Whosoever he be of the children of Israel, or of the strangers that sojourn in Israel, that giveth of his seed unto Molech; he shall surely be put to death; the people of the land shall stone him with stones. 20:3 I also will set My face against that man, and will cut him off from among his people, because he hath given of his seed unto Molech, to defile My sanctuary, and to profane My holy name. 20:4 And if the people of the land do at all hide their eyes from that man, when he giveth of his seed unto Molech, and put him not to death; 20:5 then I will set My face against that man, and against his family, and will cut him off, and all that go astray after him, to go astray after Molech, from among their people.

ב2

20:6 And the soul that turneth unto the ghosts, and unto the familiar spirits, to go astray after them, I will even set My face against that soul, and will cut him off from among his people. 20:7 Sanctify yourselves therefore, and be ye holy; for I am the LORD your God. 20:8 And keep ye My statutes, and do them: I am the LORD who sanctify you.

ג1

20:9 For whatsoever man there be that curseth his father or his mother shall surely be put to death; he hath cursed his father or his mother; his blood shall be upon him.

א2

20:10 And the man that committeth adultery with another man's wife, even he that committeth adultery with his neighbour's wife, both the adulterer and the adulteress shall surely be put to death.

20:11 And the man that lieth with his father's wife--he hath uncovered his father's nakedness--both of them shall surely be put to death; their blood shall be upon them.

20:12 And if a man lie with his daughter-in-law, both of them shall surely be put to death; they have wrought corruption; their blood shall be upon them.

20:13 And if a man lie with mankind, as with womankind, both of them have committed abomination: they shall surely be put to death; their blood shall be upon them.

20:14 And if a man take with his wife also her mother, it is wickedness: they shall be burnt with fire, both he and they; that there be no wickedness among you.

20:15 And if a man lie with a beast, he shall surely be put to death; and ye shall slay the beast.

20:16 And if a woman approach unto any beast, and lie down thereto, thou shalt kill the woman, and the beast: they shall surely be put to death; their blood shall be upon them.

ב2

20:17 And if a man shall take his sister, his father's daughter, or his mother's daughter, and see her nakedness, and she see his nakedness: it is a shameful thing; and they shall be cut off in the sight of the children of their people: he hath uncovered his sister's nakedness; he shall bear his iniquity.

20:18 And if a man shall lie with a woman having her sickness, and shall uncover her nakedness--he hath made naked her fountain, and she hath uncovered the fountain of her blood--both of them shall be cut off from among their people.

20:19 And thou shalt not uncover the nakedness of thy mother's sister, nor of thy father's sister; for he hath made naked his near kin; they shall bear their iniquity.

ג2

20:20 And if a man shall lie with his uncle's wife--he hath uncovered his uncle's nakedness--they shall bear their sin; they shall die childless.

20:21 And if a man shall take his brother's wife, it is impurity: he hath uncovered his brother's nakedness; they shall be childless.

א3

20:22 Ye shall therefore keep all My statutes, and all Mine ordinances, and do them, that the land, whither I bring you to dwell therein, vomit you not out. 20:23 And ye shall not walk in the customs of the nation, which I am casting out before you; for they did all these things, and therefore I abhorred them. 20:24 But I have said unto you: 'Ye shall inherit their land, and I will give it unto you to possess it, a land flowing with milk and honey.' I am the LORD your God, who have set you apart from the peoples.

ב3

20:25 Ye shall therefore separate between the clean beast and the unclean, and between unclean fowl and the clean; and ye shall not make your souls detestable by beast, or by fowl, or by any thing wherewith the ground teemeth, which I have set apart for you to hold unclean. 20:26 And ye shall be holy unto Me; for I the LORD am holy, and have set you apart from the peoples, that ye should be Mine.

ג3

20:27 A man also or a woman that divineth by a ghost or a familiar spirit, shall surely be put to death; they shall stone them with stones; their blood shall be upon them. {P}

Leviticus Unit XV (21:1-24)

1א

21:1 And the LORD said unto Moses: Speak unto the priests the sons of Aaron, and say unto them: There shall none defile himself for the dead among his people; 21:2 except for his kin, that is near unto him, for his mother, and for his father, and for his son, and for his daughter, and for his brother; 21:3 and for his sister a virgin, that is near unto him, that hath had no husband, for her may he defile himself. 21:4 He shall not defile himself, being a chief man among his people, to profane himself. 21:5 They shall not make baldness upon their head, neither shall they shave off the corners of their beard, nor make any cuttings in their flesh. 21:6 They shall be holy unto their God, and not profane the name of their God; for the offerings of the LORD made by fire, the bread of their God, they do offer; therefore they shall be holy.

1ב

21:7 They shall not take a woman that is a harlot, or profaned; neither shall they take a woman put away from her husband; for he is holy unto his God. 21:8 Thou shalt sanctify him therefore; for he offereth the bread of thy God; he shall be holy unto thee; for I the LORD, who sanctify you, am holy.

1ג

21:9 And the daughter of any priest, if she profane herself by playing the harlot, she profaneth her father: she shall be burnt with fire. {S}

2א

21:10 And the priest that is highest among his brethren, upon whose head the anointing oil is poured, and that is consecrated to put on the garments, shall not let the hair of his head go loose, nor rend his clothes; 21:11 neither shall he go in to any dead body, nor defile himself for his father, or for his mother; 21:12 neither shall he go out of the sanctuary, nor profane the sanctuary of his God; for the consecration of the anointing oil of his God is upon him: I am the LORD.

2ב

21:13 And he shall take a wife in her virginity. 21:14 A widow, or one divorced, or a profaned woman, or a harlot, these shall he not take; but a virgin of his own people shall he take to wife. 21:15 And he shall not profane his seed among his people; for I am the LORD who sanctify him. {S}

2ג

21:16 And the LORD spoke unto Moses, saying: 21:17 Speak unto Aaron, saying: Whosoever he be of thy seed throughout their generations that hath a blemish, let him not approach to offer the bread of his God. 21:18 For whatsoever man he be that hath a blemish, he shall not approach: a blind man, or a lame, or he that hath any thing maimed, or anything too long, 21:19 or a man that is broken-footed, or broken-handed, 21:20 or crook-backed, or a dwarf, or that hath his eye overspread, or is scabbed, or scurvy, or hath his stones crushed; 21:21 no man of the seed of Aaron the priest, that hath a blemish, shall come nigh to offer the offerings of the LORD made by fire; he hath a blemish; he shall not come nigh to offer the bread of his God. 21:22 He may eat the bread of his God, both of the most holy, and of the holy. 21:23 Only he shall not go in unto the veil, nor come nigh unto the altar, because he hath a blemish; that he profane not My holy places; for I am the LORD who sanctify them. 21:24 So Moses spoke unto Aaron, and to his sons, and unto all the children of Israel. {P}

Leviticus Unit XVI (22:1-25)

1א

22:1 And the LORD spoke unto Moses, saying: 22:2 Speak unto Aaron and to his sons, that they separate themselves from the holy things of the children of Israel, which they hallow unto Me, and that they profane not My holy name: I am the LORD.

1ב

22:3 Say unto them: Whosoever he be of all your seed throughout your generations, that approacheth unto the holy things, which the children of Israel hallow unto the LORD, having his uncleanness upon him, that soul shall be cut off from before Me: I am the LORD.

1ג

22:4 What man soever of the seed of Aaron is a leper, or hath an issue, he shall not eat of the holy things, until he be clean. And whoso toucheth any one that is unclean by the dead; or from whomsoever the flow of seed goeth out; 22:5 or whosoever toucheth any swarming thing, whereby he may be made unclean, or a man of whom he may take uncleanness, whatsoever uncleanness he hath; 22:6 the soul that toucheth any such shall be unclean until the even, and shall not eat of the holy things, unless he bathe his flesh in water. 22:7 And when the sun is down, he shall be clean; and afterward he may eat of the holy things, because it is his bread. 22:8 That which dieth of itself, or is torn of beasts, he shall not eat to defile himself therewith: I am the LORD.

2א

22:9 They shall therefore keep My charge, lest they bear sin for it, and die therein, if they profane it: I am the LORD who sanctify them.

2ב

22:10 There shall no common man eat of the holy thing; a tenant of a priest, or a hired servant, shall not eat of the holy thing. 22:11 But if a priest buy any soul, the purchase of his money, he may eat of it; and such as are born in his house, they may eat of his bread. 22:12 And if a priest's daughter be married unto a common man, she shall not eat of that which is set apart from the holy things. 22:13 But if a priest's daughter be a widow, or divorced, and have no child, and is returned unto her father's house, as in her youth, she may eat of her father's bread; but there shall no common man eat thereof. 22:14 And if a man eat of the holy thing through error, then he shall put the fifth part thereof unto it, and shall give unto the priest the holy thing. 22:15 And they shall not profane the holy things of the children of Israel, which they set apart unto the LORD; 22:16 and so cause them to bear the iniquity that bringeth guilt, when they eat their holy things; for I am the LORD who sanctify them. {P}

2ג

22:17 And the LORD spoke unto Moses, saying: 22:18 Speak unto Aaron, and to his sons, and unto all the children of Israel, and say unto them: Whosoever he be of the house of Israel, or of the strangers in Israel, that bringeth his offering, whether it be any of their vows, or any of their free-will-offerings, which are brought unto the LORD for a burnt-offering; 22:19 that ye may be accepted, ye shall offer a male without blemish, of the beeves, of the sheep, or of the goats. 22:20 But whatsoever hath a blemish, that shall ye not bring; for it shall not be acceptable for you. 22:21 And whosoever bringeth a sacrifice of peace-offerings unto the LORD in fulfilment of a vow clearly uttered, or for a freewill-offering, of the herd or of the flock, it shall be perfect to be accepted; there shall be no blemish therein. 22:22 Blind, or broken, or maimed, or having a wen, or scabbed, or scurvy, ye shall not offer these unto the LORD, nor make an offering by fire of them upon the altar unto the LORD. 22:23 Either a bullock or a lamb that hath any thing too long or too short, that mayest thou offer for a freewill-offering; but for a vow it shall not be accepted. 22:24 That which hath its stones bruised, or crushed, or torn, or cut, ye shall not offer unto the LORD; neither shall ye do thus in your land. 22:25 Neither from the hand of a foreigner shall ye offer the bread of your God of any of these, because their corruption is in them, there is a blemish in them; they shall not be accepted for you. {S}

Leviticus Unit XVII (22:26-33)

1א

22:26 And the LORD spoke unto Moses, saying: 22:27 When a bullock, or a sheep, or a goat, is brought forth, then it shall be seven days under the dam; but from the eighth day and thenceforth it may be accepted for an offering made by fire unto the LORD.

2א

22:31 And ye shall keep My commandments, and do them: I am the LORD.

1ב

22:28 And whether it be cow or ewe, ye shall not kill it and its young both in one day. 22:29 And when ye sacrifice a sacrifice of thanksgiving unto the LORD, ye shall sacrifice it that ye may be accepted. 22:30 On the same day it shall be eaten; ye shall leave none of it until the morning: I am the LORD.

2ב

22:32 And ye shall not profane My holy name; but I will be hallowed among the children of Israel: I am the LORD who hallow you, 22:33 that brought you out of the land of Egypt, to be your God: I am the LORD. {P}

Leviticus Unit XVIII (23:1-44)

1א

A i 23:1 And the LORD spoke unto Moses, saying: 23:2 Speak unto the children of Israel, and say unto them: The appointed seasons of the LORD, which ye shall proclaim to be holy convocations, even these are My appointed seasons.

ii 23:3 Six days shall work be done; but on the seventh day is a sabbath of solemn rest, a holy convocation; ye shall do no manner of work; it is a sabbath unto the LORD in all your dwellings. {P}

B i 23:4 These are the appointed seasons of the LORD, even holy convocations, which ye shall proclaim in their appointed season.
ii 23:5 In the first month, on the fourteenth day of the month at dusk, is the LORD'S passover. 23:6 And on the fifteenth day of the same month is the feast of unleavened bread unto the LORD; seven days ye shall eat unleavened bread. 23:7 In the first day ye shall have a holy convocation; ye shall do no manner of servile work. 23:8 And ye shall bring an offering made by fire unto the LORD seven days; in the seventh day is a holy convocation; ye shall do no manner of servile work. {P}

2א

A 23:23 And the LORD spoke unto Moses, saying: 23:24 Speak unto the children of Israel, saying: In the seventh month, in the first day of the month, shall be a solemn rest unto you, a memorial proclaimed with the blast of horns, a holy convocation. 23:25 Ye shall do no manner of servile work; and ye shall bring an offering made by fire unto the LORD. {S}

B 23:26 And the LORD spoke unto Moses, saying: 23:27 Howbeit on the tenth day of this seventh month is the day of atonement; there shall be a holy convocation unto you, and ye shall afflict your souls; and ye shall bring an offering made by fire unto the LORD. 23:28 And ye shall do no manner of work in that same day; for it is a day of atonement, to make atonement for you before the LORD your God. 23:29 For whatsoever soul it be that shall not be afflicted in that same day, he shall be cut off from his people. 23:30 And whatsoever soul it be that doeth any manner of work in that same day, that soul will I destroy from among his people. 23:31 Ye shall do no manner of work; it is a statute for ever throughout your generations in all your dwellings. 23:32 It shall be unto you a sabbath of solemn rest, and ye shall afflict your souls; in the ninth day of the month at even, from even unto even, shall ye keep your sabbath. {P}

1ב

A i 23:9 And the LORD spoke unto Moses saying: 23:10 Speak unto the children of Israel, and say unto them: When ye are come into the land which I give unto you, and shall reap the harvest thereof, then ye shall bring the sheaf of the first-fruits of your harvest unto the priest. 23:11 And he shall wave the sheaf before the LORD, to be accepted for you; on the morrow after the sabbath the priest shall wave it. 23:12 And in the day when ye wave the sheaf, ye shall offer a he-lamb without blemish of the first year for a burnt-offering unto the LORD. 23:13 And the meal-offering thereof shall be two tenth parts of an ephah of fine flour mingled with oil, an offering made by fire unto the LORD for a sweet savour; and the drink-offering thereof shall be of wine, the fourth part of a hin.

ii 23:14 And ye shall eat neither bread, nor parched corn, nor fresh ears, until this selfsame day, until ye have brought the offering of your God; it is a statute for ever throughout your generations in all your dwellings. {S}
B i 23:15 And ye shall count unto you from the morrow after the day of rest, from the day that ye brought the sheaf of the waving; seven weeks shall there be complete; 23:16 even unto the morrow after the seventh week shall ye number fifty days; and ye shall present a new meal-offering unto the LORD. 23:17 Ye shall bring out of your dwellings two wave-loaves of two tenth parts of an ephah; they shall be of fine flour, they shall be baked with leaven, for first-fruits unto the LORD. 23:18 And ye shall present with the bread seven lambs without blemish of the first year, and one young bullock, and two rams; they shall be a burnt-offering unto the LORD, with their meal-offering, and their drink-offerings, even an offering made by fire, of a sweet savour unto the LORD. 23:19 And ye shall offer one he-goat for a sin-offering, and two he-lambs of the first year for a sacrifice of peace-offerings. 23:20 And the priest shall wave them with the bread of the first-fruits for a wave-offering before the LORD, with the two lambs; they shall be holy to the LORD for the priest. 23:21 And ye shall make proclamation on the selfsame day; there shall be a holy convocation unto you; ye shall do no manner of servile work; it is a statute for ever in all your dwellings throughout your generations.
ii 23:22 And when ye reap the harvest of your land, thou shalt not wholly reap the corner of thy field, neither shalt thou gather the gleaning of thy harvest; thou shalt leave them for the poor, and for the stranger: I am the LORD your God. {P}

2ב

A 23:33 And the LORD spoke unto Moses, saying: 23:34 Speak unto the children of Israel, saying: On the fifteenth day of this seventh month is the feast of tabernacles for seven days unto the LORD. 23:35 On the first day shall be a holy convocation; ye shall do no manner of servile work. 23:36 Seven days ye shall bring an offering made by fire unto the LORD; on the eighth day shall be a holy convocation unto you; and ye shall bring an offering made by fire unto the LORD; it is a day of solemn assembly; ye shall do no manner of servile work. 23:37 These are the appointed seasons of the LORD, which ye shall proclaim to be holy convocations, to bring an offering made by fire unto the LORD, a burnt-offering, and a meal-offering, a sacrifice, and drink-offerings, each on its own day; 23:38 beside the sabbaths of the LORD, and beside your gifts, and beside all your vows, and beside all your freewill-offerings, which ye give unto the LORD

B 23:39 Howbeit on the fifteenth day of the seventh month, when ye have gathered in the fruits of the land, ye shall keep the feast of the LORD seven days; on the first day shall be a solemn rest, and on the eighth day shall be a solemn rest. 23:40 And ye shall take you on the first day the fruit of goodly trees, branches of palm-trees, and boughs of thick trees, and willows of the brook, and ye shall rejoice before the LORD your God seven days. 23:41 And ye shall keep it a feast unto the LORD seven days in the year; it is a statute for ever in your generations; ye shall keep it in the seventh month. 23:42 Ye shall dwell in booths seven days; all that are home-born in Israel shall dwell in booths; 23:43 that your generations may know that I made the children of Israel to dwell in booths, when I brought them out of the land of Egypt: I am the LORD your God. 23:44 And Moses declared unto the children of Israel the appointed seasons of the LORD. {P}

Leviticus Unit XIX (24:1-23)

1א

24:1 And the LORD spoke unto Moses, saying: 24:2 'Command the children of Israel, that they bring unto thee pure olive oil beaten for the light, to cause a lamp to burn continually. 24:3 Without the veil of the testimony, in the tent of meeting, shall Aaron order it from evening to morning before the LORD continually; it shall be a statute for ever throughout your generations. 24:4 He shall order the lamps upon the pure candlestick before the LORD continually. {P}

2א

24:10 And the son of an Israelitish woman, whose father was an Egyptian, went out among the children of Israel; and the son of the Israelitish woman and a man of Israel strove together in the camp. 24:11 And the son of the Israelitish woman blasphemed the Name, and cursed; and they brought him unto Moses. And his mother's name was Shelomith, the daughter of Dibri, of the tribe of Dan. 24:12 And they put him in ward, that it might be declared unto them at the mouth of the LORD. {P}

1ב

24:5 And thou shalt take fine flour, and bake twelve cakes thereof: two tenth parts of an ephah shall be in one cake. 24:6 And thou shalt set them in two rows, six in a row, upon the pure table before the LORD. 24:7 And thou shalt put pure frankincense with each row, that it may be to the bread for a memorial-part, even an offering made by fire unto the LORD. 24:8 Every sabbath day he shall set it in order before the LORD continually; it is from the children of Israel, an everlasting covenant. 24:9 And it shall be for Aaron and his sons; and they shall eat it in a holy place; for it is most holy unto him of the offerings of the LORD made by fire, a perpetual due.' {S}

2ב

24:13 And the LORD spoke unto Moses, saying: 24:14 'Bring forth him that hath cursed without the camp; and let all that heard him lay their hands upon his head, and let all the congregation stone him. 24:15 And thou shalt speak unto the children of Israel, saying: Whosoever curseth his God shall bear his sin. 24:16 And he that blasphemeth the name of the LORD, he shall surely be put to death; all the congregation shall certainly stone him; as well the stranger, as the home-born, when he blasphemeth the Name, shall be put to death. 24:17 And he that smiteth any man mortally shall surely be put to death. 24:18 And he that smiteth a beast mortally shall make it good: life for life. 24:19 And if a man maim his neighbour; as he hath done, so shall it be done to him: 24:20 breach for breach, eye for eye, tooth for tooth; as he hath maimed a man, so shall it be rendered unto him. 24:21 And he that killeth a beast shall make it good; and he that killeth a man shall be put to death. 24:22 Ye shall have one manner of law, as well for the stranger, as for the home-born; for I am the LORD your God.' 24:23 And Moses spoke to the children of Israel, and they brought forth him that had cursed out of the camp, and stoned him with stones. And the children of Israel did as the LORD commanded Moses. {P}

Leviticus Unit XX (25:1-55)

1א

25:1 And the LORD spoke unto Moses in mount Sinai, saying: 25:2 Speak unto the children of Israel, and say unto them: When ye come into the land which I give you, then shall the land keep a sabbath unto the LORD. 25:3 Six years thou shalt sow thy field, and six years thou shalt prune thy vineyard, and gather in the produce thereof. 25:4 But in the seventh year shall be a sabbath of solemn rest for the land, a sabbath unto the LORD; thou shalt neither sow thy field, nor prune thy vineyard. 25:5 That which groweth of itself of thy harvest thou shalt not reap, and the grapes of thy undressed vine thou shalt not gather; it shall be a year of solemn rest for the land. 25:6 And the sabbath-produce of the land shall be for food for you: for thee, and for thy servant and for thy maid, and for thy hired servant and for the settler by thy side that sojourn with thee; 25:7 and for thy cattle, and for the beasts that are in thy land, shall all the increase thereof be for food. {S}

1ב

25:8 And thou shalt number seven sabbaths of years unto thee, seven times seven years; and there shall be unto thee the days of seven sabbaths of years, even forty and nine years. 25:9 Then shalt thou make proclamation with the blast of the horn on the tenth day of the seventh month; in the day of atonement shall ye make proclamation with the horn throughout all your land. 25:10 And ye shall hallow the fiftieth year, and proclaim liberty throughout the land unto all the inhabitants thereof; it shall be a jubilee unto you; and ye shall return every man unto his possession, and ye shall return every man unto his family. 25:11 A jubilee shall that fiftieth year be unto you; ye shall not sow, neither reap that which groweth of itself in it, nor gather the grapes in it of the undressed vines. 25:12 For it is a jubilee; it shall be holy unto you; ye shall eat the increase thereof out of the field. 25:13 In this year of jubilee ye shall return every man unto his possession. 25:14 And if thou sell aught unto thy neighbour, or buy of thy neighbour's hand, ye shall not wrong one another. 25:15 According to the number of years after the jubilee thou shalt buy of thy neighbour, and according unto the number of years of the crops he shall sell unto thee. 25:16 According to the multitude of the years thou shalt increase the price thereof, and according to the fewness of the years thou shalt diminish the price of it; for the number of crops doth he sell unto thee. 25:17 And ye shall not wrong one another; but thou shalt fear thy God; for I am the LORD your God.

1ג

25:18 Wherefore ye shall do My statutes, and keep Mine ordinances and do them; and ye shall dwell in the land in safety. 25:19 And the land shall yield her fruit, and ye shall eat until ye have enough, and dwell therein in safety. 25:20 And if ye shall say: 'What shall we eat the seventh year? behold, we may not sow, nor gather in our increase'; 25:21 then I will command My blessing upon you in the sixth year, and it shall bring forth produce for the three years. 25:22 And ye shall sow the eighth year, and eat of the produce, the old store; until the ninth year, until her produce come in, ye shall eat the old store. 25:23 And the land shall not be sold in perpetuity; for the land is Mine; for ye are strangers and settlers with Me. 25:24 And in all the land of your possession ye shall grant a redemption for the land. {S}

2א

25:25 If thy brother be waxen poor, and sell some of his possession, then shall his kinsman that is next unto him come, and shall redeem that which his brother hath sold. 25:26 And if a man have no one to redeem it, and he be waxen rich and find sufficient means to redeem it; 25:27 then let him count the years of the sale thereof, and restore the overplus unto the man to whom he sold it; and he shall return unto his possession. 25:28 But if he have not sufficient means to get it back for himself, then that which he hath sold shall remain in the hand of him that hath bought it until the year of jubilee; and in the jubilee it shall go out, and he shall return unto his possession. {S}

2ב

25:29 And if a man sell a dwelling-house in a walled city, then he may redeem it within a whole year after it is sold; for a full year shall he have the right of redemption. 25:30 And if it be not redeemed within the space of a full year, then the house that is in the walled city shall be made sure in perpetuity to him that bought it, throughout his generations; it shall not go out in the jubilee. 25:31 But the houses of the villages which have no wall round about them shall be reckoned with the fields of the country; they may be redeemed, and they shall go out in the jubilee. 25:32 But as for the cities of the Levites, the houses of the cities of their possession, the Levites shall have a perpetual right of redemption. 25:33 And if a man purchase of the Levites, then the house that was sold in the city of his possession, shall go out in the jubilee; for the houses of the cities of the Levites are their possession among the children of Israel. 25:34 But the fields of the open land about their cities may not be sold; for that is their perpetual possession. {S}

3א

25:35 And if thy brother be waxen poor, and his means fail with thee; then thou shalt uphold him: as a stranger and a settler shall he live with thee. 25:36 Take thou no interest of him or increase; but fear thy God; that thy brother may live with thee. 25:37 Thou shalt not give him thy money upon interest, nor give him thy victuals for increase. 25:38 I am the LORD your God, who brought you forth out of the land of Egypt, to give you the land of Canaan, to be your God. {S}

3ב

25:39 And if thy brother be waxen poor with thee, and sell himself unto thee, thou shalt not make him to serve as a bondservant. 25:40 As a hired servant, and as a settler, he shall be with thee; he shall serve with thee unto the year of jubilee. 25:41 Then shall he go out from thee, he and his children with him, and shall return unto his own family, and unto the possession of his fathers shall he return. 25:42 For they are My servants, whom I brought forth out of the land of Egypt; they shall not be sold as bondmen. 25:43 Thou shalt not rule over him with rigour; but shalt fear thy God. 25:44 And as for thy bondmen, and thy bondmaids, whom thou mayest have: of the nations that are round about you, of them shall ye buy bondmen and bondmaids. 25:45 Moreover of the children of the strangers that do sojourn among you, of them may ye buy, and of their families that are with you, which they have begotten in your land; and they may be your possession. 25:46 And ye may make them an inheritance for your children after you, to hold for a possession: of them may ye take your bondmen for ever; but over your brethren the children of Israel ye shall not rule, one over another, with rigour. {S}

3ג

25:47 And if a stranger who is a settler with thee be waxen rich, and thy brother be waxen poor beside him, and sell himself unto the stranger who is a settler with thee, or to the offshoot of a stranger's family, 25:48 after that he is sold he may be redeemed; one of his brethren may redeem him; 25:49 or his uncle, or his uncle's son, may redeem him, or any that is nigh of kin unto him of his family may redeem him; or if he be waxen rich, he may redeem himself. 25:50 And he shall reckon with him that bought him from the year that he sold himself to him unto the year of jubilee; and the price of his sale shall be according unto the number of years; according to the time of a hired servant shall he be with him. 25:51 If there be yet many years, according unto them he shall give back the price of his redemption out of the money that he was bought for. 25:52 And if there remain but few years unto the year of jubilee, then he shall reckon with him; according unto his years shall he give back the price of his redemption. 25:53 As a servant hired year by year shall he be with him; he shall not rule with rigour over him in thy sight. 25:54 And if he be not redeemed by any of these means, then he shall go out in the year of jubilee, he, and his children with him. 25:55 For unto Me the children of Israel are servants; they are My servants whom I brought forth out of the land of Egypt: I am the LORD your God.

Leviticus Unit XXI (26:1-47)

1א

26:1 Ye shall make you no idols, neither shall ye rear you up a graven image, or a pillar, neither shall ye place any figured stone in your land, to bow down unto it; for I am the LORD your God.

2א

A 26:3 If ye walk in My statutes, and keep My commandments, and do them; 26:4 then I will give your rains in their season, and the land shall yield her produce, and the trees of the field shall yield their fruit. 26:5 And your threshing shall reach unto the vintage, and the vintage shall reach unto the sowing time; and ye shall eat your bread until ye have enough, and dwell in your land safely.

B 26:6 And I will give peace in the land, and ye shall lie down, and none shall make you afraid;

C and I will cause evil beasts to cease out of the land,

D neither shall the sword go through your land. 26:7 And ye shall chase your enemies, and they shall fall before you by the sword. 26:8 And five of you shall chase a hundred, and a hundred of you shall chase ten thousand; and your enemies shall fall before you by the sword.

E 26:9 And I will have respect unto you, and make you fruitful, and multiply you; and will establish My covenant with you. 26:10 And ye shall eat old store long kept, and ye shall bring forth the old from before the new. 26:11 And I will set My tabernacle among you, and My soul shall not abhor you. 26:12 And I will walk among you, and will be your God, and ye shall be My people. 26:13 I am the LORD your God, who brought you forth out of the land of Egypt, that ye should not be their bondmen; and I have broken the bars of your yoke, and made you go upright. {P}

3א

26:42 then will I remember My covenant with Jacob, and also My covenant with Isaac, and also My covenant with Abraham will I remember; and I will remember the land. 26:43 For the land shall lie forsaken without them, and shall be paid her sabbaths, while she lieth desolate without them; and they shall be paid the punishment of their iniquity; because, even because they rejected Mine ordinances, and their soul abhorred My statutes. 26:44 And yet for all that, when they are in the land of their enemies, I will not reject them, neither will I abhor them, to destroy them utterly, and to break My covenant with them; for I am the LORD their God.

1ב

26:2 Ye shall keep My sabbaths, and reverence My sanctuary: I am the LORD. {P}

2ב

A 26:14 But if ye will not hearken unto Me, and will not do all these commandments; 26:15 and if ye shall reject My statutes, and if your soul abhor Mine ordinances, so that ye will not do all My commandments, but break My covenant; 26:16 I also will do this unto you: I will appoint terror over you, even consumption and fever, that shall make the eyes to fail, and the soul to languish; and ye shall sow your seed in vain, for your enemies shall eat it. 26:17 And I will set My face against you, and ye shall be smitten before your enemies; they that hate you shall rule over you; and ye shall flee when none pursueth you.

B 26:18 And if ye will not yet for these things hearken unto Me, then I will chastise you seven times more for your sins. 26:19 And I will break the pride of your power; and I will make your heaven as iron, and your earth as brass. 26:20 And your strength shall be spent in vain; for your land shall not yield her produce, neither shall the trees of the land yield their fruit.

C 26:21 And if ye walk contrary unto Me, and will not hearken unto Me; I will bring seven times more plagues upon you according to your sins. 26:22 And I will send the beast of the field among you, which shall rob you of your children, and destroy your cattle, and make you few in number; and your ways shall become desolate.

D 26:23 And if in spite of these things ye will not be corrected unto Me, but will walk contrary unto Me; 26:24 then will I also walk contrary unto you; and I will smite you, even I, seven times for your sins. 26:25 And I will bring a sword upon you, that shall execute the vengeance of the covenant; and ye shall be gathered together within your cities; and I will send the pestilence among you; and ye shall be delivered into the hand of the enemy. 26:26 When I break your staff of bread, ten women shall bake your bread in one oven, and they shall deliver your bread again by weight; and ye shall eat, and not be satisfied. {S}

E 26:27 And if ye will not for all this hearken unto Me, but walk contrary unto Me; 26:28 then I will walk contrary unto you in fury; and I also will chastise you seven times for your sins. 26:29 And ye shall eat the flesh of your sons, and the flesh of your daughters shall ye eat. 26:30 And I will destroy your high places, and cut down your sun-pillars, and cast your carcasses upon the carcasses of your idols; and My soul shall abhor you. 26:31 And I will make your cities a waste, and will bring your sanctuaries unto desolation, and I will not smell the savour of your sweet odours. 26:32 And I will bring the land into desolation; and your enemies that dwell therein shall be astonished at it. 26:33 And you will I scatter among the nations, and I will draw out the sword after you; and your land shall be a desolation, and your cities shall be a waste. 26:34 Then shall the land be paid her sabbaths, as long as it lieth desolate, and ye are in your enemies' land; even then shall the land rest, and repay her sabbaths. 26:35 As long as it lieth desolate it shall have rest; even the rest which it had not in your sabbaths, when ye dwelt upon it. 26:36 And as for them that are left of you, I will send a faintness into their heart in the lands of their enemies; and the sound of a driven leaf shall chase them; and they shall flee, as one fleeth from the sword; and they shall fall when none pursueth. 26:37 And they shall stumble one upon another, as it were before the sword, when none pursueth; and ye shall have no power to stand before your enemies. 26:38 And ye shall perish among the nations, and the land of your enemies shall eat you up. 26:39 And they that are left of you shall pine away in their iniquity in your enemies' lands; and also in the iniquities of their fathers shall they pine away with them. 26:40 And they shall confess their iniquity, and the iniquity of their fathers, in their treachery which they committed against Me, and also that they have walked contrary unto Me. 26:41 I also will walk contrary unto them, and bring them into the land of their enemies; if then perchance their uncircumcised heart be humbled, and they then be paid the punishment of their iniquity;

3ב

26:45 But I will for their sakes remember the covenant of their ancestors, whom I brought forth out of the land of Egypt in the sight of the nations, that I might be their God: I am the LORD. 26:46 These are the statutes and ordinances and laws, which the LORD made between Him and the children of Israel in mount Sinai by the hand of Moses. {P}

Leviticus Unit XXII (27:1-34)

א1

27:1 And the LORD spoke unto Moses, saying: 27:2 Speak unto the children of Israel, and say unto them: When a man shall clearly utter a vow of persons unto the LORD, according to thy valuation, 27:3 then thy valuation shall be for the male from twenty years old even unto sixty years old, even thy valuation shall be fifty shekels of silver, after the shekel of the sanctuary. 27:4 And if it be a female, then thy valuation shall be thirty shekels. 27:5 And if it be from five years old even unto twenty years old, then thy valuation shall be for the male twenty shekels, and for the female ten shekels. 27:6 And if it be from a month old even unto five years old, then thy valuation shall be for the male five shekels of silver, and for the female thy valuation shall be three shekels of silver. 27:7 And if it be from sixty years old and upward: if it be a male, then thy valuation shall be fifteen shekels, and for the female ten shekels. 27:8 But if he be too poor for thy valuation, then he shall be set before the priest, and the priest shall value him; according to the means of him that vowed shall the priest value him. {S}

א2

A 27:16 And if a man shall sanctify unto the LORD part of the field of his possession, then thy valuation shall be according to the sowing thereof; the sowing of a homer of barley shall be valued at fifty shekels of silver. 27:17 If he sanctify his field from the year of jubilee, according to thy valuation it shall stand. 27:18 But if he sanctify his field after the jubilee, then the priest shall reckon unto him the money according to the years that remain unto the year of jubilee, and an abatement shall be made from thy valuation. 27:19 And if he that sanctified the field will indeed redeem it, then he shall add the fifth part of the money of thy valuation unto it, and it shall be assured to him. 27:20 And if he will not redeem the field, or if he have sold the field to another man, it shall not be redeemed any more. 27:21 But the field, when it goeth out in the jubilee, shall be holy unto the LORD, as a field devoted; the possession thereof shall be the priest's.
B 27:22 And if he sanctify unto the LORD a field which he hath bought, which is not of the field of his possession; 27:23 then the priest shall reckon unto him the worth of thy valuation unto the year of jubilee; and he shall give thy valuation in that day, as a holy thing unto the LORD. 27:24 In the year of jubilee the field shall return unto him of whom it was bought, even to him to whom the possession of the land belongeth. 27:25 And all thy valuations shall be according to the shekel of the sanctuary; twenty gerahs shall be the shekel.

ב1

27:9 And if it be a beast, whereof men bring an offering unto the LORD, all that any man giveth of such unto the LORD shall be holy. 27:10 He shall not alter it, nor change it, a good for a bad, or a bad for a good; and if he shall at all change beast for beast, then both it and that for which it is changed shall be holy. 27:11 And if it be any unclean beast, of which they may not bring an offering unto the LORD, then he shall set the beast before the priest. 27:12 And the priest shall value it, whether it be good or bad; as thou the priest valuest it, so shall it be. 27:13 But if he will indeed redeem it, then he shall add the fifth part thereof unto thy valuation.

ב2

A 27:26 Howbeit the firstling among beasts, which is born as a firstling to the LORD, no man shall sanctify it; whether it be ox or sheep, it is the LORD'S. 27:27 And if it be of an unclean beast, then he shall ransom it according to thy valuation, and shall add unto it the fifth part thereof; or if it be not redeemed, then it shall be sold according to thy valuation.

B 27:28 Notwithstanding, no devoted thing, that a man may devote unto the LORD of all that he hath, whether of man or beast, or of the field of his possession, shall be sold or redeemed; every devoted thing is most holy unto the LORD. 27:29 None devoted, that may be devoted of men, shall be ransomed; he shall surely be put to death.

ג1

27:14 And when a man shall sanctify his house to be holy unto the LORD, then the priest shall value it, whether it be good or bad; as the priest shall value it, so shall it stand. 27:15 And if he that sanctified it will redeem his house, then he shall add the fifth part of the money of thy valuation unto it, and it shall be his.

ג2

A 27:30 And all the tithe of the land, whether of the seed of the land, or of the fruit of the tree, is the LORD'S; it is holy unto the LORD. 27:31 And if a man will redeem aught of his tithe, he shall add unto it the fifth part thereof.

B 27:32 And all the tithe of the herd or the flock, whatsoever passeth under the rod, the tenth shall be holy unto the LORD. 27:33 He shall not inquire whether it be good or bad, neither shall he change it; and if he change it at all, then both it and that for which it is changed shall be holy; it shall not be redeemed. 27:34 These are the commandments, which the LORD commanded Moses for the children of Israel in mount Sinai. {P}

Numbers

Numbers Unit I (1:1-4:49)

1א

A 1:1 And the LORD spoke unto Moses in the wilderness of Sinai, in the tent of meeting, on the first day of the second month, in the second year after they were come out of the land of Egypt, saying: 1:2 'Take ye the sum of all the congregation of the children of Israel, by their families, by their fathers' houses, according to the number of names, every male, by their polls; 1:3 from twenty years old and upward, all that are able to go forth to war in Israel: ye shall number them by their hosts, even thou and Aaron. 1:4 And with you there shall be a man of every tribe, every one head of his fathers' house. 1:5 And these are the names of the men that shall stand with you: of Reuben, Elizur the son of Shedeur. 1:6 Of Simeon, Shelumiel the son of Zurishaddai. 1:7 Of Judah, Nahshon the son of Amminadab. 1:8 Of Issachar, Nethanel the son of Zuar. 1:9 Of Zebulun, Eliab the son of Helon. 1:10 Of the children of Joseph: of Ephraim, Elishama the son of Ammihud; of Manasseh, Gamaliel the son of Pedahzur. 1:11 Of Benjamin, Abidan the son of Gideoni. 1:12 Of Dan, Ahiezer the son of Ammishaddai. 1:13 Of Asher, Pagiel the son of Ochran. 1:14 Of Gad, Eliasaph the son of Deuel. 1:15 Of Naphtali, Ahira the son of Enan.' 1:16 These were the elect of the congregation, the princes of the tribes of their fathers; they were the heads of the thousands of Israel. 1:17 And Moses and Aaron took these men that are pointed out by name. 1:18 And they assembled all the congregation together on the first day of the second month, and they declared their pedigrees after their families, by their fathers' houses, according to the number of names, from twenty years old and upward, by their polls. 1:19 As the LORD commanded Moses, so did he number them in the wilderness of Sinai. {S}

1ב

A 1:48 And the LORD spoke unto Moses, saying: 1:49 'Howbeit the tribe of Levi thou shalt not number, neither shalt thou take the sum of them among the children of Israel; 1:50 but appoint thou the Levites over the tabernacle of the testimony, and over all the furniture thereof, and over all that belongeth to it; they shall bear the tabernacle, and all the furniture thereof; and they shall minister unto it, and shall encamp round about the tabernacle. 1:51 And when the tabernacle setteth forward, the Levites shall take it down; and when the tabernacle is to be pitched, the Levites shall set it up; and the common man that draweth nigh shall be put to death. 1:52 And the children of Israel shall pitch their tents, every man with his own camp, and every man with his own standard, according to their hosts. 1:53 But the Levites shall pitch round about the tabernacle of the testimony, that there be no wrath upon the congregation of the children of Israel; and the Levites shall keep the charge of the tabernacle of the testimony.' 1:54 Thus did the children of Israel; according to all that the LORD commanded Moses, so did they. {P}

B 1:20 And the children of Reuben, Israel's first-born, their generations, by their families, by their fathers' houses, according to the number of names, by their polls, every male from twenty years old and upward, all that were able to go forth to war; 1:21 those that were numbered of them, of the tribe of Reuben, were forty and six thousand and five hundred. {P}

1:22 Of the children of Simeon, their generations, by their families, by their fathers' houses, those that were numbered thereof, according to the number of names, by their polls, every male from twenty years old and upward, all that were able to go forth to war; 1:23 those that were numbered of them, of the tribe of Simeon, were fifty and nine thousand and three hundred. {P}

1:24 Of the children of Gad, their generations, by their families, by their fathers' houses, according to the number of names, from twenty years old and upward, all that were able to go forth to war; 1:25 those that were numbered of them, of the tribe of Gad, were forty and five thousand six hundred and fifty. {P}

1:26 Of the children of Judah, their generations, by their families, by their fathers' houses, according to the number of names, from twenty years old and upward, all that were able to go forth to war; 1:27 those that were numbered of them, of the tribe of Judah, were threescore and fourteen thousand and six hundred. {P}

1:28 Of the children of Issachar, their generations, by their families, by their fathers' houses, according to the number of names, from twenty years old and upward, all that were able to go forth to war; 1:29 those that were numbered of them, of the tribe of Issachar, were fifty and four thousand and four hundred. {P}

1:30 Of the children of Zebulun, their generations, by their families, by their fathers' houses, according to the number of names, from twenty years old and upward, all that were able to go forth to war; 1:31 those that were numbered of them, of the tribe of Zebulun, were fifty and seven thousand and four hundred. {P}

1:32 Of the children of Joseph, namely, of the children of Ephraim, their generations, by their families, by their fathers' houses, according to the number of names, from twenty years old and upward, all that were able to go forth to war; 1:33 those that were numbered of them, of the tribe of Ephraim, were forty thousand and five hundred. {P}

1:34 Of the children of Manasseh, their generations, by their families, by their fathers' houses, according to the number of names, from twenty years old and upward, all that were able to go forth to war; 1:35 those that were numbered of them, of the tribe of Manasseh, were thirty and two thousand and two hundred. {P}

1:36 Of the children of Benjamin, their generations, by their families, by their fathers' houses, according to the number of names, from twenty years old and upward, all that were able to go forth to war; 1:37 those that were numbered of them, of the tribe of Benjamin, were thirty and five thousand and four hundred. {P}

1:38 Of the children of Dan, their generations, by their families, by their fathers' houses, according to the number of names, from twenty years old and upward, all that were able to go forth to war; 1:39 those that were numbered of them, of the tribe of Dan, were threescore and two thousand and seven hundred. {P}

1:40 Of the children of Asher, their generations, by their families, by their fathers' houses, according to the number of names, from twenty years old and upward, all that were able to go forth to war; 1:41 those that were numbered of them, of the tribe of Asher, were forty and one thousand and five hundred. {P}

1:42 Of the children of Naphtali, their generations, by their families, by their fathers' houses, according to the number of names, from twenty years old and upward, all that were able to go forth to war; 1:43 those that were numbered of them, of the tribe of Naphtali, were fifty and three thousand and four hundred. {P}

C 1:44 These are those that were numbered, which Moses and Aaron numbered, and the princes of Israel, being twelve men; they were each one for his fathers' house. 1:45 And all those that were numbered of the children of Israel by their fathers' houses, from twenty years old and upward, all that were able to go forth to war in Israel; 1:46 even all those that were numbered were six hundred thousand and three thousand and five hundred and fifty. 1:47 But the Levites after the tribe of their fathers were not numbered among them. {P}

B 2:1 And the LORD spoke unto Moses and unto Aaron, saying: 2:2 'The children of Israel shall pitch by their fathers' houses; every man with his own standard, according to the ensigns; a good way off shall they pitch round about the tent of meeting. 2:3 Now those that pitch on the east side toward the sunrising shall be they of the standard of the camp of Judah, according to their hosts; the prince of the children of Judah being Nahshon the son of Amminadab, 2:4 and his host, and those that were numbered of them, threescore and fourteen thousand and six hundred; 2:5 and those that pitch next unto him shall be the tribe of Issachar; the prince of the children of Issachar being Nethanel the son of Zuar, 2:6 and his host, even those that were numbered thereof, fifty and four thousand and four hundred; 2:7 and the tribe of Zebulun; the prince of the children of Zebulun being Eliab the son of Helon, 2:8 and his host, and those that were numbered thereof, fifty and seven thousand and four hundred; 2:9 all that were numbered of the camp of Judah being a hundred thousand and fourscore thousand and six thousand and four hundred, according to their hosts; they shall set forth first. {S} 2:10 On the south side shall be the standard of the camp of Reuben according to their hosts; the prince of the children of Reuben being Elizur the son of Shedeur, 2:11 and his host, and those that were numbered thereof, forty and six thousand and five hundred; 2:12 and those that pitch next unto him shall be the tribe of Simeon; the prince of the children of Simeon being Shelumiel the son of Zurishaddai, 2:13 and his host, and those that were numbered of them, fifty and nine thousand and three hundred; 2:14 and the tribe of Gad; the prince of the children of Gad being Eliasaph the son of Reuel, 2:15 and his host, even those that were numbered of them, forty and five thousand and six hundred and fifty; 2:16 all that were numbered of the camp of Reuben being a hundred thousand and fifty and one thousand and four hundred and fifty, according to their hosts; and they shall set forth second. {S} 2:17 Then the tent of meeting, with the camp of the Levites, shall set forward in the midst of the camps; as they encamp, so shall they set forward, every man in his place, by their standards. {S} 2:18 On the west side shall be the standard of the camp of Ephraim according to their hosts; the prince of the children of Ephraim being Elishama the son of Ammihud, 2:19 and his host, and those that were numbered of them, forty thousand and five hundred; 2:20 and next unto him shall be the tribe of Manasseh; the prince of the children of Manasseh being Gamaliel the son of Pedahzur, 2:21 and his host, and those that were numbered of them, thirty and two thousand and two hundred; 2:22 and the tribe of Benjamin; the prince of the children of Benjamin being Abidan the son of Gideoni, 2:23 and his host, and those that were numbered of them, thirty and five thousand and four hundred; 2:24 all that were numbered of the camp of Ephraim being a hundred thousand and eight thousand and a hundred, according to their hosts; and they shall set forth third. {S} 2:25 On the north side shall be the standard of the camp of Dan according to their hosts; the prince of the children of Dan being Ahiezer the son of Ammishaddai, 2:26 and his host, and those that were numbered of them, threescore and two thousand and seven hundred; 2:27 and those that pitch next unto him shall be the tribe of Asher; the prince of the children of Asher being Pagiel the son of Ochran, 2:28 and his host, and those that were numbered of them, forty and one thousand and five hundred; 2:29 and the tribe of Naphtali; the prince of the children of Naphtali being Ahira the son of Enan, 2:30 and his host, and those that were numbered of them, fifty and three thousand and four hundred; 2:31 all that were numbered of the camp of Dan being a hundred thousand and fifty and seven thousand and six hundred; they shall set forth hindmost by their standards.' {P}

C 2:32 These are they that were numbered of the children of Israel by their fathers' houses; all that were numbered of the camps according to their hosts were six hundred thousand and three thousand and five hundred and fifty. 2:33 But the Levites were not numbered among the children of Israel; as the LORD commanded Moses. 2:34 Thus did the children of Israel: according to all that the LORD commanded Moses, so they pitched by their standards, and so they set forward, each one according to its families, and according to its fathers' houses. {P}

2א

A 3:1 Now these are the generations of Aaron and Moses in the day that the LORD spoke with Moses in mount Sinai. 3:2 And these are the names of the sons of Aaron: Nadab the first-born, and Abihu, Eleazar, and Ithamar. 3:3 These are the names of the sons of Aaron, the priests that were anointed, whom he consecrated to minister in the priest's office. 3:4 And Nadab and Abihu died before the LORD, when they offered strange fire before the LORD, in the wilderness of Sinai, and they had no children; and Eleazar and Ithamar ministered in the priest's office in the presence of Aaron their father. {P}

B 3:5 And the LORD spoke unto Moses, saying: 3:6 'Bring the tribe of Levi near, and set them before Aaron the priest, that they may minister unto him. 3:7 And they shall keep his charge, and the charge of the whole congregation before the tent of meeting, to do the service of the tabernacle. 3:8 And they shall keep all the furniture of the tent of meeting, and the charge of the children of Israel, to do the service of the tabernacle. 3:9 And thou shalt give the Levites unto Aaron and to his sons; they are wholly given unto him from the children of Israel. 3:10 And thou shalt appoint Aaron and his sons, that they may keep their priesthood; and the common man that draweth nigh shall be put to death.' {P}

C 3:11 And the LORD spoke unto Moses, saying: 3:12 'And I, behold, I have taken the Levites from among the children of Israel instead of every first-born that openeth the womb among the children of Israel; and the Levites shall be Mine; 3:13 for all the first-born are Mine: on the day that I smote all the first-born in the land of Egypt I hallowed unto Me all the first-born in Israel, both man and beast, Mine they shall be: I am the LORD.' {P}

2ב

A 3:14 And the LORD spoke unto Moses in the wilderness of Sinai, saying: 3:15 'Number the children of Levi by their fathers' houses, by their families; every male from a month old and upward shalt thou number them.' 3:16 And Moses numbered them according to the word of the LORD, as he was commanded. 3:17 And these were the sons of Levi by their names: Gershon, and Kohath, and Merari. 3:18 And these are the names of the sons of Gershon by their families: Libni and Shimei. 3:19 And the sons of Kohath by their families: Amram and Izhar, Hebron and Uzziel. 3:20 And the sons of Merari by their families: Mahli and Mushi. These are the families of the Levites according to their fathers' houses.

B 3:21 Of Gershon was the family of the Libnites, and the family of the Shimeites; these are the families of the Gershonites. 3:22 Those that were numbered of them, according to the number of all the males, from a month old and upward, even those that were numbered of them were seven thousand and five hundred. 3:23 The families of the Gershonites were to pitch behind the tabernacle westward. 3:24 the prince of the fathers' house of the Gershonites being Eliasaph the son of Lael, 3:25 and the charge of the sons of Gershon in the tent of meeting the tabernacle, and the Tent, the covering thereof, and the screen for the door of the tent of meeting, 3:26 and the hangings of the court, and the screen for the door of the court--which is by the tabernacle, and by the altar, round about--and the cords of it, even whatsoever pertaineth to the service thereof. {S} 3:27 And of Kohath was the family of the Amramites, and the family of the Izharites, and the family of the Hebronites, and the family of the Uzzielites; these are the families of the Kohathites: 3:28 according to the number of all the males, from a month old and upward, eight thousand and six hundred, keepers of the charge of the sanctuary. 3:29 The families of the sons of Kohath were to pitch on the side of the tabernacle southward; 3:30 the prince of the fathers' house of the families of the Kohathites being Elizaphan the son of Uzziel, 3:31 and their charge the ark, and the table, and the candlestick, and the altars, and the vessels of the sanctuary wherewith the priests minister, and the screen, and all that pertaineth to the service thereof; 3:32 Eleazar the son of Aaron the priest being prince of the princes of the Levites, and having the oversight of them that keep the charge of the sanctuary. 3:33 Of Merari was the family of the Mahlites, and the family of the Mushites; these are the families of Merari. 3:34 And those that were numbered of them, according to the number of all the males, from a month old and upward, were six thousand and two hundred; 3:35 the prince of the fathers' house of the families of Merari being Zuriel the son of Abihail; they were to pitch on the side of the tabernacle northward; 3:36 the appointed charge of the sons of Merari being the boards of the tabernacle, and the bars thereof, and the pillars thereof, and the sockets thereof, and all the instruments thereof, and all that pertaineth to the service thereof; 3:37 and the pillars of the court round about, and their sockets, and their pins, and their cords. 3:38 And those that were to pitch before the tabernacle eastward, before the tent of meeting toward the sunrising, were Moses, and Aaron and his sons, keeping the charge of the sanctuary, even the charge for the children of Israel; and the common man that drew nigh was to be put to death. 3:39 All that were numbered of the Levites, whom Moses and Aaron numbered at the commandment of the LORD, by their families, all the males from a month old and upward, were twenty and two thousand.

C {S} 3:40 And the LORD said unto Moses: 'Number all the first-born males of the children of Israel from a month old and upward, and take the number of their names. 3:41 And thou shalt take the Levites for Me, even the LORD, instead of all the first-born among the children of Israel; and the cattle of the Levites instead of all the firstlings among the cattle of the children of Israel.' 3:42 And Moses numbered, as the LORD commanded him, all the first-born among the children of Israel. 3:43 And all the first-born males according to the number of names, from a month old and upward, of those that were numbered of them, were twenty and two thousand two hundred and threescore and thirteen. {P}

3:44 And the LORD spoke unto Moses, saying: 3:45 'Take the Levites instead of all the first-born among the children of Israel, and the cattle of the Levites instead of their cattle; and the Levites shall be Mine, even the LORD'S. 3:46 And as for the redemption of the two hundred and three score and thirteen of the first-born of the children of Israel, that are over and above the number of the Levites, 3:47 thou shalt take five shekels apiece by the poll; after the shekel of the sanctuary shalt thou take them--the shekel is twenty gerahs. 3:48 And thou shalt give the money wherewith they that remain over of them are redeemed unto Aaron and to his sons.' 3:49 And Moses took the redemption-money from them that were over and above them that were redeemed by the Levites; 3:50 from the first-born of the children of Israel took he the money: a thousand three hundred and threescore and five shekels, after the shekel of the sanctuary. 3:51 And Moses gave the redemption-money unto Aaron and to his sons, according to the word of the LORD, as the LORD commanded Moses. {P}

3א

A 4:1 And the LORD spoke unto Moses and unto Aaron, saying: 4:2 'Take the sum of the sons of Kohath from among the sons of Levi, by their families, by their fathers' houses, 4:3 from thirty years old and upward even until fifty years old, all that enter upon the service, to do work in the tent of meeting. 4:4 This is the service of the sons of Kohath in the tent of meeting, about the most holy things: 4:5 when the camp setteth forward, Aaron shall go in, and his sons, and they shall take down the veil of the screen, and cover the ark of the testimony with it; 4:6 and shall put thereon a covering of sealskin, and shall spread over it a cloth all of blue, and shall set the staves thereof. 4:7 And upon the table of showbread they shall spread a cloth of blue, and put thereon the dishes, and the pans, and the bowls, and the jars wherewith to pour out; and the continual bread shall remain thereon. 4:8 And they shall spread upon them a cloth of scarlet, and cover the same with a covering of sealskin, and shall set the staves thereof. 4:9 And they shall take a cloth of blue, and cover the candlestick of the light, and its lamps, and its tongs, and its snuffdishes, and all the oil vessels thereof, wherewith they minister unto it. 4:10 And they shall put it and all the vessels thereof within a covering of sealskin, and shall put it upon a bar. 4:11 And upon the golden altar they shall spread a cloth of blue, and cover it with a covering of sealskin, and shall set the staves thereof. 4:12 And they shall take all the vessels of ministry, wherewith they minister in the sanctuary, and put them in a cloth of blue, and cover them with a covering of sealskin, and shall put them on a bar. 4:13 And they shall take away the ashes from the altar, and spread a purple cloth thereon. 4:14 And they shall put upon it all the vessels thereof, wherewith they minister about it, the fire-pans, the flesh-hooks, and the shovels, and the basins, all the vessels of the altar; and they shall spread upon it a covering of sealskin, and set the staves thereof. 4:15 And when Aaron and his sons have made an end of covering the holy furniture, and all the holy vessels, as the camp is to set forward--after that, the sons of Kohath shall come to bear them; but they shall not touch the holy things, lest they die. These things are the burden of the sons of Kohath in the tent of meeting. 4:16 And the charge of Eleazar the son of Aaron the priest shall be the oil for the light, and the sweet incense, and the continual meal-offering, and the anointing oil: he shall have the charge of all the tabernacle, and of all that therein is, whether it be the sanctuary, or the furniture thereof.' {P}

4:17 And the LORD spoke unto Moses and unto Aaron, saying: 4:18 'Cut ye not off the tribe of the families of the Kohathites from among the Levites; 4:19 but thus do unto them, that they may live, and not die, when they approach unto the most holy things: Aaron and his sons shall go in, and appoint them every one to his service and to his burden; 4:20 but they shall not go in to see the holy things as they are being covered, lest they die.' {P}

B 4:21 And the LORD spoke unto Moses saying: 4:22 'Take the sum of the sons of Gershon also, by their fathers' houses, by their families; 4:23 from thirty years old and upward until fifty years old shalt thou number them: all that enter in to wait upon the service, to do service in the tent of meeting. 4:24 This is the service of the families of the Gershonites, in serving and in bearing burdens: 4:25 they shall bear the curtains of the tabernacle, and the tent of meeting, its covering, and the covering of sealskin that is above upon it, and the screen for the door of the tent of meeting; 4:26 and the hangings of the court, and the screen for the door of the gate of the court, which is by the tabernacle and by the altar round about, and their cords, and all the instruments of their service, and whatsoever there may be to do with them, therein shall they serve. 4:27 At the commandment of Aaron and his sons shall be all the service of the sons of the Gershonites, in all their burden, and in all their service; and ye shall appoint unto them in charge all their burden. 4:28 This is the service of the families of the sons of the Gershonites in the tent of meeting; and their charge shall be under the hand of Ithamar the son of Aaron the priest. {S}

C 4:29 As for the sons of Merari, thou shalt number them by their families, by their fathers' houses; 4:30 from thirty years old and upward even unto fifty years old shalt thou number them, every one that entereth upon the service, to do the work of the tent of meeting. 4:31 And this is the charge of their burden, according to all their service in the tent of meeting: the boards of the tabernacle, and the bars thereof, and the pillars thereof, and the sockets thereof; 4:32 and the pillars of the court round about, and their sockets, and their pins, and their cords, even all their appurtenance, and all that pertaineth to their service; and by name ye shall appoint the instruments of the charge of their burden. 4:33 This is the service of the families of the sons of Merari, according to all their service, in the tent of meeting, under the hand of Ithamar the son of Aaron the priest.'

3ב

A 4:34 And Moses and Aaron and the princes of the congregation numbered the sons of the Kohathites by their families, and by their fathers' houses, 4:35 from thirty years old and upward even unto fifty years old, every one that entered upon the service, for service in the tent of meeting. 4:36 And those that were numbered of them by their families were two thousand seven hundred and fifty. 4:37 These are they that were numbered of the families of the Kohathites, of all that did serve in the tent of meeting, whom Moses and Aaron numbered according to the commandment of the LORD by the hand of Moses. {S}

B 4:38 And those that were numbered of the sons of Gershon, by their families, and by their fathers' houses, 4:39 from thirty years old and upward even unto fifty years old, every one that entered upon the service, for service in the tent of meeting, 4:40 even those that were numbered of them, by their families, by their fathers' houses, were two thousand and six hundred and thirty. 4:41 These are they that were numbered of the families of the sons of Gershon, of all that did serve in the tent of meeting, whom Moses and Aaron numbered according to the commandment of the LORD.

C 4:42 And those that were numbered of the families of the sons of Merari, by their families, by their fathers' houses, 4:43 from thirty years old and upward even unto fifty years old, every one that entered upon the service, for service in the tent of meeting, 4:44 even those that were numbered of them by their families, were three thousand and two hundred. 4:45 These are they that were numbered of the families of the sons of Merari, whom Moses and Aaron numbered according to the commandment of the LORD by the hand of Moses. 4:46 All those that were numbered of the Levites, whom Moses and Aaron and the princes of Israel numbered, by their families, and by their fathers' houses, 4:47 from thirty years old and upward even unto fifty years old, every one that entered in to do the work of service, and the work of bearing burdens in the tent of meeting, 4:48 even those that were numbered of them, were eight thousand and five hundred and fourscore. 4:49 According to the commandment of the LORD they were appointed by the hand of Moses, every one to his service, and to his burden; they were also numbered, as the LORD commanded Moses. {P}

Numbers Unit II (5:1-6:21)

1א

5:1 And the LORD spoke unto Moses, saying: 5:2 'Command the children of Israel, that they put out of the camp every leper, and every one that hath an issue, and whosoever is unclean by the dead; 5:3 both male and female shall ye put out, without the camp shall ye put them; that they defile not their camp, in the midst whereof I dwell.' 5:4 And the children of Israel did so, and put them out without the camp; as the LORD spoke unto Moses, so did the children of Israel. {P}

2א

5:11 and the LORD spoke unto Moses, saying: 5:12 Speak unto the children of Israel, and say unto them: If any man's wife go aside, and act unfaithfully against him, 5:13 and a man lie with her carnally, and it be hid from the eyes of her husband, she being defiled secretly, and there be no witness against her, neither she be taken in the act; 5:14 and the spirit of jealousy come upon him, and he be jealous of his wife, and she be defiled; or if the spirit of jealousy come upon him, and he be jealous of his wife, and she be not defiled; 5:15 then shall the man bring his wife unto the priest, and shall bring her offering for her, the tenth part of an ephah of barley meal; he shall pour no oil upon it, nor put frankincense thereon; for it is a meal-offering of jealousy, a meal-offering of memorial, bringing iniquity to remembrance. 5:16 And the priest shall bring her near, and set her before the LORD. 5:17 And the priest shall take holy water in an earthen vessel; and of the dust that is on the floor of the tabernacle the priest shall take, and put it into the water. 5:18 And the priest shall set the woman before the LORD, and let the hair of the woman's head go loose, and put the meal-offering of memorial in her hands, which is the meal-offering of jealousy; and the priest shall have in his hand the water of bitterness that causeth the curse. 5:19 And the priest shall cause her to swear, and shall say unto the woman: 'If no man have lain with thee, and if thou hast not gone aside to uncleanness, being under thy husband, be thou free from this water of bitterness that causeth the curse; 5:20 but if thou hast gone aside, being under thy husband, and if thou be defiled, and some man have lain with thee besides thy husband-- 5:21 then the priest shall cause the woman to swear with the oath of cursing, and the priest shall say unto the woman--the LORD make thee a curse and an oath among thy people, when the LORD doth make thy thigh to fall away, and thy belly to swell; 5:22 and this water that causeth the curse shall go into thy bowels, and make thy belly to swell, and thy thigh to fall away'; and the woman shall say: 'Amen, Amen.' 5:23 And the priest shall write these curses in a scroll, and he shall blot them out into the water of bitterness. 5:24 And he shall make the woman drink the water of bitterness that causeth the curse; and the water that causeth the curse shall enter into her and become bitter. 5:25 And the priest shall take the meal-offering of jealousy out of the woman's hand, and shall wave the meal-offering before the LORD, and bring it unto the altar. 5:26 And the priest shall take a handful of the meal-offering, as the memorial-part thereof, and make it smoke upon the altar, and afterward shall make the woman drink the water. 5:27 And when he hath made her drink the water, then it shall come to pass, if she be defiled, and have acted unfaithfully against her husband, that the water that causeth the curse shall enter into her and become bitter, and her belly shall swell, and her thigh shall fall away; and the woman shall be a curse among her people. 5:28 And if the woman be not defiled, but be clean; then she shall be cleared, and shall conceive seed. 5:29 This is the law of jealousy, when a wife, being under her husband, goeth aside, and is defiled; 5:30 or when the spirit of jealousy cometh upon a man, and he be jealous over his wife; then shall he set the woman before the LORD, and the priest shall execute upon her all this law. 5:31 And the man shall be clear from iniquity, and that woman shall bear her iniquity. {P}

1ב

5:5 And the LORD spoke unto Moses, saying: 5:6 Speak unto the children of Israel: When a man or woman shall commit any sin that men commit, to commit a trespass against the LORD, and that soul be guilty; 5:7 then they shall confess their sin which they have done; and he shall make restitution for his guilt in full, and add unto it the fifth part thereof, and give it unto him in respect of whom he hath been guilty. 5:8 But if the man have no kinsman to whom restitution may be made for the guilt, the restitution for guilt which is made shall be the LORD'S, even the priest's; besides the ram of the atonement, whereby atonement shall be made for him. 5:9 And every heave-offering of all the holy things of the children of Israel, which they present unto the priest, shall be his. 5:10 And every man's hallowed things shall be his: whatsoever any man giveth the priest, it shall be his. {P}

2ב

6:1 And the LORD spoke unto Moses, saying: 6:2 Speak unto the children of Israel, and say unto them: When either man or woman shall clearly utter a vow, the vow of a Nazirite, to consecrate himself unto the LORD, 6:3 he shall abstain from wine and strong drink: he shall drink no vinegar of wine, or vinegar of strong drink, neither shall he drink any liquor of grapes, nor eat fresh grapes or dried. 6:4 All the days of his Naziriteship shall he eat nothing that is made of the grape-vine, from the pressed grapes even to the grapestone. 6:5 All the days of his vow of Naziriteship there shall no razor come upon his head; until the days be fulfilled, in which he consecrateth himself unto the LORD, he shall be holy, he shall let the locks of the hair of his head grow long. 6:6 All the days that he consecrateth himself unto the LORD he shall not come near to a dead body. 6:7 He shall not make himself unclean for his father, or for his mother, for his brother, or for his sister, when they die; because his consecration unto God is upon his head. 6:8 All the days of his Naziriteship he is holy unto the LORD. 6:9 And if any man die very suddenly beside him, and he defile his consecrated head, then he shall shave his head in the day of his cleansing, on the seventh day shall he shave it. 6:10 And on the eighth day he shall bring two turtledoves, or two young pigeons, to the priest, to the door of the tent of meeting. 6:11 And the priest shall prepare one for a sin-offering, and the other for a burnt-offering, and make atonement for him, for that he sinned by reason of the dead; and he shall hallow his head that same day. 6:12 And he shall consecrate unto the LORD the days of his Naziriteship, and shall bring a he-lamb of the first year for a guilt-offering; but the former days shall be void, because his consecration was defiled. 6:13 And this is the law of the Nazirite, when the days of his consecration are fulfilled: he shall bring it unto the door of the tent of meeting; 6:14 and he shall present his offering unto the LORD, one he-lamb of the first year without blemish for a burnt-offering, and one ewe-lamb of the first year without blemish for a sin-offering, and one ram without blemish for peace-offerings, 6:15 and a basket of unleavened bread, cakes of fine flour mingled with oil, and unleavened wafers spread with oil, and their meal-offering, and their drink-offerings. 6:16 And the priest shall bring them before the LORD, and shall offer his sin-offering, and his burnt-offering. 6:17 And he shall offer the ram for a sacrifice of peace-offerings unto the LORD, with the basket of unleavened bread; the priest shall offer also the meal-offering thereof, and the drink-offering thereof. 6:18 And the Nazirite shall shave his consecrated head at the door of the tent of meeting, and shall take the hair of his consecrated head, and put it on the fire which is under the sacrifice of peace-offerings. 6:19 And the priest shall take the shoulder of the ram when it is sodden, and one unleavened cake out of the basket, and one unleavened wafer, and shall put them upon the hands of the Nazirite, after he hath shaven his consecrated head. 6:20 And the priest shall wave them for a wave-offering before the LORD; this is holy for the priest, together with the breast of waving and the thigh of heaving; and after that the Nazirite may drink wine. 6:21 This is the law of the Nazirite who voweth, and of his offering unto the LORD for his Naziriteship, beside that for which his means suffice; according to his vow which he voweth, so he must do after the law of his Naziriteship. {P}

Numbers Unit III (6:22-10:36)

א

6:22 And the LORD spoke unto Moses, saying: 6:23 'Speak unto Aaron and unto his sons, saying: On this wise ye shall bless the children of Israel; ye shall say unto them: {S} 6:24 The LORD bless thee, and keep thee; {S} 6:25 The LORD make His face to shine upon thee, and be gracious unto thee; {S} 6:26 The LORD lift up His countenance upon thee, and give thee peace. {S} 6:27 So shall they put My name upon the children of Israel, and I will bless them.' {S}

ב

7:1 And it came to pass on the day that Moses had made an end of setting up the tabernacle, and had anointed it and sanctified it, and all the furniture thereof, and the altar and all the vessels thereof, and had anointed them and sanctified them; 7:2 that the princes of Israel, the heads of their fathers' houses, offered--these were the princes of the tribes, these are they that were over them that were numbered. 7:3 And they brought their offering before the LORD, six covered wagons, and twelve oxen: a wagon for every two of the princes, and for each one an ox; and they presented them before the tabernacle. 7:4 And the LORD spoke unto Moses, saying: 7:5 'Take it of them, that they may be to do the service of the tent of meeting; and thou shalt give them unto the Levites, to every man according to his service.' 7:6 And Moses took the wagons and the oxen, and gave them unto the Levites. 7:7 Two wagons and four oxen he gave unto the sons of Gershon, according to their service. 7:8 And four wagons and eight oxen he gave unto the sons of Merari, according unto their service, under the hand of Ithamar the son of Aaron the priest. 7:9 But unto the sons of Kohath he gave none, because the service of the holy things belonged unto them: they bore them upon their shoulders.

ג

7:10 And the princes brought the dedication-offering of the altar in the day that it was anointed, even the princes brought their offering before the altar. 7:11 And the LORD said unto Moses: 'They shall present their offering each prince on his day, for the dedication of the altar.' {S} 7:12 And he that presented his offering the first day was Nahshon the son of Amminadab, of the tribe of Judah; 7:13 and his offering was one silver dish, the weight thereof was a hundred and thirty shekels, one silver basin of seventy shekels, after the shekel of the sanctuary; both of them full of fine flour mingled with oil for a meal-offering; 7:14 one golden pan of ten shekels, full of incense; 7:15 one young bullock, one ram, one he-lamb of the first year, for a burnt-offering; 7:16 one male of the goats for a sin-offering; 7:17 and for the sacrifice of peace-offerings, two oxen, five rams, five he-goats, five he-lambs of the first year. This was the offering of Nahshon the son of Amminadab. {P}

7:18 On the second day Nethanel the son of Zuar, prince of Issachar, did offer: 7:19 he presented for his offering one silver dish, the weight thereof was a hundred and thirty shekels, one silver basin of seventy shekels, after the shekel of the sanctuary; both of them full of fine flour mingled with oil for a meal-offering; 7:20 one golden pan of ten shekels, full of incense; 7:21 one young bullock, one ram, one he-lamb of the first year, for a burnt-offering; 7:22 one male of the goats for a sin-offering; 7:23 and for the sacrifice of peace-offerings, two oxen, five rams, five he-goats, five he-lambs of the first year. This was the offering of Nethanel the son of Zuar. {P}

7:24 On the third day Eliab the son of Helon, prince of the children of Zebulun: 7:25 his offering was one silver dish, the weight thereof was a hundred and thirty shekels, one silver basin of seventy shekels, after the shekel of the sanctuary; both of them full of fine flour mingled with oil for a meal-offering; 7:26 one golden pan of ten shekels, full of incense; 7:27 one young bullock, one ram, one he-lamb of the first year, for a burnt-offering; 7:28 one male of the goats for a sin-offering; 7:29 and for the sacrifice of peace-offerings, two oxen, five rams, five he-goats, five he-lambs of the first year. This was the offering of Eliab the son of Helon. {P}

7:30 On the fourth day Elizur the son of Shedeur, prince of the children of Reuben: 7:31 his offering was one silver dish, the weight thereof was a hundred and thirty shekels, one silver basin of seventy shekels, after the shekel of the sanctuary; both of them full of fine flour mingled with oil for a meal-offering; 7:32 one golden pan of ten shekels, full of incense; 7:33 one young bullock, one ram, one he-lamb of the first year, for a burnt-offering; 7:34 one male of the goats for a sin-offering; 7:35 and for the sacrifice of peace-offerings, two oxen, five rams, five he-goats, five he-lambs of the first year. This was the offering of Elizur the son of Shedeur. {P}

7:36 On the fifth day Shelumiel the son of Zurishaddai, prince of the children of Simeon: 7:37 his offering was one silver dish, the weight thereof was a hundred and thirty shekels, one silver basin of seventy shekels, after the shekel of the sanctuary; both of them full of fine flour mingled with oil for a meal-offering; 7:38 one golden pan of ten shekels, full of incense; 7:39 one young bullock, one ram, one he-lamb of the first year, for a burnt-offering; 7:40 one male of the goats for a sin-offering; 7:41 and for the sacrifice of peace-offerings, two oxen, five rams, five he-goats, five he-lambs of the first year. This was the offering of Shelumiel the son of Zurishaddai. {P}

7:42 On the sixth day Eliasaph the son of Deuel, prince of the children of Gad: 7:43 his offering was one silver dish, the weight thereof was a hundred and thirty shekels, one silver basin of seventy shekels, after the shekel of the sanctuary; both of them full of fine flour mingled with oil for a meal-offering; 7:44 one golden pan of ten shekels, full of incense; 7:45 one young bullock, one ram, one he-lamb of the first year, for a burnt-offering; 7:46 one male of the goats for a sin-offering; 7:47 and for the sacrifice of peace-offerings, two oxen, five rams, five he-goats, five he-lambs of the first year. This was the offering of Eliasaph the son of Deuel. {P}

7:48 On the seventh day Elishama the son of Ammihud, prince of the children of Ephraim: 7:49 his offering was one silver dish, the weight thereof was a hundred and thirty shekels, one silver basin of seventy shekels, after the shekel of the sanctuary; both of them full of fine flour mingled with oil for a meal-offering; 7:50 one golden pan of ten shekels, full of incense; 7:51 one young bullock, one ram, one he-lamb of the first year, for a burnt-offering; 7:52 one male of the goats for a sin-offering; 7:53 and for the sacrifice of peace-offerings, two oxen, five rams, five he-goats, five he-lambs of the first year. This was the offering of Elishama the son of Ammihud. {P}

7:54 On the eighth day Gamaliel the son of Pedahzur, prince of the children of Manasseh: 7:55 his offering was one silver dish, the weight thereof was a hundred and thirty shekels, one silver basin of seventy shekels, after the shekel of the sanctuary; both of them full of fine flour mingled with oil for a meal-offering; 7:56 one golden pan of ten shekels, full of incense; 7:57 one young bullock, one ram, one he-lamb of the first year, for a burnt-offering; 7:58 one male of the goats for a sin-offering; 7:59 and for the sacrifice of peace-offerings, two oxen, five rams, five he-goats, five he-lamb of the first year. This was the offering of Gamaliel the son of Pedahzur. {P}

7:60 On the ninth day Abidan the son of Gideoni, prince of the children of Benjamin: 7:61 his offering was one silver dish, the weight thereof was a hundred and thirty shekels, one silver basin of seventy shekels, after the shekel of the sanctuary; both of them full of fine flour mingled with oil for a meal-offering; 7:62 one golden pan of ten shekels, full of incense; 7:63 one young bullock, one ram, one he-lamb of the first year, for a burnt-offering; 7:64 one male of the goats for a sin-offering; 7:65 and for the sacrifice of peace-offerings, two oxen, five rams, five he-goats, five he-lambs of the first year. This was the offering of Abidan the son of Gideoni. {P}

7:66 On the tenth day Ahiezer the son of Ammishaddai, prince of the children of Dan: 7:67 his offering was one silver dish, the weight thereof was a hundred and thirty shekels, one silver basin of seventy shekels, after the shekel of the sanctuary; both of them full of fine flour mingled with oil for a meal-offering; 7:68 one golden pan of ten shekels, full of incense; 7:69 one young bullock, one ram, one he-lamb of the first year, for a burnt-offering; 7:70 one male of the goats for a sin-offering; 7:71 and for the sacrifice of peace-offerings, two oxen, five rams, five he-goats, five he-lambs of the first year. This was the offering of Ahiezer the son of Ammishaddai. {P}

7:72 On the eleventh day Pagiel the son of Ochran, prince of the children of Asher: 7:73 his offering was one silver dish, the weight thereof was a hundred and thirty shekels, one silver basin of seventy shekels, after the shekel of the sanctuary; both of them full of fine flour mingled with oil for a meal-offering; 7:74 one golden pan of ten shekels, full of incense; 7:75 one young bullock, one ram, one he-lamb of the first year, for a burnt-offering; 7:76 one male of the goats for a sin-offering; 7:77 and for the sacrifice of peace-offerings, two oxen, five rams, five he-goats, five he-lambs of the first year. This was the offering of Pagiel the son of Ochran. {P}

7:78 On the twelfth day Ahira the son of Enan, prince of the children of Naphtali: 7:79 his offering was one silver dish, the weight thereof was a hundred and thirty shekels, one silver basin of seventy shekels, after the shekel of the sanctuary; both of them full of fine flour mingled with oil for a meal-offering; 7:80 one golden pan of ten shekels, full of incense; 7:81 one young bullock, one ram, one he-lamb of the first year, for a burnt-offering; 7:82 one male of the goats for a sin-offering; 7:83 and for the sacrifice of peace-offerings, two oxen, five rams, five he-goats, five he-lambs of the first year. This was the offering of Ahira the son of Enan. {P}

7:84 This was the dedication-offering of the altar, in the day when it was anointed, at the hands of the princes of Israel: twelve silver dishes, twelve silver basins, twelve golden pans; 7:85 each silver dish weighing a hundred and thirty shekels, and each basin seventy; all the silver of the vessels two thousand and four hundred shekels, after the shekel of the sanctuary; 7:86 twelve golden pans, full of incense, weighing ten shekels apiece, after the shekel of the sanctuary; all the gold of the pans a hundred and twenty shekels; 7:87 all the oxen for the burnt-offering twelve bullocks, the rams twelve, the he-lambs of the first year twelve, and their meal-offering; and the males of the goats for a sin-offering twelve; 7:88 and all the oxen for the sacrifice of peace-offerings twenty and four bullocks, the rams sixty, the he-goats sixty, the he-lambs of the first year sixty. This was the dedication-offering of the altar, after that it was anointed. 7:89 And when Moses went into the tent of meeting that He might speak with him, then he heard the Voice speaking unto him from above the ark-cover that was upon the ark of the testimony, from between the two cherubim; and He spoke unto him. {P}

2א

A 8:1 And the LORD spoke unto Moses, saying: 8:2 'Speak unto Aaron, and say unto him: When thou lightest the lamps, the seven lamps shall give light in front of the candlestick.' 8:3 And Aaron did so: he lighted the lamps thereof so as to give light in front of the candlestick, as the LORD commanded Moses.

B 8:4 And this was the work of the candlestick, beaten work of gold; unto the base thereof, and unto the flowers thereof, it was beaten work; according unto the pattern which the LORD had shown Moses, so he made the candlestick. {P}

2ב

A 8:5 And the LORD spoke unto Moses, saying: 8:6 'Take the Levites from among the children of Israel, and cleanse them. 8:7 And thus shalt thou do unto them, to cleanse them: sprinkle the water of purification upon them, and let them cause a razor to pass over all their flesh, and let them wash their clothes, and cleanse themselves. 8:8 Then let them take a young bullock, and its meal-offering, fine flour mingled with oil, and another young bullock shalt thou take for a sin-offering. 8:9 And thou shalt present the Levites before the tent of meeting; and thou shalt assemble the whole congregation of the children of Israel. 8:10 And thou shalt present the Levites before the LORD; and the children of Israel shall lay their hands upon the Levites. 8:11 And Aaron shall offer the Levites before the LORD for a wave-offering from the children of Israel, that they may be to do the service of the LORD. 8:12 And the Levites shall lay their hands upon the heads of the bullocks; and offer thou the one for a sin-offering, and the other for a burnt-offering, unto the LORD, to make atonement for the Levites. 8:13 And thou shalt set the Levites before Aaron, and before his sons, and offer them for a wave-offering unto the LORD. 8:14 Thus shalt thou separate the Levites from among the children of Israel; and the Levites shall be Mine. 8:15 And after that shall the Levites go in to do the service of the tent of meeting; and thou shalt cleanse them, and offer them for a wave-offering. 8:16 For they are wholly given unto Me from among the children of Israel; instead of all that openeth the womb, even the first-born of all the children of Israel, have I taken them unto Me. 8:17 For all the first-born among the children of Israel are Mine, both man and beast; on the day that I smote all the first-born in the land of Egypt I sanctified them for Myself. 8:18 And I have taken the Levites instead of all the first-born among the children of Israel. 8:19 And I have given the Levites--they are given to Aaron and to his sons from among the children of Israel, to do the service of the children of Israel in the tent of meeting, and to make atonement for the children of Israel, that there be no plague among the children of Israel, through the children of Israel coming nigh unto the sanctuary.' 8:20 Thus did Moses, and Aaron, and all the congregation of the children of Israel, unto the Levites; according unto all that the LORD commanded Moses touching the Levites, so did the children of Israel unto them. 8:21 And the Levites purified themselves, and they washed their clothes; and Aaron offered them for a sacred gift before the LORD; and Aaron made atonement for them to cleanse them. 8:22 And after that went the Levites in to do their service in the tent of meeting before Aaron, and before his sons; as the LORD had commanded Moses concerning the Levites, so did they unto them. {S}

B 8:23 And the LORD spoke unto Moses, saying: 8:24 'This is that which pertaineth unto the Levites: from twenty and five years old and upward they shall go in to perform the service in the work of the tent of meeting; 8:25 and from the age of fifty years they shall return from the service of the work, and shall serve no more; 8:26 but shall minister with their brethren in the tent of meeting, to keep the charge, but they shall do no manner of service. Thus shalt thou do unto the Levites touching their charges.' {P}

2ג

A 9:1 And the LORD spoke unto Moses in the wilderness of Sinai, in the first month of the second year after they were come out of the land of Egypt, saying: 9:2 'Let the children of Israel keep the passover in its appointed season. 9:3 In the fourteenth day of this month, at dusk, ye shall keep it in its appointed season; according to all the statutes of it, and according to all the ordinances thereof, shall ye keep it.' 9:4 And Moses spoke unto the children of Israel, that they should keep the passover. 9:5 And they kept the passover in the first month, on the fourteenth day of the month, at dusk, in the wilderness of Sinai; according to all that the LORD commanded Moses, so did the children of Israel.

B 9:6 But there were certain men, who were unclean by the dead body of a man, so that they could not keep the passover on that day; and they came before Moses and before Aaron on that day. 9:7 And those men said unto him: 'We are unclean by the dead body of a man; wherefore are we to be kept back, so as not to bring the offering of the LORD in its appointed season among the children of Israel?' 9:8 And Moses said unto them: 'Stay ye, that I may hear what the LORD will command concerning you.' {P}

9:9 And the LORD spoke unto Moses, saying: 9:10 'Speak unto the children of Israel, saying: If any man of you or of your generations shall be unclean by reason of a dead body, or be in a journey afar off, yet he shall keep the passover unto the LORD; 9:11 in the second month on the fourteenth day at dusk they shall keep it; they shall eat it with unleavened bread and bitter herbs; 9:12 they shall leave none of it unto the morning, nor break a bone thereof; according to all the statute of the passover they shall keep it. 9:13 But the man that is clean, and is not on a journey, and forbeareth to keep the passover, that soul shall be cut off from his people; because he brought not the offering of the LORD in its appointed season, that man shall bear his sin. 9:14 And if a stranger shall sojourn among you, and will keep the passover unto the LORD: according to the statute of the passover, and according to the ordinance thereof, so shall he do; ye shall have one statute, both for the stranger, and for him that is born in the land.' {S}

א3

A 9:15 And on the day that the tabernacle was reared up the cloud covered the tabernacle, even the tent of the testimony; and at even there was upon the tabernacle as it were the appearance of fire, until morning. 9:16 So it was alway: the cloud covered it, and the appearance of fire by night. 9:17 And whenever the cloud was taken up from over the Tent, then after that the children of Israel journeyed; and in the place where the cloud abode, there the children of Israel encamped. 9:18 At the commandment of the LORD the children of Israel journeyed, and at the commandment of the LORD they encamped: as long as the cloud abode upon the tabernacle they remained encamped. 9:19 And when the cloud tarried upon the tabernacle many days, then the children of Israel kept the charge of the LORD, and journeyed not. 9:20 And sometimes the cloud was a few days upon the tabernacle; according to the commandment of the LORD they remained encamped, and according to the commandment of the LORD they journeyed. 9:21 And sometimes the cloud was from evening until morning; and when the cloud was taken up in the morning, they journeyed; or if it continued by day and by night, when the cloud was taken up, they journeyed. 9:22 Whether it were two days, or a month, or a year, that the cloud tarried upon the tabernacle, abiding thereon, the children of Israel remained encamped, and journeyed not; but when it was taken up, they journeyed. 9:23 At the commandment of the LORD they encamped, and at the commandment of the LORD they journeyed; they kept the charge of the LORD, at the commandment of the LORD by the hand of Moses. {P}

B 10:1 And the LORD spoke unto Moses, saying: 10:2 'Make thee two trumpets of silver; of beaten work shalt thou make them; and they shall be unto thee for the calling of the congregation, and for causing the camps to set forward. 10:3 And when they shall blow with them, all the congregation shall gather themselves unto thee at the door of the tent of meeting. 10:4 And if they blow but with one, then the princes, the heads of the thousands of Israel, shall gather themselves unto thee. 10:5 And when ye blow an alarm, the camps that lie on the east side shall take their journey. 10:6 And when ye blow an alarm the second time, the camps that lie on the south side shall set forward; they shall blow an alarm for their journeys. 10:7 But when the assembly is to be gathered together, ye shall blow, but ye shall not sound an alarm. 10:8 And the sons of Aaron, the priests, shall blow with the trumpets; and they shall be to you for a statute for ever throughout your generations. 10:9 And when ye go to war in your land against the adversary that oppresseth you, then ye shall sound an alarm with the trumpets; and ye shall be remembered before the LORD your God, and ye shall be saved from your enemies. 10:10 Also in the day of your gladness, and in your appointed seasons, and in your new moons, ye shall blow with the trumpets over your burnt-offerings, and over the sacrifices of your peace-offerings; and they shall be to you for a memorial before your God: I am the LORD your God.' {P}

ב3

A 10:11 And it came to pass in the second year, in the second month, on the twentieth day of the month, that the cloud was taken up from over the tabernacle of the testimony. 10:12 And the children of Israel set forward by their stages out of the wilderness of Sinai; and the cloud abode in the wilderness of Paran.-- 10:13 And they took their first journey, according to the commandment of the LORD by the hand of Moses.

B 10:14 And in the first place the standard of the camp of the children of Judah set forward according to their hosts; and over his host was Nahshon the son of Amminadab. 10:15 And over the host of the tribe of the children of Issachar was Nethanel the son of Zuar. 10:16 And over the host of the tribe of the children of Zebulun was Eliab the son of Helon. 10:17 And the tabernacle was taken down; and the sons of Gershon and the sons of Merari, who bore the tabernacle, set forward. 10:18 And the standard of the camp of Reuben set forward according to their hosts; and over his host was Elizur the son of Shedeur. 10:19 And over the host of the tribe of the children of Simeon was Shelumiel the son of Zurishaddai. 10:20 And over the host of the tribe of the children of Gad was Eliasaph the son of Deuel. 10:21 And the Kohathites the bearers of the sanctuary set forward, that the tabernacle might be set up against their coming. 10:22 And the standard of the camp of the children of Ephraim set forward according to their hosts; and over his host was Elishama the son of Ammihud. 10:23 And over the host of the tribe of the children of Manasseh was Gamaliel the son of Pedahzur. 10:24 And over the host of the tribe of the children of Benjamin was Abidan the son of Gideoni. 10:25 And the standard of the camp of the children of Dan, which was the rearward of all the camps, set forward according to their hosts; and over his host was Ahiezer the son of Ammishaddai. 10:26 And over the host of the tribe of the children of Asher was Pagiel the son of Ochran. 10:27 And over the host of the tribe of the children of Naphtali was Ahira the son of Enan. 10:28 Thus were the journeyings of the children of Israel according to their hosts.--And they set forward. {S}

ג3

A 10:29 And Moses said unto Hobab, the son of Reuel the Midianite, Moses' father-in-law: 'We are journeying unto the place of which the LORD said: I will give it you; come thou with us, and we will do thee good; for the LORD hath spoken good concerning Israel.' 10:30 And he said unto him: 'I will not go; but I will depart to mine own land, and to my kindred.' 10:31 And he said: 'Leave us not, I pray thee; forasmuch as thou knowest how we are to encamp in the wilderness, and thou shalt be to us instead of eyes. 10:32 And it shall be, if thou go with us, yea, it shall be, that what good soever the LORD shall do unto us, the same will we do unto thee.'

B 10:33 And they set forward from the mount of the LORD three days' journey; and the ark of the covenant of the LORD went before them three days' journey, to seek out a resting-place for them. 10:34 And the cloud of the LORD was over them by day, when they set forward from the camp. {S} 10:35 And it came to pass, when the ark set forward, that Moses said: 'Rise up, O LORD, and let Thine enemies be scattered; and let them that hate Thee flee before Thee.' 10:36 And when it rested, he said: 'Return, O LORD, unto the ten thousands of the families of Israel.' {P}

Numbers Unit IV (11:1-12:16)

א

A 11:1 And the people were as murmurers, speaking evil in the ears of the LORD; and when the LORD heard it, His anger was kindled; and the fire of the LORD burnt among them, and devoured in the uttermost part of the camp. 11:2 And the people cried unto Moses; and Moses prayed unto the LORD, and the fire abated. 11:3 And the name of that place was called Taberah, because the fire of the LORD burnt among them.

B 11:4 And the mixed multitude that was among them fell a lusting; and the children of Israel also wept on their part, and said: 'Would that we were given flesh to eat! 11:5 We remember the fish, which we were wont to eat in Egypt for nought; the cucumbers, and the melons, and the leeks, and the onions, and the garlic; 11:6 but now our soul is dried away; there is nothing at all; we have nought save this manna to look to.'-- 11:7 Now the manna was like coriander seed, and the appearance thereof as the appearance of bdellium. 11:8 The people went about, and gathered it, and ground it in mills, or beat it in mortars, and seethed it in pots, and made cakes of it; and the taste of it was as the taste of a cake baked with oil. 11:9 And when the dew fell upon the camp in the night, the manna fell upon it.-- 11:10 And Moses heard the people weeping, family by family, every man at the door of his tent; and the anger of the LORD was kindled greatly; and Moses was displeased.

C 11:11 And Moses said unto the LORD: 'Wherefore hast Thou dealt ill with Thy servant? and wherefore have I not found favour in Thy sight, that Thou layest the burden of all this people upon me? 11:12 Have I conceived all this people? have I brought them forth, that Thou shouldest say unto me: Carry them in thy bosom, as a nursing-father carrieth the sucking child, unto the land which Thou didst swear unto their fathers? 11:13 Whence should I have flesh to give unto all this people? for they trouble me with their weeping, saying: Give us flesh, that we may eat. 11:14 I am not able to bear all this people myself alone, because it is too heavy for me. 11:15 And if Thou deal thus with me, kill me, I pray Thee, out of hand, if I have found favour in Thy sight; and let me not look upon my wretchedness.' {P}

ב

A 11:16 And the LORD said unto Moses: 'Gather unto Me seventy men of the elders of Israel, whom thou knowest to be the elders of the people, and officers over them; and bring them unto the tent of meeting, that they may stand there with thee. 11:17 And I will come down and speak with thee there; and I will take of the spirit which is upon thee, and will put it upon them; and they shall bear the burden of the people with thee, that thou bear it not thyself alone.

B 11:18 And say thou unto the people: Sanctify yourselves against to-morrow, and ye shall eat flesh; for ye have wept in the ears of the LORD, saying: Would that we were given flesh to eat! for it was well with us in Egypt; therefore the LORD will give you flesh, and ye shall eat. 11:19 Ye shall not eat one day, nor two days, nor five days, neither ten days, nor twenty days; 11:20 but a whole month, until it come out at your nostrils, and it be loathsome unto you; because that ye have rejected the LORD who is among you, and have troubled Him with weeping, saying: Why, now, came we forth out of Egypt?'

C 11:21 And Moses said: 'The people, among whom I am, are six hundred thousand men on foot; and yet Thou hast said: I will give them flesh, that they may eat a whole month! 11:22 If flocks and herds be slain for them, will they suffice them? or if all the fish of the sea be gathered together for them, will they suffice them?' {P}

11:23 And the LORD said unto Moses: 'Is the LORD'S hand waxed short? now shalt thou see whether My word shall come to pass unto thee or not.'

ג

A 11:24 And Moses went out, and told the people the words of the LORD; and he gathered seventy men of the elders of the people, and set them round about the Tent. 11:25 And the LORD came down in the cloud, and spoke unto him, and took of the spirit that was upon him, and put it upon the seventy elders; and it came to pass, that, when the spirit rested upon them, they prophesied, but they did so no more. 11:26 But there remained two men in the camp, the name of the one was Eldad, and the name of the other Medad; and the spirit rested upon them; and they were of them that were recorded, but had not gone out unto the Tent; and they prophesied in the camp. 11:27 And there ran a young man, and told Moses, and said: 'Eldad and Medad are prophesying in the camp.' 11:28 And Joshua the son of Nun, the minister of Moses from his youth up, answered and said: 'My lord Moses, shut them in.' 11:29 And Moses said unto him: 'Art thou jealous for my sake? would that all the LORD'S people were prophets, that the LORD would put His spirit upon them!'

B 11:30 And Moses withdrew into the camp, he and the elders of Israel. 11:31 And there went forth a wind from the LORD, and brought across quails from the sea, and let them fall by the camp, about a day's journey on this side, and a day's journey on the other side, round about the camp, and about two cubits above the face of the earth. 11:32 And the people rose up all that day, and all the night, and all the next day, and gathered the quails; he that gathered least gathered ten heaps; and they spread them all abroad for themselves round about the camp.

C 11:33 While the flesh was yet between their teeth, ere it was chewed, the anger of the LORD was kindled against the people, and the LORD smote the people with a very great plague. 11:34 And the name of that place was called Kibroth-hattaavah, because there they buried the people that lusted. 11:35 From Kibroth-hattaavah the people journeyed unto Hazeroth; and they abode at Hazeroth. {P}

א2

12:1 And Miriam and Aaron spoke against Moses because of the Cushite woman whom he had married; for he had married a Cushite woman. 12:2 And they said: 'Hath the LORD indeed spoken only with Moses? hath He not spoken also with us?' And the LORD heard it.-- 12:3 Now the man Moses was very meek, above all the men that were upon the face of the earth.-- {S}

ב2

12:4 And the LORD spoke suddenly unto Moses, and unto Aaron, and unto Miriam: 'Come out ye three unto the tent of meeting.' And they three came out. 12:5 And the LORD came down in a pillar of cloud, and stood at the door of the Tent, and called Aaron and Miriam; and they both came forth. 12:6 And He said: 'Hear now My words: if there be a prophet among you, I the LORD do make Myself known unto him in a vision, I do speak with him in a dream. 12:7 My servant Moses is not so; he is trusted in all My house; 12:8 with him do I speak mouth to mouth, even manifestly, and not in dark speeches; and the similitude of the LORD doth he behold; wherefore then were ye not afraid to speak against My servant, against Moses?' 12:9 And the anger of the LORD was kindled against them; and He departed. 12:10 And when the cloud was removed from over the Tent, behold, Miriam was leprous, as white as snow; and Aaron looked upon Miriam; and, behold, she was leprous.

ג2

12:11 And Aaron said unto Moses: 'Oh my lord, lay not, I pray thee, sin upon us, for that we have done foolishly, and for that we have sinned. 12:12 Let her not, I pray, be as one dead, of whom the flesh is half consumed when he cometh out of his mother's womb.' 12:13 And Moses cried unto the LORD, saying: 'Heal her now, O God, I beseech Thee.' {P}

12:14 And the LORD said unto Moses: 'If her father had but spit in her face, should she not hide in shame seven days? let her be shut up without the camp seven days, and after that she shall be brought in again.' 12:15 And Miriam was shut up without the camp seven days; and the people journeyed not till Miriam was brought in again. 12:16 And afterward the people journeyed from Hazeroth, and pitched in the wilderness of Paran. {P}

Numbers Unit V (13:1-14:45)

1א

13:1 And the LORD spoke unto Moses, saying: 13:2 'Send thou men, that they may spy out the land of Canaan, which I give unto the children of Israel; of every tribe of their fathers shall ye send a man, every one a prince among them.' 13:3 And Moses sent them from the wilderness of Paran according to the commandment of the LORD; all of them men who were heads of the children of Israel. 13:4 And these were their names: of the tribe of Reuben, Shammua the son of Zaccur. 13:5 Of the tribe of Simeon, Shaphat the son of Hori. 13:6 Of the tribe of Judah, Caleb the son of Jephunneh. 13:7 Of the tribe of Issachar, Igal the son of Joseph. 13:8 Of the tribe of Ephraim, Hoshea the son of Nun. 13:9 Of the tribe of Benjamin, Palti the son of Raphu. 13:10 Of the tribe of Zebulun, Gaddiel the son of Sodi. 13:11 Of the tribe of Joseph, namely, of the tribe of Manasseh, Gaddi the son of Susi. 13:12 Of the tribe of Dan, Ammiel the son of Gemalli. 13:13 Of the tribe of Asher, Sethur the son of Michael. 13:14 Of the tribe of Naphtali, Nahbi the son of Vophsi. 13:15 Of the tribe of Gad, Geuel the son of Machi. 13:16 These are the names of the men that Moses sent to spy out the land. And Moses called Hoshea the son of Nun Joshua.

2א

13:25 And they returned from spying out the land at the end of forty days. 13:26 And they went and came to Moses, and to Aaron, and to all the congregation of the children of Israel, unto the wilderness of Paran, to Kadesh; and brought back word unto them, and unto all the congregation, and showed them the fruit of the land. 13:27 And they told him, and said: 'We came unto the land whither thou sentest us, and surely it floweth with milk and honey; and this is the fruit of it. 13:28 Howbeit the people that dwell in the land are fierce, and the cities are fortified, and very great; and moreover we saw the children of Anak there. 13:29 Amalek dwelleth in the land of the South; and the Hittite, and the Jebusite, and the Amorite, dwell in the mountains; and the Canaanite dwelleth by the sea, and along by the side of the Jordan.' 13:30 And Caleb stilled the people toward Moses, and said: 'We should go up at once, and possess it; for we are well able to overcome it.' 13:31 But the men that went up with him said: 'We are not able to go up against the people; for they are stronger than we.' 13:32 And they spread an evil report of the land which they had spied out unto the children of Israel, saying: 'The land, through which we have passed to spy it out, is a land that eateth up the inhabitants thereof; and all the people that we saw in it are men of great stature. 13:33 And there we saw the Nephilim, the sons of Anak, who come of the Nephilim; and we were in our own sight as grasshoppers, and so we were in their sight.' 14:1 And all the congregation lifted up their voice, and cried; and the people wept that night.

1ב

13:17 And Moses sent them to spy out the land of Canaan, and said unto them: 'Get you up here into the South, and go up into the mountains; 13:18 and see the land, what it is; and the people that dwelleth therein, whether they are strong or weak, whether they are few or many; 13:19 and what the land is that they dwell in, whether it is good or bad; and what cities they are that they dwell in, whether in camps, or in strongholds; 13:20 and what the land is, whether it is fat or lean, whether there is wood therein, or not. And be ye of good courage, and bring of the fruit of the land.'-- Now the time was the time of the first-ripe grapes.-- 13:21 So they went up, and spied out the land from the wilderness of Zin unto Rehob, at the entrance to Hamath. 13:22 And they went up into the South, and came unto Hebron; and Ahiman, Sheshai, and Talmai, the children of Anak, were there.--Now Hebron was built seven years before Zoan in Egypt.-- 13:23 And they came unto the valley of Eshcol, and cut down from thence a branch with one cluster of grapes, and they bore it upon a pole between two; they took also of the pomegranates, and of the figs.-- 13:24 That place was called the valley of Eshcol, because of the cluster which the children of Israel cut down from thence.--

2ב

14:2 And all the children of Israel murmured against Moses and against Aaron; and the whole congregation said unto them: 'Would that we had died in the land of Egypt! or would we had died in this wilderness! 14:3 And wherefore doth the LORD bring us unto this land, to fall by the sword? Our wives and our little ones will be a prey; were it not better for us to return into Egypt?' 14:4 And they said one to another: 'Let us make a captain, and let us return into Egypt.' 14:5 Then Moses and Aaron fell on their faces before all the assembly of the congregation of the children of Israel. 14:6 And Joshua the son of Nun and Caleb the son of Jephunneh, who were of them that spied out the land, rent their clothes. 14:7 And they spoke unto all the congregation of the children of Israel, saying: 'The land, which we passed through to spy it out, is an exceeding good land. 14:8 If the LORD delight in us, then He will bring us into this land, and give it unto us--a land which floweth with milk and honey. 14:9 Only rebel not against the LORD, neither fear ye the people of the land; for they are bread for us; their defence is removed from over them, and the LORD is with us; fear them not.' 14:10 But all the congregation bade stone them with stones, when the glory of the LORD appeared in the tent of meeting unto all the children of Israel. {P}

3א

A 14:11 And the LORD said unto Moses: 'How long will this people despise Me? and how long will they not believe in Me, for all the signs which I have wrought among them? 14:12 I will smite them with the pestilence, and destroy them, and will make of thee a nation greater and mightier than they.' 14:13 And Moses said unto the LORD: 'When the Egyptians shall hear--for Thou broughtest up this people in Thy might from among them-- 14:14 they will say to the inhabitants of this land, who have heard that Thou LORD art in the midst of this people; inasmuch as Thou LORD art seen face to face, and Thy cloud standeth over them, and Thou goest before them, in a pillar of cloud by day, and in a pillar of fire by night; 14:15 now if Thou shalt kill this people as one man, then the nations which have heard the fame of Thee will speak, saying: 14:16 Because the LORD was not able to bring this people into the land which He swore unto them, therefore He hath slain them in the wilderness. 14:17 And now, I pray Thee, let the power of the LORD be great, according as Thou hast spoken, saying: 14:18 The LORD is slow to anger, and plenteous in lovingkindness, forgiving iniquity and transgression, and that will by no means clear the guilty; visiting the iniquity of the fathers upon the children, upon the third and upon the fourth generation. 14:19 Pardon, I pray Thee, the iniquity of this people according unto the greatness of Thy lovingkindness, and according as Thou hast forgiven this people, from Egypt even until now.'
B 14:20 And the LORD said: 'I have pardoned according to thy word. 14:21 But in very deed, as I live--and all the earth shall be filled with the glory of the LORD-- 14:22 surely all those men that have seen My glory, and My signs, which I wrought in Egypt and in the wilderness, yet have put Me to proof these ten times, and have not hearkened to My voice; 14:23 surely they shall not see the land which I swore unto their fathers, neither shall any of them that despised Me see it. 14:24 But My servant Caleb, because he had another spirit with him, and hath followed Me fully, him will I bring into the land whereinto he went; and his seed shall possess it. 14:25 Now the Amalekite and the Canaanite dwell in the Vale; tomorrow turn ye, and get you into the wilderness by the way to the Red Sea.' {P}

4א

14:39 And Moses told these words unto all the children of Israel; and the people mourned greatly. 14:40 And they rose up early in the morning, and got them up to the top of the mountain, saying: 'Lo, we are here, and will go up unto the place which the LORD hath promised; for we have sinned.' 14:41 And Moses said: 'Wherefore now do ye transgress the commandment of the LORD, seeing it shall not prosper? 14:42 Go not up, for the LORD is not among you; that ye be not smitten down before your enemies. 14:43 For there the Amalekite and the Canaanite are before you, and ye shall fall by the sword; forasmuch as ye are turned back from following the LORD, and the LORD will not be with you.'

3ב

A 14:26 And the LORD spoke unto Moses and unto Aaron, saying: 14:27 'How long shall I bear with this evil congregation, that keep murmuring against Me? I have heard the murmurings of the children of Israel, which they keep murmuring against Me. 14:28 Say unto them: As I live, saith the LORD, surely as ye have spoken in Mine ears, so will I do to you: 14:29 your carcasses shall fall in this wilderness, and all that were numbered of you, according to your whole number, from twenty years old and upward, ye that have murmured against Me; 14:30 surely ye shall not come into the land, concerning which I lifted up My hand that I would make you dwell therein, save Caleb the son of Jephunneh, and Joshua the son of Nun. 14:31 But your little ones, that ye said would be a prey, them will I bring in, and they shall know the land which ye have rejected. 14:32 But as for you, your carcasses shall fall in this wilderness. 14:33 And your children shall be wanderers in the wilderness forty years, and shall bear your strayings, until your carcasses be consumed in the wilderness. 14:34 After the number of the days in which ye spied out the land, even forty days, for every day a year, shall ye bear your iniquities, even forty years, and ye shall know My displeasure. 14:35 I the LORD have spoken, surely this will I do unto all this evil congregation, that are gathered together against Me; in this wilderness they shall be consumed, and there they shall die.'

B 14:36 And the men, whom Moses sent to spy out the land, and who, when they returned, made all the congregation to murmur against him, by bringing up an evil report against the land, 14:37 even those men that did bring up an evil report of the land, died by the plague before the LORD. 14:38 But Joshua the son of Nun, and Caleb the son of Jephunneh, remained alive of those men that went to spy out the land.

4ב

14:44 But they presumed to go up to the top of the mountain; nevertheless the ark of the covenant of the LORD, and Moses, departed not out of the camp. 14:45 Then the Amalekite and the Canaanite, who dwelt in that hill-country, came down, and smote them and beat them down, even unto Hormah. {P}

Numbers Unit VI (15:1-31)

א1

15:1 And the LORD spoke unto Moses, saying: 15:2 Speak unto the children of Israel, and say unto them: When ye are come into the land of your habitations, which I give unto you, 15:3 and will make an offering by fire unto the LORD, a burnt-offering, or a sacrifice, in fulfilment of a vow clearly uttered, or as a freewill-offering, or in your appointed seasons, to make a sweet savour unto the LORD, of the herd, or of the flock; 15:4 then shall he that bringeth his offering present unto the LORD a meal-offering of a tenth part of an ephah of fine flour mingled with the fourth part of a hin of oil; 15:5 and wine for the drink-offering, the fourth part of a hin, shalt thou prepare with the burnt-offering or for the sacrifice, for each lamb. 15:6 Or for a ram, thou shalt prepare for a meal-offering two tenth parts of an ephah of fine flour mingled with the third part of a hin of oil; 15:7 and for the drink-offering thou shalt present the third part of a hin of wine, of a sweet savour unto the LORD. 15:8 And when thou preparest a bullock for a burnt-offering, or for a sacrifice, in fulfilment of a vow clearly uttered, or for peace-offerings unto the LORD; 15:9 then shall there be presented with the bullock a meal-offering of three tenth parts of an ephah of fine flour mingled with half a hin of oil. 15:10 And thou shalt present for the drink-offering half a hin of wine, for an offering made by fire, of a sweet savour unto the LORD. 15:11 Thus shall it be done for each bullock, or for each ram, or for each of the he-lambs, or of the kids. 15:12 According to the number that ye may prepare, so shall ye do for every one according to their number. 15:13 All that are home-born shall do these things after this manner, in presenting an offering made by fire, of a sweet savour unto the LORD.

ב1

15:14 And if a stranger sojourn with you, or whosoever may be among you, throughout your generations, and will offer an offering made by fire, of a sweet savour unto the LORD; as ye do, so he shall do. 15:15 As for the congregation, there shall be one statute both for you, and for the stranger that sojourneth with you, a statute for ever throughout your generations; as ye are, so shall the stranger be before the LORD. 15:16 One law and one ordinance shall be both for you, and for the stranger that sojourneth with you. {P}

ג1

15:17 And the LORD spoke unto Moses, saying: 15:18 Speak unto the children of Israel, and say unto them: When ye come into the land whither I bring you, 15:19 then it shall be, that, when ye eat of the bread of the land, ye shall set apart a portion for a gift unto the LORD. 15:20 Of the first of your dough ye shall set apart a cake for a gift; as that which is set apart of the threshing-floor, so shall ye set it apart. 15:21 Of the first of your dough ye shall give unto the LORD a portion for a gift throughout your generations. {S}

א2

15:22 And when ye shall err, and not observe all these commandments, which the LORD hath spoken unto Moses, 15:23 even all that the LORD hath commanded you by the hand of Moses, from the day that the LORD gave commandment, and onward throughout your generations; 15:24 then it shall be, if it be done in error by the congregation, it being hid from their eyes, that all the congregation shall offer one young bullock for a burnt-offering, for a sweet savour unto the LORD--with the meal-offering thereof, and the drink-offering thereof, according to the ordinance--and one he-goat for a sin-offering. 15:25 And the priest shall make atonement for all the congregation of the children of Israel, and they shall be forgiven; for it was an error, and they have brought their offering, an offering made by fire unto the LORD, and their sin-offering before the LORD, for their error. 15:26 And all the congregation of the children of Israel shall be forgiven, and the stranger that sojourneth among them; for in respect of all the people it was done in error. {S}

ב2

15:27 And if one person sin through error, then he shall offer a she-goat of the first year for a sin-offering. 15:28 And the priest shall make atonement for the soul that erreth, when he sinneth through error, before the LORD, to make atonement for him; and he shall be forgiven, 15:29 both he that is home-born among the children of Israel, and the stranger that sojourneth among them: ye shall have one law for him that doeth aught in error.

ג2

15:30 But the soul that doeth aught with a high hand, whether he be home-born or a stranger, the same blasphemeth the LORD; and that soul shall be cut off from among his people. 15:31 Because he hath despised the word of the LORD, and hath broken His commandment; that soul shall utterly be cut off, his iniquity shall be upon him. {P}

Numbers Unit VII (15:32-17:26)

א

15:32 And while the children of Israel were in the wilderness, they found a man gathering sticks upon the sabbath day. 15:33 And they that found him gathering sticks brought him unto Moses and Aaron, and unto all the congregation. 15:34 And they put him in ward, because it had not been declared what should be done to him. {S} 15:35 And the LORD said unto Moses: 'The man shall surely be put to death; all the congregation shall stone him with stones without the camp.' 15:36 And all the congregation brought him without the camp, and stoned him with stones, and he died, as the LORD commanded Moses. {P}

ב

15:37 And the LORD spoke unto Moses, saying: 15:38 'Speak unto the children of Israel, and bid them that they make them throughout their generations fringes in the corners of their garments, and that they put with the fringe of each corner a thread of blue. 15:39 And it shall be unto you for a fringe, that ye may look upon it, and remember all the commandments of the LORD, and do them; and that ye go not about after your own heart and your own eyes, after which ye use to go astray; 15:40 that ye may remember and do all My commandments, and be holy unto your God. 15:41 I am the LORD your God, who brought you out of the land of Egypt, to be your God: I am the LORD your God.' {P}

א2

A 16:1 Now Korah, the son of Izhar, the son of Kohath, the son of Levi, with Dathan and Abiram, the sons of Eliab, and On, the son of Peleth, sons of Reuben, took men; 16:2 and they rose up in face of Moses, with certain of the children of Israel, two hundred and fifty men; they were princes of the congregation, the elect men of the assembly, men of renown; 16:3 and they assembled themselves together against Moses and against Aaron, and said unto them: 'Ye take too much upon you, seeing all the congregation are holy, every one of them, and the LORD is among them; wherefore then lift ye up yourselves above the assembly of the LORD?' 16:4 And when Moses heard it, he fell upon his face. 16:5 And he spoke unto Korah and unto all his company, saying: 'In the morning the LORD will show who are His, and who is holy, and will cause him to come near unto Him; even him whom He may choose will He cause to come near unto Him. 16:6 This do: take you censors, Korah, and all his company; 16:7 and put fire therein, and put incense upon them before the LORD to-morrow; and it shall be that the man whom the LORD doth choose, he shall be holy; ye take too much upon you, ye sons of Levi.' 16:8 And Moses said unto Korah: 'Hear now, ye sons of Levi: 16:9 is it but a small thing unto you, that the God of Israel hath separated you from the congregation of Israel, to bring you near to Himself, to do the service of the tabernacle of the LORD, and to stand before the congregation to minister unto them; 16:10 and that He hath brought thee near, and all thy brethren the sons of Levi with thee? and will ye seek the priesthood also? 16:11 Therefore thou and all thy company that are gathered together against the LORD--; and as to Aaron, what is he that ye murmur against him?' 16:12 And Moses sent to call Dathan and Abiram, the sons of Eliab; and they said: 'We will not come up; 16:13 is it a small thing that thou hast brought us up out of a land flowing with milk and honey, to kill us in the wilderness, but thou must needs make thyself also a prince over us? 16:14 Moreover thou hast not brought us into a land flowing with milk and honey, nor given us inheritance of fields and vineyards; wilt thou put out the eyes of these men? we will not come up.' 16:15 And Moses was very wroth, and said unto the LORD: 'Respect not Thou their offering; I have not taken one ass from them, neither have I hurt one of them.' 16:16 And Moses said unto Korah: 'Be thou and all thy congregation before the LORD, thou, and they, and Aaron, to-morrow; 16:17 and take ye every man his fire-pan, and put incense upon them, and bring ye before the LORD every man his fire-pan, two hundred and fifty fire-pans; thou also, and Aaron, each his fire-pan.' 16:18 And they took every man his fire-pan, and put fire in them, and laid incense thereon, and stood at the door of the tent of meeting with Moses and Aaron.

B 16:19 And Korah assembled all the congregation against them unto the door of the tent of meeting; and the glory of the LORD appeared unto all the congregation. {S} 16:20 And the LORD spoke unto Moses and unto Aaron, saying: 16:21 'Separate yourselves from among this congregation, that I may consume them in a moment.' 16:22 And they fell upon their faces, and said: 'O God, the God of the spirits of all flesh, shall one man sin, and wilt Thou be wroth with all the congregation?' {S}

ב2

A 17:1 And the LORD spoke unto Moses, saying: 17:2 'Speak unto Eleazar the son of Aaron the priest, that he take up the fire-pans out of the burning, and scatter thou the fire yonder; for they are become holy; 17:3 even the fire-pans of these men who have sinned at the cost of their lives, and let them be made beaten plates for a covering of the altar--for they are become holy, because they were offered before the LORD--that they may be a sign unto the children of Israel.' 17:4 And Eleazar the priest took the brazen fire-pans, which they that were burnt had offered; and they beat them out for a covering of the altar, 17:5 to be a memorial unto the children of Israel, to the end that no common man, that is not of the seed of Aaron, draw near to burn incense before the LORD; that he fare not as Korah, and as his company; as the LORD spoke unto him by the hand of Moses. {P}

B 17:6 But on the morrow all the congregation of the children of Israel murmured against Moses and against Aaron, saying: 'Ye have killed the people of the LORD.' 17:7 And it came to pass, when the congregation was assembled against Moses and against Aaron, that they looked toward the tent of meeting; and, behold, the cloud covered it, and the glory of the LORD appeared. 17:8 And Moses and Aaron came to the front of the tent of meeting. {S} 17:9 And the LORD spoke unto Moses, saying: 17:10 'Get you up from among this congregation, that I may consume them in a moment.' And they fell upon their faces. 17:11 And Moses said unto Aaron: 'Take thy fire-pan, and put fire therein from off the altar, and lay incense thereon, and carry it quickly unto the congregation, and make atonement for them; for there is wrath gone out from the LORD: the plague is begun.' 17:12 And Aaron took as Moses spoke, and ran into the midst of the assembly; and, behold, the plague was begun among the people; and he put on the incense, and made atonement for the people. 17:13 And he stood between the dead and the living; and the plague was stayed. 17:14 Now they that died by the plague were fourteen thousand and seven hundred, besides them that died about the matter of Korah. 17:15 And Aaron returned unto Moses unto the door of the tent of meeting, and the plague was stayed. {P}

C 16:23 And the LORD spoke unto Moses, saying: 16:24 'Speak unto the congregation, saying: Get you up from about the dwelling of Korah, Dathan, and Abiram.' 16:25 And Moses rose up and went unto Dathan and Abiram; and the elders of Israel followed him. 16:26 And he spoke unto the congregation, saying: 'Depart, I pray you, from the tents of these wicked men, and touch nothing of theirs, lest ye be swept away in all their sins.' 16:27 So they got them up from the dwelling of Korah, Dathan, and Abiram, on every side; and Dathan and Abiram came out, and stood at the door of their tents, with their wives, and their sons, and their little ones. 16:28 And Moses said: 'Hereby ye shall know that the LORD hath sent me to do all these works, and that I have not done them of mine own mind. 16:29 If these men die the common death of all men, and be visited after the visitation of all men, then the LORD hath not sent Me. 16:30 But if the LORD make a new thing, and the ground open her mouth, and swallow them up, with all that appertain unto them, and they go down alive into the pit, then ye shall understand that these men have despised the LORD.' 16:31 And it came to pass, as he made an end of speaking all these words, that the ground did cleave asunder that was under them. 16:32 And the earth opened her mouth and swallowed them up, and their households, and all the men that appertained unto Korah, and all their goods. 16:33 So they, and all that appertained to them, went down alive into the pit; and the earth closed upon them, and they perished from among the assembly. 16:34 And all Israel that were round about them fled at the cry of them; for they said: 'Lest the earth swallow us up.' 16:35 And fire came forth from the LORD, and devoured the two hundred and fifty men that offered the incense. {S}

C 17:16 And the LORD spoke unto Moses, saying: 17:17 'Speak unto the children of Israel, and take of them rods, one for each fathers' house, of all their princes according to their fathers' houses, twelve rods; thou shalt write every man's name upon his rod. 17:18 And thou shalt write Aaron's name upon the rod of Levi, for there shall be one rod for the head of their fathers' houses. 17:19 And thou shalt lay them up in the tent of meeting before the testimony, where I meet with you. 17:20 And it shall come to pass, that the man whom I shall choose, his rod shall bud; and I will make to cease from Me the murmurings of the children of Israel, which they murmur against you.' 17:21 And Moses spoke unto the children of Israel; and all their princes gave him rods, for each prince one, according to their fathers' houses, even twelve rods; and the rod of Aaron was among their rods. 17:22 And Moses laid up the rods before the LORD in the tent of the testimony. 17:23 And it came to pass on the morrow, that Moses went into the tent of the testimony; and, behold, the rod of Aaron for the house of Levi was budded, and put forth buds, and bloomed blossoms, and bore ripe almonds. 17:24 And Moses brought out all the rods from before the LORD unto all the children of Israel; and they looked, and took every man his rod. {P}

17:25 And the LORD said unto Moses: 'Put back the rod of Aaron before the testimony, to be kept there, for a token against the rebellious children; that there may be made an end of their murmurings against Me, that they die not.' 17:26 Thus did Moses; as the LORD commanded him, so did he. {P}

Numbers Unit VIII (17:27-19:22)

א

17:27 And the children of Israel spoke unto Moses, saying: 'Behold, we perish, we are undone, we are all undone. 17:28 Every one that cometh near, that cometh near unto the tabernacle of the LORD, is to die; shall we wholly perish?' {S} 18:1 And the LORD said unto Aaron: 'Thou and thy sons and thy fathers' house with thee shall bear the iniquity of the sanctuary; and thou and thy sons with thee shall bear the iniquity of your priesthood. 18:2 And thy brethren also, the tribe of Levi, the tribe of thy father, bring thou near with thee, that they may be joined unto thee, and minister unto thee, thou and thy sons with thee being before the tent of the testimony. 18:3 And they shall keep thy charge, and the charge of all the Tent; only they shall not come nigh unto the holy furniture and unto the altar, that they die not, neither they, nor ye. 18:4 And they shall be joined unto thee, and keep the charge of the tent of meeting, whatsoever the service of the Tent may be; but a common man shall not draw nigh unto you. 18:5 And ye shall keep the charge of the holy things, and the charge of the altar, that there be wrath no more upon the children of Israel. 18:6 And I, behold, I have taken your brethren the Levites from among the children of Israel; for you they are given as a gift unto the LORD, to do the service of the tent of meeting. 18:7 And thou and thy sons with thee shall keep your priesthood in everything that pertaineth to the altar, and to that within the veil; and ye shall serve; I give you the priesthood as a service of gift; and the common man that draweth nigh shall be put to death.' {P}

ב

18:8 And the LORD spoke unto Aaron: 'And I, behold, I have given thee the charge of My heave-offerings; even of all the hallowed things of the children of Israel unto thee have I given them for a consecrated portion, and to thy sons, as a due for ever. 18:9 This shall be thine of the most holy things, reserved from the fire: every offering of theirs, even every meal-offering of theirs, and every sin-offering of theirs, and every guilt-offering of theirs, which they may render unto Me, shall be most holy for thee and for thy sons. 18:10 In a most holy place shalt thou eat thereof; every male may eat thereof; it shall be holy unto thee. 18:11 And this is thine: the heave-offering of their gift, even all the wave-offerings of the children of Israel; I have given them unto thee, and to thy sons and to thy daughters with thee, as a due for ever; every one that is clean in thy house may eat thereof. 18:12 All the best of the oil, and all the best of the wine, and of the corn, the first part of them which they give unto the LORD, to thee have I given them. 18:13 The first-ripe fruits of all that is in their land, which they bring unto the LORD, shall be thine; every one that is clean in thy house may eat thereof. 18:14 Every thing devoted in Israel shall be thine. 18:15 Every thing that openeth the womb, of all flesh which they offer unto the LORD, both of man and beast, shall be thine; howbeit the first-born of man shalt thou surely redeem, and the firstling of unclean beasts shalt thou redeem. 18:16 And their redemption-money--from a month old shalt thou redeem them--shall be, according to thy valuation, five shekels of silver, after the shekel of the sanctuary--the same is twenty gerahs. 18:17 But the firstling of an ox, or the firstling of a sheep, or the firstling of a goat, thou shalt not redeem; they are holy: thou shalt dash their blood against the altar, and shalt make their fat smoke for an offering made by fire, for a sweet savour unto the LORD. 18:18 And the flesh of them shall be thine, as the wave-breast and as the right thigh, it shall be thine. 18:19 All the heave-offerings of the holy things, which the children of Israel offer unto the LORD, have I given thee, and thy sons and thy daughters with thee, as a due for ever; it is an everlasting covenant of salt before the LORD unto thee and to thy seed with thee.' 18:20 And the LORD said unto Aaron: 'Thou shalt have no inheritance in their land, neither shalt thou have any portion among them; I am thy portion and thine inheritance among the children of Israel. {S} 18:21 And unto the children of Levi, behold, I have given all the tithe in Israel for an inheritance, in return for their service which they serve, even the service of the tent of meeting. 18:22 And henceforth the children of Israel shall not come nigh the tent of meeting, lest they bear sin, and die. 18:23 But the Levites alone shall do the service of the tent of meeting, and they shall bear their iniquity; it shall be a statute for ever throughout your generations, and among the children of Israel they shall have no inheritance. 18:24 For the tithe of the children of Israel, which they set apart as a gift unto the LORD, I have given to the Levites for an inheritance; therefore I have said unto them: Among the children of Israel they shall have no inheritance.' {P}

ג

18:25 And the LORD spoke unto Moses, saying: 18:26 'Moreover thou shalt speak unto the Levites, and say unto them: When ye take of the children of Israel the tithe which I have given you from them for your inheritance, then ye shall set apart of it a gift for the LORD, even a tithe of the tithe. 18:27 And the gift which ye set apart shall be reckoned unto you, as though it were the corn of the threshing-floor, and as the fulness of the wine-press. 18:28 Thus ye also shall set apart a gift unto the LORD of all your tithes, which ye receive of the children of Israel; and thereof ye shall give the gift which is set apart unto the LORD to Aaron the priest. 18:29 Out of all that is given you ye shall set apart all of that which is due unto the LORD, of all the best thereof, even the hallowed part thereof out of it. 18:30 Therefore thou shalt say unto them: When ye set apart the best thereof from it, then it shall be counted unto the Levites as the increase of the threshing-floor, and as the increase of the wine-press. 18:31 And ye may eat it in every place, ye and your households; for it is your reward in return for your service in the tent of meeting. 18:32 And ye shall bear no sin by reason of it, seeing that ye have set apart from it the best thereof; and ye shall not profane the holy things of the children of Israel, that ye die not.' {P}

2א

19:1 And the LORD spoke unto Moses and unto Aaron, saying: 19:2 This is the statute of the law which the LORD hath commanded, saying: Speak unto the children of Israel, that they bring thee a red heifer, faultless, wherein is no blemish, and upon which never came yoke. 19:3 And ye shall give her unto Eleazar the priest, and she shall be brought forth without the camp, and she shall be slain before his face. 19:4 And Eleazar the priest shall take of her blood with his finger, and sprinkle of her blood toward the front of the tent of meeting seven times. 19:5 And the heifer shall be burnt in his sight; her skin, and her flesh, and her blood, with her dung, shall be burnt. 19:6 And the priest shall take cedarwood, and hyssop, and scarlet, and cast it into the midst of the burning of the heifer. 19:7 Then the priest shall wash his clothes, and he shall bathe his flesh in water, and afterward he may come into the camp, and the priest shall be unclean until the even. 19:8 And he that burneth her shall wash his clothes in water, and bathe his flesh in water, and shall be unclean until the even. 19:9 And a man that is clean shall gather up the ashes of the heifer, and lay them up without the camp in a clean place, and it shall be kept for the congregation of the children of Israel for a water of sprinkling; it is a purification from sin. 19:10 And he that gathereth the ashes of the heifer shall wash his clothes, and be unclean until the even; and it shall be unto the children of Israel, and unto the stranger that sojourneth among them, for a statute for ever.

2ב

19:11 He that toucheth the dead, even any man's dead body, shall be unclean seven days; 19:12 the same shall purify himself therewith on the third day and on the seventh day, and he shall be clean; but if he purify not himself the third day and the seventh day, he shall not be clean. 19:13 Whosoever toucheth the dead, even the body of any man that is dead, and purifieth not himself--he hath defiled the tabernacle of the LORD--that soul shall be cut off from Israel; because the water of sprinkling was not dashed against him, he shall be unclean; his uncleanness is yet upon him.

2ג

19:14 This is the law: when a man dieth in a tent, every one that cometh into the tent, and every thing that is in the tent, shall be unclean seven days. 19:15 And every open vessel, which hath no covering close-bound upon it, is unclean. 19:16 And whosoever in the open field toucheth one that is slain with a sword, or one that dieth of himself, or a bone of a man, or a grave, shall be unclean seven days. 19:17 And for the unclean they shall take of the ashes of the burning of the purification from sin, and running water shall be put thereto in a vessel. 19:18 And a clean person shall take hyssop, and dip it in the water, and sprinkle it upon the tent, and upon all the vessels, and upon the persons that were there, and upon him that touched the bone, or the slain, or the dead, or the grave. 19:19 And the clean person shall sprinkle upon the unclean on the third day, and on the seventh day; and on the seventh day he shall purify him; and he shall wash his clothes, and bathe himself in water, and shall be clean at even. 19:20 But the man that shall be unclean, and shall not purify himself, that soul shall be cut off from the midst of the assembly, because he hath defiled the sanctuary of the LORD; the water of sprinkling hath not been dashed against him: he is unclean. 19:21 And it shall be a perpetual statute unto them; and he that sprinkleth the water of sprinkling shall wash his clothes; and he that toucheth the water of sprinkling shall be unclean until even. 19:22 And whatsoever the unclean person toucheth shall be unclean; and the soul that toucheth him shall be unclean until even. {P}

Numbers Unit IX (20:1-22:1)

1א

20:1 And the children of Israel, even the whole congregation, came into the wilderness of Zin in the first month; and the people abode in Kadesh; and Miriam died there, and was buried there. 20:2 And there was no water for the congregation; and they assembled themselves together against Moses and against Aaron. 20:3 And the people strove with Moses, and spoke, saying: 'Would that we had perished when our brethren perished before the LORD! 20:4 And why have ye brought the assembly of the LORD into this wilderness, to die there, we and our cattle? 20:5 And wherefore have ye made us to come up out of Egypt, to bring us in unto this evil place? it is no place of seed, or of figs, or of vines, or of pomegranates; neither is there any water to drink.' 20:6 And Moses and Aaron went from the presence of the assembly unto the door of the tent of meeting, and fell upon their faces; and the glory of the LORD appeared unto them. {P}
20:7 And the LORD spoke unto Moses, saying: 20:8 'Take the rod, and assemble the congregation, thou, and Aaron thy brother, and speak ye unto the rock before their eyes, that it give forth its water; and thou shalt bring forth to them water out of the rock; so thou shalt give the congregation and their cattle drink.' 20:9 And Moses took the rod from before the LORD, as He commanded him. 20:10 And Moses and Aaron gathered the assembly together before the rock, and he said unto them: 'Hear now, ye rebels; are we to bring you forth water out of this rock?' 20:11 And Moses lifted up his hand, and smote the rock with his rod twice; and water came forth abundantly, and the congregation drank, and their cattle. {S} 20:12 And the LORD said unto Moses and Aaron: 'Because ye believed not in Me, to sanctify Me in the eyes of the children of Israel, therefore ye shall not bring this assembly into the land which I have given them.' 20:13 These are the waters of Meribah, where the children of Israel strove with the LORD, and He was sanctified in them. {S}

2א

20:22 And they journeyed from Kadesh; and the children of Israel, even the whole congregation, came unto mount Hor. 20:23 And the LORD spoke unto Moses and Aaron in mount Hor, by the border of the land of Edom, saying: 20:24 'Aaron shall be gathered unto his people; for he shall not enter into the land which I have given unto the children of Israel, because ye rebelled against My word at the waters of Meribah. 20:25 Take Aaron and Eleazar his son, and bring them up unto mount Hor. 20:26 And strip Aaron of his garments, and put them upon Eleazar his son; and Aaron shall be gathered unto his people, and shall die there.' 20:27 And Moses did as the LORD commanded; and they went up into mount Hor in the sight of all the congregation. 20:28 And Moses stripped Aaron of his garments, and put them upon Eleazar his son; and Aaron died there in the top of the mount; and Moses and Eleazar came down from the mount. 20:29 And when all the congregation saw that Aaron was dead, they wept for Aaron thirty days, even all the house of Israel. {S}

1ב

20:14 And Moses sent messengers from Kadesh unto the king of Edom: 'Thus saith thy brother Israel: Thou knowest all the travail that hath befallen us; 20:15 how our fathers went down into Egypt, and we dwelt in Egypt a long time; and the Egyptians dealt ill with us, and our fathers; 20:16 and when we cried unto the LORD, He heard our voice, and sent an angel, and brought us forth out of Egypt; and, behold, we are in Kadesh, a city in the uttermost of thy border. 20:17 Let us pass, I pray thee, through thy land; we will not pass through field or through vineyard, neither will we drink of the water of the wells; we will go along the king's highway, we will not turn aside to the right hand nor to the left, until we have passed thy border.' 20:18 And Edom said unto him: 'Thou shalt not pass through me, lest I come out with the sword against thee.' 20:19 And the children of Israel said unto him: 'We will go up by the highway; and if we drink of thy water, I and my cattle, then will I give the price thereof; let me only pass through on my feet; there is no hurt.' 20:20 And he said: 'Thou shalt not pass through.' And Edom came out against him with much people, and with a strong hand. 20:21 Thus Edom refused to give Israel passage through his border; wherefore Israel turned away from him. {P}

2ב

21:1 And the Canaanite, the king of Arad, who dwelt in the South, heard tell that Israel came by the way of Atharim; and he fought against Israel, and took some of them captive. 21:2 And Israel vowed a vow unto the LORD, and said: 'If Thou wilt indeed deliver this people into my hand, then I will utterly destroy their cities.' 21:3 And the LORD hearkened to the voice of Israel, and delivered up the Canaanites; and they utterly destroyed them and their cities; and the name of the place was called Hormah. {P}

א3

A 21:4 And they journeyed from mount Hor by the way to the Red Sea, to compass the land of Edom; and the soul of the people became impatient because of the way. 21:5 And the people spoke against God, and against Moses: 'Wherefore have ye brought us up out of Egypt to die in the wilderness? for there is no bread, and there is no water; and our soul loatheth this light bread.' 21:6 And the LORD sent fiery serpents among the people, and they bit the people; and much people of Israel died. 21:7 And the people came to Moses, and said: 'We have sinned, because we have spoken against the LORD, and against thee; pray unto the LORD, that He take away the serpents from us.' And Moses prayed for the people. 21:8 And the LORD said unto Moses: 'Make thee a fiery serpent, and set it upon a pole; and it shall come to pass, that every one that is bitten, when he seeth it, shall live.' 21:9 And Moses made a serpent of brass, and set it upon the pole; and it came to pass, that if a serpent had bitten any man, when he looked unto the serpent of brass, he lived. 21:10 And the children of Israel journeyed, and pitched in Oboth. 21:11 And they journeyed from Oboth, and pitched at Ije-abarim, in the wilderness which is in front of Moab, toward the sun-rising. 21:12 From thence they journeyed, and pitched in the valley of Zered. 21:13 From thence they journeyed, and pitched on the other side of the Arnon, which is in the wilderness, that cometh out of the border of the Amorites.--For Arnon is the border of Moab, between Moab and the Amorites;

B21:14 wherefore it is said in the book of the Wars of the LORD: Vaheb in Suphah, and the valleys of Arnon, 21:15 And the slope of the valleys that inclineth toward the seat of Ar, and leaneth upon the border of Moab.-- 21:16 And from thence to Beer; that is the well whereof the LORD said unto Moses: 'Gather the people together, and I will give them water.' {S} 21:17 Then sang Israel this song: Spring up, O well--sing ye unto it-- 21:18 The well, which the princes digged, which the nobles of the people delved, with the sceptre, and with their staves. And from the wilderness to Mattanah; 21:19 and from Mattanah to Nahaliel; and from Nahaliel to Bamoth; 21:20 and from Bamoth to the valley that is in the field of Moab, by the top of Pisgah, which looketh down upon the desert. {P}

א4

21:31 Thus Israel dwelt in the land of the Amorites. 21:32 And Moses sent to spy out Jazer, and they took the towns thereof, and drove out the Amorites that were there.

ב3

A21:21 And Israel sent messengers unto Sihon king of the Amorites, saying: 21:22 'Let me pass through thy land; we will not turn aside into field, or into vineyard; we will not drink of the water of the wells; we will go by the king's highway, until we have passed thy border.' 21:23 And Sihon would not suffer Israel to pass through his border; but Sihon gathered all his people together, and went out against Israel into the wilderness, and came to Jahaz; and he fought against Israel. 21:24 And Israel smote him with the edge of the sword, and possessed his land from the Arnon unto the Jabbok, even unto the children of Ammon; for the border of the children of Ammon was strong. 21:25 And Israel took all these cities; and Israel dwelt in all the cities of the Amorites, in Heshbon, and in all the towns thereof. 21:26 For Heshbon was the city of Sihon the king of the Amorites, who had fought against the former king of Moab, and taken all his land out of his hand, even unto the Arnon.

B21:27 Wherefore they that speak in parables say: Come ye to Heshbon! let the city of Sihon be built and established! 21:28 For a fire is gone out of Heshbon, a flame from the city of Sihon; it hath devoured Ar of Moab, the lords of the high places of Arnon. 21:29 Woe to thee, Moab! thou art undone, O people of Chemosh; he hath given his sons as fugitives, and his daughters into captivity, unto Sihon king of the Amorites. 21:30 We have shot at them--Heshbon is perished--even unto Dibon, and we have laid waste even unto Nophah, which reacheth unto Medeba.

ב4

21:33 And they turned and went up by the way of Bashan; and Og the king of Bashan went out against them, he and all his people, to battle at Edrei. 21:34 And the LORD said unto Moses: 'Fear him not; for I have delivered him into thy hand, and all his people, and his land; and thou shalt do to him as thou didst unto Sihon king of the Amorites, who dwelt at Heshbon.' 21:35 So they smote him, and his sons, and all his people, until there was none left him remaining; and they possessed his land. 22:1 And the children of Israel journeyed, and pitched in the plains of Moab beyond the Jordan at Jericho. {S}

Numbers Unit X (22:2-25:16)

1א

22:2 And Balak the son of Zippor saw all that Israel had done to the Amorites. 22:3 And Moab was sore afraid of the people, because they were many; and Moab was overcome with dread because of the children of Israel. 22:4 And Moab said unto the elders of Midian: 'Now will this multitude lick up all that is round about us, as the ox licketh up the grass of the field.'--And Balak the son of Zippor was king of Moab at that time.-- 22:5 And he sent messengers unto Balaam the son of Beor, to Pethor, which is by the River, to the land of the children of his people, to call him, saying: 'Behold, there is a people come out from Egypt; behold, they cover the face of the earth, and they abide over against me. 22:6 Come now therefore, I pray thee, curse me this people; for they are too mighty for me; peradventure I shall prevail, that we may smite them, and that I may drive them out of the land; for I know that he whom thou blessest is blessed, and he whom thou cursest is cursed.' 22:7 And the elders of Moab and the elders of Midian departed with the rewards of divination in their hand; and they came unto Balaam, and spoke unto him the words of Balak. 22:8 And he said unto them: 'Lodge here this night, and I will bring you back word, as the LORD may speak unto me'; and the princes of Moab abode with Balaam. 22:9 And God came unto Balaam, and said: 'What men are these with thee?' 22:10 And Balaam said unto God: 'Balak the son of Zippor, king of Moab, hath sent unto me [saying]: 22:11 Behold the people that is come out of Egypt, it covereth the face of the earth; now, come curse me them; peradventure I shall be able to fight against them, and shall drive them out.' 22:12 And God said unto Balaam: 'Thou shalt not go with them; thou shalt not curse the people; for they are blessed.' 22:13 And Balaam rose up in the morning, and said unto the princes of Balak: 'Get you into your land; for the LORD refuseth to give me leave to go with you.' 22:14 And the princes of Moab rose up, and they went unto Balak, and said: 'Balaam refuseth to come with us.' 22:15 And Balak sent yet again princes, more, and more honourable than they. 22:16 And they came to Balaam, and said to him: 'Thus saith Balak the son of Zippor: Let nothing, I pray thee, hinder thee from coming unto me; 22:17 for I will promote thee unto very great honour, and whatsoever thou sayest unto me I will do; come therefore, I pray thee, curse me this people.' 22:18 And Balaam answered and said unto the servants of Balak: 'If Balak would give me his house full of silver and gold, I cannot go beyond the word of the LORD my God, to do any thing, small or great. 22:19 Now therefore, I pray you, tarry ye also here this night, that I may know what the LORD will speak unto me more.' 22:20 And God came unto Balaam at night, and said unto him: 'If the men are come to call thee, rise up, go with them; but only the word which I speak unto thee, that shalt thou do.'

2א

A 22:36 And when Balak heard that Balaam was come, he went out to meet him unto Ir-moab, which is on the border of Arnon, which is in the utmost part of the border. 22:37 And Balak said unto Balaam: 'Did I not earnestly send unto thee to call thee? wherefore camest thou not unto me? am I not able indeed to promote thee to honour?' 22:38 And Balaam said unto Balak: 'Lo, I am come unto thee; have I now any power at all to speak any thing? the word that God putteth in my mouth, that shall I speak.' 22:39 And Balaam went with Balak, and they came unto Kiriath-huzoth. 22:40 And Balak sacrificed oxen and sheep, and sent to Balaam, and to the princes that were with him. 22:41 And it came to pass in the morning that Balak took Balaam, and brought him up into Bamoth-baal, and he saw from thence the utmost part of the people. 23:1 And Balaam said unto Balak: 'Build me here seven altars, and prepare me here seven bullocks and seven rams.' 23:2 And Balak did as Balaam had spoken; and Balak and Balaam offered on every altar a bullock and a ram. 23:3 And Balaam said unto Balak: 'Stand by thy burnt-offering, and I will go; peradventure the LORD will come to meet me; and whatsoever He showeth me I will tell thee.' And he went to a bare height. 23:4 And God met Balaam; and he said unto Him: 'I have prepared the seven altars, and I have offered up a bullock and a ram on every altar.' 23:5 And the LORD put a word in Balaam's mouth, and said: 'Return unto Balak, and thus thou shalt speak.' 23:6 And he returned unto him, and, lo, he stood by his burnt-offering, he, and all the princes of Moab.

B 23:7 And he took up his parable, and said: From Aram Balak bringeth me, the king of Moab from the mountains of the East: 'Come, curse me Jacob, and come, execrate Israel.' 23:8 How shall I curse, whom God hath not cursed? And how shall I execrate, whom the LORD hath not execrated? 23:9 For from the top of the rocks I see him, and from the hills I behold him: lo, it is a people that shall dwell alone, and shall not be reckoned among the nations. 23:10 Who hath counted the dust of Jacob, or numbered the stock of Israel? Let me die the death of the righteous, and let mine end be like his!

1ב

22:21 And Balaam rose up in the morning, and saddled his ass, and went with the princes of Moab. 22:22 And God's anger was kindled because he went; and the angel of the LORD placed himself in the way for an adversary against him.--Now he was riding upon his ass, and his two servants were with him.-- 22:23 And the ass saw the angel of the LORD standing in the way, with his sword drawn in his hand; and the ass turned aside out of the way, and went into the field; and Balaam smote the ass, to turn her into the way. 22:24 Then the angel of the LORD stood in a hollow way between the vineyards, a fence being on this side, and a fence on that side. 22:25 And the ass saw the angel of the LORD, and she thrust herself unto the wall, and crushed Balaam's foot against the wall; and he smote her again. 22:26 And the angel of the LORD went further, and stood in a narrow place, where was no way to turn either to the right hand or to the left. 22:27 And the ass saw the angel of the LORD, and she lay down under Balaam; and Balaam's anger was kindled, and he smote the ass with his staff. 22:28 And the LORD opened the mouth of the ass, and she said unto Balaam: 'What have I done unto thee, that thou hast smitten me these three times?' 22:29 And Balaam said unto the ass: 'Because thou hast mocked me; I would there were a sword in my hand, for now I had killed thee.' 22:30 And the ass said unto Balaam: 'Am not I thine ass, upon which thou hast ridden all thy life long unto this day? was I ever wont to do so unto thee?' And he said: 'Nay.' 22:31 Then the LORD opened the eyes of Balaam, and he saw the angel of the LORD standing in the way, with his sword drawn in his hand; and he bowed his head, and fell on his face. 22:32 And the angel of the LORD said unto him: 'Wherefore hast thou smitten thine ass these three times? behold, I am come forth for an adversary, because thy way is contrary unto me; 22:33 and the ass saw me, and turned aside before me these three times; unless she had turned aside from me, surely now I had even slain thee, and saved her alive.' 22:34 And Balaam said unto the angel of the LORD: 'I have sinned; for I knew not that thou stoodest in the way against me; now therefore, if it displease thee, I will get me back.' 22:35 And the angel of the LORD said unto Balaam: 'Go with the men; but only the word that I shall speak unto thee, that thou shalt speak.' So Balaam went with the princes of Balak.

2ב

A 23:11 And Balak said unto Balaam: 'What hast thou done unto me? I took thee to curse mine enemies, and, behold, thou hast blessed them altogether.' 23:12 And he answered and said: 'Must I not take heed to speak that which the LORD putteth in my mouth?' 23:13 And Balak said unto him: 'Come, I pray thee, with me unto another place, from whence thou mayest see them; thou shalt see but the utmost part of them, and shalt not see them all; and curse me them from thence.' 23:14 And he took him into the field of Zophim, to the top of Pisgah, and built seven altars, and offered up a bullock and a ram on every altar. 23:15 And he said unto Balak: 'Stand here by thy burnt-offering, while I go toward a meeting yonder.' 23:16 And the LORD met Balaam, and put a word in his mouth, and said: 'Return unto Balak, and thus shalt thou speak.' 23:17 And he came to him, and, lo, he stood by his burnt-offering, and the princes of Moab with him. And Balak said unto him: 'What hath the LORD spoken?'

B 23:18 And he took up his parable, and said: Arise, Balak, and hear; give ear unto me, thou son of Zippor: 23:19 God is not a man, that He should lie; neither the son of man, that He should repent: when He hath said, will He not do it? or when He hath spoken, will He not make it good? 23:20 Behold, I am bidden to bless; and when He hath blessed, I cannot call it back. 23:21 None hath beheld iniquity in Jacob, neither hath one seen perverseness in Israel; the LORD his God is with him, and the shouting for the King is among them. 23:22 God who brought them forth out of Egypt is for them like the lofty horns of the wild-ox. 23:23 For there is no enchantment with Jacob, neither is there any divination with Israel; now is it said of Jacob and of Israel: 'What hath God wrought!' 23:24 Behold a people that riseth up as a lioness, and as a lion doth he lift himself up; he shall not lie down until he eat of the prey, and drink the blood of the slain.

3א

A 23:25 And Balak said unto Balaam: 'Neither curse them at all, nor bless them at all.' 23:26 But Balaam answered and said unto Balak: 'Told not I thee, saying: All that the LORD speaketh, that I must do?' 23:27 And Balak said unto Balaam: 'Come now, I will take thee unto another place; peradventure it will please God that thou mayest curse me them from thence.' 23:28 And Balak took Balaam unto the top of Peor, that looketh down upon the desert. 23:29 And Balaam said unto Balak: 'Build me here seven altars, and prepare me here seven bullocks and seven rams.' 23:30 And Balak did as Balaam had said, and offered up a bullock and a ram on every altar. 24:1 And when Balaam saw that it pleased the LORD to bless Israel, he went not, as at the other times, to meet with enchantments, but he set his face toward the wilderness. 24:2 And Balaam lifted up his eyes, and he saw Israel dwelling tribe by tribe; and the spirit of God came upon him.

B 24:3 And he took up his parable, and said: The saying of Balaam the son of Beor, and the saying of the man whose eye is opened; 24:4 The saying of him who heareth the words of God, who seeth the vision of the Almighty, fallen down, yet with opened eyes: 24:5 How goodly are thy tents, O Jacob, thy dwellings, O Israel! 24:6 As valleys stretched out, as gardens by the river-side; as aloes planted of the LORD, as cedars beside the waters; 24:7 Water shall flow from his branches, and his seed shall be in many waters; and his king shall be higher than Agag, and his kingdom shall be exalted. 24:8 God who brought him forth out of Egypt is for him like the lofty horns of the wild-ox; he shall eat up the nations that are his adversaries, and shall break their bones in pieces, and pierce them through with his arrows. 24:9 He couched, he lay down as a lion, and as a lioness; who shall rouse him up? Blessed be every one that blesseth thee, and cursed be every one that curseth thee.

3ב

A 24:10 And Balak's anger was kindled against Balaam, and he smote his hands together; and Balak said unto Balaam: 'I called thee to curse mine enemies, and, behold, thou hast altogether blessed them these three times. 24:11 Therefore now flee thou to thy place; I thought to promote thee unto great honour; but, lo, the LORD hath kept thee back from honour.' 24:12 And Balaam said unto Balak: 'Spoke I not also to thy messengers that thou didst send unto me, saying: 24:13 If Balak would give me his house full of silver and gold, I cannot go beyond the word of the LORD, to do either good or bad of mine own mind; what the LORD speaketh, that will I speak? 24:14 And now, behold, I go unto my people; come, and I will announce to thee what this people shall do to thy people in the end of days.'

B 24:15 And he took up his parable, and said: The saying of Balaam the son of Beor, and the saying of the man whose eye is opened; 24:16 The saying of him who heareth the words of God, and knoweth the knowledge of the Most High, who seeth the vision of the Almighty, fallen down, yet with opened eyes: 24:17 I see him, but not now; I behold him, but not nigh; there shall step forth a star out of Jacob, and a scepter shall rise out of Israel, and shall smite through the corners of Moab, and break down all the sons of Seth. 24:18 And Edom shall be a possession, Seir also, even his enemies, shall be a possession; while Israel doeth valiantly. 24:19 And out of Jacob shall one have dominion, and shall destroy the remnant from the city. 24:20 And he looked on Amalek, and took up his parable, and said: Amalek was the first of the nations; but his end shall come to destruction. 24:21 And he looked on the Kenite, and took up his parable, and said: Though firm be thy dwelling-place, and though thy nest be set in the rock; 24:22 Nevertheless Kain shall be wasted; How long? Asshur shall carry thee away captive. 24:23 And he took up his parable, and said: Alas, who shall live after God hath appointed him? 24:24 But ships shall come from the coast of Kittim, and they shall afflict Asshur, and shall afflict Eber, and he also shall come to destruction. 24:25 And Balaam rose up, and went and returned to his place; and Balak also went his way. {P}

4א

A 25:1 And Israel abode in Shittim, and the people began to commit harlotry with the daughters of Moab. 25:2 And they called the people unto the sacrifices of their gods; and the people did eat, and bowed down to their gods. 25:3 And Israel joined himself unto the Baal of Peor; and the anger of the LORD was kindled against Israel. 25:4 And the LORD said unto Moses: 'Take all the chiefs of the people, and hang them up unto the LORD in face of the sun, that the fierce anger of the LORD may turn away from Israel.' 25:5 And Moses said unto the judges of Israel: 'Slay ye every one his men that have joined themselves unto the Baal of Peor.'

B 25:6 And, behold, one of the children of Israel came and brought unto his brethren a Midianitish woman in the sight of Moses, and in the sight of all the congregation of the children of Israel, while they were weeping at the door of the tent of meeting. 25:7 And when Phinehas, the son of Eleazar, the son of Aaron the priest, saw it, he rose up from the midst of the congregation, and took a spear in his hand. 25:8 And he went after the man of Israel into the chamber, and thrust both of them through, the man of Israel, and the woman through her belly. So the plague was stayed from the children of Israel. 25:9 And those that died by the plague were twenty and four thousand. {P}

4ב

A 25:10 And the LORD spoke unto Moses, saying: 25:11 'Phinehas, the son of Eleazar, the son of Aaron the priest, hath turned My wrath away from the children of Israel, in that he was very jealous for My sake among them, so that I consumed not the children of Israel in My jealousy. 25:12 Wherefore say: Behold, I give unto him My covenant of peace; 25:13 and it shall be unto him, and to his seed after him, the covenant of an everlasting priesthood; because he was jealous for his God, and made atonement for the children of Israel.' 25:14 Now the name of the man of Israel that was slain, who was slain with the Midianitish woman, was Zimri, the son of Salu, a prince of a fathers' house among the Simeonites. 25:15 And the name of the Midianitish woman that was slain was Cozbi, the daughter of Zur; he was head of the people of a fathers' house in Midian. {P}

B 25:16 And the LORD spoke unto Moses, saying: 25:17 'Harass the Midianites, and smite them; 25:18 for they harass you, by their wiles wherewith they have beguiled you in the matter of Peor, and in the matter of Cozbi, the daughter of the prince of Midian, their sister, who was slain on the day of the plague in the matter of Peor.'

Numbers Unit XI (26:1-27:23)

1א

A 26:1 And it came to pass after the plague, {P} that the LORD spoke unto Moses and unto Eleazar the son of Aaron the priest, saying: 26:2 'Take the sum of all the congregation of the children of Israel, from twenty years old and upward, by their fathers' houses, all that are able to go forth to war in Israel.' 26:3 And Moses and Eleazar the priest spoke with them in the plains of Moab by the Jordan at Jericho, saying: 26:4 '[Take the sum of the people,] from twenty years old and upward, as the LORD commanded Moses and the children of Israel, that came forth out of the land of Egypt.' 26:5 Reuben, the first-born of Israel: the sons of Reuben: of Hanoch, the family of the Hanochites; of Pallu, the family of the Palluites; 26:6 of Hezron, the family of the Hezronites; of Carmi, the family of the Carmites. 26:7 These are the families of the Reubenites; and they that were numbered of them were forty and three thousand and seven hundred and thirty. 26:8 And the sons of Pallu: Eliab. 26:9 And the sons of Eliab: Nemuel, and Dathan, and Abiram. These are that Dathan and Abiram, the elect of the congregation, who strove against Moses and against Aaron in the company of Korah, when they strove against the LORD; 26:10 and the earth opened her mouth, and swallowed them up together with Korah, when that company died; what time the fire devoured two hundred and fifty men, and they became a sign. 26:11 Notwithstanding the sons of Korah died not. {S} 26:12 The sons of Simeon after their families: of Nemuel, the family of the Nemuelites; of Jamin, the family of the Jaminites; of Jachin, the family of the Jachinites; 26:13 of Zerah, the family of the Zerahites; of Shaul, the family of the Shaulites. 26:14 These are the families of the Simeonites, twenty and two thousand and two hundred. {S} 26:15 The sons of Gad after their families: of Zephon, the family of the Zephonites; of Haggi, the family of the Haggites; of Shuni, the family of the Shunites; 26:16 of Ozni, the family of the Oznites; of Eri, the family of the Erites; 26:17 of Arod, the family of the Arodites; of Areli, the family of the Arelites. 26:18 These are the families of the sons of Gad according to those that were numbered of them, forty thousand and five hundred. {S} 26:19 The sons of Judah: Er and Onan; and Er and Onan died in the land of Canaan. 26:20 And the sons of Judah after their families were: of Shelah, the family of the Shelanites; of Perez, the family of the Perezites; of Zerah, the family of the Zerahites. 26:21 And the sons of Perez were: of Hezron, the family of the Hezronites; of Hamul, the family of the Hamulites. 26:22 These are the families of Judah according to those that were numbered of them, threescore and sixteen thousand and five hundred. {S} 26:23 The sons of Issachar after their families: of Tola, the family of the Tolaites; of Puvah, the family of the Punites; 26:24 of Jashub, the family of the Jashubites; of Shimron, the family of the Shimronites. 26:25 These are the families of Issachar according to those that were numbered of them, threescore and four thousand and three hundred. {S} 26:26 The sons of Zebulun after their families: of Sered, the family of the Seredites; of Elon, the family of the Elonites; of Jahleel, the family of the Jahleelites. 26:27 These are the families of the Zebulunites according to those that were numbered of them, threescore thousand and five hundred. {S} 26:28 The sons of Joseph after their families: Manasseh and Ephraim. 26:29 The sons of Manasseh: of Machir, the family of the Machirites--and Machir begot Gilead; of Gilead, the family of the Gileadites. 26:30 These are the sons of Gilead: of Iezer, the family of the Iezerites; of Helek, the family of the Helekites; 26:31 and of Asriel, the family of the Asrielites; and of Shechem, the family of the Shechemites; 26:32 and of Shemida, the family of the Shemidaites; and of Hepher, the family of the Hepherites. 26:33 And Zelophehad the son of Hepher had no sons, but daughters; and the names of the daughters of Zelophehad were Mahlah, and Noah, Hoglah, Milcah, and Tirzah. 26:34 These are the families of Manasseh; and they that were numbered of them were fifty and two thousand and seven hundred. {S} 26:35 These are the sons of Ephraim after their families: of Shuthelah, the family of the Shuthelahites; of Becher, the family of the Becherites; of Tahan, the family of the Tahanites. 26:36 And these are the sons of Shuthelah: of Eran, the family of the Eranites. 26:37 These are the families of the sons of Ephraim according to those that were numbered of them, thirty and two thousand and five hundred. These are the sons of Joseph after their families. {S} 26:38 The sons of Benjamin after their families: of Bela, the family of the Belaites; of Ashbel, the family of the Ashbelites; of Ahiram, the family of the Ahiramites; 26:39 of Shephupham, the family of the Shuphamites; of Hupham, the family of the Huphamites. 26:40 And the sons of Bela were Ard and Naaman; [of Ard,] the family of the Ardites; of Naaman, the family of the Naamites. 26:41 These are the sons of Benjamin after their families; and they that were numbered of them were forty and five thousand and six hundred. {S} 26:42 These are the sons of Dan after their families: of Shuham, the family of the Shuhamites. These are the families of Dan after their families. 26:43 All the families of the Shuhamites, according to those that were numbered of them, were threescore and four thousand and four hundred. {S} 26:44 The sons of Asher after their families: of Imnah, the family of the Imnites; of Ishvi, the family of the Ishvites; of Beriah, the family of the Beriites. 26:45 Of the sons of Beriah: of Heber, the family of the Heberites; of Malchiel, the family of the Malchielites. 26:46 And the name of the daughter of Asher was Serah. 26:47 These are the families of the sons of Asher according to those that were numbered of them, fifty and three thousand and four hundred. {S} 26:48 The sons of Naphtali after their families: of Jahzeel, the family of the Jahzeelites; of Guni, the family of the Gunites; 26:49 of Jezer, the family of the Jezerites; of Shillem, the family of the Shillemites. 26:50 These are the families of Naphtali according to their families; and they that were numbered of them were forty and five thousand and four hundred. 26:51 These are they that were numbered of the children of Israel, six hundred thousand and a thousand and seven hundred and thirty. {P}

B 26:52 And the LORD spoke unto Moses, saying: 26:53 'Unto these the land shall be divided for an inheritance according to the number of names. 26:54 To the more thou shalt give the more inheritance, and to the fewer thou shalt give the less inheritance; to each one according to those that were numbered of it shall its inheritance be given. 26:55 Notwithstanding the land shall be divided by lot; according to the names of the tribes of their fathers they shall inherit. 26:56 According to the lot shall their inheritance be divided between the more and the fewer.' {S}

1ב

A 26:57 And these are they that were numbered of the Levites after their families: of Gershon, the family of the Gershonites; of Kohath, the family of the Kohathites; of Merari, the family of the Merarites. 26:58 These are the families of Levi: the family of the Libnites, the family of the Hebronites, the family of the Mahlites, the family of the Mushites, the family of the Korahites. And Kohath begot Amram. 26:59 And the name of Amram's wife was Jochebed, the daughter of Levi, who was born to Levi in Egypt; and she bore unto Amram Aaron and Moses, and Miriam their sister. 26:60 And unto Aaron were born Nadab and Abihu, Eleazar and Ithamar. 26:61 And Nadab and Abihu died, when they offered strange fire before the LORD. 26:62 And they that were numbered of them were twenty and three thousand, every male from a month old and upward; for they were not numbered among the children of Israel, because there was no inheritance given them among the children of Israel.

B 26:63 These are they that were numbered by Moses and Eleazar the priest, who numbered the children of Israel in the plains of Moab by the Jordan at Jericho. 26:64 But among these there was not a man of them that were numbered by Moses and Aaron the priest, who numbered the children of Israel in the wilderness of Sinai. 26:65 For the LORD had said of them: 'They shall surely die in the wilderness.' And there was not left a man of them, save Caleb the son of Jephunneh, and Joshua the son of Nun. {S}

אצ

A 27:1 Then drew near the daughters of Zelophehad, the son of Hepher, the son of Gilead, the son of Machir, the son of Manasseh, of the families of Manasseh the son of Joseph; and these are the names of his daughters: Mahlah, Noah, and Hoglah, and Milcah, and Tirzah. 27:2 And they stood before Moses, and before Eleazar the priest, and before the princes and all the congregation, at the door of the tent of meeting, saying: 27:3 'Our father died in the wilderness, and he was not among the company of them that gathered themselves together against the LORD in the company of Korah, but he died in his own sin; and he had no sons. 27:4 Why should the name of our father be done away from among his family, because he had no son? Give unto us a possession among the brethren of our father.' 27:5 And Moses brought their cause before the LORD. {P}

B 27:6 And the LORD spoke unto Moses, saying: 27:7 'The daughters of Zelophehad speak right: thou shalt surely give them a possession of an inheritance among their father's brethren; and thou shalt cause the inheritance of their father to pass unto them. 27:8 And thou shalt speak unto the children of Israel, saying: If a man die, and have no son, then ye shall cause his inheritance to pass unto his daughter. 27:9 And if he have no daughter, then ye shall give his inheritance unto his brethren. 27:10 And if he have no brethren, then ye shall give his inheritance unto his father's brethren. 27:11 And if his father have no brethren, then ye shall give his inheritance unto his kinsman that is next to him of his family, and he shall possess it. And it shall be unto the children of Israel a statute of judgment, as the LORD commanded Moses.' {P}

בצ

A 27:12 And the LORD said unto Moses: 'Get thee up into this mountain of Abarim, and behold the land which I have given unto the children of Israel. 27:13 And when thou hast seen it, thou also shalt be gathered unto thy people, as Aaron thy brother was gathered; 27:14 because ye rebelled against My commandment in the wilderness of Zin, in the strife of the congregation, to sanctify Me at the waters before their eyes.'--These are the waters of Meribath-kadesh in the wilderness of Zin.-- {S}

B 27:15 And Moses spoke unto the LORD, saying: 27:16 'Let the LORD, the God of the spirits of all flesh, set a man over the congregation, 27:17 who may go out before them, and who may come in before them, and who may lead them out, and who may bring them in; that the congregation of the LORD be not as sheep which have no shepherd.' 27:18 And the LORD said unto Moses: 'Take thee Joshua the son of Nun, a man in whom is spirit, and lay thy hand upon him; 27:19 and set him before Eleazar the priest, and before all the congregation; and give him a charge in their sight. 27:20 And thou shalt put of thy honour upon him, that all the congregation of the children of Israel may hearken. 27:21 And he shall stand before Eleazar the priest, who shall inquire for him by the judgment of the Urim before the LORD; at his word shall they go out, and at his word they shall come in, both he, and all the children of Israel with him, even all the congregation.' 27:22 And Moses did as the LORD commanded him; and he took Joshua, and set him before Eleazar the priest, and before all the congregation. 27:23 And he laid his hands upon him, and gave him a charge, as the LORD spoke by the hand of Moses. {P}

Numbers Unit XII (28:1-30:17)

א

A 28:1 And the LORD spoke unto Moses, saying: 28:2 Command the children of Israel, and say unto them: My food which is presented unto Me for offerings made by fire, of a sweet savour unto Me, shall ye observe to offer unto Me in its due season. 28:3 And thou shalt say unto them: This is the offering made by fire which ye shall bring unto the LORD: he-lambs of the first year without blemish, two day by day, for a continual burnt-offering. 28:4 The one lamb shalt thou offer in the morning, and the other lamb shalt thou offer at dusk; 28:5 and the tenth part of an ephah of fine flour for a meal-offering, mingled with the fourth part of a hin of beaten oil. 28:6 It is a continual burnt-offering, which was offered in mount Sinai, for a sweet savour, an offering made by fire unto the LORD. 28:7 And the drink-offering thereof shall be the fourth part of a hin for the one lamb; in the holy place shalt thou pour out a drink-offering of strong drink unto the LORD. 28:8 And the other lamb shalt thou present at dusk; as the meal-offering of the morning, and as the drink-offering thereof, thou shalt present it, an offering made by fire, of a sweet savour unto the LORD. {P}

B 28:9 And on the sabbath day two he-lambs of the first year without blemish, and two tenth parts of an ephah of fine flour for a meal-offering, mingled with oil, and the drink-offering thereof. 28:10 This is the burnt-offering of every sabbath, beside the continual burnt-offering, and the drink-offering thereof. {P}

C 28:11 And in your new moons ye shall present a burnt-offering unto the LORD: two young bullocks, and one ram, seven he-lambs of the first year without blemish; 28:12 and three tenth parts of an ephah of fine flour for a meal-offering, mingled with oil, for each bullock; and two tenth parts of fine flour for a meal-offering, mingled with oil, for the one ram; 28:13 and a several tenth part of fine flour mingled with oil for a meal-offering unto every lamb; for a burnt-offering of a sweet savour, an offering made by fire unto the LORD. 28:14 And their drink-offerings shall be half a hin of wine for a bullock, and the third part of a hin for the ram, and the fourth part of a hin for a lamb. This is the burnt-offering of every new moon throughout the months of the year. 28:15 And one he-goat for a sin-offering unto the LORD; it shall be offered beside the continual burnt-offering, and the drink-offering thereof. {S}

D 28:16 And in the first month, on the fourteenth day of the month, is the LORD'S passover. 28:17 And on the fifteenth day of this month shall be a feast; seven days shall unleavened bread be eaten. 28:18 In the first day shall be a holy convocation; ye shall do no manner of servile work; 28:19 but ye shall present an offering made by fire, a burnt-offering unto the LORD: two young bullocks, and one ram, and seven he-lambs of the first year; they shall be unto you without blemish; 28:20 and their meal-offering, fine flour mingled with oil; three tenth parts shall ye offer for a bullock, and two tenth parts for the ram; 28:21 a several tenth part shalt thou offer for every lamb of the seven lambs; 28:22 and one he-goat for a sin-offering, to make atonement for you. 28:23 Ye shall offer these beside the burnt-offering of the morning, which is for a continual burnt-offering. 28:24 After this manner ye shall offer daily, for seven days, the food of the offering made by fire, of a sweet savour unto the LORD; it shall be offered beside the continual burnt-offering, and the drink-offering thereof. 28:25 And on the seventh day ye shall have a holy convocation; ye shall do no manner of servile work. {S}

E 28:26 Also in the day of the first-fruits, when ye bring a new meal-offering unto the LORD in your feast of weeks, ye shall have a holy convocation: ye shall do no manner of servile work; 28:27 but ye shall present a burnt-offering for a sweet savour unto the LORD: two young bullocks, one ram, seven he-lambs of the first year; 28:28 and their meal-offering, fine flour mingled with oil, three tenth parts for each bullock, two tenth parts for the one ram, 28:29 a several tenth part for every lamb of the seven lambs; 28:30 one he-goat, to make atonement for you. 28:31 Beside the continual burnt-offering, and the meal-offering thereof, ye shall offer them--they shall be unto you without blemish--and their drink-offerings. {P}

F 29:1 And in the seventh month, on the first day of the month, ye shall have a holy convocation: ye shall do no manner of servile work; it is a day of blowing the horn unto you. 29:2 And ye shall prepare a burnt-offering for a sweet savour unto the LORD: one young bullock, one ram, seven he-lambs of the first year without blemish; 29:3 and their meal-offering, fine flour mingled with oil, three tenth parts for the bullock, two tenth part for the ram, 29:4 and one tenth part for every lamb of the seven lambs; 29:5 and one he-goat for a sin-offering, to make atonement for you; 29:6 beside the burnt-offering of the new moon, and the meal-offering thereof, and the continual burnt-offering and the meal-offering thereof, and their drink-offerings, according unto their ordinance, for a sweet savour, an offering made by fire unto the LORD. {S}

ב

A 30:2 And Moses spoke unto the heads of the tribes of the children of Israel, saying: This is the thing which the LORD hath commanded. 30:3 When a man voweth a vow unto the LORD, or sweareth an oath to bind his soul with a bond, he shall not break his word; he shall do according to all that proceedeth out of his mouth.

B 30:4 Also when a woman voweth a vow unto the LORD, and bindeth herself by a bond, being in her father's house, in her youth, 30:5 and her father heareth her vow, or her bond wherewith she hath bound her soul, and her father holdeth his peace at her, then all her vows shall stand, and every bond wherewith she hath bound her soul shall stand.

C 30:6 But if her father disallow her in the day that he heareth, none of her vows, or of her bonds wherewith she hath bound her soul, shall stand; and the LORD will forgive her, because her father disallowed her.

D 30:7 And if she be married to a husband, while her vows are upon her, or the clear utterance of her lips, wherewith she hath bound her soul; 30:8 and her husband hear it, whatsoever day it be that he heareth it, and hold his peace at her; then her vows shall stand, and her bonds wherewith she hath bound her soul shall stand.

E 30:9 But if her husband disallow her in the day that he heareth it, then he shall make void her vow which is upon her, and the clear utterance of her lips, wherewith she hath bound her soul; and the LORD will forgive her.

F 30:10 But the vow of a widow, or of her that is divorced, even every thing wherewith she hath bound her soul, shall stand against her. 30:11 And if a woman vowed in her husband's house, or bound her soul by a bond with an oath, 30:12 and her husband heard it, and held his peace at her, and disallowed her not, then all her vows shall stand, and every bond wherewith she bound her soul shall stand.

G29:7 And on the tenth day of this seventh month ye shall have a holy convocation; and ye shall afflict your souls; ye shall do no manner of work; 29:8 but ye shall present a burnt-offering unto the LORD for a sweet savour: one young bullock, one ram, seven he-lambs of the first year; they shall be unto you without blemish; 29:9 and their meal-offering, fine flour mingled with oil, three tenth parts for the bullock, two tenth parts for the one ram, 29:10 a several tenth part for every lamb of the seven lambs; 29:11 one he-goat for a sin-offering; beside the sin-offering of atonement, and the continual burnt-offering, and the meal-offering thereof, and their drink-offerings. {S}

H29:12 And on the fifteenth day of the seventh month ye shall have a holy convocation: ye shall do no manner of servile work, and ye shall keep a feast unto the LORD seven days; 29:13 and ye shall present a burnt-offering, an offering made by fire, of a sweet savour unto the LORD: thirteen young bullocks, two rams, fourteen he-lambs of the first year; they shall be without blemish; 29:14 and their meal-offering, fine flour mingled with oil, three tenth parts for every bullock of the thirteen bullocks, two tenth parts for each ram of the two rams, 29:15 and a several tenth part for every lamb of the fourteen lambs; 29:16 and one he-goat for a sin-offering beside the continual burnt-offering, the meal-offering thereof, and the drink-offering thereof. {S} 29:17 And on the second day ye shall present twelve young bullocks, two rams, fourteen he-lambs of the first year without blemish; 29:18 and their meal-offering and their drink-offerings for the bullocks, for the rams, and for the lambs, according to their number, after the ordinance; 29:19 and one he-goat for a sin-offering; beside the continual burnt-offering, and the meal-offering thereof, and their drink-offerings. {S} 29:20 And on the third day eleven bullocks, two rams, fourteen he-lambs of the first year without blemish; 29:21 and their meal-offering and their drink-offerings for the bullocks, for the rams, and for the lambs, according to their number, after the ordinance; 29:22 and one he-goat for a sin-offering; beside the continual burnt-offering, and the meal-offering thereof, and the drink-offering thereof. {S} 29:23 And on the fourth day ten bullocks, two rams, fourteen he-lambs of the first year without blemish; 29:24 their meal-offering and their drink-offerings for the bullocks, for the rams, and for the lambs, according to their number, after the ordinance; 29:25 and one he-goat for a sin-offering; beside the continual burnt-offering, the meal-offering thereof, and the drink-offering thereof. {S} 29:26 And on the fifth day nine bullocks, two rams, fourteen he-lambs of the first year without blemish; 29:27 and their meal-offering and their drink-offerings for the bullocks, for the rams, and for the lambs, according to their number, after the ordinance; 29:28 and one he-goat for a sin-offering; beside the continual burnt-offering, and the meal-offering thereof, and the drink-offering thereof. {S} 29:29 And on the sixth day eight bullocks, two rams, fourteen he-lambs of the first year without blemish; 29:30 and their meal-offering and their drink-offerings for the bullocks, for the rams, and for the lambs, according to their number, after the ordinance; 29:31 and one he-goat for a sin-offering; beside the continual burnt-offering, the meal-offering thereof, and the drink-offerings thereof. {S} 29:32 And on the seventh day seven bullocks, two rams, fourteen he-lambs of the first year without blemish; 29:33 and their meal-offering and their drink-offerings for the bullocks, for the rams, and for the lambs, according to their number, after the ordinance; 29:34 and one he-goat for a sin-offering; beside the continual burnt-offering, the meal-offering thereof, and the drink-offering thereof. {S} 29:35 On the eighth day ye shall have a solemn assembly: ye shall do no manner of servile work; 29:36 but ye shall present a burnt-offering, an offering made by fire, of a sweet savour unto the LORD: one bullock, one ram, seven he-lambs of the first year without blemish; 29:37 their meal-offering and their drink-offerings for the bullock, for the ram, and for the lambs, shall be according to their number, after the ordinance; 29:38 and one he-goat for a sin-offering; beside the continual burnt-offering, and the meal-offering thereof, and the drink-offering thereof. 29:39 These ye shall offer unto the LORD in your appointed seasons, beside your vows, and your freewill-offerings, whether they be your burnt-offerings, or your meal-offerings, or your drink-offerings, or your peace-offerings. 30:1 And Moses told the children of Israel according to all that the LORD commanded Moses. {P}

G30:13 But if her husband make them null and void in the day that he heareth them, then whatsoever proceeded out of her lips, whether it were her vows, or the bond of her soul, shall not stand: her husband hath made them void; and the LORD will forgive her.

H 30:14 Every vow, and every binding oath to afflict the soul, her husband may let it stand, or her husband may make it void. 30:15 But if her husband altogether hold his peace at her from day to day, then he causeth all her vows to stand, or all her bonds, which are upon her; he hath let them stand, because he held his peace at her in the day that he heard them. 30:16 But if he shall make them null and void after that he hath heard them, then he shall bear her iniquity. 30:17 These are the statutes, which the LORD commanded Moses, between a man and his wife, between a father and his daughter, being in her youth, in her father's house. {P}

Numbers Unit XIII (31:1-36:13)

A 31:1 And the LORD spoke unto Moses, saying: 31:2 'Avenge the children of Israel of the Midianites; afterward shalt thou be gathered unto thy people.' 31:3 And Moses spoke unto the people, saying: 'Arm ye men from among you for the war, that they may go against Midian, to execute the LORD'S vengeance on Midian. 31:4 Of every tribe a thousand, throughout all the tribes of Israel, shall ye send to the war.' 31:5 So there were delivered, out of the thousands of Israel, a thousand of every tribe, twelve thousand armed for war. 31:6 And Moses sent them, a thousand of every tribe, to the war, them and Phinehas the son of Eleazar the priest, to the war, with the holy vessels and the trumpets for the alarm in his hand. 31:7 And they warred against Midian, as the LORD commanded Moses; and they slew every male. 31:8 And they slew the kings of Midian with the rest of their slain: Evi, and Rekem, and Zur, and Hur, and Reba, the five kings of Midian; Balaam also the son of Beor they slew with the sword. 31:9 And the children of Israel took captive the women of Midian and their little ones; and all their cattle, and all their flocks, and all their goods, they took for a prey. 31:10 And all their cities in the places wherein they dwelt, and all their encampments, they burnt with fire. 31:11 And they took all the spoil, and all the prey, both of man and of beast. 31:12 And they brought the captives, and the prey, and the spoil, unto Moses, and unto Eleazar the priest, and unto the congregation of the children of Israel, unto the camp, unto the plains of Moab, which are by the Jordan at Jericho. {S}

B 31:13 And Moses, and Eleazar the priest, and all the princes of the congregation, went forth to meet them without the camp. 31:14 And Moses was wroth with the officers of the host, the captains of thousands and the captains of hundreds, who came from the service of the war. 31:15 And Moses said unto them: 'Have ye saved all the women alive? 31:16 Behold, these caused the children of Israel, through the counsel of Balaam, to revolt so as to break faith with the LORD in the matter of Peor, and so the plague was among the congregation of the LORD. 31:17 Now therefore kill every male among the little ones, and kill every woman that hath known man by lying with him. 31:18 But all the women children, that have not known man by lying with him, keep alive for yourselves. 31:19 And encamp ye without the camp seven days; whosoever hath killed any person, and whosoever hath touched any slain, purify yourselves on the third day and on the seventh day, ye and your captives. 31:20 And as to every garment, and all that is made of skin, and all work of goats' hair, and all things made of wood, ye shall purify.' {S}

A 32:1 Now the children of Reuben and the children of Gad had a very great multitude of cattle; and when they saw the land of Jazer, and the land of Gilead, that, behold, the place was a place for cattle, 32:2 the children of Gad and the children of Reuben came and spoke unto Moses, and to Eleazar the priest, and unto the princes of the congregation, saying: 32:3 'Ataroth, and Dibon, and Jazer, and Nimrah, and Heshbon, and Elealeh, and Sebam, and Nebo, and Beon, 32:4 the land which the LORD smote before the congregation of Israel, is a land for cattle, and thy servants have cattle.' {S}

B 32:5 And they said: 'If we have found favour in thy sight, let this land be given unto thy servants for a possession; bring us not over the Jordan.' 32:6 And Moses said unto the children of Gad and to the children of Reuben: 'Shall your brethren go to the war, and shall ye sit here? 32:7 And wherefore will ye turn away the heart of the children of Israel from going over into the land which the LORD hath given them? 32:8 Thus did your fathers, when I sent them from Kadesh-barnea to see the land. 32:9 For when they went up unto the valley of Eshcol, and saw the land, they turned away the heart of the children of Israel, that they should not go into the land which the LORD had given them. 32:10 And the LORD'S anger was kindled in that day, and He swore, saying: 32:11 Surely none of the men that came up out of Egypt, from twenty years old and upward, shall see the land which I swore unto Abraham, unto Isaac, and unto Jacob; because they have not wholly followed Me; 32:12 save Caleb the son of Jephunneh the Kenizzite, and Joshua the son of Nun; because they have wholly followed the LORD. 32:13 And the LORD'S anger was kindled against Israel, and He made them wander to and fro in the wilderness forty years, until all the generation, that had done evil in the sight of the LORD, was consumed. 32:14 And, behold, ye are risen up in your fathers' stead, a brood of sinful men, to augment yet the fierce anger of the LORD toward Israel. 32:15 For if ye turn away from after Him, He will yet again leave them in the wilderness; and so ye will destroy all this people.' {S}

C 31:21 And Eleazar the priest said unto the men of war that went to the battle: 'This is the statute of the law which the LORD hath commanded Moses: 31:22 Howbeit the gold, and the silver, the brass, the iron, the tin, and the lead, 31:23 every thing that may abide the fire, ye shall make to go through the fire, and it shall be clean; nevertheless it shall be purified with the water of sprinkling; and all that abideth not the fire ye shall make to go through the water. 31:24 And ye shall wash your clothes on the seventh day, and ye shall be clean, and afterward ye may come into the camp.' {S}

D 31:25 And the LORD spoke unto Moses, saying: 31:26 'Take the sum of the prey that was taken, both of man and of beast, thou, and Eleazar the priest, and the heads of the fathers' houses of the congregation; 31:27 and divide the prey into two parts: between the men skilled in war, that went out to battle, and all the congregation; 31:28 and levy a tribute unto the LORD of the men of war that went out to battle: one soul of five hundred, both of the persons, and of the beeves, and of the asses, and of the flocks; 31:29 take it of their half, and give it unto Eleazar the priest, as a portion set apart for the LORD. 31:30 And of the children of Israel's half, thou shalt take one drawn out of every fifty, of the persons, of the beeves, of the asses, and of the flocks, even of all the cattle, and give them unto the Levites, that keep the charge of the tabernacle of the LORD.' 31:31 And Moses and Eleazar the priest did as the LORD commanded Moses. 31:32 Now the prey, over and above the booty which the men of war took, was six hundred thousand and seventy thousand and five thousand sheep, 31:33 and threescore and twelve thousand beeves, 31:34 and threescore and one thousand asses, 31:35 and thirty and two thousand persons in all, of the women that had not known man by lying with him. 31:36 And the half, which was the portion of them that went out to war, was in number three hundred thousand and thirty thousand and seven thousand and five hundred sheep. 31:37 And the LORD'S tribute of the sheep was six hundred and threescore and fifteen. 31:38 And the beeves were thirty and six thousand, of which the LORD'S tribute was threescore and twelve. 31:39 And the asses were thirty thousand and five hundred, of which the LORD'S tribute was threescore and one. 31:40 And the persons were sixteen thousand, of whom the LORD'S tribute was thirty and two persons. 31:41 And Moses gave the tribute, which was set apart for the LORD, unto Eleazar the priest, as the LORD commanded Moses. 31:42 And of the children of Israel's half, which Moses divided off from the men that warred-- 31:43 now the congregation's half was three hundred thousand and thirty thousand and seven thousand and five hundred sheep, 31:44 and thirty and six thousand beeves, 31:45 and thirty thousand and five hundred asses, 31:46 and sixteen thousand persons-- 31:47 even of the children of Israel's half, Moses took one drawn out of every fifty, both of man and of beast, and gave them unto the Levites, that kept the charge of the tabernacle of the LORD; as the LORD commanded Moses. 31:48 And the officers that were over the thousands of the host, the captains of thousands, and the captains of hundreds, came near unto Moses; 31:49 and they said unto Moses: 'Thy servants have taken the sum of the men of war that are under our charge, and there lacketh not one man of us. 31:50 And we have brought the LORD'S offering, what every man hath gotten, of jewels of gold, armlets, and bracelets, signet-rings, ear-rings, and girdles, to make atonement for our souls before the LORD.' 31:51 And Moses and Eleazar the priest took the gold of them, even all wrought jewels. 31:52 And all the gold of the gift that they set apart for the LORD, of the captains of thousands, and of the captains of hundreds, was sixteen thousand seven hundred and fifty shekels.-- 31:53 For the men of war had taken booty, every man for himself.-- 31:54 And Moses and Eleazar the priest took the gold of the captains of thousands and of hundreds, and brought it into the tent of meeting, for a memorial for the children of Israel before the LORD. {P}

C 32:16 And they came near unto him, and said: 'We will build sheepfolds here for our cattle, and cities for our little ones; 32:17 but we ourselves will be ready armed to go before the children of Israel, until we have brought them unto their place; and our little ones shall dwell in the fortified cities because of the inhabitants of the land. 32:18 We will not return unto our houses, until the children of Israel have inherited every man his inheritance. 32:19 For we will not inherit with them on the other side of the Jordan, and forward, because our inheritance is fallen to us on this side of the Jordan eastward.' {P}

D 32:20 And Moses said unto them: 'If ye will do this thing: if ye will arm yourselves to go before the LORD to the war, 32:21 and every armed man of you will pass over the Jordan before the LORD, until He hath driven out His enemies from before Him, 32:22 and the land be subdued before the LORD, and ye return afterward; then ye shall be clear before the LORD, and before Israel, and this land shall be unto you for a possession before the LORD. 32:23 But if ye will not do so, behold, ye have sinned against the LORD; and know ye your sin which will find you. 32:24 Build you cities for your little ones, and folds for your sheep; and do that which hath proceeded out of your mouth.' 32:25 And the children of Gad and the children of Reuben spoke unto Moses, saying: 'Thy servants will do as my lord commandeth. 32:26 Our little ones, our wives, our flocks, and all our cattle, shall be there in the cities of Gilead; 32:27 but thy servants will pass over, every man that is armed for war, before the LORD to battle, as my lord saith.' 32:28 So Moses gave charge concerning them to Eleazar the priest, and to Joshua the son of Nun, and to the heads of the fathers' houses of the tribes of the children of Israel. 32:29 And Moses said unto them: 'If the children of Gad and the children of Reuben will pass with you over the Jordan, every man that is armed to battle, before the LORD, and the land shall be subdued before you, then ye shall give them the land of Gilead for a possession; 32:30 but if they will not pass over with you armed, they shall have possessions among you in the land of Canaan.' 32:31 And the children of Gad and the children of Reuben answered, saying: 'As the LORD hath said unto thy servants, so will we do. 32:32 We will pass over armed before the LORD into the land of Canaan, and the possession of our inheritance shall remain with us beyond the Jordan.' 32:33 And Moses gave unto them, even to the children of Gad, and to the children of Reuben, and unto the half-tribe of Manasseh the son of Joseph, the kingdom of Sihon king of the Amorites, and the kingdom of Og king of Bashan, the land, according to the cities thereof with their borders, even the cities of the land round about. 32:34 And the children of Gad built Dibon, and Ataroth, and Aroer; 32:35 and Atroth-shophan, and Jazer, and Jogbehah; 32:36 and Beth-nimrah, and Beth-haran; fortified cities, and folds for sheep. 32:37 And the children of Reuben built Heshbon, and Elealeh, and Kiriathaim; 32:38 and Nebo, and Baal-meon--their names being changed--and Sibmah; and gave their names unto the cities which they builded. 32:39 And the children of Machir the son of Manasseh went to Gilead, and took it, and dispossessed the Amorites that were therein. 32:40 And Moses gave Gilead unto Machir the son of Manasseh; and he dwelt therein. 32:41 And Jair the son of Manasseh went and took the villages thereof, and called them Havvoth-jair. 32:42 And Nobah went and took Kenath, and the villages thereof, and called it Nobah, after his own name. {P}

2

33:1 These are the stages of the children of Israel, by which they went forth out of the land of Egypt by their hosts under the hand of Moses and Aaron. 33:2 And Moses wrote their goings forth, stage by stage, by the commandment of the LORD; and these are their stages at their goings forth. 33:3 And they journeyed from Rameses in the first month, on the fifteenth day of the first month; on the morrow after the passover the children of Israel went out with a high hand in the sight of all the Egyptians, 33:4 while the Egyptians were burying them that the LORD had smitten among them, even all their first-born; upon their gods also the LORD executed judgments. 33:5 And the children of Israel journeyed from Rameses, and pitched in Succoth. 33:6 And they journeyed from Succoth, and pitched in Etham, which is in the edge of the wilderness. 33:7 And they journeyed from Etham, and turned back unto Pihahiroth, which is before Baal-zephon; and they pitched before Migdol. 33:8 And they journeyed from Penehahiroth, and passed through the midst of the sea into the wilderness; and they went three days' journey in the wilderness of Etham, and pitched in Marah. 33:9 And they journeyed from Marah, and came unto Elim; and in Elim were twelve springs of water, and threescore and ten palm-trees; and they pitched there. 33:10 And they journeyed from Elim, and pitched by the Red Sea. 33:11 And they journeyed from the Red Sea, and pitched in the wilderness of Sin. 33:12 And they journeyed from the wilderness of Sin, and pitched in Dophkah. 33:13 And they journeyed from Dophkah, and pitched in Alush. 33:14 And they journeyed from Alush, and pitched in Rephidim, where was no water for the people to drink. 33:15 And they journeyed from Rephidim, and pitched in the wilderness of Sinai. 33:16 And they journeyed from the wilderness of Sinai, and pitched in Kibroth-hattaavah. 33:17 And they journeyed from Kibroth-hattaavah, and pitched in Hazeroth. 33:18 And they journeyed from Hazeroth, and pitched in Rithmah. 33:19 And they journeyed from Rithmah, and pitched in Rimmon-perez. 33:20 And they journeyed from Rimmon-perez, and pitched in Libnah. 33:21 And they journeyed from Libnah, and pitched in Rissah. 33:22 And they journeyed from Rissah, and pitched in Kehelah. 33:23 And they journeyed from Kehelah, and pitched in mount Shepher. 33:24 And they journeyed from mount Shepher, and pitched in Haradah. 33:25 And they journeyed from Haradah, and pitched in Makheloth. 33:26 And they journeyed from Makheloth, and pitched in Tahath. 33:27 And they journeyed from Tahath, and pitched in Terah. 33:28 And they journeyed from Terah, and pitched in Mithkah. 33:29 And they journeyed from Mithkah, and pitched in Hashmonah. 33:30 And they journeyed from Hashmonah, and pitched in Moseroth. 33:31 And they journeyed from Moseroth, and pitched in Bene-jaakan. 33:32 And they journeyed from Bene-jaakan, and pitched in Hor-haggidgad. 33:33 And they journeyed from Hor-haggidgad, and pitched in Jotbah. 33:34 And they journeyed from Jotbah, and pitched in Abronah. 33:35 And they journeyed from Abronah, and pitched in Ezion-geber. 33:36 And they journeyed from Ezion-geber, and pitched in the wilderness of Zin--the same is Kadesh. 33:37 And they journeyed from Kadesh, and pitched in mount Hor, in the edge of the land of Edom.-- 33:38 And Aaron the priest went up into mount Hor at the commandment of the LORD, and died there, in the fortieth year after the children of Israel were come out of the land of Egypt, in the fifth month, on the first day of the month. 33:39 And Aaron was a hundred and twenty and three years old when he died in mount Hor. {S} 33:40 And the Canaanite, the king of Arad, who dwelt in the South in the land of Canaan, heard of the coming of the children of Israel.-- 33:41 And they journeyed from mount Hor, and pitched in Zalmonah. 33:42 And they journeyed from Zalmonah, and pitched in Punon. 33:43 And they journeyed from Punon, and pitched in Oboth. 33:44 And they journeyed from Oboth, and pitched in Ije-abarim, in the border of Moab. 33:45 And they journeyed from Ijim, and pitched in Dibon-gad. 33:46 And they journeyed from Dibon-gad, and pitched in Almon-diblathaim. 33:47 And they journeyed from Almon-diblathaim, and pitched in the mountains of Abarim, in front of Nebo. 33:48 And they journeyed from the mountains of Abarim, and pitched in the plains of Moab by the Jordan at Jericho. 33:49 And they pitched by the Jordan, from Beth-jeshimoth even unto Abel-shittim in the plains of Moab. {S}

גא

A 33:50 And the LORD spoke unto Moses in the plains of Moab by the Jordan at Jericho, saying: 33:51 'Speak unto the children of Israel, and say unto them: When ye pass over the Jordan into the land of Canaan, 33:52 then ye shall drive out all the inhabitants of the land from before you, and destroy all their figured stones, and destroy all their molten images, and demolish all their high places. 33:53 And ye shall drive out the inhabitants of the land, and dwell therein; for unto you have I given the land to possess it. 33:54 And ye shall inherit the land by lot according to your families--to the more ye shall give the more inheritance, and to the fewer thou shalt give the less inheritance; wheresoever the lot falleth to any man, that shall be his; according to the tribes of your fathers shall ye inherit. 33:55 But if ye will not drive out the inhabitants of the land from before you, then shall those that ye let remain of them be as thorns in your eyes, and as pricks in your sides, and they shall harass you in the land wherein ye dwell. 33:56 And it shall come to pass, that as I thought to do unto them, so will I do unto you. {P}
B 34:1 And the LORD spoke unto Moses, saying: 34:2 'Command the children of Israel, and say unto them: When ye come into the land of Canaan, this shall be the land that shall fall unto you for an inheritance, even the land of Canaan according to the borders thereof. 34:3 Thus your south side shall be from the wilderness of Zin close by the side of Edom, and your south border shall begin at the end of the Salt Sea eastward; 34:4 and your border shall turn about southward of the ascent of Akrabbim, and pass along to Zin; and the goings out thereof shall be southward of Kadesh-barnea; and it shall go forth to Hazar-addar, and pass along to Azmon; 34:5 and the border shall turn about from Azmon unto the Brook of Egypt, and the goings out thereof shall be at the Sea. 34:6 And for the western border, ye shall have the Great Sea for a border; this shall be your west border. 34:7 And this shall be your north border: from the Great Sea ye shall mark out your line unto mount Hor; 34:8 from mount Hor ye shall mark out a line unto the entrance to Hamath; and the goings out of the border shall be at Zedad; 34:9 and the border shall go forth to Ziphron, and the goings out thereof shall be at Hazar-enan; this shall be your north border. 34:10 And ye shall mark out your line for the east border from Hazar-enan to Shepham; 34:11 and the border shall go down from Shepham to Riblah, on the east side of Ain; and the border shall go down, and shall strike upon the slope of the sea of Chinnereth eastward; 34:12 and the border shall go down to the Jordan, and the goings out thereof shall be at the Salt Sea; this shall be your land according to the borders thereof round about.' 34:13 And Moses commanded the children of Israel, saying: 'This is the land wherein ye shall receive inheritance by lot, which the LORD hath commanded to give unto the nine tribes, and to the half-tribe; 34:14 for the tribe of the children of Reuben according to their fathers' houses, and the tribe of the children of Gad according to their fathers' houses, have received, and the half-tribe of Manasseh have received, their inheritance; 34:15 the two tribes and the half-tribe have received their inheritance beyond the Jordan at Jericho eastward, toward the sun-rising.' {P}

גב

A 35:1 And the LORD spoke unto Moses in the plains of Moab by the Jordan at Jericho, saying: 35:2 'Command the children of Israel, that they give unto the Levites of the inheritance of their possession cities to dwell in; and open land round about the cities shall ye give unto the Levites. 35:3 And the cities shall they have to dwell in; and their open land shall be for their cattle, and for their substance, and for all their beasts. 35:4 And the open land about the cities, which ye shall give unto the Levites, shall be from the wall of the city and outward a thousand cubits round about. 35:5 And ye shall measure without the city for the east side two thousand cubits, and for the south side two thousand cubits, and for the west side two thousand cubits, and for the north side two thousand cubits, the city being in the midst. This shall be to them the open land about the cities. 35:6 And the cities which ye shall give unto the Levites, they shall be the six cities of refuge, which ye shall give for the manslayer to flee thither; and beside them ye shall give forty and two cities. 35:7 All the cities which ye shall give to the Levites shall be forty and eight cities: them shall ye give with the open land about them. 35:8 And concerning the cities which ye shall give of the possession of the children of Israel, from the many ye shall take many, and from the few ye shall take few; each tribe according to its inheritance which it inheriteth shall give of its cities unto the Levites.' {P}

B 35:9 And the LORD spoke unto Moses, saying: 35:10 'Speak unto the children of Israel, and say unto them: When ye pass over the Jordan into the land of Canaan, 35:11 then ye shall appoint you cities to be cities of refuge for you, that the manslayer that killeth any person through error may flee thither. 35:12 And the cities shall be unto you for refuge from the avenger, that the manslayer die not, until he stand before the congregation for judgment. 35:13 And as to the cities which ye shall give, there shall be for you six cities of refuge. 35:14 Ye shall give three cities beyond the Jordan, and three cities shall ye give in the land of Canaan; they shall be cities of refuge. 35:15 For the children of Israel, and for the stranger and for the settler among them, shall these six cities be for refuge, that every one that killeth any person through error may flee thither. 35:16 But if he smote him with an instrument of iron, so that he died, he is a murderer; the murderer shall surely be put to death. 35:17 And if he smote him with a stone in the hand, whereby a man may die, and he died, he is a murderer; the murderer shall surely be put to death. 35:18 Or if he smote him with a weapon of wood in the hand, whereby a man may die, and he died, he is a murderer; the murderer shall surely be put to death. 35:19 The avenger of blood shall himself put the murderer to death; when he meeteth him, he shall put him to death. 35:20 And if he thrust him of hatred, or hurled at him any thing, lying in wait, so that he died; 35:21 or in enmity smote him with his hand, that he died; he that smote him shall surely be put to death: he is a murderer; the avenger of blood shall put the murderer to death when he meeteth him. 35:22 But if he thrust him suddenly without enmity, or hurled upon him any thing without lying in wait, 35:23 or with any stone, whereby a man may die, seeing him not, and cast it upon him, so that he died, and he was not his enemy, neither sought his harm; 35:24 then the congregation shall judge between the smiter and the avenger of blood according to these ordinances; 35:25 and the congregation shall deliver the manslayer out of the hand of the avenger of blood, and the congregation shall restore him to his city of refuge, whither he was fled; and he shall dwell therein until the death of the high priest, who was anointed with the holy oil. 35:26 But if the manslayer shall at any time go beyond the border of his city of refuge, whither he fleeth; 35:27 and the avenger of blood find him without the border of his city of refuge, and the avenger of blood slay the manslayer; there shall be no bloodguiltiness for him; 35:28 because he must remain in his city of refuge until the death of the high priest; but after the death of the high priest the manslayer may return into the land of his possession. 35:29 And these things shall be for a statute of judgment unto you throughout your generations in all your dwellings. 35:30 Whoso killeth any person, the murderer shall be slain at the mouth of witnesses; but one witness shall not testify against any person that he die. 35:31 Moreover ye shall take no ransom for the life of a murderer, that is guilty of death; but he shall surely be put to death. 35:32 And ye shall take no ransom for him that is fled to his city of refuge, that he should come again to dwell in the land, until the death of the priest. 35:33 So ye shall not pollute the land wherein ye are; for blood, it polluteth the land; and no expiation can be made for the land for the blood that is shed therein, but by the blood of him that shed it. 35:34 And thou shalt not defile the land which ye inhabit, in the midst of which I dwell; for I the LORD dwell in the midst of the children of Israel.' {P}

C 34:16 And the LORD spoke unto Moses, saying: 34:17 'These are the names of the men that shall take possession of the land for you: Eleazar the priest, and Joshua the son of Nun. 34:18 And ye shall take one prince of every tribe, to take possession of the land. 34:19 And these are the names of the men: of the tribe of Judah, Caleb the son of Jephunneh. 34:20 And of the tribe of the children of Simeon, Shemuel the son of Ammihud. 34:21 Of the tribe of Benjamin, Elidad the son of Chislon. 34:22 And of the tribe of the children of Dan a prince, Bukki the son of Jogli. 34:23 Of the children of Joseph: of the tribe of the children of Manasseh a prince, Hanniel the son of Ephod; 34:24 and of the tribe of the children of Ephraim a prince, Kemuel the son of Shiphtan. 34:25 And of the tribe of the children of Zebulun a prince, Eli-zaphan the son of Parnach. 34:26 And of the tribe of the children of Issachar a prince, Paltiel the son of Azzan. 34:27 And of the tribe of the children of Asher a prince, Ahihud the son of Shelomi. 34:28 And of the tribe of the children of Naphtali a prince, Pedahel the son of Ammihud. 34:29 These are they whom the LORD commanded to divide the inheritance unto the children of Israel in the land of Canaan.' {P}

C 36:1 And the heads of the fathers' houses of the family of the children of Gilead, the son of Machir, the son of Manasseh, of the families of the sons of Joseph, came near, and spoke before Moses, and before the princes, the heads of the fathers' houses of the children of Israel; 36:2 and they said: 'The LORD commanded my lord to give the land for inheritance by lot to the children of Israel; and my lord was commanded by the LORD to give the inheritance of Zelophehad our brother unto his daughters. 36:3 And if they be married to any of the sons of the other tribes of the children of Israel, then will their inheritance be taken away from the inheritance of our fathers, and will be added to the inheritance of the tribe whereunto they shall belong; so will it be taken away from the lot of our inheritance. 36:4 And when the jubilee of the children of Israel shall be, then will their inheritance be added unto the inheritance of the tribe whereunto they shall belong; so will their inheritance be taken away from the inheritance of the tribe of our fathers.' 36:5 And Moses commanded the children of Israel according to the word of the LORD, saying: 'The tribe of the sons of Joseph speaketh right. 36:6 This is the thing which the LORD hath commanded concerning the daughters of Zelophehad, saying: Let them be married to whom they think best; only into the family of the tribe of their father shall they be married. 36:7 So shall no inheritance of the children of Israel remove from tribe to tribe; for the children of Israel shall cleave every one to the inheritance of the tribe of his fathers. 36:8 And every daughter, that possesseth an inheritance in any tribe of the children of Israel, shall be wife unto one of the family of the tribe of her father, that the children of Israel may possess every man the inheritance of his fathers. 36:9 So shall no inheritance remove from one tribe to another tribe; for the tribes of the children of Israel shall cleave each one to its own inheritance.' 36:10 Even as the LORD commanded Moses, so did the daughters of Zelophehad. 36:11 For Mahlah, Tirzah, and Hoglah, and Milcah, and Noah, the daughters of Zelophehad, were married unto their father's brothers' sons. 36:12 They were married into the families of the sons of Manasseh the son of Joseph, and their inheritance remained in the tribe of the family of their father. 36:13 These are the commandments and the ordinances, which the LORD commanded by the hand of Moses unto the children of Israel in the plains of Moab by the Jordan at Jericho. {P}

Deuteronomy

Deuteronomy Unit 1 (1:1-3:23)

1

1:1 These are the words which Moses spoke unto all Israel beyond the Jordan; in the wilderness, in the Arabah, over against Suph, between Paran and Tophel, and Laban, and Hazeroth, and Di-zahab. 1:2 It is eleven days journey from Horeb unto Kadesh-barnea by the way of mount Seir. 1:3 And it came to pass in the fortieth year, in the eleventh month, on the first day of the month, that Moses spoke unto the children of Israel, according unto all that the LORD had given him in commandment unto them; 1:4 after he had smitten Sihon the king of the Amorites, who dwelt in Heshbon, and Og the king of Bashan, who dwelt in Ashtaroth, at Edrei; 1:5 beyond the Jordan, in the land of Moab, took Moses upon him to expound this law, saying: 1:6 The LORD our God spoke unto us in Horeb, saying: 'Ye have dwelt long enough in this mountain; 1:7 turn you, and take your journey, and go to the hill-country of the Amorites and unto all the places nigh thereunto, in the Arabah, in the hill-country, and in the Lowland, and in the South, and by the sea-shore; the land of the Canaanites, and Lebanon, as far as the great river, the river Euphrates. 1:8 Behold, I have set the land before you: go in and possess the land which the LORD swore unto your fathers, to Abraham, to Isaac, and to Jacob, to give unto them and to their seed after them.'

2א

1:9 And I spoke unto you at that time, saying: 'I am not able to bear you myself alone; 1:10 the LORD your God hath multiplied you, and, behold, ye are this day as the stars of heaven for multitude.-- 1:11 The LORD, the God of your fathers, make you a thousand times so many more as ye are, and bless you, as He hath promised you!-- 1:12 How can I myself alone bear your cumbrance, and your burden, and your strife? 1:13 Get you, from each one of your tribes, wise men, and understanding, and full of knowledge, and I will make them heads over you.' 1:14 And ye answered me, and said: 'The thing which thou hast spoken is good for us to do.' 1:15 So I took the heads of your tribes, wise men, and full of knowledge, and made them heads over you, captains of thousands, and captains of hundreds, and captains of fifties, and captains of tens, and officers, tribe by tribe. 1:16 And I charged your judges at that time, saying: 'Hear the causes between your brethren, and judge righteously between a man and his brother, and the stranger that is with him. 1:17 Ye shall not respect persons in judgment; ye shall hear the small and the great alike; ye shall not be afraid of the face of any man; for the judgment is God's; and the cause that is too hard for you ye shall bring unto me, and I will hear it.' 1:18 And I commanded you at that time all the things which ye should do.

3א

2:2 And the LORD spoke unto me, saying: 2:3 'Ye have compassed this mountain long enough; turn you northward. 2:4 And command thou the people, saying: Ye are to pass through the border of your brethren the children of Esau, that dwell in Seir; and they will be afraid of you; take ye good heed unto yourselves therefore; 2:5 contend not with them; for I will not give you of their land, no, not so much as for the sole of the foot to tread on; because I have given mount Seir unto Esau for a possession. 2:6 Ye shall purchase food of them for money, that ye may eat; and ye shall also buy water of them for money, that ye may drink. 2:7 For the LORD thy God hath blessed thee in all the work of thy hand; He hath known thy walking through this great wilderness; these forty years the LORD thy God hath been with thee; thou hast lacked nothing.' 2:8 So we passed by from our brethren the children of Esau, that dwell in Seir, from the way of the Arabah, from Elath and from Ezion-geber. {S}

2ב

1:19 And we journeyed from Horeb, and went through all that great and dreadful wilderness which ye saw, by the way to the hill-country of the Amorites, as the LORD our God commanded us; and we came to Kadesh-barnea. 1:20 And I said unto you: 'Ye are come unto the hill-country of the Amorites, which the LORD our God giveth unto us. 1:21 Behold, the LORD thy God hath set the land before thee; go up, take possession, as the LORD, the God of thy fathers, hath spoken unto thee; fear not, neither be dismayed.' 1:22 And ye came near unto me every one of you, and said: 'Let us send men before us, that they may search the land for us, and bring us back word of the way by which we must go up, and the cities unto which we shall come.' 1:23 And the thing pleased me well; and I took twelve men of you, one man for every tribe; 1:24 and they turned and went up into the mountains, and came unto the valley of Eshcol, and spied it out. 1:25 And they took of the fruit of the land in their hands, and brought it down unto us, and brought us back word, and said: 'Good is the land which the LORD our God giveth unto us.' 1:26 Yet ye would not go up, but rebelled against the commandment of the LORD your God; 1:27 and ye murmured in your tents, and said: 'Because the LORD hated us, He hath brought us forth out of the land of Egypt, to deliver us into the hand of the Amorites, to destroy us. 1:28 Whither are we going up? our brethren have made our heart to melt, saying: The people is greater and taller than we; the cities are great and fortified up to heaven; and moreover we have seen the sons of the Anakim there.' 1:29 Then I said unto you: 'Dread not, neither be afraid of them. 1:30 The LORD your God who goeth before you, He shall fight for you, according to all that He did for you in Egypt before your eyes; 1:31 and in the wilderness, where thou hast seen how that the LORD thy God bore thee, as a man doth bear his son, in all the way that ye went, until ye came unto this place. 1:32 Yet in this thing ye do not believe the LORD your God, 1:33 Who went before you in the way, to seek you out a place to pitch your tents in: in fire by night, to show you by what way ye should go, and in the cloud by day.'

3ב

And we turned and passed by the way of the wilderness of Moab. 2:9 And the LORD said unto me: 'Be not at enmity with Moab, neither contend with them in battle; for I will not give thee of his land for a possession; because I have given Ar unto the children of Lot for a possession.-- 2:10 The Emim dwelt therein aforetime, a people great, and many, and tall, as the Anakim; 2:11 these also are accounted Rephaim, as the Anakim; but the Moabites call them Emim. 2:12 And in Seir dwelt the Horites aforetime, but the children of Esau succeeded them; and they destroyed them from before them, and dwelt in their stead; as Israel did unto the land of his possession, which the LORD gave unto them.-- 2:13 Now rise up, and get you over the brook Zered.' And we went over the brook Zered. 2:14 And the days in which we came from Kadesh-barnea, until we were come over the brook Zered, were thirty and eight years; until all the generation, even the men of war, were consumed from the midst of the camp, as the LORD swore unto them. 2:15 Moreover the hand of the LORD was against them, to discomfit them from the midst of the camp, until they were consumed.

2ג

1:34 And the LORD heard the voice of your words, and was wroth, and swore, saying: 1:35 'Surely there shall not one of these men, even this evil generation, see the good land, which I swore to give unto your fathers, 1:36 save Caleb the son of Jephunneh, he shall see it; and to him will I give the land that he hath trodden upon, and to his children; because he hath wholly followed the LORD.' 1:37 Also the LORD was angry with me for your sakes, saying: Thou also shalt not go in thither; 1:38 Joshua the son of Nun, who standeth before thee, he shall go in thither; encourage thou him, for he shall cause Israel to inherit it. 1:39 Moreover your little ones, that ye said should be a prey, and your children, that this day have no knowledge of good or evil, they shall go in thither, and unto them will I give it, and they shall possess it. 1:40 But as for you, turn you, and take your journey into the wilderness by the way to the Red Sea.' 1:41 Then ye answered and said unto me: 'We have sinned against the LORD, we will go up and fight, according to all that the LORD our God commanded us.' And ye girded on every man his weapons of war, and deemed it a light thing to go up into the hill-country. 1:42 And the LORD said unto me: 'Say unto them: Go not up, neither fight; for I am not among you; lest ye be smitten before your enemies.' 1:43 So I spoke unto you, and ye hearkened not; but ye rebelled against the commandment of the LORD, and were presumptuous, and went up into the hill-country. 1:44 And the Amorites, that dwell in that hill-country, came out against you, and chased you, as bees do, and beat you down in Seir, even unto Hormah. 1:45 And ye returned and wept before the LORD; but the LORD hearkened not to your voice, nor gave ear unto you. 1:46 So ye abode in Kadesh many days, according unto the days that ye abode there. 2:1 Then we turned, and took our journey into the wilderness by the way to the Red Sea, as the LORD spoke unto me; and we compassed mount Seir many days. {S}

3ג

2:16 So it came to pass, when all the men of war were consumed and dead from among the people, {S} 2:17 that the LORD spoke unto me saying: 2:18 'Thou art this day to pass over the border of Moab, even Ar; 2:19 and when thou comest nigh over against the children of Ammon, harass them not, nor contend with them; for I will not give thee of the land of the children of Ammon for a possession; because I have given it unto the children of Lot for a possession.-- 2:20 That also is accounted a land of Rephaim: Rephaim dwelt therein aforetime; but the Ammonites call them Zamzummim, 2:21 a people great, and many, and tall, as the Anakim; but the LORD destroyed them before them; and they succeeded them, and dwelt in their stead; 2:22 as He did for the children of Esau, that dwell in Seir, when He destroyed the Horites from before them; and they succeeded them, and dwelt in their stead even unto this day; 2:23 and the Avvim, that dwelt in villages as far as Gaza, the Caphtorim, that came forth out of Caphtor, destroyed them, and dwelt in their stead.--

אד

2:24 Rise ye up, take your journey, and pass over the valley of Arnon; behold, I have given into thy hand Sihon the Amorite, king of Heshbon, and his land; begin to possess it, and contend with him in battle. 2:25 This day will I begin to put the dread of thee and the fear of thee upon the peoples that are under the whole heaven, who, when they hear the report of thee, shall tremble, and be in anguish because of thee.' 2:26 And I sent messengers out of the wilderness of Kedemoth unto Sihon king of Heshbon with words of peace, saying: 2:27 'Let me pass through thy land; I will go along by the highway, I will neither turn unto the right hand nor to the left. 2:28 Thou shalt sell me food for money, that I may eat; and give me water for money, that I may drink; only let me pass through on my feet; 2:29 as the children of Esau that dwell in Seir, and the Moabites that dwell in Ar, did unto me; until I shall pass over the Jordan into the land which the LORD our God giveth us.' 2:30 But Sihon king of Heshbon would not let us pass by him; for the LORD thy God hardened his spirit, and made his heart obstinate, that He might deliver him into thy hand, as appeareth this day. {S} 2:31 And the LORD said unto me: 'Behold, I have begun to deliver up Sihon and his land before thee; begin to possess his land.' 2:32 Then Sihon came out against us, he and all his people, unto battle at Jahaz. 2:33 And the LORD our God delivered him up before us; and we smote him, and his sons, and all his people. 2:34 And we took all his cities at that time, and utterly destroyed every city, the men, and the women, and the little ones; we left none remaining; 2:35 only the cattle we took for a prey unto ourselves, with the spoil of the cities which we had taken. 2:36 From Aroer, which is on the edge of the valley of Arnon, and from the city that is in the valley, even unto Gilead, there was not a city too high for us: the LORD our God delivered up all before us. 2:37 Only to the land of the children of Ammon thou camest not near; all the side of the river Jabbok, and the cities of the hill-country, and wheresoever the LORD our God forbade us.

בד

3:1 Then we turned, and went up the way to Bashan; and Og the king of Bashan came out against us, he and all his people, unto battle at Edrei. 3:2 And the LORD said unto me: 'Fear him not; for I have delivered him, and all his people, and his land, into thy hand; and thou shalt do unto him as thou didst unto Sihon king of the Amorites, who dwelt at Heshbon.' 3:3 So the LORD our God delivered into our hand Og also, the king of Bashan, and all his people; and we smote him until none was left to him remaining. 3:4 And we took all his cities at that time; there was not a city which we took not from them; threescore cities, all the region of Argob, the kingdom of Og in Bashan. 3:5 All these were fortified cities, with high walls, gates, and bars; beside the unwalled towns a great many. 3:6 And we utterly destroyed them, as we did unto Sihon king of Heshbon, utterly destroying every city, the men, and the women, and the little ones. 3:7 But all the cattle, and the spoil of the cities, we took for a prey unto ourselves. 3:8 And we took the land at that time out of the hand of the two kings of the Amorites that were beyond the Jordan, from the valley of Arnon unto mount Hermon-- 3:9 which Hermon the Sidonians call Sirion, and the Amorites call it Senir-- 3:10 all the cities of the plain, and all Gilead, and all Bashan, unto Salcah and Edrei, cities of the kingdom of Og in Bashan.-- 3:11 For only Og king of Bashan remained of the remnant of the Rephaim; behold, his bedstead was a bedstead of iron; is it not in Rabbah of the children of Ammon? nine cubits was the length thereof, and four cubits the breadth of it, after the cubit of a man.--

גד

3:12 And this land we took in possession at that time; from Aroer, which is by the valley of Arnon, and half the hill-country of Gilead, and the cities thereof, gave I to the Reubenites and to the Gadites; 3:13 and the rest of Gilead, and all Bashan, the kingdom of Og, gave I unto the half-tribe of Manasseh; all the region of Argob--all that Bashan is called the land of Rephaim. 3:14 Jair the son of Manasseh took all the region of Argob, unto the border of the Geshurites and the Maacathites, and called them, even Bashan, after his own name, Havvoth-jair, unto this day.-- 3:15 And I gave Gilead unto Machir. 3:16 And unto the Reubenites and unto the Gadites I gave from Gilead even unto the valley of Arnon, the middle of the valley for a border; even unto the river Jabbok, which is the border of the children of Ammon; 3:17 the Arabah also, the Jordan being the border thereof, from Chinnereth even unto the sea of the Arabah, the Salt Sea, under the slopes of Pisgah eastward. 3:18 And I commanded you at that time, saying: 'The LORD your God hath given you this land to possess it; ye shall pass over armed before your brethren the children of Israel, all the men of valour. 3:19 But your wives, and your little ones, and your cattle--I know that ye have much cattle--shall abide in your cities which I have given you; 3:20 until the LORD give rest unto your brethren, as unto you, and they also possess the land which the LORD your God giveth them beyond the Jordan; then shall ye return every man unto his possession, which I have given you. 3:21 And I commanded Joshua at that time, saying: 'Thine eyes have seen all that the LORD your God hath done unto these two kings; so shall the LORD do unto all the kingdoms whither thou goest over. 3:22 Ye shall not fear them; for the LORD your God, He it is that fighteth for you.' {S}

5

3:23 And I besought the LORD at that time, saying: 3:24 'O Lord GOD, Thou hast begun to show Thy servant Thy greatness, and Thy strong hand; for what god is there in heaven or on earth, that can do according to Thy works, and according to Thy mighty acts? 3:25 Let me go over, I pray Thee, and see the good land that is beyond the Jordan, that goodly hill-country, and Lebanon.' 3:26 But the LORD was wroth with me for your sakes, and hearkened not unto me; and the LORD said unto me: 'Let it suffice thee; speak no more unto Me of this matter. 3:27 Get thee up into the top of Pisgah, and lift up thine eyes westward, and northward, and southward, and eastward, and behold with thine eyes; for thou shalt not go over this Jordan. 3:28 But charge Joshua, and encourage him, and strengthen him; for he shall go over before this people, and he shall cause them to inherit the land which thou shalt see.' 3:29 So we abode in the valley over against Beth-peor. {P}

Deuteronomy Unit II (4:1-49)

א1

4:1 And now, O Israel, hearken unto the statutes and unto the ordinances, which I teach you, to do them; that ye may live, and go in and possess the land which the LORD, the God of your fathers, giveth you. 4:2 Ye shall not add unto the word which I command you, neither shall ye diminish from it, that ye may keep the commandments of the LORD your God which I command you. 4:3 Your eyes have seen what the LORD did in Baal-peor; for all the men that followed the Baal of Peor, the LORD thy God hath destroyed them from the midst of thee. 4:4 But ye that did cleave unto the LORD your God are alive every one of you this day.

א2

4:9 Only take heed to thyself, and keep thy soul diligently, lest thou forget the things which thine eyes saw, and lest they depart from thy heart all the days of thy life; but make them known unto thy children and thy children's children; 4:10 the day that thou stoodest before the LORD thy God in Horeb, when the LORD said unto me: 'Assemble Me the people, and I will make them hear My words that they may learn to fear Me all the days that they live upon the earth, and that they may teach their children.' 4:11 And ye came near and stood under the mountain; and the mountain burned with fire unto the heart of heaven, with darkness, cloud, and thick darkness. 4:12 And the LORD spoke unto you out of the midst of the fire; ye heard the voice of words, but ye saw no form; only a voice. 4:13 And He declared unto you His covenant, which He commanded you to perform, even the ten words; and He wrote them upon two tables of stone. 4:14 And the LORD commanded me at that time to teach you statutes and ordinances, that ye might do them in the land whither ye go over to possess it.

א3

4:21 Now the LORD was angered with me for your sakes, and swore that I should not go over the Jordan, and that I should not go in unto that good land, which the LORD thy God giveth thee for an inheritance; 4:22 but I must die in this land, I must not go over the Jordan; but ye are to go over, and possess that good land.

א4

4:25 When thou shalt beget children, and children's children, and ye shall have been long in the land, and shall deal corruptly, and make a graven image, even the form of any thing, and shall do that which is evil in the sight of the LORD thy God, to provoke Him; 4:26 I call heaven and earth to witness against you this day, that ye shall soon utterly perish from off the land whereunto ye go over the Jordan to possess it; ye shall not prolong your days upon it, but shall utterly be destroyed. 4:27 And the LORD shall scatter you among the peoples, and ye shall be left few in number among the nations, whither the LORD shall lead you away. 4:28 And there ye shall serve gods, the work of men's hands, wood and stone, which neither see, nor hear, nor eat, nor smell. 4:29 But from thence ye will seek the LORD thy God; and thou shalt find Him, if thou search after Him with all thy heart and with all thy soul. 4:30 In thy distress, when all these things are come upon thee, in the end of days, thou wilt return to the LORD thy God, and hearken unto His voice; 4:31 for the LORD thy God is a merciful God; He will not fail thee, neither destroy thee, nor forget the covenant of thy fathers which He swore unto them.

א5

4:41 Then Moses separated three cities beyond the Jordan toward the sunrising; 4:42 that the manslayer might flee thither, that slayeth his neighbour unawares, and hated him not in time past; and that fleeing unto one of these cities he might live: 4:43 Bezer in the wilderness, in the table-land, for the Reubenites; and Ramoth in Gilead, for the Gadites; and Golan in Bashan, for the Manassites.

ב1

4:5 Behold, I have taught you statutes and ordinances, even as the LORD my God commanded me, that ye should do so in the midst of the land whither ye go in to possess it. 4:6 Observe therefore and do them; for this is your wisdom and your understanding in the sight of the peoples, that, when they hear all these statutes, shall say: 'Surely this great nation is a wise and understanding people.' 4:7 For what great nation is there, that hath God so nigh unto them, as the LORD our God is whensoever we call upon Him? 4:8 And what great nation is there, that hath statutes and ordinances so righteous as all this law, which I set before you this day?

ב2

4:15 Take ye therefore good heed unto yourselves--for ye saw no manner of form on the day that the LORD spoke unto you in Horeb out of the midst of the fire-- 4:16 lest ye deal corruptly, and make you a graven image, even the form of any figure, the likeness of male or female, 4:17 the likeness of any beast that is on the earth, the likeness of any winged fowl that flieth in the heaven, 4:18 the likeness of any thing that creepeth on the ground, the likeness of any fish that is in the water under the earth; 4:19 and lest thou lift up thine eyes unto heaven, and when thou seest the sun and the moon and the stars, even all the host of heaven, thou be drawn away and worship them, and serve them, which the LORD thy God hath allotted unto all the peoples under the whole heaven. 4:20 But you hath the LORD taken and brought forth out of the iron furnace, out of Egypt, to be unto Him a people of inheritance, as ye are this day.

ב3

4:23 Take heed unto yourselves, lest ye forget the covenant of the LORD your God, which He made with you, and make you a graven image, even the likeness of any thing which the LORD thy God hath forbidden thee. 4:24 For the LORD thy God is a devouring fire, a jealous God. {P}

ב4

4:32 For ask now of the days past, which were before thee, since the day that God created man upon the earth, and from the one end of heaven unto the other, whether there hath been any such thing as this great thing is, or hath been heard like it? 4:33 Did ever a people hear the voice of God speaking out of the midst of the fire, as thou hast heard, and live? 4:34 Or hath God assayed to go and take Him a nation from the midst of another nation, by trials, by signs, and by wonders, and by war, and by a mighty hand, and by an outstretched arm, and by great terrors, according to all that the LORD your God did for you in Egypt before thine eyes? 4:35 Unto thee it was shown, that thou mightest know that the LORD, He is God; there is none else beside Him. 4:36 Out of heaven He made thee to hear His voice, that He might instruct thee; and upon earth He made thee to see His great fire; and thou didst hear His words out of the midst of the fire. 4:37 And because He loved thy fathers, and chose their seed after them, and brought thee out with His presence, with His great power, out of Egypt, 4:38 to drive out nations from before thee greater and mightier than thou, to bring thee in, to give thee their land for an inheritance, as it is this day; 4:39 know this day, and lay it to thy heart, that the LORD, He is God in heaven above and upon the earth beneath; there is none else. 4:40 And thou shalt keep His statutes, and His commandments, which I command thee this day, that it may go well with thee, and with thy children after thee, and that thou mayest prolong thy days upon the land, which the LORD thy God giveth thee, for ever. {P}

ב5

4:44 And this is the law which Moses set before the children of Israel; 4:45 these are the testimonies, and the statutes, and the ordinances, which Moses spoke unto the children of Israel, when they came forth out of Egypt; 4:46 beyond the Jordan, in the valley over against Beth-peor, in the land of Sihon king of the Amorites, who dwelt at Heshbon, whom Moses and the children of Israel smote, when they came forth out of Egypt; 4:47 and they took his land in possession, and the land of Og king of Bashan, the two kings of the Amorites, who were beyond the Jordan toward the sunrising; 4:48 from Aroer, which is on the edge of the valley of Arnon, even unto mount Sion--the same is Hermon-- 4:49 and all the Arabah beyond the Jordan eastward, even unto the sea of the Arabah, under the slopes of Pisgah. {P}

Deuteronomy Unit III (5:1-6:3)

1א

5:1 And Moses called unto all Israel, and said unto them: Hear, O Israel, the statutes and the ordinances which I speak in your ears this day, that ye may learn them, and observe to do them.

2א

A 5:6 I am the LORD thy God, who brought thee out of the land of Egypt, out of the house of bondage. Thou shalt have no other gods before Me. 5:7 Thou shalt not make unto thee a graven image, even any manner of likeness, of any thing that is in heaven above, or that is in the earth beneath, or that is in the water under the earth. 5:8 Thou shalt not bow down unto them, nor serve them; for I the LORD thy God am a jealous God, visiting the iniquity of the fathers upon the children, and upon the third and upon the fourth generation of them that hate Me, 5:9 and showing mercy unto the thousandth generation of them that love Me and keep My commandments. {S}
B 5:10 Thou shalt not take the name of the LORD thy God in vain; for the LORD will not hold him guiltless that taketh His name in vain. {S}

3א

A 5:16 Thou shalt not murder. {S}
B Neither shalt thou commit adultery. {S}
C Neither shalt thou steal. {S}

4א

A 5:18 These words the LORD spoke unto all your assembly in the mount out of the midst of the fire, of the cloud, and of the thick darkness, with a great voice, and it went on no more. And He wrote them upon two tables of stone, and gave them unto me.

B 5:19 And it came to pass, when ye heard the voice out of the midst of the darkness, while the mountain did burn with fire, that ye came near unto me, even all the heads of your tribes, and your elders; 5:20 and ye said: 'Behold, the LORD our God hath shown us His glory and His greatness, and we have heard His voice out of the midst of the fire; we have seen this day that God doth speak with man, and he liveth. 5:21 Now therefore why should we die? for this great fire will consume us; if we hear the voice of the LORD our God any more, then we shall die. 5:22 For who is there of all flesh, that hath heard the voice of the living God speaking out of the midst of the fire, as we have, and lived? 5:23 Go thou near, and hear all that the LORD our God may say; and thou shalt speak unto us all that the LORD our God may speak unto thee; and we will hear it and do it.'
C 5:24 And the LORD heard the voice of your words, when ye spoke unto me; and the LORD said unto me: 'I have heard the voice of the words of this people, which they have spoken unto thee; they have well said all that they have spoken. 5:25 Oh that they had such a heart as this alway, to fear Me, and keep all My commandments, that it might be well with them, and with their children for ever! 5:26 Go say to them: Return ye to your tents. 5:27 But as for thee, stand thou here by Me, and I will speak unto thee all the commandment, and the statutes, and the ordinances, which thou shalt teach them, that they may do them in the land which I give them to possess it.'

1ב

5:2 The LORD our God made a covenant with us in Horeb. 5:3 The LORD made not this covenant with our fathers, but with us, even us, who are all of us here alive this day. 5:4 The LORD spoke with you face to face in the mount out of the midst of the fire-- 5:5 I stood between the LORD and you at that time, to declare unto you the word of the LORD; for ye were afraid because of the fire, and went not up into the mount--saying: {S}

2ב

A 5:11 Observe the sabbath day, to keep it holy, as the LORD thy God commanded thee. 5:12 Six days shalt thou labour, and do all thy work; 5:13 but the seventh day is a sabbath unto the LORD thy God, in it thou shalt not do any manner of work, thou, nor thy son, nor thy daughter, nor thy man-servant, nor thy maid-servant, nor thine ox, nor thine ass, nor any of thy cattle, nor thy stranger that is within thy gates; that thy man-servant and thy maid-servant may rest as well as thou. 5:14 And thou shalt remember that thou was a servant in the land of Egypt, and the LORD thy God brought thee out thence by a mighty hand and by an outstretched arm; therefore the LORD thy God commanded thee to keep the sabbath day. {S}
B 5:15 Honour thy father and thy mother, as the LORD thy God commanded thee; that thy days may be long, and that it may go well with thee, upon the land which the LORD thy God giveth thee. {S}

3ב

A Neither shalt thou bear false witness against thy neighbour. {S}
B 5:17 Neither shalt thou covet thy neighbour's wife; {S}
C neither shalt thou desire thy neighbour's house, his field, or his man-servant, or his maid-servant, his ox, or his ass, or any thing that is thy neighbour's. {S}

4ב

A 5:28 Ye shall observe to do therefore as the LORD your God hath commanded you; ye shall not turn aside to the right hand or to the left. 5:29 Ye shall walk in all the way which the LORD your God hath commanded you, that ye may live, and that it may be well with you, and that ye may prolong your days in the land which ye shall possess.
B 6:1 Now this is the commandment, the statutes, and the ordinances, which the LORD your God commanded to teach you, that ye might do them in the land whither ye go over to possess it-- 6:2 that thou mightest fear the LORD thy God, to keep all His statutes and His commandments, which I command thee, thou, and thy son, and thy son's son, all the days of thy life; and that thy days may be prolonged.

C 6:3 Hear therefore, O Israel, and observe to do it; that it may be well with thee, and that ye may increase mightily, as the LORD, the God of thy fathers, hath promised unto thee--a land flowing with milk and honey. {P}

Deuteronomy Unit IV (6:6-8:18)

א1

A 6:4 Hear, O Israel: the LORD our God, the LORD is one.

B 6:5 And thou shalt love the LORD thy God with all thy heart, and with all thy soul, and with all thy might.

C 6:6 And these words, which I command thee this day, shall be upon thy heart; 6:7 and thou shalt teach them diligently unto thy children, and shalt talk of them when thou sittest in thy house, and when thou walkest by the way, and when thou liest down, and when thou risest up. 6:8 And thou shalt bind them for a sign upon thy hand, and they shall be for frontlets between thine eyes. 6:9 And thou shalt write them upon the door-posts of thy house, and upon thy gates. {S}

א2

A 6:20 When thy son asketh thee in time to come, saying: 'What mean the testimonies, and the statutes, and the ordinances, which the LORD our God hath commanded you? 6:21 then thou shalt say unto thy son:

B 'We were Pharaoh's bondmen in Egypt; and the LORD brought us out of Egypt with a mighty hand. 6:22 And the LORD showed signs and wonders, great and sore, upon Egypt, upon Pharaoh, and upon all his house, before our eyes. 6:23 And He brought us out from thence, that He might bring us in, to give us the land which He swore unto our fathers. 6:24 And the LORD commanded us to do all these statutes, to fear the LORD our God, for our good always, that He might preserve us alive, as it is at this day.

C 6:25 And it shall be righteousness unto us, if we observe to do all this commandment before the LORD our God, as He hath commanded us.' {S}

ב1

A 6:10 And it shall be, when the LORD thy God shall bring thee into the land which He swore unto thy fathers, to Abraham, to Isaac, and to Jacob, to give thee--great and goodly cities, which thou didst not build, 6:11 and houses full of all good things, which thou didst not fill, and cisterns hewn out, which thou didst not hew, vineyards and olive-trees, which thou didst not plant, and thou shalt eat and be satisfied-- 6:12 then beware lest thou forget the LORD, who brought thee forth out of the land of Egypt, out of the house of bondage.

B 6:13 Thou shalt fear the LORD thy God; and Him shalt thou serve, and by His name shalt thou swear. 6:14 Ye shall not go after other gods, of the gods of the peoples that are round about you; 6:15 for a jealous God, even the LORD thy God, is in the midst of thee; lest the anger of the LORD thy God be kindled against thee, and He destroy thee from off the face of the earth. {S}

C 6:16 Ye shall not try the LORD your God, as ye tried Him in Massah. 6:17 Ye shall diligently keep the commandments of the LORD your God, and His testimonies, and His statutes, which He hath commanded thee. 6:18 And thou shalt do that which is right and good in the sight of the LORD; that it may be well with thee, and that thou mayest go in and possess the good land which the LORD swore unto thy fathers, 6:19 to thrust out all thine enemies from before thee, as the LORD hath spoken. {S}

ב2

A 7:1 When the LORD thy God shall bring thee into the land whither thou goest to possess it, and shall cast out many nations before thee, the Hittite, and the Girgashite, and the Amorite, and the Canaanite, and the Perizzite, and the Hivite, and the Jebusite, seven nations greater and mightier than thou; 7:2 and when the LORD thy God shall deliver them up before thee, and thou shalt smite them; then thou shalt utterly destroy them; thou shalt make no covenant with them, nor show mercy unto them; 7:3 neither shalt thou make marriages with them: thy daughter thou shalt not give unto his son, nor his daughter shalt thou take unto thy son. 7:4 For he will turn away thy son from following Me, that they may serve other gods; so will the anger of the LORD be kindled against you, and He will destroy thee quickly. 7:5 But thus shall ye deal with them: ye shall break down their altars, and dash in pieces their pillars, and hew down their Asherim, and burn their graven images with fire.

B 7:6 For thou art a holy people unto the LORD thy God: the LORD thy God hath chosen thee to be His own treasure, out of all peoples that are upon the face of the earth. 7:7 The LORD did not set His love upon you, nor choose you, because ye were more in number than any people--for ye were the fewest of all peoples-- 7:8 but because the LORD loved you, and because He would keep the oath which He swore unto your fathers, hath the LORD brought you out with a mighty hand, and redeemed you out of the house of bondage, from the hand of Pharaoh king of Egypt.

C 7:9 Know therefore that the LORD thy God, He is God; the faithful God, who keepeth covenant and mercy with them that love Him and keep His commandments to a thousand generations; 7:10 and repayeth them that hate Him to their face, to destroy them; He will not be slack to him that hateth Him, He will repay him to his face.

3א

A **7:11** Thou shalt therefore keep the commandment, and the statutes, and the ordinances, which I command thee this day, to do them. {P}
7:12 And it shall come to pass, because ye hearken to these ordinances, and keep, and do them, that the LORD thy God shall keep with thee the covenant and the mercy which He swore unto thy fathers, 7:13 and He will love thee, and bless thee, and multiply thee; He will also bless the fruit of thy body and the fruit of thy land, thy corn and thy wine and thine oil, the increase of thy kine and the young of thy flock, in the land which He swore unto thy fathers to give thee. 7:14 Thou shalt be blessed above all peoples; there shall not be male or female barren among you, or among your cattle. 7:15 And the LORD will take away from thee all sickness; and He will put none of the evil diseases of Egypt, which thou knowest, upon thee, but will lay them upon all them that hate thee. 7:16 And thou shalt consume all the peoples that the LORD thy God shall deliver unto thee; thine eye shall not pity them;

B neither shalt thou serve their gods; for that will be a snare unto thee. {S}

4א

A **8:1** All the commandment which I command thee this day shall ye observe to do, that ye may live, and multiply, and go in and possess the land which the LORD swore unto your fathers.
B 8:2 And thou shalt remember all the way which the LORD thy God hath led thee these forty years in the wilderness, that He might afflict thee, to prove thee, to know what was in thy heart, whether thou wouldest keep His commandments, or no. 8:3 And He afflicted thee, and suffered thee to hunger, and fed thee with manna, which thou knewest not, neither did thy fathers know; that He might make thee know that man doth not live by bread only, but by every thing that proceedeth out of the mouth of the LORD doth man live. 8:4 Thy raiment waxed not old upon thee, neither did thy foot swell, these forty years.

C 8:5 And thou shalt consider in thy heart, that, as a man chasteneth his son, so the LORD thy God chasteneth thee. 8:6 And thou shalt keep the commandments of the LORD thy God, to walk in His ways, and to fear Him. 8:7 For the LORD thy God bringeth thee into a good land, a land of brooks of water, of fountains and depths, springing forth in valleys and hills; 8:8 a land of wheat and barley, and vines and fig-trees and pomegranates; a land of olive-trees and honey; 8:9 a land wherein thou shalt eat bread without scarceness, thou shalt not lack any thing in it; a land whose stones are iron, and out of whose hills thou mayest dig brass. 8:10 And thou shalt eat and be satisfied, and bless the LORD thy God for the good land which He hath given thee.

3ב

A **7:17** If thou shalt say in thy heart: 'These nations are more than I; how can I dispossess them?' 7:18 thou shalt not be afraid of them; thou shalt well remember what the LORD thy God did unto Pharaoh, and unto all Egypt: 7:19 the great trials which thine eyes saw, and the signs, and the wonders, and the mighty hand, and the outstretched arm, whereby the LORD thy God brought thee out; so shall the LORD thy God do unto all the peoples of whom thou art afraid. 7:20 Moreover the LORD thy God will send the hornet among them, until they that are left, and they that hide themselves, perish from before thee. 7:21 Thou shalt not be affrighted at them; for the LORD thy God is in the midst of thee, a God great and awful. 7:22 And the LORD thy God will cast out those nations before thee by little and little; thou mayest not consume them quickly, lest the beasts of the field increase upon thee. 7:23 But the LORD thy God shall deliver them up before thee, and shall discomfit them with a great discomfiture, until they be destroyed. 7:24 And He shall deliver their kings into thy hand, and thou shalt make their name to perish from under heaven; there shall no man be able to stand against thee, until thou have destroyed them.
B 7:25 The graven images of their gods shall ye burn with fire; thou shalt not covet the silver or the gold that is on them, nor take it unto thee, lest thou be snared therein; for it is an abomination to the LORD thy God. 7:26 And thou shalt not bring an abomination into thy house, and be accursed like unto it; thou shalt utterly detest it, and thou shalt utterly abhor it; for it is a devoted thing. {P}

4ב

A **8:11** Beware lest thou forget the LORD thy God, in not keeping His commandments, and His ordinances, and His statutes, which I command thee this day;
B 8:12 lest when thou hast eaten and art satisfied, and hast built goodly houses, and dwelt therein; 8:13 and when thy herds and thy flocks multiply, and thy silver and thy gold is multiplied, and all that thou hast is multiplied; 8:14 then thy heart be lifted up, and thou forget the LORD thy God, who brought thee forth out of the land of Egypt, out of the house of bondage; 8:15 who led thee through the great and dreadful wilderness, wherein were serpents, fiery serpents, and scorpions, and thirsty ground where was no water; who brought thee forth water out of the rock of flint; 8:16 who fed thee in the wilderness with manna, which thy fathers knew not, that He might afflict thee, and that He might prove thee, to do thee good at thy latter end; 8:17 and thou say in thy heart: 'My power and the might of my hand hath gotten me this wealth.'
C 8:18 But thou shalt remember the LORD thy God, for it is He that giveth thee power to get wealth, that He may establish His covenant which He swore unto thy fathers, as it is this day. {P}
8:19 And it shall be, if thou shalt forget the LORD thy God, and walk after other gods, and serve them, and worship them, I forewarn you this day that ye shall surely perish. 8:20 As the nations that the LORD maketh to perish before you, so shall ye perish; because ye would not hearken unto the voice of the LORD your God. {P}

Deuteronomy Unit V (9:1-10:11)

1א

9:1 Hear, O Israel: thou art to pass over the Jordan this day, to go in to dispossess nations greater and mightier than thyself, cities great and fortified up to heaven, 9:2 a people great and tall, the sons of the Anakim, whom thou knowest, and of whom thou hast heard say: 'Who can stand before the sons of Anak?' 9:3 Know therefore this day, that the LORD thy God is He who goeth over before thee as a devouring fire; He will destroy them, and He will bring them down before thee; so shalt thou drive them out, and make them to perish quickly, as the LORD hath spoken unto thee. 9:4 Speak not thou in thy heart, after that the LORD thy God hath thrust them out from before thee, saying: 'For my righteousness the LORD hath brought me in to possess this land'; whereas for the wickedness of these nations the LORD doth drive them out from before thee. 9:5 Not for thy righteousness, or for the uprightness of thy heart, dost thou go in to possess their land; but for the wickedness of these nations the LORD thy God doth drive them out from before thee, and that He may establish the word which the LORD swore unto thy fathers, to Abraham, to Isaac, and to Jacob.

2א

A 9:8 Also in Horeb ye made the LORD wroth, and the LORD was angered with you to have destroyed you. 9:9 When I was gone up into the mount to receive the tables of stone, even the tables of the covenant which the LORD made with you, then I abode in the mount forty days and forty nights; I did neither eat bread nor drink water. 9:10 And the LORD delivered unto me the two tables of stone written with the finger of God; and on them was written according to all the words, which the LORD spoke with you in the mount out of the midst of the fire in the day of the assembly. 9:11 And it came to pass at the end of forty days and forty nights, that the LORD gave me the two tables of stone, even the tables of the covenant. 9:12 And the LORD said unto me: 'Arise, get thee down quickly from hence; for thy people that thou hast brought forth out of Egypt have dealt corruptly; they are quickly turned aside out of the way which I commanded them; they have made them a molten image.' 9:13 Furthermore the LORD spoke unto me, saying: 'I have seen this people, and, behold, it is a stiffnecked people; 9:14 let Me alone, that I may destroy them, and blot out their name from under heaven; and I will make of thee a nation mightier and greater than they.'

B 9:15 So I turned and came down from the mount, and the mount burned with fire; and the two tables of the covenant were in my two hands. 9:16 And I looked, and, behold, ye had sinned against the LORD your God; ye had made you a molten calf; ye had turned aside quickly out of the way which the LORD had commanded you. 9:17 And I took hold of the two tables, and cast them out of my two hands, and broke them before your eyes. 9:18 And I fell down before the LORD, as at the first, forty days and forty nights; I did neither eat bread nor drink water; because of all your sin which ye sinned, in doing that which was evil in the sight of the LORD, to provoke Him. 9:19 For I was in dread of the anger and hot displeasure, wherewith the LORD was wroth against you to destroy you. But the LORD hearkened unto me that time also. 9:20 Moreover the LORD was very angry with Aaron to have destroyed him; and I prayed for Aaron also the same time. 9:21 And I took your sin, the calf which ye had made, and burnt it with fire, and beat it in pieces, grinding it very small, until it was as fine as dust; and I cast the dust thereof into the brook that descended out of the mount.--

3א

A 9:25 So I fell down before the LORD the forty days and forty nights that I fell down; because the LORD had said He would destroy you. 9:26 And I prayed unto the LORD, and said: 'O Lord GOD, destroy not Thy people and Thine inheritance, that Thou hast redeemed through Thy greatness, that Thou hast brought forth out of Egypt with a mighty hand. 9:27 Remember Thy servants, Abraham, Isaac, and Jacob; look not unto the stubbornness of this people, nor to their wickedness, nor to their sin; 9:28 lest the land whence Thou broughtest us out say: Because the LORD was not able to bring them into the land which He promised unto them, and because He hated them, He hath brought them out to slay them in the wilderness. 9:29 Yet they are Thy people and Thine inheritance, that Thou didst bring out by Thy great power and by Thy outstretched arm.' {P}

B 10:1 At that time the LORD said unto me: 'Hew thee two tables of stone like unto the first, and come up unto Me into the mount; and make thee an ark of wood. 10:2 And I will write on the tables the words that were on the first tables which thou didst break, and thou shalt put them in the ark.' 10:3 So I made an ark of acacia-wood, and hewed two tables of stone like unto the first, and went up into the mount, having the two tables in my hand. 10:4 And He wrote on the tables according to the first writing, the ten words, which the LORD spoke unto you in the mount out of the midst of the fire in the day of the assembly; and the LORD gave them unto me. 10:5 And I turned and came down from the mount, and put the tables in the ark which I had made; and there they are, as the LORD commanded me.--

4א

10:10 Now I stayed in the mount, as at the first time, forty days and forty nights; and the LORD hearkened unto me that time also; the LORD would not destroy thee.

1ב

9:6 Know therefore that it is not for thy righteousness that the LORD thy God giveth thee this good land to possess it; for thou art a stiffnecked people. 9:7 Remember, forget thou not, how thou didst make the LORD thy God wroth in the wilderness; from the day that thou didst go forth out of the land of Egypt, until ye came unto this place, ye have been rebellious against the LORD.

2ב

A 9:22 And at Taberah, and at Massah, and at Kibroth-hattaavah, ye made the LORD wroth.

B 9:23 And when the LORD sent you from Kadesh-barnea, saying: 'Go up and possess the land which I have given you'; then ye rebelled against the commandment of the LORD your God, and ye believed Him not, nor hearkened to His voice. 9:24 Ye have been rebellious against the LORD from the day that I knew you.--

3ב

A 10:6 And the children of Israel journeyed from Beeroth-benejaakan to Moserah; there Aaron died, and there he was buried; and Eleazar his son ministered in the priest's office in his stead.

B 10:7 From thence they journeyed unto Gudgod; and from Gudgod to Jotbah, a land of brooks of water.-- 10:8 At that time the LORD separated the tribe of Levi, to bear the ark of the covenant of the LORD, to stand before the LORD to minister unto Him, and to bless in His name, unto this day. 10:9 Wherefore Levi hath no portion nor inheritance with his brethren; the LORD is his inheritance, according as the LORD thy God spoke unto him.--

4ב

10:11 And the LORD said unto me: 'Arise, go before the people, causing them to set forward, that they may go in and possess the land, which I swore unto their fathers to give unto them.' {P}

Deuteronomy Unit VI (10:12-11:32)

1א

10:12 And now, Israel, what doth the LORD thy God require of thee, but to fear the LORD thy God, to walk in all His ways, and to love Him, and to serve the LORD thy God with all thy heart and with all thy soul; 10:13 to keep for thy good the commandments of the LORD, and His statutes, which I command thee this day? 10:14 Behold, unto the LORD thy God belongeth the heaven, and the heaven of heavens, the earth, with all that therein is. 10:15 Only the LORD had a delight in thy fathers to love them, and He chose their seed after them, even you, above all peoples, as it is this day. 10:16 Circumcise therefore the foreskin of your heart, and be no more stiffnecked. 10:17 For the LORD your God, He is God of gods, and Lord of lords, the great God, the mighty, and the awful, who regardeth not persons, nor taketh reward. 10:18 He doth execute justice for the fatherless and widow, and loveth the stranger, in giving him food and raiment. 10:19 Love ye therefore the stranger; for ye were strangers in the land of Egypt. 10:20 Thou shalt fear the LORD thy God; Him shalt thou serve; and to Him shalt thou cleave, and by His name shalt thou swear. 10:21 He is thy glory, and He is thy God, that hath done for thee these great and tremendous things, which thine eyes have seen. 10:22 Thy fathers went down into Egypt with threescore and ten persons; and now the LORD thy God hath made thee as the stars of heaven for multitude.

2א

11:13 And it shall come to pass, if ye shall hearken diligently unto My commandments which I command you this day, to love the LORD your God, and to serve Him with all your heart and with all your soul, 11:14 that I will give the rain of your land in its season, the former rain and the latter rain, that thou mayest gather in thy corn, and thy wine, and thine oil. 11:15 And I will give grass in thy fields for thy cattle, and thou shalt eat and be satisfied. 11:16 Take heed to yourselves, lest your heart be deceived, and ye turn aside, and serve other gods, and worship them; 11:17 and the anger of the LORD be kindled against you, and He shut up the heaven, so that there shall be no rain, and the ground shall not yield her fruit; and ye perish quickly from off the good land which the LORD giveth you. 11:18 Therefore shall ye lay up these My words in your heart and in your soul; and ye shall bind them for a sign upon your hand, and they shall be for frontlets between your eyes. 11:19 And ye shall teach them your children, talking of them, when thou sittest in thy house, and when thou walkest by the way, and when thou liest down, and when thou risest up. 11:20 And thou shalt write them upon the door-posts of thy house, and upon thy gates; 11:21 that your days may be multiplied, and the days of your children, upon the land which the LORD swore unto your fathers to give them, as the days of the heavens above the earth. {S}

1ב

11:1 Therefore thou shalt love the LORD thy God, and keep His charge, and His statutes, and His ordinances, and His commandments, alway. 11:2 And know ye this day; for I speak not with your children that have not known, and that have not seen the chastisement of the LORD your God, His greatness, His mighty hand, and His outstretched arm, 11:3 and His signs, and His works, which He did in the midst of Egypt unto Pharaoh the king of Egypt, and unto all his land; 11:4 and what He did unto the army of Egypt, unto their horses, and to their chariots; how He made the water of the Red Sea to overflow them as they pursued after you, and how the LORD hath destroyed them unto this day; 11:5 and what He did unto you in the wilderness, until ye came unto this place; 11:6 and what He did unto Dathan and Abiram, the sons of Eliab, the son of Reuben; how the earth opened her mouth, and swallowed them up, and their households, and their tents, and every living substance that followed them, in the midst of all Israel; 11:7 but your eyes have seen all the great work of the LORD which He did.

2ב

11:22 For if ye shall diligently keep all this commandment which I command you, to do it, to love the LORD your God, to walk in all His ways, and to cleave unto Him, 11:23 then will the LORD drive out all these nations from before you, and ye shall dispossess nations greater and mightier than yourselves. 11:24 Every place whereon the sole of your foot shall tread shall be yours: from the wilderness, and Lebanon, from the river, the river Euphrates, even unto the hinder sea shall be your border. 11:25 There shall no man be able to stand against you: the LORD your God shall lay the fear of you and the dread of you upon all the land that ye shall tread upon, as He hath spoken unto you. {S}

1ג

11:8 Therefore shall ye keep all the commandment which I command thee this day, that ye may be strong, and go in and possess the land, whither ye go over to possess it; 11:9 and that ye may prolong your days upon the land, which the LORD swore unto your fathers to give unto them and to their seed, a land flowing with milk and honey. {S} 11:10 For the land, whither thou goest in to possess it, is not as the land of Egypt, from whence ye came out, where thou didst sow thy seed, and didst water it with thy foot, as a garden of herbs; 11:11 but the land, whither ye go over to possess it, is a land of hills and valleys, and drinketh water as the rain of heaven cometh down; 11:12 a land which the LORD thy God careth for; the eyes of the LORD thy God are always upon it, from the beginning of the year even unto the end of the year. {S}

2ג

11:26 Behold, I set before you this day a blessing and a curse: 11:27 the blessing, if ye shall hearken unto the commandments of the LORD your God, which I command you this day; 11:28 and the curse, if ye shall not hearken unto the commandments of the LORD your God, but turn aside out of the way which I command you this day, to go after other gods, which ye have not known. {S} 11:29 And it shall come to pass, when the LORD thy God shall bring thee into the land whither thou goest to possess it, that thou shalt set the blessing upon mount Gerizim, and the curse upon mount Ebal. 11:30 Are they not beyond the Jordan, behind the way of the going down of the sun, in the land of the Canaanites that dwell in the Arabah, over against Gilgal, beside the terebinths of Moreh? 11:31 For ye are to pass over the Jordan to go in to possess the land which the LORD your God giveth you, and ye shall possess it, and dwell therein. 11:32 And ye shall observe to do all the statutes and the ordinances which I set before you this day.

Deuteronomy Unit VI (10:12-11:32)

א1

10:12 And now, Israel, what doth the LORD thy God require of thee, but to fear the LORD thy God, to walk in all His ways, and to love Him, and to serve the LORD thy God with all thy heart and with all thy soul; 10:13 to keep for thy good the commandments of the LORD, and His statutes, which I command thee this day? 10:14 Behold, unto the LORD thy God belongeth the heaven, and the heaven of heavens, the earth, with all that therein is. 10:15 Only the LORD had a delight in thy fathers to love them, and He chose their seed after them, even you, above all peoples, as it is this day. 10:16 Circumcise therefore the foreskin of your heart, and be no more stiffnecked. 10:17 For the LORD your God, He is God of gods, and Lord of lords, the great God, the mighty, and the awful, who regardeth not persons, nor taketh reward. 10:18 He doth execute justice for the fatherless and widow, and loveth the stranger, in giving him food and raiment. 10:19 Love ye therefore the stranger; for ye were strangers in the land of Egypt. 10:20 Thou shalt fear the LORD thy God; Him shalt thou serve; and to Him shalt thou cleave, and by His name shalt thou swear. 10:21 He is thy glory, and He is thy God, that hath done for thee these great and tremendous things, which thine eyes have seen. 10:22 Thy fathers went down into Egypt with threescore and ten persons; and now the LORD thy God hath made thee as the stars of heaven for multitude.

ב1

11:1 Therefore thou shalt love the LORD thy God, and keep His charge, and His statutes, and His ordinances, and His commandments, alway. 11:2 And know ye this day; for I speak not with your children that have not known, and that have not seen the chastisement of the LORD your God, His greatness, His mighty hand, and His outstretched arm, 11:3 and His signs, and His works, which He did in the midst of Egypt unto Pharaoh the king of Egypt, and unto all his land; 11:4 and what He did unto the army of Egypt, unto their horses, and to their chariots; how He made the water of the Red Sea to overflow them as they pursued after you, and how the LORD hath destroyed them unto this day; 11:5 and what He did unto you in the wilderness, until ye came unto this place; 11:6 and what He did unto Dathan and Abiram, the sons of Eliab, the son of Reuben; how the earth opened her mouth, and swallowed them up, and their households, and their tents, and every living substance that followed them, in the midst of all Israel; 11:7 but your eyes have seen all the great work of the LORD which He did.

א2

11:8 Therefore shall ye keep all the commandment which I command thee this day, that ye may be strong, and go in and possess the land, whither ye go over to possess it; 11:9 and that ye may prolong your days upon the land, which the LORD swore unto your fathers to give unto them and to their seed, a land flowing with milk and honey. {S} 11:10 For the land, whither thou goest in to possess it, is not as the land of Egypt, from whence ye came out, where thou didst sow thy seed, and didst water it with thy foot, as a garden of herbs; 11:11 but the land, whither ye go over to possess it, is a land of hills and valleys, and drinketh water as the rain of heaven cometh down; 11:12 a land which the LORD thy God careth for; the eyes of the LORD thy God are always upon it, from the beginning of the year even unto the end of the year. {S}

ב2

11:13 And it shall come to pass, if ye shall hearken diligently unto My commandments which I command you this day, to love the LORD your God, and to serve Him with all your heart and with all your soul, 11:14 that I will give the rain of your land in its season, the former rain and the latter rain, that thou mayest gather in thy corn, and thy wine, and thine oil. 11:15 And I will give grass in thy fields for thy cattle, and thou shalt eat and be satisfied. 11:16 Take heed to yourselves, lest your heart be deceived, and ye turn aside, and serve other gods, and worship them; 11:17 and the anger of the LORD be kindled against you, and He shut up the heaven, so that there shall be no rain, and the ground shall not yield her fruit; and ye perish quickly from off the good land which the LORD giveth you. 11:18 Therefore shall ye lay up these My words in your heart and in your soul; and ye shall bind them for a sign upon your hand, and they shall be for frontlets between your eyes. 11:19 And ye shall teach them your children, talking of them, when thou sittest in thy house, and when thou walkest by the way, and when thou liest down, and when thou risest up. 11:20 And thou shalt write them upon the door-posts of thy house, and upon thy gates; 11:21 that your days may be multiplied, and the days of your children, upon the land which the LORD swore unto your fathers to give them, as the days of the heavens above the earth. {S}

א3

11:22 For if ye shall diligently keep all this commandment which I command you, to do it, to love the LORD your God, to walk in all His ways, and to cleave unto Him, 11:23 then will the LORD drive out all these nations from before you, and ye shall dispossess nations greater and mightier than yourselves. 11:24 Every place whereon the sole of your foot shall tread shall be yours: from the wilderness, and Lebanon, from the river, the river Euphrates, even unto the hinder sea shall be your border. 11:25 There shall no man be able to stand against you: the LORD your God shall lay the fear of you and the dread of you upon all the land that ye shall tread upon, as He hath spoken unto you. {S}

ב3

11:26 Behold, I set before you this day a blessing and a curse: 11:27 the blessing, if ye shall hearken unto the commandments of the LORD your God, which I command you this day; 11:28 and the curse, if ye shall not hearken unto the commandments of the LORD your God, but turn aside out of the way which I command you this day, to go after other gods, which ye have not known. {S} 11:29 And it shall come to pass, when the LORD thy God shall bring thee into the land whither thou goest to possess it, that thou shalt set the blessing upon mount Gerizim, and the curse upon mount Ebal. 11:30 Are they not beyond the Jordan, behind the way of the going down of the sun, in the land of the Canaanites that dwell in the Arabah, over against Gilgal, beside the terebinths of Moreh? 11:31 For ye are to pass over the Jordan to go in to possess the land which the LORD your God giveth you, and ye shall possess it, and dwell therein. 11:32 And ye shall observe to do all the statutes and the ordinances which I set before you this day.

Deuteronomy Unit VII (12:1-21:9)

א

A **12:1** These are the statutes and the ordinances, which ye shall observe to do in the land which the LORD, the God of thy fathers, hath given thee to possess it, all the days that ye live upon the earth. **12:2** Ye shall surely destroy all the places, wherein the nations that ye are to dispossess served their gods, upon the high mountains, and upon the hills, and under every leafy tree. **12:3** And ye shall break down their altars, and dash in pieces their pillars, and burn their Asherim with fire; and ye shall hew down the graven images of their gods; and ye shall destroy their name out of that place. **12:4** Ye shall not do so unto the LORD your God. **12:5** But unto the place which the LORD your God shall choose out of all your tribes to put His name there, even unto His habitation shall ye seek, and thither thou shalt come; **12:6** and thither ye shall bring your burnt-offerings, and your sacrifices, and your tithes, and the offering of your hand, and your vows, and your freewill-offerings, and the firstlings of your herd and of your flock; **12:7** and there ye shall eat before the LORD your God, and ye shall rejoice in all that ye put your hand unto, ye and your households, wherein the LORD thy God hath blessed thee.

Bi **12:8** Ye shall not do after all that we do here this day, every man whatsoever is right in his own eyes; **12:9** for ye are not as yet come to the rest and to the inheritance, which the LORD your God giveth thee.

ii **12:10** But when ye go over the Jordan, and dwell in the land which the LORD your God causeth you to inherit, and He giveth you rest from all your enemies round about, so that ye dwell in safety; **12:11** then it shall come to pass that the place which the LORD your God shall choose to cause His name to dwell there, thither shall ye bring all that I command you: your burnt-offerings, and your sacrifices, your tithes, and the offering of your hand, and all your choice vows which ye vow unto the LORD. **12:12** And ye shall rejoice before the LORD your God, ye, and your sons, and your daughters, and your men-servants, and your maid-servants, and the Levite that is within your gates, forasmuch as he hath no portion nor inheritance with you.

iii **12:13** Take heed to thyself that thou offer not thy burnt-offerings in every place that thou seest; **12:14** but in the place which the LORD shall choose in one of thy tribes, there thou shalt offer thy burnt-offerings, and there thou shalt do all that I command thee.

ב

A **12:28** Observe and hear all these words which I command thee, that it may go well with thee, and with thy children after thee for ever, when thou doest that which is good and right in the eyes of the LORD thy God. {S} **12:29** When the LORD thy God shall cut off the nations from before thee, whither thou goest in to dispossess them, and thou dispossessest them, and dwellest in their land; **12:30** take heed to thyself that thou be not ensnared to follow them, after that they are destroyed from before thee; and that thou inquire not after their gods, saying: 'How used these nations to serve their gods? even so will I do likewise.' **12:31** Thou shalt not do so unto the LORD thy God; for every abomination to the LORD, which He hateth, have they done unto their gods; for even their sons and their daughters do they burn in the fire to their gods. **13:1** All this word which I command you, that shall ye observe to do; thou shalt not add thereto, nor diminish from it. {P}

Bi **13:2** If there arise in the midst of thee a prophet, or a dreamer of dreams--and he give thee a sign or a wonder, **13:3** and the sign or the wonder come to pass, whereof he spoke unto thee--saying: 'Let us go after other gods, which thou hast not known, and let us serve them'; **13:4** thou shalt not hearken unto the words of that prophet, or unto that dreamer of dreams; for the LORD your God putteth you to proof, to know whether ye do love the LORD your God with all your heart and with all your soul. **13:5** After the LORD your God shall ye walk, and Him shall ye fear, and His commandments shall ye keep, and unto His voice shall ye hearken, and Him shall ye serve, and unto Him shall ye cleave. **13:6** And that prophet, or that dreamer of dreams, shall be put to death; because he hath spoken perversion against the LORD your God, who brought you out of the land of Egypt, and redeemed thee out of the house of bondage, to draw thee aside out of the way which the LORD thy God commanded thee to walk in. So shalt thou put away the evil from the midst of thee. {S}

ii **13:7** If thy brother, the son of thy mother, or thy son, or thy daughter, or the wife of thy bosom, or thy friend, that is as thine own soul, entice thee secretly, saying: 'Let us go and serve other gods,' which thou hast not known, thou, nor thy fathers; **13:8** of the gods of the peoples that are round about you, nigh unto thee, or far off from thee, from the one end of the earth even unto the other end of the earth; **13:9** thou shalt not consent unto him, nor hearken unto him; neither shall thine eye pity him, neither shalt thou spare, neither shalt thou conceal him; **13:10** but thou shalt surely kill him; thy hand shall be first upon him to put him to death, and afterwards the hand of all the people. **13:11** And thou shalt stone him with stones, that he die; because he hath sought to draw thee away from the LORD thy God, who brought thee out of the land of Egypt, out of the house of bondage. **13:12** And all Israel shall hear, and fear, and shall do no more any such wickedness as this is in the midst of thee. {S}

iii **13:13** If thou shalt hear tell concerning one of thy cities, which the LORD thy God giveth thee to dwell there, saying: **13:14** 'Certain base fellows are gone out from the midst of thee, and have drawn away the inhabitants of their city, saying: Let us go and serve other gods, which ye have not known'; **13:15** then shalt thou inquire, and make search, and ask diligently; and, behold, if it be truth, and the thing certain, that such abomination is wrought in the midst of thee; **13:16** thou shalt surely smite the inhabitants of that city with the edge of the sword, destroying it utterly, and all that is therein and the cattle thereof, with the edge of the sword. **13:17** And thou shalt gather all the spoil of it into the midst of the broad place thereof, and shall burn with fire the city, and all the spoil thereof every whit, unto the LORD thy God; and it shall be a heap for ever; it shall not be built again. **13:18** And there shall cleave nought of the devoted thing to thy hand, that the LORD may turn from the fierceness of His anger, and show thee mercy, and have compassion upon thee, and multiply thee, as He hath sworn unto thy fathers; **13:19** when thou shalt hearken to the voice of the LORD thy God, to keep all His commandments which I command thee this day, to do that which is right in the eyes of the LORD thy God. {S}

C 12:15 Notwithstanding thou mayest kill and eat flesh within all thy gates, after all the desire of thy soul, according to the blessing of the LORD thy God which He hath given thee; the unclean and the clean may eat thereof, as of the gazelle, and as of the hart. 12:16 Only ye shall not eat the blood; thou shalt pour it out upon the earth as water.

Di 12:17 Thou mayest not eat within thy gates the tithe of thy corn, or of thy wine, or of thine oil, or the firstlings of thy herd or of thy flock, nor any of thy vows which thou vowest, nor thy freewill-offerings, nor the offering of thy hand; 12:18 but thou shalt eat them before the LORD thy God in the place which the LORD thy God shall choose, thou, and thy son, and thy daughter, and thy man-servant, and thy maid-servant, and the Levite that is within thy gates; and thou shalt rejoice before the LORD thy God in all that thou puttest thy hand unto. 12:19 Take heed to thyself that thou forsake not the Levite as long as thou livest upon thy land. {S}

ii 12:20 When the LORD thy God shall enlarge thy border, as He hath promised thee, and thou shalt say: 'I will eat flesh', because thy soul desireth to eat flesh; thou mayest eat flesh, after all the desire of thy soul. 12:21 If the place which the LORD thy God shall choose to put His name there be too far from thee, then thou shalt kill of thy herd and of thy flock, which the LORD hath given thee, as I have commanded thee, and thou shalt eat within thy gates, after all the desire of thy soul. 12:22 Howbeit as the gazelle and as the hart is eaten, so thou shalt eat thereof; the unclean and the clean may eat thereof alike. 12:23 Only be stedfast in not eating the blood; for the blood is the life; and thou shalt not eat the life with the flesh. 12:24 Thou shalt not eat it; thou shalt pour it out upon the earth as water. 12:25 Thou shalt not eat it; that it may go well with thee, and with thy children after thee, when thou shalt do that which is right in the eyes of the LORD. 12:26 Only thy holy things which thou hast, and thy vows, thou shalt take, and go unto the place which the LORD shall choose; 12:27 and thou shalt offer thy burnt-offerings, the flesh and the blood, upon the altar of the LORD thy God; and the blood of thy sacrifices shall be poured out against the altar of the LORD thy God, and thou shalt eat the flesh.

C 14:1 Ye are the children of the LORD your God: ye shall not cut yourselves, nor make any baldness between your eyes for the dead. 14:2 For thou art a holy people unto the LORD thy God, and the LORD hath chosen thee to be His own treasure out of all peoples that are upon the face of the earth. {S} 14:3 Thou shalt not eat any abominable thing. 14:4 These are the beasts which ye may eat: the ox, the sheep, and the goat, 14:5 the hart, and the gazelle, and the roebuck, and the wild goat, and the pygarg, and the antelope, and the mountain-sheep. 14:6 And every beast that parteth the hoof, and hath the hoof wholly cloven in two, and cheweth the cud, among the beasts, that ye may eat. 14:7 Nevertheless these ye shall not eat of them that only chew the cud, or of them that only have the hoof cloven: the camel, and the hare, and the rock-badger, because they chew the cud but part not the hoof, they are unclean unto you; 14:8 and the swine, because he parteth the hoof but cheweth not the cud, he is unclean unto you; of their flesh ye shall not eat, and their carcasses ye shall not touch. {S} 14:9 These ye may eat of all that are in the waters: whatsoever hath fins and scales may ye eat; 14:10 and whatsoever hath not fins and scales ye shall not eat; it is unclean unto you. {S} 14:11 Of all clean birds ye may eat. 14:12 But these are they of which ye shall not eat: the great vulture, and the bearded vulture, and the ospray; 14:13 and the glede, and the falcon, and the kite after its kinds; 14:14 and every raven after its kinds; 14:15 and the ostrich, and the night-hawk, and the sea-mew, and the hawk after its kinds; 14:16 the little owl, and the great owl, and the horned owl; 14:17 and the pelican, and the carrion-vulture, and the cormorant; 14:18 and the stork, and the heron after its kinds, and the hoopoe, and the bat. 14:19 And all winged swarming things are unclean unto you; they shall not be eaten. 14:20 Of all clean winged things ye may eat. 14:21 Ye shall not eat of any thing that dieth of itself; thou mayest give it unto the stranger that is within thy gates, that he may eat it; or thou mayest sell it unto a foreigner; for thou art a holy people unto the LORD thy God. Thou shalt not seethe a kid in its mother's milk. {P}

Di 14:22 Thou shalt surely tithe all the increase of thy seed, that which is brought forth in the field year by year. 14:23 And thou shalt eat before the LORD thy God, in the place which He shall choose to cause His name to dwell there, the tithe of thy corn, of thy wine, and of thine oil, and the firstlings of thy herd and of thy flock; that thou mayest learn to fear the LORD thy God always.

ii 14:24 And if the way be too long for thee, so that thou art not able to carry it, because the place is too far from thee, which the LORD thy God shall choose to set His name there, when the LORD thy God shall bless thee; 14:25 then shalt thou turn it into money, and bind up the money in thy hand, and shalt go unto the place which the LORD thy God shall choose. 14:26 And thou shalt bestow the money for whatsoever thy soul desireth, for oxen, or for sheep, or for wine, or for strong drink, or for whatsoever thy soul asketh of thee; and thou shalt eat there before the LORD thy God, and thou shalt rejoice, thou and thy household. 14:27 And the Levite that is within thy gates, thou shalt not forsake him; for he hath no portion nor inheritance with thee. {S}

2א

A 14:28 At the end of every three years, even in the same year, thou shalt bring forth all the tithe of thine increase, and shalt lay it up within thy gates. 14:29 And the Levite, because he hath no portion nor inheritance with thee, and the stranger, and the fatherless, and the widow, that are within thy gates, shall come, and shall eat and be satisfied; that the LORD thy God may bless thee in all the work of thy hand which thou doest. {S}

B 15:1 At the end of every seven years thou shalt make a release. 15:2 And this is the manner of the release: every creditor shall release that which he hath lent unto his neighbour; he shall not exact it of his neighbour and his brother; because the LORD'S release hath been proclaimed. 15:3 Of a foreigner thou mayest exact it; but whatsoever of thine is with thy brother thy hand shall release. 15:4 Howbeit there shall be no needy among you--for the LORD will surely bless thee in the land which the LORD thy God giveth thee for an inheritance to possess it-- 15:5 if only thou diligently hearken unto the voice of the LORD thy God, to observe to do all this commandment which I command thee this day. 15:6 For the LORD thy God will bless thee, as He promised thee; and thou shalt lend unto many nations, but thou shalt not borrow; and thou shalt rule over many nations, but they shall not rule over thee. {S}

C 15:7 If there be among you a needy man, one of thy brethren, within any of thy gates, in thy land which the LORD thy God giveth thee, thou shalt not harden thy heart, nor shut thy hand from thy needy brother; 15:8 but thou shalt surely open thy hand unto him, and shalt surely lend him sufficient for his need in that which he wanteth. 15:9 Beware that there be not a base thought in thy heart, saying: 'The seventh year, the year of release, is at hand'; and thine eye be evil against thy needy brother, and thou give him nought; and he cry unto the LORD against thee, and it be sin in thee. 15:10 Thou shalt surely give him, and thy heart shall not be grieved when thou givest unto him; because that for this thing the LORD thy God will bless thee in all thy work, and in all that thou puttest thy hand unto. 15:11 For the poor shall never cease out of the land; therefore I command thee, saying: 'Thou shalt surely open thy hand unto thy poor and needy brother, in thy land.' {S}
D 15:12 If thy brother, a Hebrew man, or a Hebrew woman, be sold unto thee, he shall serve thee six years; and in the seventh year thou shalt let him go free from thee. 15:13 And when thou lettest him go free from thee, thou shalt not let him go empty; 15:14 thou shalt furnish him liberally out of thy flock, and out of thy threshing-floor, and out of thy winepress; of that wherewith the LORD thy God hath blessed thee thou shalt give unto him. 15:15 And thou shalt remember that thou wast a bondman in the land of Egypt, and the LORD thy God redeemed thee; therefore I command thee this thing to-day. 15:16 And it shall be, if he say unto thee: 'I will not go out from thee'; because he loveth thee and thy house, because he fareth well with thee; 15:17 then thou shalt take an awl, and thrust it through his ear and into the door, and he shall be thy bondman for ever. And also unto thy bondwoman thou shalt do likewise. 15:18 It shall not seem hard unto thee, when thou lettest him go free from thee; for to the double of the hire of a hireling hath he served thee six years; and the LORD thy God will bless thee in all that thou doest. {P}

2ב

A 15:19 All the firstling males that are born of thy herd and of thy flock thou shalt sanctify unto the LORD thy God; thou shalt do no work with the firstling of thine ox, nor shear the firstling of thy flock. 15:20 Thou shalt eat it before the LORD thy God year by year in the place which the LORD shall choose, thou and thy household. 15:21 And if there be any blemish therein, lameness, or blindness, any ill blemish whatsoever, thou shalt not sacrifice it unto the LORD thy God. 15:22 Thou shalt eat it within thy gates; the unclean and the clean may eat it alike, as the gazelle, and as the hart. 15:23 Only thou shalt not eat the blood thereof; thou shalt pour it out upon the ground as water. {P}
B 16:1 Observe the month of Abib, and keep the passover unto the LORD thy God; for in the month of Abib the LORD thy God brought thee forth out of Egypt by night. 16:2 And thou shalt sacrifice the passover-offering unto the LORD thy God, of the flock and the herd, in the place which the LORD shall choose to cause His name to dwell there. 16:3 Thou shalt eat no leavened bread with it; seven days shalt thou eat unleavened bread therewith, even the bread of affliction; for in haste didst thou come forth out of the land of Egypt; that thou mayest remember the day when thou camest forth out of the land of Egypt all the days of thy life. 16:4 And there shall be no leaven seen with thee in all they borders seven days; neither shall any of the flesh, which thou sacrificest the first day at even, remain all night until the morning. 16:5 Thou mayest not sacrifice the passover-offering within any of thy gates, which the LORD thy God giveth thee; 16:6 but at the place which the LORD thy God shall choose to cause His name to dwell in, there thou shalt sacrifice the passover-offering at even, at the going down of the sun, at the season that thou camest forth out of Egypt. 16:7 And thou shalt roast and eat it in the place which the LORD thy God shall choose; and thou shalt turn in the morning, and go unto thy tents. 16:8 Six days thou shalt eat unleavened bread; and on the seventh day shall be a solemn assembly to the LORD thy God; thou shalt do no work therein. {S}

C 16:9 Seven weeks shalt thou number unto thee; from the time the sickle is first put to the standing corn shalt thou begin to number seven weeks. 16:10 And thou shalt keep the feast of weeks unto the LORD thy God after the measure of the freewill-offering of thy hand, which thou shalt give, according as the LORD thy God blesseth thee. 16:11 And thou shalt rejoice before the LORD thy God, thou, and thy son, and thy daughter, and thy man-servant, and thy maid-servant, and the Levite that is within they gates, and the stranger, and the fatherless, and the widow, that are in the midst of thee, in the place which the LORD thy God shall choose to cause His name to dwell there. 16:12 And thou shalt remember that thou wast a bondman in Egypt; and thou shalt observe and do these statutes. {P}

D 16:13 Thou shalt keep the feast of tabernacles seven days, after that thou hast gathered in from thy threshing-floor and from thy winepress. 16:14 And thou shalt rejoice in thy feast, thou, and thy son, and thy daughter, and thy man-servant, and thy maid-servant, and the Levite, and the stranger, and the fatherless, and the widow, that are within thy gates. 16:15 Seven days shalt thou keep a feast unto the LORD thy God in the place which the LORD shall choose; because the LORD thy God shall bless thee in all thine increase, and in all the work of thy hands, and thou shalt be altogether joyful. 16:16 Three times in a year shall all thy males appear before the LORD thy God in the place which He shall choose; on the feast of unleavened bread, and on the feast of weeks, and on the feast of tabernacles; and they shall not appear before the LORD empty; 16:17 every man shall give as he is able, according to the blessing of the LORD thy God which He hath given thee. {S}

אג

Ai 16:18 Judges and officers shalt thou make thee in all thy gates, which the LORD thy God giveth thee, tribe by tribe; and they shall judge the people with righteous judgment.

ii 16:19 Thou shalt not wrest judgment; thou shalt not respect persons; neither shalt thou take a gift; for a gift doth blind the eyes of the wise, and pervert the words of the righteous. 16:20 Justice, justice shalt thou follow, that thou mayest live, and inherit the land which the LORD thy God giveth thee. {S}

Bi 16:21 Thou shalt not plant thee an Asherah of any kind of tree beside the altar of the LORD thy God, which thou shalt make thee.

ii 16:22 Neither shalt thou set thee up a pillar, which the LORD thy God hateth. {S}

iii 17:1 Thou shalt not sacrifice unto the LORD thy God an ox, or a sheep, wherein is a blemish, even any evil thing; for that is an abomination unto the LORD thy God. {S}

Ci 17:2 If there be found in the midst of thee, within any of thy gates which the LORD thy God giveth thee, man or woman, that doeth that which is evil in the sight of the LORD thy God, in transgressing His covenant, 17:3 and hath gone and served other gods, and worshipped them, or the sun, or the moon, or any of the host of heaven, which I have commanded not; 17:4 and it be told thee, and thou hear it, then shalt thou inquire diligently, and, behold, if it be true, and the thing certain, that such abomination is wrought in Israel; 17:5 then shalt thou bring forth that man or that woman, who have done this evil thing, unto thy gates, even the man or the woman; and thou shalt stone them with stones, that they die. 17:6 At the mouth of two witnesses, or three witnesses, shall he that is to die be put to death; at the mouth of one witness he shall not be put to death. 17:7 The hand of the witnesses shall be first upon him to put him to death, and afterward the hand of all the people. So thou shalt put away the evil from the midst of thee. {P}
ii 17:8 If there arise a matter too hard for thee in judgment, between blood and blood, between plea and plea, and between stroke and stroke, even matters of controversy within thy gates; then shalt thou arise, and get thee up unto the place which the LORD thy God shall choose. 17:9 And thou shall come unto the priests the Levites, and unto the judge that shall be in those days; and thou shalt inquire; and they shall declare unto thee the sentence of judgment. 17:10 And thou shalt do according to the tenor of the sentence, which they shall declare unto thee from that place which the LORD shall choose; and thou shalt observe to do according to all that they shall teach thee. 17:11 According to the law which they shall teach thee, and according to the judgment which they shall tell thee, thou shalt do; thou shalt not turn aside from the sentence which they shall declare unto thee, to the right hand, nor to the left.
iii
17:12 And the man that doeth presumptuously, in not hearkening unto the priest that standeth to minister there before the LORD thy God, or unto the judge, even that man shall die; and thou shalt exterminate the evil from Israel. 17:13 And all the people shall hear, and fear, and do no more presumptuously. {S}

בג

Ai 17:14 When thou art come unto the land which the LORD thy God giveth thee, and shalt possess it, and shalt dwell therein; and shalt say: 'I will set a king over me', like all the nations that are round about me'; 17:15 thou shalt in any wise set him king over thee, whom the LORD thy God shall choose; one from among thy brethren shalt thou set king over thee; thou mayest not put a foreigner over thee, who is not thy brother. 17:16 Only he shall not multiply horses to himself, nor cause the people to return to Egypt, to the end that he should multiply horses; forasmuch as the LORD hath said unto you: 'Ye shall henceforth return no more that way.' 17:17 Neither shall he multiply wives to himself, that his heart turn not away; neither shall he greatly multiply to himself silver and gold.
ii 17:18 And it shall be, when he sitteth upon the throne of his kingdom, that he shall write him a copy of this law in a book, out of that which is before the priests the Levites. 17:19 And it shall be with him, and he shall read therein all the days of his life; that he may learn to fear the LORD his God, to keep all the words of this law and these statutes, to do them; 17:20 that his heart be not lifted up above his brethren, and that he turn not aside from the commandment, to the right hand, or to the left; to the end that he may prolong his days in his kingdom, he and his children, in the midst of Israel. {S}
Bi 18:1 The priests the Levites, even all the tribe of Levi, shall have no portion nor inheritance with Israel; they shall eat the offerings of the LORD made by fire, and His inheritance. 18:2 And they shall have no inheritance among their brethren; the LORD is their inheritance, as He hath spoken unto them. {S}
ii 18:3 And this shall be the priests' due from the people, from them that offer a sacrifice, whether it be ox or sheep, that they shall give unto the priest the shoulder, and the two cheeks, and the maw. 18:4 The first-fruits of thy corn, of thy wine, and of thine oil, and the first of the fleece of thy sheep, shalt thou give him. 18:5 For the LORD thy God hath chosen him out of all thy tribes, to stand to minister in the name of the LORD, him and his sons for ever. {S}
iii 18:6 And if a Levite come from any of thy gates out of all Israel, where he sojourneth, and come with all the desire of his soul unto the place which the LORD shall choose; 18:7 then he shall minister in the name of the LORD his God, as all his brethren the Levites do, who stand there before the LORD. 18:8 They shall have like portions to eat, beside that which is his due according to the fathers' houses. {S}
Ci 18:9 When thou art come into the land which the LORD thy God giveth thee, thou shalt not learn to do after the abominations of those nations. 18:10 There shall not be found among you any one that maketh his son or his daughter to pass through the fire, one that useth divination, a soothsayer, or an enchanter, or a sorcerer, 18:11 or a charmer, or one that consulteth a ghost or a familiar spirit, or a necromancer. 18:12 For whosoever doeth these things is an abomination unto the LORD; and because of these abominations the LORD thy God is driving them out from before thee. 18:13 Thou shalt be whole-hearted with the LORD thy God. 18:14 For these nations, that thou art to dispossess, hearken unto soothsayers, and unto diviners; but as for thee, the LORD thy God hath not suffered thee so to do.

ii 18:15 A prophet will the LORD thy God raise up unto thee, from the midst of thee, of thy brethren, like unto me; unto him ye shall hearken; 18:16 according to all that thou didst desire of the LORD thy God in Horeb in the day of the assembly, saying: 'Let me not hear again the voice of the LORD my God, neither let me see this great fire any more, that I die not.' 18:17 And the LORD said unto me: 'They have well said that which they have spoken. 18:18 I will raise them up a prophet from among their brethren, like unto thee; and I will put My words in his mouth, and he shall speak unto them all that I shall command him. 18:19 And it shall come to pass, that whosoever will not hearken unto My words which he shall speak in My name, I will require it of him.

iii 18:20 But the prophet, that shall speak a word presumptuously in My name, which I have not commanded him to speak, or that shall speak in the name of other gods, that same prophet shall die.' 18:21 And if thou say in thy heart: 'How shall we know the word which the LORD hath not spoken?' 18:22 When a prophet speaketh in the name of the LORD, if the thing follow not, nor come to pass, that is the thing which the LORD hath not spoken; the prophet hath spoken it presumptuously, thou shalt not be afraid of him. {S}

מח

Ai 19:1 When the LORD thy God shall cut off the nations, whose land the LORD thy God giveth thee, and thou dost succeed them, and dwell in their cities, and in their houses; 19:2 thou shalt separate three cities for thee in the midst of thy land, which the LORD thy GOD giveth thee to possess it. 19:3 Thou shalt prepare thee the way, and divide the borders of thy land, which the LORD thy God causeth thee to inherit, into three parts, that every manslayer may flee thither.

ii 19:4 And this is the case of the manslayer, that shall flee thither and live: whoso killeth his neighbour unawares, and hated him not in time past; 19:5 as when a man goeth into the forest with his neighbour to hew wood, and his hand fetcheth a stroke with the axe to cut down the tree, and the head slippeth from the helve, and lighteth upon his neighbour, that he die; he shall flee unto one of these cities and live; 19:6 lest the avenger of blood pursue the manslayer, while his heart is hot, and overtake him, because the way is long, and smite him mortally; whereas he was not deserving of death, inasmuch as he hated him not in time past. 19:7 Wherefore I command thee, saying: 'Thou shalt separate three cities for thee.'

iii 19:8 And if the LORD thy God enlarge thy border, as He hath sworn unto thy fathers, and give thee all the land which He promised to give unto thy fathers-- 19:9 if thou shalt keep all this commandment to do it, which I command thee this day, to love the LORD thy God, and to walk ever in His ways--then shalt thou add three cities more for thee, beside these three; 19:10 that innocent blood be not shed in the midst of thy land, which the LORD thy God giveth thee for an inheritance, and so blood be upon thee. {P}

iv 19:11 But if any man hate his neighbour, and lie in wait for him, and rise up against him, and smite him mortally that he die; and he flee into one of these cities; 19:12 then the elders of his city shall send and fetch him thence, and deliver him into the hand of the avenger of blood, that he may die. 19:13 Thine eye shall not pity him, but thou shalt put away the blood of the innocent from Israel, that it may go well with thee. {S}

B 19:14 Thou shalt not remove thy neighbour's landmark, which they of old time have set, in thine inheritance which thou shalt inherit, in the land that the LORD thy God giveth thee to possess it. {S}

C 19:15 One witness shall not rise up against a man for any iniquity, or for any sin, in any sin that he sinneth; at the mouth of two witnesses, or at the mouth of three witnesses, shall a matter be established. 19:16 If an unrighteous witness rise up against any man to bear perverted witness against him; 19:17 then both the men, between whom the controversy is, shall stand before the LORD, before the priests and the judges that shall be in those days. 19:18 And the judges shall inquire diligently; and, behold, if the witness be a false witness, and hath testified falsely against his brother; 19:19 then shall ye do unto him, as he had purposed to do unto his brother; so shalt thou put away the evil from the midst of thee. 19:20 And those that remain shall hear, and fear, and shall henceforth commit no more any such evil in the midst of thee. 19:21 And thine eye shall not pity: life for life, eye for eye, tooth for tooth, hand for hand, foot for foot. {S}

מט

Ai 20:1 When thou goest forth to battle against thine enemies, and seest horses, and chariots, and a people more than thou, thou shalt not be afraid of them; for the LORD thy God is with thee, who brought thee up out of the land of Egypt. 20:2 And it shall be, when ye draw nigh unto the battle, that the priest shall approach and speak unto the people, 20:3 and shall say unto them: 'Hear, O Israel, ye draw nigh this day unto battle against your enemies; let not your heart faint; fear not, nor be alarmed, neither be ye affrighted at them; 20:4 for the LORD your God is He that goeth with you, to fight for you against your enemies, to save you.'

ii 20:5 And the officers shall speak unto the people, saying: 'What man is there that hath built a new house, and hath not dedicated it? let him go and return to his house, lest he die in the battle, and another man dedicate it. 20:6 And what man is there that hath planted a vineyard, and hath not used the fruit thereof? let him go and return unto his house, lest he die in the battle, and another man use the fruit thereof. 20:7 And what man is there that hath betrothed a wife, and hath not taken her? let him go and return unto his house, lest he die in the battle, and another man take her.' 20:8 And the officers shall speak further unto the people, and they shall say: 'What man is there that is fearful and faint-hearted? let him go and return unto his house, lest his brethren's heart melt as his heart.' 20:9 And it shall be, when the officers have made an end of speaking unto the people, that captains of hosts shall be appointed at the head of the people. {S}

iii 20:10 When thou drawest nigh unto a city to fight against it, then proclaim peace unto it. 20:11 And it shall be, if it make thee answer of peace, and open unto thee, then it shall be, that all the people that are found therein shall become tributary unto thee, and shall serve thee. 20:12 And if it will make no peace with thee, but will make war against thee, then thou shalt besiege it. 20:13 And when the LORD thy God delivereth it into thy hand, thou shalt smite every male thereof with the edge of the sword; 20:14 but the women, and the little ones, and the cattle, and all that is in the city, even all the spoil thereof, shalt thou take for a prey unto thyself; and thou shalt eat the spoil of thine enemies, which the LORD thy God hath given thee. 20:15 Thus shalt thou do unto all the cities which are very far off from thee, which are not of the cities of these nations.

iv 20:16 Howbeit of the cities of these peoples, that the LORD thy God giveth thee for an inheritance, thou shalt save alive nothing that breatheth, 20:17 but thou shalt utterly destroy them: the Hittite, and the Amorite, the Canaanite, and the Perizzite, the Hivite, and the Jebusite; as the LORD thy God hath commanded thee; 20:18 that they teach you not to do after all their abominations, which they have done unto their gods, and so ye sin against the LORD your God. {S}

B 20:19 When thou shalt besiege a city a long time, in making war against it to take it, thou shalt not destroy the trees thereof by wielding an axe against them; for thou mayest eat of them, but thou shalt not cut them down; for is the tree of the field man, that it should be besieged of thee? 20:20 Only the trees of which thou knowest that they are not trees for food, them thou mayest destroy and cut down, that thou mayest build bulwarks against the city that maketh war with thee, until it fall. {P}

C 21:1 If one be found slain in the land which the LORD thy God giveth thee to possess it, lying in the field, and it be not known who hath smitten him; 21:2 then thy elders and thy judges shall come forth, and they shall measure unto the cities which are round about him that is slain. 21:3 And it shall be, that the city which is nearest unto the slain man, even the elders of that city shall take a heifer of the herd, which hath not been wrought with, and which hath not drawn in the yoke. 21:4 And the elders of that city shall bring down the heifer unto a rough valley, which may neither be plowed nor sown, and shall break the heifer's neck there in the valley. 21:5 And the priests the sons of Levi shall come near--for them the LORD thy God hath chosen to minister unto Him, and to bless in the name of the LORD; and according to their word shall every controversy and every stroke be. 21:6 And all the elders of that city, who are nearest unto the slain man, shall wash their hands over the heifer whose neck was broken in the valley. 21:7 And they shall speak and say: 'Our hands have not shed this blood, neither have our eyes seen it. 21:8 Forgive, O LORD, Thy people Israel, whom Thou hast redeemed, and suffer not innocent blood to remain in the midst of Thy people Israel.' And the blood shall be forgiven them. 21:9 So shalt thou put away the innocent blood from the midst of thee, when thou shalt do that which is right in the eyes of the LORD. {S}

Deuteronomy Unit VIII (21:10-25:4)

א

Ai 21:10 When thou goest forth to battle against thine enemies, and the LORD thy God delivereth them into thy hands, and thou carriest them away captive, 21:11 and seest among the captives a woman of goodly form, and thou hast a desire unto her, and wouldest take her to thee to wife; 21:12 then thou shalt bring her home to thy house; and she shall shave her head, and pare her nails; 21:13 and she shall put the raiment of her captivity from off her, and shall remain in thy house, and bewail her father and her mother a full month; and after that thou mayest go in unto her, and be her husband, and she shall be thy wife. 21:14 And it shall be, if thou have no delight in her, then thou shalt let her go whither she will; but thou shalt not sell her at all for money, thou shalt not deal with her as a slave, because thou hast humbled her. {S}

ii 21:15 If a man have two wives, the one beloved, and the other hated, and they have borne him children, both the beloved and the hated; and if the first-born son be hers that was hated; 21:16 then it shall be, in the day that he causeth his sons to inherit that which he hath, that he may not make the son of the beloved the first-born before the son of the hated, who is the first-born; 21:17 but he shall acknowledge the first-born, the son of the hated, by giving him a double portion of all that he hath; for he is the first-fruits of his strength, the right of the first-born is his. {S}

ב

Ai 22:13 If any man take a wife, and go in unto her, and hate her, 22:14 and lay wanton charges against her, and bring up an evil name upon her, and say: 'I took this woman, and when I came nigh to her, I found not in her the tokens of virginity'; 22:15 then shall the father of the damsel, and her mother, take and bring forth the tokens of the damsel's virginity unto the elders of the city in the gate. 22:16 And the damsel's father shall say unto the elders: 'I gave my daughter unto this man to wife, and he hateth her; 22:17 and, lo, he hath laid wanton charges, saying: I found not in thy daughter the tokens of virginity; and yet these are the tokens of my daughter's virginity.' And they shall spread the garment before the elders of the city. 22:18 And the elders of that city shall take the man and chastise him. 22:19 And they shall fine him a hundred shekels of silver, and give them unto the father of the damsel, because he hath brought up an evil name upon a virgin of Israel; and she shall be his wife; he may not put her away all his days. {S} 22:20 But if this thing be true, that the tokens of virginity were not found in the damsel; 22:21 then they shall bring out the damsel to the door of her father's house, and the men of her city shall stone her with stones that she die; because she hath wrought a wanton deed in Israel, to play the harlot in her father's house; so shalt thou put away the evil from the midst of thee. {S}

ii 22:22 If a man be found lying with a woman married to a husband, then they shall both of them die, the man that lay with the woman, and the woman; so shalt thou put away the evil from Israel. {S} 22:23 If there be a damsel that is a virgin betrothed unto a man, and a man find her in the city, and lie with her; 22:24 then ye shall bring them both out unto the gate of that city, and ye shall stone them with stones that they die: the damsel, because she cried not, being in the city; and the man, because he hath humbled his neighbour's wife; so thou shalt put away the evil from the midst of thee. {S} 22:25 But if the man find the damsel that is betrothed in the field, and the man take hold of her, and lie with her; then the man only that lay with her shall die. 22:26 But unto the damsel thou shalt do nothing; there is in the damsel no sin worthy of death; for as when a man riseth against his neighbour, and slayeth him, even so is this matter. 22:27 For he found her in the field; the betrothed damsel cried, and there was none to save her. {S} 22:28 If a man find a damsel that is a virgin, that is not betrothed, and lay hold on her, and lie with her, and they be found; 22:29 then the man that lay with her shall give unto the damsel's father fifty shekels of silver, and she shall be his wife, because he hath humbled her; he may not put her away all his days. {S} 23:1 A man shall not take his father's wife, and shall not uncover his father's skirt. {S}

ג

Ai 24:1 When a man taketh a wife, and marrieth her, then it cometh to pass, if she find no favour in his eyes, because he hath found some unseemly thing in her, that he writeth her a bill of divorcement, and giveth it in her hand, and sendeth her out of his house, 24:2 and she departeth out of his house, and goeth and becometh another man's wife, 24:3 and the latter husband hateth her, and writeth her a bill of divorcement, and giveth it in her hand, and sendeth her out of his house; or if the latter husband die, who took her to be his wife; 24:4 her former husband, who sent her away, may not take her again to be his wife, after that she is defiled; for that is abomination before the LORD; and thou shalt not cause the land to sin, which the LORD thy God giveth thee for an inheritance. {S}

ii 24:5 When a man taketh a new wife, he shall not go out in the host, neither shall he be charged with any business; he shall be free for his house one year, and shall cheer his wife whom he hath taken. 24:6 No man shall take the mill or the upper millstone to pledge; for he taketh a man's life to pledge. {S}

Bi 21:18 If a man have a stubborn and rebellious son, that will not hearken to the voice of his father, or the voice of his mother, and though they chasten him, will not hearken unto them; 21:19 then shall his father and his mother lay hold on him, and bring him out unto the elders of his city, and unto the gate of his place; 21:20 and they shall say unto the elders of his city: 'This our son is stubborn and rebellious, he doth not hearken to our voice; he is a glutton, and a drunkard.' 21:21 And all the men of his city shall stone him with stones, that he die; so shalt thou put away the evil from the midst of thee; and all Israel shall hear, and fear. {S}

ii 21:22 And if a man have committed a sin worthy of death, and he be put to death, and thou hang him on a tree; 21:23 his body shall not remain all night upon the tree, but thou shalt surely bury him the same day; for he that is hanged is a reproach unto God; that thou defile not thy land which the LORD thy God giveth thee for an inheritance. {S}

Ci 22:1 Thou shalt not see thy brother's ox or his sheep driven away, and hide thyself from them; thou shalt surely bring them back unto thy brother. 22:2 And if thy brother be not nigh unto thee, and thou know him not, then thou shalt bring it home to thy house, and it shall be with thee until thy brother require it, and thou shalt restore it to him. 22:3 And so shalt thou do with his ass; and so shalt thou do with his garment; and so shalt thou do with every lost thing of thy brother's, which he hath lost, and thou hast found; thou mayest not hide thyself. {S}

ii 22:4 Thou shalt not see thy brother's ass or his ox fallen down by the way, and hide thyself from them; thou shalt surely help him to lift them up again. {S}

Bi 23:2 He that is crushed or maimed in his privy parts shall not enter into the assembly of the LORD. {S} 23:3 A bastard shall not enter into the assembly of the LORD; even to the tenth generation shall none of his enter into the assembly of the LORD. {S} 23:4 An Ammonite or a Moabite shall not enter into the assembly of the LORD; even to the tenth generation shall none of them enter into the assembly of the LORD for ever; 23:5 because they met you not with bread and with water in the way, when ye came forth out of Egypt; and because they hired against thee Balaam the son of Beor from Pethor of Aram-naharaim, to curse thee. 23:6 Nevertheless the LORD thy God would not hearken unto Balaam; but the LORD thy God turned the curse into a blessing unto thee, because the LORD thy God loved thee. 23:7 Thou shalt not seek their peace nor their prosperity all thy days for ever. {S} 23:8 Thou shalt not abhor an Edomite, for he is thy brother; thou shalt not abhor an Egyptian, because thou wast a stranger in his land. 23:9 The children of the third generation that are born unto them may enter into the assembly of the LORD. {S}

ii 23:10 When thou goest forth in camp against thine enemies, then thou shalt keep thee from every evil thing. 23:11 If there be among you any man, that is not clean by reason of that which chanceth him by night, then shall he go abroad out of the camp, he shall not come within the camp. 23:12 But it shall be, when evening cometh on, he shall bathe himself in water; and when the sun is down, he may come within the camp. 23:13 Thou shalt have a place also without the camp, whither thou shalt go forth abroad. 23:14 And thou shalt have a paddle among thy weapons; and it shall be, when thou sittest down abroad, thou shalt dig therewith, and shalt turn back and cover that which cometh from thee. 23:15 For the LORD thy God walketh in the midst of thy camp, to deliver thee, and to give up thine enemies before thee; therefore shall thy camp be holy; that He see no unseemly thing in thee, and turn away from thee. {S}

Ci 23:16 Thou shalt not deliver unto his master a bondman that is escaped from his master unto thee; 23:17 he shall dwell with thee, in the midst of thee, in the place which he shall choose within one of thy gates, where it liketh him best; thou shalt not wrong him. {S}

ii 23:18 There shall be no harlot of the daughters of Israel, neither shall there be a sodomite of the sons of Israel. 23:19 Thou shalt not bring the hire of a harlot, or the price of a dog, into the house of the LORD thy God for any vow; for even both these are an abomination unto the LORD thy God. {S}

Bi 24:7 If a man be found stealing any of his brethren of the children of Israel, and he deal with him as a slave, and sell him; then that thief shall die; so shalt thou put away the evil from the midst of thee. {S}

ii 24:8 Take heed in the plague of leprosy, that thou observe diligently, and do according to all that the priests the Levites shall teach you, as I commanded them, so ye shall observe to do. 24:9 Remember what the LORD thy God did unto Miriam, by the way as ye came forth out of Egypt. {S}

Ci 24:10 When thou dost lend thy neighbour any manner of loan, thou shalt not go into his house to fetch his pledge. 24:11 Thou shalt stand without, and the man to whom thou dost lend shall bring forth the pledge without unto thee. 24:12 And if he be a poor man, thou shalt not sleep with his pledge; 24:13 thou shalt surely restore to him the pledge when the sun goeth down, that he may sleep in his garment, and bless thee; and it shall be righteousness unto thee before the LORD thy God. {S}

ii 24:14 Thou shalt not oppress a hired servant that is poor and needy, whether he be of thy brethren, or of thy strangers that are in thy land within thy gates. 24:15 In the same day thou shalt give him his hire, neither shall the sun go down upon it; for he is poor, and setteth his heart upon it: lest he cry against thee unto the LORD and it be sin in thee. {S}

Di 22:5 A woman shall not wear that which pertaineth unto a man, neither shall a man put on a woman's garment; for whosoever doeth these things is an abomination unto the LORD thy God. {P}

ii 22:6 If a bird's nest chance to be before thee in the way, in any tree or on the ground, with young ones or eggs, and the dam sitting upon the young, or upon the eggs, thou shalt not take the dam with the young; 22:7 thou shalt in any wise let the dam go, but the young thou mayest take unto thyself; that it may be well with thee, and that thou mayest prolong thy days. {S}

Ei 22:8 When thou buildest a new house, then thou shalt make a parapet for thy roof, that thou bring not blood upon thy house, if any man fall from thence. 22:9 Thou shalt not sow thy vineyard with two kinds of seed; lest the fulness of the seed which thou hast sown be forfeited together with the increase of the vineyard. {S}
ii 22:10 Thou shalt not plow with an ox and an ass together. 22:11 Thou shalt not wear a mingled stuff, wool and linen together. {S} 22:12 Thou shalt make thee twisted cords upon the four corners of thy covering, wherewith thou coverest thyself. {S}

Di 23:20 Thou shalt not lend upon interest to thy brother: interest of money, interest of victuals, interest of any thing that is lent upon interest. 23:21 Unto a foreigner thou mayest lend upon interest; but unto thy brother thou shalt not lend upon interest; that the LORD thy God may bless thee in all that thou puttest thy hand unto, in the land whither thou goest in to possess it. {S}
ii 23:22 When thou shalt vow a vow unto the LORD thy God, thou shalt not be slack to pay it; for the LORD thy God will surely require it of thee; and it will be sin in thee. 23:23 But if thou shalt forbear to vow, it shall be no sin in thee. 23:24 That which is gone out of thy lips thou shalt observe and do; according as thou hast vowed freely unto the LORD thy God, even that which thou hast promised with thy mouth. {S}
Ei 23:25 When thou comest into thy neighbour's vineyard, then thou mayest eat grapes until thou have enough at thine own pleasure; but thou shalt not put any in thy vessel. {S}

ii 23:26 When thou comest into thy neighbour's standing corn, then thou mayest pluck ears with thy hand; but thou shalt not move a sickle unto thy neighbour's standing corn. {S}

Di 24:16 The fathers shall not be put to death for the children, neither shall the children be put to death for the fathers; every man shall be put to death for his own sin. {S}

ii 24:17 Thou shalt not pervert the justice due to the stranger, or to the fatherless; nor take the widow's raiment to pledge. 24:18 But thou shalt remember that thou wast a bondman in Egypt, and the LORD thy God redeemed thee thence; therefore I command thee to do this thing. {S}

Ei 24:19 When thou reapest thy harvest in thy field, and hast forgot a sheaf in the field, thou shalt not go back to fetch it; it shall be for the stranger, for the fatherless, and for the widow; that the LORD thy God may bless thee in all the work of thy hands. {S}

ii 24:20 When thou beatest thine olive-tree, thou shalt not go over the boughs again; it shall be for the stranger, for the fatherless, and for the widow. 24:21 When thou gatherest the grapes of thy vineyard, thou shalt not glean it after thee; it shall be for the stranger, for the fatherless, and for the widow. 24:22 And thou shalt remember that thou wast a bondman in the land of Egypt; therefore I command thee to do this thing. {S} 25:1 If there be a controversy between men, and they come unto judgment, and the judges judge them, by justifying the righteous, and condemning the wicked, 25:2 then it shall be, if the wicked man deserve to be beaten, that the judge shall cause him to lie down, and to be beaten before his face, according to the measure of his wickedness, by number. 25:3 Forty stripes he may give him, he shall not exceed; lest, if he should exceed, and beat him above these with many stripes, then thy brother should be dishonoured before thine eyes. 25:4 Thou shalt not muzzle the ox when he treadeth out the corn. {S}

Deuteronomy Unit IX (25:5-27:26)

א

A 25:5 If brethren dwell together, and one of them die, and have no child, the wife of the dead shall not be married abroad unto one not of his kin; her husband's brother shall go in unto her, and take her to him to wife, and perform the duty of a husband's brother unto her. 25:6 And it shall be, that the first-born that she beareth shall succeed in the name of his brother that is dead, that his name be not blotted out of Israel. 25:7 And if the man like not to take his brother's wife, then his brother's wife shall go up to the gate unto the elders, and say: 'My husband's brother refuseth to raise up unto his brother a name in Israel; he will not perform the duty of a husband's brother unto me.' 25:8 Then the elders of his city shall call him, and speak unto him; and if he stand, and say: 'I like not to take her'; 25:9 then shall his brother's wife draw nigh unto him in the presence of the elders, and loose his shoe from off his foot, and spit in his face; and she shall answer and say: 'So shall it be done unto the man that doth not build up his brother's house.' 25:10 And his name shall be called in Israel the house of him that had his shoe loosed. {S}

B 25:11 When men strive together one with another, and the wife of the one draweth near to deliver her husband out of the hand of him that smiteth him, and putteth forth her hand, and taketh him by the secrets; 25:12 then thou shalt cut off her hand, thine eye shall have no pity. {S}

C 25:13 Thou shalt not have in thy bag diverse weights, a great and a small. 25:14 Thou shalt not have in thy house diverse measures, a great and a small. 25:15 A perfect and just weight shalt thou have; a perfect and just measure shalt thou have; that thy days may be long upon the land which the LORD thy God giveth thee. 25:16 For all that do such things, even all that do unrighteously, are an abomination unto the LORD thy God. {P}

ב

A 25:17 Remember what Amalek did unto thee by the way as ye came forth out of Egypt; 25:18 how he met thee by the way, and smote the hindmost of thee, all that were enfeebled in thy rear, when thou wast faint and weary; and he feared not God. 25:19 Therefore it shall be, when the LORD thy God hath given thee rest from all thine enemies round about, in the land which the LORD thy God giveth thee for an inheritance to possess it, that thou shalt blot out the remembrance of Amalek from under heaven; thou shalt not forget. {P}

B 26:1 And it shall be, when thou art come in unto the land which the LORD thy God giveth thee for an inheritance, and dost possess it, and dwell therein; 26:2 that thou shalt take of the first of all the fruit of the ground, which thou shalt bring in from thy land that the LORD thy God giveth thee; and thou shalt put it in a basket and shalt go unto the place which the LORD thy God shall choose to cause His name to dwell there. 26:3 And thou shalt come unto the priest that shall be in those days, and say unto him: 'I profess this day unto the LORD thy God, that I am come unto the land which the LORD swore unto our fathers to give us.' 26:4 And the priest shall take the basket out of thy hand, and set it down before the altar of the LORD thy God. 26:5 And thou shalt speak and say before the LORD thy God: 'A wandering Aramean was my father, and he went down into Egypt, and sojourned there, few in number; and he became there a nation, great, mighty, and populous. 26:6 And the Egyptians dealt ill with us, and afflicted us, and laid upon us hard bondage. 26:7 And we cried unto the LORD, the God of our fathers, and the LORD heard our voice, and saw our affliction, and our toil, and our oppression. 26:8 And the LORD brought us forth out of Egypt with a mighty hand, and with an outstretched arm, and with great terribleness, and with signs, and with wonders. 26:9 And He hath brought us into this place, and hath given us this land, a land flowing with milk and honey. 26:10 And now, behold, I have brought the first of the fruit of the land, which Thou, O LORD, hast given me.' And thou shalt set it down before the LORD thy God, and worship before the LORD thy God. 26:11 And thou shalt rejoice in all the good which the LORD thy God hath given unto thee, and unto thy house, thou, and the Levite, and the stranger that is in the midst of thee. {S}

C 26:12 When thou hast made an end of tithing all the tithe of thine increase in the third year, which is the year of tithing, and hast given it unto the Levite, to the stranger, to the fatherless, and to the widow, that they may eat within thy gates, and be satisfied, 26:13 then thou shalt say before the LORD thy God: 'I have put away the hallowed things out of my house, and also have given them unto the Levite, and unto the stranger, to the fatherless, and to the widow, according to all Thy commandment which Thou hast commanded me; I have not transgressed any of Thy commandments, neither have I forgotten them. 26:14 I have not eaten thereof in my mourning, neither have I put away thereof, being unclean, nor given thereof for the dead; I have hearkened to the voice of the LORD my God, I have done according to all that Thou hast commanded me. 26:15 Look forth from Thy holy habitation, from heaven, and bless Thy people Israel, and the land which Thou hast given us, as Thou didst swear unto our fathers, a land flowing with milk and honey.' {S}

2א

A 26:16 This day the LORD thy God commandeth thee to do these statutes and ordinances; thou shalt therefore observe and do them with all thy heart, and with all thy soul.

B 26:17 Thou hast avouched the LORD this day to be thy God, and that thou wouldest walk in His ways, and keep His statutes, and His commandments, and His ordinances, and hearken unto His voice. 26:18 And the LORD hath avouched thee this day to be His own treasure, as He hath promised thee, and that thou shouldest keep all His commandments; 26:19 and to make thee high above all nations that He hath made, in praise, and in name, and in glory; and that thou mayest be a holy people unto the LORD thy God, as He hath spoken. {P}

3א

27:9 And Moses and the priests the Levites spoke unto all Israel, saying: 'Keep silence, and hear, O Israel; this day thou art become a people unto the LORD thy God. 27:10 Thou shalt therefore hearken to the voice of the LORD thy God, and do His commandments and His statutes, which I command thee this day.' {S}

4א

A 27:15 Cursed be the man that maketh a graven or molten image, an abomination unto the LORD, the work of the hands of the craftsman, and setteth it up in secret. And all the people shall answer and say: Amen. {S} 27:16 Cursed be he that dishonoureth his father or his mother. And all the people shall say: Amen. {S}

B 27:17 Cursed be he that removeth his neighbour's landmark. And all the people shall say: Amen. {S}

C 27:18 Cursed be he that maketh the blind to go astray in the way. And all the people shall say: Amen. {S} 27:19 Cursed be he that perverteth the justice due to the stranger, fatherless, and widow. And all the people shall say: Amen.

2ב

A 27:1 And Moses and the elders of Israel commanded the people, saying: 'Keep all the commandment which I command you this day. 27:2 And it shall be on the day when ye shall pass over the Jordan unto the land which the LORD thy God giveth thee, that thou shalt set thee up great stones, and plaster them with plaster. 27:3 And thou shalt write upon them all the words of this law, when thou art passed over; that thou mayest go in unto the land which the LORD thy God giveth thee, a land flowing with milk and honey, as the LORD, the God of thy fathers, hath promised thee. B 27:4 And it shall be when ye are passed over the Jordan, that ye shall set up these stones, which I command you this day, in mount Ebal, and thou shalt plaster them with plaster. 27:5 And there shalt thou build an altar unto the LORD thy God, an altar of stones; thou shalt lift up no iron tool upon them. 27:6 Thou shalt build the altar of the LORD thy God of unhewn stones; and thou shalt offer burnt-offerings thereon unto the LORD thy God. 27:7 And thou shalt sacrifice peace-offerings, and shalt eat there; and thou shalt rejoice before the LORD thy God. 27:8 And thou shalt write upon the stones all the words of this law very plainly.' {S}

3ב

27:11 And Moses charged the people the same day, saying: 27:12 'These shall stand upon mount Gerizim to bless the people, when ye are passed over the Jordan: Simeon, and Levi, and Judah, and Issachar, and Joseph, and Benjamin; 27:13 and these shall stand upon mount Ebal for the curse: Reuben, Gad, and Asher, and Zebulun, Dan, and Naphtali. 27:14 And the Levites shall speak, and say unto all the men of Israel with a loud voice: {S}

4ב

A 27:20 Cursed be he that lieth with his father's wife; because he hath uncovered his father's skirt. And all the people shall say: Amen. {S} 27:21 Cursed be he that lieth with any manner of beast. And all the people shall say: Amen. {S} 27:22 Cursed be he that lieth with his sister, the daughter of his father, or the daughter of his mother. And all the people shall say: Amen. {S} 27:23 Cursed be he that lieth with his mother-in-law. And all the people shall say: Amen. {S}
B 27:24 Cursed be he that smiteth his neighbour in secret. And all the people shall say: Amen. {S} 27:25 Cursed be he that taketh a bribe to slay an innocent person. And all the people shall say: Amen. {S}
C 27:26 Cursed be he that confirmeth not the words of this law to do them. And all the people shall say: Amen.' {P}

Deuteronomy Unit X (28:1-68)

1א

A 28:1 And it shall come to pass, if thou shalt hearken diligently unto the voice of the LORD thy God, to observe to do all His commandments which I command thee this day, that the LORD thy God will set thee on high above all the nations of the earth. 28:2 And all these blessings shall come upon thee, and overtake thee, if thou shalt hearken unto the voice of the LORD thy God.

B 28:3 Blessed shalt thou be in the city, and blessed shalt thou be in the field. 28:4 Blessed shall be the fruit of thy body, and the fruit of thy land, and the fruit of thy cattle, the increase of thy kine, and the young of thy flock. 28:5 Blessed shall be thy basket and thy kneading-trough. 28:6 Blessed shalt thou be when thou comest in, and blessed shalt thou be when thou goest out.

C 28:7 The LORD will cause thine enemies that rise up against thee to be smitten before thee; they shall come out against thee one way, and shall flee before thee seven ways.

1ב

A 28:8 The LORD will command the blessing with thee in thy barns, and in all that thou puttest thy hand unto; and He will bless thee in the land which the LORD thy God giveth thee.

B 28:9 The LORD will establish thee for a holy people unto Himself, as He hath sworn unto thee; if thou shalt keep the commandments of the LORD thy God, and walk in His ways. 28:10 And all the peoples of the earth shall see that the name of the LORD is called upon thee; and they shall be afraid of thee.

C 28:11 And the LORD will make thee over-abundant for good, in the fruit of thy body, and in the fruit of thy cattle, and in the fruit of thy land, in the land which the LORD swore unto thy fathers to give thee.

1ג

A 28:12 The LORD will open unto thee His good treasure the heaven to give the rain of thy land in its season, and to bless all the work of thy hand; and thou shalt lend unto many nations, but thou shalt not borrow.

B 28:13 And the LORD will make thee the head, and not the tail.

C and thou shalt be above only, and thou shalt not be beneath; if thou shalt hearken unto the commandments of the LORD thy God, which I command thee this day, to observe and to do them; 28:14 and shalt not turn aside from any of the words which I command you this day, to the right hand, or to the left, to go after other gods to serve them. {P}

2א

A 28:15 But it shall come to pass, if thou wilt not hearken unto the voice of the LORD thy God, to observe to do all His commandments and His statutes which I command thee this day; that all these curses shall come upon thee,

B 28:16 Cursed shalt thou be in the city, and cursed shalt thou be in the field. 28:17 Cursed shall be thy basket and thy kneading-trough. 28:18 Cursed shall be the fruit of thy body, and the fruit of thy land, the increase of thy kine, and the young of thy flock. 28:19 Cursed shalt thou be when thou comest in, and cursed shalt thou be when thou goest out.

C 28:20 The LORD will send upon thee cursing, discomfiture, and rebuke, in all that thou puttest thy hand unto to do, until thou be destroyed, and until thou perish quickly; because of the evil of thy doings, whereby thou hast forsaken Me.

D 28:21 The LORD will make the pestilence cleave unto thee, until He have consumed thee from off the land, whither thou goest in to possess it.

E 28:22 The LORD will smite thee with consumption, and with fever, and with inflammation, and with fiery heat, and with drought, and with blasting, and with mildew; and they shall pursue thee until thou perish. 28:23 And thy heaven that is over thy head shall be brass, and the earth that is under thee shall be iron.

F 28:24 The LORD will make the rain of thy land powder and dust; from heaven shall it come down upon thee, until thou be destroyed.

G 28:25 The LORD will cause thee to be smitten before thine enemies; thou shalt go out one way against them, and shalt flee seven ways before them; and thou shalt be a horror unto all the kingdoms of the earth. 28:26 And thy carcasses shall be food unto all fowls of the air, and unto the beasts of the earth, and there shall be none to frighten them away.

2ב

A 28:27 The LORD will smite thee with the boil of Egypt, and with the emerods, and with the scab, and with the itch, whereof thou canst not be healed.

B G 28:28 The LORD will smite thee with madness, and with blindness, and with astonishment of heart. 28:29 And thou shalt grope at noonday, as the blind gropeth in darkness, and thou shalt not make thy ways prosperous; and thou shalt be only oppressed and robbed alway, and there shall be none to save thee.

C 28:30 Thou shalt betroth a wife, and another man shall lie with her; thou shalt build a house, and thou shalt not dwell therein; thou shalt plant a vineyard, and shalt not use the fruit thereof. 28:31 Thine ox shall be slain before thine eyes, and thou shalt not eat thereof; thine ass shall be violently taken away from before thy face, and shall not be restored to thee; thy sheep shall be given unto thine enemies; and thou shalt have none to save thee.

D 28:32 Thy sons and thy daughters shall be given unto another people, and thine eyes shall look, and fail with longing for them all the day; and there shall be nought in the power of thy hand.

E 28:33 The fruit of thy land, and all thy labours, shall a nation which thou knowest not eat up; and thou shalt be only oppressed and crushed away: 28:34 so that thou shalt be mad for the sight of thine eyes which thou shalt see.

F 28:35 The LORD will smite thee in the knees, and in the legs, with a sore boil, whereof thou canst not be healed, from the sole of thy foot unto the crown of thy head.

G 28:36 The LORD will bring thee, and thy king whom thou shalt set over thee, unto a nation that thou hast not known, thou nor thy fathers; and there shalt thou serve other gods, wood and stone. 28:37 And thou shalt become an astonishment, a proverb, and a byword, among all the peoples whither the LORD shall lead thee away.

2ג

A 28:38 Thou shalt carry much seed out into the field, and shalt gather little in; for the locust shall consume it.

B 28:39 Thou shalt plant vineyards and dress them, but thou shalt neither drink of the wine, nor gather the grapes; for the worm shall eat them.

C 28:40 Thou shalt have olive-trees throughout all thy borders, but thou shalt not anoint thyself with the oil; for thine olives shall drop off.

D 28:41 Thou shalt beget sons and daughters, but they shall not be thine; for they shall go into captivity.

E 28:42 All thy trees and the fruit of thy land shall the locust possess.

F 28:43 The stranger that is in the midst of thee shall mount up above thee higher and higher; and thou shalt come down lower and lower. 28:44 He shall lend to thee, and thou shalt not lend to him; he shall be the head, and thou shalt be the tail.

G 28:45 And all these curses shall come upon thee, and shall pursue thee, and overtake thee, till thou be destroyed; because thou didst not hearken unto the voice of the LORD thy God, to keep His commandments and His statutes which He commanded thee. 28:46 And they shall be upon thee for a sign and for a wonder, and upon thy seed for ever; 28:47 because thou didst not serve the LORD thy God with joyfulness, and with gladness of heart, by reason of the abundance of all things; 28:48 therefore shalt thou serve thine enemy whom the LORD shall send against thee, in hunger, and in thirst, and in nakedness, and in want of all things; and he shall put a yoke of iron upon thy neck, until he have destroyed thee.

‏ג‎א

28:49 The LORD will bring a nation against thee from far, from the end of the earth, as the vulture swoopeth down; a nation whose tongue thou shalt not understand; 28:50 a nation of fierce countenance, that shall not regard the person of the old, nor show favour to the young. 28:51 And he shall eat the fruit of thy cattle, and the fruit of thy ground, until thou be destroyed; that also shall not leave thee corn, wine, or oil, the increase of thy kine, or the young of thy flock, until he have caused thee to perish. 28:52 And he shall besiege thee in all thy gates, until thy high and fortified walls come down, wherein thou didst trust, throughout all thy land; and he shall besiege thee in all thy gates throughout all thy land, which the LORD thy God hath given thee. 28:53 And thou shalt eat the fruit of thine own body, the flesh of thy sons and of thy daughters whom the LORD thy God hath given thee; in the siege and in the straitness, wherewith thine enemies shall straiten thee.

‏ד‎א

28:58 If thou wilt not observe to do all the words of this law that are written in this book, that thou mayest fear this glorious and awful Name, the LORD thy God; 28:59 then the LORD will make thy plagues wonderful, and the plagues of thy seed, even great plagues, and of long continuance, and sore sicknesses, and of long continuance. 28:60 And He will bring back upon thee all the diseases of Egypt, which thou wast in dread of; and they shall cleave unto thee. 28:61 Also every sickness, and every plague, which is not written in the book of this law, them will the LORD bring upon thee, until thou be destroyed. 28:62 And ye shall be left few in number, whereas ye were as the stars of heaven for multitude; because thou didst not hearken unto the voice of the LORD thy God. 28:63 And it shall come to pass, that as the LORD rejoiced over you to do you good, and to multiply you; so the LORD will rejoice over you to cause you to perish, and to destroy you; and ye shall be plucked from off the land whither thou goest in to possess it.

‏ג‎ב

28:54 The man that is tender among you, and very delicate, his eye shall be evil against his brother, and against the wife of his bosom, and against the remnant of his children whom he hath remaining; 28:55 so that he will not give to any of them of the flesh of his children whom he shall eat, because he hath nothing left him; in the siege and in the straitness, wherewith thine enemy shall straiten thee in all thy gates.

‏ד‎ב

28:64 And the LORD shall scatter thee among all peoples, from the one end of the earth even unto the other end of the earth; and there thou shalt serve other gods, which thou hast not known, thou nor thy fathers, even wood and stone. 28:65 And among these nations shalt thou have no repose, and there shall be no rest for the sole of thy foot; but the LORD shall give thee there a trembling heart, and failing of eyes, and languishing of soul. 28:66 And thy life shall hang in doubt before thee; and thou shalt fear night and day, and shalt have no assurance of thy life. 28:67 In the morning thou shalt say: 'Would it were even!' and at even thou shalt say: 'Would it were morning!' for the fear of thy heart which thou shalt fear, and for the sight of thine eyes which thou shalt see.

‏ג‎ג

28:56 The tender and delicate woman among you, who would not adventure to set the sole of her foot upon the ground for delicateness and tenderness, her eye shall be evil against the husband of her bosom, and against her son, and against her daughter; 28:57 and against her afterbirth that cometh out from between her feet, and against her children whom she shall bear; for she shall eat them for want of all things secretly; in the siege and in the straitness, wherewith thine enemy shall straiten thee in thy gates.

‏ד‎ג

28:68 And the LORD shall bring thee back into Egypt in ships, by the way whereof I said unto thee: 'Thou shalt see it no more again'; and there ye shall sell yourselves unto your enemies for bondmen and for bondwoman, and no man shall buy you. {S}

Deuteronomy Unit XI (28:69-30:20)

1א

A 28:69 These are the words of the covenant which the LORD commanded Moses to make with the children of Israel in the land of Moab, beside the covenant which He made with them in Horeb. {P}

B 29:1 And Moses called unto all Israel, and said unto them: Ye have seen all that the LORD did before your eyes in the land of Egypt unto Pharaoh, and unto all his servants, and unto all his land; 29:2 the great trials which thine eyes saw, the signs and those great wonders; 29:3 but the LORD hath not given you a heart to know, and eyes to see, and ears to hear, unto this day. 29:4 And I have led you forty years in the wilderness; your clothes are not waxen old upon you, and thy shoe is not waxen old upon thy foot. 29:5 Ye have not eaten bread, neither have ye drunk wine or strong drink; that ye might know that I am the LORD your God.

C 29:6 And when ye came unto this place, Sihon the king of Heshbon, and Og the king of Bashan, came out against us unto battle, and we smote them. 29:7 And we took their land, and gave it for an inheritance unto the Reubenites, and to the Gadites, and to the half-tribe of the Manassites. 29:8 Observe therefore the words of this covenant, and do them, that ye may make all that ye do to prosper. {P}

2א

A 29:21 And the generation to come, your children that shall rise up after you, and the foreigner that shall come from a far land, shall say, when they see the plagues of that land, and the sicknesses wherewith the LORD hath made it sick; 29:22 and that the whole land thereof is brimstone, and salt, and a burning, that it is not sown, nor beareth, nor any grass groweth therein, like the overthrow of Sodom and Gomorrah, Admah and Zeboiim, which the LORD overthrew in His anger, and in His wrath; 29:23 even all the nations shall say 'Wherefore hath the LORD done thus unto this land? what meaneth the heat of this great anger?' 29:24 then men shall say: 'Because they forsook the covenant of the LORD, the God of their fathers, which He made with them when He brought them forth out of the land of Egypt; 29:25 and went and served other gods, and worshipped them, gods that they knew not, and that He had not allotted unto them; 29:26 therefore the anger of the LORD was kindled against this land, to bring upon it all the curse that is written in this book; 29:27 and the LORD rooted them out of their land in anger, and in wrath, and in great indignation, and cast them into another land, as it is this day'.--

B 29:28 The secret things belong unto the LORD our God; but the things that are revealed belong unto us and to our children for ever, that we may do all the words of this law. {S}

3א

30:15 See, I have set before thee this day life and good, and death and evil, 30:16 in that I command thee this day to love the LORD thy God, to walk in His ways, and to keep His commandments and His statutes and His ordinances; then thou shalt live and multiply, and the LORD thy God shall bless thee in the land whither thou goest in to possess it. 30:17 But if thy heart turn away, and thou wilt not hear, but shalt be drawn away, and worship other gods, and serve them; 30:18 I declare unto you this day, that ye shall surely perish; ye shall not prolong your days upon the land, whither thou passest over the Jordan to go in to possess it.

1ב

A 29:9 Ye are standing this day all of you before the LORD your God: your heads, your tribes, your elders, and your officers, even all the men of Israel, 29:10 your little ones, your wives, and thy stranger that is in the midst of thy camp, from the hewer of thy wood unto the drawer of thy water; 29:11 that thou shouldest enter into the covenant of the LORD thy God--and into His oath--which the LORD thy God maketh with thee this day; 29:12 that He may establish thee this day unto Himself for a people, and that He may be unto thee a God, as He spoke unto thee, and as He swore unto thy fathers, to Abraham, to Isaac, and to Jacob. 29:13 Neither with you only do I make this covenant and this oath; 29:14 but with him that standeth here with us this day before the LORD our God, and also with him that is not here with us this day--

B 29:15 for ye know how we dwelt in the land of Egypt; and how we came through the midst of the nations through which ye passed; 29:16 and ye have seen their detestable things, and their idols, wood and stone, silver and gold, which were with them-- 29:17 lest there should be among you man, or woman, or family, or tribe, whose heart turneth away this day from the LORD our God, to go to serve the gods of those nations;

C lest there should be among you a root that beareth gall and wormwood; 29:18 and it come to pass, when he heareth the words of this curse, that he bless himself in his heart, saying: 'I shall have peace, though I walk in the stubbornness of my heart--that the watered be swept away with the dry'; 29:19 the LORD will not be willing to pardon him, but then the anger of the LORD and His jealousy shall be kindled against that man, and all the curse that is written in this book shall lie upon him, and the LORD shall blot out his name from under heaven; 29:20 and the LORD shall separate him unto evil out of all the tribes of Israel, according to all the curses of the covenant that is written in this book of the law.

2ב

A 30:1 And it shall come to pass, when all these things are come upon thee, the blessing and the curse, which I have set before thee, and thou shalt bethink thyself among all the nations, whither the LORD thy God hath driven thee, 30:2 and shalt return unto the LORD thy God, and hearken to His voice according to all that I command thee this day, thou and thy children, with all thy heart, and with all thy soul; 30:3 that then the LORD thy God will turn thy captivity, and have compassion upon thee, and will return and gather thee from all the peoples, whither the LORD thy God hath scattered thee. 30:4 If any of thine that are dispersed be in the uttermost parts of heaven, from thence will the LORD thy God gather thee, and from thence will He fetch thee. 30:5 And the LORD thy God will bring thee into the land which thy fathers possessed, and thou shalt possess it; and He will do thee good, and multiply thee above thy fathers. 30:6 And the LORD thy God will circumcise thy heart, and the heart of thy seed, to love the LORD thy God with all thy heart, and with all thy soul, that thou mayest live. 30:7 And the LORD thy God will put all these curses upon thine enemies, and on them that hate thee, that persecuted thee. 30:8 And thou shalt return and hearken to the voice of the LORD, and do all His commandments which I command thee this day. 30:9 And the LORD thy God will make thee over-abundant in all the work of thy hand, in the fruit of thy body, and in the fruit of thy cattle, and in the fruit of thy land, for good; for the LORD will again rejoice over thee for good, as He rejoiced over thy fathers; 30:10 if thou shalt hearken to the voice of the LORD thy God, to keep His commandments and His statutes which are written in this book of the law; if thou turn unto the LORD thy God with all thy heart, and with all thy soul. {S}

B 30:11 For this commandment which I command thee this day, it is not too hard for thee, neither is it far off. 30:12 It is not in heaven, that thou shouldest say: 'Who shall go up for us to heaven, and bring it unto us, and make us to hear it, that we may do it?' 30:13 Neither is it beyond the sea, that thou shouldest say: 'Who shall go over the sea for us, and bring it unto us, and make us to hear it, that we may do it?' 30:14 But the word is very nigh unto thee, in thy mouth, and in thy heart, that thou mayest do it. {S}

3ב

30:19 I call heaven and earth to witness against you this day, that I have set before thee life and death, the blessing and the curse; therefore choose life, that thou mayest live, thou and thy seed; 30:20 to love the LORD thy God, to hearken to His voice, and to cleave unto Him; for that is thy life, and the length of thy days; that thou mayest dwell in the land which the LORD swore unto thy fathers, to Abraham, to Isaac, and to Jacob, to give them. {P}

Deuteronomy Unit XII (31:1-32:47)

1א

A 31:1 And Moses went and spoke these words unto all Israel. 31:2 And he said unto them: 'I am a hundred and twenty years old this day; I can no more go out and come in; and the LORD hath said unto me: Thou shalt not go over this Jordan. 31:3 The LORD thy God, He will go over before thee; He will destroy these nations from before thee, and thou shalt dispossess them; and Joshua, he shall go over before thee, as the LORD hath spoken. 31:4 And the LORD will do unto them as He did to Sihon and to Og, the kings of the Amorites, and unto their land; whom He destroyed. 31:5 And the LORD will deliver them up before you, and ye shall do unto them according unto all the commandment which I have commanded you. 31:6 Be strong and of good courage, fear not, nor be affrighted at them; for the LORD thy God, He it is that doth go with thee; He will not fail thee, nor forsake thee.' {S}

B 31:7 And Moses called unto Joshua, and said unto him in the sight of all Israel: 'Be strong and of good courage; for thou shalt go with this people into the land which the LORD hath sworn unto their fathers to give them; and thou shalt cause them to inherit it. 31:8 And the LORD, He it is that doth go before thee; He will be with thee, He will not fail thee, neither forsake thee; fear not, neither be dismayed.'

2א

A 31:14 And the LORD said unto Moses: 'Behold, thy days approach that thou must die; call Joshua, and present yourselves in the tent of meeting, that I may give him a charge.' And Moses and Joshua went, and presented themselves in the tent of meeting. 31:15 And the LORD appeared in the Tent in a pillar of cloud; and the pillar of cloud stood over the door of the Tent. 31:16 And the LORD said unto Moses: 'Behold, thou art about to sleep with thy fathers; and this people will rise up, and go astray after the foreign gods of the land, whither they go to be among them, and will forsake Me, and break My covenant which I have made with them. 31:17 Then My anger shall be kindled against them in that day, and I will forsake them, and I will hide My face from them, and they shall be devoured, and many evils and troubles shall come upon them; so that they will say in that day: Are not these evils come upon us because our God is not among us? 31:18 And I will surely hide My face in that day for all the evil which they shall have wrought, in that they are turned unto other gods.

B 31:19 Now therefore write ye this song for you, and teach thou it the children of Israel; put it in their mouths, that this song may be a witness for Me against the children of Israel. 31:20 For when I shall have brought them into the land which I swore unto their fathers, flowing with milk and honey; and they shall have eaten their fill, and waxen fat; and turned unto other gods, and served them, and despised Me, and broken My covenant; 31:21 then it shall come to pass, when many evils and troubles are come upon them, that this song shall testify before them as a witness; for it shall not be forgotten out of the mouths of their seed; for I know their imagination how they do even now, before I have brought them into the land which I swore.' 31:22 So Moses wrote this song the same day, and taught it the children of Israel. 31:23 And he gave Joshua the son of Nun a charge, and said: 'Be strong and of good courage; for thou shalt bring the children of Israel into the land which I swore unto them; and I will be with thee.'

1ב

A 31:9 And Moses wrote this law, and delivered it unto the priests the sons of Levi, that bore the ark of the covenant of the LORD, and unto all the elders of Israel. 31:10 And Moses commanded them, saying: 'At the end of every seven years, in the set time of the year of release, in the feast of tabernacles, 31:11 when all Israel is come to appear before the LORD thy God in the place which He shall choose, thou shalt read this law before all Israel in their hearing.

B 31:12 Assemble the people, the men and the women and the little ones, and thy stranger that is within thy gates, that they may hear, and that they may learn, and fear the LORD your God, and observe to do all the words of this law; 31:13 and that their children, who have not known, may hear, and learn to fear the LORD your God, as long as ye live in the land whither ye go over the Jordan to possess it.' {P}

2ב

A 31:24 And it came to pass, when Moses had made an end of writing the words of this law in a book, until they were finished, 31:25 that Moses commanded the Levites, that bore the ark of the covenant of the LORD, saying: 31:26 'Take this book of the law, and put it by the side of the ark of the covenant of the LORD your God, that it may be there for a witness against thee. 31:27 For I know thy rebellion, and thy stiff neck; behold, while I am yet alive with you this day, ye have been rebellious against the LORD; and how much more after my death?

B 31:28 Assemble unto me all the elders of your tribes, and your officers, that I may speak these words in their ears, and call heaven and earth to witness against them. 31:29 For I know that after my death ye will in any wise deal corruptly, and turn aside from the way which I have commanded you; and evil will befall you in the end of days; because ye will do that which is evil in the sight of the LORD, to provoke Him through the work of your hands.' 31:30 And Moses spoke in the ears of all the assembly of Israel the words of this song, until they were finished: {P}

3א

32:1 Give ear, ye heavens, and I will speak; and let the earth hear the words of my mouth. 32:2 My doctrine shall drop as the rain, my speech shall distil as the dew; as the small rain upon the tender grass, and as the showers upon the herb. 32:3 For I will proclaim the name of the LORD; ascribe ye greatness unto our God. 32:4 The Rock, His work is perfect; for all His ways are justice; a God of faithfulness and without iniquity, just and right is He. 32:5 Is corruption His? No; His children's is the blemish; a generation crooked and perverse. 32:6 Do ye thus requite the LORD, O foolish people and unwise? is not He thy father that hath gotten thee? hath He not made thee, and established thee? 32:7 Remember the days of old, consider the years of many generations; ask thy father, and he will declare unto thee, thine elders, and they will tell thee. 32:8 When the Most High gave to the nations their inheritance, when He separated the children of men, He set the borders of the peoples according to the number of the children of Israel. 32:9 For the portion of the LORD is His people, Jacob the lot of His inheritance. 32:10 He found him in a desert land, and in the waste, a howling wilderness; He compassed him about, He cared for him, He kept him as the apple of His eye. 32:11 As an eagle that stirreth up her nest, hovereth over her young, spreadeth abroad her wings, taketh them, beareth them on her pinions-- 32:12 The LORD alone did lead him, and there was no strange god with Him. 32:13 He made him ride on the high places of the earth, and he did eat the fruitage of the field; and He made him to suck honey out of the crag, and oil out of the flinty rock; 32:14 Curd of kine, and milk of sheep, with fat of lambs, and rams of the breed of Bashan, and he-goats, with the kidney-fat of wheat; and of the blood of the grape thou drankest foaming wine. 32:15 But Jeshurun waxed fat, and kicked--thou didst wax fat, thou didst grow thick, thou didst become gross--and he forsook God who made him, and contemned the Rock of his salvation. 32:16 They roused Him to jealousy with strange gods, with abominations did they provoke Him. 32:17 They sacrificed unto demons, no-gods, gods that they knew not, new gods that came up of late, which your fathers dreaded not. 32:18 Of the Rock that begot thee thou wast unmindful, and didst forget God that bore thee.

3ב

32:19 And the LORD saw, and spurned, because of the provoking of His sons and His daughters. 32:20 And He said: 'I will hide My face from them, I will see what their end shall be; for they are a very froward generation, children in whom is no faithfulness. 32:21 They have roused Me to jealousy with a no-god; they have provoked Me with their vanities; and I will rouse them to jealousy with a no-people; I will provoke them with a vile nation. 32:22 For a fire is kindled in My nostril, and burneth unto the depths of the nether-world, and devoureth the earth with her produce, and setteth ablaze the foundations of the mountains. 32:23 I will heap evils upon them; I will spend Mine arrows upon them; 32:24 The wasting of hunger, and the devouring of the fiery bolt, and bitter destruction; and the teeth of beasts will I send upon them, with the venom of crawling things of the dust. 32:25 Without shall the sword bereave, and in the chambers terror; slaying both young man and virgin, the suckling with the man of gray hairs. 32:26 I thought I would make an end of them, I would make their memory cease from among men; 32:27 Were it not that I dreaded the enemy's provocation, lest their adversaries should misdeem, lest they should say: Our hand is exalted, and not the LORD hath wrought all this.' 32:28 For they are a nation void of counsel, and there is no understanding in them. 32:29 If they were wise, they would understand this, they would discern their latter end. 32:30 How should one chase a thousand, and two put ten thousand to flight, except their Rock had given them over and the LORD had delivered them up? 32:31 For their rock is not as our Rock, even our enemies themselves being judges. 32:32 For their vine is of the vine of Sodom, and of the fields of Gomorrah; their grapes are grapes of gall, their clusters are bitter; 32:33 Their wine is the venom of serpents, and the cruel poison of asps. 32:34 'Is not this laid up in store with Me, sealed up in My treasuries? 32:35 Vengeance is Mine, and recompense, against the time when their foot shall slip; for the day of their calamity is at hand, and the things that are to come upon them shall make haste. 32:36 For the LORD will judge His people, and repent Himself for His servants; when He seeth that their stay is gone, and there is none remaining, shut up or left at large. 32:37 And it is said: Where are their gods, the rock in whom they trusted; 32:38 Who did eat the fat of their sacrifices, and drank the wine of their drink-offering? let him rise up and help you, let him be your protection. 32:39 See now that I, even I, am He, and there is no god with Me; I kill, and I make alive; I have wounded, and I heal; and there is none that can deliver out of My hand. 32:40 For I lift up My hand to heaven, and say: As I live for ever, 32:41 If I whet My glittering sword, and My hand take hold on judgment; I will render vengeance to Mine adversaries, and will recompense them that hate Me. 32:42 I will make Mine arrows drunk with blood, and My sword shall devour flesh; with the blood of the slain and the captives, from the long-haired heads of the enemy.' 32:43 Sing aloud, O ye nations, of His people; for He doth avenge the blood of His servants, and doth render vengeance to His adversaries, and doth make expiation for the land of His people. {P}

4א

32:44 And Moses came and spoke all the words of this song in the ears of the people, he, and Hoshea the son of Nun.

4ב

32:45 And when Moses made an end of speaking all these words to all Israel, 32:46 he said unto them: 'Set your heart unto all the words wherewith I testify against you this day; that ye may charge your children therewith to observe to do all the words of this law. 32:47 For it is no vain thing for you; because it is your life, and through this thing ye shall prolong your days upon the land, whither ye go over the Jordan to possess it.' {P}

Deuteronomy Unit XIII (32:48-34:12)

1א

32:48 And the LORD spoke unto Moses that selfsame day, saying: 32:49 'Get thee up into this mountain of Abarim, unto mount Nebo, which is in the land of Moab, that is over against Jericho; and behold the land of Canaan, which I give unto the children of Israel for a possession; 32:50 and die in the mount whither thou goest up, and be gathered unto thy people; as Aaron thy brother died in mount Hor, and was gathered unto his people. 32:51 Because ye trespassed against Me in the midst of the children of Israel at the waters of Meribath-kadesh, in the wilderness of Zin; because ye sanctified Me not in the midst of the children of Israel. 32:52 For thou shalt see the land afar off; but thou shalt not go thither into the land which I give the children of Israel.' {P}

2א

A 33:6 Let Reuben live, and not die in that his men become few. {S}

B 33:7 And this for Judah, and he said: Hear, LORD, the voice of Judah, and bring him in unto his people; his hands shall contend for him, and Thou shalt be a help against his adversaries. {P}

3א

33:13 And of Joseph he said: Blessed of the LORD be his land; for the precious things of heaven, for the dew, and for the deep that coucheth beneath, 33:14 And for the precious things of the fruits of the sun, and for the precious things of the yield of the moons, 33:15 And for the tops of the ancient mountains, and for the precious things of the everlasting hills, 33:16 And for the precious things of the earth and the fulness thereof, and the good will of Him that dwelt in the bush; let the blessing come upon the head of Joseph, and upon the crown of the head of him that is prince among his brethren. 33:17 His firstling bullock, majesty is his; and his horns are the horns of the wild-ox; with them he shall gore the peoples all of them, even the ends of the earth; and they are the ten thousands of Ephraim, and they are the thousands of Manasseh. {S}

4א

A 33:20 And of Gad he said: Blessed be He that enlargeth Gad; he dwelleth as a lioness, and teareth the arm, yea, the crown of the head. 33:21 And he chose a first part for himself, for there a portion of a ruler was reserved; and there came the heads of the people, he executed the righteousness of the LORD, and His ordinances with Israel. {S}
B 33:22 And of Dan he said: Dan is a lion's whelp, that leapeth forth from Bashan.

5א

33:26 There is none like unto God, O Jeshurun, who rideth upon the heaven as thy help, and in His excellency on the skies. 33:27 The eternal God is a dwelling-place, and underneath are the everlasting arms; and He thrust out the enemy from before thee, and said: 'Destroy.' 33:28 And Israel dwelleth in safety, the fountain of Jacob alone, in a land of corn and wine; yea, his heavens drop down dew. 33:29 Happy art thou, O Israel, who is like unto thee? a people saved by the LORD, the shield of thy help, and that is the sword of thy excellency! And thine enemies shall dwindle away before thee; and thou shalt tread upon their high places. {S}

1ב

33:1 And this is the blessing wherewith Moses the man of God blessed the children of Israel before his death. 33:2 And he said: The LORD came from Sinai, and rose from Seir unto them; He shined forth from mount Paran, and He came from the myriads holy, at His right hand was a fiery law unto them. 33:3 Yea, He loveth the peoples, all His holy ones--they are in Thy hand; and they sit down at Thy feet, receiving of Thy words. 33:4 Moses commanded us a law, an inheritance of the congregation of Jacob. 33:5 And there was a king in Jeshurun, when the heads of the people were gathered, all the tribes of Israel together.

2ב

A 33:8 And of Levi he said: Thy Thummim and Thy Urim be with Thy holy one, whom Thou didst prove at Massah, with whom Thou didst strive at the waters of Meribah; 33:9 Who said of his father, and of his mother: 'I have not seen him'; neither did he acknowledge his brethren, nor knew he his own children; for they have observed Thy word, and keep Thy covenant. 33:10 They shall teach Jacob Thine ordinances, and Israel Thy law; they shall put incense before Thee, and whole burnt-offering upon Thine altar. 33:11 Bless, LORD, his substance, and accept the work of his hands; smite through the loins of them that rise up against him, and of them that hate him, that they rise not again. {S}
B 33:12 Of Benjamin he said: The beloved of the LORD shall dwell in safety by Him; He covereth him all the day, and He dwelleth between his shoulders. {S}

3ב

33:18 And of Zebulun he said: Rejoice, Zebulun, in thy going out, and, Issachar, in thy tents. 33:19 They shall call peoples unto the mountain; there shall they offer sacrifices of righteousness; for they shall suck the abundance of the seas, and the hidden treasures of the sand. {S}

4ב

A 33:23 And of Naphtali he said: O Naphtali, satisfied with favour, and full with the blessing of the LORD: possess thou the sea and the south. {S}

B 33:24 And of Asher he said: Blessed be Asher above sons; let him be the favoured of his brethren, and let him dip his foot in oil. 33:25 Iron and brass shall be thy bars; and as thy days, so shall thy strength be.

5ב

34:1 And Moses went up from the plains of Moab unto mount Nebo, to the top of Pisgah, that is over against Jericho. And the LORD showed him all the land, even Gilead as far as Dan; 34:2 and all Naphtali, and the land of Ephraim and Manasseh, and all the land of Judah as far as the hinder sea; 34:3 and the South, and the Plain, even the valley of Jericho the city of palm-trees, as far as Zoar. 34:4 And the LORD said unto him: 'This is the land which I swore unto Abraham, unto Isaac, and unto Jacob, saying: I will give it unto thy seed; I have caused thee to see it with thine eyes, but thou shalt not go over thither.' 34:5 So Moses the servant of the LORD died there in the land of Moab, according to the word of the LORD. 34:6 And he was buried in the valley in the land of Moab over against Beth-peor; and no man knoweth of his sepulchre unto this day. 34:7 And Moses was a hundred and twenty years old when he died: his eye was not dim, nor his natural force abated. 34:8 And the children of Israel wept for Moses in the plains of Moab thirty days; so the days of weeping in the mourning for Moses were ended. 34:9 And Joshua the son of Nun was full of the spirit of wisdom; for Moses had laid his hands upon him; and the children of Israel hearkened unto him, and did as the LORD commanded Moses. 34:10 And there hath not arisen a prophet since in Israel like unto Moses, whom the LORD knew face to face; 34:11 in all the signs and the wonders, which the LORD sent him to do in the land of Egypt, to Pharaoh, and to all his servants, and to all his land; 34:12 and in all the mighty hand, and in all the great terror, which Moses wrought in the sight of all Israel. {P}